CONTEMPORARY IMMIGRATION IN AMERICA

CONTEMPORARY IMMIGRATION IN AMERICA

A State-by-State Encyclopedia

VOLUME 2

MONTANA–WYOMING

Kathleen R. Arnold, Editor

 GREENWOOD

AN IMPRINT OF ABC-CLIO, LLC

Santa Barbara, California • Denver, Colorado • Oxford, England

Library of Congress Cataloging-in-Publication Data

Contemporary immigration in America : a state-by-state encyclopedia /
   Kathleen R. Arnold, editor.
     pages cm
   Includes bibliographical references and index.
   ISBN 978-0-313-39917-6 (hard copy : alk. paper) — ISBN 978-0-313-39918-3 (ebook)
1. United States—Emigration and immigration—Encyclopedias.
2. Immigrants—United States—Encyclopedias.   I. Arnold, Kathleen R., 1966– editor.
   JV6465.C745   2014
   304.8'73003—dc23   2014039672

ISBN: 978-0-313-39917-6
EISBN: 978-0-313-39918-3

19 18 17 16 15   1 2 3 4 5

This book is also available on the World Wide Web as an eBook.
Visit www.abc-clio.com for details.

Greenwood
An Imprint of ABC-CLIO, LLC

ABC-CLIO, LLC
130 Cremona Drive, P.O. Box 1911
Santa Barbara, California 93116–1911

This book is printed on acid-free paper ∞

Manufactured in the United States of America

Contents

VOLUME 2

26
MONTANA

William P. Kladky

CHRONOLOGY

1682	Montana is claimed, as part of the territory of Louisiana, by the French explorer René-Robert Cavelier, sieur de La Salle.
1743	The sons of French-Canadian trader Pierre Gaultier de Varennes (1685–1749), sieur de La Vérendrye, see the Big Horn Mountains of Montana and Wyoming.
1805–1806	The Lewis and Clark Expedition crosses Montana.
1807	Spanish explorer Manuel Lisa (1772–1820) builds the first fur fort in Montana on the Yellowstone River.
1828	Fort Union, an American Fur Company post, is built at the mouth of the Yellowstone River.
1841	Jesuit missionary Father Pierre-Jean de Smet (1801–1873) establishes St. Mary's Mission in the Bitterroot Valley near Stevensville.
1853	John "Johnny" F. Grant (1831–1907) starts the first beef herd in the Deer Lodge Valley.
1857	The first sheep ranching begins in the Bitterroot Valley.
1860	The first steamboat reaches Fort Benton.
1862	Placer miners rush to a gold strike on the Grasshopper Creek (Bannack).
1864	The Montana Vigilantes hang Bannack sheriff Henry Plummer (1832–1864) and other "Innocents." The U.S. Congress creates the Montana Territory. The area's first newspaper, *The Montana Post*, begins publication in Virginia City.
1870	The open-range cattle industry begins on the Montana prairies.

1872	The U.S. Congress creates Yellowstone National Park.
1876	The army of General George A. Custer (1839–1876) is annihilated by a coalition of American Indian tribes at the Battle of the Little Big Horn: "Custer's Last Stand."
1877	Significant copper mining begins in Butte.
1880	The Utah and Northern Railroad enters Montana.
1883	The Northern Pacific Railroad is completed through Montana. Marcus Daly (1841–1900) establishes the town of Anaconda and a smelter works.
1889	Montana becomes the 41st state.
1890	The first hydroelectric dam is built in Great Falls.
1893	The Great Northern Railway is completed through Montana.
1894	Helena wins an election to become the permanent capital of Montana.
1909	The Chicago, Milwaukee, St. Paul and Pacific Railroad ("Milwaukee Road") is completed through Montana.
1910	The U.S. Congress establishes Glacier National Park.
1910–1918	The homesteading boom peaks on Montana's plains.
1911–1925	Some 25 new Montana counties are created.
1914	Montana women receive the right to vote.
1916	Jeannette P. Rankin (1880–1973) of Missoula is elected as the first woman in the U.S. Congress.
1917	Congresswoman Rankin votes against U.S. entry into World War I. The Industrial Workers of the World labor organizer Frank Little (1879–1917) is lynched in Butte.
1919	The first of severe agricultural depressions (extending into the early 1940s) begins in Montana. Oil is discovered in the Cat Creek field.
1922	KDYS (Great Falls), Montana's first licensed radio station, begins broadcasting.
1930	The tourist industry begins in Montana.
1933	The construction of Fort Peck Dam begins. Many federal Civilian Conservation Corps camps are established across Montana.
1935	The federal Works Progress Administration begins several projects in Montana.
1936	The Rural Electrification Act begins work in Montana.
1941	Congresswoman Rankin votes against U.S. entry into World War II.
1950	Great Falls replaces Butte as Montana's largest city.
1951	A petroleum boom begins in eastern Montana.
1952	Michael "Mike" J. Mansfield (1903–2001) is elected to the U.S. Senate (D) for the first time.
1953	KOOK-TV (Billings), Montana's first licensed television station, begins broadcast.
1955	Aluminum plant begins processing in Columbia Falls. The Berkley Pit copper operation starts in Butte.
1961	The Malmstrom Air Force Base in Great Falls becomes the site of the nation's first Intercontinental ballistic missile command.

1964	The U.S. Congress passes the federal Wilderness Act.
1967	The Bell Creek petroleum field is discovered. The longest and costliest labor strike in Montana history occurs in Butte.
1968	The Yellowtail Dam is completed, and work begins on the Libby Dam.
1969	The largest-scale strip mining of coal begins at Colstrip.
1970	Consolidation creates the Burlington Northern Railroad.
1972	Montana's voters approve a new state constitution.
1980	Billings replaces Great Falls as Montana's largest city.
1981	The "Milwaukee Road" railroad line declares bankruptcy.
1982	Copper-mining operations cease at Butte's Berkeley Pit.
1986	Limited underground mining resumes in Butte. Some high-tech gold mining reopens in Montana's mountains.
1987	The last gaps in the federal interstate highway system in Montana are completed.
1988	The United States and Canada sign a Free-Trade Agreement, directly affecting Montana's economy.
1990	While the state's timber industry declines, tourism and specialized mining thrive.
1992	As a result of the 1990 U.S. Census, Montana loses one of its two representatives in Congress.
1993	Robert Redford's film, *A River Runs through It*, stimulates additional tourism and immigration to the state.
2010	The Pew Hispanic Center estimates that undocumented immigrants make up less than 0.5 percent of the state's population.
2013	The foreign-born are estimated to comprise about 2 percent of the state's population, with about half being naturalized citizens.

HISTORICAL OVERVIEW

MONTANA BEFORE 1862

Before white explorers found the area, Montana was occupied by the Flathead Indians, one of the Salishan-speaking tribes. Cooperative and peaceful, they periodically hunted buffalo with the Nez Percé tribe of Idaho. Eventually, they were driven westward toward the mountains by the Shoshoni Indians. In the desert south and west, the Shoshonis had established their territory by the end of the seventeenth century by wars with various Plains Indians. In turn, the Shoshonis were forced to move by the fierce Blackfeet tribe of the Algonquian language. The various tribes—including Sioux, Bannocks, Crows, Chippewas, Cree, and others—competed for the hunting areas, migrating for food or because of war.

The first white men to enter Montana were probably French and Spanish explorers in the seventeenth century. Montana was included in the gigantic French

John Jacob Astor (1763–1848) standing on the shore of a lake with a rifle and his foot on a punt, buying furs from American Indians in western New York. Undated illustration. (Bettmann/Corbis)

territory of Louisiana, explored by René-Robert Cavelier, sieur de La Salle in 1682. In 1809–1810, the explorer David Thompson, as a Hudson Bay Company employee, visited several areas in Montana. Other parties explored different parts of the state, including Alexander Ross from Scotland leading a North-West Company party, including Canadians, Iroquois Indians, and Hawaiians. Major Andrew Henry of the Rocky Mountain Fur Company built Fort Henry and explored Great Falls. The area also was hunted extensively as well as productively traded with the American Indians by the American Fur Company, owned by John Jacob Astor (1763–1848). Some French and Scots came as fur traders. Missionaries began to arrive in Montana during this period. The Flathead and Nez Percé tribes asked for missionaries to be sent.

The United States acquired most of what is now Montana as part of the Louisiana Purchase. The northwestern part was gained by treaty with Britain in 1846. At various times, parts of Montana were in the territories of Louisiana, Missouri, Nebraska, Dakota, Oregon, Washington, and Idaho.

Montana Gold Rush (1862)

The Montana Gold Rush changed everything. In 1862, prospectors found gold in Grasshopper Creek in the southwestern part of the state. Other gold strikes followed, and a number of wild mining camps grew around the gold fields. These included Bannack, Diamond City, Virginia City, and many others.

The miners could reach the mines because the U.S. military previously had constructed the 624-mile Mullan Road, which ran from Walla Walla to Fort Benton and was opened in 1863. After 1860, people could access this road by taking a steamboat up the Missouri River during the high water months. The military's Fort Benton quickly grew to become a regional transportation center. The boats going back downstream for St. Louis hauled hides, furs, gold, and those who had given up their dreams of avarice—at least in this way.

Most miners took the four major overland routes, which were rugged but cheaper than traveling by steamboat and followed the age-old Native American paths. The northern route followed Indian trails across North Dakota. The Corinne Road from Utah brought so many prospectors from the South that, according to Jesuit missionary Father Pierre-Jean de Smet, "not a blade of grass can shoot up on account of the continual passing." Many came from the southern states, including from Confederate U.S. Civil War Army units. One of the major gold fields was called Confederate Gulch because three Southerners discovered it (Billington and Ridge 1982; Montana Historical Society 2008).

They came to Montana from many areas, including those who have originally gone to Oregon and California in the 1850s. Within one year, Virginia City swelled to 4,000 men. Quickly built to amuse the men were eight billiard halls, five gambling dens, three "hurdy-gurdies" (i.e., dance halls), some prostitution houses, many bars, and—perhaps in competition—two churches. Contrary to popular belief, some historians hold that the level of dissipation was not markedly higher in miners' camps than in the general population (Malone and Roeder 1976, 67).

With this booming population influx came businessmen who included some Jewish merchants like Julius Basinski, who was successful in several towns and cities. The missionaries reportedly passed a tin cup for gold dust at services instead of collection plates. Virginia City, Bozeman, and Helena were sizable towns by 1865. Attracted by the miners' demand for food, farmers soon arrived to cultivate the fertile mountain valleys near the mines.

Most of the miners were American migrants from the East and the Midwest, though the Butte silver and copper ledges were mined by mostly German and Irish immigrants. The miners tolerated some ethnic groups except for Native Americans, African Americans, and Chinese—and there were many Chinese who immigrated to work. The state's Chinese population grew to 2,070 by 1870, and was composed of almost one-third of Butte's residents. The 1880 U.S. Census found that 65 percent of German Gulch residents were born in China, a dramatic increase from only five Chinese-born residents in 1870, though underreporting of Chinese-born residents could explain the startling difference.

The hiring of Chinese immigrants for work at substandard wages, the perceived torrent of immigration, and competition for claims and jobs all spiked

U.S. representative Steve Daines, left, and Montana attorney general Tim Fox discuss the security of Montana's driver's licenses in Helena, Montana, on February 13, 2014. Daines's bill proposes to strike a portion of a 2005 antiterrorism law that sets national standards for driver's licenses and identification cards. (AP Photo/Matt Volz)

racial tensions. In Virginia City, Chinese settlers were required to live in separate areas. Job discrimination against them was prevalent. They were relegated to the jobs nobody else wanted: laundry, menial work, restaurants, and the poorest-quality mining claims. The Montana territorial legislature even outlawed Chinese ownership of mining claims. Their 1872 Alien Law, which forbade foreign-born ownership of Montana placer mining claims, was specifically designed to legally stop Chinese control. Later in 1872, however, a lawsuit resulted in the law being overturned by the Territorial Montana Supreme Court because it conflicted with federal law promoting development. Understandably, given this level of official and unofficial harassment, after the gold rush ended, few Chinese took up permanent Montana residence. Almost 50 percent had left by 1900.

Several additional gold mining strikes occurred between 1860 and 1885, one in 1866 drawing roughly 5,000 miners. When the surface of the ore lodes was exhausted, most left for other prospects in other territories. This continual search for riches by the prospectors eventually drove them to the Dakotas's Black Hills and deeper into Native American territory, creating conflicts there. Military authorities made some attempts to preserve the area as Native American reservations, but the fervid rush in 1875–1876 forced more the American Indian removal and suffering.

Montana Becomes a Territory

Eventually, the commotion and the chaos of the thinly organized camps, as well as the population surge, necessitated a more permanent law-and-order and organized government. At this time, Montana was legally part of the Idaho Territory, but it was largely ignored, hundreds of rough miles from the territorial capitol in Lewiston. Montana previously had been part of the territories of Oregon, Washington, Nebraska, and Dakota. Law was enforced, but unevenly and in a biased manner. The only courts were run by the miners, and the judges were usually poorly educated, leading to varied standards. Leading the effort to impose better order was Sidney Edgerton (1818–1900)—the ex-Congressman—who was appointed chief justice of Idaho. After petition, Edgerton was chosen by the locals to go to Washington, D.C., to lobby for splitting the Territory of Idaho into two to form Montana.

When the creation of the Montana Territory came to the floor of the U.S. House of Representatives, there was a spirited, very partisan debate over what should be the proper name for this new territory. Democrats wanted to name it "Jefferson" to commemorate President Thomas F. Jefferson (1743–1826) or "Douglas" to honor the Illinois senator Stephen A. Douglas (1813–1861). One Congressman suggested "Shoshone" for the Native American tribe, but withdrew it when he was told that the word translated as "snake." Another Democrat proposed "Abyssinia," a taunt about the Republicans' support for African American causes. Finally, the House agreed on "Montana," and sent it to the Senate. After some discussion about a Native American name being more appropriate, it passed as "Montana." Montana thus became a territory on May 26, 1864, and Edgerton was appointed by President Abraham Lincoln (1809–1865) as the territorial governor (Malone and Roeder 1976, 72–73).

Soon, Montana Democrats became interested in statehood both because they grew frustrated with being ruled by Washington-appointed (mostly Republican) territorial governors and because they felt they could dominate the state. Although Montana legally did not have sufficient population to become a state, advocates argued that Congress had bent the rules to admit Nevada in 1864. In 1866, acting governor Thomas F. Meagher (1823–1867), a Democrat, called a constitutional convention. The Republicans were outraged and easily persuaded the Radical Republicans then in control of the U.S. Congress to declare the Montana legislative act authorizing the convention as illegal. The illegal convention eventually produced a constitution for Montana, but according to legend it ignominiously was lost or burnt in a fire.

During this time, transportation improvements continued with both positive and negative impacts. The construction of the Bozeman Trail from the Oregon Trail to Montana went across Crow and Sioux territories helping the state's development, but provoking the destructive Indian Wars from 1860 to 1875. The wars included two of the most famous Native American campaigns in American history: "Custer's Last Stand" on June 25, 1876, near the Little Bighorn River in southeastern Montana, and the two-day battle at Big Hole in southwestern Montana when Colonel Nelson A. Miles (1839–1925) captured Chief Joseph's Nez Percé Native Americans near the Canadian border.

The first cattle herd was brought from Oregon to Montana in the 1850s, but when Nelson Story (1838–1926) drove 1,000 longhorn cattle from Texas to Montana in 1866, the cattle industry truly commenced. With the Native Americans removed or subdued, farmers in the 1870s moved from the mountain valleys to eastern Montana's rich grasslands with its many nurturing streams. The Montana Territory began advertising for settlers in 1869. Pamphlets on the territory were distributed in Germany and the Scandinavian countries. The federal government's Oregon and California grant program helped this considerably. The state received the most acres of public domain. Montana received 263,000 acres, mainly in the form of 60 miles on each side of the tracks of the Northern Pacific Railroad. Ranches sprouted and the population increased.

In the U.S. Civil War, Montana resident Thomas F. Meagher (1823–1867) became famous as the leader of the hard-fighting Irish Brigade. As a result of his heroics, Meagher in 1865 was appointed secretary of the Montana Territory by President Andrew Johnson (1808–1875). According to the 1870 U.S. Census, Montana's population consisted of 18,306 Anglos; 1,949 Chinese; 183 African Americans; and an estimated 19,300 Native Americans. Immigration societies were set up in Helena (1872) and Bozeman (1875) to draw more settlers as well as to assist those who arrived. For example, the Bozeman Society tried to bring immigrants into Big Horn and Yellowstone counties.

The so-called Dakota Boom during the 1870s and 1880s drew many new settlers to the Dakotas and Montana. From having no cattle in 1860, Montana had 428,279 by 1880. Cowhands came in from many regions, including Civil War veterans, Mexican Americans ("vaqueros"), and African Americans. Many of the ranchers were also women. Struggling eastern farmers were attracted by magazine and newspaper stories of waiting riches.

This turned into a torrent of new settlers after the 1881–1883 opening of the Northern Pacific Railroad's network to the eastern markets, driven by Canadian American financier James J. Hill (1838–1916). The railroad brought European immigrants to work, and created towns through its determined colonization program that included free transportation for homeowners. Immigrants from northern Europe particularly were targeted because of the similar climate. In 1882, an English colony was set up in Helena and the Yellowstone Valley. In the early 1890s, some French settled in Missoula County, a couple of Dutch families came to the Gallatin Valley, and several Finnish lumbermen migrated east of Missoula. There were also new Italian and German settlers in Fergus and Park counties, as well as numerous Germans who had come from North Dakota and Canada. Most of the sheepmen and many cattlemen were English and Scottish, but the Germans owned the cattle. After the Civil War ended, some African Americans also arrived to work. These new migrants mostly settled along the railroad and created towns like Glendive and Billings.

Seeing a commercial opening, several corporations rushed in to consolidate small ranches into 100,000-head enterprises. Eastern capital also funded mechanized mining operations to extract the deep riches during the 1870s and 1880s.

STATEHOOD

As a result of this activity, the population of Montana grew from about 39,000 to nearly 143,000 during the 1880s. The state's population leapt a phenomenal 365 percent during the 1880s, its historically largest growth rate. Much of the state's growth was due to numerous immigrants who came to work the major strikes at the mines around Butte. After the earliest strikes produced gold, silver was found in Butte Hill, and then miners discovered large copper veins. As Butte Hill became known as the "Richest Hill on Earth," these riches drew miners from Ireland, England, and other European nations. Smelters were built in Anaconda and Great Falls, and more men were hired to operate them. Railroad development in western Montana in the early 1880s made additional silver ore deposits easier to reach, and the boom intensified. In 1883, Montana ranked as the second-largest silver producer in the United States. This rank continued through the mid-1890s, except in 1887 when the state was the largest producer.

The Montana Territory tried again to appeal for statehood in 1884, but this time was defeated by the Democrats. This changed after Benjamin Harrison (1833–1901) was elected in 1888 and the Republicans achieved majorities in both the U.S. House of Representatives and the Senate. In 1889, the new Congress authorized Montana, North and South Dakota, and Washington to develop constitutions. After Montana's voters subsequently approved a constitution, it became the 41st state on November 8, 1889. Later in 1889, Joseph K. Toole (1851–1929) of Helena was elected the first governor.

The new state continued to flourish via development of its natural resources. Marcus Daly (1841–1900) and William A. Clark (1839–1925) led the development of Butte copper. Daly built Anaconda and spent lavishly to try to make it the state capital. However, Clark favored Helena and after raucous campaigning, ballot stuffing, and two votes, the voters chose Helena.

Scandinavians, Irish, and "Cousin Jacks" from Cornwall in southeastern England came to work at the smelters and mills of Daly's Anaconda Copper Mining Company located in Anaconda and Great Falls. Butte was dominated by the Irish and "Cousin Jacks," who fought over religious differences but helped celebrate each other's holidays. They, along with men from Devon and Wales, joined other experienced miners from Nevada, Colorado, Utah, and California. Many immigrant workers from the Balkan countries came after 1900. There also were Chinese, English, Finns, and Germans. Irish, Poles, and Italians labored in the coal mines in Cascade, Carbon, and Musselshell counties. The mines and their surrounding hamlets and towns (e.g., Butte, East Helena, and Great Falls) then somewhat became a test "melting pot" of the many nationalities of the workers.

But they continued to feel ethnic and class bias against the Chinese. Eventually, some 2,000 Chinese placer miners worked and lived in German Gulch, French Gulch, Rocker, Pioneer City, Bannack, and Alder Gulch. Forced out of mining by discriminatory taxation, violent threats, and onerous ordinances stemming from the fear of cheap labor, the Chinese opened service-oriented businesses such as laundries and mercantile in booming Butte, a supply hub for surrounding communities. The economic depressions of the 1870s and the 1890s exacerbated anti-Chinese tensions, leading to riots and the boycotting of Chinese businesses across the United States, including Montana. In 1895, Butte labor unions and the chamber of commerce conducted a boycott of Chinese-owned businesses. Their livelihood threatened, Chinese businessmen sued the labor unions and eventually won in court, though they received no compensation for their lost business.

Population of the eastern part of the state grew relatively slowly because big cattlemen and big sheepmen had assembled such large parcels that small farmers could not afford to buy land. This changed when these large landowners started selling or giving quarter sections (i.e., 160 acres) to small cattle and crop farmers in the 1890s. With that, eastern Montana's population surged. The 1880s and 1890s were the peak of the cattle-raising industry.

1900–1945

Montana's population had grown from 143,000 in 1890 to 243,000 by 1900. With a population density of 1.7 persons per square mile, the state was technically a "frontier" according to the U.S. Census's definition. The state then produced 61 percent of the copper in the United States and 23 percent of the world's. In 1906, a federal religion survey discovered that 74 percent of Montana's residents were Catholic, twice the national average. There were 11,343 Native Americans in the state.

During the early 1900s, new dams were built to harness the rivers and to provide water for irrigation and electric power for industry. The extension of the railroads assisted the processing industries. New plants refined sugar, milled flour, and processed meat. In 1910, Congress created Glacier National Park, which became an attraction for the tourists.

Farmers rushed in after the enactment of the Enlarged Homestead Act of 1909 which doubled maximum claims from 160 to 320 acres. These new migrants came despite evidence that the lands were drought-plagued. The rural eastern part of the state increased from virtually no population in 1901 to almost 60,000 by 1917. Many immigrants arrived through the New York City port or from Canada's ports of Sweetgrass (began as a port of entry in 1903), Gateway (1908), and Roosville (1930). Thousands of Germans and Scandinavians immigrants who came to settle the dryland areas of the north and east-central began to prosper. Some came in community groups: Dutch in the Gallantin Valley, French near Missoula, and Belgians outside of Valier.

In 1910, Montana's African American population reached its highest point at 1,834. Over 25 percent of the state's population was foreign-born in 1910, with most from Canada, Ireland, Germany, and Scotland. These groups were joined by large groups of Finns and Italians, as well as some Greeks, Bulgarians, Rumanians, Serbs, Croatians, Poles, and Czechs, who worked the railroads and the mines around Butte.

It was a period of migratory churn. Between 70,000 and 80,000 came to the eastern and central parts of the state during 1909–1918 period, but over 60,000 left before 1922. This happened primarily because of lack of skills. A study discovered that 70 percent of those settlers without previous farming experience failed, compared to 48 percent of the farmer veterans.

Jeannette Rankin of Missoula, a leader in the campaign for women's rights, was elected to the U.S. House of Representatives in 1916. She was the first woman to serve in Congress. The 1900–1916 period was extremely fruitful for large crop harvesting in Montana, but the good times ended with the 1917–1920 drought. This problem was compounded by very harsh winters, which killed crops; the national economic recession; and the worldwide plummet of agricultural prices. The state lost populations in the 1920s, as thousands of settlers were overcome by the harsh climate that sometimes seemed to only feature drought, blizzards, and windstorms. Many small towns that had been established by the railroads declined into dust. For example, Coburg began in the 1880s as a stop on the Great Northern. By 1917, it had 50 families. It kept growing until the financial recession. Coburg only had three families, a depot, a hotel, one store, and a few small buildings by the late 1920s. These buildings were razed after the Great Northern stops in the 1930s, and Coburg—and human habitation—vanished for 200 square miles.

More positively, the rise of the sugar industry attracted new immigrants. The industry was stimulated by the development of irrigation for sugar-beet growing in 1906. Japanese immigrants were the initial beet field workers, followed by Russians and Germans, and then Mexicans after World War I.

The World War stimulated nativism, leading to prejudice and discrimination against such perceived "pro-Germans" as Finns, Irish, and Poles. Responding, many of the immigrant population announced their opposition to war. There even was a large anti-war parade by the Irish Pearse-Connolly Club in Butte on March 17, 1918. As the parade began, the police arrested 54 men for "plotting against the U.S. Government" and held them on $10,000 bond each. Also during the war, the Montana Council of Defense banned the use of the German language. This resulted in hundreds of German Mennonite families fleeing to Canada.

The state had a population growth spurt during the 1920s, partly abetted by increased immigration. Mexicans arrived to work in the sugar industry around Billings, then the third-largest Montana city (Federal Writers' Project 1949, 128). As of 1930, the foreign-born constituted 45.2 percent of the state's population. Germans were the largest (30,377), followed by Norwegians (29,386), English (18,915), Irish (17,940), Swedes (16,226), Russians (13,761), and Yugoslavs (9,278). There also was a smattering of Danes, Italians, Finns, and Czechoslovakians, among many others. The U.S. Census also discovered that during the 1920s Asians and African Americans had declined in population.

Arresting this increase, Montana had severe droughts in five of the years of the 1930s. Some 10,000 farms (or 18 percent) closed. The state's population was still predominantly male during the 1930s. It was also rather stagnant. Most farmers were staying in place, with few-if any-coming to the state to farm. Two small population migrations occurred, one from the smaller villages to the larger towns and cities, and the other from the dryland areas to irrigated (or irrigable) valleys. The Irish, English, Germans, Finns, and Italians were mostly in the industrialized cities, Norwegians and Danes primarily farmed the state's northeastern section, and French-Canadians lived in the northwestern section.

Like most, Montana suffered during the Great Depression of the 1930s. Demand for the state's metals dropped because of the nationwide lag in production. Drought contributed to the drop in farm income brought on by the Depression. Montana needed sizable federal assistance to emerge from the Depression. State and federal programs helped develop the state's resources. The 1940 building of the giant Fort Peck Dam provided jobs and badly needed water for irrigation. Other extremely helpful federal Public Works Administration and Works Progress Administration projects included insect control, irrigation, rural electrification, and soil conservation. Essential parks, recreational areas, and roads were also constructed. The state needed the help. In 1935, Montana had one of the West's highest rates (27.7 percent) of tenant farmers, an indication of the precariousness of the farming industry.

Montana's mostly rural (66.2 percent) 1940 population was 559,456, a tiny 1.9 percent increase since 1920s 548,889. In the 1940s, Montana was one of the least-populated states, with only 3.7 people per square mile compared to the national 41.3 average. The tourist industry (including dude ranches) was growing steadily but had not made stimulated strong population growth. The U.S. Census found that Montana had 16,841 American Indians; 1,120 African Americans; 508 Japanese; and 258 Chinese. Some 8,569 of the population had been born in Canada; 6,896 in Norway; 4,401 in Germany; and 4,084 in the Soviet Union.

Montana congresswoman Rankin won fame in 1941 as the only member of Congress to vote against U.S. entry into World War II. Rankin said she did not believe in war and could not vote for it. During 1943–1947, Montana had an influx of Hutterites (German-speaking Anabaptists) as a result of discriminatory legislation in Canada. They founded 22 communities with a population around 2,000. This group originally had been driven out of Russia because of military laws that did not respect their religious beliefs.

Butte, then the state's largest city with its 1945 population of 39,532, had a mix of ethnic groups compared to most other localities. This was mostly due to it being a mining center that was first settled in the 1860s by Irish, Welsh, and Cornish miners. Later, many other nationalities also came to work, especially from the Balkan nations. Butte then had prosperous neighborhoods of Chinese, Italians, Finns, and Germans. At this time, Great Falls had sizable populations of Yugoslavs and Scots. These cities markedly contrasted with Helena, the state capitol, whose 1945 population of 11,803 included very few foreign-born.

Montana's economy boomed during World War II (1939–1945). The state's meat and grain were in great demand, and its copper and other metals were utilized in the war effort. After the war, though, lower prices for grain greatly reduced agricultural income and the economy sagged. As a result, many moved from farming areas to the towns and cities to find jobs. Some small farming towns were abandoned and the state experienced out-migration.

Montana's Current Ancestry

In the twenty-first century, Montana has had a much higher percentage of Native Americans than most other states. This group's population has been steadily growing in the twentieth century compared to the general state population stagnation. By 1970, the American Indian population had grown to 27,130. In 2012, most lived on and adjacent to one of the state's seven reservations, and are the majority in most of these counties. Representing a mixed heritage, Montana's Native Americans are from 12 ethnolinguistic groups.

The state now remains primarily native-born. There are only 19,488 foreign-born residents of the state's 989,415 total in 2010, with the most born in Europe (33.7

percent) and Asia (27.3 percent). Almost 90 percent of residents are of European descent. German ancestry is the largest and Scandinavian ancestry dominates some northern and eastern prairie regions. Irish and English are the second- and third-largest European ancestries. Western Montana (e.g., Butte) has more varied ethnicity. There are also about 3,000 people with Filipino ancestry, the largest number of Asian Americans. Montana still has a large settlement of Hutterites, the nation's second most populous. The state's Hispanic population is mostly in the Billings area, where Mexican Americans have been for many years.

TOPICAL ESSAYS

RECENT POPULATION TRENDS

By most yardsticks, recent immigration to the state has been minimal. In the 1950s and 1960s, several large federal projects were built in Montana. Minuteman missiles were set up around Great Falls, and a number of dams were constructed on the Missouri River. None of these projects significantly increased the level of permanent population.

There were some positive trends. Urbanization had been continuing, albeit on a rather small scale. The loss of farming families from the eastern part of the state was slightly offset during this period by the growth of Havre, Glendive, and Billings. The state also went through a natural increase boom and had the country's eighth-highest birth rate in 1960.

Further, the state's downward population trend was also slowed by net in-migration. Montana had a fossil fuel deposits boom after the late 1970s international oil crisis. Prosperous coal strip mines stimulated boomtowns similar to earlier gold strikes. This could continue because 50 of the state's 56 counties had coal deposits.

Unfortunately, Montana's mining and smelting industry collapsed in the early 1980s. In 1980, the Anaconda smelter closed and many jobs ended. This helped to cause the state to lose population during the 1960–1987 period. This was typical of the Great Plains states, which were experiencing out-migration to the Sun Belt as well as the coastal and border states.

This falling trend was reversed somewhat in the late 1980s when a slump in California's economy led many to migrate to other western states like Montana. Partially as a result, Billings became a regional center again and gained population during the 1990s. The state's eastern section's ranching and farming areas merely maintained their population.

The state's population was not predicted to grow much in the next decades, and will get progressively grayer. According to some projections, in 2030, Montana will be one of the 10 states that has more individuals who are 65 and older than under 18. Montana also is projected to be one of only six where over one-fourth will be over 65 in 2030. The U.S. Census Bureau estimates the state's total population in 2030 to be 1,044,898. For the future, this fourth-largest state with the 44th-lowest population, as for many decades, will be dependent upon net natural increase and especially immigration for its subsistence and vitality.

Twenty-First Century Immigration Controversies

By all measures, legal and undocumented immigration to Montana in the past decade has been minimal. According to the U.S. Department of Homeland Security, legal immigrant admission to the state for 2001–2010 was 5,007. After 1965, the number of "green card" recipients who intended to reside in Montana constituted 33.2 percent of the admissions. During the 1965–1969 period, annual admissions averaged about 395 persons. The total admissions for 1965–2010 were 19,816, though the 1989–1991 data included former undocumented immigrants amnestied in 1986. According to 1991 Immigration and Naturalization Service data, there were 227 amnesty applicants from Montana (87 pre-1982 residents and 140 agricultural workers). During 2005–2010 period, annual admissions to Montana averaged 527. During the 1996–2005 period, the most immigrants to the state for residence came from Mexico (2,748), India (2,175), China (1,792), and the Soviet Union (1,258), according to the conservative, anti-immigrant group Federation for American Immigration Reform (FAIR).

The impact of these immigrants has, if anything, been very positive. In 2005, only 13.9 percent of immigrants had incomes below the poverty level, which is slightly below the state's 14.4 percent. Montana is one of 28 states to have a median household income below the national average: $39,301 compared to $46,326, and also below most other western states.

Refugee admission for 2000–2009 was granted to only 95 persons. Montana had only eight refugees in 2009, including one for asylum. This low level of refugee resettlement is because of lack of funding and relative absence of necessary institutions. The state's undocumented immigrant population was estimated by the conservative, anti-immigration group FAIR in 2010 to be approximately 5,000.

The only evidence that Montana is disadvantaged by foreign-born immigration stems chiefly from the state's not being a primary destination. A study in 2003 by the conservative, anti-immigrant group Center for Immigration Studies found Montana was one of the 16 states to lose one congressional seat in federal electoral reapportionment because of higher immigration elsewhere. Montana actually failed to gain a seat it would otherwise have gained through net natural increase. Immigrants are defined as naturalized American citizens, legal permanent residents, undocumented aliens, and those with long-term temporary visas.

Despite these relatively low levels of immigration and refugee resettlement, there have been recent protests and agitation. A 2010 Rasmussen Poll found that 65 percent of state's residents would support local passage of a version of Arizona's restrictive Senate Bill 1070 and 27 percent would oppose. A 2006 Montana State University Billings poll discovered that 68 percent believe that the government's efforts were not sufficient to prevent undocumented immigrants from entering the nation, and 68 percent disagree with legalizing the status of undocumented immigrants. The major statewide organization advocating immigration reform is the Montanans for Immigration Law Enforcement, located in Bozeman.

Unsurprisingly, Montana has joined the national embrace of ID cards. In 2011, by a two-to-one vote the Montana legislature passed House Bill 0178 requiring legal presence for driver's license applicants. This was a reversal of the legislature's voting unanimously to not implement REAL ID in 2008. The state also registered in 2011 with the U.S. Department of Homeland Security's Systematic Alien Verification for Entitlements (SAVE) system. SAVE is maintained to determine legal immigration status for benefit-issuing agencies, institutions, and licensing bureaus so that only those applicants entitled to benefits receive them.

The anti-undocumented immigrant advocates were incensed by the 2012 decision by the federal Customs and Border Protection agency to close nine Border Patrol stations including one in Billings. Citing financial constraints and the need to consolidate operations, the agency would relocate agents and support staffers closer to the border. The anti-immigrant group FAIR objected that the interior stations are a necessary "second line of defense" to catch undocumented immigrants who get beyond international borders. It remains to be seen whether the state will continue to move in this direction or will embrace immigration as it has done, however fitfully, in its history.

NOTABLE GROUPS

Montana Immigrant Justice Alliance

The Montana Immigrant Justice Alliance (MIJA) is a pro-immigrant group concerned about the growth of anti-immigrant sentiment since 2001, both in the state and nationwide. The acronym "MIJA" is similar to "mi hija" in Spanish (my daughter), indicating their commitment to keeping families intact. The group provides public education on issues affecting immigrants—particularly how recent state and local policies affect immigrants—and legal advocacy. Unlike other advocacy groups in the nation, this particular alliance takes a stronger, more critical stance against issues like racial profiling by the Montana police, human rights issues regarding immigrants in detention, and state and local laws that are unconstitutional. This group of legal advocates has filed suits against institutions violating equal protection and habeas corpus rights, for instance, and their website effectively documents immigrants' stories about these issues. Through a combination of pro bono legal services, lobbying, and direct service referral, this group also aims to help immigrants know their rights and to understand current legislation. Perhaps most importantly, while state and local discourse in the 2010s has been critical of immigrants, this group shifts the narrative and challenges these negative assessments, reminding all residents of the states about democracy and human rights.

BIBLIOGRAPHY

Astle, John. "Century of Butte Stories: St. Patrick's Day Riot in 1918." Coppercity.com. 2002. http://www.coppercity.com/memories/johnastle/st_patrick_day_1918.htm. Accessed March 25, 2014.

Barkwell, Lawrence. "John 'Johnny' Francis Grant, 1831–1907." http://www.scribd.com/doc/17259550/John-Francis-Grant-Metis-Rancher. Accessed March 25, 2014.

Billington, Ray Allen, and Martin Ridge. *Westward Expansion: A History of the American Frontier*. New York: Macmillan Publishing Company, 1982.

Camarota, Steven A., Dudley L. Poston Jr., and Amanda K. Baumle. "Remaking the Political Landscape: The Impact of Illegal and Legal Immigration on Congressional Apportionment." Center for Immigration Studies, 2003. http://www.cis.org/ImmigrationEffectCongressionalApportionment. Accessed March 25, 2014.

Cratty, Carol. "Nine Border Patrol Stations to Close; 41 Agents to Move to Posts Closer to Borders." CNN.com, 2012, http://articles.cnn.com/2012–07–09/us/us_border-patrol-stations_1_border-patrol-apprehensions-of-illegal-border-interior-stations. Accessed March 25, 2014.

Federal Writers' Project. *Montana: A State Guide Book*. New York: Hastings House, 1949.

Federation for American Immigration Reform. "Immigration Facts." FAIR, 2012. http://www.fairus.org/states/montana. Accessed March 25, 2014.

Federation for American Immigration Reform. "Montana Poll Data." FAIR, 2012. http://www.fairus.org/facts/states/poll_MT. Accessed March 25, 2014.

Fritz, Harry W., and Katherine Hansen. "A Brief History of Montana." Montana Historical Society. http://mhs.mt.gov/education/studentguide/HistoryOfMontana.asp. Accessed March 25, 2014.

Kephart, Janice. "Montana Adopts Legal-Presence Requirement of REAL ID Act." Center for Immigration Reform, 2011. http://www.cis.org/kephart/montana-real-id-legal-presence. Accessed March 25, 2014.

Kephart, Janice. "REAL ID Implementation Annual Report." Center for Immigration Reform, 2012. http://www.cis.org/real-id-implementation-report#7. Accessed March 25, 2014.

Levinson, Robert E. "Julius Basinski: Pioneer Montana Merchant." *Montana* 22 (Winter 1972): 60–68.

Malone, Michael P., and Richard B. Roeder. *Montana: A History of Two Centuries*. Seattle: University of Washington Press, 1976.

McManus, Sheila. "Mapping the Alberta-Montana Borderlands: Race, Ethnicity and Gender in the Late Nineteenth Century." *Journal of American Ethnic History* 20, no. 3 (2001): 71.

Merritt, Christopher W. "The Coming Man from Canton: Chinese Experience in Montana (1862–1943)." Unpublished Doctoral dissertation, University of Montana, 2010. http://etd.lib.umt.edu/theses/available/etd-06142010–161744/unrestricted/Merritt_Dissertation_Final.pdf. Accessed March 25, 2014.

Meyer, Garren. "A Culture History of the German Gulch Chinese." Unpublished Master of Arts Thesis, University of Montana, Department of Anthropology, 2001. http://etd.lib.umt.edu/theses/available/etd-06192012–215531/unrestricted/Norman_William_Thesis_FINAL.pdf. Accessed March 25, 2014.

Montana Historical Society. "Montana: Stories of the Land." 2008. http://mhs.mt.gov/education/textbook/Introduction1.asp. Accessed March 25, 2014.

Montana Immigrant Justice Alliance (MIJA). Montana Immigrant Justice Alliance (MIJA) Website. http://www.mija.org/. Accessed February 22, 2014.

Nugent, Walter. *Into the West: The Story of Its People.* New York: Alfred A. Knopf, 1999.

Proximity. "State Demographic Projections to 2030." Proximityone.com, 2012. http://proximityone.com/st0030.htm. Accessed March 25, 2014.

Radford, Dwight A. "History of Montana." *Red Book: American State, County, and Town Sources.* Ancestry.com, 2010. http://www.ancestry.com/wiki/index.php?title=Montana_Family_History_Research. Accessed March 25, 2014.

Reichert, Christiane. "Returning and New Montana Migrants: Socio-Economic and Motivational Differences." *Growth and Change* 32, no. 4 (2001): 447.

Schlesinger, Andrea Batista. "Pro-Immigrant Populism." *Nation* 284, no. 9 (2007): 6–8.

Schmalzbauer, Leah. "'Doing Gender,' Ensuring Survival: Mexican Migration and Economic Crisis in the Rural Mountain West." *Rural Sociology* 76, no. 4 (2011): 441–60.

Schmalzbauer, Leah. "Family Divided: The Class Formation of Honduran Transnational Families." *Global Networks* 8, no .3 (2008): 329–46.

Schneider, Carrie. "Remembering Butte's Chinatown." *Montana: The Magazine of Western History* 54, no. 2 (Summer 2004): 67–69.

Schwartz, J. "More Are Moving to Montana." *American Demographics* 14, no. 5 (1992): 12.

Thompson, Warren S., and P. K. Whelpton. "Changes in Regional and Urban Patterns of Population Growth." *American Sociological Review* 5, no. 6 (1940): 921–29.

Toole, K. Ross. *Twentieth-Century Montana: A State of Extremes.* Norman: University of Oklahoma Press, 1972.

U.S. Bureau of the Census. "American FactFinder." 2012. http://factfinder2.census.gov/faces/nav/jsf/pages/index.xhtml. Accessed March 25, 2014.

U.S. Bureau of the Census. "Characteristics of the Population." 2012. http://www2.census.gov/prod2/decennial/documents/33973538v2p4ch5.pdf. Accessed March 25, 2014.

U.S. Bureau of the Census and the U.S. Department of Commerce. "Median Income for 4-Person Families, by State." 2011. http://www.census.gov/hhes/www/income/data/statistics/4person.html. Accessed March 25, 2014.

U.S. Citizenship and Immigration Services. "SAVE." U.S. Department of Homeland Security, 2012. http://www.uscis.gov/portal/site/uscis/menuitem.eb1d4c2a3e5b9ac89243c6

a7543f6d1a/?vgnextoid=1721c2ec0c7c8110VgnVCM1000004718190aRCRD&vgn
extchannel=1721c2ec0c7c8110VgnVCM1000004718190aRCRD. Accessed March
25, 2014.

U.S. Department of Health and Human Services, Office of Refugee Resettlement.
"State Profiles 2007–2009: Montana." http://www.acf.hhs.gov/programs/orr/data
/StateProfiles07–09.pdf. Accessed March 25, 2014.

U.S. Department of Homeland Security. *2010 Yearbook of Immigration Facts*. Washington,
DC: Government Printing Office, 2011. http://www.dhs.gov/yearbook-immigration-
statistics. Accessed March 25, 2014.

27

NEBRASKA

Samantha Bryant

CHRONOLOGY

1803	The United States acquires land from France in the Louisiana Purchase, expanding the territorial possession of the United States from west of the Mississippi River to the border of the Rocky Mountains.
1854	Congress passes the Kansas-Nebraska Act, overturning the Missouri Compromise of 1820 and establishing the territories of Kansas and Nebraska. The Nebraska Territory holds a population of approximately 2,730 persons.
1854	Omaha is established. The city is incorporated in 1857 and serves as the territorial capital of Nebraska until statehood.
1864	The state legislature passes an act to incorporate the Nebraska Immigrant Association.
1867	United States admits Nebraska as a state.
1867	The state legislature moves the state capital from Omaha to Lincoln. Rail lines link Chicago to Omaha.
1869	The state legislature supports a charter establishing the state's flagship institution, the University of Nebraska.
1869–1870	In efforts to acquire cheap labor, the railroad company Union Pacific urges immigrant groups to relocate to Nebraska. Immigrants from Sweden and Nova Scotia and Russian German peoples settle in several Nebraskan counties such as Polk, Saunders, Colfax, and Sutton. Nebraska's vast agrarian landscape and homesteading opportunities lead to a rise in European immigration throughout the nineteenth century.

1870	Building begins on a rail line connecting Plattsmouth and Lincoln supported by the Burlington and Missouri River Railroad. Railroad companies as well as the state seek to facilitate commerce between rural, agricultural areas to budding urban centers to accrue profit. The Board of Immigration is created in an attempt to monitor state immigration.
1871	The state's House of Representatives votes in favor of impeaching Governor David Butler. Butler's opponents accuse him of accepting bribes and misappropriating funds for the university's construction.
1873	The Union Pacific Missouri River Bridge opens.
1873	The state legislature passes an act to establish a state bureau of immigration.
1890s	Nebraskan support for the People's Party significantly increases, appealing to immigrant and native laborers during a period of economic deflation and agricultural overproduction. In 1892, the People's Party National Convention meets in Omaha.
1898	Omaha hosts the Trans-Mississippi Exposition in order to demonstrate its urban growth and attract investment.
1909	A riot breaks out in South Omaha over the increased population of Greek immigrants laboring in the city's packing plants.
1910	Nebraska's German American Alliance is formed in an attempt to proliferate and facilitate German culture and community in the state.
1910	First sugar factory opens in Western Nebraska, employing largely Mexican and Mexican American laborers, or betabeleros.
1913	The state legislature approves the Mockett Law which enforces foreign language study in Nebraskan public, urban schools on an elective basis.
1917	In light of the United States' entrance in World War I in 1914, the Nebraska State Council of Defense is established following approval from the state legislature. The council places heavy restrictions on the display and cultivation of German identity in Nebraska. Loyalty oaths are enforced on immigrants of German descent in addition to the burning of German literature.
1918	The state legislature repeals the Mockett Law due to anti-German sentiment.
1920s	Ku Klux Klan groups emerge in response to postwar immigration, Catholicism, and sociocultural changes.
1943–1964	The Great Western Sugar Company contracts Mexican and Mexican American laborers under the Bracero Program.
1972	The state legislature approves the formation of the Nebraska Commission on Mexican Americans in an effort to aid the state's growing Latino/a American population.

1975	Farmland Foods, a pork-processing company opens, attracting an increased number of immigrant workers to Crete, Nebraska.
2000	The state legislature approves the creation of the Task Force on the Productive Integration of the Immigration Workforce Population in order to evaluate Nebraska's public policy concerning immigrant labor and communities.
2006	Legislative Bill (LB) 239 passes, giving undocumented immigrant students who qualify access to in-state tuition rates.
2009	The state legislature passes LB 403 which authorizes federal background checks on all individuals applying for state benefits. This law aims to check applicants' immigration status.
2010	Fremont passes an ordinance on undocumented immigration. The ban includes immigrant employment and the renting of property.
2013	The Nebraska Supreme Court votes in favor of undocumented immigrants' reception of worker's compensation benefits.
2013	An anti-immigrant protest is held in Omaha.

HISTORICAL OVERVIEW

"Beautiful Nebraska, Peaceful Prairieland"

Located in the American heartland, Nebraska has long attracted immigrants due to the state's history of economic development and opportunities for land acquisition. Since its admission to statehood in 1867, immigration in Nebraska remains a weighty issue economically and politically. Urban areas such as Omaha exhibit demographically diverse populations, a sharp contrast to the state's largely ethnically homogenous rural communities. The historic presence of multiple ethnic groups centers on employment opportunities in agricultural, cattle-raising, and meatpacking industries. Immediately following World War II, Nebraska's largely agricultural-based economy recovered due to improvements in crop production techniques and technologies. Soybean and sorghum production grew during the postwar period. In addition, the raising of livestock increased, attracting industries such as Farmland Foods to the state in 1975. However, the state's rural population and the number of farms experienced a decline, leading to the development of urban fringe communities along the immediate outskirts of the cities. Urban areas became sites for emergent manufacturing industries in the 1950s and 1960s. Cities like Omaha and Lincoln experienced population increases by 30 to 50 percent and served as centers for cultural and ethnic diversity. The decreasing number of farms in Nebraska from the World War II era to the 1970s attracted foreign-born populations to the state's major cities due to employment and housing opportunities.

During the postwar period, the demographics of Nebraska's foreign-born population shifted from persons of European origins prominent in the late nineteenth

On May 20, 1862, President Abraham Lincoln signed the Homestead Act, giving 160 acre freehold farms from the public domain to citizens who would live on them for five years. Settlers, like the family shown here in Custer County, Nebraska, left the East to pioneer in frontier country. Between 1862 and 1900, possibly 400,000 families received cheap land from the government. Opportunities such as these attracted European immigrants to this area. (Bettmann/Corbis)

century to that of Latin America and Asia. In 2000, Latino/as comprised 53.6 percent of the state's foreign-born population and Asians comprised 25.7 percent. Of Nebraska's total immigrant population, 57 percent hailed from El Salvador, Mexico, Central America, and the Caribbean islands. Overall, the foreign-born population in Nebraska has increased over the past decade according to estimates provided in the 2000 and 2010 U.S. Census from 74,638 to approximately 109,472 persons. Recent state legislation has sought to approach issues stemming from the diverse cultural, economic, and political needs of the new immigrant populations. These efforts seek to provide services such as immigrant access to policy benefits and legal counsel for undocumented immigrants. Federal legislation and political trends have inspired debates concerning the relationship between the foreign-born and native-born populations as well as the role of diversity on the state and local levels.

The following section is designed to contextualize immigration politics and economic development in Nebraska since 1945. Discussions surround the complexity of state and local developments on immigration in accordance with federal policies. The first half of the section establishes the changing nature of the foreign-born population in Nebraska in addition to the rural–urban divide present in the state's approach to immigration and ethnic diversity. Urban measures increasingly seek to incorporate immigrant populations into the local community with the creation of commissions to represent minority groups in the state legislature. The relationship between history and contemporary politics receives significant focus. The second half of the section delves into the more recent developments of state and local immigration legislation during the late 1990s and 2000s. The involvement of local communities on Nebraska's immigration policy points to the rural–urban divide concerning diversification. The results of state and local government actions have a direct impact on the reception of foreign-born populations in Nebraska's sociocultural and political landscapes.

CHANGING TIDES: IMMIGRATION IN NEBRASKA SINCE 1945

Throughout the nineteenth century, European immigration to Nebraska remained consistently high. The transcontinental railroad and agricultural sectors drew populations such as Czechs, Germans, and the Swedish to rural areas. Between 1910 and 1920, however, Nebraska experienced a decrease in its total foreign-born population by approximately 14 percent (U.S. Census Bureau 1920). Particularly, the 1910 "foreign-born white," or native European/Mexican, population consisted of 175,865, dropping to 149,652 in 1920. In 1920, immigrant groups deemed "non-white," such as populations from India, China, and Japan, composed of 3,911 peoples. The largest groups within the foreign-born community came from Germany, Sweden, Czechoslovakia, Denmark, and Russia.

A correlation between urban space and the concentration of immigrant populations began to emerge between the 1920s and 1930s due largely to the Great Depression. In Omaha, 35,381 of the total 191,601 population consisted of "foreign-born whites" with only 240 identifying as non-white foreign-born individuals, according to the 1920 U.S. Census. However, a comparison in 1930 yielded 10.1 percent of the state's total urban population comprising of immigrants with 7.4 percent residing in rural areas. The U.S. Census further deconstructed the rural population into farm and non-farm categories. More "foreign-born whites" resided in non-farm sectors rather than on actual farms despite the role of farms as places of employment. Between the 1930s and 1940s, the Mexican immigrant population in Nebraska remained relatively small, actually decreasing from 3,943 in 1930 to 1,773 in 1940. Due to the ecological and economic devastation in the Midwest from the 1920s through the 1940s, farms became unreliable as sources of work for immigrant laborers. In addition, federal immigration legislation placed constraints on which immigrant groups entered the United States.

After World War II, Nebraska's manufacturing, construction, retail trade, and service industries began to boom. Between 1940 and 1950, Lincoln's total population increased by 20.6 percent and Omaha's by 12.2 percent. In all, Nebraska's urban inhabitants steadily increased during the immediate postwar period, contrasting with the national trend. Urbanized yet incorporated fringe communities grew in an effort to accommodate the population shift, particularly in the counties of Lancaster, Sapry, and Douglas near Lincoln and Omaha. Rural territory increasingly declined in populace from 1940 to 1960.The number of farms and farm residencies dropped after World War II. In contrast to the national development of suburb communities, Nebraska experienced a reverse trend with individuals moving to the cities of Lincoln and Omaha in order to find employment and housing.

The demographic landscape of Nebraska has shifted notably since the 1960s. As the state population continued to diversify from the 1980s through the 2000s, the number of immigrants entering Nebraska with U.S. citizenship decreased noticeably. Prior to 1980, an estimated 84.1 percent of the foreign-born population entered as citizens while, in 2011, this number dropped to 15.5 percent. Similar changes are reflected nationally with a gradual decrease in immigrants entering the United States without citizenship. The foreign-born population in Nebraska experienced a 55.6 percent increase between the years 2000 and 2011. Despite this growth, the immigrant population consisted of only 6.3 percent of the total state population. Between the years 1990 and 2011, the country of origin for the most populous immigrant groups in Nebraska has also changed from Mexico (14.6 percent), Germany (9.3 percent), and Soviet Russia (7.6 percent) to Mexico (41.1 percent), Vietnam (6.6 percent), and El Salvador (3.7 percent). Nationally in 2011, Nebraska ranked 27th out of the 50 states and the District of Columbia in the percentage of immigrant population within the total population.

State and local government discussions concerning immigration policy emphasize the cost of immigration in areas such as "education, healthcare, and law enforcement systems" (Ashford and Trout 2008). The immigrant population in Nebraska contributes significantly to the state's service economy. In 2000, 80.4 percent of the meat-processing industry employed foreign-born laborers. While Nebraska spent $1.6 million on the state's immigrant population, the hypothetical loss of the entire foreign-born population on the state's economy would cost approximately $13.4 million. State spending largely occurred in the urban regions of Lancaster, Sarpy, and Douglas counties during the mid-2000s. The clear presence of immigrant labor on the state's economy has presented questions for state and local governments, specifically regarding the immigrant population's sociocultural incorporation to local communities and their access to public benefits. In 2006, the foreign-born population remained 8.75 percent of Nebraska's production, accounting for 7.4 percent "of total income earners" in the state (Ashford and Trout 2008). While immigrants comprise 51.6 percent of the total working-age population without high-school degrees, 4.5 percent of immigrants acquired a college education. However, approximately 20.7 percent of college-educated immigrants in Nebraska remained underutilized, employed in unskilled occupations such as housekeeping. Studies conducted by the state legislature revealed relationship between a larger immigrant labor pool and positive contributions to the market.

In 2006, the Nebraska state legislature enacted LB 239, a modified application of the federal government's Development, Relief, and Education for Alien Minors Act. While the state approved undocumented immigrants' access to in state tuition rates, stipulations remained intact such as residency, guardian's residency, and the signing of a pledge to apply for "permanent residen[cy] as soon as he or she was eligible" (Ashford and Trout 2008). Approximately 10.5 percent of the immigrant population in Nebraska consisted of minors with a growing number of minors living with "at least one immigrant parent or guardian in 2011" (Migration Policy Institute, "Social and Demographic Characteristics" 2013). Documentation of immigrant status persists in the application status for state healthcare and human services benefits such as Medicaid and food stamps.

TOPICAL ESSAYS

Latino/a Immigrant Community

The Latino/a community serves as Nebraska's fastest-growing immigrant group between the mid-1980s and the 2000s. Specifically, the population grew during the years 2000 and 2010 by 70 percent (Ramos et al. 2013, 1). The Latino/a immigrant population increased by 11 percent between the periods of 1980 to 1984 and 1985 to 1989. Demographically, the Latino/a immigrant population in Nebraska remains younger in age when compared to other immigrant groups with a median age of 22.8. In terms of birth countries, "approximately three-fourths of the . . . Latino population is of Mexican origin followed by people from Central America and the Caribbean" (Ramos et al. 2013, 4). Largely, immigrants from Mexico have arrived to the state from rural communities in Mexico and comprise a great proportion of the state's farm-working population. The growing presence of the Latino/a foreign-born population in Nebraska has had a notable impact on the demographic composition of the state, political discourse, and economic growth.

In the 1990s, the correlation between farm jobs and economic prosperity dropped significantly, reflected in part by the employment of low-skill Latino/a immigrant laborers. The driving forces of rural poverty revolve around meager wages and the temporary nature of farmwork in the United States. The position of these immigrant laborers has led to discussion by groups affiliated with the University of Nebraska-Lincoln as well as the Latino American Commission concerning the health and safety of Latino/a immigrant farmworkers, particularly on issues of injury and illness. Since the 1990s, structural changes in rural economies such as the increasing use of technological devices and the corresponding loss of rural jobs, while more were available in urban service and management positions, have contributed to an increase in homelessness among Latino working-age males in rural areas. Of Nebraska's working age Latino/a immigrant population, 50.3 percent work in the fields of production, natural resources, construction, maintenance, and meatpacking. Despite these setbacks, the Latino/a immigrant population remains a dominant force in the growing economic prosperity of the state, specifically in the aforementioned sectors. The city of Lexington, Nebraska, attracts a large number of immigrant laborers with its Iowa Beef Processors plant, turning a tide from the 1980s that led to a sharp decrease in population. Between the years 1990 and 1992, the Latino/a community encompassed approximately 44 percent of the Iowa Beef Processors's new hires in Lexington, most of them males. In 2011, approximately 24.7 percent of Nebraska's foreign-born population from Latin American countries lived below the poverty line. Linguistically, 26.6 percent of households that only spoke Spanish lived in poverty. Comparatively, the median income gap between Latino/as and non-Latino whites in 2010 remained approximately $12,916. Unemployment in the Latino/a community between 2009 and 2010 increased from 8.30 to 11.30 percent. The nature and conditions of certain occupations that largely employ Latino/a immigrant population has led to questions surrounding the group's access to healthcare benefits, education, and everyday life necessities.

Organizations such as the Latino American Commission have sought to address the political and cultural needs of the immigrant group given its significant presence in Nebraska. The organization, created in 1972 under LB 1081, was designed as an advocacy group for Latino/a immigrants and Latino Americans—the first of its kind in the United States. Following World War II, Latino/a immigrants found growing opportunities for employment in Nebraska with the state's increasing number of sugar beet factories, meatpacking plants, and railroad centers. Thus, the population moved from the outskirts of the state to urban and rural areas in the state. The influence of Cesar Chavez's migrant labor movement during the 1960s and 1970s influenced advocacy and political mobilization of the Latino/a immigrant population in the Midwest. The purpose of the commission centered on addressing the place of the Latino/a community in state and local government issues such as public benefits, healthcare, and education. Currently, the commission offers programs, training, and legal counsel for the population. Other advocacy groups like Proteus, Nebraska Equal Rights Commission, and the American Civil Liberties Union, Nebraska, have also sought to focus on the interests of the Latino/a immigrant and Latino American communities in the state. Education, family resources, and healthcare benefits have become the focus of contested legal and public issues in Nebraska, especially during the mid-1990s and 2000s with the increasing visibility of the foreign-born population.

The growing presence of the Latino/a immigrant population in Nebraska has also made an important impact on the state's public education systems.

Language proficiency remained a matter of attention in 2011 when 74.2 percent of Spanish-speaking persons over the age of five maintained limited English language skills. Limited English language proficiency presents problems in regard to educational attainment and employment. According to 2011 U.S. Census data, individuals speaking exclusively Spanish in their household remained least likely—in comparison to other language groups—to graduate from high school. Approximately 49.6 percent did not finish high school, 23.2 percent completed their high school education, 16.2 percent acquired some college education, and only 10.9 percent of Spanish speakers acquired a bachelor's degree in 2011. Compared with native Indo-European, Asian, Pacific Island, and English language speakers, Spanish speakers remained least likely to acquire a college education. With 35.0 percent of the foreign-born, Spanish-speaking population in Nebraska maintaining limited English proficiency, state and local governments have sought to provide language training and programs to urban and rural communities in order to address the issue. In 2000, over 71.8 percent of Nebraska's foreign-born Latino/a population did not graduate from high school as opposed to 26.3 percent of U.S. born Latino/as. Linguistic and cultural awareness serve as key elements in increasing the rate of educational attainment in the Latino immigrant community.

Asian Immigrant Community

Between the years 2005 and 2007, the Asian foreign-born population in Nebraska increased by 35 percent, almost 19 percent higher than the national average in 2006. The largest groups within the population consist of Vietnamese, Chinese, Asian Indian, Filipino/a, Japanese, and Korean persons. The Asian immigrant population increased from 1.3 percent in 2000 to 1.7 percent in 2007 with a growth in 7,789 individuals within that time frame. The Vietnamese, Chinese, and Asian Indian community comprise 71 percent of the entire Asian population in the state. In 2006, the U.S. Census Bureau reported that the Vietnamese population in Nebraska consisted of 30.7 percent in comparison to the national 11.3 percent estimate. Within the foreign-born population, approximately 32.3 percent of Nebraska's Asian immigrant population was naturalized, while 38.2 percent did not acquire citizenship status. These numbers have made the Asian community the second-fastest-growing immigrant group behind the Latino/a population in the state.

In terms of population distribution, the Second Congressional District contained a vast majority of the state's Asian population with First Congressional District coming in second. The Second Congressional District includes the city of Omaha and Congressional District consists of the state capital of Lincoln. In 2006, 58.1 percent of the state's Vietnamese population resided in First

Congressional District, 35.5 percent in the rural Third Congressional District, and 8.5 percent in Second Congressional District. The Second Congressional District maintained a high population of Chinese (29.9 percent) and Asian Indian (26.5 percent) peoples. The rural region of Nebraska only included 12.4 percent of the state's total Asian foreign-born population. Urban districts containing Omaha and Lincoln remained significantly higher in Asian immigrant residency.

Nebraska's Asian population remains a notable presence in the state's workforce, especially in management and professional occupations. In the mid-2000s, 50.1 percent of the state's Asian population aged 16 and older acquired employment in the field of management and 26.1 percent in "production, transportation, and material moving" (Schaefer et al. 2008, 21). In comparison to the Latino/a community, the Asian population in Nebraska did not constitute a high proportion of workers in occupations such as fishing, construction, farming, and maintenance work. Approximately 74 percent of the state's Asian population remained in the workforce in 2006, while roughly 5 percent were unemployed. In 2011, the Asian immigrant population comprised 24.5 percent of Nebraska's total foreign-born and civilian employed labor force.

The growth of the Asian immigrant population in Nebraska has also had an impact on the demographics of the state's public education system and institutions of higher education. In regard to language skills, Japanese and Chinese immigrant groups maintain the highest percentage of English proficiency in non-English-dominant households among persons aged five and older. The Vietnamese population in Nebraska, however, retains over 59.7 percent of persons with limited English proficiency in non-English households. In 2011, 73.7 percent of foreign-born workers that utilized Asian and Pacific Islands languages in their household were part of the Nebraska workforce. Language attainment plays a significant role on the level of education obtained by the Asian immigrant population in the state. In general, the distribution of the Asian population within the Nebraska educational system consisted of 7.4 percent enrollment in nursery school and kindergarten, 30.0 percent in elementary school, 20.8 percent in high school, and 41.8 percent in college and graduate school. Approximately 17 percent of the Asian population did not complete their secondary education, according to the 2006 American Community Survey. A gender gap exists in the population aged 25 and over concerning the attainment of secondary education: 23.9 percent of females in the population did not complete high school as compared to 9.9 percent of males. In addition, 76.1 percent of females in the group graduated "high school or higher" with 90.1 percent of males achieving the same level of education. Gender, language, and cultural outreach remain key factors in addressing the educational needs of Nebraska's foreign-born Asian population and its diverse communities.

CZECH IMMIGRANT COMMUNITY

The Czech population in Nebraska has served as a fixture in the state's foreign-born population even after World War II despite no longer reaching such high numbers once exhibited at the turn of the century. Drought, immigration legislation, and economic depression during the 1920s and 1930s led to a decrease in the Czech population in rural regions. In 1948, a communist coup took hold in Czechoslovakia, leading to modest immigration to the state's urban areas. In 1950, Douglas County housed a vast percentage of the Czech immigrant population, demonstrating the eastward movement of the Czech community in Nebraska away from the farmland of rural areas to the urbanized East. During the 1960s, heritage chapters emerged which were dedicated to preserving the history, language, and traditions of the Czech population after successful festivals in Omaha and Wilbur such as the formation of Nebraska Czechs Incorporated in 1963. Immigration from Central and Eastern Europe reduced significantly during the postwar period in favor of a vastly growing foreign-born population hailing from different countries within Latin America.

The rise of computerized technology and mass media outlets has contributed to the loss of ethnic cultures and traditions, specifically within the Czech community. As the demographics of the Nebraskan immigrant community changes, the Old World communities from Central and Eastern Europe have largely disseminated into the foreground. The Czech language has also decreased in the state. Slavic speakers consisted of approximately 1.6 percent of Nebraska's foreign-born population over the age of five in 2011. However, in comparison to numerous Spanish-speaking immigrants in Nebraska, Slavic language speakers express a high proficiency in English, approximately 81.2 percent. In contrast to other foreign-born communities, Czech immigrants do not remain as isolated in terms of language, especially since Czech households also utilize English. However, rural communities appear to preserve Czech culture more so than in urban areas due to the isolation of rural communities. According to the 1990 U.S. Census, a high proportion of the Czech population resided in the eastern half of the state with 25 percent of five counties in the state identifying largely as Czech.

FREMONT IMMIGRATION ORDINANCE

In June 2010, a petition circulated and was passed by the residents of Fremont, Nebraska, launching community discussion and action concerning immigration in the city. The ordinance in question, Ordinance No. 5165, "prohibit[s] the harboring of illegal aliens or hiring of undocumented aliens, providing definitions, making provision for occupancy licenses, providing judicial process, [and] repealing conflicting provisions" (Ordinance No. 5165). The ordinance targeted the undocumented, foreign-born population and the group's access to employment and property. Particularly, the resolution targeted businesses in Fremont and encouraged the utilization of the E-Verify Program in making employment decisions. The Immigration Reform and Control Act of 1985 and the Illegal Immigration Reform and Immigration Responsibility Act of 1996 served as the legal basis of ordinance's provisions on businesses' employment of undocumented immigrant laborers. Provisions surrounding property leasing and rentership targeted landlords and businesses that knowingly allowed undocumented immigrants to reside in a city-dwelling unit (Ordinance No. 5165). The amendments described in the ordinance were passed on February 28, 2012. While the provisions concerning housing required federal approval, the business portion of the resolution took effect on March 5, 2012. On June 28, 2013, the U.S. Eighth Circuit Court of Appeals ruled in favor of the Fremont ordinance on immigration.

Despite the ordinance's approval by a majority of the city's voters, civil rights and immigrant rights organizations voiced their opposition, seeking to appeal the resolution. Three groups, the Fair Housing Center of Nebraska-Iowa, the National Fair Housing Alliance, and National Council of La Raza, filed a court brief in September 2012 opposing the ordinance's anti-immigrant language and its violation of the Fair Housing Act. The American Civil Liberties Union and the Mexican American Legal Defense and Educational Fund have continued their legal battle after the June 2013 U.S. Court of Appeals decision. Attorneys for the groups requested an "en banc" rehearing of the case, declaring that the ordinance targets the Latino/a community in Fremont. The Latino/a community is the city's foreign-born group in terms of population.

Immigrant Population Outlook

Cultural awareness and community-based organizations have increased from the 1960s into the 2000s in an effort to meet the growing needs of diverse ethnic groups. Specifically, federal research and departments such as the Office of Minority Health revealed goals in a 1999 report that planned to raise cultural and linguistic awareness in the public health sector. Organizations in Nebraska like the Community Action Partnership of Mid-Nebraska and the Community Action Partnership of Western Nebraska addressed the healthcare and housing needs of the immigrant community. In an effort to meet the National Culturally and Linguistically Appropriate Services standards, the Community Action Partnership of Mid-Nebraska began offering the Clinic of Good Health service in Gibbon and Lexington, Nebraska. The service provided a culturally and linguistically educated staff and maintained strategies in effort to reach the immigrant population in the region. However, issues regarding funding led to the service shutting down in 2011, leaving 500 to 600 patrons without access to affordable, culturally

State senator Charlie Jansssen of Fremont, second left, Jeremy Jensen, third left, and John Wiegert, center, celebrate with other activists in Fremont, Nebraska, on February 11, 2014, after city voters decided by voting "no" to uphold the law designed to bar immigrants from renting homes if they don't have legal permission to be in the United States. (AP Photo/ Nati Harnik)

oriented health care. Funding and grants continue to serve as the linchpin for many immigrants in receiving appropriate healthcare and community services, especially in light of the recession of the late 2000s.

Language proficiency in English has remained a goal for state and local governments, pointing to the increase in linguistic diversity in Nebraska. The 2011 Limited English Proficiency Plan sought to identify immigrants with low English language skills in order to improve access to employment and education. The primary language groups that the government plan targets are Spanish and Vietnamese speakers. Based on the results of the 2010 American Community Survey, 52,371 Spanish speakers and 3,917 Vietnamese speakers reported that their household solely utilized their native tongue, speaking English "less than very well" (American Community Survey, "Nebraska," 2010). The number of languages represented/offered by the state plan has increased from four languages in 2000 to eleven languages in 2009. With the increase in immigration, linguistic isolation serves as a problem in the workforce population. Between the years 2005 and 2009, the workforce in Lincoln comprised 10,470 immigrant laborers that only spoke their native language. The largest of these groups remains the Latino/a community. Lincoln reported a 98 percent increase and Omaha reported a 91 percent increase in the number of Spanish-speaking workers between 2000 and 2010. In turn, the state's Workforce Training Program has increased its grant funding to include Spanish, English as a second language, and cultural awareness programs and training.

Nebraska's public education system reflects the growing presence of the foreign-born community as well as the state and local governments' need to address the specific concerns of the immigrant community in the classroom. According to the state's yearly report card, student membership has increased within the Latino/a community from the 2010–2011 school year (47,836) to the 2012–2013 school year (51,017). Within the same year, the Asian student population in the Nebraska public school system also increased from approximately 6,000 students to 6,621. The percentage of the state's students receiving English as second language aid dropped slightly from 2011–2012 (6.47 percent) to 2012–2013 (5.96 percent) due to government cutbacks. Despite the drop, English Language Learners (ELLs) between grades 3rd and 11th increased their proficiency in reading from the 2009–2010 (36 percent) to the 2012–2013 (54 percent) academic years. Science scores for the population, however, remained low between the 2011–2012 (27 percent) and 2012–2013 (26 percent) academic years. Projections based on data trends between 1995 and 2005 indicate the narrowing of the gender gap among female and male foreign-born students in the state's public and private postsecondary institutions. Full-time enrollment has steadily decreased among male foreign-born students from 61.9 percent in 1995 to 57.0 percent in 2005. The opposite is revealed from full-time female foreign-born students from 38.1 percent to 43.0 percent between 1995 and 2005. The gender gap among female and male foreign-born students remains smaller in terms of part-time enrollment in the state's postsecondary institutions. In 2005, male enrollment consisted of approximately 56.0 percent and female enrollment 44.0 percent among foreign-born students. The overall percentage of foreign-born college degree recipients in Nebraska between the years 2000 and 2011 grew by roughly 67.6 percent. Despite overall growth, state government studies reflect a rising need for language and educational programs to prevent the retention of immigrant students as well as training the population for the workforce.

Organizations and institutions around the state have sought to answer the need for legal counsel and training sessions regarding state and federal immigration legislation. As federal, state, and local governments approach immigration legislation differently, facilities like the Immigration Clinic at the University of Nebraska-Lincoln offer legal counsel and information concerning resources and agencies for low-income immigrant families and individuals. Many church organizations provide social services for immigrants such as language services, representation in asylum cases, and assistance with legal paperwork and forms. Most notably, the nonprofit organization Nebraska Appleseed serves as a vocal advocate of immigration reform, specifically surrounding issues of economic justice, health care, child welfare, and workers' rights.

As the immigrant population continues to grow, the foreign-born population will become more politicized and mobilized. As a dominant presence in the immigrant population, the Latino/a community have formed commissions, organizations, and labor unions in an effort to vocalize advocacy for immigration reform. In the 2004 general election, the Latino/a population eligible to vote turned out by roughly 70 percent. Voter registration and civic engagement remain key elements in establishing an immigrant voice in Nebraskan politics. According to census-based projections, the Latino/a community in Nebraska will grow to represent roughly 20 percent of the state's total population by 2025 as compared to only 7 percent in 2006. The Asian-born population entering Nebraska between 1990 and 1999 comprised 41.9 percent and in the 2000s an additional 29.9 percent increased. In 2006, the Vietnamese population (6.9 percent) and the Chinese population (4.7 percent) largely encompassed the total Asian foreign-born community. The significant increase in the immigrant population from 1990 to 2006 remained so dramatic that Nebraska ranked seventh in the nation for percentage increase in its foreign-born population. Thus, politicization, particularly on immigrant rights and legislation, has grown noticeably since the 1990s and is expected to continue.

NOTABLE GROUPS

HEARTLAND WORKERS CENTER

For approximately 20 years, the Heartland Workers Center has served the Latino/a immigrant community in Omaha and throughout the Midwest. The center's mission centers on encouraging worker equality, cultural preservation of the Latino/a community, and civic leadership. The organization offers programs and workshops providing the laborer community with a skill set necessary to facilitate meetings and conduct research on issues relating to their community and livelihood. In addition, the Heartland Workers Center provides workshops and training on immigrant voting rights as well as gender-specific issues. The center is also a member of the National Alliance of Latin American and Caribbean Communities. In recent years, the Heartland Workers Center participated in a rally for immigration reform in Lincoln on April 4, 2013. Specifically, the organization along with an estimated 40 others sought to approach the issue of citizenship for un-naturalized immigrants currently residing in Nebraska. Throughout the year, the center supports events and rallies such as family marches. Family marches serve as a means of protest on issues of deportation, improving immigration reform, and keeping immigrant families in Nebraska and the United States together.

BIBLIOGRAPHY

American Community Survey. "Nebraska." 2010. http://factfinder2.census.gov/faces/nav /jsf/pages/community_facts.xhtml#none. Accessed October 18, 2013.

Anders, Tisa. "*Betabeleros* and the Western Nebraska Sugar Industry: An Early Twentieth-Century History." In L. Allegro, and A. G. Wood, eds. *Latin American Migration to the U.S. Heartland: Changing Social Landscapes in Middle America.* Urbana: University of Illinois Press, 2013, pp. 42–66.

Ashford, Brad (Senator), and Stacey Trout. "Review of State and Local Approaches to Immigration Policy." 2008. http://nlcs1.nlc.state.ne.us/epubs/L3750/B054–2008.pdf. Accessed October 9, 2013.

Beck, Margery A. "3 Groups Join in Opposing Fremont Immigration Law." *Lincoln Journal Star,* September 6, 2012. http://journalstar.com/news/state-and-regional/govt-and-politics/groups-join-in-opposing-fremont-immigration-law /article_19e202e4–58ba-5f20-ac3b-9ba6c02a491e.html. Accessed October 5, 2013.

Benjamin-Alvarado, Jonathan. "Latino Political Participation in Nebraska: The Challenge of Enhancing Voter Mobilization and Representation." Office of Latino/Latin American Studies. 2006. http://nlcs1.nlc.state.ne.us/epubs/U7090/B002.0003–2006.pdf. Accessed October 7, 2013.

Bitzes, John G. "The Anti-Greek Riot of 1909—South Omaha." *Nebraska History* 51 (1970): 199–224.

Coordinating Commission for Postsecondary Education. "Total Enrollment by Race/Ethnicity and by Gender." 2006. http://www.ccpe.state.ne.us/PublicDoc/Ccpe/Reports /FactLook/95–05/SectionA/text/FL_95–05_Sec_A.5_TotCt_by_Race-Gender.pdf. Accessed October 5, 2013.

"Court: Undocumented Immigrant Entitled to Workers' Comp." *World-Herald Bureau,* January 5, 2013. http://www.immigrationadvocates.org/nonprofit/news /article.458431-Court_Undocumented_immigrant_entitled_to_workers_comp. Accessed October 7, 2013.

Davis, Roger P. "'Service Not Power': The Early Years of the Nebraska Commission on Mexican-Americans, 1971–1975." *Nebraska History* 89 (2008): 67–83.

Dillingham, William P. "Reports of the Immigration Commission." U.S. Government Printing Office. 1911. http://www.ebrary.com/stanford/Dillingham1.html. Accessed October 11, 2013.

Ference, Gregory C. "Slovak Immigration to the United States in Light of American, Czech, and Slovak History." *Nebraska History* 74, nos. 3 and 4 (Fall/Winter 1993): 130–35.

Gaber, Sharon L., and Rodrigo Cantarero. "Hispanic Migrant Laborer Homelessness in Nebraska: Examining Agricultural Restructuring as One Path to Homelessness." *Social Thought & Research* 20, no. 1/2 (1997): 55–72.

Gouveia, Lourdes, and Donald D. Stull. "Latino Immigrants, Meatpacking, and Rural Communities: A Case Study of Lexington, Nebraska." Julian Samora Research Institute.

1997. http://www.jsri.msu.edu/upload/research-reports/rr26.pdf. Accessed October 7, 2013.

Gouveia, Lourdes, and Mary Ann Powell, with research assistance by Esperance Camargo, data analysis by Jerry Deichert. "Educational Achievement and the Successful Integration of Latinos in Nebraska: A Statistical Profile to Inform Policies and Programs." Office of Latino/Latin American Studies. 2005. http://nlcs1.nlc.state.ne.us/epubs/M1500/B010–2005.pdf. Accessed October 11, 2013.

Heartland Workers Center. 2011. http://www.heartlandworkerscenter.org/. Accessed October 4, 2013.

Heineman, Dave (Governor). "Undocumented Immigration Bill Takes Effect Later This Year." 2009. http://www.governor.nebraska.gov/columns/2009/04_09/17_Immigration_Takes_Effect.html. Accessed September 22, 2013.

Hovey, Art. "Fremont and Nebraska Look Ahead after Immigration Vote." *Lincoln Journal Star*, June 23, 2010. http://journalstar.com/news/state-and-regional/nebraska/fremont-and-nebraska-look-ahead-after-immigration-vote/article_106539b0–7e5a-11df-9b48–001cc4c03286.html. Accessed October 7, 2013.

Latino American Commission. 2011. http://www.latinoac.nebraska.gov/about.htm. Accessed October 11, 2013.

Library of Congress. "Kansas-Nebraska Act: Primary Documents in American History." 2010. http://www.loc.gov/rr/program/bib/ourdocs/kansas.html. Accessed September 19, 2013.

Luebke, Frederick C. "The German-American Alliance in Nebraska, 1910–1917." *Nebraska History* 49 (1968): 165–85.

Luebke, Frederick C. *Nebraska: An Illustrated History*. 2nd ed. Lincoln: University of Nebraska Press, 2005.

Martin, Philip, and J. Edward Taylor. "Farm Employment, Immigration, and Poverty: A Structural Analysis." *Journal of Agricultural and Resource Economics* 28, no. 2 (August 2003): 349–63.

Migration Policy Institute. "Nebraska: Income & Poverty." *MPI Data Hub*. 2013. http://www.migrationinformation.org/datahub/state4.cfm?ID=NE. Accessed October 5, 2013.

Migration Policy Institute. "Nebraska: Language & Education." *MPI Data Hub*. 2013. http://www.migrationinformation.org/datahub/state2.cfm?ID=NE. Accessed October 5, 2013.

Migration Policy Institute. "Nebraska: Social & Demographic Characteristics." *MPI Data Hub*. 2013. http://www.migrationinformation.org/datahub/state.cfm?ID=NE. Accessed October 5, 2013.

Migration Policy Institute. "Nebraska: Workforce." *MPI Data Hub*. 2013. http://www.migrationinformation.org/datahub/state3.cfm?ID=NE. Accessed October 5, 2013.

Nebraska Department of Education. "2012–2013 State of the Schools Report: A Report on Nebraska Public Schools." 2013. http://reportcard.education.ne.gov/Default_State.aspx?AgencyID=00–0000–000. Accessed October 5, 2013.

Olson, James C., and Ronald C. Naugle. *History of Nebraska*. 3rd ed. Lincoln: University of Nebraska Press, 1997.

"Omaha Rally Protests Immigration Policies." *Lincoln Journal Star*, September 13, 2013. http://journalstar.com/news/state-and-regional/nebraska/omaha-rally-protests-immigration-policies/article_f3bb3c7c-58e2–5c3f-bdf0–4965e0d717e3.html. Accessed October 5, 2013.

Pilger, Lori, and Art Hovey. "Fremont Immigration Law Ruled Legal." *Lincoln Journal Star*, June 28, 2013. http://journalstar.com/news/state-and-regional/nebraska/fremont-immigration-law-ruled-legal/article_937e7b95–53f1–5104-ac3a-fb0ef6157872.html. Accessed October 5, 2013.

Ramos, Athena, Shireen Rajaram, Lourdes Gouveia, Yuriko Doku, Drissa Toure, Anthony Zhang, and Sondra Manske. "Health Profile of Nebraska's Latino Population." 2013. http://dhhs.ne.gov/publichealth/Documents/Health%20Profile%20Latino%20Report%202013.pdf. Accessed October 11, 2013.

Schaefer, Joann, Jacquelyn Miller, Sue Medinger, Raponzil Drake, and Anthony Zhang. "The Socioeconomic Status of Nebraska Asians." Department of Health and Human Services. 2008. http://dhhs.ne.gov/publichealth/Documents/SESofAsians.pdf. Accessed October 9, 2013.

Task Force on the Productive Integration of Immigrant Workforce Population. "The Dream Lives On: New Immigrants/New Opportunities for Nebraska." 2001. http://nlcs1.nlc.state.ne.us/epubs/L3790/B063–2001.pdf. Accessed September 23, 2013.

Tomkins, Alan J., Tarik Abdel-Monem, and Angel Rivera-Colon. "Immigration Controversies in Nebraska: Policies, Politics, and Public Perspectives." University of Nebraska Public Policy Center, 2009. http://ppc.nebraska.edu/userfiles/file/Documents/projects/ImmigrationControversiesinNE—PoliciesPoliticsandPublicPerspectives.pdf.Accessed September 21, 2013.

U.S. Census Bureau. *Census of Population and Housing Characteristics*. "Summary of Population and Housing Characteristics: Nebraska." 2010. http://www.census.gov/prod/www/decennial.html. Accessed October 18, 2013.

U.S. Census Bureau. *Census of Population and Housing. Volume 1: Characteristics of the Population, Nebraska*. 1960. http://www.census.gov/prod/www/decennial.html. Accessed October 18, 2013.

U.S. Census Bureau. *Census of Population and Housing. Volume 2: Characteristics of the Population, Part 4: Minnesota—New Mexico*. 1943. http://www.census.gov/prod/www/decennial.html. Accessed October 18, 2013.

U.S. Census Bureau. *Census of Population and Housing. Volume 2: Characteristics of the Population, Nebraska*. 1950. http://www.census.gov/prod/www/decennial.html. Accessed October 18, 2013.

U.S. Census Bureau. *Census of Population and Housing. Volume 3: Population, 1920. Composition and Characteristics of the Population by States*. 1920. http://www.census.gov/prod/www/decennial.html. Accessed October 18, 2013.

U.S. Census Bureau. *State and County QuickFacts: Nebraska*. 2013. http://quickfacts.census.gov/qfd/states/31000.html. Accessed October 18, 2013.

U.S. Department of Health and Human Services. *National Standard for Culturally and Linguistically Appropriate Services in Health Care: Executive Summary*. 2001. http://minority health.hhs.gov/assets/pdf/checked/executive.pdf.Accessed October 11, 2013.

University of Nebraska-Lincoln. "By the People: Introduction: Immigration and Nebraska."
2007. http://ppc.unl.edu/files/ByThePeople/relateddocs/Nebraska20Background%20
Document%20on%20Immigration.pdf. Accessed October 11, 2013.

University of Nebraska-Lincoln, College of Journalism and Mass Communications. "Strate
gic Discussions for Nebraska: Immigration in Nebraska." 2008. http://www.prairiefire
newspaper.com/files/201301-immigration-in-nebraska.pdf.   Accessed   October
10, 2013.

Walton, Don. "Capitol Crowd Urges Support for Immigration Reform." *Lincoln Journal Star*, April 4, 2013. http://journalstar.com/news/state-and-regional/federal
-politics/capitol-crowd-urges-support-for-immigration-reform/article_8e3b3c9f
-c54d-59ad-820a-fba0715030e5.html. Accessed October 7, 2013.

Zavadil, Chris. "Immigrant Ordinance Opponents Ask to Be Heard by Full
Court." *Fremont Tribune*, August 13, 2013. http://fremonttribune.com/news
/local/immigrant-ordinance-opponents-ask-to-be-heard-by-full-court/article
_ac9dc0b9-e037–5ea2-ad0e-45171577dba6.html. Accessed October 7, 2013.

Zhang, Anthony. *Racial/Ethnic Minority Population Growth State of Nebraska Fact Book*.
Department of Health and Human Services. 2009. http://dhhs.ne.gov/publichealth
/Documents/Nebraska%20Minority%20Population%20Growth%20FB.pdf. Accessed
October 14, 2013.

28

NEVADA

Maryam Stevenson and John Tuman

CHRONOLOGY

1776	Nevada is believed to have been discovered by Spanish Franciscan missionary, Father Garces, and two Indian guides.
1822	The Nevada area is transferred to the new Republic of Mexico.
1848	The Treaty of Guadalupe-Hidalgo ends the Mexican–American War, after which the United States purchases Nevada from Mexico. Mexican residents are allowed to remain but are subjected to public and private discrimination.
1849	Chinese immigrants move to Nevada to work in local mines. State statutes prohibit Chinese nationals from owning property.
1850	Mormon settlement begins in the western Utah Territory (now Nevada).
1860s	Latina/os begin immigrating to the state to work in mining, the service industry, and ranching.
1861	Nevada separates from the Utah Territory. Nevada Territory is established by Congress.
1864	Nevada gains statehood and passes a state constitution.
1865	The permanent settlement of Las Vegas (originally called Los Vegas Rancho) begins.
1867–1869	Chinese immigration increases during construction of the Central Pacific Railroad. Anglos view them as threats to their own livelihoods and to the unions. Racism is widespread.
1870	In this year, 44.2 percent of Nevada's population is foreign-born, the highest percentage in any state and over three times the national percentage of foreign-born immigrants.

1882, 1907, 1921, 1924 In these years, various federal acts and two important Supreme Court decisions (the Chinese Exclusion cases) lead to the establishment of strict immigration quotas, based on eugenic studies and particularly limiting Chinese immigration to the United States and, consequently, to Nevada.

1940   The federal government eases restrictions on Chinese immigration to the United States.

1959   The Nevada legislature repeals employment prohibitions against the Chinese.

1960s   The Communist revolution in Cuba forces Cuban exiles with experiences in the Havana casinos to settle in Nevada to seek jobs in the casino industry. Puerto Ricans begin immigrating to Nevada from the East Coast.

1995   Senate Bill (SB) 475 is passed, which requires the courts to disclose information relating to a defendant's criminal background conducted by the state's Division of Parole and Probation to the United States Immigration and Naturalization Service (INS) for the purpose of deportation of foreigners.

1999   Senate Joint Resolution Number 19 is passed, which is designed to urge the U.S. Congress to mitigate the consequences of an entry and exit control system to track all foreign visitors to the United States. The state legislature is concerned that this system could impact travel and tourism within the state.

2001   Assembly Bill 500 is passed, which makes racial profiling by a peace officer on the basis of race, ethnicity, or national origin as a basis for a traffic stop or initiating other action to be unlawful.

2006   Immigration reform protests in response to House Report 4437 are held throughout the spring in Las Vegas, Carson City, and Reno (along with other major cities in the United States).

2012   The 2013 Nevada legislative session considers proposed legislation that includes the portions of Arizona's SB1070 law that were upheld by the U.S. Supreme Court.

HISTORICAL OVERVIEW

Much like the rest of the United States, the state of Nevada and particularly the city of Las Vegas have been largely shaped by the immigration to the United States over the past two centuries. Immigration to the United States in the early years of the republic primarily occurred from western and northern European states to the Atlantic coast and predominantly New York City. By the 1920s, Congress imposed eugenic per country quotas to shift the ethnic composition of immigrants, but nevertheless immigrants from the South and the West (including Mexico, China, Japan, and the Philippines) allegedly began entering the United

States through western ports of entry, particularly San Francisco and other coastal cities. Nevada also experienced a small scale of the European immigration during this period.

By the 1950s, Congress began to reform a number of immigration laws in an attempt to address Cold War concerns. These new reforms, combined with a number of push factors in countries around the world, including Civil War, revolution, poverty, political oppression, and religious persecution, maintained previous quotas and the country experienced relatively low levels of immigration. Nevertheless, there was some unexplained inflow of Asians, Latina/os, and Africans to the United States. These new immigrants arrived from areas farther away from Europe, and as a result, entry to the United States no longer came via the Atlantic. In fact, over time, western cities suddenly became important ports of entry. Specifically, after 1965, Phoenix, Albuquerque, and Los Angeles became significant ports of entry for these new immigrants.

As a result of these new immigrants, the demographic landscape throughout the southwest began to change. Cities such as El Paso, Albuquerque, Phoenix, Tucson, San Diego, and Las Vegas experienced an inflow of Latina/o and Asian immigrants throughout the mid-twentieth century. While a number of factors influenced individual decisions of where to settle, many came to Las Vegas in search of employment in the new gaming center.

Today, Clark County is one of America's fastest-growing areas and the most ethnically diverse and populous area in the state. Unlike other states where a number of cities may have significant areas of population, the population of Nevada is largely clustered in Clark County and Washoe County. In comparing these two counties, according to the 2010 U.S. Census, the population of Clark County was around 2 million, compared to just less than 500,000 in Washoe County. The foreign-born population accounted for 21 percent of Clark County's total population (420,000 people) and 15 percent of Washoe County (75,000 people). As a result, because the greater majority of immigrants in Nevada resided in Clark County, the remaining analysis in this section will focus on migration to the Las Vegas Valley. This is also in line with the scholarly work conducted on immigration in the state.

Throughout the first half of the twentieth century, Las Vegas was primarily a railroad town and while Nevada re-legalized casino gambling in 1931, it was not until World War II when gambling became Las Vegas's main industry. In 1941, the El Rancho Vegas opened on the Strip (a departure from the small downtown gambling clubs), and was followed by the Last Frontier, Fabulous Flamingo, and Thunderbird casinos throughout the 1940s, and the Desert Inn, Sands, Sahara, Riviera, Dunes, and Starburst by the end of the 1950s, creating new jobs and a demand for unskilled labor. This demand was met by an increase in Latina/os to Clark County from 578 in 1960 to 9,937 in 1970, to nearly 35,000 by 1980 and

83,000 by 1990. Asians also increased in number from 9,207 in 1980 to 25,153 in 1990 as the casino industry boomed in the center of town. Thus, by 2000, the U.S. Census listed Clark County's Latina/o population as 302,000, or 21.9 percent of the total population of Las Vegas. Additionally, there were 78,959 Asian-Pacific Islanders, or 5.7 percent of the total population. This increase included not only new immigration but also an internal migration from other areas in the United States, such as Europeans from the north and eastern states, and Latina/os from the southwestern region of the United States.

The population of Clark County increased in similar fashion throughout the second half of the twentieth century by Anglos and African Americans. And while the gaming industry certainly could explain the general increase in population, there were other factors that could also explain the increase in the immigrant population. First, the relatively recent crackdowns throughout the 2000s by Border Patrol agents throughout Arizona, Texas, and California and the saturation of Mexicans of the unskilled market in these states over time made Nevada, and particularly Las Vegas, an attractive location for settlers. Additionally, Moehring (2005) argues that a lower cost of living, availability of work without high school educational requirements, low-cost entertainment, and established ethnic subcultures have also contributed to the increase in foreign-born, particularly Latino immigrants to the Clark County region.

TOPICAL ESSAYS

Bilingual Related and Other Specialized Services

In 2010, the American Community Survey estimated that 20.0 percent of Nevadans speak Spanish or Spanish Creole at home. Of these, 54.4 percent indicated they speak English "very well" and 45.6 percent indicated they speak English less than "very well." This perhaps translates into approximately 10 percent of the Nevada population, or more than 250,000 people that speak very little English across the state.

As a result, a market has been created to meet the needs of this substantial non-English-speaking and/or bilingual population. Within the court system, for example, according to KNPR Nevada Public Radio, 30 percent of cases handled by public defenders in Clark County are made up of Spanish-speaking individuals who do not speak English.

Additionally, the Clark County Court Interpreter's Office, which was established in 1975, has seen requests for interpreters increase by 1,617 percent between 1981 and 2000. In 1981, 1,655 court cases required interpreters from 25 languages. By 1994, 12,317 cases required interpreters, and by 2000, 26,773 required the use of 320 certified interpreters for 79 different languages.

A professional association (Nevada Interpreters and Translators Association [NITA]) for translators and interpreters also exists within the state that, according to their website, is designed to improve the availability of language services in Nevada. NITA provides a directory of language professionals for organizations or individuals in need of translation services. Of the 33 individual and corporate members who offer interpreter and/or translation services in Nevada, 24 specifically offer Spanish-language services.

Additionally, the Clark County School District, the fifth-largest school district in the country, has the second-largest English language-learner population in the country (second only to the Los Angeles Unified School District). Furthermore, Latina/o students outnumber Anglo students in the Clark County schools by nearly 33 percent with Latina/os accounting for 137,003, or 44 percent of the total student population, and Anglo students accounting for 91,448, or 29.4 percent of the total population. Between the 1992–1994 and 2000–2001 school years, the number of students enrolled in the ELL program increased by 245 percent to 35,296. By 2010, 90,295 of the total 299,854 students enrolled in the Clark County School District were enrolled in ELL program. These students spoke 134 different languages and came from 150 various countries (as a point of reference, the U.S. Department of State recognizes a total of 195 countries throughout the world).

Other specialized services have also increased since the 1980s. The number of immigration attorneys has increased from only one full-time immigration law specialist in the early 1980s to 54 members of the Nevada Chapter of the American Immigration Lawyers Association in 2011. In 1987, immigration cases by Nevada residents were heard at immigration court in Phoenix by a single immigration judge. By 1996, an immigration court opened in Las Vegas and currently has two full-time immigration judges. Nevada immigrants were served at a branch office in Phoenix by INS, the predecessor to the current U.S. Citizenship and Immigration Service. In 2001, INS opened a full service field office in Las Vegas.

2010 IMMIGRANT PROFILE AND VARIOUS IMPACTS

Taking a step back again to look at the state as a whole, the foreign-born immigrant population makes up roughly 20 percent (or 1 in 5) of all Nevadans and the share of immigrants in the Nevada population has been steadily increasing over time. According to the U.S. Census, in 1990, the foreign-born population was 8.7 percent. By 2000, that percentage increased to 15.8 percent and up to 18.8 percent by 2010 for a total of 508,458 immigrants, compared to the national figure of 12.9 percent.

Of these foreign-born in 2010, 57.2 percent were from Latin America, 29.8 percent were from Asia, 8.5 percent were from Europe, 1.7 percent were from Canada,

2.3 percent were from Africa, and 0.5 percent were from Oceania. Latino/as clearly comprise the majority of the foreign-born population in Nevada, and their numbers have steadily been increasing over time. In 1990, Latino/as comprised 10.4 percent of Nevada's population, growing to 19.7 percent in 2000 and 26.6 percent in 2010 for a total of 719,435. The Asian population has grown from 2.9 percent in 1990, to 4.5 percent in 2000, to 7.3 percent in 2010 for a total of 197,439.

Over time, immigrants have been much more involved in the political system on both national and local levels. Of the abovementioned foreign-born immigrants in Nevada (508,458), 41.8 percent are naturalized U.S. citizens. As Latino/as and Asians comprise over one-third of all Nevadans, their share of the voting population is greatest. In the 2008 presidential elections, Latinos comprised 11.6 percent of Nevadan voters, while Asians comprised 3.4 percent. This recent influx of immigrant naturalized voters, particularly Latino voters, has resulted in a shift in voting behavior on a macro level for the state. Once a consistently red state, Nevada has since the 2008 election been an important swing state, due largely to this shift in demographics.

Economically, immigrants (both documented and undocumented) have been an important component of the state's economy as workers and taxpayers. According to the U.S. Census Bureau, in 2010, immigrants comprised 24.5 percent of the state's workforce. Latino immigrants paid approximately $2.6 billion in

President Barack Obama, to the right, facing the crowd, shakes hands after speaking about immigration at Del Sol High School in Las Vegas on January 29, 2013. (AP Photo/Carolyn Kaster)

federal taxes and $1.6 billion in state and local taxes in 2005, according to a report by the Progressive Leadership Alliance of Nevada.

Additionally, according to the Pew Hispanic Center, undocumented immigrants comprised 10 percent of the state's workforce in 2010, amounting to 140,000 workers throughout the state. Data from the Institute for Taxation and Economic Policy indicates that these undocumented immigrants paid a total of $133.5 million in state and local taxes in 2010, including $117.4 million in sales tax and $16.1 million in property taxes.

Public Opinion in Nevada on Immigration

According to a 2011 Pew Hispanic Center study, Nevada has the largest percentage of undocumented immigrants per capita in the nation. The study found that undocumented immigrants make up 7.2 percent of Nevada's total population compared to 6.8 percent in California and 6.7 percent in Texas. Combined with the domestic problems associated with the economic recession in the late 2000s, including high levels of unemployment and foreclosure rates, and the fiscal problems currently plaguing the state, one might expect public opinion in Nevada on undocumented immigrants to be quite low. The poll results, however, indicate that public opinion is split based on the type of policy in question.

A number of polls have been conducted in the state of Nevada in the past several years centering on immigration and the issue of undocumented immigrants. Over time, Nevada citizens have consistently largely been in favor of stricter enforcement and against amnesty for undocumented immigrants. The most recent public opinion surveys were conducted between May 2007 and September 2010. The results of these polls are provided in the following paragraphs.

A Mason-Dixon poll conducted in May 2007 interviewed 625 registered Nevada voters. Of those polled, 262 were registered Republicans, 259 Democrats, and 104 independents. The poll revealed that an astounding majority supported decreasing public services to undocumented immigrants and more stringent law enforcement measures, regardless of party affiliation, gender, or region of residence. Of those polled, 72 percent indicated that undocumented immigrants graduating from Nevada high schools should not be eligible for the Millennium scholarship. The scholarship provides up to four years of tuition to graduates of Nevada high schools to state public colleges and/or universities. About 77 percent indicated that state documents and election ballots should not be printed in any language other than English. Additionally, 81 percent said that Nevada businesses should be punished for employing undocumented immigrants.

In October 2007, another Mason-Dixon poll of 625 registered voters found that 59 percent of registered voters believed that a "tough approach to immigration" is preferable to a guest worker program. Additionally, 36 percent of those polled were in favor of an amnesty plan and the balance of the remaining 64 percent was undecided.

A February 2009 statewide public opinion poll by the Zogby International polling organization indicated that a majority of residents (62 percent) believed that undocumented immigration is either negatively or somewhat negatively affecting the state, 67 percent indicated that the estimated 200,000 undocumented immigrants living in Nevada have either a very negative or somewhat negative impact on the state's budge.

With regard to amnesty, 55 percent oppose a legalization or amnesty plan for undocumented immigrants and support government enforcement and strengthening of existing laws to return immigrants home, while 34 percent support granting amnesty. Additionally, 60 percent agreed with the statement that "granting amnesty to the estimated 200,000 illegal immigrants now living in Nevada would harm American workers, add to the state's fiscal crisis, and lead to more illegal immigration" compared to 19 percent who agreed with the statement that granting amnesty would benefit the earlier-mentioned American workers, ease the state's fiscal crisis, and solve the problem of undocumented immigration once and for all and 19 percent who did not agree with either statement.

On the heels of the passage of Arizona's SB 1070 bill on undocumented immigrants, a May 2010 Mason-Dixon poll ordered by the *Las Vegas Review-Journal* asked GOP primary voters whether they would support or oppose a similar law enacted in Nevada. Of those polled, only 8 percent opposed the measure and 7 percent were undecided. The telephone poll had a margin of error of plus or minus 4.5 percentage points.

In July 2010, a Rasmussen poll surveying 750 likely Nevada voters indicated that 65 percent favored passage of a law similar to Arizona's SB 1070, 28 percent opposed, and 7 percent were unsure. Additionally, 63 percent disagreed with the Justice Department's decision to challenge the legality of Arizona's SB 1070 in federal court, while 29 percent agreed with the decision. Finally, when asked if they agree or disagree with the statement: "some people believe that the goal of immigration policy should be to keep out national security threats, criminals and those who would come here to live off our welfare system. Beyond that, all immigrants would be welcome"; 62 percent agreed, 22 percent disagreed, and 16 percent were unsure.

Finally, a September 2010 poll of adults in Nevada conducted by the *Law Vegas Review-Journal* and CBS 8 News NOW found that 89 percent believed there should be stricter penalties on employers hiring undocumented immigrants. About 54 percent believed that undocumented immigrants take jobs away from U.S. citizens, while 31 percent disagreed that they take jobs from citizens. Additionally, 57 percent of those polled believed that children born in the United

States to undocumented immigrants should not be able to become U.S. citizens, while 29 percent did.

Recent State Legislative Immigration Measures

Since 1995, the Nevada legislature has passed only three immigration-related bills in all regular and special sessions between 1995 and 2011. The consequence of these bills has been relatively trivial and made few changes to existing law. Additionally, while a number of immigration-related bills have been introduced (largely dealing with the status of undocumented aliens and verification of status by employers), none have passed within the state legislature since 2001.

In 2001, Assembly Bill 500 made racial profiling by a peace officer based on race, ethnicity, or national origin as a basis for a traffic stop or initiating other action unlawful. Senate Joint Resolution Number 19 passed in 1999 was designed to urge the U.S. Congress to mitigate the consequences of an entry and exit control system to track all foreign visitors to the United States. The state legislature was concerned that this system could impact travel and tourism within the state. Finally SB 475, which was passed in 1995, required the courts to disclose information relating to a defendant's criminal background conducted by the state's Division of Parole and Probation to the U.S. INS for the purpose of deportation of foreigners.

Prospects for the Future

The 2010 Census indicated that the share of foreign-born immigrants has been steadily increasing in Nevada over time and is higher than the national figure. In 1990, for example, the foreign-born population was 8.7 percent. By 2000 that percentage increased to 15.8 percent and was up to 18.8 percent by 2010 for a total of 508,458 immigrants, compared to the national figure of 12.9 percent. Because immigration has occurred on a large scale within a relatively short period of time in Nevada, many needs are still not being met; for example, English language facilities for adults are inadequate, health care is difficult for many casino workers to obtain, housing for some immigrants is substandard, and poverty is a growing problem for some.

These issues were among those currently discussed in the recent post-presidential debate on comprehensive immigration reform in 2013. Congress debated reform as recently as 2006, 2007, and 2008, but these attempts failed. To date, reform has not been introduced in the midst of economic recession. Should Congress come to an agreement on what to do with the millions of undocumented immigrants currently in the United States, there is likely to be a significant impact on the state of Nevada as these immigrants may be able to enter the workforce in more significant ways and participate in the economy of the state to a much greater degree.

Additionally, the problem of undocumented immigration plaguing the rest of the country is of particular concern in areas such as Las Vegas that have high numbers of Latina/os. A number of states have implemented their own restrictive immigration legislation to address this problem (e.g., Arizona's SB 1070). In following these states, the 2013 Nevada legislative session will consider a submitted bill that includes portions of Arizona's SB1070 law that were upheld by the U.S. Supreme Court earlier in 2012.

The future of immigration in Nevada and Las Vegas rests on the success and/ or failure of these state and national policies. Regardless, the fact remains that immigration has been a significant factor in the economic and social make up of both the state and the Las Vegas Valley and is likely to continue to do so in the near future.

Various Communities

While the earlier sections focus on the large share of the population that comprise Latina/o and Asian immigrants, the state (and particularly Las Vegas) is a relatively ethnically diverse area. Unlike other metropolitan areas, the presence of a rich and diverse ethnic culture is not as prevalent in Las Vegas. As mentioned earlier, between the 1900s and the 1970s, Nevada, and particularly Las Vegas, benefitted from European immigration in the early part of the century and Mexican, Chinese, and Japanese immigration beginning in the mid- to late twentieth century. By the 1980s and 1990s, a new internal migration occurred, with Europeans moving west from northern and eastern states, and Latina/os moving from the southwestern states.

Refugee resettlement has also played a role in the ethnic diversification of Nevada. Since the 1970s, refugees have settled in Las Vegas through the assistance of Catholic Charities of Southern Nevada, the Franciscan Center, Episcopal Migration Services, and the Jewish Family Services Agency. Since the 1990s, the economy and high number of available low-skilled jobs made Las Vegas an attractive port of entry for refugees. Between 1995 and 2001, for example, Catholic Charities, the largest sponsor of refugee resettlement, sponsored 5,168 refugees from 32 countries, including Cuba, Bosnia, Iran, Vietnam, Sudan, Serbia, and Somalia.

Currently, Clark County boasts immigrants from every Latin American country, with the greatest numbers coming from Mexico and Central America. Among Asians, Filipinos, Chinese, and Koreans, respectively, make up the largest populations of Clark County foreign residents.

Bob Fulkerson, executive director of the Progressive Leadership Alliance (PLA) of Nevada, introduces Reno mayor Bob Cashell at a news conference in the parish of the Trinity Episcopal Church in Reno, Nevada, on February 13, 2014. The PLA is an umbrella group that includes the Nevada Immigrant Coalition. (AP Photo/Scott Sonner)

NOTABLE GROUPS

Progressive Leadership Alliance of Nevada

The Progressive Leadership Alliance of Nevada is an umbrella group encompassing the Nevada Immigrant Coalition (which was established in 2008) and challenging the anti-immigration legislation that has become more prevalent in states in this region. This group works on a wide range of issues for groups that have been subject to discrimination and marginalization: from LBGQT (lesbian, bisexual, gay, queer, and transgendered) politics and marriage equity to workers' rights. At the level of immigration, they have compiled an in-depth study on the contribution that immigrant labor makes to the state, from 2006 to 2008. They have successfully helped in challenging nearly every anti-immigrant proposal at the state and local levels and provide public education advocating on behalf of immigrants. In 2010, they sponsored a "Latino Day at the Legislature" and in 2011, successfully challenged the state's consideration of the use of E-Verify. While E-Verify would seemingly help employers to hire only immigrants who are legally authorized to work, the program's effects overreach this narrow intention and make both workers and employers more vulnerable. The group is critical about Arizona's attempts at enforcing harsh, anti-immigration policies and like many other state and local groups, is challenging the Secure Communities (S-Comm) Program because of its failure to adhere to its mission: identifying and capturing dangerous immigrant criminals and instead undermining the well-being of thousands of noncriminal immigrants and creating a negative context of reception. Through a blend of public education, lobbying, and legal advocacy, this statewide group is fighting on behalf of the rights of all persons resident in the state.

BIBLIOGRAPHY

Arreola, Daniel D. *Hispanic Spaces, Latino Places: Community and Cultural Diversity in Contemporary America*. Austin: University of Texas Press, 2004.

Barkan, Elliot. "New Origins, New Homeland, New Region: American Immigration and the Emergence of the Sunbelt, 1955–1985." In Raymond A. Mohl, ed. *Searching for the Sunbelt: Historical Perspectives on a Region*. Knoxville: University of Tennessee Press, 1990, pp. 124–48.

Bowers, Michael W. *The Sagebrush State*. 3rd ed. Las Vegas: University of Nevada Press, 2006.

Daniels, Roger. *Coming to America: A History of Immigration and Ethnicity in American Life*. New York: Harper Collins, 1990.

Haines, David W., and Carol A. Mortland, eds. *Manifest Destinies: Americanizing Immigrants and Internationalizing Americans*. Westport, CT: Praeger, 2001.

Haines, David W. *Refugees in America in the 1990s: A Reference Handbook*. Westport, CT: Greenwood Press, 1996.

Immigration Policy Center. "New Americans in Nevada: The Economic and Political Power of Immigrants, Latinos, and Asians in the Silver State." Washington, DC: American Immigration Council, 2012.

Miranda, M. L. *A History of Hispanics in Southern Nevada*. Reno: University of Nevada Press, 1989.

Miranda, M. L. "The Mexicans: The Ethnic Diversification of Las Vegas." In Jerry Simich and Thomas C. Wright, eds. *The Peoples of Las Vegas*. Reno: University of Nevada Press, 2005, pp. 56–77.

Moehring, Eugene P. "The Ethnic Diversification of Las Vegas." In Jerry Simich, and Thomas C. Wright, eds. *The Peoples of Las Vegas*. Reno: University of Nevada Press, 2005. pp. 1–17.

Moehring, Eugene P., and Michael S. Green. *Las Vegas: A Centennial History*. Reno and Las Vegas: University of Nevada Press, 2005.

Nevada Department of Education. *Student Enrollment and Licensed Personnel Information*. Research Bulletin. Vol. 51. Carson City: Nevada State Department of Education, 2011. http://www.doe.nv.gov/Resources/Bulletin-FY2011.pdf. Accessed April 15, 2013.

Portes, Alejandro, and Ruben G. Rumbaut. *Immigrant America: A Portrait*. 2nd ed. Berkeley: University of California Press, 1996.

Progressive Leadership Alliance of Nevada. Progressive Leadership Alliance of Nevada Webpage. http://www.planevada.org/our-work/immigration/. Accessed February 22, 2014.

Shepperson, John B., and Ronald M. James, eds. *Uncovering Nevada's Past: A Primary Source History of the Silver State*. Reno and Las Vegas: University of Nevada Press, 2004.

Shepperson, Wilbur S. *Restless Strangers: Nevada's Immigrants and Their Interpreters*. Reno: University of Nevada Press, 1970.

Simich, Jerry, and Thomas C. Wright, eds. *More Peoples of Las Vegas*. Reno and Las Vegas: University of Nevada Press, 2010.

Simich, Jerry, and Thomas C. Wright, eds. *The Peoples of Las Vegas*. Reno and Las Vegas: University of Nevada Press, 2005.

Titus, Dina, and Thomas C. Wright. "The Ethnic Diversification of Las Vegas." In Jerry Simich, and Thomas C. Wright, eds. *The Peoples of Las Vegas*. Reno: University of Nevada Press, 2005, pp. 18–36.

Tuman, John P. *Latin American Migrants in the Las Vegas Valley: Civic Engagement and Political Participation*. Washington, DC: Woodrow Wilson International Center for Scholars, 2009.

U.S. Census Bureau. *1980, 1990, 2000, 2010 Census of Population*. Washington, DC: U.S. Census Bureau.

Wright, Thomas, John P. Tuman, and Maryam T. Stevenson. "Immigration and Ethnic Diversity in Nevada." In Dmitri N. Shalin, ed. *The Social Health of Nevada: Leading Indicators and Quality of Life in the Silver State*. Las Vegas: UNLV Center for Democratic Culture, 2012. http://cdclv.unlv.edu/mision/index.html. Accessed April 15, 2013.

29

NEW HAMPSHIRE

William P. Kladky

CHRONOLOGY

Pre-1600	Various Algonquian (Pennacook) tribes inhabit the area before European settlement.
1603	The region is first explored by Europeans by Martin Pring (1603) and Samuel de Champlain (1605).
1620	The Council for New England, formerly the Plymouth Company, receives a royal grant of land between latitudes 40°N and 48°N.
1623	Under an English land grant, Captain John Smith sends settlers to establish a fishing colony at the base of the Piscataqua River, near Rye and Dover.
1629/1630	The area between the Piscataqua and the Merrimack is named New Hampshire by Captain John Mason, who helps found Portsmouth (which is incorporated in 1653) and is captain of the port of Portsmouth, England, in the county of Hampshire.
1641	Through claims based on a misinterpretation of its charter, Massachusetts annexes New Hampshire.
1679	New Hampshire is made a separate royal colony, with Portsmouth as the capital.
1741	Benning Wentworth is made the first governor of New Hampshire alone. Previously, the crown had appointed a single man to govern both colonies.
1776 (July 4)	New Hampshire delegates are the first to vote for the Declaration of Independence.
1784 (June 2)	New Hampshire adopts a constitution using Massachusetts as guide.

1788	New Hampshire becomes the ninth and last necessary state to ratify the new U.S. Constitution.
1807	The national embargo against trade with Britain decimates trade with Canada.
1809	Benjamin Prichard and others build a cotton spinning mill operated by water power on the Merrimack.
1812	There is some agitation within New England for secession, as merchants oppose war with their largest trading partner.
1828	The first women's strike in the nation occurs at Dover's Cocheco Mills.
1827/1830	The first public high schools in the state are established in Portsmouth.
1842	New Hampshire's northern boundary is fixed when the Webster-Ashburton Treaty sets the line between Canada and the United States.
1853–1857	Term of Franklin Pierce, the only U.S. president from New Hampshire.
1861–1865	New Hampshire strongly supports the Northern cause during the Civil War, contributing many troops.
1908	Monsignor Pierre Hevey organizes the nation's first credit union in Manchester for helping mill workers save and borrow money.
1911	A bill is passed to protect big rivers by creating forest reserves at their headwaters.
1930s	The Great Depression severely impacts the state's economy, especially in one-industry towns.
1952	After New Hampshire simplifies its ballot access laws in 1949 seeking to boost voter turnout, it becomes the location of the nation's first modern presidential primary.
1961 (May 5)	Alan Shepard (1923–1998) of Derry becomes the first American in space.
1985	Christa McAuliffe (1948–1986) of Concord becomes the first private citizen selected to venture into space. She dies with her six space shuttle *Challenger* crewmates on January 28, 1986, when *Challenger* explodes shortly after launch.
2007	New Hampshire becomes "the first state to recognize same-sex unions without a court order or the threat of one."
2008	The state begins offering same-sex civil unions.
2010	Same-sex marriage becomes legal in New Hampshire.
2012	The Internal Affairs Committee of the New Hampshire State Senate votes 2–1 to kill a proposed resolution supporting the tough Arizona immigration law.

HISTORICAL OVERVIEW

SEVENTEENTH AND EIGHTEENTH CENTURIES

From its beginnings, New Hampshire had very porous borders both with its New England neighboring states and French-speaking Quebec in Canada. The colony that became the state of New Hampshire was founded on the division in 1629 of a 1622 land grant by the Council for New England to Captain John Mason and Sir Ferdinando Gorges (who founded Maine).

Various Algonquian (Pennacook) tribes had inhabited the area prior to European settlement, ranging widely over the region. One of the first tribes to encounter European colonists, the Pennacook were decimated by diseases. Before then, they were attracted to the area because of the many waterways. The area around Concord, the modern state capital, was originally settled by a branch of the Abenaki Indians called the Pennacook. The tribe thrived by fishing for migrating salmon, sturgeon, and alewives with their nets across the Merrimack River. The streams were the transportation route for their birchbark canoes to venture from sizable Lake Winnipesaukee to the Atlantic Ocean.

It still is disputed whether the first European settlement in the state was at Portsmouth or Dover. Most agree that the state was first settled in 1623 by Europeans at Odiorne's Point in Rye (near Portsmouth) by English fishermen, three years after the pilgrims arrived at Plymouth. The first native New Hampshirite, John Thompson, was born there. New Hampshire was one of the original 13 colonies.

Early settlement was confined to the port region along the state's narrow coastline. Lumbering played an important role from the start. In 1631, 8 Danish men and 22 women settled near Portsmouth, and the men sawed lumber and made potash. The Province shipped 20,000 "tons of boards and staves, and ten cargoes of masts" for the king's navy by 1671. In 1631, Captain Thomas Wiggin served as the first governor of the Upper Plantation.

Aside from this Danish group, almost all state residents throughout this period were of British origin. Most of the towns were derived from Old England names (e.g., Bath, Bristol, and Dover). The Scotch Irish were the second-largest group, mostly concentrated around Manchester "Derryfield", Londonderry, and Derry.

Almost immediately, conflicts with Massachusetts began. Although the towns united in 1639, Massachusetts had also claimed the territory. In 1641, an agreement was made for the area to come under Massachusetts's jurisdiction, with town home rule permitted. Throughout the seventeenth century, the area was also a refuge for exiles from the various oppressions of Puritan Massachusetts.

The relationship between Massachusetts and the independent New Hampshirites was controversial and tense, made more so by the land claims of the heirs of John Mason. After disputes continued, King Charles II separated New Hampshire from Massachusetts in 1679, issuing a charter for the royal Province of New Hampshire, with John Cutt as governor. New Hampshire was absorbed into the Dominion of New England in 1686, which collapsed in 1689. After a brief period without formal government (the settlements were de facto ruled by Massachusetts), William and Mary issued a new provincial charter in 1691. From 1699 to

1741, the governors of Massachusetts were also commissioned as governors of New Hampshire.

Immigrants from England continued to trickle in, with occasional bursts that changed the nature of the state. Some 1,000 Scotch Irish settlers came to Londonderry in 1719 direct from Londonderry, Ireland. In short time, they brought the potato, grew flax, and started linen manufacturing which became New England's first major textile industry.

Portsmouth thrived during this colonial period, primarily because of its shipbuilding industry. The USS *Constitution*, for instance, was built from timber from Allenstown, located but 50 miles from Portsmouth's yards. The state's many lumbering firms made this possible, and immigrants were drawn to the work. In 1741, New Hampshire returned to its royal provincial status with a governor of its own, Benning Wentworth, who was its governor from 1741 to 1766.

New Hampshire was one of the Thirteen Colonies that revolted against the British rule in the American Revolution. In January 1776, it became the first colony to set up an independent government and the first to establish a constitution. The state raised three regiments for the Continental army: the first, second, and third New Hampshire regiments. New Hampshire Militia units fought at the Battle of Bunker Hill, the Battle of Bennington, during the Saratoga Campaign, and the Battle of Rhode Island. John Paul Jones's ship, the sloop-of-war USS *Ranger*, and the frigate USS *Raleigh* were built in Portsmouth.

On January 5, 1776, the Congress of New Hampshire, meeting in Exeter, ratified the first state constitution in the United States, six months before the signing of the Declaration of Independence. After independence, the state thrived. By 1800, New Hampshire's population was 183,858, found across the state. Immigrants continued to arrive, drawn by the steady development of industries across the state. Again, the many waterways proved very attractive and crucial for progress. While farming was prevalent, there were sawmills and gristmills supported by water power, and of course fishing continued to be a major occupation and industry.

Nineteenth Century

In 1800, Portsmouth Navy Yard was established as the first federal navy yard. This led to Portsmouth being one of the nation's busiest ports and shipbuilding cities throughout the nineteenth century and a major employment center attracting immigrants and in-migrants from nearby states. The first cotton-goods factory in the state was built in 1803, at New Ipswich, nearby the Souhegan River from which it got its power.

The state's major towns began becoming cities. Concord was named the state capital in 1808. Following Blodgett's suggestion, Derryfield was renamed

Manchester in 1810, the year the mill was incorporated as the Amoskeag Cotton and Woolen Manufacturing Company. The company was purchased in 1825 by entrepreneurs from Massachusetts, expanding to three mills in 1826, and then incorporated, in 1831, as the Amoskeag Manufacturing Company. Immigrants soon arrived to become its employees. Despite this industrial development, in 1830 some 83 percent of the state's workers were still in farming.

The various industries took off later in the new nineteenth century, aided by the considerable technological and transportation improvements. The Industrial Revolution spurred economic growth in New Hampshire mill towns, such as Dover, Keene, Laconia, Manchester, Nashua, and Rochester, where rivers provided power for the mills. It shifted growth to the new mill towns. Oppositionally, the port of Portsmouth declined as other ports like New York and Philadelphia gathered business.

New Hampshire industries became nationally known and the destination for many seeking work. For example, the Abbot and Downing Company in Concord manufactured wagons and coaches, which between 1813 and the Civil War were the main means of transportation on the overland trails of the West.

But most of the jobs were in the mills. The ensuing rapid growth of textile manufacturing in New England caused a shortage of workers. Recruiters were hired by mill agents to bring young women and children from the countryside to work in the factories. Between 1830 and 1860, transportation improvements such as the stagecoach and railroad services made it easier for large numbers of workers to travel. Many female workers came from farm towns in northern New England.

As the textile industry grew, immigration also expanded, especially from Quebec (the "French Canadians") and Ireland. As the number of Irish workers in the mills increased, the number of young women working in the mills declined. Mill employment of women caused a population boom in urban centers. Many of the mill jobs had opened because many of the native young people did not want such work.

Resultantly, in the 1820s and 1830s, New Hampshire had a number of Irish immigrants. The usual trip was that they first arrived at the Boston or New York ports, and then migrated to New England cities and mill towns where there was a need for labor. In Portsmouth, the Irish became a significant presence. Most were laborers, though some worked in ocean-related jobs. In the state, as elsewhere, the Irish immigrant to survive took any job for any wage, which contributed to the racialized stereotyping and ridiculing of Irish as menial laborers. Irish workers did hard labor on infrastructure such as railways, streets, sewers, water works; in residential, commercial, public buildings; and single women often worked in mills, replacing discontented mill girls and many female Irish worked as domestic servants in the homes of the growing wealthy middle class. The approximately 50 Irish immigrants in Dover, by 1830, were different from Irish in other towns because they had brought industrial skills useful in cotton factories. By 1840, many had left the factories and opened businesses or had bought land.

On the Merrimack River, a planned model company town was built by Amoskeag engineers and architects and was founded in 1838. Incorporated as a city in 1846, Manchester would become home to the largest cotton mill in the world. Other products manufactured include shoes, cigars, and paper. The Amoskeag foundry made rifles, sewing machines, textile machinery, fire engines, and locomotives.

With the population growth and diversification, conflicts inevitably arose. Abolitionists from Dartmouth College founded an experimental Noyes Academy in Canaan in 1835 that also was interracial. Before the end of the year, rural opponents destroyed and burned the school to protest integrated education.

The northern boundary of the state finally was settled by the Webster–Ashburton Treaty with Great Britain in 1842. Due to ambiguous terms in the 1783 Treaty of Paris—which settled the American Revolutionary War—there were three possible definitions of "the northwestern most head of the Connecticut River." The area around the three tributaries that flowed into the head of the river was either under the jurisdiction of the United States or Canada. This led to the formation of the Indian Stream Republic (1832–1835). When the states could not agree, both countries sent in tax-collectors and debt-collecting sheriffs. This double taxation greatly angered the residents, and the republic was formed. The republic voluntarily ended in 1835 when it voted to rejoin the United States. Britain then gave up its claim in January 1836, and American jurisdiction was finalized in May 1836. The area still was called Indian Stream in the 1840 U.S. Census on June 1, 1840.

During this period, New England was the most industrialized part of the country. By 1850, over 25 percent of all manufacturing value in the country and over a third of its industrial workforce were in New England. In New Hampshire, industrialization was concentrated in the South and East. The northern parts of the state produced lumber and the mountains provided tourist attractions and some employment.

Racial and ethnic tensions surrounding the new immigrants continued. After 1850, most Irish immigrants were unskilled and poor, and worked in the mills. In Manchester, on July 3–4, 1854, Irish youths and Protestants rioted following the legal arraignment of a Protestant stable owner for an Irishman's death that resulted from a fight over a rental of a horse and buggy. In the riot, Catholics destroyed private property, Protestants stoned the new St. Anne's Catholic Church, and both sustained personal injuries before the fire chief and mayor quelled the clashes.

In the 1860s, the state recorded its only decadal decrease in population until the twentieth century, as many citizens joined the nation's westward movement.

However, this population loss was reversed in the 1870s and 1880s as industry flourished because of improved transportation and water-power advancements. Many cities were incorporated, including Keene (1873), Rochester (1891), Somersworth and Laconia (1893), Franklin (1895), and Berlin 1897. This renewed population boom was assisted by the state's formation of a Department of Public Instruction in 1867, a State Board of Health in 1881, a library commission in 1891, and St. Anselm College in 1893.

The continuing influx of foreign-born workers changed the state's population, which went from 95.2 percent native in 1850 to 19.2 percent foreign-born in 1890. Nativistic resentment continued. For example, one nativist prophesized in 1874 that, "In a half century . . . not a vestige of pure, original New Hampshire blood will be left" (Fogg, quoted in Federal Writing Project 1938, 77).

In the 1890s, a number of Greeks immigrated to Manchester and Nashua, the start of a large wave to the state between 1890 and 1920. Most of the 350,000 were unskilled men hoping to work, save money, and return home. Because about 80 percent were from rural backgrounds, most were barely literate and almost none could speak English.

Many of these French Canadian, Irish, and Greek immigrants found their first jobs in New Hampshire as unskilled factory laborers or as lumberjacks in the heavily forested regions of the state. However, as they became better established, they began their own small businesses in increasing numbers.

The state also began to develop voluntary social organizations to serve old and new residents. In the late 1800s and early 1900s, social clubs (i.e., fraternal organizations) had become an important part of most communities. For those with eighteenth-century-and-older ancestors, the Grange and the Masons were popular.

Faced with exclusion from established social life, New Hampshire immigrants began their own groups and associations. These brotherhood organizations supported a sense of community among those with a common language and cultural ties. For instance, L'Association Catholique de Jeunesse Franco-Américaine was a youth group similar to ones in Quebec.

French Canadian immigrants in the late 1800s were economically motivated. Farming, the traditional basis of Quebec's economy, had always been difficult due to marginal soil and a short growing season. The farmland where French Canadian immigrants came from was not productive enough to sustain its population. A plunge in Quebec's wheat production and a potato blight during 1827–1844 caused many to leave. By the late 1800s, large textile-manufacturing companies relied heavily on French Canadian immigrants to fill many of the unskilled jobs in their mills. In addition to low pay and sometimes dangerous working conditions, these immigrants also had to endure long workdays that ranged between 12 and 16 hours per day.

1900 TO 1945

The largest immigrant group, French Canadians, numbered 76,000 in New Hampshire in 1900, and were somewhat established. Unfortunately, a new wave of Greek immigrants produced resentment and fear by Irish immigrants especially over job loss. There was open confrontation at times in Nashua. When, in 1901, the Brackett Shoe Company tried to hire Greek workers to replace strikers, the striking Irish workers "brandishing of knives and guns to frighten off the Greeks." There were also clashes between Greeks and Irish in Manchester in 1906.

In 1907–1908, many young, healthy, Russian farm people immigrated to New Hampshire, drawn by employment possibilities and good wages. They mainly went to Claremont, and found work in the mills and shoe shops. With their success at saving money, they brought their families to settle permanently. One of their major employers was the Sullivan Machinery Company, famous as a manufacturer of mining, industrial, and quarrying machinery. In 1908, the first bituminous roadway was constructed near Nashua. A diverse network of roads soon followed, easing migration of all types. The state's railroad system was established.

The French Canadian immigration had been largely by railroad. They were very slow in acculturation—which helped to fuel nativistic fears and resentments—because of their comparative isolation within American society: Catholic and French-speaking, served by priests from Quebec, and few intermarried (a 1926 study discovered that only 11 percent had intermarried). In addition, because so many crossed and re-crossed national borders in search of work and family, their political impact was minimal. Many traveled to New Hampshire by way of mill towns in southern New England, especially Massachusetts. In 1912, the Greek immigrants became the only large European group of which more than 50 percent returned to their original home country when many returned to Greece to fight in the Balkan Wars.

During the infamous "Red Scare" raids between 1919 and 1920, Russian immigrant social clubs were targeted. In Claremont during the arrests, "anarchistic literature" was seized which, when translated, proved to be religious pamphlets and newspapers. The *Claremont Daily Eagle* reported that innocents were arrested, probably due to their unfamiliarity with the English language. Three of the 23 arrested in Claremont were deported. Other arrests and releases without public trial resulted in continued suspicions, as well as significant damage to people's reputations and businesses. This also negatively and unfairly affected the labor movement in the state, for in Claremont, an American Federation of Labor organizer was driven from town and many workers would not support labor reform for fear of being labeled communists or socialists.

Despite this tension, many immigrants stayed. By 1920, there were 3,000 Greeks in Manchester. Greek male and female workers made up about 10 percent of Amoskeag's workers. However, continuing ethnic discrimination and a rather weak support system caused some Greek men to opt for other employment choices, such as shoe shops and service industries. Unfortunately, the passage and enforcement of the harsh U.S. Immigration Act in 1924 severely curtailed immigration to the country, and New Hampshire was no exception.

Despite the immigration curtailment, the state's population continued to grow 3.1 percent during the 1920s to 465,293. The numbers of foreign-born, however, declined from being 22.4 percent in 1910 to 20.6 percent in the 1920s, to 17.8 percent by 1930. In 1922, the textile trades struck in New England—in the state largely in the Amoskeag Mills—was the largest in the state's history, with 60,000–80,000 idle for nine months. Nativists, of course, blamed the immigrant groups.

To dispel anti-Greek sentiment that had arisen mostly due to employment fears, two defensive organizations, the American Hellenic Educational Progressive Association (1922) and the Greek American Progressive Association (1923), were started. Both of these organizations focused on preserving their traditional customs, promoting assimilation into American society, and teaching their members about democratic norms.

The New Hampshire textile industry also was hit hard by the 1929–1936 national Depression, as well as the growing competition from southern mills. The industrial centers especially suffered. The closing of the Amoskeag Mills in 1935 was a major blow to Manchester and Hillsborough County.

As of the late 1930s, New Hampshire was somewhat divided between its farms and cities. Some 71 percent of the farm population was native-born, compared to the heavy ethnic concentration in industrial towns like Manchester, where one-third of the population was French Canadian. French Canadians also were the major group in Nashua, seconded by Greeks. Concord was British. Berlin was bilingual, with a large group of Norwegians.

1945 TO THE PRESENT

The post–World War II decades had seen New Hampshire recover from the decline of its industrial and manufacturing base. The bankruptcy of the Brown Company paper mill in Berlin in the 1940s and the closing of the former Nashua Manufacturing Company mill in Nashua in 1949 were typical failures. The changes first resulted in population declines, but New Hampshire emerged as a net population draw from both domestic and foreign areas. The state's porous borders had been an invaluable asset in this process.

Like many states, World War II proved a boon to economic recovery. During the war, the Portsmouth Navy Yard flourished as a center for shipbuilding, especially submarines, small boats, and warship repair. Employment and population stabilized and increased, drawing migrants from other states and foreign countries.

Also similar to other states, the federal development of the nation's highway system during and after the war facilitated economic development in New Hampshire. Aiding the development was an increase in the state's economic and cultural links with the greater Boston, Massachusetts, region. This reflected a national trend, in which improved highway networks had helped metropolitan areas expand into formerly rural areas or small nearby cities.

Aided by federally funded transportation improvements, the rise of new technology heralded the change in the state's economic and demographic fortunes. The replacement of the Nashua textile mills with the defense electronics contractor Sanders Associates in 1952 and the arrival of the minicomputer manufacturer Digital Equipment Corporation in the 1970s were signal events that typify the emergence of southern New Hampshire as a high-tech branch of Massachusetts's pulsing Route 128 corridor. Interstate-95, Interstate-495, and the variety of other federal-funded interstate highways were essential ingredients. All of this spectacular growth led to New Hampshire having the lowest state unemployment ever recorded in 1988: a tiny 2.0 percent. The Manchester-Nashua-Portsmouth area was known as the "Golden Triangle."

As Massachusetts migrants arrived in seeming droves to claim the high-tech jobs, this influx of new residents inspired NIMBY-ism (Not in My Backyard) against growth, such as in Hollis. Long-simmering tensions with nearby Massachusetts—especially the political gulf between staunch Republicans and liberal Democrats—exacerbated this.

It is important to note that the runaway aspect of the state's southern development was somewhat limited and crested within two decades. One major reason cited for this inherent plateau has been its distance from a major airport, in this case, Logan Airport in Boston. New Hampshire has continued to attract migrants from other states such as Massachusetts but in reduced numbers.

The postwar years also saw the rise in importance of New Hampshire's political primary for president of the United States, which as the first actual voting primary in the quadrennial campaign season draws enormous domestic and international media attention. It all began innocently enough. In an attempt to boost voter turnout, the state legislature simplified its ballot access laws in 1949. In the process, the state became the location for the nation's first modern presidential primary.

Since 1952, New Hampshire became the most important testing grounds for candidates for the Republican and Democratic nominations. In a recent election cycle, the media gave New Hampshire and Iowa almost 50 percent of all the attention paid to all states in the primary process. By many accounts, this has magnified the state's decision powers and created repeated efforts by other states to change their primaries.

State law permits a town with fewer than 100 residents to open its polls at midnight, and close when all registered citizens have cast their ballots. Dixville Notch in Coos County and Hart's Location in Carroll County, among other towns, have implemented these. Resultantly, Dixville Notch and Hart's Location are traditionally the first places in both New Hampshire and the nation to vote in presidential primaries and elections.

In many respects, New Hampshire continues to be atypical of New England during the 1990s. For instance, the 2000 Census found New Hampshire was the fastest-growing state within the Northeast for the fourth straight decade—up an impressive 11 percent since 1990.

The U.S. Census discovered that a significant percentage of the state's residents have emigrated from other states. This was different from most states. Of New Hampshire's population in 2000 (1,235,786), 43.3 percent were born in New Hampshire. Significant in-migration from neighboring Massachusetts—escaping "Tax-achusetts"—had been the major factor. A dominant 24.8 percent are born in Massachusetts (307,078), followed by New York (60,557), Maine (38,518), Connecticut (29,661), Vermont (29,397), New Jersey (21,053), and Pennsylvania (19,403). Some 11,492 were born outside the nation, and 54,154 were foreign-born. The percentage born in other states decreased to 51.0 percent, but still was the third-highest percentage in the entire nation.

The U.S. Census Bureau estimated that the population of New Hampshire was 1,318,194 on July 1, 2011, a 0.13 percent increase since the 2010 Census (U.S. Census Bureau 2011a). The center of population has moved south 12 miles (19 km) since 1950, a reflection of the fact that the fastest growth in the state has been along its southern border, which was within commuting range of Boston and other Massachusetts cities.

Like the nation as a whole, the state's migration has slowed in recent decades. New Hampshire has continued to grow at a slower rate than the nation but more than most nearby states. The 24.8 percent growth rate in the 1980s declined to 11.4 percent in the 1990s and 6.5 percent in the 2000–2010 period. From July 1, 2010 to July 1, 2011, for instance, the state grew 1,387 with a surplus of births over deaths accounting for the increase. Net international immigration was 1,165, but domestic migration was a negative with 2,763. Hillsborough continued to be the leading county for growth during this time.

Part of this has been a net out-migration from the state during the first decade of the twenty-first century. Domestic in-migration during 2000–2010 to New Hampshire was primarily from Massachusetts (17,810), Maine (29,140), Florida (23,856), Vermont (22,068), and New York (19,347) (Internal Revenue Service 2011). Dwarfing this, out-migration from the state during the same period was to Maine (87,016), Florida (44,299), Maine (35,575), Vermont (21,884), and New York (16,614).

In addition, there is evidence that the recent mortgage default crisis resulted in more out-migration for the state. Of those states with comparable mortgage equity problems, New Hampshire had the highest rate of moving during 2006–2009 period.

In the twenty-first century, New Hampshire continues to be known for its somewhat individualistic, idiosyncratic culture and government. Aside from its French Canadian heritage, which is not atypical of polyglot America, New Hampshire has virtually no minorities, no seatbelt law for persons over 18 years of age, no helmet law for motorcyclists, no mandatory auto-insurance law, and has neither an income tax nor a sales tax. Part of the state's curious reputation stems from the state's prominence in the presidential primary process and historically the well-known, pugnacious conservative political views of the Manchester *Union Leader* newspaper's long-time editor William Loeb (1905–1981).

The state, though, also typifies a shared New England heritage and culture primarily shaped by waves of immigration from Europe. As we have seen, in contrast to other American regions, many of New England's earliest Puritan settlers came from eastern England, contributing to the region's distinctive accents, foods, customs, and social structures. This has continued to the present. Most agree that a cultural gap exists between urban New Englanders along the populated coastline, and rural denizens in western Massachusetts, northwestern Connecticut, Vermont, New Hampshire, and Maine, where population density comparatively is low. This cultural divide is readily apparent in the recent citizen objections to the relatively low numbers of refugee settlement.

New Hampshire, typical of New England, has largely preserved its regional character, especially in its historic places and in its northern section. The enduring European influence is apparent: the use of traffic rotaries; the bilingual French and English towns of northern Vermont, Maine, and New Hampshire; the occasional usage of British spelling; the prevalence of English town and county names; and its unique, often non-rhotic coastal dialect reminiscent of southeastern England. At least in New Hampshire, the more things change, the more they have remained—somewhat—the same.

TOPICAL ESSAYS

A White State Getting Slightly Less White

In terms of race (and of culture), New Hampshire is one of the whitest states in the country. In 1790, it was 99.4 percent white; in 1900, it was 99.0 percent white; in 1960, it was 99.7 percent white; and in 2010: 93.9 percent are white (92.3 percent non-Latino white), 2.2 percent are Asian, 1.1 percent are black or African American, and 0.2 percent are Native American/American Indian. Currently, the largest ancestry groups in New Hampshire are estimated at 24.5 percent French and French Canadian, 21.5 percent Irish, 17.6 percent English, 10.3 percent Italian, 8.4 percent German, 5.4 percent American, 4.4 percent Scottish, 4.2 percent Polish, 2.0 percent Swedish, 1.6 percent Greek, 1.4 percent Portuguese, and 1.1 percent Scotch Irish.

New Hampshire has the highest percentage (24.5 percent of the population) of residents of French/French Canadian/Acadian ancestry of any U.S. state. This is the primary reason why the state also has a significant portion of residents who speak another language at home. According to the 2000 U.S. Census, 3.4 percent of the population aged 5 and older speaks French at home, while 1.6 percent speaks Spanish. In the state's northern-most Coös County, 16.2 percent of the population speaks French at home. However, the long-term trend was a decline. For the state, this decreased between 2000 and 2005 to 33,304 from 39,545 French-speaking at home. The sole exception was for Spanish-speaking emigrants. Those speaking Spanish at home increased during the same period from 18,645 to 20, 789, respectively.

THE NEW IMMIGRATION

New Hampshire has not had large waves of immigration since the early twentieth century. The percentage of state residents who are foreign-born had declined steadily from its high of 22.5 percent in 1910 to a tiny 3.7 percent in 1990. Since then, it rose slowly to 4.4 percent in 2000. This was significantly below the nation's average of 7.9 percent in 1990 and 11.1 percent in 2000, as well as New England's 9.9 percent in 2000.

Unlike many states, New Hampshire had not experienced a surge in undocumented immigration during the 1990–2010 period. While the estimated number had technically tripled from less than 5,000 in 1990 to about 15,000 in 2005, it remained comparatively and absolutely rather low. The estimated "illegal" population remained below 1.6 percent of the state's total population, a percentage that was typical of northern New England but below that of the Northeast in general.

On the other hand, there was ample evidence that another type of immigration since 1980 has been met with increased opposition by those with nativistic sentiment. The state recently has been the destination of a number of international refugees. In the 1997–2009 period, international refugees primarily settled in Manchester (1,807), Concord (778), Laconia (260), and Nashua (70). A state government study found that between 228 and 643 refugees annually had been settled in the state between 1996 and 2000. Some 70.8 percent were from Europe, 16.2 percent were from Africa, and 12.1 percent were from Asia. Previously, 841 had come in 1990; 1,993 had come in 1995; 2,856 had come in 1998; and a higher 4,532 had come in 2000.

Chuda Niroula, a native of Bhutan, poses in his apartment with his country's flag and the United States flag, in Manchester, New Hampshire, on May 8, 2013. Almost two years ago he arrived in Manchester as one of the 60,000 to 80,000 refugees taken in each year by the United States. (AP Photo/Jim Cole)

According to the state government, about 300 to 400 refugees annually are resettled in New Hampshire by two agencies, Lutheran Social Services of New Hampshire and the International Institute of New Hampshire. To assist, these nonprofit agencies received the U.S. Department of State's Bureau of Population and Migration funding and resettled a certain number of refugees based on their ability to provide services for new arrivals coming into the United States. Added funds were provided by the Federal Office of Refugee Resettlement to aid self-sufficiency services.

Despite this support, this relatively small influx has inspired protests and hate crimes. Public sentiment even has led to laws being introduced to control this type of immigration. On March 15, 2012, the state's House of Representatives passed a bill that would allow the city of Manchester to ask for a moratorium on refugee resettlement. Under the bill, New Hampshire towns could ask for a one-year moratorium on new refugee resettlements. The bill's opponents say the state does not have the authority to do this. Manchester representative Phil Greazzo, a Republican, said the resettlement agency was not doing a good job helping refugees integrate into society, and the city's social services were overwhelmed. In light of the state's overall net out-migration trend, the impact of any resettlement curtailment probably would further reduce New Hampshire's population.

NOTABLE GROUPS

CATHOLIC CHARITIES

As in many states, Catholic Charities is an important group aiding immigrants and refugees. They are headquartered in Manchester, New Hampshire, and provide legal advocacy for a wide range of needs. This includes helping resident undocumented children apply for Deferred Action for Childhood Arrivals, helping workers fill out the necessary paper work for legal authorization of employment, and helping victims of domestic violence obtain a U-Visa, for example. In addition to these individualized services, they also run more general education workshops for immigrants and provide some social services and social service referrals. While this organization has been operating since the 1940s, the branch that deals with immigration and refugees was established in 1979 to help Vietnamese refugees arriving after the Vietnam War. When this refugee flow began to decrease, the services expanded to help a broader range of immigrants and refugees settling in the state. Because of its Catholic mission, it is particularly dedicated to keeping families together and helping poor workers. The group also works with state and local food banks to help feed the poor and is particularly concerned about preventing detention and deportation.

BIBLIOGRAPHY

Anderson, Robert Charles. *The Great Migration Begins: Immigrants to New England, 1620–1633*. Vol. 3. Boston: New England Historic Genealogical Society, 1995.

"Below Is a Guide of All 50 States to View Your State Minimum Requirements and Regulations." Autoinsuranceremedy.com. http://www.autoinsuranceremedy.com/new-hampshire-auto-insurance.html. Accessed March 25, 2014.

Brown, Roger Hamilton. *The Struggle for the Indian Stream Territory*. Cleveland: Western Reserve University Press, 1955.

Carlson, Lynn. "New England Population History." Brown University, 2011. http://www.brown.edu/Research/Earthlab/lulchistory/nepopulationgrowth.htm. Accessed March 25, 2014.

Daniels, Roger. *Coming to America: A History of Immigration and Ethnicity in American Life*. 2nd ed. New York: HarperCollins, 2002.

Daniels, Roger. *Guarding the Golden Door: American Immigration Policy and Immigrants since 1882*. New York: Hill and Wang, 2004.

Doan, Daniel. *Indian Stream Republic: Settling a New England Frontier, 1785–1842*. Lebanon, NH: University Press of New England, 1997.

Dublin, Thomas. *Transforming Women's Work: New England Lives in the Industrial Revolution*. Ithaca, NY: Cornell University Press, 1995.

Evans-Brown, Sam. "NH House Passes Refugee Moratorium Bill." NHPR News: New Hampshire, 2012. http://news.nhpr.org/post/nh-house-passes-refugee-moratorium-bill. Accessed March 25, 2014.

Fischer, David Hackett. *Albion's Seed: Four British Folkways in America*. New York: Oxford University Press, 1991.

Fogg, Alonzo J. *The Statistics and Gazetteer of New-Hampshire*. Concord, NH: D. L. Guernsey, 1874.

Garreau, Joel. *Edge City: Life on the New Frontier*. New York: Random House, 1991.

Gibson, Campbell, and Kay Jung. *Historical Census Statistics on the Foreign-Born Population: 1850 to 2000*. Population Division, Working Paper No. 81. Washington, DC: U.S. Census Bureau, 2006.

Gibson, Campbell, and Kay Jung. *Historical Census Statistics on Population Totals by Race, 1790 to 1990, and by Hispanic Origin, 1970 to 1990, for the United States, Regions, Divisions, and States*. Population Division, Working Paper No. 76. Washington, DC: U.S. Census Bureau, 2002.

Governors Highway Safety Association. "Seatbelt Laws." 2012. http://www.ghsa.org/html/stateinfo/laws/seatbelt_laws.html. Accessed March 25, 2014.

Governor's Office of Energy and Community Services. *New Hampshire Refugee Office: Statistical Abstract 2000*. 2000. http://www.nh.gov/oep/programs/refugee/documents/report_master.pdf. Accessed March 25, 2014.

Hansen, Kristin A. *Geographic Mobility: March 1993 to March 1994*. Current Population Reports, P20–485. Washington, DC: U.S. Census Bureau, 1995.

He, Wan, and Jason P. Schachter. *Internal Migration of the Older Population: 1995 to 2000*. Census 2000 Special Reports, CENSR-10. Washington, DC: U.S. Census Bureau, 2003.

"Helmet Law Statutes by State, State of New Hampshire. Age Requirement." Bikersrights. com. http://www.bikersrights.com/states/newhampshire/newhampshire.html. Accessed March 25, 2014.

"Historical Census Data for 1850." University of Virginia, http://fisher.lib.virginia.edu/cgi-local/censusbin/census/cen.pl?year=850. Accessed March 25, 2014.

Hoefer, John P. *New England's Crises and Cultural Memory*. Cambridge: Cambridge University Press, 2004.

Hoefer, John Sribner. *The Isles of Shoals: An Historical Sketch*. New York: Hurd and Houghton, 1873.

Hoefer, Michael, Nancy Rytina, and Bryan C. Baker. *Estimates of the Unauthorized Immigrant Population Residing in the United States: January 2010*. Washington, DC: Office of Immigration Statistics, Policy Directorate, U.S. Department of Homeland Security, 2011.

Internal Revenue Service. "SOI Tax Stats: Migration Data-New Hampshire." 2011. http://www.irs.gov/taxstats/article/0,,id=213891,00.html. Accessed March 25, 2014.

Lyford, James O., Amos Hadley, Will B. Howe, and City History Commission. *History of Concord, New Hampshire: From the Original Grant in Seventeen Hundred and*

Twenty-five to the Opening of the Twentieth Century. Vol. 1. Concord, NH: The Rumford Press, 1896.

Modern Language Association. "MLA Language Map Data Center." 2007. Mla.org. Accessed March 25, 2014.

Molloy, Raven, Christopher L. Smith, and Abigail Wozniak. "Internal Migration in the United States." *Journal of Economic Perspectives* 25, no.3 (2011): 17–96.

New Hampshire Catholic Charities. New Hampshire Catholic Charities Website. http://www.nh-cc.org/what-we-do/immigration-refugee-services.aspx. Accessed February 22, 2014.

New Hampshire Department of Revenue Administration. "Does NH Have an Income Tax or Sales Tax?" 2012. http://www.revenue.nh.gov/faq/gti-rev.htm. Accessed March 25, 2014.

New Hampshire Historical Society. "Greeks in New Hampshire." New Hampshire's Immigrants: Notes and Facts, 2012. http://www.nhhistory.org/edu/support/nhimmigration/nhimmgreek.pdf. Accessed March 25, 2014.

New Hampshire Historical Society. "Irish in New Hampshire." New Hampshire's Immigrants: Notes and Facts, 2012. http://www.nhhistory.org/edu/support/nhimmigration/nhimmirish.pdf. Accessed March 25, 2014.

New Hampshire Historical Society. "New Hampshire's French-Canadian Americans." New Hampshire's Immigrants: Notes and Facts, 2012. http://www.nhhistory.org/edu/support/nhimmigration/nhfrenchcanadians.pdf. Accessed March 26, 2014.

New Hampshire Historical Society. "Russians in New Hampshire." New Hampshire's Immigrants: Notes and Facts, 2012. http://www.nhhistory.org/edu/support/nhimmigration/nhimmrussian.pdf. Accessed March 36, 2014.

New Hampshire Office of Energy and Planning. "New Hampshire Refugee Program: Program Services." 2012. http://www.nh.gov/oep/programs/refugee/services.htm. Accessed March 26, 2014.

New Hampshire Office of Energy and Planning. "Population Center of New Hampshire, 1950–2000." October 2007.

Palermo, Sarah. "Refugee Homes Targeted: Malicious Graffiti Called Hate Crime." *Concord Monitor*, September 20, 2011. http://www.concordmonitor.com/news/4541141-95/graffiti-refugees-manesseengendahayo. Accessed August 22, 2014.

Passel, Jeffrey S., and D'Vera Cohn. "Unauthorized Immigrant Population: National and State Trends, 2010." Pew Hispanic Center, 2011. http://pewhispanic.org/files/reports/133.pdf. Accessed March 26, 2014.

"The Peterborough Town Library." Libraryhistorybuff.org. Accessed March 26, 2014.

Porter, Douglas R. "Deflecting Growth in Exurban New Hampshire." *Urban Land* (June 1989): 34–35.

Ren, Ping. *Lifetime Mobility in the United States: 2010.* American Community Survey Briefs, ACSBR10–07. Washington, DC: U.S. Census Bureau, 2011.

Smith, Helen Ainsley. *The Thirteen Colonies: Virginia, Massachusetts, New Hampshire, New York.* New York: Knickerbocker Press, 1901.

U.S. Census Bureau. *2005 American Community Survey & Census 2000.* Summary File 3, STP 258. Washington, DC: U.S. Census Bureau, 2011.

U.S. Census Bureau. 2010 *American Community Survey 1-Year Estimates: State-to-State Migration Flows*. Washington, DC: U.S. Census Bureau, 2010.

U.S. Census Bureau. *Annual Estimates of the Resident Population for the United States, Regions, States, and Puerto Rico: April 1, 2010 to July 1, 2011*. 2011 Population Estimates. Washington, DC: U.S. Census Bureau, Population Division, 2011a.

U.S. Census Bureau. *Cumulative Estimates of the Components of Resident Population Change for Counties: April 1, 2010 to July 1, 2011*. Washington, DC: U.S. Census Bureau, 2011b.

U.S. Census Bureau. *Immigrants, Outmigrants, and Net Migration between 1985 and 1990 and Movers from Abroad, for States: 1990*. Table 5. Washington, DC: U.S. Census Bureau, 1992.

U.S. Census Bureau. *Population*. Washington, DC: U.S. Census Bureau, 1910.

U.S. Census Bureau. *Resident Population Data: Population Change*. Washington, DC: U.S. Census Bureau, 2012.

U.S. Census Bureau. *State of Residence in 2000 by State of Birth: 2000*. Census 2000 Brief, PHC-T38. Washington, DC: U.S. Census Bureau, 2005.

U.S. Department of Homeland Security. *Estimates of the Unauthorized Immigrant Population Residing in the United States: 1990 to 2000*. 2003. http://www.dhs.gov/xlibrary /assets/ statistics/publications/Ill_Report_1211.pdf. Accessed March 25, 2014.

U.S. Department of Homeland Security. *Persons Naturalized by State or Territory of Residence: Fiscal Years 2001 to 2010, Yearbook of Immigration Statistics*, Table 22, 2011.

Veblen, Eric. *The Manchester Union Leader in New Hampshire Elections*. New York: HarperCollins, 1975.

Vorhees, Mara, Gregor Clark, Ned Friary, Paula Hardy, and Caroline Sieg. *New England Lonely Planet*. London: Lonely Planet, 2008.

Wang, Beverley. "State Senate Approves Civil Unions for Same-Sex Couples." *Concord Monitor*, April 26, 2007. http://www.concordmonitor.com/article/state-senate-approves-civil-unions-for-same-sex-couples. Accessed August 7, 2014.

Workers of Federal Writing Project of the Works Progress Administration (Federal Writing Project). *New Hampshire: A Guide to the Granite State*. Boston: Houghton Mifflin, 1938.

30

New Jersey

Karey Leung

CHRONOLOGY

Pre-Founding	The Ramapough Lenape, Nanticoke Lenni-Lenape Tribal, and Powhatan Renape Nation are the original peoples of New Jersey. As part of the Algonquin nation, the Lenni-Lenape tribe is known for its peaceful ways and mediation of conflicts within the Algonquin nation.
1524	New Jersey coastline is explored by early Europeans.
1609	Henry Hudson arrives in Newark Bay.
1638	Swedish colony is established on the Delaware River.
1655	The Dutch settle in the Swedish colony.
1660	The Dutch establish the first European town (Bergen) in what is now New Jersey.
1676	This early colony is divided between East Jersey and West Jersey.
1683	The English colonize land by force from the Lenni-Lenape tribe in the area known today as Freehold, beginning in 1683. At this time, almost half of the people in New Jersey are English immigrants. The Dutch comprise the second-largest immigrant group and a fifth of the people, followed by Swedes and Finns who move along the Delaware River, and the Scots who settle in East Jersey.
1702	East Jersey and West Jersey are united to form one colony.
1721	The village of "Trent's Town" (now Trenton) is established.
1746	Princeton University is established.
1766	Rutgers University is founded.
1787	New Jersey becomes the third state to ratify the U.S. Constitution.

1790	New Jersey is the first signatory on the Bill of Rights.
1790–1840	First significant wave of immigration occurs after the United States is formed; most immigrants come from England, Ireland, Germany, and France. Nativist hostility directed against the working class, largely Catholic immigrants from Ireland and Germany is based on fears of their "clannishness" as well as public drinking. In a time of economic hardship, earlier Protestant immigrants fear Catholics; people also feel that recent immigrants would compete for low-skilled jobs and stereotype the new arrivals as immoral, carriers of disease, and prone to criminal activity. The Order of United Americans, an early variant of the Know-Nothing Party, promotes anti-Catholicism in the state.
1804	The state provides for the "Gradual Abolition of Slavery."
1807	The franchise (vote) is limited to free, white, male citizens.
1844	The New Jersey Constitution disqualifies Catholics from holding public office. Suffrage restrictions are based largely on class as voting is restricted to tax-paying property owners.
1844–1855	While the New Jersey Supreme Court reinterprets "taxable inhabitant" to coincide with federal law in restricting voting to white male citizens in 1844, noncitizens vote in local and school board elections until the superintendent sues North Brunswick township to annul the results of a school board election in 1855.
1860	The Underground Railroad is active in New Jersey.
1863	The draft riots occur in Newark and other major cities; these riots are now viewed as anti-Irish and were often harmful to African Americans.
1865–1915	First- and second-generation immigrants comprise most of the work force during the industrial period of growth in the 50 years after the Civil War.
1870s	Chinese laborers eventually organize strikes as well to fight for better working conditions and wages. To attract immigrants to fill the labor shortage from westward expansion, New Jersey's Commissioner of Immigration, also the local realtor, actively recruits immigration to the state's undeveloped agricultural areas in the south.
1870	After California bars the Chinese after construction of the transcontinental railroads, a New Jersey steam laundry factory recruits Chinese laborers from San Francisco to break up a Knights of Labor strike of Irish women workers in Belleville.
1871	The American working class in urban areas comprise mostly of noncitizens.
1880s–1910s	During the second wave of immigration from the 1880s to 1910s, southern Italians are the largest group of immigrants in New Jersey, followed by Russians, Austrians, Hungarians, Czechs, Polish, and Slovaks. While these immigrants may have been professionals or

	skilled laborers in their home countries, many had to work in manual labor or semiskilled jobs to survive.
1881–1915	While Jewish peddlers have been in Monmouth County since 1716, Russian Jews escaping the pogroms of 1881–1915 settle in two agricultural colonies in Alliance and Woodbine in southern New Jersey with resources from Jewish philanthropists.
1892	Ellis Island Immigration Station is established.
1913	New Jersey silk strike occurs in Paterson.
1915	Standard Oil Strike, Bayonne occurs.
1919	Textile workers strike for a 44-hour week in Paterson.
1933	German citizen Albert Einstein visits the United States for the first time and the Nazis establish their power while he is traveling. His cottage and boat are confiscated by the Nazis and a bounty is set by the Nazis. His books are burned and by the end of the year he travels back to the United States. Einstein becomes one of the first scholars in residence at the Institute for Advanced Studies, established the same year at Princeton.
1934	Seabrook Farms strike occurs.
1935	Albert Einstein applies for U.S. citizenship, remaining at Princeton for the rest of his life.
1948	The Displaced Persons Act of 1948 brings immigrants to New Jersey.
1949	New Jersey passes the Civil Rights Act.
1965	Hart-Celler Act is passed.
1976	Migrant worker program is established.
1980s	Central American refugees arrive in New Jersey, receiving mixed status.
1998	The U.S. Supreme Court rules that New Jersey controls the majority of Ellis Island (versus New York).
2001 (September 11)	Terrorist attacks and their consequences affect the New York and New Jersey area significantly.
2011	An immigration report by the Pew Hispanic Trust shows that the number of illegal immigrants in New Jersey remained steady between 2007 and 2010, though New Jersey was still among the states with the highest number of undocumented immigrants, with about 550,000, or about 6 percent of the state's population.
2014	A bill is introduced in the New Jersey legislature to extend driving privileges to undocumented immigrants.

HISTORICAL OVERVIEW

New Jersey prospered during the postwar decades. Economic prosperity was due in part to growth in agricultural, manufacturing, technical, and research-based industries. To support the growth of these industries, New Jersey businesses actively hired immigrants and encouraged migrations of people to work in farms and factories in the post–world war years.

Seabrook Farms

After a strike of 500 African American and Italian workers organizing for higher wages was broken up by local police and state troopers who fired tear gas bombs to stop the protest in 1934 (*New York Times* 1934), the owner of Seabrook Farms, Charles F. Seabrook, started the practice of contracting labor from detained prisoners of war. After the war, to replace German prisoners of war who left for Germany, Seabrook contracted Japanese Americans and Japanese Peruvians detained in U.S. internment camps in the West. Roughly 3,000 Japanese Americans settled in the area north of Bridgeton which at the time had the largest population of Japanese Americans in any town in the United States. Besides contracting those interned in detention camps, Seabrook Farms also recruited West Indian, Jamaican, and Puerto Rican laborers. Following the Displaced Persons Act of 1948 which made Estonian "displaced persons" available for labor on U.S. soil, the frozen foods-processing factory also sponsored Estonian refugees escaping Soviet occupation to work 12-hour shifts at the Bridgeton factory. Other farms in south Jersey took advantage of Mexican labor during the guest worker Bracero Program. Campbell Soup in Camden and Glassboro Farm contracted labor from Puerto Rico during and after World War II. Between 1920 and 1950, the Latino population increased sixfold from 1,684 to 11,387—mostly due to the growth of the Puerto Rican, Central and South Americans communities.

U.S. Representative Peter Rodino's Immigration Bills

Newark congressman and chair of the House Judiciary Committee Peter W. Rodino was one of the proponents to reform immigration policy in 1965. After the federal government abolished the quota system in the Immigration and Nationality Act of 1965 in which employment and family reunification preferences were established, most immigrants arrived from the Americas and Asia. In 1973, Rodino also sponsored a federal immigration bill to curb undocumented immigration and punish businesses for knowingly hiring undocumented workers. He sought to reform immigration procedures to cut down on lengthy waits for immigrants from countries in the Western Hemisphere seeking to reunite with families in 1976.

Migrant Farmworkers

In 1976, Glassboro Association joined by Green Giant Farms headquartered in Vineland contracted with the Commonwealth of Puerto Rico to bring

4,000 temporary farmers to work in rural farms and nurseries. The pact raises the minimum wage by 10 cents to $2.40 per hour for agricultural workers and $2.45 per hour for nursery workers. Besides these official efforts to recruit migrant farm labor, there were incidents of informal recruitment of contract labor from Puerto Rico by private farms in which worker abuse and wage theft was reported. In June 1975, young Puerto Rican migrant farmworkers employed at Sorbello vegetable farm in Gloucester County alleged involuntary servitude by crew leader Marcos Portalatin. The resulting legal case of enslavement was a first in New Jersey and a first in the United States for over 100 years. When legal advocates from the American Civil Liberties Union (ACLU), state assemblyman Byron M. Baer (D-Bergen), and reporters from *The Star-Ledger* tried to conduct an investigation into the abuses at Sorbello by interviewing workers, the investigators were violently pushed out of the farm. Migrant workers at Sorbello farms worked 10- to 14-hour days, 7 days a week. They told of physical abuse, withheld wages, and forced purchasing of provisions at the company store. Some workers were taking home a few cents for a whole week of work.

The practice of hiring migrant farm labor continued to the present period. In 2010, the rural areas of Vineland, Bridgeton, and Millville in south Jersey helped Cumberland County reach "majority-minority" status with Latinos, African Americans, and Asians comprising 50.1 percent of the population according to the U.S. Census Bureau. Essex County, home to residents of Brazilian and Portuguese descent is New Jersey's other majority-minority county.

Central American Refugees

During the 1980s, the New Jersey Central American Network and the New Jersey Inter-Religious Task Force, made up of disarmament and asylum rights groups supporting refugees from El Salvador, Guatemala, and Nicaragua, publically protested President Reagan's involvement with Nicaraguan contras. Speaking at the groups' rally at Montclair, Sister Darlene Nicgorski, one of the 11 defendants on trial in Arizona for helping undocumented immigrants from Central America during the refugee crisis noted the discrepancy in the treatment of political refugees from Soviet countries and those from Central America. Church groups gave sanctuary to Central American refugees who were refused political asylum status by the U.S. government. New Jersey churches joined the sanctuary movement of close to 200 churches around the country to shelter undocumented asylum seekers from arrests by U.S. immigration authorities. During the height of the refugee crisis, there were an estimated 10,000 to 25,000 undocumented Central American refugees sheltered in churches and communities in mainly Essex, Hudson, and Union counties. The New Jersey Center for Central American Refugees in Plainfield assisted undocumented refugees with basic survival needs as well as offered legal aid to those facing deportation proceedings.

IMMIGRATION AND NATURALIZATION SERVICE TREATMENT OF LATINOS

In February 1980, the case of wrongfully deported American citizen Norberto Gautier to Guatemala revealed the ways in which the INS in U.S. colony Puerto Rico may have abused their authority in seeking deportations of suspected undocumented immigrants. When Gautier was about to board a plane from San Juan back to Newark, INS authorities charged Gautier of being a Guatemala citizen based on his accent. When Gautier showed his social security card to prove his U.S. citizenship, INS officers refused to accept the document claiming the card was forged. Gautier's lawyer, Jeffrey Fogel from the Urban Legal Clinic of Rutgers University Law School argued that Gautier was detained and interrogated for three days during which time he was pressured to sign a voluntary deportation order. After efforts by Gautier's brother, members of the ACLU of New Jersey, and U.S. senator Bill Bradley, Gautier was released from a Guatemalan prison although consulate officials in Guatemala resisted his release.

WELFARE REFORM OF 1996

In 1996, Governor Christie Whitman proposed an overhaul of the state welfare system by replacing Family Development Program and Aid to Families with Dependent Children with Work First New Jersey. Following the provisions of the federal Personal Responsibility and Work Opportunity and Reconciliation Act of 1996, Governor Whitman's plan would end state-level welfare to legal permanent residents (LPRs) if they arrived after the passage of the federal law on August 22, 1996. The final version of the bill passed on January 29, 1997 barred LPRs from receiving benefits from the Work First New Jersey program after six months unless they could prove they were on the path to citizenship. According to the provisions of the law, LPRs must have had either passed the civics and English portion of the citizenship exam or were in the final stages of the naturalization process (P.L. 1997, c.14 [S38; A15]).

PUNITIVE MEASURES AGAINST BUSINESSES

A 1996 bill was introduced in the state legislature stating that all public contracts could be terminated if the employer does not abide by the rules as stated in the Immigration and Nationality Act. If the employer employed a person not lawfully permitted to work in the United States, then the company would be barred from entering into public contracts or grants with the state. Companies would be responsible for fines up to $10,000 for every undocumented worker hired. This bill would have raised the fines that U.S. congressman Rodino set in 1973 tenfold.

Red Bank

In 1999, a xenophobic flier attacking immigrants was posted in the town of Red Bank. The flier read "Did you simply ignore the problem or were you too busy trying to get that little worm out of the tequila bottle? Wake up and smell the tacos, U.S. citizens! Red Bank can no longer afford to wait for the U.S. Federal Government to pass immigration laws. We Must Act Now!!!" The flier further dehumanized undocumented immigrants: "This infestation of IA's [illegal aliens] has recently started to spread east of Broad Street." Mayor Pasquale Menna called the flier "racist" and stated that immigration policing is a federal issue. Police spokesman captain Stephen McCarthy supports Menna's denunciation of the racist sign (Burton 1999).

Post-9/11 Anti-Immigrant Legislation

Introduced by District 9 assemblymen Christopher J. Connors and Jeffrey W. Moran on February 11, 2002, an anti-immigration bill urged Congress to reform immigration policies in line with the "national interest." Drawn up in the aftermath of 9/11, the language of the bill paints both undocumented and legal immigration as "threatening America's foundation." Seeking to roll back immigration levels to pre-1965 levels which the bill calls "traditional levels" of 300,000 people per year, the bill supports the funding and enactment of the federal Illegal Reform and Immigration Responsibility Act of 1986. Among the anti-immigrant provisions of the bill were calls to require schools to report foreign students if they did not begin classes; bar entry of visitors, immigrants, and refugees from countries "known to pose a terrorist threat"; and withdrawal of federal funds from cities who pass "immigrant protection ordinances." The most controversial portion of the bill sought a constitutional amendment to ban birthright citizenship for those whose parents were not citizens or LPRs (Legal Permanent Residents). Despite unsuccessful attempts, the bill has been repeatedly reintroduced into the state senate and assembly since 2002.

Day Laborers' Rights—Freehold

In 2003, upon pressure from an anti-immigrant group Pressing Our Elected Officials to Protect Our Living Environment, which endorsed candidates who introduce anti-immigrant ordinances, the officials at Freehold voted to prevent laborers from finding work by a day-laborer site outside of town. Joseph B. Bellina, borough administrator for Freehold did not want Freehold to be a magnet for day laborers, many of whom he claimed do not reside in the township. Moreover, residents of Freehold have complained that laborers litter and urinate in public without public facilities nearby. The mayor of Freehold equated undocumented immigrants as carriers of disease. When Freehold first forbade workers from congregating at "las vías," Rev. Dr. Andre McGuire offered the Second Baptist Church to serve as a temporary day labor-hiring site. The church catalogued the workers' skills and matched them with employers' needs. The Reverend McGuire argued from a human rights perspective: "[t]o jump up and cut off a man's livelihood is inhumane" (Peterson 2003). He acknowledged that his solution was a temporary measure that ultimately should require a more permanent solution. The Reverend McGuire sought collaboration with surrounding communities where day laborers reside.

One year later in 2004, day laborers fought against Freehold residents in reclaiming public space in which to solicit work. National Day Laborer Organizing Network and other immigrant rights groups supported the day laborers in Freehold. After a lawsuit was filed by the Puerto Rican Legal Defense and Education Fund (PRLDEF), Mexican day laborers were allowed back in "las vías." Casa Freehold, a nonprofit organization that fought for migrants' rights and provided language and basic aid to migrants, helped in the struggle to reestablish the day-labor site. Migrants interviewed by researchers and activists complained of harassment by police and local residents. Some workers worked without breaks, food, water, or were denied pay after working. In one incident, a researcher witnessed the Freehold police ordering migrants away from a shaded area under the trees and forced migrants to stand in the officially sanctioned area on a particularly hot day.

In January 2011, a Seton Hall Law School study interviewing 113 day laborers at seven day-laborer sites in New Jersey found abuse (26 percent), wage theft (54 percent), unsafe conditions (43 percent), and injuries (26 percent) on the job. Of those who faced assaults by their employers, only 14 percent filed a report with the police. About 35 percent of the subjects reported being abandoned at the worksite, while very few day laborers reported wage losses to the Department of Labor and Workforce Development (Immigrants' Rights/International Human Rights Clinic 2011, 2). A summit sponsored by federal labor authorities claimed that close to 25 percent of all work-related deaths occur to Latino workers. New Jersey's migrant farmworkers and day laborers are particularly vulnerable to casualties and injuries on the job.

Anti-Immigrant Legislation in Response to Violent Crime

After the murder of two brothers, Karlo Gonzalez and Zabdiel Gonzalez, 14 and 7 years old, respectively, by undocumented immigrant Richard Toledo in Stafford

Township in 2006, senators Connors and Oroho introduced a resolution to urge Congress to enact comprehensive immigration reform. Linking undocumented immigrants with a rise in violent crime and terrorism, the resolution chastised Mexico for encouraging unlawful entry of Mexican citizens across the U.S. border by allegedly publishing "how-to" manuals. The resolution explicitly referred to the Gonzalez's murders as impetus for the resolution. Also, in May 2007, an unsuccessful terrorist attempt to kill Fort Dix soldiers by a group comprising three undocumented immigrants and three legal immigrants prompted state lawmakers to plead to Washington for tightening federal immigration policy. New Jersey's Office of Homeland Security gave testimony to the Assembly Homeland Security and Preparedness Committee in which legislators warned against the threat of "homegrown terrorism" from what was considered as lax federal immigration enforcement.

TOPICAL ESSAYS

287(G) Agreements

In reaction to a murder of three Newark college students by a group of suspects, one of whom was an undocumented immigrant released on bail, New Jersey's attorney general Anne Milgram issued executive order Law Enforcement Directive No. 2007–3 to deputize local law enforcement officers to report those arrested and suspected of undocumented status to Immigration and Customs Enforcement (ICE). The directive gives instructions to state, county, and state law enforcement officers to inquire into the immigration status of detained suspects. The order is similar to 287(g) state and local immigration enforcement agreements across the country in which authority is delegated to local enforcement agencies to enforce immigration law. The directive seeks to report criminal immigrants to ICE if there is reason to believe that the suspect may be undocumented. The directive is meant to report only suspects of serious crimes or drunken driving offenses. However, a Seton Hall University study found that an overwhelming number of those reported to ICE and later detained did not commit serious crimes nor were driving while intoxicated. The study found that 72 percent of the 68 interviewees reported to ICE were detained for minor traffic violations unrelated to driving while intoxicated. While the executive order, "explicitly restricts law enforcement from inquiring into or investigating the immigration status of any victim, witness, or person requesting assistance from the police" (Department of Law and Public Safety 4), a number of detained respondents were passengers in vehicles or questioned while a victim or witness to a crime. About 28 percent of the suspects in custody reported having never been arrested for a crime but were apprehended on the street for no other reason except they were suspected of undocumented status. According to the report, between September 2007 and March 2008, only 1,417 of

The U.S. Immigration and Customs Enforcement officers take a man into custody in New Jersey on March 28, 2012. In 1996, the United States implemented a mass detention and deportation system, implicating thousands of immigrants whose only crime was often working in the United States. Families have been separated and individuals returned to countries where they may never have lived. Since Barack Obama was elected, this system has only been strengthened. (AP Photo/U.S. Immigration and Customs Enforcement)

the 10,000 individuals reported to ICE by law enforcement officers had civil immigration violations. Roughly a third of those referred to ICE in the first six months of the directive's implementation were either U.S. citizens or legal residents of the country. The report notes that the selective criteria for arrests and detention provide evidence that the directive encourages racial profiling in a state that has a high percentage of naturalized citizens and Latino immigrants. Scholars, legal advocates, and public officials have protested the program for violating the equal protection and due process clause of the Fourteenth Amendment.

Since the directive, local counties have tried to implement 287(g) agreements in their communities. Morristown local police applied to be trained by ICE agents to spot and detain those who are perceived to be without documentation. In 2007, immigrant rights groups protested Morristown's mayor Donald Cresitello's plan to implement the 287(g) program in conflating local police functions with non-criminal civil violation enforcement. Groups opposing Morristown's operation of

287(g) included the New Jersey Immigration Policy Network, American Friends Service Committee (Newark), Latino Alliance of New Jersey, Morris County Hispanic American Chamber of Commerce, Wind of the Spirit Immigration resource center in Morristown, ACLU, American Jewish Committee, and the Jersey Battered Women's Service. In November 2009, the new mayor Tim Dougherty successfully ran against Cresitello during the primaries by opposing the implementation of 287(g) which he claimed was ripe for abuse as police may unfairly target those who look Latino as well as dampen the trust between the immigrant community and local police.

In 2009, Monmonth County went beyond the 2007 statewide directive to inquire into the immigration status of all those incarcerated in the county jail regardless of the crime committed. Winning her campaign on the promise to implement the 287(g) program, Monmouth County sheriff Kim Guadagno praised the program for increasing public safety in the county. However, the chair of the Monmouth County chapter of the Latino Leadership Alliance of New Jersey, Frank Argote-Freyre criticized Guadagno for pandering to anti-immigrant beliefs to gain political traction as the Monmouth County Jail had less than 1 percent of undocumented immigrants (Celano 2009). As of 2012, Hudson County Department of Corrections (since 2008) and Monmouth County Sheriff's Office (since 2009) are listed as participating localities that participate in the 287(g) program.

COMMUNITY IDENTIFICATION CARDS

After a brutally beaten man was found dead and unidentified for over a week in 2008, the Latin American Legal Defense and Education Fund (LALDEF) of Princeton with the support of the Princeton Police Department decided to introduce community ID cards to give added protection to a vulnerable population as well as allow individuals to use the local library and receive medical care at hospitals. The photo ID card is recognized by police, clinics, hospitals, libraries, parks, and schools in the greater Mercer County area. While the community ID card was originally issued based on the needs of the undocumented population, the card also helps those who find it difficult to receive a photo ID card such as the homeless and those on probation or in re-entry programs. One-tenth of the cards are issued to American citizens. In 2009, Tremendously Trenton Coalition and LALDEF worked to establish a similar community identification card program in Trenton.

DEPORTATION

Activists and legal advocates are fighting to stay the deportation of two brothers who are eligible to apply for legal permanent residency under the Development,

Relief, and Education for Alien Minors Act provisions. Residents of Paterson, Michell D. Valle and Yasser S. Valle, known as the Valle brothers, came to the United States at age 6 and 5 years, respectively, and have received high school and college diplomas. They are due for deportation after one year (Michell D. Valle) and three months (Yasser S. Valle) in detention. The Newark ICE office refused the Stay of Removal requested by the Valle brothers' lawyer. Since the Valle brothers have been in the United States since they were young children and pose no threat to national security, supporters argue that the Valle brothers should be considered for a stay in the final order of removal as outlined by the Morton memorandum, written by ICE's director, John Morton. Over 1,000 people have signed a petition to the Newark ICE office to exercise prosecutorial discretion in the Valle brothers' deportation cases.

DETENTION CENTERS

The New Jersey Advocates for Immigrant Detainees (NJAID) protested Essex County's five-year contract with ICE signed in 2011 to build a new 2,700 bed detention center. NJAID warned that the projected revenue from the contract failed to take into account the role of a third party for-profit prison company, a subsidiary of GEO Group. According to the members of NJAID, "[o]f the $108 per day that Essex will receive from ICE, $78 per day will be paid directly to the private company, a corporation with a checkered history" (Gottlieb et al. 2012). NJAID contend that the public was not properly informed of the profits that would be directly absorbed by GEO group, which had been cited for human rights violations at their other private immigrant detention facilities in other parts of the country. In a report published on March 23, 2012, New York University law school's immigrant rights clinic found that conditions at Essex County detention centers were not up to the safety standards of ICE's nonbinding guidelines. Despite the so-called reforms, facilities still failed to meet ICE standards: "[e]very indicator of the conditions and treatment of immigrant detainees in Essex County shows a detention system that is failing to meet the bare minimum of humane treatment and due process" (Freeman and Major 2012, 3). Most of the immigrants detained in Essex County violated only civil charges and have no criminal record. At the Bergen County Jail, a 22-year-old immigrant detainee committed suicide due to the lack of medical services to ameliorate the detainee's pain from a preexisting medical condition. Despite recommendation to change human rights violations at New Jersey's detention centers, little has been done. Across the board, over 75 percent of the 1,500 detainees in New Jersey were not represented by a lawyer in 2009. Other violations vary across detention facilities. At some locations, visitation hours are limited to 30 minutes; there are a lack of contact visits with friends and family; the elderly, mentally ill, and disabled are held without adequate medical personnel and facilities to treat such populations; and access to legal materials is restricted to only 45 minutes a week (Monmouth County Jail). After one year from the first report, there have been more cases of physical and verbal abuse at the Essex County Jail and inattention to detainees' grievances have been reported at Hudson County Jail.

E-Verify

In May 2010, Assemblywoman McHose, Senator Steve Oroho, and Assemblyman Gary Chiusano sponsored legislation to enforce the use of E-Verify concurrently in the senate and assembly. Businesses could be fined between $100 and $1000 for each undocumented worker hired and could lose their business licenses temporarily or permanently for repeat offenders. Political scientist Michael Rodriguez at Richard Stockton College calls the targeting of businesses by federal and statewide auditing as "silent raids" as businesses were often unaware of immigration audits until the last moment when employers have little time to seek legal help or ensure their hiring records are in order (Rodriguez 2012, 13). Businesses in the agricultural, landscaping, restaurant, and resort industries complain that E-Verify unfairly burdens employers who are finding it difficult to staff jobs that most Americans do not want to do.

Higher Education/Tuition Equity

In February 2011, the County College of Morris (CCM) voted to overturn its nine-year policy of denying undocumented students admission to the college after the terrorist attacks of 9/11. Within two months, CCM backed out of its decision to charge in-state prices for undocumented students when the county's freeholders and conservative group Judicial Watch sent a letter to the trustees threatening to sue the county college based on its violation of a 1996 federal law to prohibit undocumented immigrants from receiving public services. One of the trustees justified his reversal of the decision: "I'm not in favor of defending in court a vote of ours that might cost tens of thousands of dollars in legal fees" (*The Huffington Post* 2011).

In December 2011, pro-immigrant Democratic assemblyman Angel Fuentes representing Audobon, Camden, and Woodbury counties sponsored a bill that would make taxpaying residents eligible for the New Jersey Better Educational Savings program. To apply, one need only a taxpayer ID number or a social security number to receive a possible scholarship of up to $1,500 in a New Jersey college or university. This allows those without a social security number access to a college savings plan that would help undocumented immigrants pay for their children's higher education expenses. The bill also set up a New Jersey Dream Fund

Commission made up of nine members appointed by the governor to further help advance the educational opportunities of children of immigrants (A4401).

The New Jersey legislature rejected the Higher Education Citizenship Equality Act, a tuition bill that would allow undocumented college students to pay in-state tuition in January 2012. Americans for Legal Immigration, an anti-illegal immigration group, helped to lobby against the bill. New Jersey is the only state among the top five most populous states for immigration that does not offer in-state tuition to undocumented students.

In early 2012, a New Jersey high-school student who is an American citizen was denied state financial aid for college because her mother was an undocumented immigrant. The ACLU and Rutgers Litigation lawyers argued that the student was denied rights that all native-born citizens should receive under the Fourteenth Amendment. The New Jersey Supreme Court ruled that the applicant was wrongfully denied state aid due to a 2005 bureaucratic rule that required the student's parents to provide documents such as a driver's license if the student was under 24 years of age and still lived with the parents. This change in regulations could affect hundreds to thousands of U.S. citizens who are denied aid because their parents could not provide the official documentation required for the state aid application. A bill introduced in the state senate would ensure that U.S. citizens of undocumented immigrants would have the same access to in-state tuition rates as other citizens and legal immigrants.

Highland Park

Following the tradition of the national church sanctuary movement to protect Central American refugees from deportation in the 1980s, the Reformed Church of Highland Park currently acts as a sanctuary for Indonesian Christian refugees who are facing deportation orders from ICE. Indonesian Christians face persecution if returned to the mostly Muslim nation. Those who are in the ICE databases have been denied asylum because they applied too late upon arrival in the country. In 2009, Rev. Seth Kaper-Dale made arrangements with ICE supervisors to allow 72 Indonesian Christians to receive temporary work permits to remain in the United States. After two years, ICE changed its mind and deported five Indonesian Christians back to their home country. The Reverend Kaper-Dale along with immigrant rights activists have been lobbying Congress to pass legislation to allow Indonesian Christian asylum seekers to reapply for asylum status even if they had missed the previous deadline.

Illegal Immigration Relief Act Ordinance in Riverside

Riverside was one of the towns following in the footsteps of Hazleton, Pennsylvania, to pass a version of the Illegal Immigration Relief Act (IIRA) ordinance.

After the ACLU, PRLDEF, People for the American Way, several businesses, and landlords successfully won a lawsuit against the town's ordinance, Riverside paid $82,000 in legal fees to Immigration Reform Law Institute (IRLI) lawyers in the fight to uphold the ordinance. The legal extension of the anti-immigration group Federation for American Immigration Reform, IRLI also defends the IIRA ordinance in other towns across the county. In *Riverside Coalition v. Riverside*, the plaintiffs sought to dismiss the ordinance for suspending business licenses for up to five years and fining businesses and landlords $2,000 for knowingly hiring or renting to undocumented immigrants, respectively. Responding to grassroots political pressure from anti-immigrant groups, Riverside's mayor Charles Hilton supported the restrictionist policy for pushing illegal immigrants out of Riverside. He said that "[t]he business district is fairly vacant now, but it's not the legitimate businesses that are gone. . . . It's all the ones that were supporting the illegal immigrants, or, as I like to call them, the criminal aliens." Many businesses are suffering from the flight of immigrants from the town (Belson and Capuzzo 2007). "The ordinance almost authorizes a vigilante-type of attitude," said David Verduin, a Riverside business owner and a plaintiff. "Everyone lives in fear." He added, "Immigration is too complicated an issue for us to make a judgment on. Even federal agents need a court's help in deciding who is here illegally" ("Businesses Sue Riverside" 2006). Current mayor George Conard has changed his mind after voting for the ordinance.

Morristown Anti-Crowding Ordinance

Due to pressures from the neighborhood association and concerned residents who claimed they do not allow their children to play on the street because the day laborers were perceived to be a threat to neighborhood safety, the former mayor Jay Delaney increased enforcement of single-family use ordinance violations. Delaney hired two more housing inspectors as well as created another municipal court specifically to prosecute housing violators of the anti-crowding ordinance. Landlords could be charged $30,000 and spend time in jail for "stacked housing" in which 18–20 men would pay up to $500 to share a portion of the house.

Besides stepping up enforcement of anti-crowding laws, Mayor Cresitello wanted to make conditions for day laborers more difficult, alleging that the move would help reduce crime. One of the scare tactics Cresitello practiced was to instruct the Morristown police to survey day laborers every morning. Day laborers who sought out contractors by blocking the entrance of local businesses were told they would be reported to the Department of Labor. Cresitello noted that this may be an empty threat: "[w]ho knows if the state will actually do something . . . much less the Feds, but maybe it'll be a deterrent" (Rockland 2008). On May 1, 2008, hundreds of day laborers in Morristown joined the national protest "A Day without Immigrants."

Post-9/11 Surveillance

Despite previous denials that New Jersey authorities worked alongside the New York Police Department (NYPD) in investigating terrorism cases in New Jersey, a NYPD Intelligence Division report published in July 2012 confirmed involvement of New Jersey law enforcement agencies in working with the NYPD in infiltrating the Islamic Center of Passaic County in Paterson. Newark police and state police officers were also notified of NYPD surveillance of New Jersey's "ethnic hotspots" in Paterson, Jersey City, and Edison. Governor Christie originally denied knowledge of NYPD surveillance of New Jersey residents of Arab descent. New Jersey state police involvement with NYPD investigations came to light during Imam Dr. Mohammad Ahmad Hasan Qatanani's deportation trial based on an appeal of the immigration ruling that granted him legal permanent residency status in 1999. The NYPD contracted an informant through the New Jersey Office of Counter-Terrorism to gain access to the Islamic Center. In a city with the second-largest Muslim population in the United States, Imam Qatanani heads one of the largest Muslim mosques in the country. Born in Palestine, Imam Qatanani has a doctorate in Islamic Jurisprudence from the Jordanian University and has given over 100 speeches at churches and synagogues in New Jersey. He was the 2010 Heinburg Civic Fellow at Rutgers-Newark College of Arts and Sciences. Interfaith supporters of the spiritual leader claim that his contributions to the Muslim and larger community especially his attempts at building interfaith dialogue toward tolerance and peace immediately following the attacks of 9/11 should count toward his stay of deportation. Since July 2006, the Imam and his family have been in removal proceedings for failing to disclose his time in detention by Israeli authorities in his 1999 application for LPR status. Imam Qatanani's lawyer disputes the perjury claim as detention of Palestinians by Israel was a routine procedure especially during the first intifada in 1993 when Qatanani was held and was not charged for any crime.

Protests and Activists

Alfredo Lopez, a day laborer from Freehold spoke out at the national day laborer assembly in Los Angeles. He said that he would not do day laborer work if he had the language skills and legal status: "We don't have a choice but to do this kind of work. . . . Only those who are here legally, who speak English, and who have better skills stay out of the streets and get better jobs." Another day laborer from Oregon expressed the following: "There's dignity in work. . . . People should be allowed to make a living, here and everywhere. It shouldn't even be considered a threat for a community because it's also service. You're helping your community" (Guidi and Juliano 2012). Alejandro Abarca started Workers Committee for

Progress and Social Welfare. Abarca and other activists fought to raise the minimum wage of day laborers to $10 an hour.

In Lakewood, a group led by resident Diane Reaves planned to rally against illegal immigration in August 2007. She claimed that the group's First-Amendment rights were denied as police refused to offer added protection for what was considered a private function. Fearing "gangs" would threaten members of the rally, Reaves waged a public campaign against the police department as well as several groups who promised support and then reneged on their decision.

RAIDS AND DEPORTATION

In the first public report that documents violations made by ICE agents in home raids, the Benjamin N. Cardozo School of Law studied the extent to which ICE agents did not follow due process or obtain search warrants to raid the homes of mostly Latinos in New York and New Jersey. In 2008, for example, ICE agents in Patterson held a Guatemalan family at gunpoint during an ICE raid of a father who had LPR status and his nine-year-old son who was a U.S. citizen. About 66 percent of the targeted suspects by ICE agents were Latino, while 87 percent of "collateral" arrests were Latino in New Jersey. The study urged that there should be oversight or official documentation of home raids to ensure that agents comply with federal law. About 25 percent of ICE agents did not receive permission to enter the homes. No written reason on why an individual was targeted or questioned was found in two-thirds of the arrest reports (Chiu et al. 2009). According to the report, there was a large difference between New York and New Jersey rates of obtaining consent to enter homes: 86 percent of raids were conducted without consent in New York, while 24 percent of raids were without consent in New Jersey. The researchers provided evidence that the New Jersey ICE Office may have concocted consent where there was none or mistook what consent legally means. The discrepancy was noted in the following report that was recorded as "Subject gave consent": "[t]he Newark Fugitive Operation team . . . gained access into apartment [redacted] by way of knocking, thus the door was opened from the intensity of the banging. Upon slowly entering the apartment at [redacted] I noticed that [redacted] was approaching the doorway" (Chiu et al. 2009, 10). In the New Jersey dataset, 63 percent of ICE arrests were "collateral" arrests made at the site of targeted suspects' homes. ICE agents violated the Fourth Amendment which guarantees against unreasonable search and seizures in 67 percent of the cases. An overwhelmingly large percentage (90 percent) of collateral arrests without a reasonable ground for suspicion was Latino.

In response to the likelihood of arrest violations by ICE agents in New Jersey, the NJ May 1 Coalition and the New Jersey Civil Rights Defense Committee provided resources to set up a Rapid Response Network Hotline for people to call for assistance during an ICE raid. The Rapid Response Network in Princeton gives translation services and information over the phone as well as sends volunteers to local ICE raids to act as potential witnesses.

SANCTUARY CITIES

Anti-immigrant groups specified Hightstown, Bridgeton, Trenton, and Newark as "sanctuary cities" that the groups claim have refused cooperation with ICE raids of undocumented immigrants. Conservative websites sought punitive measures such as withdrawing federal funds from these cities for non-cooperation with immigration authorities while portraying sanctuary cities as havens actively welcoming the undocumented. A proposed law (ACR. 88 2002) sought to end federal funding for cities that failed to report employers who knowingly hired undocumented immigrants.

Bader Qarmont, a candidate for U.S. Senate in 2012, is running on an anti-immigration campaign that attacks his opponent for being inactive on the issue of sanctuary cities. Qarmont is challenging incumbent Joe Kyrillos for his

Senator Robert Menendez, D-New Jersey, speaks during an immigration rally on the National Mall in Washington, D.C., on October 8, 2013. Menendez called on the House Republican leadership to pass comprehensive immigration reform with a path to citizenship. (AP Photo/Jose Luis Magana)

silence on immigration matters which Qarmont equates with granting amnesty to and creating sanctuary cities for undocumented immigrants. According to Qarmont's campaign manager, RoseAnn Salanitri, Qarmont is proposing an active "punitive" platform to deal with undocumented immigration. The plan is as follows: "It is comprised of several steps that start with securing the border, deporting illegal aliens with a criminal record, finger printing and registering the rest, and imposing a significant fine that can be paid weekly over a 10-year period. The plan also comes with a back of the line period where illegals cannot vote or receive entitlements for 10-years. After 10 years they can apply for a Green Card but still cannot vote" (Salanitri 2012). Salanitri calls Qarmont brave for adopting stricter measures to punish undocumented immigrants. Salanitri wards off critics who claim that Qarmont is not tough enough to take back driver's licenses from undocumented immigrants. Salanitri blames Kyrillos for not enforcing tighter scrutiny on issuing such driver's licenses to undocumented immigrants in the first place. The site claims that tea party activists have already withdrawn support for Kyrillos in Monmouth County.

Secure Communities

In early 2012, New Jersey began its cooperation with the federal program, S-Comm that requires local law enforcement to share fingerprint data of detained criminal suspects with ICE. A fingerprint match with ICE's database of individuals with potential immigration violations automatically gives ICE the authority to issue a detainer on the individual for up to 2 days not including weekends and holidays. Before the suspect is released from jail, local police must contact ICE who will determine if the individual should be detained for immigration offenses. Civil rights advocates argue that S-Comm deports undocumented immigrants who do not pose a public threat to the community. Often parents of U.S. citizen children are deported regardless of their ties to family or community members. State and city officials, citizens, legal advocates, and academics have resisted S-Comm through rallies and petitions to the governor. U.S. senator Robert Menendez has spoken out against the program's implementation as counterproductive to stopping criminal activity. A significant percentage of deported noncitizens have never been convicted of a crime or were held for minor criminal offenses. Moreover, immigrant rights advocates warn that the program works against the intended functions of law enforcement by making survivors of crimes less likely to report to the police out of fear of deportation. The New Jersey State Advisory Committee published a report that found that local law enforcement and immigration authorities have conflicting interests in securing communities against crime as victims and witnesses would be less likely to report crime if coming out would make them vulnerable to immigration inquiries.

Upon hearing complaints by state and local police departments, Governor Christie did not approve of state compliance with the fingerprint-sharing technology. Immigrant advocate and program director of the American Friends Service Committee Immigrant Rights Program in Newark, Amy Gottlieb was highly vocal in the fight against the implementation of S-Comm and early on warned that ICE can implement S-Comm whether or not there was consent from the state. Despite the lobbying and grassroots efforts by immigrant activists to urge Governor Christie to resist the program, a federal mandate overrode the need for Christie's approval. S-Comm is now activated in all 21 counties as of February 22, 2012. In the four months since the statewide initiation of S-Comm, ICE has deported 59 individuals labeled as "criminal aliens." ("Activated Jurisdictions" 2012, 14) In fiscal year 2011, a total of 5,305 undocumented immigrants have been deported in New Jersey.

TRU-ID

New Jersey's version of the 2005 federal Real ID program, TRU-ID, has been stalled in the courts as of May 2012. The ACLU of New Jersey brought a last-minute legal challenge against the implementation of the program which required social security documents for renewing a driver's license. ACLU argued that the new requirements would unduly burden those without social security cards such as the homeless. The ACLU claimed that New Jersey already has a stringent system of identity verification for driver's licenses and does not need additional documents which would increase the likelihood of identity theft. The Motor Vehicle Commission claimed that they are trying to meet the federal guidelines by the 2014 deadline. Anti-immigrant groups have called the resistance against the federal Real ID program a "Real ID rebellion."

NOTABLE GROUPS

New Jersey Advocates for Immigrant Detainees

Responding to the establishment of a mass detention and deportation system, beginning in 1996, the New Jersey Advocates for Immigrant Detainees provides public education about specific detainees to raise public awareness of the effects of detention and deportation on families and communities. These stories also evoke public sympathy for an area of the law that is less than transparent. The group is composed of a number of civic and religious groups that are working to improve conditions in the current detention system and aiming to reduce or eliminate the broad use of these two punitive mechanisms in the future. In conjunction with efforts by the American Friends Service Committee, for example, they have questioned the methods by which private contractors have won awards for building and running detention centers. Part of their concern is that this public–private partnership often results in significant human rights violations, particularly toward would-be refugees who have fled dangerous conditions in their own country only to be confined in centers with no basic legal or criminal rights.

BIBLIOGRAPHY

"Abuse Detailed at Slavery Trial of Migrant Boss." *The Star-Ledger*, June 18, 1975, 1.

"Activated Jurisdictions." U.S. Immigration and Customs Enforcement, June 5, 2012. http://www.ice.gov/doclib/secure-communities/pdf/sc-activated.pdf. Accessed July 12, 2013.

Adely, Hannan. "N.J. Cops Helped Spy on Iman in NYPD Muslim Surveillance." NorthJersey.com, July 10, 2012. http://www.northjersey.com/news/State_denies_NJ_cops_helped_spy_on_imam.html?page=all. Accessed July 12, 2013.

Belson, Ken, and Jill P. Capuzzo. "Towns Rethink Laws against Illegal Immigrants." *The New York Times*, September 26, 2007. http://www.nytimes.com/2007/09/26/nyregion/26riverside.html?pagewanted=all. Accessed July 12, 2013.

Bernstein, Nina. "Officials Hid Truth of Immigrant Deaths in Jail." *The New York Times*, January 9, 2010. http://www.nytimes.com/2010/01/10/us/10detain.html?ref=incustody deaths. Accessed July 12, 2013.

"Broadening the Franchise." *New Jersey Law Journal* 740 (May 20, 1996): 28.

Burton, John. "Anonymous Flier Targets Illegal Aliens—Writer Blames Borough Officials, Business Owners for Inaction on Immigration Issues." *Two River Times*, Week of November 30–December 7, 1999. http://www.trtnj.com/issues/091016/news3.php. Accessed July 12, 2013.

"Businesses Sue Riverside, NJ Over Vague, Discriminatory Anti-Immigrant Ordinance." American Civil Liberties Union, October 18, 2006. www.aclu.org/immigrants-rights/businesses-sue-riverside-nj-over-vague-discriminatory-anti-immigrant-ordinance. Accessed July 12, 2013.

Carpenter, Amanda. " 'Sanctuary Cities' Embrace Illegal Immigrants." Human Events, Powerful Conservative Voices, May 4, 2007. http://www.humanevents.com/2007/05/04/sanctuary-cities-embrace-illegal-immigrants/. Accessed July 12, 2013.

Celano, Clare Marie. "Freehold Mayor Take Illegal Aliens to Task." Freehold News Transcript, May 10, 2006. http://newstranscript.gmnews.com/news/2006/0510/Front_page/114.html. Accessed July 12, 2013.

Celano, Clare Marie. "Opinions Differ on Need for Immigration Checks: Monmouth Sheriff Gains OK to Examine Status of Individuals in Jail." News Transcript, July 29, 2009. http://nt.gmnews.com/news/2009-07–29/front_page/005.html. Accessed July 12, 2013.

Chiu, Bess, Lynly Egyes, Peter L. Markowitz, and Jaya Vasandani. *Constitution on ICE: A Report on Immigration Home Raid Operations, Cardozo Immigration Justice Clinic*. New York, 2009. http://www.cardozo.yu.edu/uploadedFiles/Cardozo/Profiles/immigrationlaw-741/IJC_ICE-Home-Raid-Report%20Updated.pdf. Accessed July 12, 2013.

Cleaveland, Carol, and Laura Kelly. "Shared Social Space and Strategies to Find Work: An Exploratory Study of Mexican Day Laborers in Freehold, NJ." *Social Justice* 35, no 4 (2008): 51–65.

Cottin, Heather. "Day Laborer Organizer 'Served the People.'" July 7, 2008. http://www .workers.org/2008/us/abarca_0710/. Accessed July 12, 2013.

"County College of Morris Trustees Vote to Charge Undocumented Students Out-of-State Tuition." *The Huffington Post*, April 22, 2011. http://www.huffington post.com/2011/04/22/county-college-of-morris-_n_852661.html. Accessed July 12, 2013.

Farbenblum, Bassina, and Jessica Jansyn. "Crossing the Line: Damaging Immigration Enforcement Practices by New Jersey Police Following Attorney General Law Enforcement Directive 2007–3." The Center for Social Justice, Seton Hall University School of Law, April 2009. http://law.shu.edu/ProgramsCenters/PublicIntGovServ/upload /crossing_the_line.pdf. Accessed July 12, 2013.

"Federal Labor Officials Host Summit on Latino, Immigrant Worker Safety." *The Associated Press*, June 5, 2011. http://ndlon.org/en/by-issue/665-federal-labor-officials-host-summit-on-latino-immigrant-worker-safety. Accessed July 12, 2013.

Freeman, Semuteh, and Lauren Major. "Immigration Incarceration: The Expansion and Failed Reform of Immigration Detention in Essex County, NJ." New York University School of Law Immigrant Rights Clinic in Cooperation with New Jersey Advocates for Immigrant Detainees, March 2012. http://www.afsc.org/sites/afsc.civicactions. net/files/documents/ImmigrationIncarceration2012.pd. Accessed July 12, 2013.

Gottlieb, Amy, Cynthia Mellon, and Joseph Thomas-Berger. "NJ Advocates for Immigrant Detainees Issued Opinion Piece Denouncing Essex County Detention Contract." American Friends Service Committee Website, 2012. http://afsc.org/story /nj-advocates-immigrant-detainees-issued-opinion-piece-denouncing-essex-county-detention-contra. Accessed July 12, 2013.

Guidi, Ruxandra, and Michael Juliano. "300 Day Laborers from around the Country Meet in LA to Talk Immigration." 89.3 KPCC Southern California Public Radio, February 21, 2012. http://www.scpr.org/news/2012/02/21/31322/300-day-laborers-around-country-meet-la-talk-immig/. Accessed July 12, 2013.

"4 Hurt as Strikers Renew Farm Fight: Tear Gas Bombs End Battle with Police and Workers at Bridgeton, N.J." *Special to The New York Times*, July 7, 1934, p. 3.

Immigrants' Rights/International Human Rights Clinic. "All Work and No Pay: Day Laborers, Wage Theft, and Workplace Justice in New Jersey." Center for Social Justice, Seton Hall University School of Law, January 2011. http://www.windofthespirit.net /All_Work_No_Pay_SHU-2011.pdf. Accessed July 12, 2013.

Lurie, Maxine N., Marc Mappen, and Michael Siegel. *Encyclopedia of New Jersey*. New Brunswick, NJ: Rutgers University Press, 2004.

Matza, Michael. "Cumberland County, N.J., Joins 'Majority Minority Trend.'" *The Philadelphia Inquirer*, June 28, 2012. http://articles.philly.com/2012–06–28 /news/32442072_1_majority-minority-poverty-rate-population. Accessed July 12, 2013.

"Migrants Sign Pact." *The Star-Ledger*, March 14, 1976, Sec. I, 31.

New Jersey Advocates for Immigrant Detainees. New Jersey Advocates for Immigrant Detainees Webpage. http://njaid.blogspot.com/. Accessed February 22, 2014.

"One Year Progress Update on Immigration Detention in New Jersey." New Jersey Advocates for Immigrant Detainees, April 29, 2011. http://afsc.org/sites/afsc.civicactions.net/files/documents/One%20year%20Locked%20Up%20final.pdf. Accessed July 12, 2013.

Peterson, Iver. "Hispanic Day Laborers Sue Freehold, Claiming Right to Gather to Seek Work." *The New York Times*, December 31, 2003. http://www.nytimes.com/2003/12/31/nyregion/hispanic-day-laborers-sue-freehold-claiming-right-to-gather-to-seek-work.html?pagewanted=2&src=pm. Accessed July 12, 2013.

"Puerto Rico Deports U.S. Citizen Because of Accent." *The New York Times News Service*, February 14, 1980, p. 2-c.

Riverside Coalition v. Riverside, No. l:06-cv-03842-RMB-AMD (N.J. Super. Ct. Law Div., filed Oct. 18, 2006). http:clearinghouse.wustl.edu/chDocs/public/IM-NJ-000 1–0001.pdf. Accessed July 12, 2013.

RocklandMichael Aaron. "Those People." *New Jersey Monthly*, January 30, 2008. http://njmonthly.com/articles/lifestyle/people/those-people.html. Accessed July 12, 2013.

Rodriguez, Michael. "Immigration Policy: Understanding the Impact of a Changing Policy Environment on Local Businesses." William J. Hughes Center for Public Policy, The Richard Stockton College of New Jersey, April 2012. http://intraweb.stockton.edu/eyos/hughescenter/content/docs/Publications/Immigration%20brief%20Rodriguez.pdf. Accessed July 12, 2013.

Salanitri, RoseAnn. "Kyrillos Supports Sanctuary Cities in Monmouth County Says Qarmout, While Qarmout Says No to Amnesty." PR Web, May 23, 2012. http://www.prweb.com/releases/2012/5/prweb9527053.htm. Accessed July 12, 2013.

Semple, Kirk. "A Sanctuary amid Fears of Persecution at Home." *The New York Times*, May 16, 2012. http://www.nytimes.com/2012/05/17/nyregion/reformed-church-gives-sanctuary-to-indonesians-ordered-to-be-deported.html. Accessed July 12, 2013.

Squires, Patricia. "Aiding Contras Opposed." *The New York Times*, March 16, 1986, 695.

Squires, Patricia. "Peace Efforts on Rise." *The New York Times*, April 13, 1986, NJ 13.

Taylor, Stuart Jr. "16 Indicted by U.S. in Bid to End Church Smuggling of Latin Aliens." *Special to the New York Times*, January 15, 1985, A1.

31

NEW MEXICO

William P. Kladky

CHRONOLOGY

1200s-1500s	The Pueblo Indians establish villages along the Rio Grande.
1536	Álvar Núñez Cabeza de Vaca (1488/1490–1587/1588), Estevan the Moor (ca. 1500–1539), and two others reach Culiacan, Mexico, after possibly crossing what is now southern New Mexico, and begin rumors of the Seven Cities of Cibola, as described by Franciscan friar Fray Marcos de Niza (1495–1558).
1539	Fray Marcos de Niza and Estevan lead an expedition to find Cibola and reach the Zuni village of Hawikuh.
1540–1542	Francisco Vásquez de Coronado (1510–1554), governor of the Kingdom of Nueva Galicia (New Galicia—a province of New Spain northwest of Mexico and comprising the Mexican states of Jalisco, Sinaloa, and Nayarit—explores the area from Gulf of California to Kansas) discovers the Grand Canyon.
1580–1581	Fray Agustin Rodriguez (d. 1582) leads an expedition to New Mexico.
1582–1583	Fray Bernardino Beltran and Fray Antonio de Espejo (1560–?) travel to New Mexico to search for survivors of the Rodriguez group.
1598	With 500 Spanish settlers and soldiers and 7,000 head of livestock, Juan de Oñate (1550–1626) travels from Zacatecas, Mexico, and establishes the first Spanish capital of San Juan de los Caballeros at the Tewa village of Ohke north of present-day Espanola.
1600	San Gabriel, the second capital of New Mexico, is founded at the intersection of the Rio Grande and the Chama River.

1601	There is a mass desertion of San Gabriel by colonists. Subsequently, new recruits from Spain and Mexico are sent to reinforce the colony.
1605	Oñate leads an expedition to the Colorado River, visits El Morro, and leaves a message on Inscription Rock.
1608	Oñate is removed as governor and sent to Mexico City to be tried for mistreating the American Indians and abuse of power. The Spanish Crown decides to continue settlement of New Mexico as a royal province.
1609–1610	Governor Pedro de Peralta (1584–1666) establishes a new capital at Santa Fe. Construction begins on the Palace of the Governors. Gaspar de Villagra publishes an epic history on the founding of New Mexico, the first book printed about any area in the modern United States.
1626	The Spanish Inquisition is established in New Mexico.
1641	Governor Luis de Rosas is assassinated by colonists during a conflict between the church and state.
1680	The Pueblo Indian Revolt Spanish survivors flee to El Paso. At the time of the Pueblo revolt, the New Mexico Spanish population was about 2,500.
1692–1693	Don Diego de Vargas recolonizes Santa Fe, as Spanish civilization returns to New Mexico.
1695	Santa Cruz de la Cañada (Canada) is founded.
1706	While developing Santa Fe as a trade center, the returning settlers found the old town of San Francisco de Albuquerque in 1706, naming it after the viceroy of New Spain, Francisco Fernández de la Cueva, the 10th Duke of Albuquerque (1666–1724).
1743	French trappers reach Santa Fe and begin a limited trade with the Spanish.
1776	Franciscan friars Francisco Atanasio Dominguez (ca. 1740–1805/1807) and Silvestre Vélez de Escalante (1750–1780) try to find a route from Santa Fe, New Mexico to Spanish missions in California.
1786	Spanish New Mexico governor Juan Bautista de Anza (1736–1788) makes peace with the Comanches.
1807	American lieutenant Zebulon M. Pike (1778–1813) leads the first Anglo-American expedition into New Mexico.
1817	The Spanish population of New Mexico reaches 27,000.
1821	Mexico declares its independence from Spain. The Santa Fe Trail is opened to international trade.
1828	The first major gold discovery in the western United States is made in the Ortiz Mountains south of Santa Fe.
1829–1830	The Old Spanish Trail—a difficult pack-animal route—opens, linking Los Angeles to Santa Fe and the Camino Real.

1830s	Black slaves were among the immigrants to the area in the 1830s.
1841	Texas soldiers invade New Mexico and claim all land east of the Rio Grande. Their efforts are thwarted by Gov. Manuel Armijo (1793–1853).
1846	The Mexican-American War begins. U.S. army colonel Stephen Watts Kearny (1794–1848) annexes New Mexico to the United States.
1848	The Treaty of Guadalupe Hidalgo ends the Mexican-American War. The United States pays Mexico $15 million for California, New Mexico, Arizona, Nevada, Utah, and parts of Wyoming and Colorado.
1850	The influx of Anglo-Americans first begins to New Mexico, when the Santa Fe Trail was used by many on their way to the California gold fields.
1851	French Roman Catholic bishop Jean-Baptiste Lamy (1814–1888) arrives in New Mexico and establishes schools, hospitals, and orphanages throughout the territory.
1853	The Surveyor of General Claims Office is established in New Mexico, though claims by Mexican Americans cannot be processed fast enough to prevent takeovers.
1854	The Gadsden Purchase from Mexico adds 45,000 square miles to the territory.
1861	Confederates invade New Mexico front Texas. The Confederate Territory of Arizona is declared with the capital at La Mesilla.
1863–1868	Known as the "Long Walk," Navajos and Apaches are relocated to Bosque Redondo.
1870s	Colorado ranchers and Mormon colonists settle in San Juan Valley in the northwest corner of the state. More Germans arrive.
1878	The Atchison, Topeka, and Santa Fe Railroad is completed, opening full-scale trade and migration from the East and Midwest.
1880s	The state's southwestern corner attracts miners from other states. Swiss entrepreneurs and settlers put down roots.
1881	The Southern Pacific Railroad is completed, encouraging the great cattle boom of the 1880s and the development of cow towns.
1882	The wagon or *carreta* (large two-wheel ox cart) route in New Mexico is discontinued after a branch of the Santa Fe Railroad links Albuquerque to El Paso.
1890s	Many immigrants come from various places such as Italy, Germany, Poland, Russia, England, France, and Asia. They join Mexicans coming to New Mexico to work in cattle and sheep grazing and agriculture.
1900–1910	A steady stream of U.S. migrants raise New Mexico's population to over 325,000, mainly in the eastern and southern regions.

	Significant Mexican immigration continues, aided by lax enforcement of the border.
1903	The first laws restricting immigration across the Mexican border are enacted.
1906	The people of New Mexico and Arizona vote on the issue of joint statehood, with New Mexico voting in favor and Arizona against.
1910	The New Mexico Constitution is drafted in preparation for statehood. At the New Mexican constitutional convention, Mexican American delegates mandate that both Spanish and English be used for all state business; to support the conditions of the 1848 Treaty of Guadalupe Hidalgo.
1912	New Mexico is admitted to the Union as the 47th state.
1923–1924	Oil is discovered on the Navajo Reservation.
1930–1932	Stricter border enforcement led to over 6,000 Mexicans being deported to Mexico.
1930–1943	The Great Depression forces Mexican out-migration because of the huge decrease in jobs in agriculture, cattle raising, and mining.
1945	The world's first atomic bomb is detonated at Trinity Site in southern New Mexico after its development at Los Alamos.
Post-1945	The state becomes a center for nuclear, solar, and geothermal energy research and development, and many highly educated scientists and engineers move to the state.
1990s	New Mexico's Mexican-born immigrant populations increased from 50,043 in 1990 to 71,760 in 1998, most coming for jobs in agriculture, construction, and the service industry.
2001–2011	The leading countries of origin of "green card" admissions to New Mexico are Mexico (2,748), India (2,175), China (1,792), Philippines (884), Canada (750), and Germany (541).
2005	About 11.65 percent of the state's employment was derived directly or indirectly from military spending. With a Native American population of 207,400 in 2005, New Mexico still ranks as an important center of American Indian culture. The Apache and Ute live on federal reservations within the state.
2006	Some 72.8 percent of immigrants residing in the state of New Mexico are Mexican-born. New Mexico is the fastest-growing state in the United States and has the largest increase in population size.
2007–2010	New Mexico's undocumented immigrant population increases from 80,000 to 85,000, or 4.3 percent of the total population.
2010	Susana Martinez (1959–) is elected as the first woman governor of New Mexico, as well as the first Latino/a woman governor in the united States.
2013	The foreign-born are estimated to comprise one-tenth of the population of New Mexico.

HISTORICAL OVERVIEW

Pre-1800

By European exploration in the sixteenth century, New Mexico had Pueblo peoples and groups of Navajo, Apache and Ute Indians. Spanish conquistador Francisco Vásquez de Coronado (1510–1554) led an expedition in 1540–1542 to find the mystical Seven Golden Cities of Cibola as described by Cabeza de Vaca. The Spaniards discovered some pueblos and the first of the Seven Cities of Cibola in 1541, but no golden cities. After other expeditions similarly failed to find any rich cities, Coronado and his men left New Mexico.

The first permanent European settlement in New Mexico was founded by Juan de Oñate (1550–1626) as the San Juan colony on the Rio Grande in 1598. Oñate came via El Camino Real, a 700-mile trail from New Spain to San Juan, which friendly American Indians helped him build. The northern part of the trail was heavily used from the 1830s to about 1884. Juan Griego, or John the Greek, was among Oñate's colonists.

Oñate's colony became the province's first capital and was very racially mixed. Although half of the 129 soldiers who first colonized New Mexico in 1598 had been born in Spain, by 1680, 9 out of 10 residents were native-born. Pueblo Indians and *genízaros*, the formerly enslaved Apaches and Navajos who were free, intermarried with non-Indians.

In 1609, Pedro de Peralta (ca. 1584–1666) established Santa Fe. From 1610 to 1680, many settlers came to farm and raise cattle, and Franciscan missionaries arrived to convert the American Indians. To encourage Spanish settlement, reward patrons, and create a buffer zone between the American Indians and settlers, Spain awarded an *encomienda*—a land grant to an individual, group, or town—to selected settlers. Of these 295 grants, 141 were made to individuals, and the remaining 154 were made to communities (e.g., Las Vegas, New Mexico, in 1835), including 23 grants made by Spain to indigenous Indian pueblos (villages) to recognize lands that the pueblos had held before the settlers arrived. Disputes arose during the New Mexico land grant confirmation process in the early 1900s because only 24 percent of the acreage claimed in New Mexico was awarded, compared to 73 percent in California.

Hating the *encomienda* and the missionaries, the usually fractious pueblos united under the pope (ca. 1630–ca. 1690), a Tewa medicine man, in a revolt against the Spanish in 1680. Many Spanish settlers were killed and the survivors went south to El Paso, along with some Christianized Indians and mestizos (with both Spanish and Indian blood). After the pope's death, Diego de Vargas (1643–1704) returned the region to Spanish rule.

Some of the colonists who settled in the seventeenth and eighteenth centuries were descendants of forced Jewish converts who had fled the Spanish Inquisition.

They were forced to convert to Catholicism but privately kept Jewish practices. In the eighteenth century, the sparsely settled region slowly gained population. In 1706, settlers founded Albuquerque, named after the viceroy of New Spain, the Duke of Albuquerque. French trappers reached Santa Fe in 1754 and traded with the Spanish but had no political impact. To impose some order upon its far-flung settlements, the Spanish colonial administration was reorganized in 1776 and united New Mexico, Texas, Arizona, and Mexico's northern states. Also in 1776, Franciscan friars Francisco Atanasio Domínguez (ca. 1740–1805/1807) and Silvestre Vélez de Escalante (1750–1780) tried to find a route from Santa Fe to the Spanish missions in California. Their trek became the Spanish Trail, and many traveled its 1,800 difficult miles. Some progress also occurred regarding relations with the American Indians. In 1786, Spanish New Mexico governor Juan Bautista de Anza (1736–1788) made peace with the Comanches.

Nineteenth Century

After its 1810–1821 War of Independence, the Mexican authorities assumed control of the large province containing New Mexico. Mexican authority and investment was minimal during their 26 years of control because the area was so poor and resources meager. At first, the Spanish authorities forbade U.S. trappers to trade. However, when trader William Becknell returned to the United States in 1821 with news that Mexico welcomed trade through Santa Fe, it inspired more to come.

Santa Fe's central location was important and by the 1820s, it had emerged as the center of various trading routes linking much of the Southwest. Many utilized the Santa Fe Trail, from Independence, Missouri, to Santa Fe. A number of traders were from Tennessee and Kentucky. The successful Santa Fe Trail trading company set up its first trading post in 1826, and in 1833 built an adobe fort and trading post called Bent's Fort on the Arkansas River. Located 200 miles east of Taos, it was the only place settled by Anglos along the trail. The 2,400-mile pack-train Spanish Trail from Los Angeles to Santa Fe was primarily used by Latino/as, white traders, and ex-trappers after 1829. The wagon trains along the trail brought more Americans. Because the area was controlled by Mexico, customs fees varied considerably, and friction was often present. Some of the travelers stayed, married Mexicans, and became farmers or townspeople.

Black slaves were among the immigrants arriving in the 1830s. Some 5,000 black slaves (6 percent of population) had been brought by Cherokees, Choctaws, Chickasaws, Creeks, and Seminoles when they relocated to Indian Territory. Many black slaves escaped. Since Mexico had outlawed slavery in 1829, New Mexico represented freedom—if they could get there. In 1845, there was a minor incident when five black slaves arrived with comancheros in Taos and the U.S.

diplomatic representative demanded their return—unsuccessfully. Other blacks lived as trappers.

The 1830s and 1840s were unsettled. After 1836, the Plains Indian nations of Comanches, Kiowas, and Cheyennes allied to prevent "immigrant tribes" from encroaching upon their bison lands. In 1837, fearing that their livelihoods would be disturbed, the Pueblo Indians and some New Mexicans briefly overthrew the Mexican regional government. Throughout, relations with the American Indian tribes were generally hostile. There were reports of Lipan Apache attacks on German immigrants on the Santa Fe Trail in 1849.

In the 1840s, attempting to encourage settlement in the northern region, the Mexican governor made the 1.7 million acre Maxwell Land Grant, which became the largest tract of land held by a single owner in U.S. history. Mexico reasoned that Mexican settlers would rush in and resist any influx from Anglo-Americans. But American and other settlers continued to arrive, like the Canadians and Germans who set up shops and became ranchers in Valencia County, Albuquerque, and Las Vegas.

After the Mexican-American War (1846–1848) and the Treaty of Guadalupe Hidalgo in 1848, Mexico ceded its sparsely settled northern section—including New Mexico—to the United States. Almost immediately afterward, New Mexico residents were interested in statehood. However, with the Congressional Compromise of 1850, New Mexico's bid for statehood with an anti-slavery constitution was postponed. The Congressional Compromise also included Texas transferring eastern New Mexico to the federal government, ending a boundary dispute. With this compromise, the U.S. government established the Territory of New Mexico in 1850. In 1851, the territory—including most of Arizona, New Mexico, and part of Colorado—established Santa Fe as its capital. New Mexico was sparsely populated and mostly consisted of Spanish-speaking, agricultural communities. Except in larger towns like Santa Fe, the English language and American customs were unknown.

The United States offered citizenship to Mexicans living there. Piles of stones were set up to mark the southern border. A subsequent treaty in 1853 altered the border by adding 47 more boundary markers to the original six, with most just piles of stones. Over time, markers were moved or destroyed, leading to two agreements in 1882 and 1889 to more clearly define the boundaries. Photographers then documented the location of the markers.

When statehood was being debated, some felt New Mexico was hardly worth the effort. It was called "the Siberia of America" by the *Chicago Tribune*, and the *Milwaukee Sentinel* called its inhabitants "half-breeds, greasers, outlaws." New Mexico's statehood was also opposed because some thought that its mainly Latino/a and Indian population was too foreign and too Catholic. Others wondered if these recently conquered people would be loyal to their new country. To counter, there was discussion about whether changing the name would help attain statehood with Navajo and Lincoln suggested but rejected. The worry was misplaced. The territory soon became increasingly Anglo with the United States in control after 1850, utilizing mostly Anglo appointed officials. This cultural shift further increased after 1880 when the railroads brought an influx of Anglo settlers, many openly contemptuous of the "Mexicans."

Black Indians, freed slaves, and free mulattoes were among the 22 "free Negroes" discovered in New Mexico's first territorial census in 1850. The acquisition of New Mexico by the United States meant the end of free blacks. In 1857, the legislature banned "free Negroes" as well as racial intermarriage. A pro-Southern bias took over, as evidenced by the passage of a slave code in 1859 very similar to the national 1850 Fugitive Slave Act.

The discovery of gold and silver in New Mexico led to a temporary population upsurge during the 1840s through the 1880s, but the lack of adequate water frustrated efforts and prospectors moved on to other areas. Some—from Italy, China, Poland, Germany, Britain, Austria, Croatia, Finland, Sweden, Mexico, and Greece—miners, along with many Texans, did settle. More Germans arrived in the 1870s, and Swiss entrepreneurs and settlers came in the 1880s.

With the 29,670 square mile Gadsden Purchase of 1853, the United States acquired from Mexico the southwestern part of New Mexico and southern Arizona. This purchase was done to facilitate a non-mountainous route for a proposed transcontinental railroad which eventually was built by the Southern Pacific Railroad in 1881. Soon, the territory attracted new settlers, and New Mexico's non-Indian population increased 51.9 percent from 1850s 61,547 to 93,516 in 1860. The territory of Arizona was split off as a separate territory in 1863. In 1867, it was estimated that there were 1,500 to 3,000 American Indian slaves.

In the 1860s, New Mexico did not receive the rush of American homesteaders like Oregon and California partly because most of the best land had been claimed before and because many areas were not safe for settlers because of American Indian troubles. There was ongoing conflict between the Apache, the Navajo, and Spanish Mexican settlements in the territory. Federal control began to be asserted in 1864 when the Navajo were forced on reservations, and returned to their lands in an 1868 treaty. While some moved to reservations, the Apache wars continued until Geronimo (1829–1909) surrendered in 1886. With all of the American Indian tribes relocated to reservations, Anglo settlement accelerated.

Railroad improvements made immigration and development feasible. In 1878, the Atchison, Topeka, and Santa Fe Railroads were completed, followed by the Southern Pacific Railroad in 1881. By 1885, over 1,100 miles of track had been constructed in New Mexico. Albuquerque became a railroad boom town. These railways enabled the cattle boom of the 1880s and the development of cow towns.

Within a few years, homesteaders and squatters arrived and fenced in and plowed the lands. There was a steady black migration during this period, from only 22 in 1850 to 85 blacks in 1860, and 172 in 1870, reaching 1,015 in 1880 and then 1,956 in 1890. In the 1870s and 1880s, the trains brought settlers from Iowa, Missouri, and Arkansas to become farmers in eastern and western New Mexico. In 1890, 93.8 percent of the territory was rural.

Other community institutions soon appeared to serve the new settlers. While there were no banking institutions in New Mexico in 1870, by 1890, 46 banks operated. Immigration and migration to New Mexico was further stimulated by its reputation as a healthy place to live. For instance, tuberculosis's emergence in the 1890s and early 1900s led to the development of many hospitals devoted to its cure. At one time, there were 17 sanatoriums in Albuquerque.

The modern tourist era began in New Mexico in 1881 when the Santa Fe Railroad built the Montezuma Hotel near Las Vegas in 1881. The national interstate highway system has brought many more tourists and migrants for tourism-industry jobs, and tourism remains New Mexico's leading industry. In the late nineteenth and early twentieth century, New Mexico changed from being tri-cultural—Anglo, Latino/a, and Indian—to multicultural. Many immigrants came from various places: Italy, German Jews, Poland, Russia, England, France, and Asia. They joined the Mexicans coming to New Mexico to work in cattle and sheep grazing and agriculture. The expansion of the coal, copper, iron, and silver mines also created a demand for cheap and available labor, drawing many Mexicans. The first Greeks started coming to Albuquerque around the late 1890s, many working on the railroad. Even more Mexican immigration was driven by the post-1910 precarious political situation in Mexico, as the economy declined and poverty climbed.

1900 TO 1950

As of 1900, the New Mexico Territory's population was only about 300,000, sparsely settled by ranchers, irrigation farmers, and some townspeople along the Santa Fe and Southern Pacific Railroads. Between 1900 and 1910, a steady stream of U.S. migrants raised the population to over 325,000, mainly in the East and South. The U.S. Census also found 6,649 foreign-born Mexicans. Less than 10 percent of the population lived in towns, and over 90 percent had been born in New Mexico. Aside from the farmers, most worked for railroads, mining companies, printers, and lumber mills.

New Mexico took much longer than the rest of the Mexican territory to gain statehood, largely because it was the only one that remained predominantly Mexican/Latino/a even after Anglo settlers arrived. Individuals feared the large Latino/a (and Catholic) population's influence on the multicultural state. Ironically, the Spanish-American War increased New Mexico's statehood chances.

More of Theodore Roosevelt's Rough Riders came from New Mexico and Arizona than any other area, and Roosevelt eventually advocated statehood.

In 1912, the U.S. Congress admitted New Mexico as the 47th state, after unsuccessfully trying to limit the enabling act language to "English only." Its constitution included women's suffrage, direct primaries, and other democratic policies. The New Mexico Constitution made both English and Spanish official languages. It also guaranteed equal rights and education to all New Mexicans regardless of language, religion, or race. After statehood, artists, oil, and nuclear power stimulated migration and immigration to the state. In 1917, an arts patron began inviting artists to Taos, and the town became an artist colony, drawing tourists, migrants, and immigrants.

Significant Mexican immigration continued, aided by lax enforcement of the border. In 1910, there were 11,918 foreign-born Mexicans, which increased to 20,272 by 1920. Many initially settled in Grant and Doña Aña counties and moved to other areas for employment in the copper, coal, and metal industries. About 31 percent of miners were Mexicans by 1930. There were 2,000 in Albuquerque by the early 1920s, drawn to the major port of U.S. entry for Mexican workers. Many mutual aid societies were founded to assist the new immigrants. Founded in 1894, the Alianza Hispano Americana helped both immigrants and native Nuevomexicanos with their economic, political, and social needs. Some towns established *comisiones honoríficas* to assist the immigrants with civil rights issues.

In the 1920s, oil and natural gas were discovered on the Navajo reservation in the state. This stimulated more immigration, as workers arrived. However, the U.S. government began controlling immigration after 1917. While the Border Patrol was started in 1924, it did not really begin tightening the border until 1929.

By 1928, New Mexico included sufficient Catholics and Jews to generate the formation of a Ku Klux Klan branch in the Roswell area. They mostly hated a recent influx of migrants from the Southern states. Fortunately, the Klan was opposed by almost the rest of the state. Coal mining was an important job and wealth source in New Mexico in the 1920s through the 1940s. At its peak, it employed almost 5,000 in 61 mines. By the 1950s, the industry was in steep decline.

The installation of irrigation systems produced an agricultural boom. Land owners planted cotton, citrus, and beet crops, and needed labor to harvest the fields. This drew Mexicans in sizable numbers attracted by the higher wages. Though Mexicans were about 80 percent of migrant agricultural laborers, they were not arriving in the numbers going to other states like California. As late as 1920, when the Mexican-born population of the United States reached nearly 500,000, New Mexico's share amounted to less than 20,000, most living near the southern border. The Mexican immigrants were disparaged as *suramatos*—workers from the South.

Mexican immigration continued to grow until 1929 when the Great Depression forced out-migration because of the huge decrease in jobs in agriculture, cattle raising, and mining. Growers turned to poor American families—now willing to work for low wages—rather than Mexicans to harvest the crops. Identified as economic competition, Mexicans began to return to Mexico. New Mexico's population was 423,317 in 1930, now including immigrants from the Philippines and India. There also were nearly 7,800 foreign-born whites. The number born in Mexico had declined 21.2 percent from 1920s 20,272 to 15,983 in 1930. Stricter border enforcement led to over 6,000 Mexicans being deported to Mexico between 1930 and 1932. Deportation was also utilized by the government to combat labor agitation, with many leaders of the Liga Obrera de Habla Española and Chihuahuita expelled in 1936. This typified the hostility and discrimination directed at Mexican immigrants during this period.

A high birth rate and steady migration reduced the Spanish and Native American population percentages in New Mexico. In 1940, approximately half the population had Spanish surnames. This dropped to 36.5 percent in 1950 and to 25 percent in 1960. The American Indian population has held steady at about 5 percent through this period.

By the early 1940s, the state was becoming increasingly urban and more diverse. Almost one-third was urban, and the state's population had leaped 270 percent from 1,900 to 531,818. Additional immigration and migration to New Mexico was stimulated when the U.S. government built the Los Alamos Research Center in 1943.

In 1942, a plan to colonize between 40,000 and 60,000 Japanese Americans in Maxwell drew immediate outcry, prompting the governor to challenge the effort. During World War II, there were several internment camps in New Mexico. The ones at Santa Fe and Lordsburg held U.S. residents of Japanese descent, German and Italian soldiers were at Lordsburg, and Roswell held Germans.

1950 TO THE PRESENT

After 1950, New Mexico became increasingly more diverse and urbanized. The black population more than doubled from 8,408 in 1950 to 17,063 in 1960. The percentage living in rural areas declined from 66.8 percent in 1940 to 49.8 percent in 1950 and then 34.1 percent by 1960.

This largely occurred because of changes in the state's industry. After World War II, the state emerged as a leader in nuclear, solar, and geothermal energy research and development. The Sandia National Laboratories (founded 1949) conducted nuclear research and special weapons development at Kirtland Air Force Base south of Albuquerque. Hundreds of highly educated scientists and engineers moved in, and by the 1960s New Mexico had a higher percentage of people holding a PhD than any other state. The development of modern manufacturing (defense weaponry and electronic equipment), uranium mining, military installations, and oil and gas production expansion has brought more jobs and migrants to work. The previously dominant industries of farming and ranching have declined steadily. Agricultural mechanization has pushed many to the towns and cities or commuting to work. In the southeastern part of the state, migrants from Texas have settled in many towns. They are Baptists rather than Catholics and have little in common with the state's Spanish-Indian heritage.

The state is now very racially mixed and demographically the only minority-majority state. According to the 2000 U.S. Census, the most commonly claimed ancestry groups in New Mexico were Spanish (18.7 percent), Mexican (16.3 percent), American Indian (10.3 percent), and German (9.8 percent). Additionally, the Asian share of the state's population increased from 0.9 percent in 1990 to 1.1 percent in 2000 to 1.2 percent (24,791) in 2010.

Most recent Mexican immigrants and the foreign-born live in the southern part of the state. In 2010, New Mexico's 46 percent of Latino/as was the nation's highest, and 10 percent were American Indian. The majority of Latino/as have Spanish ancestry, especially in the North. These people are the descendants of Spanish colonists who arrived during the sixteenth, seventeenth, and eighteenth centuries.

In the twenty-first century, New Mexico has 207,400 Native Americans, second to Alaska, and is an important center of American Indian culture. The Apache and some Ute live on federal reservations. The Navajo nation's 16 million acre reservation is the largest in the country. Pueblo Indians are scattered across the state. The state has 19 pueblos, each governed autonomously.

TOPICAL ESSAYS

Recent Immigration History

Despite the Immigration Act of 1965 putting a numerical limit upon immigrants allowed to enter the United States from the Western Hemisphere, many Mexican families continued migrating north for short-term employment. New Mexico's Mexican-born immigrants increased from 50,043 in 1990 to 71,760 in 1998. Most came for jobs in agriculture, construction, and the service industry. Many immigrants work in restaurants, hotels, and landscaping. Some own restaurants, bakeries, clothing, music, auto, shoe repair, and other shops.

New Mexico's foreign-born population has grown significantly from 5.3 percent in 1990 to 8.2 percent in 2000, and 9.9 percent in 2010. Comparatively, though, the state ranks in the middle. Its total was significantly lower than the national 12.9 percent, and its 1990–2010 154.8 percent increase was only the 26th-highest. The state's 205,141 immigrants (2010) stay longer than others. In 2010, its average stay for immigrants—defined as foreign-born—was 20.6 years compared to 19.1 nationally. About 73 percent of children in immigrant families have parents who have lived in the United States over 10 years. Some 33.9 percent of immigrants (69,511) in the state were naturalized U.S. citizens in 2010.

During the past five years, annual admissions of "green card" recipients who intend to reside in New Mexico averaged about 3,568 persons. This was much higher than the 1,025 average of the 1960s. According to the Federation for American Immigration Reform (FAIR), an anti-immigration group, the leading countries of origin in 2012 of the 21,145 admissions in the previous 10 years were Mexico (2,748), India (2,175), China (1,792), Philippines (884), Canada (750), and Germany (541).

By most measurements, New Mexico is a settled community for Mexican immigrants in 2013 because new immigrants are largely going to other states. Most recent immigrants have a higher level of education and have settled in the urban areas of the state. A total of 21.5 percent of the foreign-born who were naturalized U.S. citizens in 2009 had a bachelor's or

New Mexico governor Susana Martinez looks toward the gallery as she prepares to address a joint session of the House and Senate during the first day of the Legislature in Santa Fe, New Mexico, on January 17, 2012. She is the first woman governor in New Mexico and the first Latina governor in the United States. (AP Photo/Susan Montoya Bryan)

higher degree, compared to 11.5 percent of noncitizens, and the number of immigrants with a college degree increased 53.9 percent between 2000 and 2009. Some 79 percent of children with immigrant parents were "English proficient" in 2009.

Many immigrants are employed in the construction and service industries, and a significant number are in poverty. Language is a problem, for 34 percent of children in immigrant families live in a linguistically isolated household, with 17 percent in families with parents having less than a ninth-grade education. Some 37 percent of immigrant children live in poverty, compared with 24 percent of children in U.S.-born families. In the Albuquerque metro and surrounding northern New Mexico, an estimated 24–29 percent of children live in immigrant families.

Many live in colonias—very poor, rural desert Mexican settlements with scarce infrastructure and unsafe housing. There are also many colonias or slums on both sides of the border. Colonias especially developed after the North American Free-Trade Agreement in 1994, which stimulated a large increase in low-skilled jobs through the *maquiladora* industry (the Border Industrial Program). The *maquiladora* industry is manufacturing in a free-trade zone and now employs over 1.3 million Mexicans in about 3,000 *maquiladoras*. There are 37 colonias in Doña Aña County, and 140 in the rest of the state. New Mexico has also received 1,965 refugees during the 1999–2009 period. Consent of the state government is needed for refugee settlement, the only immigration program with this requirement (FAIR 2012).

UNDOCUMENTED IMMIGRATION

New Mexico's 180-mile international border is an open desert and generally uninhabited. According to the anti-immigrant group FAIR, the undocumented population in New Mexico in 2005 was 73,000. This number is 87.1 percent above the U.S. government estimate of 39,000 in 2000, and 265 percent above the 1990 estimate of 20,000 (granted that this group is considered biased). From 2007 to 2010, the state's undocumented immigrants population increased an estimated from 80,000 to 85,000, or 4.3 percent of the total population. It was approximately 20,000 in 1990. New Mexico is one of three states in which 90 percent of the undocumented population has their origins in Mexico. In 2010, 5.6 percent of the state's labor force (50,000 of 709,000) was undocumented, the 11th-highest in the nation.

Undocumented immigration has become a much contested political issue in New Mexico, with some areas pro-immigrant and others vehemently opposed. For example, Santa Fe is designated a "sanctuary city" by its local government. However, some local law enforcement agencies have collaborated in arrest and detainment activities with immigration enforcement agencies along the border.

In 2007, Albuquerque and Santa Fe school personnel were barred from putting information about a child's immigration status in records or sharing it with outside agencies, including federal immigration authorities. Personnel are also told to deny any request from immigration officials to enter a school to search for information or seize students. School officials instead would determine whether to grant access.

A much-criticized 2013 FAIR study estimates that undocumented immigration costs state taxpayers about $717 million annually. The average household annually paid $1,000 to cover the costs associated with undocumented immigrants. The anti-immigrant group FAIR estimates that undocumented workers pay about $34 million in taxes to the state annually, less than 5 percent of their cost, and the state would likely get greater tax revenues if jobs held by undocumented individuals were by American-born and legal resident workers.

RECENT ANTI-IMMIGRANT ADVOCACY AND ACTIONS

During most of its history, New Mexico has been a model of balancing a push for border security with coping with undocumented immigrants. For instance, the state passed a law in 2005 that allows undocumented immigrants to pay the same tuition rate as legal, in-state residents, and in 2009, it was the 23rd state to ban racial profiling. The major reason for this approach is that New Mexico has the highest percentage of Latino/as of any state (45 percent), and they historically have had significant political power. The current New Mexico legislature is 44 percent Latino/a. Since becoming a state, New Mexico has had five Latino governors.

This climate has been changing, however. Influential factors include the cost of undocumented immigrants and the fierce competition for jobs in a recession. New Mexico's coffers have been strained by the many drug trafficking and immigration cases' impact on the federal judicial and corrections system. The U.S. District Court in New Mexico has the highest case load per judgeship in the nation and has the fourth-busiest court nationally. Resultantly, the state is very short of jail space.

A group of protesters at a rally on January 24, 2012, at the state capitol building in Santa Fe, New Mexico. The group, Somos Un Pueblo Unido, We Are a United people, organized the rally protesting the proposed repeal of issuing driver's licenses to undocumented immigrants, a move supported by Governor Susana Martinez. (AP Photo/J. R. Oppenheim)

In line with this, in 2009, the mayor of Albuquerque was elected after vowing to give the city police more power to check offenders' immigration status. A 2010 poll by Research and Polling Inc. (derived from the anti-immigrant group FAIR) of Albuquerque found that 72 percent of New Mexicans, including 69 percent of Latino/as, opposed the state's law allowing undocumented aliens to get driver's licenses.

In 2010, Susana Martinez (1959–), a Doña Ana County, New Mexico prosecutor, was elected New Mexico governor—but with only 38 percent of the Latino vote. In 2011, she alleged that the state's liberal driver's license law had turned New Mexico into a magnet for people from other states wanting a license. New Mexico and Washington are the only two states that grant unrestricted driver's license to undocumented immigrants. Accordingly, the state's Taxation and Revenue Department has prosecuted a number of people. Martinez argued that New Mexico residents would need passports in order to board planes and enter federal buildings because the state's driver's license law does not impose the citizenship and immigration restrictions required by the REAL ID Act. As of January 2013, a passport is required for domestic flights. In addition, Martinez has tried in the 2013 legislative session to get the state's 2003 driver's license law repealed.

NOTABLE GROUPS

Somos Un Pueblo Unido

The group *Somos Un Pueblo Unido* was established in 1995 and defends immigrants' rights in New Mexico. The original mission of the group was to challenge California's anti-immigrant Proposition 187, which was passed in 1995, but later deemed partly unconstitutional. This group spans the state but is community-based and led by immigrants, particularly aiming at workers' protections and rights (including protection against wage theft) and "racial justice." They connect the recent criminalization of immigration and profiling policies to racism, opposing questions about immigration status in municipal business transactions. In 2009, they have continued this campaign by targeting racial profiling practices and other discriminatory practices by the police. The group is headquartered in Santa Fe and is active in promoting public education, resources for immigrants, and staging public protests. Some recent issues they have worked on are: providing driver's license for all, supporting the Development, Relief, and Education for Alien Minors Act, and supporting in-state tuition for children raised in the United States.

BIBLIOGRAPHY

Albuquerque Historical Society. "Tricentennial Teachers Resource Guide." 2013. http://www.albuqhistsoc.org/. Accessed March 17, 2013.

Archibold, Randal C. "Side by Side, but Divided over Immigration." *New York Times*, May 11, 2010. http://www.nytimes.com/2010/05/12/us/12newmexico .html?pagewanted=all&_r=0. Accessed August 7, 2014.

Beck, Warren A. *New Mexico: A History of Four Centuries.* Norman: University of Oklahoma Press, 1962.

Billington, Ray Allen, and Martin Ridge. *Westward Expansion: A History of the American Frontier.* New York: Macmillan Publishing Co., 1982.

Boggs, Johnny D. "Southwest Style." *Wild West* 24 (2012): 42.

Brooks, James F. *Captives & Cousins: Slavery, Kinship, and Community in the Southwest Borderlands.* Williamsburg, VA: Omohundro Institute of Early American History and Culture, 2002.

Camarota, Steven A. "Immigrants in the United States, 2010: A Profile of America's Foreign-Born Population." Center for Immigration Studies, 2012. http://cis .org/2012-profile-of-americas-foreign-born-population. Accessed March 17, 2013.

Cañas, Jesús, Roberto A. Coronado, Robert W. Gilmer, and Eduardo Saucedo. *The Impact of the Maquiladora Industry on U.S. Border Cities,* Working Paper 1107. Dallas: Federal Reserve Bank of Dallas, 2011.

Center for Social and Demographic Analysis. "Children in Immigrant Families in New Mexico: Fact Sheet." Annie Casey Foundation, 2009. http://www.aecf.org/~/media/Pubs/ Topics/Special%20Interest%20Areas/Immigrants%20and%20Refugees/Childrenin ImmigrantFamiliesinNewMexico/AECF_immigrant_families_brief_new_mexico.pdf. Accessed March 17, 2013.

Clarke, Kevin. "Another America: A Look at 'Poverty Homesteading' in New Mexico." *U.S. Catholic* 68 (2003): 36.

Correia, David. "'Retribution Will Be Their Reward': New Mexico's Las Gorras Blancas and the Fight for the Las Vegas Land Grant Commons." *Radical History Review* 108 (2010): 49–72.

DeMark, Judith Boyce. "Introduction." In Judith Boyce DeMark, ed. *Essays in Twentieth-Century New Mexico History.* Albuquerque: University of New Mexico Press, 1994, pp. 1–12.

Ebright, M. *Land Grants and Lawsuits in Northern New Mexico.* Albuquerque: University of New Mexico Press, 1994.

Federation for American Immigration Reform (FAIR). "Immigration Facts: New Mexico." 2012. http://www.fairus.org/states/new-mexico?A=SearchResult&SearchID=379592 7&ObjectID=5121347&ObjectType=35. Accessed March 17, 2013.

Fergusson, Erna. *New Mexico: A Pageant of Three Peoples.* Albuquerque: University of New Mexico Press, 1951.

Finno, Megan, and Maryellen Bearzi. "Child Welfare and Immigration in New Mexico: Challenges, Achievements, and the Future." *Journal of Public Child Welfare* 4 (2010): 306–24.

García-Acevedo, María Rosa. "The Forgotten Diaspora: Mexican Immigration to New Mexico." In Erlinda Gonzales-Berry, and David R. Maciel, eds. *The Contested Homeland: A Chicano History of New Mexico.* Albuquerque: University of New Mexico Press, 2000, pp. 215–38.

Immigration Policy Center. "The Political and Economic Power of Immigrants, Latinos, and Asians in the Land of Enchantment." American Immigration Council, 2012. http://www.immigrationpolicy.org/just-facts/new-americans-new-mexico. Accessed March 17, 2013.

Johnson, Kenneth M., and Daniel T. Lichter. "Natural Increase: A New Source of Population Growth in Emerging Hispanic Destinations in the United States." *Population & Development Review* 34 (2008): 327–46.

Jones-Correa, Michael, and Diana Hernández. "Commonalities, Competition and Linked Fate: On Latinos Immigrants in New and Traditional Receiving Areas." Conference Papers—American Sociological Association, 2007. http://research.allacademic.com/meta/asa07_p_index.html?filter=C. Accessed March 17, 2013.

Lichter, Daniel T., Domenico Parisi, Michael C. Taquino, and Steven Michael Grice. "Residential Segregation in New Hispanic Destinations: Cities, Suburbs, and Rural Communities Compared." *Social Science Research* 39 (2010): 215–30.

Montgomery, Charles. "Becoming 'Spanish-American': Race and Rhetoric in New Mexico Politics, 1880–1928." *Journal of American Ethnic History* 20 (2001): 59–84.

Moody, Terry, and Clarence Fielder. "African-American Settlement of Southern New Mexico." New Mexico State Record Center and Archives, 2013. http://www.newmexicohistory.org/filedetails.php?fileID=21173. Accessed March 17, 2013.

New Mexico Humanities Council. "Homesteaders 1862." Atlas of Historic New Mexico Maps, 2013. http://atlas.nmhum.org/atlas.php?phndl=themes&BIMSID=ee275qgmsiqj8t4cuqqhl35st5&t=1362697271. Accessed March 17, 2013.

New Mexico Jewish Historical Society. "Crypto-Jews." 2013. http://www.nmjhs.org/crypto-jews.html. Accessed March 17, 2013.

Passel, Jeffrey, and D'Vera Cohn. "Unauthorized Immigrant Population: National and State Trends, 2010." Pew Research Hispanic Center, 2011. http://www.pewhispanic.org/2011/02/01/v-workers/. Accessed March 17, 2013.

Pomonis, Katherine. "Greeks in Albuquerque: The History of Greeks in Albuquerque, 1900–1952." New Mexico State Record Center and Archives, 2013. http://www.newmexicohistory.org/filedetails.php?fileID=24488. Accessed March 17, 2013.

Price, Paxton P. *Mesilla Valley Pioneers 1823–1912*. Las Cruces, NM: Yucca Tree Press, 2005.

Sawtelle, Susan D. "Treaty of Guadalupe Hidalgo: Findings and Possible Options Regarding Longstanding Community Land Grant Claims in New Mexico: GAO-04-59." GAO Reports, 2004, 1.

Somos Un Pueblo Unido. Somos Un Pueblo Unido Webpage. http://somosunpueblounido.org/mainpage.php. Accessed February 23, 2014.

Stamatov, Susan. "Japanese-American Internment Camps: Japanese-American Internment Camps in New Mexico 1942–1946." New Mexico Office of the State Historian, 2012. http://www.newmexicohistory.org/filedetails.php?fileID=453. Accessed March 17, 2013.

Torrez, Robert J. "A Cuarto Centennial History of New Mexico." *Official New Mexico Blue Book, Cuarto Centennial Edition, 1598–1998*. Albuquerque: Office of the New Mexico Secretary of State, 1998. http://www.nmgs.org/artcuar7.htm. Accessed March 17, 2013.

Valdes, Gustavo. "New Mexico Governor Takes Aim at Immigrant Driver's Licenses." CNN.com, January 24, 2013. http://www.cnn.com/2013/01/23/us/new-mexico-immigrant-licenses. Accessed March 17, 2013.

Zehr, Mary Ann. "With Immigrants, Districts Balance Safety, Legalities." *Education Week* 27 (2007): 1.

32

NEW YORK

Miriam Jiménez

CHRONOLOGY

1609	Henry Hudson claims land previously inhabited by native Iroquois and Algonquians. In the following years, the Dutch establish some forts and concentrate their activities on the trade of furs.
1623	The Dutch start the formal colonization of New Amsterdam. Wallons (French Protestants) settle first, Hollanders, Swedes, Norwegians, Germans, English, and Scots arrive soon after.
1626	The first African slaves are brought.
1647–1664	Peter Stuyvesant's successful administration of the colony attracts increasing migration. New Amsterdam's population includes Germans French, Swedish, and Finish, among others.
1654	The first Jews arrive to the colony.
1664	The British occupy New Amsterdam and name it New York. The British respect the ethnic and religious diversity that they find, although some of them feel unhappy regarding the "mixture of nations" that they encounter.
1790	New York with a total population of 340,120 persons ranks fifth among all states, according to the first census. One half of the state residents are of English descent, whereas only one-fifth is of Dutch descent. New York City, with only one borough, Manhattan, is the second-largest city of the Union with a population of 33,131 persons.
1820	New York State becomes the most populous state of the Union. It will remain in this position until the 1960s.

1830	In the following years, New York becomes the nation's most important port and industrial center, attracting millions of European immigrants.
1845–1854	About 3 million immigrants arrive to the state. These are the years of peak migration of the Irish, many of whom are Catholic. They have left Ireland for both political and economic reasons related to the potato famine. An influx German immigration also arrives then; Germans become the largest foreign-born group in upstate cities like Rochester and Buffalo during the following decade.
1855	Castle Garden, in the southern tip of Manhattan, becomes an immigrant station. It will operate until its closing in 1890.
1880–World War I (1914–1918)	A new massive wave of immigration takes place. The newcomers are Eastern and Southern Europeans: Italian, Polish, Greek, and Russian, and Eastern European Jewish immigrants arrive.
1890	The federal government assumes control of immigration and allocates funds for the construction of the first federal immigration station on Ellis Island.
1892	Ellis Island starts its operations on January 1.
1910	The immigrant share of New York City's population reaches a peak of 41 percent—the highest in the twentieth century. New York City's population is 2,331,542, which represents a 70-fold increase in 120 years.
1921–1924	The Immigrant Quota Act of 1921 and the National Origins Act of 1924 restrict immigration to the United States and end the wave of mass immigration into New York between 1921 and 1924.
1930	The immigrant population in New York City drops to one-third of the total population. However, between 1930 and 1960, one out of six foreign-born person of the country lives in New York City.
1954	Ellis Island definitely closes its operation as an immigration station. Between 1892 and 1954, more than 12 million immigrants pass through Ellis Island.
1965	The amendments to the 1952 McCarran-Walter Immigration and Naturalization Act will mark the beginning of a new wave of immigration to the state. Latin American, Caribbean, and Asian immigrants will change, once more, the demographic and cultural face of the state.
2001 (September 11)	The World Trade Center is attacked by terrorists in New York City.
2011	New York governor Andrew Cuomo announces that the state will no longer participate in the Secure Communities immigration enforcement program.
2011	Immigrant rights groups and the New York Civil Liberties Union accuse the upstate New York Border Patrol of abusing their power by questioning the citizenship of train and bus passengers.
2013	The foreign-born are estimated to comprise about one-fifth of the state's population.

HISTORICAL OVERVIEW

If historian Oscar Handlin is right when he says that the history of immigration in the United States is the history of the country, the focus on New York is a necessary one. This state, which has been diverse since its creation, still ranks second to all in the proportion of the foreign population that it hosts, being only surpassed by California. Some scholars (e.g., Klein 1991) consider that the state actually summarizes the larger national experience of immigration. New York City, in particular, is the archetypical case of cosmopolitanism and diversity in the United States. The city has been the most important and iconic port of entry for immigrants to the United States for a long time and the experience of those who arrives to the big metropolis during different times often resounds outside its boroughs. Through history, about 85 percent of the immigrants who arrived to the state settled in New York City.

Although the salience of New York City has often overshadowed other local or regional developments, the Empire State cannot simply be considered a reflection of the events that take place in the big urban center. Those immigrants who came to settle in other parts of the state and those who eventually relocated to its suburban areas have also made their own history. Within 54,475 square miles, the state's landscape includes large cities; suburbs; rural areas; and, in short, a complex natural, social, and political geography. Immigrants in the state have found various contexts of reception and there are local cases of particular groups that openly defy generalizations that are useful to describe and understand the trends that have been observed in New York City. In addition to this, careful demographic analyses have consistently demonstrated that the immigrant population upstate and downstate present significantly different profiles in terms of education, country of origin, and participation in the labor market, among other indicators. As historian Carl Carmer once said, with much reason, "New York State is a country" (Klein 2001) and the picture of immigration in the state is more complex than it was assumed for some time.

In 2010, according to updated Census Bureau estimates, there were 4,297,612 immigrants in the New York State. They represented almost 22 percent of the state's population and less than 11 percent of total immigrant population in the United States. Currently, six states alone account for 66 percent of the total foreign-born population of the United States and New York is, evidently, one of them—the other five are California, Florida, Texas, Illinois, and New Jersey. The foreign-born population in New York has features that openly defy easy preconceptions or about immigration. For example, despite the large historical flows of international migration to the state—or precisely because of that—the majority of foreign-born persons in New York today are fully documented immigrants.

The immigrant population has an active participation in the economy of the state: in 2007, immigrants produced $229 billion in economic output, that is, 22.4 percent of the state's gross domestic product. Historically, immigrant labor built the infrastructure of the city, including its subway system and its impressive skyscrapers. Immigrants have played a substantial role in areas that range from the provision of services to the advancement of scientific research within the prestigious universities that the state houses. Moreover, several scholars have documented the process through which immigrants have reactivated particular sectors of the economy, such as the garment industry at different times. And the arrival of foreign immigration has also offset population losses caused by lower birth rates and the out-migration of segments of native New Yorkers, particularly between 1970 and 1990.

The history of the foreign-born population in the state is long and rich. When the Dutch colonized the area, New York's population included French-speaking Walloons, Flemish, Scandinavians, and Germans; African slaves, Jews, and the British arrived later. Then, there were varying nationalities and classes in the following two centuries, that is, German farmers and entrepreneurs; Irish politicians and poor peasants; Italian artists, and landless migrants. This, in short, is a story about the Welsh, Norwegians, Greeks, Poles, Slaves, Chinese, Russians, Ukrainians, Mexicans, Central Americans, Jamaicans, Koreans, Asian Indians, Dominicans, Haitians, Pakistanis, Ghanaians, and Canadians, among many, many others. Furthermore, this is a story of immigrants who came under different legal categories and therefore includes the voices of elite-university doctors; small entrepreneurs; agricultural workers; global professionals; undocumented immigrants; and that of the refugees from Burma, Iraq, and Afghanistan, who live in the state today. Additionally, any overview of the topic must include not only the analysis of massive waves of foreign immigration but also the study of several cases of internal migration: Yankees who relocated from New England in the seventeenth century, blacks who left the South during the first part of the twentieth century, and Puerto Ricans who came in different waves particularly during the mid-twentieth century were among them. Some chapters of this story still have to be written because the analysis of immigration beyond New York City's metropolitan area has largely been neglected until relatively recent years.

In a federal system, states have limited powers to influence immigration policies; they cannot determine who arrives or the requirements or conditions to do so. States, however, play a critical role shaping the context and environment where immigrants live. The government of the state of New York has traditionally been considered generous in the availability of services that it has provided to documented foreign-born persons—and those services may often be accessible in languages different than English. In the critical area of education, official representatives often show concern with the need to educate the inhabitants of the state, regardless their legal status.

In the context of national politics, New York has a tradition of reformers and it is generally considered one of the most liberal states of the union. That, however, does not necessarily make the state an immigrant haven. For example, the political environment in Albany, the capital, is more conservative than in New York City. Moreover, the alternate party control of the governorship, a normally divided state legislature, and economic distress may create political conditions that are not necessarily favorable to immigrants. A good case to illustrate this is the heated debate that took place during the fall of 2007 regarding the state government's intention to provide driver's licenses to undocumented persons. The plan was abandoned shortly.

Voices of conservatism are present throughout the state, but they coexist with academic communities, media outlets, immigrant organizations, activists, and with think tanks across the state that raise concerns about policy issues involved in immigration processes, which challenge simplistic anti-immigrant perceptions, and use sophisticated methods to assess and underline the contributions that immigrants make to the life of state.

TOPICAL ESSAYS

The following sections present a condensed, analytical perspective of the multidimensional factors and events that have shaped the context and patterns of immigration to the state from the mid-twentieth century to the present time. Because of this contemporary focus, the intense and now often romanticized story of the massive wave of immigrants who have arrived to Ellis Island 100 years ago, for instance, has been necessarily constrained to the modest limits of the chronology included at the beginning of this chapter. The experience of those immigrants, however, are still important for understanding the current immigration debates, and precisely for that reason, it is necessary to review the standard assumptions that we have held regarding the process through which they reached mainstream circles of power.

Perhaps the struggles of today's immigrants will also be seen through romanticized lenses in some future. After all, New York has absorbed and incorporated multiple generations of immigrants through its history. And New York City in particular—dynamic and resilient as ever—it is still there, offering room for dreams and the perceived possibilities of opportunity that big urban spaces manage to offer, in one way or another.

The Post–World War II Years (1940–1970)

During the World War II and postwar years, the foreign migration to the country continued to be highly restricted by the quota system fully established between

1921 and 1924; this immigration policy largely continued until 1965. In New York, however, a modest, but important immigration resurgence took place during the mid-century decades. It was particularly remarkable that the two most-important groups of immigrants that arrived to the state during the 1940s share one essential feature: Southern blacks and Puerto Ricans were internal migrants, as opposed to foreign immigrants. In addition to them, there were also some small groups of refugees that came to the state for causes related to World War II and to the subsequent Cold War.

During the 1940s, Southern blacks left behind the depressed agricultural conditions that the cotton belt region experienced during the previous decade and sought the job opportunities that wartime conditions had created in defense plants located in cities like Detroit, Chicago, New York, and Philadelphia. Their presence in the North was not new; some Southern blacks had migrated to northern destinations since the end of the Civil War. During the last years of the nineteenth century, their migration increased and by the 1910s, this movement acquired the large proportions of what is now known as the "Great Migration." The result could be appreciated through the years: in the 1860s, 92 percent of the country's black population lived in the South, but at the end of the following century, during the 1990s, only 53 percent did so. By then, this group had become predominantly urbanized, with 86 percent of them living in cities. Some scholars had considered that such process of urbanization was one underlying factor that made the Civil Rights Movement possible in the 1960s.

About two-thirds of the African American migrants who arrived to the state of New York between the end of the nineteenth century and the 1910s settled in Manhattan. They found, upon their arrival, some conditions that at first look very promising but that did not prosper in the short term. The state then had formally abolished segregation in public facilities, had repealed an old anti-miscegenation law, and had put into place a ward system of schools to replace the previous one based on separate facilities. But negative reactions developed quickly when this migration increased and despite the official policy, racial housing segregation soon became the standard in the city. It was then when black ghettoes and slums began to form in the North.

One of those ghettoes was Harlem, in uptown Manhattan. In the 1920s, in an interesting development, this neighborhood became the very center of the Harlem Renaissance, a movement that included the vibrancy of jazz music, several novelists, and various different artistic manifestations of black pride. In later years, it was in Harlem, too, when a riot occurred that targeted white-owned and Jewish businesses. The 1935 Harlem Riot illustrated ongoing economic tensions and ethnic conflicts in the neighborhood and expressed the frustration of African Americans who largely suffered from segregation, job exclusion, and low quality of education.

The migration of Southern African Americans to New York State increased again in the 1940s, after a noticeable decline that took place during the Depression years. Approximately 3.2 million blacks left the South between 1940 and 1950; one-quarter of them settled in the state and predominantly in New York City. They occupied well-defined areas of different boroughs, including Harlem in Manhattan, Morrisania in the Bronx, South Jamaica in Queens, and Bedford-Stuyvesant in Brooklyn. Upstate, in the Buffalo area, there had been at least a small settlement of blacks since the 1920s, which remained largely marginal for some years. Then, between 1940 and 1950, the black population in Buffalo tripled, reaching as many as 79,000 persons. They were confined to a ghetto formed on the city's East Side. African Americans were also present in other northern cities like Rochester (particularly in the Baden-Osmond and Clarissa streets) and in Syracuse's Fifth Ward.

Puerto Ricans, on their side, traveled to the mainland from the Caribbean island which had been ceded to the United States in 1898 as a result of the Spanish-American War. The status of the island's inhabitants in relation to the United States was undefined for almost two decades; it was not until 1917, when the passage of the Jones Act eventually granted them citizenship rights. Consequently, Puerto Ricans did not require a visa or authorization to travel to the mainland. Nevertheless, the incorporation of Puerto Rico to the United States took place in a context of political and economic dependency and migrants to the mainland; Puerto Ricans experienced the conditions of "second class citizens," that is, housing segregation, discrimination, and the restricted job opportunities that often confined them to marginal positions of surplus labor (Martínez 2005).

During the first decades of the twentieth century, some groups of contracted workers had been taken to different areas, including Hawaii, to perform heavy agricultural labor; a few others traveled to the mainland sporadically. This changed during the postwar years. In 1940, only 1,000 Puerto Ricans migrated, but in 1953, almost 75,000 did so. In the 1950s, approximately 20 percent of the population relocated to the mainland. The large majority of them (approximately 80 percent) resided in the New York metropolitan area. The migration of Puerto Ricans reached a peak in the 1950s: their move to the mainland was then higher than the migration totals of any other single country. Because of their significant concentration in New York City, other small communities attracted less attention. One of them developed in Brentwood, Long Island, during the 1950s.

Puerto Ricans were clearly a distinctive group among Latinos/as. They arrived in the first airborne migration from abroad. As opposed to the journeys that previous migrants endure across the Atlantic Ocean, Puerto Ricans took advantage of a time when the abundance of aircrafts made the trip from the island affordable and considerably accessible. These possibilities would also facilitate the patterns of circular migration that the group showed in later decades, particularly the 1960s.

In New York City, Puerto Ricans also settled in well-defined neighborhoods: El Barrio in East Harlem, areas of Washington Heights in uptown Manhattan, and in the South Bronx area. Puerto Ricans were then the only significant Latino/a presence in the state. Their numbers made them the third most-important minority group in the country at that time, right after African Americans and Mexicans. The economic status of the group continued to be intriguing because of its high levels of poverty and their concentration in low-skilled jobs. Politically, they were able to access the coalitions of power in the city during the 1970s.

The in-migration of African Americans and Puerto Ricans made more diverse the socio-demographic face of New York City, which was of European descent until the 1950s, granted that neither groups were immigrants. By 1960, there were more than 1 million African Americans and half-a-million Puerto Ricans in New York City alone, all making approximately 22 percent of the city's population. Then, after 1965, more significant changes took place with the arrival of Caribbean, Latin American, and Asian immigrants.

During the mid-century decades, the share of population with immigrant roots increased in other areas of the state, for different reasons. Economic affluence, new transportation facilities, and the construction of housing projects triggered a dynamic process of suburbanization. At a time when the authorities in New York City undertook an aggressive wave of construction works that destroyed several old neighborhoods, increasing numbers of Italians, Irish, and Jews who were experiencing high levels of social mobility after World War II moved to the suburbs of the state. Long Island illustrated this situation well. There, the foreign-born population jumped from 126,000 to 193,000 between 1950 and 1970—the U.S.-born population increased by 1½ million. Suburbs were largely maintained as segregated preserves.

World War II and the Cold War also influenced some aspects of immigration, particularly in the category of displaced persons. During the war, several European countries accepted large numbers of Jews whose lives were threatened by the Nazi regime, but the United States did not articulate any special policy beyond the existing limits of the quota system. It was not until 1944 when President Roosevelt, in what has been considered a mostly symbolic gesture, decided to admit 1,000 non-Italian persons in the United States. The selected group of 982 persons that eventually came included men, women, and children. Most of them were Jewish and many had already been in detention camps in Europe. After the transoceanic voyage, they were sent upstate, and placed in an internment center at Fort Ontario, in the city of Oswego, New York. Since the category of refugee had not been precisely defined in those years, these persons had, at first, a peculiarly undefined status: they were accepted under the condition that they would return to their countries of origin at the end of the war and therefore were not registered as resident aliens. The camp at Forth Ontario was placed under the responsibility of the War Relocation Authority, which was the same agency that oversaw the internment of Japanese Americans into camps after the Japanese attack to Pearl Harbor. In 1946, the refugees of Fort Ontario were eventually granted the possibility to apply for U.S. citizenship.

In times of Cold War, other displaced persons arrived, among them Hungarians and then middle-class Cuban refugees who left after the 1959 Revolution and settled on parts of Long Island. In 1948, the Displaced Persons Act recognized for the first time the category of refugee, although more concrete aspects of this immigration status would be defined in subsequent decades.

New Immigration and Demographic Change in the Late Twentieth Century (1970–2000)

The last quarter of the twentieth century brought new transformations to the state. They were largely defined by two important events: the beginning of a new massive wave of international immigration and the decrease of the state population caused by the combined results of low fertility rates and the migration of native New Yorkers out of the state.

In 1965, the amendments to the 1952 McCarran-Walter Immigration and Naturalization Act became a watershed in the history of immigration to the United States. The new policy ended the eugenic quota system established in 1924, which favored northern and western European countries. With the 1965 changes, barriers to the immigration from Asian and African countries were eliminated and English-speaking Caribbean countries were no longer restricted by small quotas. The new policy also defined family reunification and occupational skills as the main criteria for admission, as opposed to country of birth. Interestingly, these changes occurred at a time when countries like China, the Soviet Union, or Dominican Republic were, for different reasons in each case, also softening restrictions to the out-migration of their citizens. Shortly after, a new wave of immigration to the United States began.

What followed is now history. Since the 1970s, a large number of immigrants arrived and they were predominantly from Latin American and Asian countries. While the share of foreign-born population in the state had been declining since 1930, it increased again after 1980. In 1930, there were 3,193,932 foreign-born persons in the state, representing 25.3 percent of total population. In 1970, by contrast, 2,109,776, immigrants accounted for a share of only 11.5 percent of the Empire State's population. In the year of 1980, it was clear that the foreign-born population was increasing: 2,388,938 immigrants in the state accounted for 13.6 percent of the total population. In New York City alone, the foreign-born population grew from 1,437,100 to 1,670,200 between 1970 and 1980, that is, from a share of 18.2 percent of the city's population to 23.6 percent. Nearly 85 percent of the persons who were legally admitted during that time settled in New York City, adding new cultural influences to the life of the metropolis.

One of the salient characteristics of this wave of immigration was its composition. In contrast to the influx of immigrants who came to the United States during the nineteenth and early twentieth centuries, the majority of the new comers in the past decades were not from European countries. In a conscientious analysis about the immigrant population New York State, scholar Nadia Youssef could already identify a "gradual, though persistent" consolidation of a set of sending countries to the state in the year 1992. They were, by rank, from the Dominican Republic, Jamaica, Guyana Haiti, and China. India and Korea followed with some distance. In New York City, the largest groups came from Dominican Republic, China, and Jamaica.

Instead of a booming economy, the new immigrants found conditions of inflation and stagnant growth in the state. Global competition affected segments of the industrial and service sectors dramatically and firms sought to maximize their gains by seeking lower taxes and cheaper sources of labor in other countries—with obvious adverse effects on the levels of employment in the state. For the first time in the history of New York, factory wages actually fell behind the national averages in those years. The financial crisis of New York City made headlines in 1975, but the city was not alone in this kind of troubles. The whole state had to accept a degree of austerity and politics of retrenchment that some considered a real breakdown of the New Deal-Great Society policies.

The declining economic opportunities of those years, combined with lower birth rates, resulted in a problem previously unknown in the state: the loss of population. And it was precisely the factor of foreign immigrants' arrival that helped to offset such loss.

A detailed analysis by scholars Richard D. Alba and Michael D. Batutis (1984) provided a comprehensive picture of the important demographic changes that took place in the state at that time. New York State and Rhode Island were the only two states that had net population losses during the 1970s. New York experienced the most serious one: its total population fell by almost 700,000. Only during the first part of the decade, in the years comprehended between 1970 and 1975, the state experienced a loss of 650,000 persons, when 1,070,000 entered and 1,720,000 left their residences in the state. The state's out-migrants went predominantly to Florida and other southern states along the Atlantic coast; to other Northeast states, particularly New Jersey; and to California.

The out-migrants tended to be young adults between the age of 20–34, and retirees aged 55 and older. Although population losses occurred in different degrees across the state's regions, the metropolitan areas were the most affected ones. Whereas New York City did not attract a large number of persons from other states, those who did come to the state settled predominantly in the city.

The in-migration to the state was, more than in any other state in the United States, of foreign origin. Among the groups of immigrants who helped offset the state's population loss, there were 50,000 Puerto Ricans and 80,000 immigrants from other Caribbean countries; 60,000 Central Americans and South Americans; 85,000 Asians, and 13,000 persons from Middle Eastern countries. In addition to this, 80,000 in-migrants were European, and 50,000 were American-born.

The immigrants who arrived to the city through the years transformed the face of many neighborhoods—some through expansion and some through ethnic succession. Immigrants infused youth and compensated for the aging population of the state, and made some segments of both the formal and informal economy grow. Illustrating the latter, the International Ladies Garment Workers' Union estimated that unregulated sweatshops went from approximately 200 in the 1970s to 3,000 in the following decade.

By the 1990s, the presence of new immigrants was evident and diverse analysts were examining the differences among immigrants in terms of length of stay, legal status, and class. Immigrants were not born equal; while some had experienced the tremendously difficult conditions of New York City's tight housing market, established professionals and business persons enjoyed the comforts of expensive accommodations or suburban houses.

New York City completed its transition to a postindustrial economy in the 1980s; that decade showed a process of important recovery. Although there were some levels of population loss in the two subsequent decades, they were pale in comparison to the critical situation of the 1970s. The state also found some balance. In the 1990s, the local-born population fell by only 10,000, while the number of foreign-born residents increased by 20,000.

As the century ended, tourism and foreign investment increased. Then, New York City entered fully into the modern dynamics of commerce, service, and financial markets to become a global city. And it was more ethnically diverse than ever. Whites had Anglo, Irish, Italian, of Greek descent; Europeans who arrived after the fall of communism also were included there. Blacks were African Americans, West Indians, of Africans; Latinos were Puerto Ricans, Dominicans, or Mexicans, among others. Asians were Chinese, Korean, and Indian.

IMMIGRATION AT THE START OF THE TWENTY-FIRST CENTURY

New York State is still an attractive destination for migrants who come from different parts of the world. Although immigrants are not arriving in the same numbers as before, it is likely that many will continue to settle there for many different reasons. The dual structure of work that the state has is one among the reasons because it requires specialized professionals and skillful technicians, along with workers who can perform manual and service jobs. The former is needed to fill positions in sectors of banking, finance, and corporative positions demanded by global markets and services and the latter keeps fully fueled subsectors of services, construction, and industrial production.

Nearly 11 percent of the total foreign-born population in the United States lives in the state; that is a little over 1 in 10 immigrants at the national level. Almost three-quarters of them reside in New York City. They are a critical component of the economy of the state, with an economic contribution of $229 billion, that is, 22.4 percent of the state's economic output.

In 2009, immigrants represented 26.9 percent of the total civilian workforce in the state. Statistics showed, overall, that the foreign-born population of the state was in better conditions compared to other states. In general, New Yorker immigrants showed higher levels of education, were more likely to have health insurance, and less likely to have entered the country without full authorization. The income differential between native and foreign-born residents was also smaller than the national average.

Beyond the big picture, there is considerable diversity in the foreign-born population of the state. In terms of income, for instance, one-third of the state immigrants had yearly earnings or $50,000 of more, whereas 29.3 percent earned less than $26,000.While two-thirds of the immigrants who lived in downstate and upstate suburbs owned their houses at that time, others endured horrifying conditions of living in basement accommodations—or worse.

In terms of education, 27.9 percent of the state immigrants had completed a college degree in 2010, whereas 26.8 percent had not finished high school. Approximately 24.3 percent of the college-educated immigrant population was affected by some degree of "skill underutilization," that is, they were either unemployed of working in unskilled jobs.

In New York City, the foreign-born population more than doubled between 1970 and 2008, reaching 3 million persons, while the native-born population declined by more than 1 million. Immigrants represented 36.4 percent of the city's population that year (twice the 1970 share). They had an active presence in the economy of the metropolis: the 1.9 million who were employed in the city that year represented as much as 43 percent of the city's workforce and generated $215 billion—32 percent of the city's gross product. Many of them were actually self-employed: 49 percent of self-employed persons in the city and 25 percent of self-employed persons in the state were immigrants (at the national level, the immigrant's share of self-employed persons of only 12 percent). Moreover, 10 of the New York City neighborhoods with the highest level of immigrant residents had the stronger economic growth between 2000 and 2007.

The city had, as a document by a Department of City Planning pointed out, "a very dynamic population." Several hundred thousand people came and went each year. Some degree of out-migration continues, and the international migration continued to upset the loss (2011). The differences between downstate and upstate immigrant population were remarkable.

Latinos/as represented 50 percent of the immigrant population in New York City, but their upstate share was only 13 percent. About 40 percent of upstate immigrants came from European countries (including Bosnia and Herzegovina, Russia, and Ukraine). Another 30 percent was originally born in Asian countries (including India), and 10 percent migrated from Canada. Canada was one of the top 10 sending countries upstate area—and the top one in Buffalo.

If the profile of immigrants in New York City defies standard conceptions, their counterpart upstate do it even more. For instance, upstate immigrants tend to be highly educated: the percentage of those who have attained a college or a graduate degree is higher than even native-born persons in the area, and they are notoriously concentrated in scientific, medical, and computer-related fields. But among immigrants, there is also a significant number that does not have a high-school degree.

New York state senator Adriano Espaillat, center, declares his race with long-time Congressman Charles Rangel too close to call in the Democratic primary for the 13th Congressional District on June 24, 2014, in New York. Espaillat, a Dominican-born legislator who lost in the 2012 primary, ran against Rangel in the majority Hispanic district that includes Harlem. (AP Photo/Jason DeCrow)

Undocumented persons represent only 13 percent of the immigrant population in the state, which is considerably below the 65 percent share in Arizona, 50 percent share of Texas, or 23 percent of New Jersey.

THE STATE: IMMIGRATION POLITICS AND POLICIES

Notwithstanding that immigration policy and the criteria for admissions of foreign-born persons are under the exclusive jurisdiction of the federal government (except for the 1996 devolution), states clearly matter. They have the power to affect the lives of immigrants directly making important services available to them, for example, education, health, and welfare. They also collaborate with federal agencies exchanging information and following deportation procedures, and they also decide the directives that the state police follows.

In principle, New York does not deny its immigrant past. Throughout the state, there is a relatively prevalent—although by no means unanimous—rhetoric of acceptance of immigrants, particularly noticeably in New York City. Public figures openly acknowledge their ethnic background, participate in ethnic pride parades, and talk about the initiative and strong work ethics that immigrants invest in the life of the state. Official documents recognize that immigrants not only helped building the state's infrastructure and kept it running but also showed the inventiveness to create business that grew into corporations. Michael Bloomberg, mayor of New York City, businessman, media billionaire, tried to start a discussion among presidential candidates about immigration plans and perspectives in the summer of 2012. Mayor Bloomberg maintained that the country needs immigrants for their creativity, to perform necessary work that other Americans would not do, and to bring their world experience to the country.

This rhetoric also exists at the level of the state government, in the more conservative political context of the capital of the state, Albany. Special reports have observed that immigrants have alleviated shortages of labor in fields such as medicine and engineering, made innovations in business and sciences, and provided a steady supply of labor, and that despite that, they have been scapegoated, particularly in times of economic downturn. Even a document released in 1996 by a group of state senators who wanted to assess possible expenses that the existing federal immigration law had caused to the state candidly recognized that most members of the taskforce had immigrant roots and that their goal was to assess costs, not ban immigration to the state. They actually considered the immigrant debates that were taking place in California at that time as "emotional," rather than rational. The debates in question were regarding California's now defunct Proposition 187, which sought to deny benefits to undocumented immigrants.

These immigrant-friendly perspectives have often run across party lines, which explained why some Republican politicians in the state, particularly moderate ones, could sometimes act on behalf of the immigrants who lived in the state. In this context, it is possible to understand the announcement that Governor George Pataki made in 1997, regarding the extension of five months that his administration had obtained from the federal government in order to allow immigrants to collect the documents that proved their eligibility for welfare benefits. This was the longest waiver granted for that purpose of any state. Many activists praised the reasonableness of the measure, although some pointed out that this benevolence was relatively cost-free for the state.

Yet, the rhetoric of acceptance to immigrants also has limits, as a heated debate that took place in 2007 showed. In September of that year, Governor Elliot Spitzer announced his decision to issue driver's licenses to New Yorkers regardless of their immigrant status; they could present a passport and apply, even lacking a social security card. The plan was presented in pragmatic terms: the governor considered that issuing driver's licenses regardless of the applicant's status would allow more people to get car insurance, would reduce premiums, and would result in higher road safety. He also said that the plan would allow the New York Department of Motor Vehicles to collect some vital statistics. This idea was new to the state, but not to the country; seven states had already implemented similar policies at that time: Hawaii, Maine, Maryland, Michigan, New Mexico, Oregon, and Washington. Utah, additionally, provided what they called "driver privilege cards," which were not issued as documents to prove identification.

Governor Spitzer modified some aspects of his proposal the following month, after a meeting with Michael Chertoff, secretary of the Department of Homeland Security. Basically, the agreement after the meeting was that the licenses issued to undocumented persons would not be used for traveling or as a form of identification, and they would be flagged "not for federal purposes." (Terraza and Macias 2007) Opposition to the measure was immediately expressed from different perspectives. Conservatives in the state—and beyond—criticized the plan as an inappropriate policy in the context of counterterrorism; others rejected what they considered as a reward to persons who could not prove a legal status and most surely had circumvented the law. From another perspective, Mayor Bloomberg saw it as a measure that would devalue state licenses; county clerks asked the governor to reverse the plan. Additionally, after the announced modifications to the plan in October, specialty media editors—serving ethnic audiences—observed that flagged licenses would be equivalent to a scarlet letter, underlining the shame of an undocumented status. Governor Spitzer finally abandoned the proposal in November.

In the context of public policy matters, education deserves a special mention. Although the history of education in the state has had its points of contention, the state law currently mandates free public education for all residents aged 5 to 21. School districts may require documents that prove age and residency (e.g., rental leases, birth certificates, utilities bills, or consular identification cards) but they are not supposed to ask for immigration-related documents.

In recent years, however, the New York Civil Liberties Union found that about 20 percent of the 139 state school districts have actually been requiring children's immigration papers in order to enroll them, or asking for information that undocumented persons could not provide. Although no cases are known of children who were denied enrollment for lack of immigration paperwork, the organization considers that such requirements not only might deter undocumented families from enrolling their children but also violate federal laws. They asked the State Department of Education to stop the practices to no avail. When a *New York Times* correspondent published an article that made reference to this situation in July 2010, several school districts turned to the Department of Education for guidance. The department responded by sending a memorandum written in consultation with its lawyers and the New York Civil Liberties Union that strongly recommended suspending such documentation requirements upon the basis of a 1982 Supreme Court decision (*Plyler v. Doe*) which recognized the right of all children to attend public school, regardless of their immigrant status, as long as they satisfy age and residency requirements.

The State University of New York and The City University of New York, the state and city public systems of college education, currently offer access to children of immigrants who do not possess regularized documents, paying in-residence tuition rates. The problem is that these students still lack access to financial aid, state assistance, or scholarships to pay for their education; moreover, their irregular status often confines them to menial jobs that do not provide them with adequate resources to pursue a college degree. Given that the U.S. Congress has repeatedly failed to approve several versions of the Development, Relief, and Education for Alien Minors Act which would target this issue, several officials and organization within the state are currently working on alternative measures or considering different paths of action. Some state legislators have introduced bills meant to help the students, whereas top state education officials have announced their intention to put more pressure on Congress (Santos 2011a). The State Department of Education, extrapolating various data sources, has even made an estimate of what funding undocumented students' college education would cost the state ($627,428 per year, as of December 2011). The department estimates that 4,550 children of undocumented immigrants graduate from the state high schools and calculates that only 5 percent of them would be willing to pursue college education, if the opportunity is offered.

In other aspects of education, advocacy groups in the state maintain after-school programs and provide tutoring for children of immigrants. Others try to develop college-readiness programs and counseling for students and parents alike. Some activist organizations are particularly concerned with presenting role models that inspire children of immigrants to continue their studies. Nonetheless, many of them still consider these efforts modest in view of the requirements of the task.

Language is another important aspect of public policy. It is particularly notice-able that the state facilitates the access to services in languages other than English. It is important to mention, however, that the use of foreign languages has a basis in federal law, as it is considered among the policies that provide help to persons with disabilities.

In New York City, immigrants have generally been free of fears of detention or deportation based on their looks. Any subway rider who detaches from the frantic rhythm of the metropolis or from his/her own self-thoughts for a moment, is likely to find a mixture of cultural backgrounds in any small group of people that randomly coincide on a train's seat. But different events punctuate this situation and introduce variables of change. For instance, due to the circumstances that resulted from the attacks to the World Trade Center in September 11, 2001, several activist organizations denounced violations to the constitutional rights of persons of Middle Eastern descent in the context of the war on terrorism. In other cases, there have been well-documented cases of racial profiling from the police. And the state is clearly not exempt from hate crimes in areas that have experienced a growing influx of immigrants or that is absent.

Recently, some organizations have perceived increasing arrests of dark-skinned and Latino men in close relation to the federal program known as Secure Communities, an important enforcement tool of the Obama administration. The program requires that local and state police share fingerprinting with the Federal Bureau of Investigation (FBI) for criminal history checks and with Homeland Security Office agencies—particularly the Immigration and Customs Enforcement (ICE)—which in turn determine whether the person is subject to deportation procedures. In July 2011, Governor Andrew Cuomo tried to withdraw the state from the program, observing that there was considerable evidence that showed that the program was ineffective in targeting serious criminals and instead, largely affected persons who had no previous criminal record. Mayor Bloomberg also announced that the city would not share the fingerprints of detainees who did not have a previous criminal record. Activist organizations strongly opposed the program which, in their perspective, failed to identify a terrorist threat and instead, had a disruptive effect on many families. Yet, the FBI and the ICE stated that, after Governor Cuomo's announcement, the counties who were already participating could not withdraw.

Soon after, federal officials determined that they did not require consent from cities or states to implement the program because the antiterrorism legislation that Congress passed in 2002 gave them the authority that was required. Despite strong opposition, Secure Communities was eventually extended throughout the state in May 2012. Between January 2011 and March 2012, ICE deported 816 people from New York State.

NOTABLE GROUP

New Immigrant Community Empowerment

The New Immigrant Community Empowerment group is one of several in New York City (Jackson Heights, Queens) fighting on behalf of immigrants' rights. The group works to prevent wage theft, helping immigrants who were affected by Hurricane Sandy (particularly wage theft that occurred during and after this time), identifying and stopping predatory groups disguised as immigrant services, and promoting a policy for a pathway to the naturalization of all immigrants. The group was established in 1999 in response to anti-immigrant billboards sponsored by Project USA. The group works on local policy, advocating for equal communication between local government and all constituents. They also help promote public education, including about civil rights, racism, and legal issues.

BIBLIOGRAPHY

Alba, Richard D., and Michael J. Batutis. "The Impact of Migration on New York State. Summary of Findings." A Report Completed for the Public Policy Institute and the Job Training Partnership Council by the Center for Social and Demographic Analysis at the State University of New York at Albany, September, 1984.

Bilotta, James D. "Reflections on an African American on His Life in the Greater Buffalo Area." In Wendell Tripp, ed. *Coming and Becoming, Pluralism in New York State History*. Cooperstown: New York State Historical Society, 2005, pp. 409–16.

Binder, Frederick M., and David Reimers. "New York as an Immigrant City." In Silvia Pedraza, and Rubén G. Rumbaut, eds. *Origins and Destinies. Immigration, Race, and Ethnicity in America*. Belmont, CA: Wadsworth Publishing Company, 1996, pp. 334–45.

Dao, James. "New York Wins an Extension on Food Stamps for Immigrants." *The New York Times*, May 12, 1997. http://www.nytimes.com/1997/03/12/nyregion/new-york-wins-an-extension-on-food-stamps-for-immigrants.html. Accessed March 26, 2014.

DiNapoli, Thomas P., and Kenneth B. Bleiwas (Office of the State Comptroller). "The Role of Immigrants in the New York City Economy." Report 17–2010, January, 2010.

Fiscal Policy Institute. "Working for a Better Life. A Profile of Immigrants in New York State Economy." 2007. http://www.fiscalpolicy.org/publications2007/FPI_ImmReport_WorkingforaBetterLife. Accessed March 26, 2014.

Fitzpatrick, J. P. *Puerto Rican Americans: The Meaning of Migration to the Mainland*. Englewood Cliffs, NJ: Prentice-Hall, 1971.

Foner, Nancy. *From Ellis Island to JFK. New York's Two Great Waves of Immigration*. London and New York: Yale University Press and Russell Sage Foundation, 2000.

Guanill, Elizabeth. "Puerto Ricans in Brentwood." In Wendell Tripp, ed. *Coming and Becoming, Pluralism in New York State History*. Cooperstown: New York State Historical Society, 2005, pp. 427–36.

Handlin, Oscar. *The Uprooted: The Epic Story of the Great Migration that Made the American People*. Boston: Little Brown, [1951] 1973.

Jiménez, Miriam. "Inventive Politicians and Ethnic Ascent from a Micro Approach. Italian Americans and Mexican Americans in the U.S. Congress." PhD Dissertation, Graduate School and University Center, City University of New York, 2010.

Kandel, William (Congressional Research Service). "The Foreign-Born Population: Trends and Selected Characteristics." CRS Report for Congress, January 18, 2011.

Khallick, David Dyssegaard. "Immigration's Impacts on Long Island Economy." *Regional Labor Review* 13, no. 1 (Fall 2010). http://www.hofstra.edu/pdf/Academics/Colleges/HCLAS/CLD/cld-rlr-fall10-immigrationimpacts-kallick.pdf. Accessed August 7, 2014.

Klein, Milton M., ed. *The Empire State. A History of New York*. Ithaca, NY: Cornell University Press with the New York State Historical Association, 2005.

Klein, Milton M. "Shaping the American Tradition: The Microcosm of Colonial New York." In Wendell Tripp, ed. *Coming and Becoming, Pluralism in New York State History*. Cooperstown: New York State Historical Society, 1991, pp. 5–29.

Macionis, John J., and Vincent N. Parrillo. *Cities and Urban Life*. Boston: Prentice Hall, 2010.

Martínez, Miranda J. "The Nuyorican Movement: Community Struggle against Blocked Mobility." In John P. Myers, ed. *Minority Voices. Linking Personal Ethnic History and the Sociological Imagination*. Boston: Pearson Education, Inc., 2005, pp. 288–305.

Massey, Douglas S., and Nancy A. Denton. "The Construction of the Ghetto." In Norman R. Yetman, ed. *Majority and Minority, the Dynamics of Race and Ethnicity in American Life*. Boston: Allyn and Bacon, 1999, pp. 178–202.

Merger, Martin N. *Race and Ethnic Relations. American and Global Perspectives*. Belmont, CA: Wadsworth Cengage Learning, 2009.

Mollenkopf, John Hull. *A Phoenix in the Ashes: The Rise and Fall of the Koch Coalition on New York City Politics*. Princeton, NJ: Princeton University Press, 1992.

Morosoff, Ellen. "Immigration Policy and Labor Force in New York State." A Report from the Chair, New York State Legislative Commission on Skills Development and Vocational Education, October, 1991.

Migration Policy Institute (MPI). "New York. Income and Poverty." Data HUB; Migration Facts, Stats, and Maps, 2010. http://migrationinformation.org/datahub/state4.cfm?ID=NY. Accessed March 27, 2014.

MPI. "New York. Language and Education." Data HUB; Migration Facts, Stats, and Maps, 2010. http://migrationinformation.org/datahub/state2.cfm?ID=NY. Accessed March 27, 2014.

MPI. "New York. Workforce Characteristics." Data HUB; Migration Facts, Stats, and Maps, 2010. http://migrationinformation.org/datahub/state3.cfm?ID=NY. Accessed February 23, 2014.

New Immigrant Community Empowerment. New Immigrant Community Empowerment Webpage. http://www.nynice.org/. Accessed February 23, 2014.

"New York City." In Carl L. Bankston III, ed. *Encyclopedia of American Immigration*. Vol. 2. Pasadena, CA: Salem Press, 2010, *Gale Virtual Reference Library*, pp. 783–87. http://

go.galegroup.com/ps/i.do?id=GALE%7CCX2503700397&v=2.1&u=columbiau&it=r &p=GVRL&sw=w. Accessed March 27, 2014.

New York City Department of City Planning. "Current Estimates of New York City's Population for July 2011." 2011. http://www.nyc.gov/html/census/popcur.shtml. Accessed March 27, 2014.

Orr, James, Susan Weiler, and Joseph Pereira. "The Foreign-Born Population in Upstate New York." Federal Reserve Bank of New York 13, no. 9 (October 2007). http://www.newyorkfed.org/research/current_issues/ci13–9/ci13–9.html. Accessed March 27, 2014.

Passel, Jeffrey S., and Rebecca L. Clark. "Immigrants in New York. Their Legal Status, Incomes, and Taxes." Urban Institute, April 1, 1998. http://www.urban.org/publications /407432.html. Accessed March 27, 2014.

Paumgarten, Nick. "The Humbling of Eliot Spitzer. The Governor's Rocky Rookie Season." *The New Yorker*, December 10, 2007. http://www.newyorker.com /reporting/2007/12/10/071210fa_fact_paumgarten?printable=true&currentPage=3#i xzz24KCBiz95. Accessed March 27, 2014.

Piven, Frances Fox, and Richard Cloward. *Poor People's Movement: Why they Succeed, How they Fail*. New York: Random, 1979.

Preston, Julia. "Despite Opposition, Immigration Agency to Expand Fingerprint Program." *The New York Times*, May 12, 2012. http://www.nytimes.com/2012/05/12/us /ice-to-expand-secure-communities-program-in-mass-and-ny.html. Accessed March 27, 2014.

Santos, Fernanda. "Regents Plan Push for Aid to Illegal Immigrants." *The New York Times*, October, 2011a. http://www.nytimes.com/2011/10/15/nyregion/new-york-regents -plan-a-push-for-the-dream-act.html. Accessed March 27, 2014.

Santos, Fernanda. "State Puts a Precise Cost on Helping Illegal Immigrant Students." *The New York Times*, December 8, 2011b. http://www .nytimes.com/schoolbook/2011/12/08/state-puts-a-precise-cost-on-helping-illegal- immigrant-students/?scp=21&sq=new%20york%20state%20immigrants&st=cse. Accessed March 27, 2014.

Semple, Kirk. "Cuomo Ends State's Role in Checking Immigrants." *The New York Times*, January 25, 2011. http://www.nytimes.com/2011/06/02/nyregion/cuomo-pulls- new-york-from-us-fingerprint-checks.html. Accessed March 27, 2014.

Semple, Kirk. "In New York, Mexicans Lag in Education." *The New York Times*, July 1, 2010. http://www.nytimes.com/2010/09/01/nyregion/01immig.html. Accessed March 27, 2014.

Semple, Kirk. "New York Asks Schools to Avoid Pupil Immigration Status." *The New York Times*, September 31, 2010. http://www.nytimes.com/2010/09/01/nyregion/01immig. html. Accessed March 27, 2014.

Soyer, Daniel. *A Coat of Many Colors: Immigration, Globalism, and Reform in the New York City Garment Industry*. New York: Fordham University Press, 1995.

Taylor, Kate. "Bloomberg Taking Immigration Issue to Obama's and Romney's Campaigns." *The New York Times*, August 13, 2012, A 15.

Terraza, Aaron Matteo, and Trinidad Macias. "New York Governor Abandons Driver's Licenses for the Unauthorized." Migration Information Source (Migration Policy Institute, MPI), November 15, 2007. http://www.migrationinformation.org/feature/display.cfm?ID=. Accessed March 27, 2014.

Vogel, Carole Garbuny. "Oswego, New York: Wartime Haven for Jewish Refugees." *Avotaynu* (Winter 1998). http:www.recognitionscience.com/cgv/Oswego.htm. Accessed March 27, 2014.

Yetman, Norman R. "African Americans." In *Majority and Minority, The Dynamics of Race and Ethnicity in American Life*. Boston: Allyn and Bacon, 1999, pp. 101–09.

Youssef, Nadia H. *The Demographics of Immigration. A Socio-Demographic Profile of the Foreign-Born Population in New York State*. New York: Center for Migration Studies, 1992.

33

NORTH CAROLINA

Darlene Xiomara Rodriguez

CHRONOLOGY

1500s	The area that is now North Carolina is first discovered by European settlers.
1660s	First permanent European settlements in North Carolina occur. Land granted by the king of England to men he was rewarding was deemed a "kingdom" and the owners would rule over it on behalf of the monarch.
1663	William Hilton explores Cape Fear.
1669	Fundamental Constitutions of Carolina established. There is indentured servitude, slavery, and conflict with Native Americans during this time period.
1677	Outbreak of Culpeper's Rebellion, which was a challenge to the rather arbitrary and feudal power arrangements of the time.
1680s–1865	Slavery is legal in North Carolina
1700s	British, Swiss, and German (Palatine) immigrants settle on the coast. Quakers arrive, hoping to escape religious intolerance and persecution in England. Quakers have strong communities and political activity through the 1760s. Tuscarora War occurs, involving European settlers and several tribes, beginning in 1711 and the Yamasee War of 1715 follows.
1707	An Act to Encourage the Settlement of This Country is established, encouraging permanent settlement and warning against pirates.
1729	North Carolina becomes a royal colony under King George II.

Mid-1700s	European immigrants first settle in Pennsylvania and eventually settle in Piedmont. Many are German and Scotch Irish. Highland Scots emigration to this area begins.
1771	Battle of Alamance Creek takes place.
Late 1700s	Increasing displacement of Native Americans occurs.
1800s	North Carolina has very low levels of immigration.
1808	The slave trade is ended in the United States, although the institution continues.
1816–1830s	Quakers in this state participate in anti-slavery movements and the Underground Railroad construction begins.
1830s–1860s	Out-migration from North Carolina to Missouri, Illinois, and Indiana occurs.
1861	Along with 10 other southern states, North Carolina secedes from the Union.
1865	Civil War ends and Reconstruction begins.
1890s	Racism becomes prevalent in politics and civil society (notably, the Ku Klux Klan).
1900	Approximately 4,500 foreign-born individuals live in North Carolina.
1918–1919	Flu epidemic strikes the state and the country.
1933–1977	North Carolina Eugenics Board is in operation.
1960s	North Carolina Agricultural and Technical State University (NC A&T) in Greensboro is recognized as a destination school for students from developing countries, especially those in Africa. This begins the development of African communities around Greensboro.
1960	Total recorded immigration in the United States is 2,515,479.
1961	In a series of modifications to the 1952 Immigration Act, the quota ceiling of 2,000 for the Asia-Pacific Triangle is lifted, with a quota of 100 for each newly independent nation.
1965	The second wave of Cuban refugees begins to reach the United States, starting with 5,000 evacuated from sea from Camarioca, and with many more being evacuated by a U.S. financed airlift. More than 250,000 refugees reach the United States from 1965 to 1972. The Hart-Celler Act opens up immigration from Asia, Africa, and Latin America.
1966–1977	First wave of Asian Indian migration into North Carolina occurs, primarily male professionals working in high-tech fields concentrated around Research Triangle Park.
1967	Palestinian refugees and immigrants come to North Carolina, settling in Guilford County.
1979	Ethnic Vietnamese are resettled in North Carolina for the first time.
1980	Federal Refugee Resettlement Act is passed, streamlining and redefining the refugee and asylee application process. Lutheran Family Services opens its first resettlement office in Greensboro.

Mid-1980s	Cuban refugees begin resettling in the Greensboro area.
1983	The U.S. Office of Refugee Resettlement moves first Cambodian refugee families to Greensboro.
1986	First set of Montagnard/Dega refugees are resettled in Greensboro, Charlotte, and Raleigh. The community around Greensboro eventually will become the largest community of Montagnard/Dega outside of Vietnam.
1987	Hmong refugees originally resettled by the U.S. government in California and other more urban areas are resettled by the U.S. government in the North Carolina mountains, as these areas are seen to be more like the homelands of the Hmong. Other Hmong begin moving in voluntarily due to family connections and more job opportunities.
1990	Major wave of Hispanic/Latino migration begins throughout the state.
1994	Immigrants from the former Yugoslavia begin arriving as refugees in the Greensboro area; Somali refugees of the Bendhir Tribe arrive in Greensboro.
1998	Former governor Jim Hunt creates the governor's Office of Hispanic/Latino Affairs and the Advisory Council for Hispanic/Latino Affairs to track the needs of the state's fastest-growing population.
2001	Center for New North Carolinians is established by an executive order from Governor Mike Easley and established at the University of North Carolina at Greensboro. Dr. Raleigh Bailey serves as its first executive director.
2006	Four laws are passed in the North Carolina General Assembly restricting undocumented immigration: one requiring all applicants for driver's licenses to have a valid social security number, one requiring citizenship status checks for all state employees, another allowing the extension of 287(g) laws allowing local police to enforce immigration laws under contract from the federal government, and a law regulating human trafficking. More deportations and fear of deportation causes retreats in the undocumented Latino community over the next few years.
2010	The Advisory Council for Hispanic/Latino Affairs is reestablished.
2011	The Raleigh *News and Observer* reports in March that Latino/Hispanic migration has slowed, due to slowdown in construction and other Latino-dominated activities. Only reported migration is farmers on H2A tobacco visas.

HISTORICAL OVERVIEW

North Carolina is a state of immigrants; not just in post-1960 era, which is the scope of this chapter, but from before the birth of the United States. Latin American, Africa, and Europe provided waves of immigration first. In the post-1960s era, Asian immigrants and refugees joined the ranks of new migrants to North Carolina. Immigration in North Carolina fell into three patterns: refugee resettlement, migrant workers, professional workers, and entrepreneurial minority activity, as described by Portes and Rumbaut (2006). In addition, the state government has enacted several laws and created offices and task forces to manage new immigrant populations. These organizations work with and create challenges for all immigrants.

Demographics of North Carolina Immigrants

The 2010 Census had the population of North Carolina at 9 million people. In 2000, 430,000 people were foreign-born, which was 5.4 percent of the population, while the percentage of foreign-born between 2008 and 2012 was 7.5 percent (U.S. Census, n.d.). Of this foreign born population, just under a quarter were naturalized U.S. citizens. By region of the world, 60,222 were born in Europe, 93,133 were born in Asia, 20,369 were born in Africa, 239,853 were born in Asia, 14,598 were born in Northern America (Canada), and 1,825 were born in Oceana. The majority of all foreign-born residents who entered between 1990 and 2000 were not citizens. Also, the majority of Latin American, Asian, and African foreign-born citizens entered North Carolina between 1990 and 2000. Most were concentrated in the urban areas of Charlotte, the Piedmont Triad, and the Triangle. However, many, mostly Hispanic/Latinos and Hmong were settling in rural and mountain areas.

Demographically by race and nationality, Latino immigration far outpaced other immigrant groups. The Pew Hispanic Center in 2008 estimated the Latino population in North Carolina at 678,000. The U.S. Census had the Latino population at just over 800,000. Of the 2008 number, nearly equal numbers of residents were native- and foreign-born. Although the majority of this group was Mexican, immigrants and refugees from Cuba, Nicaragua, El Salvador, Guatemala, the Dominican Republic, and Puerto Rico were present. However the Puerto Ricans were already U.S. citizens. The Asian population in 2010 was 208,962. Vietnamese (ethnic Vietnamese, Montagnard/Dega and Hmong) immigrants made up the largest number of Asians in North Carolina. However, Asian Indians made up another significant population. Additionally, Chinese, Japanese, Korean, Thai, Pakistani, Cambodian, and Laotian immigrants were calling North Carolina home. The U.S. Census counted the Middle East as Asia; therefore, this group also included the Palestinians, Israelis, and Lebanese in the state as well. Although the 2000 Census had Asians as only 1.4 percent of the North Carolina population, they were a large presence in high-tech, hotel management, and small ethnic market businesses. Of the new European migration, the largest numbers had been from Eastern European countries, especially those of the former Yugoslavia. Africans were lumped with black Americans in the U.S. Census, but the Center for New North Carolinians had estimated the total African population in the Piedmont Triad area (Greensboro, High Point and Winston Salem areas) to be around 12,000. African nations represented were Ghana, Nigeria, Sierra Leone, Liberia, Somalia, Rwanda, Burundi, Congo, Sudan, Ethiopia, Senegal, Cameroon, Ivory Coast, Togo, Burkina Faso, Zambia, Uganda, Kenya, Morocco, Ethiopia, Egypt, Algeria, and Tunisia.

TOPICAL ESSAYS

REFUGEE RESETTLEMENT

In 1980, the federal Refugee Resettlement Act streamlined the process of refugee resettlement. Instead of a case-by-case basis refugee approval, which favored countries that were under Communist regimes, the refugee system was streamlined and contracted out to several different agencies throughout the state. In North Carolina, the first of these agencies, Lutheran Family Services, opened in 1980 in Greensboro. This was an extension of the orphanage and other child welfare services they already provided. Currently, six agencies were contracted to provide refugee resettlement: Church World Service, World Relief, African Services Coalition, Jewish Family Services, Faith Action International House, and the Motagnard/Dega Association. In addition to these six agencies, faith organizations across North Carolina assisted with these organizations. According to Bailey (2005), many houses of worship in North Carolina had values in their holy books that prescribe helping newcomers. These values made the faith communities strong advocates to refugee resettlement. The organizations had offices in Greensboro, High Point, Raleigh, Asheville, New Bern, and Charlotte. Over the past 31 years, several different nationalities from Asia, Europe, and Africa, as well as a few Central American nationalities had resettled as immigrants in the area. Asian refugees made up the largest number of resettled refugees in North Carolina. Montagnard/Dega and Hmong were the largest groups of North Carolina refugees. Guilford County (Greensboro) was the epicenter of refugee resettlement in the state.

Montagnard Refugees

The first waves of Montagnard (French for mountain people) were resettled in 1986, after the changes in federal law. They preferred to be known as the Dega. The initial 200 settled in Greensboro and experienced cultural shock. They had fought next to U.S. soldiers in Vietnam. In addition, they were people of an indigenous culture, with no modern conveniences. After the Vietnam War, many converted to Christianity and were forced in re-education camps by the Communist government. In addition, U.S. soldiers promised they would be rescued after the war. However, many were stranded and in subsequent waves of resettlement, many reported believing they were still at war against the ethnic Vietnamese. In Greensboro, their Christian faith and their ties as veterans encouraged support from the faith communities. Currently, the population of this community exceeds 7,000 statewide, 5,000 just in the Greensboro area. This makes North Carolina the largest settlement area for Montagnards outside of Vietnam.

Hmong Refugees

A major source of secondary migration (defined in this case by migration from an initial resettlement supported by the government) into North Carolina were the Hmong refugees. Originally settled in California, the U.S. government agreed to resettle a group of these immigrants in the North Carolina Mountains. The mountains were seen as very similar to the Hmong homeland, which help these refugees adjust and recover from the drama of their resettlement. While initially most worked in low-wage agricultural and factory labor, a few younger Hmong are pursuing higher education. As of 2007, at least 10 Hmong students were enrolled at the University of North Carolina Chapel Hill. A group of thesis students, the Hmong Student Association, along with two non-Hmong advocates were sponsoring college outreach tours for Hmong high-school students encouraging them to pursue higher education. However, Hmong women note that as a culture, they are expected to marry young and pursuing higher education would be a challenge. The Hmong regularly hold cultural festivals in the North Carolina mountains, which attract Hmong refugees from all over the United States. In addition, they have a mutual aid and advocacy group, the United Hmong Association.

Other refugee groups in North Carolina included Cubans, Sudanese, Somali, Liberians, Kosovars, Bosnians, Serbians, Croatians, Haitians, and others from African and Middle Eastern countries. In addition, some of these same migrant groups, among others have applied applying for asylum, as they have entered the United Stated without documents or overstayed visas, but felt they qualified for refugee status. Cuban refugees are small in number and tend to be professionals. Some moved back to South Florida after their original resettlement, but there is a community of about 500 around the Greensboro area. The majority of the Eastern European refugees have moved on as well; however, Bosnians still constitute a large number of residents in the Greensboro area. Somali refugees came from the Bendhir tribe, a very conservative Muslim group. These refugees often clash with healthcare providers, educators, employers, and church groups over their cultural practices, especially those that affect women. As a result, some of these refugees have also moved on to other areas where there are more Somali refugees. Sudanese refugees have come in multiple waves; however, most recently, some of

Military personnel raise their hands during a naturalization ceremony for the military at Pope Air Force Base, North Carolina, on October 23, 2008. The ceremony included the oath of citizenship for 40 soldiers, sailors, and marines stationed throughout North Carolina. (Logan Mock-Bunting/Getty Images)

the "Lost Boys" who were found in refugee camps and featured in the news media resettled in North Carolina (Bailey 2005).

Entrepreneurial and Professional Immigrants

While many immigrants are thought of as being entrepreneurial in a sense, Portes and Rumbaut (2006) describe a special type of immigrant as entrepreneurial. This immigrant is defined as someone who creates business opportunities for themselves either in "ethnic enclaves" or in neighborhoods near working-class and poor native-born Americans. Professional immigrants are those who are defined by the federal government as "priority workers, professionals with advanced degrees or aliens of exceptional ability." Both classes of workers are hypothetically able to bypass economic issues by coming into high-paying jobs or business opportunities. Professional immigrants are often some of the top scholars in their fields and have to prove such before they are admitted. Entrepreneurial immigrants often help others in their nationality group move ahead by providing services in their language and selling businesses to newcomers to provide them with a source of income. However, some undocumented migrants and refugees also fit these categories. Some of the professionals choose to practice without licensure and others build businesses they risk losing if their undocumented status is discovered. In North Carolina, the first wave of this immigrant class came after the Hart-Celler Act of 1965. Intended to equalize national quotas and open up immigration for family members of naturalized citizens, it also resulted in an influx of immigrants from Asia and Africa.

African Immigrants in North Carolina

African citizens were attracted by the university system, especially NC A&T. This university has been recognized by developing countries as a valuable resource and it has drawn immigrants from Ghana, Nigeria, Sierra Leone, Liberia, and other African nations. However, it was not until the 1990s that African migrants would become significant again. This time, educated migrants from West, Central, and East African countries would come as willing migrants and as refugees. While some would continue their education, others would come and work as cab drivers and other low-skilled workers for the opportunity to send money home and bring family members over. However, many began starting businesses of their own including restaurants, cab driving and hair braiding. As discussed earlier, some African refugees have difficulty adjusting to the Southern culture. There have been notable criminal cases involving African immigrants in North Carolina, as well as an immigrant falsely accused of being a part of the Duke Lacrosse scandal in 2005. One African U.S. soldier was killed in the line of duty in 2004 before having the chance to obtain citizenship. However, despite these legal issues, Africans have been working their way into the North Carolina fabric. They have been finding Southern dishes to be similar to their own. They have established groups such as the African Services Coalition, which are now resettling refugees through contracts with the state of North Carolina. One African immigrant is even running a business selling Asian cars with American features back to friends and family in Nigeria. The immigrant who is charged in connection with the Duke Lacrosse scandal was acquitted and was rewarded by *Readers Digest* as an American hero.

Asian Indian Immigrants in North Carolina

Asian Indian immigrants have been present in North Carolina as early as the 1950s, as professors on university campuses. However, the major wave of Asian Indian migration began after Hart-Celler Act as well. Initially, these were single male professional immigrants, with work visas from companies in the Research

Triangle Park. However, starting in the 1980s, these immigrants were often family members of the initial class of immigrants. Asian Indian immigrants largely avoided being categorized with black Southerners, despite their skin color, due to what Subramanian (2000) has described as southern hospitality toward those perceived as foreign-born, such as Asian Indians. Plus, many Asian Indian migrants were already of the highest social caste and status, and worked to maintain high class and non-racially defined status as they settled in the Triangle area. In recent years, they have been more willing to embrace their culture publicly, building a Hindu temple in Morrisville, a town just east of the Research Triangle Park complex in Wake County. Cultural festivals, movies, and other activities compete with each other as they are held in towns throughout the region. Asian Indians also speak of a word, *desi*, which gauges a person who typifies an Asian Indian who has both American aspirations and ties to the home country. Asian Indians and Pakistanis in North Carolina are friends, whereas they are enemies back home. Student groups of Indians are very present at the Triangle area universities. However, this group is not without challenges. One migrant, on the more temporary H1B work visa many new Asian Indian arrivals arrive on, failed in his attempt to gain permanent status under the aliens of exceptional ability provision, despite being a researcher at North Carolina State University. His family was also thrown in limbo. A daughter who was visiting relatives in India had her visa canceled when the family was not granted permanent status. While she was able to reunite with her American-bound relatives, they would all have to return to India soon. Also, although some Asian Indian immigrants have been successful in starting high-tech businesses, Vipin Garg, a serial entrepreneur in a 2008 *News and Observer* article notes that support and money for Indian tech entrepreneurs is low.

Additional Facts about the Professional and Entrepreneurial Immigrant Class

Lastly, North Carolina has many other professional and entrepreneurial immigrants. Chinese and Korean business people have started a number of small businesses throughout the state. A Puerto Rican had started a trucking company based in Wilmington. Griffith (2005) describes how Mexican grocery stores were present in towns with at least 15,000 people and a significant Mexican population. He also notes that these stores have enhanced urban neighborhoods that were in decline, much like Portes and Rumbaut's (2006) analysis of this category of immigrant. He has also represented the Wilmington area in the state house. Many other Latino/as work in professional positions across the state, from the healthcare and education industries as translators to small construction-related businesses. Other professional migrants have had trouble with immigration-related rules. A Pakistani doctor was detained in

Pakistan for failing to register with the State Department before traveling. The rule was instituted after the 9/11 attacks on immigrants of Muslim countries. Like similar efforts to stigmatize undocumented Mexican migrants, this appears to be selective enforcement, thus maintaining bias in the immigration system. The next section will detail the struggles and successes of migrant workers, primarily Mexicans, in North Carolina.

LATINOS IN NORTH CAROLINA—IMMIGRANTS AND UNDOCUMENTED MIGRANTS

The Latino population in North Carolina is a unique population that has elements of both immigrant groups discussed earlier and dominates the definition of the migrant worker. Bean and Lowell (2007) distinguish between immigrants (those who have been given legal entry to a country) and international migrants (those who have undocumented or fraudulent entry into a country). Three-fifths of all undocumented migrants to the United States come from Mexico. About a tenth of undocumented migrants come from El Salvador. Honduras, Guatemala, and Costa Rica are also some of the immigrant-sending countries to North Carolina. These migrants only tell part of the Latino/a story in North Carolina. Since the early 1980s, Cuban refugees have been resettled in North Carolina, particularly around Greensboro. Although some of these immigrants have now left the area, a vibrant, but small community of second- and third-generation Cubans has remained. There are also pockets of affluent Puerto Ricans (who are already U.S. citizens, but not from an official state) and South Americans who have migrated for professional and educational opportunities. Some migrant workers are using the Seasonal Agricultural Workers Program and the H-2A visas, which allow them to come work legally for a season, pending the employer has proven that there is not enough demand for local workers in the industry.

Between 2000 and 2010, the Latino population grew by approximately 420,000 according to the U.S. Census. The Pew Hispanic Center estimated the 2008 population in North Carolina to be 678,000. There was nearly an even split between natives and foreign-born Latino/as. Bailey (2005) believes that the Census Bureau has underreported these numbers, as many Latino/as are undocumented, earn low income, and live in rental units and may not be counted. North Carolina was cited in 2000 as being the number one in-migration state for Latino/as. While the urban areas have the largest numbers of Latinos, rural areas often attract higher percentages. Siler City, an area just 40 miles southeast of Greensboro and about 50 miles southwest of Raleigh is about 50 percent Latino. If it were not for the Latino influx into the poultry and manufacturing industry concentrated in the area, the area would have declined. A 2008 interview of the producers of the documentary *Nuevo South* on the WUNC program *The State of Things* confirms this fact. A new elementary school was profiled, where classes have been taught in both

English and Spanish. It is also noted that the school would have not been built had it not been for the influx.

The majority of Latino workers in the state have been able to take advantage of changing patterns in manufacturing and agriculture, not just in North Carolina but nationwide. While migrant workers have been coming to the United States since the Bracero Program in the 1940s and 1950s, it was believed that any migrants coming to North Carolina were either coming from Western States such as Texas, Florida or coming directly from Mexico. Currently, most migrants are coming directly from Mexico, primarily Mexican states in the central part of the nation. Also, most farms in North Carolina are family farms run by Anglo owners. These farms were staffed primarily by the owners and their relatives, as well as African American residents of the area. However, beginning in the early 1980s, some of these farmers began losing their original source of labor to better labor opportunities. Farmers and manufacturers from others states began to come in and standardized processing of livestock and planted crops. These new standardized operations have been employing Mexican labor and brought similar practices to North Carolina. Lax enforcement of undocumented labor laws prior to the 1986 Immigration Reform and Control Act and stated preferences for rural areas by Mexican migrants created a steady stream of labor in eastern North Carolina.

Although it is believed that Mexicans and other migrants will work for far lower wages and in worse conditions, efforts have been made to create better working conditions. Many of these efforts have been championed by the North Carolina Growers Association, along with Latino advocacy groups. In 2004, Mexican workers at the Mt. Olive Pickle plant, many who hold H-2A visas, were allowed to organize. In 1989, the state of North Carolina passed the first set of laws mandating conditions at migrant worker camps attached to agricultural-processing plants and large-scale farms. In urban areas, many Latino/as have been working in fast food, construction, janitorial services, and other low-wage activities. In mountain counties, Latino/as have been employed on Christmas tree farms, as well as holding permits to pick galax, a plant found in the forest areas used in floral arrangements. Although these jobs are low-paying by U.S. standards, they pay many times more than the minimum wages in Mexico and remittances can be sent back home.

Several churches, especially Catholic and Pentecostal denominations, have risen to serve the spiritual and social needs of Mexican immigrants. In addition, festivals such as the Fiesta del Pueblo at the State Fairgrounds attract thousands of Latinos and non-Latinos to share their culture. Many professional organizations, such as the Society for Hispanic Professionals, the Hispanic Chamber of Commerce, and the Society of Hispanic Professional Engineers have chapters in the state and on university campuses. Additionally, the Mexican consulate has a Raleigh office. Private social service groups also come to the aid of these residents, as many are not eligible for government aid, even if they have legal residency. Depending on the area of the state, native-born Anglos and African Americans either embrace or show hostility to the Latino/a newcomers. Most of the opposition is centered on fears of losing jobs and a changing cultural base.

The state government, as well as local governments, has been faced with new challenges and needs to help not just this population, but all immigrant populations. The next sections detail ways in which the state has responded to immigrants, as well as new challenges faced by the immigrants themselves.

THE STATE'S RESPONSE TO IMMIGRATION

The state of North Carolina has responded to immigrants and migrants in a number of positive and negative ways. While it has been very open to legal immigration, undocumented migrants are not favored outside of the employment community. Some restrictive activities have been the participation in the 287(g) program, as well as a number of bills and laws from the general assembly. The general assembly and the governor's office have been very receptive to other efforts. They work with the federal Department of Health and Human Services to provide aid and assistance to refugee resettlement organizations. They have created two major organizations, the Office of Hispanic/Latino Affairs and the Center for New North Carolinians, to work with all immigrants to provide solutions, support, and research for immigrants and native North Carolinians. There are efforts to improve health care and education for all immigrants. This section will cover in detail many of these efforts throughout the state.

287(g) Immigration and Customs Enforcement AmeriCorps Accessing Cross-Cultural Education Service Systems Program

In 2007, eight counties and one city in North Carolina joined efforts with the Immigration and Customs Enforcement (ICE) Service to create the 287(g) ICE AmeriCorps Accessing Cross-Cultural Education Service Systems (ACCESS) program, more commonly known as 287(g). This program, along with a similar one called Secure Communities, allowed the federal government to partner with state law enforcement agencies to enforce immigration laws, based on a provision in the 1996 Illegal Immigration Reform and Immigrant Responsibility Act. 287(g) allows officers to run checks on non-citizens who have violated the law. In addition, the Secure Communities provision allows for law enforcement to fingerprint anyone charged with a crime and run all prints against an ICE database of those suspected of being in the country illegally. While 287(g) was intended to just prosecute and deport those guilty of felonies, some municipalities have taken the spirit of the law beyond its original intention. Of the eight counties and one city involved, only 13.8 percent of the arrests were felony charges. The majority of charges were misdemeanors. In addition, while some lawmakers have stated that these programs were fully paid for by the federal government, Nguyen and Gill (2010) showed that these programs cost taxpayers millions and provided examples of municipalities in other states who were suffering fiscal crises and reduction in other police and fire services due to funding for 287(g) enforcement. In North Carolina, Alamance County has been the most aggressive in enforcing the law, even adding to its jail to accommodate more immigration-related arrests. As a result, many communities reported decreased cooperation with police, reduced numbers of Latino residents, and other residents who now live in constant fear of deportation. Nguyen and Gill (2010) recommended that municipalities limit the arrests and deportations to those who are suspected of felonies; as the U.S. ICE has reiterated in re-signing agreements with municipalities, municipalities should consider the recommendations of immigration lawyers, refugee resettlement agencies, and others concerned with human rights violations and to find alternatives to rehabilitate immigrants and Latino/as who are targeted under this law. While popular opinion has pinned arrests to Latinos, people from Africa and even England have been arrested in and deported from North Carolina under this law also.

Bills and Laws in the General Assembly

Since the passage of the federal Immigration Reform and Control Act in 1986, a number of state statutes and bills have been raised that affect the conditions and climate of immigrants and migrant workers in the state. While some, such as the Migrant Workers Act of 1989 have been beneficial, others, such as recent efforts to change the constitution to make English the official language, the reduction of documents acceptable to use at state Department of Motor Vehicles (DMV) offices to obtain driver's licenses, and an effort to ban undocumented migrants from attending state community colleges and universities have had adverse effects on the immigrant community. While immigrants are attracted to certain areas in North Carolina based on lax enforcement of immigration laws, many of these new statutes make living in rural areas impossible.

Alternatively, the Migrant Housing Act of North Carolina and its subsequent amendments require business owners to provide heat and air conditioning, mattresses, clean and working kitchens, and clean and working bathroom facilities for migrant workers. It also allows for migrant workers to organize for better working conditions.

The first of the negative laws was passed in the late 1980s. An amendment to Section 145 of the North Carolina General Statutes established English as the official language in all state government dealings. This prohibited documents such as driving tests and social service program applications from being printed in other languages. However, this ruling was challenged by the American Civil Liberties Union and rescinded in 1996 such that documents can now be printed in other languages. In 2006, multiple bills and statutes were passed limiting access to government services for undocumented migrants. The first was a measure that reduced the amount of documentation that state's DMV would accept to issue and renew driver's licenses. This would in effect ban identification documents from foreign countries and individual taxpayer identification numbers from being used. Many undocumented migrants had used these numbers in lieu of having a valid social security number to obtain driver's licenses. The legislation also canceled current driver's licenses of those who had used fraudulent social security numbers and prevented all residents from using a social security card as proof of identity. Also, bills were introduced supporting U.S. constitutional amendments making English the official language of the United States, supporting using intensified efforts by the Department of Homeland Security to enforce immigration law violations, and advocating for strong language denouncing companies that have hired undocumented immigrants at the expense of hiring American-born citizens and purportedly threatening the economic development of communities.

In the current general assembly session, laws are on the table to completely ban undocumented migrants from North Carolina community colleges and state universities, as well amending the state constitution to make English the official language of the state of North Carolina. Also, a bill is currently in debate prohibiting consulate documents from the Mexican embassy from being used as proof of residency. In Durham and other cities in North Carolina, these documents have been accepted as proof of residence for access to city services.

Office for Hispanic/Latino Affairs

One of the most positive activities undertaken by the state government is the creation of the Office for Hispanic/Latino Affairs. This is a state agency headed by an appointed director of Hispanic/Latino Affairs who sits in the executive cabinet of the governor of North Carolina. In addition, an Advisory Council of Hispanic/Latino Affairs was created to supplement the work of the government agency. Its members are made up of 25 leaders of Hispanic/Latino descent and other state and local leaders from other nationalities and backgrounds from nonprofit, religious, business, and other non-governmental sectors, with 10 ex-officio members who are state of North Carolina agency heads. The office provides information on immigration laws, social services, census data, economic development, and other issues related to the well-being of Latinos in the state. The director also meets with Latino groups throughout the state to discuss issues of concern. Initially, the advisory council outlined 60 issues of importance to Hispanic/Latinos, which have been narrowed into eight subject areas: education; human relations; health and human services; workers' rights; immigration, licensing and documentation; economic development; political representation; and crime control and public safety. In addition, the original mission of the advisory council was to "advise the governor on matters concerning the Hispanic community; to work on issues of race, ethnicity and human relations and to see that Hispanics are represented in all facets of government." Although, according to McClain (2006), the last goal of including Hispanics in all facets of government was dropped in 2004. The advisory council has opposed general assembly bills and general statutes that restrict community college and state university access to Latino/as. Current governor Bev Purdue recently has named a new director of the office and has reestablished the advisory council.

Center for New North Carolinians

The Center for New North Carolinians was established on April 12, 2001, by the board of governors of the University of North Carolina System. Its initial mission was to "provide research, training, and evaluation for the state of North Carolina in addressing immigrant issues; collaboration with government and social organizations to enhance responsiveness to immigrant needs; and community support to provide training and workshops" (Center for New North Carolinians, "History of the CNNC" n.d.). There were two channels to its formation. First, founding director Raleigh Bailey worked with the federal government to create the ACCESS project in 1994. As one of the first AmeriCorps programs, it attracted members of the North Carolina immigrant community to serve one-year terms helping fellow immigrants find access to health care and make cross-cultural connections. In addition, the ACCESS project trained interpreters for healthcare facilities. When Bailey became the first director of the Center for New North Carolinians, he brought these programs into the new organization. The additional source of funding was former University of North Carolina Greensboro (UNCG) chancellor Patricia Sullivan. She recognized a need for the university community to recognize the changing demographics brought on by the refugee, immigrant and migrant communities. After convening a task force in 1997 on the UNCG campus, she petitioned the board of governors of the University of North Carolina

Health Care and Education

Scholars have applauded efforts that North Carolina has made to improve healthcare systems for immigrants, but agree that education systems are in need of work. In the healthcare realm, the state has taken a number of actions to ensure that immigrants, migrants, and other non-English speakers have the care they need. As mentioned earlier, the Center for New North Carolinians, through the

ACCESS project has been working to train healthcare educators and interpreters to reach out to Latino/a, Asian, and African communities. These educators have come from these communities and have been able to relate to the challenges and needs faced by these different ethnic groups. In 1993, the state Office of Minority Heath recognized a need to begin translating documents into Spanish. However, this has not been enough, as many migrants do not read well in Spanish or English. Accordingly, the state began to train field interpreters and healthcare workers. In 1995, several state agencies and departments combined to form the North Carolina Training for Health Care Interpreters program. In 1999, the Office of Minority Health created the "Nosotros: Latino Culture and Public Health and Human Services" program to educate healthcare providers on the cultural needs of Latino patients. These programs were later merged into the North Carolina Area Health Education Centers Spanish Language and Cultural Training Initiative. For migrant workers, North Carolina created four federally funded migrant worker health clinics in Henderson, Sampson, Duplin, and Nash counties. For migrant workers who did not live near these clinics, the Migrant Health Fee-for-Service program was created to reimburse health providers in other counties for treating migrant workers. Migrant workers also paid a copayment to use these facilities. However, the funding for these facilities and the reimbursement program were reduced in 2005. Combined with this reduction and rising healthcare costs, healthcare programs were at further risk of being scaled down due to lack of adequate funding.

The education system in North Carolina has not been as proactive in providing new services for Latino/as and other immigrants. Although the North Carolina Department of Public Instruction recognizes the need for services for limited English proficient students, the general assembly has been hesitant in supporting such initiatives. Another issue in education is the lack of licensure programs in North Carolina for English as second language (ESL) teachers. While there are more programs being added to the state university system, school systems are recruiting faculty through the Visiting International Faculty program to deal with the shortage of non-English-speaking teachers. There is also a marked difference between rural and urban populations. This also extends to the climate in the home country. Bailey notes anecdotal evidence that Montagnard and Hmong students have been less likely to continue their education than Bosnian or African students who have more support in continuing their education (Bailey 2005, 73). However, at the individual school system level, educators have been succeeding at helping students learn English and adapt. Kandel and Parrado (2006) examined an elementary school in an urban North Carolina school district that successfully engaged its students drawing on their own cultures and North Carolina culture. The Guilford County School System opened its Doris Henderson Newcomers School in 2007. The school served students in grades 3 to 12, who were in their first year

Touger Vang, right, feeds livestock while his cousin Choua Vang, left, and nephew Scott Vang, center, open bags of feed at the family farm just outside Greensboro, North Carolina, on March 22, 2009. Touger Vang is a Hmong refugee from Laos who has fought hard over the years to maintain his Hmong heritage of working with the land and promotes it with younger generations. (AP Photo/News & Record, Lynn Hey)

of school in the United States. The students spent a year learning in a bilingual environment, then transferred to the school in their home district. In addition to the classes for students, English classes were offered for any community member who needed help learning English.

CHALLENGES FOR NEW IMMIGRANTS

A combination of both laws and government practices that have helped and harmed immigrants presents challenges to both these populations and the native-born population. As stated in the previous section, laws such as 287(g), and proposals such as banning undocumented migrants from public universities have created a context of fear and hostility, thus impinging on the public safety of all immigrants and the native-born.

The first set of challenges has been in the workforce. In 2006, communities across the country, including in North Carolina, witnessed demonstrations where many Latino workers, immigrants of other nationalities, and native-born citizens walked off of jobs to show how much the U.S. workforce was dependent on immigrants and yet, was denying this fact. If more workers were politically active like those at the

Mt. Olive pickle plant, many employers and workers would be held to new standards in pay, attempts to generate legal status and conditions of the workplace.

In health care, more Latino/as have been born in the state than outside, causing higher birth rates in areas that for years were seeing declines. Rural immigrants, especially refugees who still do not speak sufficient English and have not been required to for naturalization will perhaps add to healthcare costs of rural hospitals (granted that there are no classes provided to aid in this endeavor). Morrison et al. (2007) reported that in Guilford County, which is the third-largest area in the state, there is more work needed to be done to reach immigrant communities who were at risk of untreated health problems due to food insecurity and limited access and affordability of healthcare facilities. As mentioned before, rising health costs have also prevented some immigrants and migrants from receiving adequate health care.

Challenges in education will continue to rise. If undocumented migrants are banned from colleges and universities, high school dropout rates will perhaps rise, due to students discouraged by inability to finish their education. Currently, the state law limiting in-state tuition to legal residents has been creating financial burdens on students who were also not eligible for federal financial aid. Already, this law has raised the dropout rate and threatens to add to the debt load of many other students. Other educational challenges are the need for more school facilities to educate children of immigrants, more faculty trained in languages of immigrant-sending countries, and ESL techniques. With fiscal crises affecting school systems, some of these programs are at risk of being reduced or completely eliminated in some counties across the state.

While government agencies, lawmaking bodies, nonprofit organizations, and universities are creating challenges, they could also help immigrants. The Research Triangle still attracts high numbers of foreign students and is beginning to see an increase of students whose parents were born abroad but who were born and raised in the state, such as the Hmong, Indian, and Latino/a populations. Organizations such as the Office for Hispanic/Latino Affairs, refugee resettlement groups, and the Center for New North Carolinians continue to provide resources and direction for immigrants and migrant workers to receive the aid they need to fully integrate into the United States and North Carolina.

NOTABLE GROUPS

IMMIGRANT AND REFUGEE RIGHTS PROJECT

The Immigrant and Refugee Rights Project is part of the North Carolina Justice Center, which broadly advocates on behalf of the poor in this state. In particular, this group helps those who cannot afford legal counsel and who have been treated badly by employers. The group provides direct legal counseling to immigrants, helping them fill out the proper paperwork for legal status and authorization to work, helping to fill out credible fear applications for refugees, and protecting against discriminatory treatment in public policy and employment. They also advocate on behalf of rural workers' rights, a group that is often neglected and isolated. The Raleigh-based group aids youth in applying for Deferred Action, provides legal information and more generally public education, and provides policy statements on state and local proposals. This group opposes House Bill (HB) 786, the "RECLAIM NC" Act because of its punitive nature and fundamental misunderstandings about the nature of immigration and alleged criminality. The group supports HB 904, which would provide in-state tuition to all residents of the state, regardless of legal status. The group is an important defender of personhood rights and ensuring that immigrants are not treated in a biased or exploitative manner.

BIBLIOGRAPHY

Associated Press. "INS Quick-Response Team Targets Illegals That Commit Crimes; the Six Agents Operating in Eastern N.C., One of 45 Teams in the U.S., Have Brought in about 100 for Deportation Hearings." *The Herald-Sun*, June 1, 2000, C5.

Avery, S. "World's Fare." *The News and Observer*, November 26, 1999, E1.

Bailey, Raleigh. "New Immigrant Communities in the North Carolina Piedmont Triad: Integration Issues and Challenges." In E. Gozdziak, and S. F. Martin, eds. *Beyond the Gateway: Immigrants in a Changing America*. Latham, MD: Lexington Books, 2005, pp. 57–85.

Banks, M. M. "Montagnards' Helpers Put Good Will into Action—Sponsors Make a World of Difference to the Refugees Being Resettled in Greensboro." *The News and Record*, August 11, 2002, A1.

Bean, Frank D., and B. Lindsay Lowell. "Unauthorized Migration." In M. C. Waters, ed. *The New Americans: A Guide to Immigration since 1965*. Cambridge, MA: Harvard University Press, 2007, pp. 70–82.

Bickley, R. "Independence Festival Brings Familiarity." *The News and Observer*, August 20, 2000, B1.

Bonner, Lynn. "Social Issues May Get More Traction." *The News and Observer*, January 23, 2011. http://www.newsobserver.com/2011/01/23/938092/social-issues-may-get-more-traction.html. Accessed February 24, 2014.

Bonner, P. "Bull City of Many Tongues; More Linguistically Diverse than 2/3 of Nation, We're No. 2 in Hawaiian Pidgin." *The Herald-Sun*, March 16, 2005, A1.

Center for New North Carolinians. "History of the CNNC." Center for New North Carolinians. http://cnnc.uncg.edu/about/history.htm. Accessed March 27, 2014.

Center for New North Carolinians. "Newcomers to Guilford County." Center for New North Carolinians. http://cnnc.uncg.edu/pdfs/newcomerstoguilfordcounty.pdf. Accessed March 27, 2014.

Center for New North Carolinians. "Regions of the World that Contribute to Our Local Population." Center for New North Carolinians. http://cnnc.uncg.edu/immigrants/demo graphics.htm. Accessed March 27, 2014.

Cohen, Deborah. *Braceros: Migrant Citizens and Transnational Subjects in the Postwar United States and Mexico.* Chapel Hill: University of North Carolina Press, 2011.

Collins, K. "For Family from India, a Life in Limbo; Father's Green Card Rejection Strands Daughter." *The News and Observer,* August 4, 2007, A1.

Cravey, Altha J. "Transnationality, Social Spaces, and Parallel Worlds." In H. A. Smith, and Owen J. Furuseth, eds. *Latinos in the New South: Transformations of Place.* Aldershot, UK: Ashgate, 2006, pp. 217–33.

DePriest, J. "Angels Give Family a Place to Land-Long Winding Road Started in Laos and Ended in Belmont." *Charlotte Observer,* January 12, 2003, 1L.

Diner, Hasia. "Immigration in U.S. History." *North Carolina Digital History* (U.S. Department of State). http://www.learnnc.org/lp/editions/nchist-newsouth/5690. Accessed September 8, 2013.

Donato, Katharine M., Charles Tolbert, Alfred Nucci, and Yukio Kawano. "Changing Faces, Changing Places: The Emergence of New Non-Metropolitan Immigrant Gateways." In D. S. Massey, ed. *New Faces in New Places: The Changing Geography of American Immigration.* New York: Russell Sage Foundation, 2008, pp. 75–98.

Donato, Katharine, and C. L. Bankston. "The Origins of Employer Demand for Immigrants in a New Destination: The Salience of Soft Skills." In D. S. Massey, ed. *New Faces in New Places: The Changing Geography of American Immigration.* New York: Russell Sage Foundation, 2008, pp. 124–48.

Doris Henderson Newcomers School. "Frequently Asked Questions (FAQ)." Doris Henderson Newcomers School Website. http://schoolcenter.gcsnc.com/education/school /school.php?sectiondetailid=158403&. Accessed March 27, 2014.

Edgers, J. "Passage from India." *The News and Observer,* August 29, 1999, G1.

Emery, Marla R., Clare Ginger, and J. Chamberlain. "Migrants, Markets, and the Transformation of Natural Resources Management: Galax Harvesting in Western North Carolina." In H. A. Smith, ed. *Latinos and the New South: Transformations of Place.* Aldershot, UK: Ashgate, 2006, pp. 69–85.

Fegans, B. "Second Language, First Priority; Population Boom; Agencies Scrambling to Accommodate Hispanics." *Morning Star,* April 5, 2001, 1A, 6A.

Firesheets, Tina. "He Walks the Walk." *The News and Record,* January 10, 2010.

Funk, T., and D. Coto. "Entry into U.S. Not Same for All—Foreign Policy, Clout Can Be Heavy, Influences on Immigration Rules." *Charlotte Observer,* August 13, 2006, 1A.

Gill, Hannah. *The Latino Migration Experience in North Carolina.* Chapel Hill: University of North Carolina Press, 2010.

Glascock, N. "Local Asians Live in Peace." *The News and Observer,* January 6, 2002, B4.

Gordon, M. "The Ancient Way Is Alive." *The Charlotte Observer,* June 5, 1999, 1G.

Griffith, David. "New Midwesterners, New Southerners: Immigration Experiences in Four Rural American Settings." In D. A. Massey, ed. *New Faces in New Places: The Changing Geography of American Immigration.* New York: Russell Sage Foundation, 2008, pp. 179–210.

Griffith, David. "Rural Industry and Mexican Immigration." In V. Zuniga, and R. Hernadez-Leon, eds. *New Destinations: Mexican Immigration in the United States.* New York: Russell Sage Foundation, 2005, pp. 50–75.

Howe, Eleanor. "Helping Hispanics in Transition: An Interview with H. Nolo Martinez." *Popular Government* (Fall 1999): 13–17.

Immigrant and Refugee Rights Project. North Carolina Justice Center Webpage. http://www.ncjustice.org/?q=immigrants-and-refugees. Accessed February 24, 2014.

Johnson, J. H., K. D. Johnson-Webb, and W. Farrell. "A Profile of Hispanic Newcomers to the Triangle." *Popular Government* (Fall 1999): 2–12.

Johnson, M. "Exhibit Documents Rebuilding of Refugee Community—WFU Museum Shows; Photos of Cambodian Life, Culture Blossoming in Greensboro." *Winston-Salem Journal*, September 4, 2002, B1.

"Judge Orders Sudanese Held; Mekki, Charged with Falsifying Documents, Is Called Flight Risk." *Winston-Salem Journal*, September 24, 2002, A1.

Kandel, William K., and Emilio A. Parrado. "Hispanic Population Growth and Public School Response in Two New South Immigrant Destinations." In H. A. Smith, and O. J. Furuseth, eds. *Latinos in the New South: Transformations of Place.* Aldershot, UK: Ashgate, 2006, pp. 111–34.

Lavender, C. "County Decision Draws Bad Reaction: Resolution Passed Backing Arizona Immigration Law." *The Times-News*, July 24, 2010.

Lavender, C. "County Pleased with ICE Program." *Times-News*, February 24, 2011.

"Lawmaker Files Bill to Stop Accepting Photo ID from Mexican Consulate." *Associated Press. Rocky Mount Telegram*, March 16, 2011. http://www.rockymounttelegram.com/news/ncwire/lawmaker-files-bill-stop-accepting-photo-id-mexican-consulate-353484. Accessed February 24, 2014.

Lee, D. "'What a Hero, What a Soldier'; Family, Friends and Fellow Service Members Remember Spc. Justin Onwordi." *The News and Observer*, August 20, 2004, B1.

Liu-Beers, C. "Immigration Done Wisely." *The Herald-Sun*, February 10, 2011, A7.

Massey, Douglas S., and Chiara Capoferro. "The Geographic Diversification of American Immigration." In D. A. Massey, ed. *New Faces in New Places: The Changing Geography of American Immigration*. New York: Russell Sage Foundation, 2008, pp. 1–21.

Matthews, K. "Illegal Immigrants Line up at Last Minute for 'Papers.'" *The Herald-Sun*, May 1, 2001, A1.

McClain, Paula. "North Carolina's Response to Latino Immigrants and Immigration." In G. J. Anrig, and T. A. Wang, eds. *Immigration's New Frontiers: Experiences from the Emerging Gateway States*. New York: The Century Foundation Press, 2006, pp. 7–32.

McDonald, T. "A Fixer-Upper Here; a Treasure in Nigeria; Restored U.S. Cars Find Market Thanks to Triangle Resident." *The News and Observer*, July 5, 2006, A1.

Morrison, Sharon D., Lauren Hadleman, Sudha Shuda, Kenneth Gruber, and Raleigh Bailey. "Cultural Adaptation Resources for Nutrition and Health." *Immigrant Minority Health* 9 (2007): 205–12.

Mott, Tamar E. "African Refugee Resettlement in the US: the Role and Significance of Voluntary Agencies." *Journal of Cultural Geography* 27, no. 1 (2010): 1–31.

Nguyen, Mai Thi, and Hannah Gill. *The 287(g) Program, the Costs and Consequences of Local Immigration Enforcement in North Carolina Communities*. Chapel Hill: University of North Carolina at Chapel Hill, 2010.

"North Carolina—2010 Census Results: Total Population by County." U.S. Census Bureau, March 2, 2011. http://2010.census.gov/news/pdf/cb11cn61_nc_totalpop_2010map.pdf. Accessed March 27, 2014.

Onge, Peter, and Tim Funk. "Flawed Immigration Laws Pose Risks to Everyone-Stolen Social Security Numbers Used to Get Jobs as Agencies Stay Silent." *Charlotte Observer*, April 23, 2006, 1A.

Pecquet, J. "Durham Volunteers Prepare for Refugees; Churches Work to Ease Montagnards' Entry into the American Way of Life." *The Herald-Sun*, June 5, 2002, A1.

Pecquet, J. "Half a World Away." *The Herald-Sun*, August 18, 2002, A1.

Pew Hispanic Center. "Estimates of the Size and Characteristics of the Undocumented Population." Washington, DC: Pew Hispanic Center, 2005.

Portes, Alejandro, and Ruben Rumbaut. *Immigrant America: A Portrait*. Berkley: University of California Press, 2006.

Quinllin, M. "Job Market Is Shrinking for Hispanics in N.C.—Immigration Law Enforcement Stricter, Americans Desperate for Jobs." *The News and Observer*, March 5, 2011, 1A.

Railey, J. "Liberia: Pastor Faces Agonizing Trip Back Home." *Winston-Salem Journal*, December 13, 2003, B7.

Railey, J. "Waiting, Hoping—Flood of Refugees to Triad Down since Sept. 11, Leaving Families Separated." *Winston-Salem Journal*, February 11, 2002, A1.

Raynor, D. "Influential Immigrants." *News and Observer*, March 29, 2000, A1.

Shimron, Y. "New Immigration Law Exiles Roxboro Doctor." *The News and Observer*, May 23, 2003, A1.

Smith, B. "Cleveland Files Bill to Bar Illegal Immigrants from N.C. Public Colleges." *The Times-News*, January 28, 2011. http://intheloop.freedomblogging.com/2011/01/28/cleveland-files-bill-to-bar-illegal-immigrants-from-n-c-public-colleges/1998/. Accessed August 7, 2014.

Smith, Heather A., and Owen J. Furuseth. "Making Real the Mythical Latino Community in Charlotte, North Carolina." In H.A. Smith, and O.J. Furuseth, eds. *Latinos in the New South: Transformations of Place*. Aldershot, UK: Ashgate, 2006, pp. 191–213.

Subramanian, Ajantha. "Indians in North Carolina: Race, Class, and Culture in the Making of Immigrant Identity." *Comparative Studies of South Asia, Africa and the Middle East* xx, nos. 1 & 2 (2000): 105–14.

Swaminathan, R. "Desi—a Word of Their Own; for South Asians in the Triangle, One Term Embraces Many Meanings." *The News and Observer*, September 12, 2006, E1.

Thompson, C.D. "Lessons Learned on Immigration." *The Herald-Sun*, April 18, 2007, A13.

Torres, Rebecca, M.E. Jeffrey Popke, and Holly Hapke. "The South's Silent Bargain: Rural Restructuring, Latino Labor and the Ambiguities of Migrant Experience." In H.A. Smith, and O.J. Furuseth, eds. *Latinos in the New South: Transformations of Place*. Aldershot, UK: Ashgate, 2006, pp. 37–67.

Upchurch, K. "Many Deportees Aren't Criminals." *The Herald-Sun*, April 3, 2011, A1.

U.S. Census Bureau. "Nativity, Citizenship, Year of Entry, and Region of Birth." American Fact Finder, 2000. http://factfinder2.census.gov/faces/tableservices/jsf/pages/productview .xhtml?pid=DEC_00_SF3_QTP14&prodType=table. Accessed March 27, 2014.

U.S. Census Bureau, "North Carolina Quick Facts," n.d. http://quickfacts.census.gov/qfd /states/37000.html. Accessed August 7, 2014.

U.S. Census Bureau. "Race, Hispanic or Latino, Age, and Housing Occupancy: 2010 Census Redistricting Data (Public Law 94-171) Summary File." American Fact Finder, 2010. http://factfinder2.census.gov/faces/tableservices/jsf/pages/productview .xhtml?pid=DEC_10_PL_QTPL&prodType=table. Accessed March 27, 2010.

U.S. Census Bureau. "Race and Hispanic or Latino: 2010-State—County/County Equivalent 2010 Census Redistricting Data (Public Law 94–171) Summary File." American Fact Finder, 2010. http://factfinder2.census.gov/faces/tableservices/jsf/pages /productview.xhtml?pid=DEC_10_PL_GCTPL1.ST05&prodType=table.   Accessed March 27, 2014.

U.S. Census Bureau. "Race and Hispanic or Latino: 2010-State—Place 2010 Census Redistricting Data (Public Law 94–171) Summary File." American Fact Finder, 2010.   http://factfinder2.census.gov/faces/tableservices/jsf/pages/productview. xhtml?pid=DEC_10_PL_GCTPL1.ST13&prodType=table. Accessed March 27, 2014.

U.S. Census Bureau. "U.S. Census Bureau Population Estimates." Incorporated Places and Minor Civil Divisions: North Carolina, 2009. http://www.census.gov/popest /cities/tables/SUB-EST2009–04–37.xls. Accessed March 27, 2014.

Way, D. E. "Magazine Names Cabbie Hero of the Year; Immigrant Who Stood up in Duke Lacrosse Case Says 'I Feel Really Good' about." The Herald-Sun, March 15, 2008, B1.

Weigl, A. "African Connections; Immigrants Find Dishes and Techniques in Common with Southern Cooking." The News and Observer, March 12, 2008, E1.

Wilson, A. "UNC Hmong Community Small, But Close-Knit." Chapel Hill Herald, February 28, 2007, 1.

Wood, L. Maren. "Quakers." North Carolina Digital History (U.S. Department of State). http://www.learnnc.org/lp/editions/nchist-newsouth/5690.   Accessed   September 8, 2013.

Young, M. "Hmong Blend Culture to Save It." The Charlotte Observer, November 25, 2006, B5.

Zebrowski, J. "New Citizens Pledge Allegiance." The News and Observer, July 12, 2003, B3.

Zerwick, P. "Secrets: Sudanese Man Hoped for Fairness." Winston-Salem Journal, October 1, 2002, B1.

34

NORTH DAKOTA

Sarah Garding

CHRONOLOGY

1762	France turns over the territory of present-day North Dakota to Spain, which administers the region from its base in New Orleans.
1800	French acquire Spanish American territories, including present-day North Dakota.
1803	The Louisiana Purchase gives control of present-day North Dakota to the United States.
1861	The U.S. Congress establishes Dakota Territory.
1872–1873	Northern Pacific Railway reaches the Missouri River, fueling a settlement boom. New railroad towns, like Fargo and Bismarck, develop along the rail lines.
1879	Population settlement boom in North Dakota begins. Over 100,000 people would settle over the course of seven years.
1889	North Dakota becomes the 39th state of the United States.
1889	Nonpartisan League forms, backed by Norwegians and Germans from Russia.
1890	The State Agricultural College is founded in Fargo, which would eventually become North Dakota State University.
1903	Fort Lincoln, near Bismarck, is constructed. It would be the state militia's training base, and later an internment camp during World War II.
1905	Second population boom occurs in North Dakota; population swells from 191,000 in 1890 to 647,000 in 1920.
1912	Populist measures are introduced, including constitutional changes to allow referenda.

1915	The Nonpartisan League is formed. It would grow to have over 40,000 members within a year. Norwegian and German farmers strongly backs it.
1916	The Nonpartisan League wins control of executive and legislative branches in North Dakota.
1920	Wartime surge in commodities prices collapses and the Depression comes early to North Dakota.
1926	American Beet Sugar Company opens a sugar beet plant in East Grand Forks, Minnesota, just across the border from Grand Forks. It draws a small community of people of Mexican origin.
1929	North Dakota has its driest June on record, setting the stage for the Dust Bowl conditions that devastated the economy during the Great Depression. Tens of thousands would leave during the ensuing decade.
1933	Governor Langer issues a moratorium on foreclosure sales and on exporting commodities from the state, which would later be struck down by a federal judge.
1936	Another year of severe drought wreaks havoc on crops.
1942	Fort Lincoln, south of Bismarck, becomes an internment camp, housing approximately 4,000 people of varying nationalities, the majority being Japanese, including many U.S.-born Japanese.
1945	Commodity prices surge and many farms are able to pay off debt; North Dakota has highest per capita bank deposits in the United States.
1965	North Dakota's first sugar beet refinery opens near Drayton.
1972	The North Dakota Migrant Council is created to help seasonal farm laborers, many of whom are foreign-born. The council would become the North Dakota Rural Development three years later.
1978	Oil crisis prompts oil exploration in the western portion of North Dakota. The populations of western cities like Williston and Dickinson explode as workers and capital flock to the towns.
1982–2011	Refugee resettlement increasingly occurs in this state.
1987	High oil and cattle prices boost the state's economy.
2013	The Greater North Dakota Chamber calls for Congress to enact immigration reform.

HISTORICAL OVERVIEW

HISTORICAL SETTLEMENT

The state of North Dakota was carved out of Dakota Territory in 1889. With a primarily agricultural economy and challenging climactic conditions, the state has long struggled to maintain its population, and it remains one of the least densely populated states in the country. In 1900, the total population of North

Dakota was 319,146, of which 35 percent was foreign-born. Additionally, the state was overwhelmingly rural, with 92.7 percent of the population living outside of the few cities that existed. Its largest city, Fargo, had 9,589 inhabitants, of which 27 percent were immigrants. The vast, flat plains and sparse settlement nurture semi-isolated, rural enclaves colonized by immigrants from the same regions of origin.

The settlement of North Dakota was intertwined with the westward expansion of the country's railway network after the Civil War. After the tracks were laid in North Dakota's windswept plains, the Northern Pacific Railroad, for instance, had approximately 10 miles of land on either side of the tracks to dispose of. By stimulating the settlement and cultivation of the lands adjacent to the railroad grid, the companies were building up their future customer base, as farmers would inevitably use the railroads to transport grain. In the 1870s, the Northern Pacific Railroad owned more than 10 million acres of land, or roughly a quarter of the state's terrain. The Northern Pacific, Great Northern, and other railroad companies launched extensive advertising campaigns in American and foreign newspapers, touting economic opportunities in North Dakota, and they dispatched land agents to Europe, the East Coast, and other destinations to lure settlers to the northern plains. For instance, during the 1880s, the Northern Pacific Railroad had over 800 agents in Britain and 124 in Northern Europe, along with hundreds of subagents working beneath the general agents.

In numerous instances, associations based on religious sect or region of origin were formed to sponsor a colonization mission. The association would attract members, collect fees, recruit more members, send scouts to find a settlement location, and then build a town from scratch on the prairie. For instance, the German Evangelical Colonization Society of Chicago, sponsored by the German Evangelical Synod of North America, was formed in 1882 to organize settlements with the hopes of broadening the church's base in the United States. By 1883, after existing for just over a year, the German Evangelical Colonization Society had 311 members signed on. They bought a 320-acre tract of land and created the town of New Salem. One Great Northern land agent was particularly successful in convincing the German Brethren population in the United States to send settlement colonies to North Dakota. He attended the Anabaptist movement's convention in 1893 and gained audience with elders. Within several years, there were thousands of Brethren settlers living in colonies along the railroad lines in the northern part of the state between Devils Lake and Minot. Although the circumstances were vastly different, in some ways the logics of migration were seen in the early settlement colonies and contemporary refugee resettlement in the state were broadly similar in that an institutional actor brings in small populations of immigrants with backgrounds that were quite different from white, mainstream Christian society that prevailed in the state.

A second precursor to the Dakota population boom came in the form of advances in flour-milling techniques, which whetted the American public's appetite for fine, white flours, and generated huge demand for hard spring wheat that was well-suited to North Dakota's short growing season and semi-arid climate. The population swelled from 16,000 to 191,000 between 1878 and 1890.

Two periods of population boom took place in the 1880s and the early 1900s. In 1890, immigrants comprised 43 percent of the state's population. Many of the foreign-born settlers came via initial settlements in Illinois, Iowa, Minnesota, and Wisconsin. The immigrant population in North Dakota peaked at 156,158 in 1910, when it comprised 27 percent of the state's total population. At that time, Norwegians accounted for 29.4 percent of the foreign-born population, followed by Canadians (13.5), Russian Germans (20 percent), Germans (10.1 percent), and Swedes (7.8 percent). In 1920, a fifth of the state's 646,872 inhabitants were immigrants. Norwegians remained the largest foreign-born population (29 percent) in 1920, followed by Russian Germans (22.5 percent), Canadians (11.9 percent), Germans (9.1 percent), and Swedes (8 percent). In Fargo, 36.4 percent of the foreign-born population was Norwegian in 1920, followed by Canadians (16.4 percent) and Swedes (15.2 percent).

Norwegian immigrants come to the state early on and settled in large numbers in the Red River Valley along the state's eastern border, and in the northwestern quadrant of the state. The Russian Germans settled in the middle portion of the state. Despite the allure of cheap land and open prairie, the harsh climate and relative isolation of life on the plains drove many settlers away and deterred many more from ever coming. The forces of nature—unpreventable disasters like drought, dust storms, prairie fires, floods, and blizzards—added an element of instability to life. For many European immigrants, the openness and emptiness of the terrain could be overwhelming and lonely. In many townships, over half of the settlers, who came in the nineteenth century, left, leaving within several decades of homesteading and portending the ongoing demographic decline that has challenged the state for the bulk of its existence.

There were smaller immigrant communities that work for the railroad companies. Many of them were transient laborers, but some of them remained in North Dakota and took on permanent railroad employment. The Northern Pacific and Great Northern railroads used Japanese, Chinese, Armenian, and Greek laborers from the 1890s through the 1920s, and very small communities of them were scattered in towns along the railroad lines. A handful of Chinese-operated laundries could be found in several North Dakota towns in the nineteenth century. Several hundred Lebanese, Syrians, and Turks homesteaded in the state, and one of the first mosques in U.S. history was built in Ross, North Dakota in 1929.

STRUCTURAL FACTORS SHAPING CONTEMPORARY IMMIGRATION TO NORTH DAKOTA

In many respects, climate and geography have both fueled and hindered North Dakota's population growth. The availability of plentiful, cheap land sparked the settlement boom in the 1880s. In the nineteenth and early twentieth centuries, millions of immigrants to the United States, mostly from Northern and Western Europe, participated in the land drive. North Dakota's fertile, cheap, untilled, and sparsely settled land lured more than 100,000 immigrant settlers, mostly from Norway, Germany, Russia, and Sweden. The prospect of building new societies from the ground up on the remote northern plains appealed to religious minorities who had been persecuted in Europe. With the exception of the fertile Red River Valley on the state's eastern border with Minnesota, the short growing season and distance from major markets meant that most of the agricultural lands were best suited for cattle grazing and the cultivation of small grains that could be transported long distances.

If rural settlement fueled North Dakota's population boom in the nineteenth and early twentieth centuries, the wheat-dominant nature of its economy stifled further immigration. Although farm labor was necessary to harvest wheat historically, the mechanization of farming and more efficient techniques reduce the labor intensity of farming. Dependence on capricious commodity prices, moreover, made the state's economy particularly sensitive to booms and busts, and it was hit particularly hard during the Great Depression.

While the state's demography and economy were a good fit with the land fever that characterized a sizable subset of immigration in the nineteenth and early twentieth centuries, they did not cater to the types of immigration that prevailed today. Nationwide, rural migration gave way to urban migration in the late nineteenth and early twentieth centuries as the U.S. economy industrialized, and as the source countries shifted from Northern Europe to Southern and Eastern Europe, whose emigrants settled in industrial metropolises like Chicago and Cleveland. Contemporary immigration, too, is an overwhelmingly urban phenomenon. Large cities offer a broad range of jobs in a wealth of economic sectors catering to all levels of skills and education. In 1993, over 95 percent of immigrants went to urban areas, and over half of urban immigrants settled in just 10 urban metropolises. North Dakota has few cities, and those cities that do exist do not offer the breadth and quantity of opportunities to attract a range of contemporary immigrants. Only five cities in the state have a population of greater than 20,000, and only Fargo, with its population of 105,000, exceeds 100,000.

Another reason for North Dakota's dearth of immigrants is the nature of its economy. The economic structure that grows out of nineteenth- and twentieth-century settlement was overwhelmingly agricultural, likened by some to a typical colonial economy that exports raw, unprocessed commodities and imports capital and finished goods. The climate and topography of the state, as well as its distance from major markets, restricts the kinds of agricultural ventures that are viable. Wheat, soybeans, and cattle are the mainstay of North Dakota's agricultural economy. In 1900, 80 percent of North Dakota's population was engaged in farming, and 80 percent of income generated by farming came from wheat. Until the 1950s, tens of thousands of migratory farmworkers would journey each year to North Dakota to harvest wheat; however, these were transient workers who travel from farm to farm and state to state for employment, and by the 1950s, combine threshing eliminated the need for them. The same is true of sugar beet farming, which was introduced in the Red River Valley in the early twentieth century. For many decades it was a labor-intensive endeavor, and seasonal migrant workers journeyed each year from Texas and Mexico, often working for the same families year after year. However, the growing mechanization of agriculture, particularly after World War II, made beet production less labor-intensive. If six to seven workers were needed per acre in beet production in 1930, by the 1980s one human laborer was needed per acre. The peak of migrant labor in the sugar beet industry was in 1954 when nearly 7,000 migrants worked in the Red River Valley. In sum, then, although some types of contemporary agricultural production remained labor-intensive, the types of commodities that dominated North Dakota's agricultural production have grown more mechanized, capital-intensive, and efficient, creating few jobs for migrant laborers.

The dependence on commodity exports and the weakness of the industrial sector have persisted to the present day. Although the state government has fostered a friendly business climate with tax incentives and subsidies, the small local markets, relatively small labor force, aging population, remote location, and dearth of local capital continue to impede industrial development and manufacturing. Agriculture remains the largest sector of the economy, accounting for roughly a third of the economic base when federal payments are excluded. Agricultural production, processing, and related manufacturing constitute about 44 percent of the goods and services exported from North Dakota, and the state is the eighth-largest agricultural commodities exporter in the United States. High-tech industry in North Dakota has a few bright spots, including a Microsoft campus in the Fargo area that employs several thousands, but it is still a small subset of the economy. For the most part, as Danbom notes, "agriculture is more diverse than it was a century ago, and lignite and oil have provided another economic dimension, but the economy remains colonial. North Dakota exports raw fossil fuels, unfinished farm products, and young people and imports finished products and capital" (Danbom 1988, 109).

Another problem is the small size of existing immigrant networks. Immigrants tend to settle in areas where they can draw on the social and economic support of networks of co-ethnics. In other words, immigration settlement has a snowballing dynamic in that existing immigrant communities draw more immigrants, and the larger the immigrant community, the stronger the pull. North Dakota's foreign-born population steadily decreased in the nineteenth and early twentieth centuries as European settlers died off or moved away. The foreign-born stock was not replenished between the 1920s and 1965 because of the stringent immigration laws in place at the national level. With the 1965 Immigration Act, immigration was liberalized, but the source countries overwhelmingly shifted to Asia and Latin America. North Dakota lacked existing ethnic networks to draw new immigrants from these regions, as well as the cities and diversified professional opportunities that are so important to modern immigration.

Population loss and aging have been perennial problems for North Dakota. After peaking at 681,000 in 1930, the state's population decreased by 20 percent between 1930 and 1944. The population shrank by 3.5 percent between 1940 and 1950. Only one other state experienced a similar population loss during both of these decades. For the remainder of the twentieth century, the population vacillated between modest growth and moderate population loss. In 1950, the population stood at 620,000. After modest growth between 1950 and 1960, by 1970, the population was down to 618,000. A decade later it grew by 5.7 percent to 652,717, yet by 1990, the population was down to 638,000.In the year 2000, population was 642,200, and the most recent U.S. Census puts the population at 672,591, or a 4.7 percent increase over the past 10 years (U.S. Census Bureau 2010). Nevertheless, the state population has yet to top its 1930 high of 681,000. Even when economic times are good, as they undoubtedly have been over the past decade, educated youth continue to leave for big cities in other states. One study estimated that roughly 45,000 college graduates left North Dakota between 1989 and 1999. While agriculture, low-skilled and blue-collar jobs pay roughly the national average, professional jobs pay 20–50 percent less.

In 1950, nearly three-quarters of the population lived in rural areas, and only two cities had a population with more than 25,000. In 2000, 44 percent of the population lived in rural areas, and 39 out of the state's 53 counties were completely rural. Only 15 locations in the state were designated urban areas or clusters (U.S. Census Bureau 2000). As young, educated people continued to migrate out of North Dakota, population aging was an attendant problem. Rural-to-urban migration has been ongoing in North Dakota for many decades. Between 1990 and 2000, only 6 of 53 counties in North Dakota experienced population growth (North Dakota State Data Center 2011). Between 2000 and 2010, only 11 counties had population growth. In nearly half of the 53 counties, the population decreased by 10 percent or higher during the same time period.

Contemporary Migration

The combination of ongoing out-migration from North Dakota and the restrictive immigration laws instituted in the 1920s led to steady drops in the immigrant population of North Dakota. Between 1940 and 1950, the foreign-born population decreased by 51 percent. By 1980, the foreign-born population dwindled to

14,818, just 2 percent of the state's total population. Of the foreign-born population, over half immigrated before 1950, 74 percent were naturalized citizens, 48 percent were aged 60 and above, and 12 percent were aged 85 and above. The data have suggested a graying immigrant population with little replenishment. About 37 percent of the foreign-born population is European, while 23 percent is Canadian. The U.S. Census recorded just 247 Mexican immigrants. A small but growing subset of the foreign-born population came from Asia (1,975 or 13 percent), a reflection of refugee resettlement programs that brought in hundreds of Vietnamese and other refugees from communist countries. While the foreign-born population in the United States increased from 14 million to nearly 20 million between 1980 and 1990, in North Dakota, the immigrant population decreased to 9,388 by 1990, the lowest in the century. In terms of numbers, only South Dakota and Wyoming had fewer immigrants.

Yet, while nearly a third of the foreign-born in 1990 had immigrated prior to 1950, there was evidence that newer, younger cohorts of immigrants were also growing. About 31 percent had immigrated after 1979, and 17 percent immigrated between 1987 and 1990. The cohort that immigrated after 1979 was overwhelmingly urban, with 86 percent of them residing in cities, especially Fargo and Grand Forks. After Europeans and Canadians, the next largest foreign-born group was the Asian population of 2,125. While nationwide the Mexican immigrant population was the fastest-growing, in North Dakota, there were fewer than 200 Mexican immigrants counted. In 2000, the foreign-born population increased for the first time in many decades, but at 12,114 (1.9 percent of the total population), it was still a modest figure. Over half of the immigrant population arrived during the 1990s. In Fargo, the state's most populous city, an estimated three-quarter of the 3,587 foreign-born individuals entered in the 1990s. About 54 percent (1,929) entered between 1995 and March 2000. Statewide, the top countries of birth were Canada (just over 3,000), Germany (910), Bosnia-Herzegovina (740), India (715), and Mexico (580).

The most recent data, based on the American Community Survey's 2006–2010 5-Year Estimates, indicate a population of roughly 16,000 foreign-born individuals in North Dakota, or 2 percent of the total population. It should be noted, however, that the small size of the foreign-born population makes it difficult to accurately estimate its parameters, and the data for North Dakota's foreign-born population should be treated with caution.

In sharp contrast to historical immigration to the state, the largest region of origin is Asia (an estimated 5,000 Asian immigrants or 31 percent of the foreign-born population), of which the largest groups come from China, India, Vietnam, and the Philippines. Of the state's estimated 3,500 European-born immigrants, most come from Germany and Bosnia-Herzegovina. Over 3,000 immigrants were born in Canada. The third-largest region of origin is Africa (2,464), where the majority came from East Africa, followed by Latin America (1,528). The Mexican-born population is just estimated to be roughly 800.

The profile of the immigrant population highlights the contributions that more widespread immigration could make to North Dakota's demographic dilemmas. Again, the data should be treated with caution because of the population's small size. About 57 percent of the foreign-born population falls into the 18–44 age range. Among the native-born population, just 37 percent of the population falls in this range. Among the foreign-born, the median age is 33.4, compared to the median age of 37.3 among the native-born population. The foreign-born population also has higher educational attainment levels than the native-born population. While 26 percent of the native-born population has a bachelor's degree or higher, 37 percent of the foreign-born population has a bachelor's degree or higher. An impressive 20.4 percent of the immigrant population has a graduate or professional degree. Despite the discrepancies in the level of education, the median household income among the native-born is $46,943, while for the foreign-born, it is $39,282. While 12.1 percent of the native-born population lives below the poverty level, 21.3 percent of the foreign-born population lives below the poverty line.

TOPICAL ESSAYS

North Dakota's Miniature United Nations: Refugee Resettlement in the State of Plenty

North Dakota's unique configuration of economic, demographic, and geographic traits makes it an interesting, albeit idiosyncratic, case study of contemporary immigration to the United States. On the one hand, with just 672,000 inhabitants counted in the 2010 Census, North Dakota ranks 48th among the 50 states in terms of total population. Immigrants constitute just 2 percent of the state's total population, compared to 12.5 percent at the national level. Equally striking is the composition of the foreign-born population in North Dakota, which is an unusual blend of the last remnants of earlier European migration and contemporary refugee resettlement. While the foreign-born population is led by Mexican, Asian Indian, and Filipino immigrants at the national level, in North Dakota the largest foreign-born groups include, among others, Bosnians and Vietnamese. At the same time, with the introduction of new hydraulic fracturing ("fracking") and horizontal drilling techniques to extract oil from the massive Bakken field in western North Dakota, the state has been a haven of growth in an economic maelstrom. It has had the country's lowest unemployment rate for several years running, its highest growth rate in 2010, and a recent state budget surplus of $1 billion.

With its low unemployment rate and ongoing population decline, will North Dakota become a new immigration hotspot? Having briefly discussed historical settlement earlier, this chapter describes the demographic and economic factors that have historically hampered widespread immigration to the state below. It then turns to two thematic topics—the Latino population in North Dakota and the resettlement of refugees in the state.

THE LATINO/A POPULATION

The Latino/a population in North Dakota has always been small. The 1900 Census listed just 13 Mexican-born residents, and only 27 were recorded in 1920. With the introduction of sugar beet farming on the northern plains after World War I, a number of Latino agricultural workers came to the Red River Valley from Texas and Mexico. Sugar beet production was labor-intensive; however, the American Beet Sugar Company's fields and plants were concentrated in the Minnesota portion of the Red River Valley. Nevertheless, a number of workers appear to have resided on the North Dakota side of the border in Grand Forks and Fargo. The 1930 Census tallied just over 600 North Dakotans of Mexican origin, most of them concentrated in the Red River Valley and working in the East Grand Forks, Minnesota plant. The Bracero labor agreements between the United States and Mexican governments during World War II brought hundreds and possibly thousands of Mexican workers to the Red River Valley beet fields. However, sugar beet production became much less labor-intensive after World War II, eliminating many of the jobs and prompting migrant farmworkers to move onward. Some of the seasonal workers ended up remaining in the Red River Valley, and a small population of former migrant workers returned to the region when the economy soured in the 1970s and 1980s.

At the national level, the Latino/a population has surged over the past several decades. Currently, more than half of the foreign-born population is from Latin America. North Dakota goes against the grain in two respects. First, its Latino/a population is small. Second, the share of foreign-born among the Latino/a population is also smaller than the national average. In 2000, just fewer than 8,000 people in North Dakota were identified as being of Latino/a origin, or 1.2 percent of the total population. North Dakota had the smallest foreign-born Latino population in 2000 after Vermont. In 2010, the Latino/a population stood at 13,500, or 2 percent of the total population. The cities with the largest concentrations of Latino/as were Fargo (2,308, or 2 percent of the city's population), Grand Forks (1,473, or 2.7 percent of the city's population), and Minot (1,117, or 2.7 percent of the population).Although the population's growth was numerically small, Latino/as were nevertheless one of the fastest-growing population subsets in the state. Between 2000 and 2010, the Latino/a population grew by nearly 75 percent, and an estimated one out of every five people added to the state's total population were of Latino/a origin.

Refugees from Iraq, Amar Hussein, right, his wife Ruqia Marzok, left, and their one-year-old daughter Noof Ali pose in their Fargo, North Dakota, apartment on March 31, 2009. Battered by a flood and a blizzard, Fargo residents were quick to credit friends, family, and faith for getting them through. For Fargo's newest arrivals, refugees from Iraq, Somalia, Serbia, and other hard-hit places, the web of support can be far more frail. (AP Photo/ Charles Rex Arbogast)

REFUGEE RESETTLEMENT

If the data suggest something of a miniature United Nations feel to North Dakota's small foreign-born population, the principal cause is refugee resettlement. Each year, the state department's Bureau of Population, Refugees, and Migration settles tens of thousands of refugees across the United States, using the services of 10 voluntary resettlement agencies. The refugees are distributed among U.S. states, with each state receiving anywhere from a handful to upward of 10,000. North Dakota receives roughly 400 per year. For the majority of states, the number of refugees brought in through federal programs comprises a small portion of the foreign-born population. In North Dakota, where non-refugee immigration has been sluggish for decades, the foreign-population by and large *is* the refugee population. Similarly, although North Dakota only receives several hundred refugees per year, the state's low total population means that it has one of the highest rates of refugees per capita.

The refugee countries of origin have varied over the years. Before the 1990s, the majority of refugees came from the Communist countries. Between 1982 and 1989, 1,066 refugees were resettled in North Dakota, of which just over half were from Southeast Asia, and most of the remainder from Eastern Europe. In the first half of the 1990s, an additional 762 Southeast Asian refugees arrived, along with 583 from the Middle East, 550 from the former USSR and Eastern Europe, several hundred from Latin America, and several dozen from Africa. The majority of these refugees were settled in Fargo, followed by Bismarck and Grand Forks.

All told, roughly 8,650 refugees were resettled in North Dakota between 1982 and 2011. Lutheran Social Services (LSS) was the agency that had organized refugee resettlement in the state for many decades. Of the 8,650 refugees resettled over the past three decades, about 2,030 came from the former Yugoslavia (mostly from Bosnia-Herzegovina), 1,040 from Iraq, 910 from Somalia, 810 from Bhutan, 600 from Sudan, 250 from Liberia, and 180 from Burundi. Between 1997 and 2011, 80 percent of the refugees were settled in the Fargo area, 10 percent in Grand Forks, 9 percent in Bismarck, and the remainder in other small cities. Over the past several years, the largest groups have come from Bhutan and Iraq. In 2009, nearly half of the refugees were Nepali from Bhutan, and one-quarter were from Iraq. There were another 150 secondary refugees; that is, refugees originally resettled in other states who moved to North Dakota (Child and Family Services Division 2010). In 2011, 273 out of 354 refugees came from Bhutan, 30 from Iraq, and 14 respectively from Congo and Eritrea.

The state agency tasked with refugee services is the Department of Health Services' Child and Family Services Division. LSS is the only refugee resettlement organization in North Dakota that has been approved by the federal government. In 2010, the department transferred the bulk of its refugee services to LSS. LSS, in turn, subcontracts services like English-language instruction, translation, health services, employment services, and counseling to other organizations. The funding for refugee resettlement comes mostly from the federal government, with some private donations.

Fargo, situated on North Dakota's eastern border with Minnesota and part of the Fargo-Moorhead region that encompasses the two border cities, received the largest share of the state's refugees. Between 1991 and 2000, LSS of North Dakota resettled more than 3,000 refugees in Fargo, over three-quarters of the total number of refugees settled in the state during that period. When secondary migrant refugees were included, the refugee population of the city was estimated to be roughly 5,500 by 2000. In 2000, 17 percent of the foreign-born population came from Bosnia-Herzegovina, the largest group.

Refugee resettlement has diversified the city of Fargo. In 1980, 98 percent of Fargo's population was Anglo- and American-born, while only 1.9 percent of the city's population was foreign-born. In 2010, those figures have changed to 90.2 percent and 5 percent, respectively. Asian and East African specialty shops, Mexican delis, a mosque, and other trappings of cities of immigration have recently increased the foreign-born population's visibility in the city. There are already indications that these small, existing communities of refugees have drawn secondary refugee migrants from the same countries of origin, such as Somali refugees relocating from Minneapolis to Fargo.

As the immigrant and refugee population has grown, a number of organizations have become active in community life and refugee service provision, such as the Immigrant Development Council in Fargo-Moorhead, which helps immigrants gain business skills, and Giving+Learning, an organization that pairs senior citizens mentors with new immigrants. Refugee communities, too, have formed associations, such as the New Sudanese Community Association of Fargo-Moorhead. There has been some local backlash against the refugee presence, and many native-born North Dakotans believe that the refugees are a drain on local resources, schools, and jobs.

Grand Forks, the second-largest city in North Dakota and located in the Red River Valley on the North Dakota–Minnesota border, has the second-highest population of refugees. It received roughly 650 people between 1991 and 2011. Here too, Bosnians were the dominant group in the 1990s. In Grand Forks, the Refugee Resettlement Coalition was formed in 1993 to assist refugees by furnishing apartments and transporting refugees to classes and appointments. In 2002, the city created a Refugee Advisory Board to coordinate refugee community services. In Grand Forks, the spike in the refugee immigrant population was seen in the school system. The number of foreign-born children enrolled in the Grand Forks school district's ELL program increased nearly twofold from the 2007 to 2008 academic year, when 141 immigrant students were enrolled, to 262 immigrants in 2009 to 2010.

Conclusion

As this section has shown, the interplay of population trends and economic development has often yielded contradictory results. Though the state's economy remains heavily dependent upon agriculture, the growing size of farms and the efficiency of production have fueled a slow but steady exodus from rural areas to urban areas. While unemployment remains low, North Dakota's urban areas do not offer the breadth or quantity of economic opportunities for educated professionals, making it difficult to retain college graduates. Even in good economic times, such as the 2000s, the state has battled to retain its population. While the flush of oil money to the state budget could help fuel new programs, it seems unlikely that the state will experience a dramatic demographic turnaround or become an immigration hotspot.

NOTABLE GROUPS

Grand Forks Immigrant Integration Initiative

Grand Forks participated in a pilot program established by the National League of Cities to help cities with immigration increases, improving diversity awareness and offering "citizen academies" where foreign-born population can take classes on participating in local governance, doing business, and opening a bank account. The city's public–private Grand Forks Immigrant Integration Initiative is composed of nonprofit sector organizations like LSS; the Global Friends Coalition; and representatives from the police department, school district, and city government. The goal of the program is to assist immigrants with naturalization, stimulate civic participation, improve cross-cultural communication in the broader community, and help direct immigrants to the appropriate social and community services. The city's refugee population comes from Bosnia, Burundi, Bhutan, Ethiopia, Iraq, Liberia, Somalia, Sudan, and Uganda. Around 30 refugees were resettled in Grand Forks in 2007, 60 in 2008, and approximately 90 per year since then. Additionally, an unspecified number of secondary refugees relocated to the city after initial settlement in other parts of the United States.

BIBLIOGRAPHY

American Community Survey. *American Community Survey 5-Year Estimates: 2006–2010.* 2010. http://factfinder2.census.gov/faces/nav/jsf/pages/index.xhtml. Accessed March 27, 2014.

Bjorke, C. "Little Hub on the Prairie." *Bismarck Tribune*, December 6, 2010. http://bismarcktribune.com/news/local/article_946e21ac-ff2b-11df-82b0–001cc4c03286 .html. Accessed March 28, 2014.

Bureau of Population, Refugees, and Migration. "Fact Sheet: U.S. Refugee Admissions Program Reception and Placement Program Agencies FY 2011." U.S. Department of State, May 6, 2011. http://www.state.gov/g/prm/rls/fs2011/162824.htm. Accessed March 28, 2014.

Cauchon, D. "Big Cities Lure Away North Dakota Youth." *USA Today*, February 23, 2004. http://www.usatoday.com/news/nation/2004–02–23-north-dakota-cover_x.htm. Accessed March 28, 2014.

Cauchon, D. "North Dakota Economy Booms, Population Soars." *USA Today*, March 17. 2011. http://www.usatoday.com/news/nation/census/2011–03–16-north-dakota-census_N. htm. Accessed March 28, 2014.

Child and Family Services Division. *FFY 2008/2009 Children and Family Services Statistical Bulletin.* 2010. http://www.nd.gov/dhs/info/pubs/family.html. Accessed March 28, 2014.

City of Fargo. *Consolidated Plan: Housing and Community Development. Strategic Plan for Years 2010–2014.* 2010. http://cityoffargo.org/ . . . /Consolidated%20Plan%20 10–14%20-%20final.pdf. Accessed March 28, 2014.

City of Grand Forks. "Grand Forks Immigrant Integration (GFII)." 2011. http://www.grand forksgov.com/gfgov/home.nsf/Pages/Immigrant+Integration. Accessed March 28, 2014.

Danbom, D. B. "North Dakota: The Most Midwestern State." In J. H. Madison, ed. *Heartland: Comparative Histories of the Midwestern States.* Bloomington: Indiana University Press, 1988, pp. 107–26.

Global Friends Coalition. "Frequently Asked Questions." 2011. http://www.gfcoalition.org/FAQs.html. Accessed March 28, 2014.

Haga, C. "Brown to Speak at National Immigration Conference." *Grand Forks Herald*, September 28, 2010. Accessed March 28, 2014; http://www.grandforksherald.com/content/grand-forks-mayor-mike-brown-speak national-immigration-conference Accessed August 7, 2014. Haga, C. "City, Agencies Work to Help Ease Transition for Refugees." *Grand Forks Herald*, August 20, 2010. Accessed March 28, 2014; retrieved through Newsbank.

Hansen, D. A. "Bosnian Refugees' Adjustments to Resettlement in Grand Forks, North Dakota." *Great Plains Research* 13 (Fall 2003): 271–90.

Harman, D. "Fargo's Newest Pioneers." *The Christian Science Monitor*, November 12, 2003. http://www.csmonitor.com/2003/1112/p18s02-lihc.html. Accessed March 28, 2014.

Henke, W. A. "Reichsdeutsche (Germans)." In W. C. Sherman, and P. V. Thorson, eds. *Plains Folk: North Dakota's Ethnic History*. Fargo: North Dakota Institute for Regional Studies at North Dakota State University, 1988, pp. 61–116.

Lutheran Social Services New American Services. "Frequently Asked Questions about Refugee Resettlement in North Dakota." 2011. www.lssnd.org/newamericans/NASfaq.pdf. Accessed March 28, 2014.

Milovanovic, S. Director of New American Services of Lutheran Social Services of North Dakota, Personal communication with author, January 1, 2012.

North Dakota Department of Human Services. *North Dakota Child & Family Services Plan. 2011 Annual Progress and Services Report, October 1, 2010–September 30, 2011.* 2011. http://www.nd.gov/dhs/info/pubs/family.html. Accessed March 28, 2014.

North Dakota Farm Bureau. "Agriculture's Role in the North Dakota Economy." Bismarck: North Dakota Farm Bureau, April 1, 2009. http://www.ndfb.org/?id=63. Accessed March 28, 2014.

North Dakota State Data Center. "Current Population Trends in North Dakota." Fargo: North Dakota State University, 2011. http://www.ndsu.edu/sdc/data/population-trends.htm. Accessed March 28, 2014.

Portes, Alejandro, and Ruben G. Rumbaut. *Immigrant America: A Portrait*. Berkeley: University of California Press, 1996.

Robinson, E. B. *History of North Dakota*. Lincoln: University of Nebraska Press, 1966.

Sherman, W. C. "The Dakota Environment." In W. C. Sherman, and P. V. Thorson, eds. *Plains Folk: North Dakota's Ethnic History*. Fargo: North Dakota Institute for Regional Studies at North Dakota State University, 1988, pp. 3–8.

Sherman, W. C. "The Settlement Process: Railroad and Land Company Activity." In W. C. Sherman, and P. V. Thorson, eds. *Plains Folk: North Dakota's Ethnic History*. Fargo: North Dakota Institute for Regional Studies at North Dakota State University, 1988, pp. 9–13.

Sherman, W. C. "Special Groups." In W. C. Sherman, and P. V. Thorson, eds. *Plains Folk: North Dakota's Ethnic History*. Fargo: North Dakota Institute for Regional Studies at North Dakota State University, 1988, pp. 333–406.

Tenamoc, M. J. "Aging Is Everyone's Business. Changes in Population: Implications for Data Use and Service Delivery." Bismarck: North Dakota Department of Human Services, Decision Support Services, 2010.

U.S. Census Bureau. *Census of the Population. Volume 2: Characteristics of the Population. Part 34: North Dakota.* 1950. http://www.census.gov/prod/www/abs/decennial/1950cenpopv2.html. Accessed March 28, 2014.

U.S. Census Bureau. *Census of Population and Housing. Volume 1: Characteristics of the Population. Part 36: North Dakota.* 1980. http://www.census.gov/prod/www/abs/decennial/1980cenpopv1.html.Accessed March 28, 2014.

U.S. Census Bureau. *Census of Population and Housing. Volume 3: Composition and Characteristics of the Population by States.*1920. http://www.census.gov/prod/www/abs/decennial/1920.html. Accessed March 28, 2014.

U.S. Census Bureau. *Census of Population and Housing. Volume 3: Reports by States, Showing the Composition and Characteristics of the Population for Counties, Cities, and Townships or Other Minor Civil Divisions.* 1930. http://www.census.gov/prod/www/abs/decennial/1930.html. Accessed March 28, 2014.

U.S. Census Bureau. *Census of Population: Social and Economic Characteristics (1990 CP-2–36): North Dakota.* 1990. http://www.census.gov/prod/cen1990/cp2/cp-2.html. Accessed March 28, 2014.

U.S. Census Bureau. *Census 2000 Summary File 1 (SF 1).* 2000. http://factfinder2.census.gov/faces/nav/jsf/pages/index.xhtml. Accessed March 28, 2014.

U.S. Census Bureau. *Census 2010 Summary File 1 (SF 1).* 2010. http://factfinder2.census.gov/faces/nav/jsf/pages/index.xhtml. Accessed March 28, 2014.

U.S. Census Bureau. *Census of the United States. Volume 3: Population by States, Nebraska-Wyoming.* 1910.http://www.census.gov/prod/www/abs/decennial/1910.html. Accessed March 28, 2014.

U.S. Census Bureau. "The Newly Arrived Foreign-Born Population of the United States: 2010." *American Community Survey Briefs,* November, 2011. www.census.gov/prod/2011pubs/acsbr10–16.pdf. Accessed March 28, 2014.

U.S. Office of Refugee Resettlement. *Office of Refugee Resettlement Annual Report to Congress FY 2008.* http://www.acf.hhs.gov/programs/orr/data/arc.htm. Accessed March 28, 2014.

Valencia, C. "Univision Insights: Hispanic Population Boom Continues—2010 Census Figures for Florida, Georgia, Montana, New Mexico, Kentucky, Alaska, Minnesota, North Dakota and Tennessee Show Hispanic Growth Pattern Continues." *Reuters,* March 18, 2011. http://www.reuters.com/article/2011/03/18/idUS198405+18-Mar-2011+BW20110318. Accessed March 28, 2014.

Wirtz, R. A. "Plugging the Brain Drain." *Fedgazette,* Federal Reserve Bank of Minneapolis. January 1, 2003. http://www.minneapolisfed.org/publications_papers/pub_display.cfm?id=1860. Accessed March 27, 2014.

35

OHIO

William P. Kladky

CHRONOLOGY

1670	René-Robert Cavelier, sieur de La Salle (1643–1687), a French explorer and the first European in the Ohio Country, discovers the Ohio River.
1748	The Ohio Company forms in Virginia to settle in the Ohio River Valley.
1754–1763	In the settlement of the French and Indian War, France cedes all rights to the Ohio Country to the British in the Treaty of Paris of 1763.
1768	According to the Treaty of Fort Stanwix, the Iroquois transfers all lands south and east of the Ohio River to the British.
1783	The Treaty of Paris officially ends the American Revolution. England recognizes American independence and ceded all lands in the Ohio Country.
1785	The Land Ordinance of 1785 establishes the methods for surveying and dividing land in the Ohio Country.
1786	The Ohio Company of Associates forms in Massachusetts to sell land in southeast Ohio.
1787	The Confederation Congress appoints Arthur St. Clair (1736–1818) as the first governor of the Northwest Territory.
1787	Congress enacts the Northwest Ordinance, establishing the Northwest Territory, which includes modern-day Ohio.
1788	The Ohio Company founds Marietta, the first permanent white settlement in the Northwest Territory and Ohio. John Cleves Symmes (1742–1814) purchases 311,682 acres in Ohio from the U.S. Congress.

1795	The Treaty of Greenville is signed to end the Ohio Indian Wars. The Miami, Wyandot, Shawnee, Delaware, and other American Indian nations move to northwestern Ohio.
1800	Chillicothe becomes the capital of the Northwest Territory.
1802	The Enabling Act enables residents of the eastern Northwest Territory to form the state of Ohio and seek admission to the Union.
1803	President Thomas Jefferson (1743–1826) signs the legislation making Ohio the 17th state of the Union.
1804	The Ohio General Assembly charters Ohio University in Athens, which opens in 1808 with three students.
1812	The city of Columbus is founded and designated as the new state capital.
1825	Work on the National Road and the canal system in Ohio begins.
1833	Oberlin College, the first coeducational college in the United States, is founded.
1833	The Canal Commission completes the Ohio and Erie Canal, connecting Akron with the Cuyahoga River and Cleveland, and later with the Ohio River and other canal systems in Pennsylvania and Ohio.
1835–1836	A bitter boundary dispute between Michigan and Ohio leads to the bloodless Toledo War.
1840	The nation elects Ohioan William Henry Harrison (1773–1841) of North Bend as the ninth president of the United States.
1842	A treaty with the Wyandots, also known as the Treaty of Upper Sandusky, is signed. The Wyandots, Ohio's last Indian tribe, agree to surrender all claims to land in the state.
1845	The 301-mile Miami and Erie Canal connecting the Ohio River in Cincinnati with Lake Erie in Toledo is completed.
1851	The Ohio Constitution of 1851 is adopted.
1852	The publication of *Uncle Tom's Cabin*, written in Ohio by Harriet Beecher Stowe (1811–1896), strongly condemns slavery.
1862	President Abraham Lincoln (1809–1865) issues the Emancipation Proclamation.
1863	Following a six-week siege, Confederate forces surrender Vicksburg to federal troops led by Ulysses S. Grant (1822–1885) of Point Pleasant, Ohio.
1863	The only Civil War battle in Ohio, the Battle of Buffington Island (also known as the St. Georges Creek Skirmish) is fought in Meigs County.
1864	President Lincoln promotes Ulysses S. Grant to be the supreme commander of all Union forces.
1864	Union forces under the leadership of William T. Sherman (1820–1891) of Lancaster, Ohio, capture Atlanta.
1868	Voters elect Ohioan Ulysses S. Grant to his first of two terms as the 18th president of the United States.

1870	Originally known as the Ohio Agricultural and Mechanical College, the Ohio State University is chartered as a land-grant university by the Ohio General Assembly. It opens in 1873 with 24 students.
1876	Rutherford B. Hayes (1822–1893) of Delaware, Ohio, is elected the 19th U.S. president.
1879	Thomas A. Edison (1847–1931) of Milan, Ohio, invents the electric light bulb.
1880	Ohioan James A. Garfield (1831–1881) of Moreland Hills is elected the 20th president of the United States.
1881	Charles J. Guiteau (1841–1882) shoots President Garfield, who dies three months later, in Washington, D.C.
1888	Ohioan Benjamin Harrison (1833–1901) of North Bend—the grandson of William Henry Harrison, the ninth president—is elected the 23rd president of the United States.
1896	William McKinley (1843–1901) of Niles, Ohio, is elected to his first of two terms as the 25th U.S. president.
1901	Leon Czolgosz (1873–1901) assassinates President McKinley in Buffalo, New York.
1902	The Ohio General Assembly officially adopts Ohio's state flag.
1903	Ohioans Orville (1871–1948) and Wilbur Wright (1867–1912) of Dayton complete the first successful flight of a powered airplane.
1908	William H. Taft (1857–1930) of Cincinnati, Ohio, is elected the 27th president of the United States.
1917	The U.S. Army constructs Camp Sherman near Chillicothe to train World War I troops.
1920	Ohioan Warren G. Harding (1865–1923) of Blooming Grove is elected the 29th U.S. president.
1935	Ohio's first sales tax is instituted.
1953	Finally realizing an oversight, and acting on a resolution from Ohio Republican congressman George Bender of Chagrin Falls, the U.S. Congress *viva voce* passes a resolution officially recognizing Ohio statehood and declaring Ohio's date of entry into the Union as March 1, 1803.
1955	The 241-mile Ohio Turnpike—officially the James W. Shocknessy Ohio Turnpike—is completed, having begun construction in 1949.
1958	The completion of the St. Lawrence Seaway connects Ohio cities on Lake Erie to international destinations.
1959	The state's general assembly enacts the Fair Employment Practices Legislation to outlaw racial discrimination (Section 4112.01 of the Ohio Revised Code) and creates the Ohio Civil Rights Commission.
1962	Astronaut John H. Glenn Jr. (1921–) of Cambridge, Ohio, becomes the first American to orbit the earth.

1963	William O. Walker (1896–1981) of Cleveland is named by Republican governor James Rhodes (1909–2001) as Ohio's first African American cabinet member.
1967	Carl B. Stokes (1927–1996) is elected to be the first African American mayor of a major U.S. city, Cleveland.
1969	Astronaut Neil A. Armstrong (1930–2012) of Wapakoneta, Ohio, becomes the first person to walk on the moon.
1973	Ohio voters approve the Ohio Lottery.
1979	The Columbus, Dayton, and Cleveland public schools begin busing pupils to eliminate segregation.
1986	Astronaut Judith A. Resnik (1949–1986), of Akron, dies in the Space Shuttle *Challenger* (mission STS-51-L) explosion.
1991	In their ruling in *DeRolph v. State of Ohio*, the Ohio Supreme Court declares Ohio's school funding program unconstitutional because it "fails to provide for a thorough and efficient system of common schools."
1995	International negotiations at the Wright-Patterson Air Force Base near Dayton lead to the Bosnian Peace Agreement (also known as the Dayton Agreement) ending the three-year war in Bosnia in the former Yugoslavia.
2001	Terrorist attacks on September 11 in New York City and Washington, D.C., lead to a flurry of anti-terrorist activities in Ohio and the country.
2012	Undocumented immigration becomes the fasted-growing federal arrest offense in Ohio.

HISTORICAL OVERVIEW

Before 1800

Perhaps the best explanation for the name Ohio is that it is from the Iroquoian word in its Mohawk and Cayugan dialects, *O-hē-yo*, meaning "Great River." Approximately 15,000 American Indians from the Miami, Shawnee, Ottawa, Wyandot, and Delaware nations lived in Ohio before Europeans began settlement. The American Indians had cultivated some of the lands, growing corn, tobacco, and vegetables. The Delawareans cleared 3,000 acres in one region, and the Wyandots had large cornfields in northern Ohio. Moravian missionaries helped the Delawareans build 60 houses, rail fences, and sizable agricultural clearings.

In the seventeenth century, French fur traders and missionaries entered Ohio, coming from Canada along the St. Lawrence River. They went along Lake Erie, the Ohio Valley, and into Kentucky. Most historians agree that the first European was French explorer René-Robert Cavelier, sieur de La Salle (1643–1687), who discovered the Ohio River in 1670. The French called it *La Belle Riviére*, "the beautiful river." Abbé Galinée and his Sulpicians were among the first missionaries who trekked across northern Ohio. In 1663, the "Ohio Country" became part of New France and was a royal province of the French Empire. Fort Miami (Toledo) was built in 1680 by New France governor general Louis de Buade de Frontenac (1622–1698).

The French set up trading posts to control the fur trade in the region, linked to their settlements in Canada and what they called the Illinois Country along the Mississippi River. They also built Fort Sandusky (1750) and Fort Junandat (1754), the latter probably a corruption of "Wyandot." Few English settlers ventured into this area, intimidated by the difficult route over the Appalachians. More extensive French settlement was very limited because of the hazardous water trek from Quebec, with most settlers taking the easier route along the Great Lakes to Michigan, Wisconsin, and Minnesota.

Europeans, especially the British, became much more interested in the region during the mid-eighteenth century. Hearing some English fur traders' reports of fertile land and rich resources, British settlers moved in via the many rivers as well as the multitude of Indian trails and traces. In 1748, the Ohio Company was formed in Virginia to settle in the Ohio River Valley. Britain's victory in the French and Indian War led to France conceding its entire claim to the Ohio Country in 1763. With English settlers demanding land, Indian removal began around this time. The 1768 Treaty of Fort Stanwix forced the Iroquois to give all of its lands south and east of the Ohio River to the British.

At the end of the century, emigrants from the established British colonies along the Atlantic began to arrive. Virginia, Massachusetts, and Connecticut all claimed that under their Royal Charters they owned portions of the Ohio area. Most migrants were American-born who came to Ohio from New England, the Mid-Atlantic, and the Upland South. New Englanders settled mostly in the northeastern section, as well as in Marietta, Putnam, Granville, and Worthington. They brought their own culture: towns with a central greens and commons area, Greek revival-style buildings, and the Protestant faith (e.g., the Congregational Christian Church). Maryland settlers came over the Cumberland Road, Virginians via the Wilderness Trail, and New Englanders over land across Pennsylvania along the Mohawk Trail. The first settlers tended to locate in the heavy forests in the river bottoms. They constructed housing from the timber, and distilled and exported potash.

The national Ordinance of 1785 created a barrier to small settlers, with a 640-acre minimum tract size for purchase of public lands. Land speculators and large organizations thus were favored, and settlement was slow. Military districts played an important role in Ohio's early settlement. The U.S. military district was a 2.5 million acre land tract in central Ohio established by the U.S. Congress by a 1780 resolution to compensate veterans of the American Revolutionary War for their service. The Virginia Military District of 4.2 million south-central acres was reserved by Virginia as payment for veterans of the American Revolutionary War. Settlers from Virginia and Kentucky moved into this area, but many veterans sold their grants for a fraction to speculators.

The Connecticut Western Reserve was a strip of land originally claimed by Connecticut in northeastern Ohio. In 1786, Virginia and Connecticut gave up their claims to most Ohio and western land claims in exchange for federal assumption of its American Revolutionary War debt. Connecticut finally gave up its last claim in 1800. Many New Englanders moved into the Connecticut Western Reserve, and the Puritan influence persisted.

In 1787, Congress enacted the Northwest Ordinance, specifying that this large area would eventually be divided into individual states and banning slavery north of the Ohio River. The original line drawn to divide the Ohio Territory from the Indiana Territory went to the Canadian border. In 1802, after discovering a surveying error for the northern boundary, Congress adjusted the border to Ohio's favor.

Settlement of the rest of Ohio was still minimal because of the land sale dilemma. Two 1796 public land bills attempted to fix this but did not help. Unable to get land legally, squatters moved in, creating another type of problem. Finally, the Land Act of 1800 reduced land prices while extending low credit plans, and the land rush was on. The first permanent American colony in the territory was Marietta, an island on the Ohio River, founded in 1788 by settlers from the Massachusetts colony. There followed a rush of migrants from Virginia, Kentucky, and Pennsylvania comprising largely second- and third-generation Scotch Irish. The first true immigrants to settle in the Ohio territory were the 600 French who had been victimized by a land scheme in France. Gallipolis, the colony they founded on the Ohio River in 1790, drew immigrants for decades.

In 1795, the Treaty of Greenville was signed to end the Ohio Indian Wars. Under its terms, the Miami, Wyandot, Shawnee, Delaware, and other nations moved to northwestern Ohio. Afterward, General Moses Cleaveland led 70 from the New York Hudson River area to settle in the Connecticut Western Reserve. New settlers arrived slowly, such as the founders of Youngstown.

Speculators played an important role in the rapid settlement of many towns during the 1790s. Israel Ludlow, one speculator, founded Hamilton and Dayton in 1795. Nathaniel Massie set up a site that grew into Manchester and another into Chillicothe. Columbus, Portsmouth, Xenia, Caesarville, and several others founded during the 1796–1803 period also began as a land speculator's dream.

Nineteenth Century

By the 1800s U.S. Census, Ohio had a population of 45,365 and 7 counties. While the counties along the Ohio River had most of the population, the northern section was also growing. The settlement founded by Moses Cleaveland that was to become Cleveland had a population of 1,203. Aside from its fertile lands, the state was strategically situated to attract settlement. The Ohio River was a major route for the South- and West-bound migrants.

With the added population came the interest in better governance and statehood, for the huge Northwest Territory distances had proven prohibitive for law and order. Although Chillicothe became the capital of the Northwest Territory in 1800, residents of the Ohio area wanted statehood. Attracted by the three additional electoral votes they assumed would ensue, congressional Republicans invited Ohio in 1802 to draft a constitution. As a sweetener, they joined Ohio to the eastern states by extending the National Road. The 1802 federal Enabling Act allowed these residents to form Ohio, the first to be created from the Northwest Territory.

The state's first constitution was modeled after Tennessee's, which eliminated property requirements for voting and placed effective power in the legislature with a two-year weak governor. It also recognized the rights of only white men, limiting office holders to white males over 21 years. In 1803, President Thomas Jefferson (1743–1826) signed the legislation making Ohio the 17th state of the Union.

With statehood, migration to Ohio quickened. Over 250,000 lived in the state by 1812. Most new settlers bought their land from the government land offices, though some went to speculators offering titles from the U.S. or Virginia Military Districts or the Refugee Tract which the U.S. Congress had established for Canadians who helped the American Revolution. The migration was encouraged by the federal Land Law of 1820, which made land in the public domain for sale at an 80-acre minimum at $1.25 an acre.

The state's 227,843 population had shifted further northward by the 1810 Census. Following the War of 1812, Amish and Mennonite migrants from Pennsylvania began arriving. Most were German and spoke a German dialect called Pennsylvania Dutch. Several Quakers were among these early settlers, particularly in the east and south.

Not all immigration or residence was encouraged. In 1817, the Ohio Supreme Court decided that unnaturalized residents could not vote. Later that year, the government informed representatives of the six American Indian nations still owning land in Ohio that they had to cede their claims and move to either a reservation or land across the Mississippi.

Black rights in Ohio were strictly curtailed by the so-called Black Laws of 1804 and 1807. Free blacks were forbidden to join the military, to testify against a white man, and (mostly) to attend public school. Newspapers carried ads for the return of runaway slaves. Blacks who entered the state were even required to post a $500 bond. Most blacks did unskilled labor for white employers because they were excluded from office or skilled craft work. A very few were small farmers. Some went north to Cleveland and Sandusky for railroad, dock, hotel, and barber jobs.

Despite this, the black population continued to grow. The 1820 U.S. Census found 4,723 free "colored" persons in Ohio, representing a 148.7 percent jump from 1810. The state ranked 12th in the number of free blacks in 1820 and 6th in 1850 with 25,279. That the black percentage of the total population remained miniscule did not matter and prejudice grew.

The state passed its first school law in 1821, beginning a curious practice that featured passing new laws annually and then undoing them the next year. Public education was extended to African Americans by an 1848 law.

Other members of religious sects arrived. Shakers moved into Lebanon and Shaker Heights, Cleveland. The Church of Jesus Christ of Latter-Day Saints (Mormons) moved to Kirtland from New York in 1831, and their number increased to about 25,000 by 1838. Hostility against the Mormons arose, aided by questionable land speculation and unchartered banking activities by some of the Mormons. This was aggravated by the Panic of 1837s dire economic impact. Fearing public wrath and official sanction, the Mormons hastily moved to Missouri in 1838, leaving a few ex-converts behind.

In 1825, construction of the 363-mile Erie Canal was completed, linking New York City and the eastern seaboard to the Great Lakes. The canal was a major route for trade and migration, and farm products from Ohio now could be shipped more economically to markets than via the Mississippi River. Port cities like Buffalo eventually grew into metropolises. Beginning around the mid-1820s, Ohio led other states in building canals, authorizing the Ohio Canal and the Miami and Erie Canal (which opened in 1833 and 1834, respectively). Numerous small feeder canals were also constructed, giving much of Ohio waterway access to the multitude of distant markets.

Before 1825, the Irish who had immigrated to Ohio were mostly Ulster Protestants, mainly Scotch Irish. A large influx of Catholics from southern Ireland came after 1830, primarily because of political unrest aggravated by famine. Many first worked on the Ohio and Erie Canal and the Miami and Erie Canal. Once railroads arrived, many Irish helped lay the track. Comprising some 22 percent of pre-1850 immigration traffic, Irish immigration tended to settle in towns and cities, primarily the southern lowlands. Catholic nuns from Europe arrived after 1824 to help in education, charities, and nursing. By 1850, the Irish were the second-largest immigrant group in Cincinnati. Prejudice soon arose, and the "Papists" were targets of discrimination. Some neighborhoods saw Protestants leaving after Catholic families moved in.

Most immigrants concentrated in one section. The English mainly settled in the Western Reserve, the French immigrants massed in southeastern Ohio, the Swiss in the Pennsylvania Dutch regions as well as Monroe and Tuscarawas counties, and the Canadians went from the Refugee Tract to other areas with existent English-speaking communities. Early Ohio settlers also included many former New Jersey residents, who migrated to lands that were part of the ill-fated 1788 Symmes Purchase (also known as the Miami Purchase), a 311,682-acre real estate venture in southwestern Ohio led by New Jersey judge John Cleves Symmes (1742–1814). Many of the southern migrants were from Virginia and settled in the west-central region. Similar to the New England influence, there were many large farms here, primarily the I-house style of dwelling (long brick houses with a double porch), many Scotch Irish, and Presbyterian in religion. German immigrants moved to the Scioto and Miami valleys and in Auglaize, Stark, and Tuscarawas counties. Cincinnati, Cleveland, and other large cities also received many German immigrants.

White residents alarmed by the increase in the African American population led a race riot in Cincinnati in 1829. Later that year, Cincinnati's government considered reviving the almost-dormant 1807 state legislation that required a $500 bond for any free African American to stay in Ohio. Although a public meeting voted not to give funds to African Americans to leave, many did leave for other states and Canada. This racism is especially ironic given the extensive advocacy for abolition during this period.

German emigrants began arriving following the 1830 and 1848 German revolutions and were purchasing their own homes by 1840. By 1850, Germans constituted 23 percent of Cincinnati, then Ohio's largest city. Many Germans also settled in Columbus, Lancaster, Chillicothe, and Marietta. In most of these communities, German names in gold letters were displayed over the names of retail stores. Other European immigrants, particularly from eastern Europe, began arriving soon after.

In the 1830s and 1840s, there was much confusion and agitation caused by some religious groups' advocacy of temperance and anti-slavery. In the Ohio legislature, a committee made a report recommending federal support for colonization society and stricter state law against free black settlement in the state.

The city of Cincinnati prospered as it became an important industrial and meatpacking center in the early 1830s. Its economy was extremely diversified, manufacturing shoes, steam engines, steamboats, furniture, and the like. The city was the leading furniture-manufacturing center by the 1840s, as well as one of the largest brewing and distilling centers. German immigrants formed mutual-aid societies, among several occupational groups. In 1840, Cincinnati had almost one-half of all capital invested in manufacturing in Ohio and was the main production center for readymade clothing, employing over 9,000 women doing piecework at home. Unfortunately, the crowded conditions and primitive hygiene helped a particularly bad plague devastate Cincinnati and Columbus in 1833.

During this period, the remainder of Ohio's Native American population was forced to migrate. Their numbers had been reduced to approximately 2,000 by one 1831 estimate. In the 1830s, even the reservations came under extreme pressure, and the 1842 closing of the Wyandot Reservation at Upper Sandusky was the last in the state.

Ohio's population and economic development was aided by the construction of railroads to crisscross the state between 1847 and 1853. By 1855, most of the state's interior sections were within a railroad trip to Lake Erie. With all of the changes in the state, many began agitating for a new constitution. The subsequently adopted 1851 constitution granted the right to vote to all white male citizens with one year's residence, with blacks being counted for representational apportionment only.

The 1850 Census found a state population of 1,980,329. Some 61.6 percent were Ohio-born, 27.1 percent had been born in other states (200,634 in Pennsylvania), and foreign-born comprised 11.1 percent. Of the foreign-born, the most numerous nationalities were German (111,257 or 5.6 percent of the state's population), Irish (51,562), English (25,660), French (7,375), Welsh (5,849), and Scotch (5,232). The state's people were young, large families were predominant, over 30 percent were under 10, and a fractional 1.3 percent were older than 70 years. Ohio was still primarily an agricultural state. In 1849, it ranked first in corn and wool production and second in wheat.

In 1850, Ohio had the sixth-highest number of blacks, with 25,279 or 1.3 percent of the total population. Most were employed as unskilled laborers, and some worked in the wharves along the Ohio River. While most blacks lived in southern Ohio, there was a significant increase of black population in the North beginning in the 1840s. Many came to work in growing industrial towns like Cleveland and Sandusky. There were 1,233 blacks in Columbus (6 percent of the total), and 3,172 in Cincinnati, or about 3 percent of its population.

Ohio was changed profoundly by the national Industrial Revolution of 1850–1880. Already ranking fourth in the value of its manufactured goods in 1850, the state became increasingly industrialized, urbanized, and ethnically diversified. But these changes also stimulated prejudice and reaction.

Tremendous advances in transportation made the development possible. There was a boom in railroad construction in the 1850s, with the total miles of track increasing 10-fold. During this railroad development, there were significant battles over rates, right of ways, administration, and taxation. The canals were rendered obsolete. Ohio River traffic was high during the early 1850s, but frozen during the Civil War and though it never totally recovered, it continued through subsidy and revival. Several cities were transformed into major industrial centers. Cleveland became the largest oil-refining center in the nation, and its population ballooned from 17,034 in 1850 to 160,146 in 1880. Similarly, Columbus turned into an industrial-commercial center after its railroad and canal links were completed. Springfield and Dayton grew into agricultural implement-manufacturing centers. The northeastern cities of Akron, Canton, and Youngstown were part of the development of one of the major iron and steel areas in the country.

The drastic changes stimulated reaction. During the 1850s, many white state residents joined the new Know-Nothing (American) Party, which was strongly opposed to new immigration, especially Irish. This led to many Ohio towns passing ordinances that required dead Irish Americans to be buried in segregated, Irish-only cemeteries. This rise in prejudice also again targeted Blacks. A stricter "black law" also was enacted in 1859, changing voting requirements from "white" defined as more than half white by blood to "white" not with "a distinct and visible admixture of African blood." Though the law later was declared unconstitutional by the state's Supreme Court, the prejudice and discrimination continued.

Perhaps because of this anti-immigrant surge, the percentage of immigrants declined in the second half of the nineteenth century. In 1860, 328,249 immigrants lived in Ohio or about 14 percent of the state's population. This fell to 11 percent by 1900, though the number of immigrants had risen to 458,734.

The anti-immigrant surge was also stimulated by a change in the origination of those arriving. After 1880, most came from southern and eastern Europe and were less educated and skilled than previous immigrants. Further, there were a number of blacks who migrated from the South to Ohio during the latter part of the nineteenth century. The 1890 Census counted 87,113 blacks in the state, and this grew to 96,901 by 1900. British immigration also continued, as the Welsh came to work in industry in Gallia and Jackson counties as well as in the charcoal iron industry of southern Ohio. Some also engaged in farming.

The anti-Catholic movement was an important factor in the 1891 Ohio gubernatorial election. Governor James E. Campbell was defeated by Republican William McKinley, future U.S. president, with the backing of the anti-Catholic American Protective Association.

1900 TO 1945

Immigration became increasingly diverse around the beginning of the twentieth century, though the old groups kept arriving. For example, many Irish continued to immigrate and comprised over 13 percent of all immigrants by 1900. But the overall trend for the immigrants' home country to be southern or eastern Europe accelerated after 1900. Many from Poland, Italy, Hungary, and Russia had arrived by 1920 to take jobs in the greatly expanding industrial cities, coming because of political and economic pressures overseas and the growing opportunities in the expanding economy. This rapid influx of new immigrant groups especially went to the larger northeastern urban areas. In Cleveland, 75.5 percent of the city's population was either foreign-born or first-generation descendents of foreign-born in 1900. Cleveland had the largest Slovak community and the second-largest Hungarian community, as well as receiving many arrivals from Italy, Russia, and Poland. This huge influx changed the city's cultural life, with a profusion of Roman Catholic parishes, Eastern Orthodox churches, Jewish synagogues, social halls, and cultural gardens. In 1910, Ohio had the sixth-highest percentage of foreign-born population.

Italians also came in a wave, from about 11,000 in 1900 to 60,658, a sixfold increase, by 1920. Most settled along Lake Erie, especially in Cleveland, and took low-paying work in factories or in restaurants. Some set up businesses selling traditional Italian goods to other migrants; a few established clothing or construction companies.

Other industrializing Ohio cities, particularly Toledo and Youngstown, also had a rapid rise of eastern European immigrant groups. And although Germans and Irish continued to dominate immigration to Cincinnati, the mix of groups diversified and now included Hungarians, Italians, and Greeks. The black population also increased, and by 1900 it comprised 4.4 percent of Cincinnati's total. The state's black population grew from 111,452 in 1910 to 186,187 in 1920. Cleveland became a magnet for many immigrants because of its rapidly expanding industrial base, requiring large numbers of unskilled and semiskilled laborers. Census data for 1910 listed 14,332 Slovenes in Cleveland, making it then the third-largest Slovene city in the world.

Some of the cities formally tried to help the new arrivals. In Cleveland, an Immigration Bureau was established in 1913 to help and protect immigrants, set up after an investigation by the Cleveland Immigration League found that immigrants arriving at its train depots, especially young women, were "at the mercy of any who would misuse and misdirect them." The bureau sent officers to make certain that people greeting the new arrivals were friends and relatives, to assist with their luggage, to tag and group them by destination, and to either escort or arrange passage. Officers also registered the children and informed truant officers to guarantee school attendance (*Encyclopedia of Cleveland History* 1997).

Restrictive national legislation after World War I—such as the Literacy Act of 1917, the National Origins Act of 1921 (also called the Emergency Quota Act), and the Immigration Act of 1924—outlawed large-scale immigration and enforced quotas greatly reducing the number of Southern and Eastern Europeans who could emigrate. The 1920 Census found 678,697 foreign-born in Ohio, comprising 11.8 percent of the total state population, a decrease from the 14.0 percent discovered in the 1860 Census.

The black population continued to grow rapidly in Ohio during the 1920–1950 period, doubling in percentage terms from 3.2 percent in 1920 to 6.5 percent in 1950. This was primarily, almost exclusively, in the large cities. Cleveland's black population leaped from 34,815 in 1920s to 147,847 in 1950, Cincinnati from 30,150 to 78,196, and Columbus from 22,310 to 46,692, respectively. By 1936, Columbus, a long-time center of American Methodism, had more black Baptist than Methodist churches. After the war, when the provinces of Transylvania and Bucovina became part of Greater Romania, nearly half of the immigrant popu lation returned to their native land. In the 1920s, only about 6,000 Romanians were left in Cleveland. In the 1920s, the initial Spanish-speaking immigrants from Mexico arrived in Cleveland. The Great Depression, as well as World War II, curtailed almost all immigration.

IMMIGRATION BETWEEN 1945 AND 1999

There was substantial immigration to Ohio immediately after World War II, but it slowed considerably. When immigration again significantly increased later, the new arrivals came from very different countries. Although the National Origins Act remained in force after World War II, there were several special congressional acts that allowed the immigration of some displaced persons from Europe. After 1948, approximately 2,000 Romanians immigrated to Cleveland, almost all political refugees, displaced persons, and expatriates. Many were skilled, and came from Transylvania and Banat. Cleveland also received many Ukrainian immigrants. In the late 1940s, Cleveland's Puerto Rican population also surged, originally drawn by wartime work in the Lorain steel mills.

In the 1960s, the second and third generations of Italian immigrants joined numerous others in the suburban exodus, and so by 1980 only 11,890 native-born Italians lived in Cleveland. Suburban Italians tended to replicate their urban experience. For example, Italian Village in Columbus became a prosperous suburb for Italian immigrants working in stone quarries, construction, and trade. Cleveland's west side Romanians also moved to the suburbs. Immigration to other large Ohio cities also declined.

Other immigrants and migrants arrived in the cities to replace those headed for suburbia. After slowly trickling in, Mexican immigration expanded substantially after the 1959 Cuban Revolution, especially to Cleveland. Cleveland's black population exceeded 251,000 by 1960. Many migrants came from depressed Appalachia. The repeal of the National Origins (Quota) Act in 1965 stimulated migration to Cleveland, among many other destinations. Chinese, Koreans, Indians (Asian), and Pakistanis arrived after restrictions were lessened on Asian immigration in the 1960s, drawn by Cleveland's colleges and medical and research industries.

During the 1970s and 1980s, wars and economic hardships in Southeast Asia, Central and South America, and the Middle East stimulated Vietnamese, Guatemalans, and Palestinians immigration to Cleveland. After the Vietnam War ended, about 13,500 Vietnamese immigrated, and the Greater Cleveland's Vietnamese population was 1,900 in 1995.

The 1990 Census discovered that over 50 percent of the foreign-born in the metro had European origins. Traditional older European groups, such as Poles and Italians, were still numerous. After the collapse of the Soviet Union, the city received its immigrants. Economic problems and ethnic conflicts in Eastern Europe pushed more immigrants, such as the Bosnian refugees that came in the early 1990s. In that decade, Ohio's foreign-born population increased 30.7 percent, but this was the seventh-lowest increase among all states. Cleveland welcomed new immigrants from the Pacific Rim, Mexico, and South America.

POST-2000 IMMIGRATION TRENDS

The end of the twentieth century brought a wave of non-European immigrants to Ohio, mostly from Latin America. Since 2000, the foreign-born population has grown substantially more diverse. Most have been legal, for a 2000 study found that less than 20 percent of Ohio's foreign-born are undocumented. In 2002, there were an estimated 50–75,000 undocumented immigrants in the state.

Supporters of providing a path to citizenship for immigrants deliver petitions to Speaker Boehner's Ohio district office during an immigration rally in west Chester, Ohio, on September 4, 2013. The umbrella group Alliance for Citizenship says it has collected hundreds of thousands of petitions urging Boehner to bring up immigration reform for a vote. (AP Photo/ Tom Uhlman)

As of the 2010 Census, Latino immigrants were over a fifth of Ohio's total foreign-born population. Many were from Mexico. Asians were now the largest immigrant group, comprising 36.6 percent of foreign-born residents, with Europeans next with 28.1 percent and Africans with 10.1 percent. The 2010 Census discovered that over 190,000 are of Asian descent. Some 6 percent of residents speak a language at home other than English.

Immigration continues to be a fertile source of new Ohio residents. One of the largest recent sources of immigrants is refugees from Somalia. Since war broke out in Somalia in the early 1990s, Somalis have settled across the United States, and the Columbus area has one of the highest concentrations. Some 45,000 Somalis have settled in central Ohio between 2000 and 2009.

Another of Ohio's fastest-growing ethnic groups is the Spanish-speaking population. The 2010 Census found that over 350,000 residents were of Hispanic descent, a 40 percent increase from 2000. Most of the Spanish-speaking population is located in the larger cities.

TOPICAL ESSAYS

Undocumented Immigration Controversy

The national debate over undocumented immigration has been going on for some years. In 2007, Republican state legislator Bob Latta won the Fifth District because he criticized his opponent for supporting healthcare that would cover undocumented immigrants. A 2007 Quinnipiac University poll found that residents opposed to allowing undocumented immigrants to have driver's licenses, in favor of constructing a fence along the Mexican–U.S. border and creating a national ID card for legal residents and citizens, and opposed to giving free public education to children of undocumented immigrants.

In 2009, Ohio announced that drivers who cannot provide adequate identification to police may go to jail, undocumented immigrants could be deported, and the state could cancel the registrations of vehicles driven by undocumented immigrants. This policy subsequently was upheld by a Franklin County Common Pleas Court Magistrate later that year.

Ohio, though, was one of just a few states that did not pass an anti-immigration law in 2010 or 2011. Among those proposed was House Concurrent Resolution 11, which would have sent a message of "support" to Arizona, presumably in support of that state's strict Senate Bill 1070. Also, the Ohio Immigration Reform Initiative—which would have authorized police to question a person's immigration status if there are any suspicions that they are undocumented immigrants—did not make Ohio's November 2011 ballot. This non-action was despite a 2010 poll which found 67 percent would support a state bill strengthening border security; fining companies for employing undocumented immigrants;

Somali immigrants Saida Said, left, and Asha Mohamed, both 10, share a laugh with a fellow Somali student during their fifth grade homeroom at the Highland Avenue Elementary School in Columbus, Ohio, on June 2, 1999. A century that began with immigrants flocking to Ohio's northeast ended with a migration to the state capital. Led by thousands of Hispanics and refugees from conflicts in Africa, newcomers took advantage of low rents, low unemployment, and plenty of work in central Ohio. (AP Photo/ Mike Elicson)

and requiring undocumented immigrants to register, learn English and pay taxes or be deported.

In 2011–2012, the debate often has publicly been about the cost of undocumented immigrants. The conservative, anti-immigrant group Federation for American Immigration Reform released a 2012 study that allegedly found providing education, health care, law enforcement, and social and government services to undocumented immigrants and their dependents cost Ohio taxpayers $878 million. The report estimates that about 110,000 undocumented immigrants resided in the state in 2010, almost three times as in 2000, including over 25,000 U.S.-born children of undocumented parents eligible for all means-tested programs and benefits. It is expected that similar anti- undocumented immigration bills will be proposed for 2012–2013 and beyond.

In 2012, President Barack Obama's "Deferred Action for Childhood Arrivals" announced policy—permitting as many as 1.7 million undocumented immigrants, who immigrated as children, to get Social Security and employment—authorization cards, as well as a deportation reprieve—prompted Ohio to announce that youth who receive deferred action will also be eligible for driver's licenses.

For the future, all signs indicate that other anti-undocumented immigration bills will continue to be proposed. It will be interesting to see the degree to which Ohio—which has been the birthplace or home to eight U.S. presidents, one Whig, and seven Republicans—will mirror general American trends regarding immigration policy and reception.

NOTABLE GROUPS

CENTRAL OHIO IMMIGRANT JUSTICE

The Central Ohio Immigrant Justice (COIJ) is a Columbus-based group established in 2010. It serves the local immigrant community, particularly advocating on behalf of low-wage workers. They provide information about legal rights, referrals to services, and advocate on behalf of human rights. They have created know-your-rights brochures in this region, published in several languages, and are providing advice about how to interact with law personnel. In particular, they oppose the number of noncriminal detention and deportations that have occurred in this region and help provide immigrants with information to deal with those situations. They also oppose the Secure Communities Initiative, which establishes a relationship between U.S. Immigration and Customs Enforcement (ICE) and local authorities. This group holds that if immigrants knew their rights, many would not be unjustly detained or deported. Their public information campaign is supported by the Ohio Hispanic Coalition and some Latino-owned businesses. They have also partnered with other groups, including interfaith organizations working on social justice issues, to provide training sessions for anyone who could be stopped or detained by ICE.

BIBLIOGRAPHY

Billington, Ray Allen, and Martin Ridge. *Westward Expansion: A History of the American Frontier*. 5th ed. New York: Macmillan Publishing, 1982.

Bond, Beverley W. Jr. *The Foundations of Ohio. The History of the State of Ohio, Volume I*. Columbus: Ohio State Archeological and Historical Society, 1941.

Cesar (Post by). "Ohio Anti-Immigrant Bills Proposed." Crimmigration.com, 2011. http://crimmigration.com/2011/04/20/ohio-anti-immigrant-bills-proposed.aspx. Accessed March 29, 2014.

Encyclopedia of Cleveland History. "Immigration Bureau." *Encyclopedia of Cleveland History*, 1997. http://ech.case.edu/ech-cgi/article.pl?id=IB. Accessed March 29, 2014.

Ferroni, Charles. "Italians." *Encyclopedia of Cleveland History*, 1998. http://ech.case.edu/ech-cgi/article.pl?id=I7. Accessed March 29, 2014.

Fix, Michael E., and Jeffrey S. Passel. "Immigration and Immigrants: Setting the Record Straight." Washington, DC: Urban Institute, 2004. http://www.urban.org/publications/305184.html#fig8. Accessed March 29, 2014.

Gizzi, John. "Immigration, Taxes Fuel Latta's Big Win in Ohio." *Human Events* 63, no. 43 (2007). www.blnz.com/news/2008/05/13/Immigration_Taxes_Fuel_Lattas_Ohio… Accessed August 8, 2014.

Gordon, Ian, and Tasneem Raja. "164 Anti-Immigration Laws Passed Since 2010? A MoJo Analysis." *MotherJones*, March/April 2012. http://www.motherjones.com/politics /2012/03/anti-immigration-law-database. Accessed March 29, 2014.

Grabowski, John J. "Immigration and Migration." *Encyclopedia of Cleveland History*, 1998. http://ech.case.edu/ech-cgi/article.pl?id=IAM. Accessed March 29, 2014.

Hategan, Fr. Vasile. "Romanians." *Encyclopedia of Cleveland History*, 2002. http://ech.case .edu/ech-cgi/article.pl?id=R6. Accessed March 29, 2014.

Havighurst, Walter. *Ohio: A Bicentennial History*. New York: W. W. Norton & Company, 1976.

McDougall, W. A. *Freedom Just around the Corner: A New American History 1585–1828*. New York: HarperCollins Publishers, 2004.

Ohio Historical Society. "Irish Ohioans." Ohio History Central: An Online Encyclopedia of Ohio History, 2012. http://www.ohiohistorycentral.org/entry.php?rec=596. Accessed March 29, 2014.

Ohio History Central. "Italian Ohioans." *An Online Encyclopedia*, Ohio Historical Society, 1996. http://www.ohiohistorycentral.org/entry.php?rec=599. Accessed March 29, 2014.

Ohio Secretary of State. "Immigrants in Ohio." Profile Ohio, Ohio Secretary of State, 2011. http://www.sos.state.oh.us/SOS/ProfileOhio/ImmigrantsinOhio.aspx. Accessed March 29, 2014.

Palm-Houser, Steve. "Central Ohio Immigrant Justice Launches 'Know Your Rights' Initiative." *Columbus Unitarian Universalist Examiner*, May 5, 2011. http://www.examiner .com/article/central-ohio-immigrant-justice-launches-know-your-rights-initiative. Accessed February 24, 2014.

Passel, Jeffrey S., Randolph Capps, and Michael E. Fix. "Undocumented Immigrants: Facts and Figures." Washington, DC: Urban Institute, 2004. http://www.urban.org/publications /1000587.htm. Accessed March 29, 2014.

PR Newswire. "New Report from FAIR Finds that Illegal Immigration Costs Ohio $878 Million a Year." *PR Newswire US*, *Regional Business News*, EBSCOhost, April 20, 2012. Accessed March 29, 2014. http://www.fairus.org/news/new-report-from-fair-finds-that-illegal-immigration-costs-ohio-878-million-a-year. Accessed August 22, 2014.

Quinnipiac University Polling Institute. "November 13, 2007-Ohio Voters Reject 7–1 Driver's Licenses for Illegal Aliens, Quinnipiac University Poll Finds; but Most Would Not Deport Illegal Immigrants." Quinnipiac University, November 13, 2007. http://www.quinnipiac .edu/institutes-and-centers/polling-institute/ohio/release-detail?ReleaseID=1119. Accessed March 29, 2014.

Roseboom, Eugene H., and Francis P. Weisenburger. *A History of Ohio*. Columbus: Ohio State Archeological and Historical Society, 1953.

Stein, Mark. *How the States Got Their Shapes*. New York: Harper, 2008.

Susel, Rudolph M. "Slovenes." *Encyclopedia of Cleveland History*, 1998. http://ech.case .edu/ech-cgi/article.pl?id=S16. Accessed March 29, 2014.

Sweigart, Josh. "Poll: Ohioans Back Immigration Reform." *Middletown Journal*, 2010. http://www.middletownjournal.com/news/news/local/poll-ohioans-back-immigration -reform/nNTTY/. Accessed March 29, 2014.

Toman, James. "Vietnamese." *Encyclopedia of Cleveland History*, 1998. http://ech.case.edu/ ech-cgi/article.pl?id=V. Accessed March 29, 2014.

10TV.com. "Magistrate Sides with Ohio over Immigrant Drivers." 10TV.com, 2009. http:// www.10tv.com/content/stories/2009/12/08/story-columbus-judge-denies-lulac -lawsuit.html. Accessed March 29, 2014.

Weisenburger, Francis P. *The History of the State of Ohio*. Vol. 3. Columbus: Ohio State Archeological and Historical Society, 1941.

Wilhelm, Hubert G. H., and Allen G. Noble. "Immigration and Ethnic Heritage in Ohio to 1903: The Trek of the Immigrants." Essays presented to Carl Wittke. Rock Island, IL: Augustana College Library, 1964.

36

OKLAHOMA

Elizabeth M. McCormick

CHRONOLOGY

1541   Spanish general Francisco Vásquez de Coronado leads an expedition from Mexico through the western plains of the United States, including present-day Oklahoma, in search of Gran Quivira, a fabled city of gold and silver.

1601   Spanish explorer Don Juan de Oñate leads an expedition east from New Mexico along the Canadian river through present-day northwest Oklahoma in search of Gran Quivira.

1682'   René-Robert Cavelier, sieur de La Salle, claims the Louisiana Territory, which includes present-day Oklahoma, for France.

1719   French explorer Jean-Baptiste Bénard de La Harpe leads the first known French expedition into Oklahoma, traveling north from Louisiana up the Red River and establishes trade with the local Native American tribes.

1762   The Treaty of Fontainbleu is signed and France secretly cedes the Louisiana Territory to Spain.

1790   Congress passes the Naturalization Act of 1790, the first federal law restricting immigration to the United States.

1803   Oklahoma, having been alternately under French and Spanish rule for more than a century, becomes part of the United States following the Louisiana Purchase from France.

1830   Indian Removal Act of 1830 results in the forced relocation of Native Americans living east of the Mississippi River to the Indian Territory, a largely unsettled area west of the Mississippi River that

	includes present-day Oklahoma and Kansas, and parts of Colorado, Nebraska, and Wyoming. In exchange for their relocation, Native American tribes are promised that they will be able to live in Indian Territory without fear of further encroachment of white settlement.
1871	The Missouri Texas and Kansas Railway is laid by a substantially Irish-born work force through Indian Territory.
1872	Irish priest Michael Smyth establishes St. Patrick's Church, Oklahoma's first Catholic Church, to serve Irish rail workers settled at Atoka.
1873	Immigrant coal miners from England, Scotland, Wales, and Ireland, followed later by immigrants from Italy, Poland, Russian, and Lithuania, begin to migrate in substantial numbers to work in coal fields in the Indian Territory near McAlester, Oklahoma.
1882	Congress passes the Chinese Exclusion Act, suspending further immigration of Chinese laborers for 10 years and prohibiting Chinese nationals from becoming U.S. citizens.
1886	Chinese laborers come to Oklahoma to work on the transcontinental railroad.
1889	President William Henry Harrison issues a proclamation officially opening the Oklahoma District to non-Indian settlement and one month later 50,000 non-Indian settlers, including thousands of immigrants, enter Indian Territory to lay claim to tracts of land in the Oklahoma or Unassigned District, opened by the U.S. government for homesteading. The immigrant settlers participating in the land run of 1889 mirror the quantity and diversity of immigrants—German, Irish, Scottish, Italian, Czech, English, French, Belgian, Canadian, and Danish—coming to the United States at that time.
1889	The first Chinese immigrants settle in Guthrie, Oklahoma District, following the land run of April 1889.
1890	The federal census records 2,753 foreign-born residents in Oklahoma, 4.4 percent of the population in the Oklahoma Territory, the highest proportion of foreign-born residents in the state until 2006. The proportion of foreign-born residents in the United States that year is 14.8 percent, the highest rate ever in U.S. history.
1891	During the second Oklahoma land run, 10 Polish families stake claims and establish homesteads just east of Oklahoma City in what would later become the city of Harrah and Oklahoma's largest and most enduring Polish community.
1900–1914	German refugees fleeing religious and linguistic persecution in Russia arrive in the United States, with many settling in the western part of Oklahoma, where they form Mennonite and Lutheran communities.
1907 (November 16)	Oklahoma Territory and Indian Territory, the Twin Territories, are combined and Oklahoma becomes the 46th state of the United States.

1907–1914	As part of the Galveston Plan, thousands of Jewish refugees fleeing persecution and economic hardship in Eastern Europe are diverted from overcrowded and poverty-stricken immigrant communities in Eastern cities to Galveston, Texas, where they then disperse throughout the southwest, many settling in cities and towns in Oklahoma where they work in a variety of occupations, prosper economically and build strong cultural and social networks.
1910	The federal census records 40,084 foreign-born residents in Oklahoma, about 2.8 percent of the state's population.
1918	Multiple attacks and incidents of intimidation and persecution are carried out against the German Russian Mennonite community in Oklahoma, who are targeted because of their use of the German language and their fundamental religious opposition to war, which together are perceived as signs of disloyalty to the United States. By mid-1918, large numbers of Mennonites have left Oklahoma and migrate to Canada.
1930–1940	More than 2,000 Mexican-born residents of Oklahoma, three-quarters of the Mexican immigrants living in Oklahoma, including some legal residents and U.S. citizens, leave the state during a nationwide Mexican repatriation campaign of deportation and so-called voluntary repatriation.
1942–1945	A number of prison camps are established and operated throughout Oklahoma to detain German prisoners of war and Japanese and Italian non-combatant "enemy aliens." At one time, there are more than 30 camps holding more than 20,000 detainees.
1947	Polish freedom fighter and future justice of the Oklahoma Supreme Court Marian Peter Opala (1921–2010) immigrates to the United States and settles in Oklahoma City.
1970–1980	The number of Mexican-born residents of Oklahoma and of the United States as a whole more than doubles.
1975	The first wave of Vietnamese refugees arrives in Oklahoma following the fall of Saigon, with most settling in Oklahoma City.
1989	Nadia Comaneci, Romanian gymnast, five-time Olympic gold medalist, and first female gymnast to earn a perfect score of 10 in an Olympic event, defects from Romania and travels to the United States where she eventually settles in Oklahoma and establishes a gymnastics academy with her husband, Olympic gymnast Bart Connor.
1990	The federal census records 65,489 foreign-born residents in Oklahoma, about 2.1 percent of the state's population.
1996	Governor Frank Keating establishes the governor's Advisory Council on Latin American and Hispanic Affairs. The council is charged with "coordinating, assisting and cooperating with the efforts of state agencies to serve the needs of Hispanics, especially in the areas of culture, education, employment, health, housing, and recreation."

2000	The federal census records 131,747 foreign-born residents in Oklahoma, about 3.8 percent of the state's population. Mexicans and Mexican Americans comprised 8.1 percent of the population of Oklahoma City; 5.4 percent of the population of Tulsa; 12.6 percent of the population of Altus, the location of a major meat-processing plant; and 28.1 percent of the population of Guymon, the location of a massive corporate hog slaughterhouse and processing plant.
2006	The federal census records 175,987 foreign-born residents in Oklahoma, about 4.9 percent of the state's population.
2007 (June 29)	The Tulsa City Council passes a resolution recommending that the mayor of Tulsa direct the Tulsa Police Department to conduct immigration status checks of individuals arrested and charged with felony and misdemeanor crimes and to report those with unlawful immigration status to federal immigration authorities.
2007 (July 9)	The U.S. Immigration and Customs Enforcement (ICE) and the Tulsa County Sherriff's Office enter into an agreement authorizing certain sheriff's department officials to enforce federal immigration law.
2007 (November 1)	The Oklahoma Taxpayer and Citizen Protection Act (House Bill [HB] 1804) is enacted.
2008	U.S. ICE establishes a permanent office in Tulsa.
2011	The federal census records 208,857 foreign-born residents in Oklahoma, about 5.5 percent of the state's population.

HISTORICAL OVERVIEW

Early Years to World War II

The history of immigration to and immigrants in Oklahoma is a story with two distinct parts. The first chapter of Oklahoma immigration history is a story of primarily European immigration that took place in a series of brief episodes of large-scale migration into Oklahoma's vast and largely unpopulated territory. At the end of the Civil War, the discovery of the plentiful coal resources in southeast Oklahoma led to a new wave of nonnative immigrants coming to work in the mines and coalfields. In the beginning, most of these laborers were Scottish, Irish, English, and Welsh who came to Oklahoma from mining operations in Pennsylvania. As the industry grew and the demand for labor increased, immigrant miners from southern and eastern Europe also began to arrive, first from other mines in the eastern United States and eventually directly from their native lands. In 1890, Mexican immigrants began to arrive in Oklahoma to find work in the mines, many having left their jobs in Mexican coal and silver mines and on railroad work crews in the United States for better wages in the Oklahoma mines. From the beginning, the majority of Oklahoma coal miners were either foreign-born or second-generation immigrants, and this continued to be the case through the opening of Indian Territory to non-Indian settlement in 1889 and Oklahoma statehood in 1907, when 55 percent of Oklahoma coal miners were foreign-born. In addition, as a growing number of the nonnative miners made arrangements for family members to join them and made permanent homes in Oklahoma, the size of the immigrant population in cities and towns throughout the coal-mining region of southeastern Oklahoma grew significantly.

Throughout the early years of statehood, the immigrant population in Oklahoma was quite diverse but primarily European, with the greatest number of immigrants coming from Germany to the farmlands in the northern part of the state. Large numbers of Russian, Italian, Irish, English, and Austrian immigrants also arrived in Oklahoma, some drawn by opportunities in farming and ranching, and others looking for work in the coal mines and oil fields, on the railroad, and in the growing manufacturing sector. In addition to the immigrants attracted to Oklahoma by economic opportunities, many immigrants arrived in Oklahoma after fleeing persecution and oppression in their home countries. Second- and third-generation descendants of the Italian, German, Irish, Czech, Russian, Scottish, and Mexican immigrants who settled in Oklahoma in the late nineteenth and early twentieth centuries still remain in Oklahoma today and continue to contribute to the rich cultural heritage of the state. The significant role played by these pioneer immigrant communities in the early history of the state is memorialized in the many cities and towns bearing names that reflect the diverse immigrant origins of the state: Prague, Erin Springs, Shamrock, Poteau, Verdigris, Cimarron, Berlin, and Choteau. Additionally, cultural festivals and other celebrations around the state regularly pay tribute to this heritage.

European immigration to Oklahoma declined sharply over the twentieth century, and though well over half of Oklahoma residents claimed European ancestry in the 2010 Census, currently fewer than one-half of 1 percent of Oklahoma residents are European-born. In fact, from 1890 to 1970, the percentage of foreign-born residents of Oklahoma continued to decline and during that time the composition of the immigrant population began to shift as fewer Europeans and greater numbers of Latin American, especially Mexican, and Asian newcomers made their homes in Oklahoma.

Significant numbers of Mexican immigrants first began arriving in Oklahoma in the early twentieth century. In response to social and economic conditions following the 1910 Revolution in Mexico, thousands of Mexicans came to Oklahoma where they worked in the cotton fields, coal mines, oil fields, slaughterhouses, quarries, and a variety of other, unskilled jobs in the state. Many Mexicans also worked on the railroads where from 1900 until the late 1920s, the majority of the maintenance crews were Mexicans. Initially, Mexican immigrants in Oklahoma were primarily single men who moved to follow largely seasonal work, and frequently crossed back and forth across the border to visit families at home. The transitory lifestyle of the Mexican laborer was considered an asset by many, who believed that Mexicans made less desirable citizens and were less likely to integrate into American society. Eventually employers came to realize that a more stable, permanent workforce was an asset, so they began to help workers bring their families from Mexico to settle in Oklahoma near their worksites. By 1930, there were approximately 7,500 Mexicans living in Oklahoma, and small Mexican communities had been established in Oklahoma City, Tulsa, Sapulpa, and other towns along the railroad.

U.S. immigration officials did little to interrupt the inflow of Mexican workers into the railroad yards, mines, farms, and meatpacking plants of Oklahoma until 1929. "Cheap Mexican labor was in great demand by a host of America's burgeoning industries. The railroads, mining companies and agribusinesses sent agents to greet immigrants at the border, where they extolled the rewards of their respective enterprises. Border officials felt no duty to impede the labor flow into the southwest" (Boisson 2006). In addition, restrictive federal immigration laws of 1917 and 1924 did little to hinder the flow of Mexican immigration into the United States. Nevertheless, the Depression brought increased hostility toward Mexican workers, along with complaints that Mexicans were taking jobs and social services from needy Americans, and eventually led to a government plan to remove as many Mexicans as possible from the United States. The plan was jointly implemented by federal, state, and local government officials through a pervasive campaign of intimidation, harassment, deportation, and "voluntary repatriation" (Johnson 2005, 55).Immigration agents, often in cooperation with local law enforcement, targeted areas with the highest concentrations of Mexican residents where they rounded up Mexicans and Mexican Americans and returned them to Mexico. The extent to which the Mexican Repatriation campaign impacted Mexican residents of Oklahoma is not known, but there is no doubt that deliberate efforts to drive Mexicans from the state were made. Oklahoma City was the target of immigration raids in 1933 and 1934 that led to the deportation of an unknown number of Mexicans. There are also records of trainloads of allegedly voluntary repatriates departing from Oklahoma City, many of whom were enticed by city officials offering to pay their train fares. Other Mexicans were undoubtedly driven from Oklahoma by a combination of the dire economic situation, the unavailability of work, and a prevalent anti-Mexican sentiment. At the end of the decade, three-quarters of the Mexican residents of Oklahoma were gone.

World War II to the Present

During the labor shortages of World War II, Mexicans were brought back to Oklahoma to work on the railroad (Driscoll 1999, 143) or in meatpacking plants and cotton fields as part of the Bracero Program. Many more are believed to have come illegally during the 20 years of the Bracero Program with a new wave of undocumented Mexican migrants coming to the United States in response to a demand for agricultural and other unskilled workers that far outstripped the number of available legal *braceros*. In the 1960s, significant numbers of Mexicans and Mexican Americans escaped mistreatment and discrimination in agricultural jobs in the Texas Rio Grande Valley and moved north to Oklahoma to secure more stable, year-round employment. Still, the number of Mexican-born residents of Oklahoma did not again reach 1930s levels until 1980, following a decade in which the total population of Mexicans living in the United States more than doubled. Mexican immigration to Oklahoma continued to increase throughout the 1980s despite a weak economy that led large numbers of native-born Oklahoma residents to leave the state.

With the passage of the Immigration Reform and Control Act (IRCA) of 1986, thousands of Mexicans living in Oklahoma took advantage of the opportunity to legalize their status, and Oklahoma was one of 10 states with the greatest number of immigrants applying for legal status under IRCA's amnesty provisions. By 1990, according to the Pew Hispanic Center (2008), Mexicans had become the largest immigrant group in Oklahoma, and that remains true today. As they had in the past, the Mexican residents who arrived in Oklahoma in the 1980s and 1990s settled primarily in Oklahoma City and Tulsa, but smaller concentrations could be found in small towns and rural areas near the farms, ranches, and processing plants where they found work.

By 2006, almost 50 percent of the immigrants living in Oklahoma were Mexican, placing Oklahoma eighth in the nation in the percentage of its foreign-born residents born in Mexico, and well above the representation of Mexicans in the total foreign-born population of the United States. Of the approximately 85,000 Mexican immigrants residing in Oklahoma in 2006, roughly one in four entered the United States after 1990, with up to 54,000 of these believed to be undocumented.

Although the most recent arrivals among Asian immigrants in Oklahoma, Vietnamese immigrants have been the second-largest immigrant group and the largest Asian American group in the state since 1990. In the 2010 Census, more than 16,000 Oklahoma residents were of Vietnamese ancestry. Before the arrival of thousands of Indochinese refugees in Oklahoma in the mid-1970s, the total foreign-born Asian population of Oklahoma had never exceeded 1,000. In the next decade, more than 20,000 immigrants from across Asia, including substantial numbers from China, Korea, India, the Philippines, and Japan, moved to Oklahoma. Following the U.S. Military withdrawal from Vietnam in 1975 and the passage of the Indochinese Migration and Refugee Act of 1975, the first wave of Vietnamese refugees began to arrive in Oklahoma; many were educated professionals fleeing persecution in Vietnam. Many in that initial wave were brought to Oklahoma from Fort Chafee, Arkansas, by Vietnam veteran and future Oklahoma state treasurer Ellis Edwards and general Clyde Watkins, who together sponsored hundreds of Vietnamese refugees, helped them find jobs, homes, and other services to help them resettle in and around Oklahoma City. The Vietnamese settled in an area of Oklahoma City, now known as Little Saigon, which grew into a thriving commercial district with grocery stores, restaurants, and other businesses. While Oklahoma City is still home to the state's largest Vietnamese community, today there are Vietnamese residing in towns and cities throughout the state.

According to estimates of the U.S. Census Bureau, the foreign-born population of Oklahoma grew more than threefold between 1990 and 2011, from 65,489 to 208,857. Those numbers represent an increase in the percentage of foreign-born Oklahoma residents from 2.1 percent to 5.2 percent of the total population. While these increases are striking, because the overall foreign-born population of the United States grew at an unprecedented rate between 1990 and 2011, Oklahoma's overall ranking in terms of its percentage of foreign-born residents and total number of foreign-born residents did not experience dramatic shifts during that period. In 2011, Oklahoma was home to approximately one-half of 1 percent of the total foreign-born population of the United States.

Oklahoma's immigrant community consists of a diversity of nationalities and ethnic groups, but the vast majority of the foreign-born residents are Latino/a. Latino/as are also the fastest-growing minority group in Oklahoma. Between 1990 and 2010, Oklahoma's Latino/a population—including both citizens and noncitizens—more than quadrupled, with the percentage of Latino/a residents growing from 2.7 to 8.9 over a decade. This increase reflects both an increase in Latino/a migration into the state and to an above-average birth rate among immigrant and nonimmigrant Latino/a residents.

The extent to which undocumented immigration has contributed to the growth in Oklahoma's immigrant population since 1990 is unclear. However, of the approximately 209,000 foreign-born residents of Oklahoma in 2010, it is estimated that between 55,000 and 95,000—as many as 45 percent—were unlawfully present in the United States, a rate that exceeds the national average of approximately 28 percent of the total foreign-born population. Moreover, as is true throughout the United States, it is estimated that the majority of the undocumented immigrants residing in Oklahoma are Mexicans who arrived in the United States after 1990, but Oklahoma has not experienced the decline in the number of undocumented immigrants since 2007, which has been experienced nationally. The greatest concentrations of undocumented immigrants are in and around the Oklahoma City and Tulsa metropolitan areas. However, other far less populated areas also have seen significant growth in their undocumented immigrant populations.

The sharp increase in the immigrant population of Oklahoma impacted communities throughout the state that faced increased demands on school districts, healthcare systems, law enforcement agencies, and other service providers. Many of these communities, unaccustomed to having large numbers of immigrant residents, were often, at least initially, poorly equipped to meet the needs of a growing and diverse immigrant population. During the 1990s, community groups and social service agencies throughout Oklahoma began offering English classes, job placement services, and other immigration-related services to help immigrants integrate into their new communities. In many locations, such programs and services did not exist, so community groups worked to institute them in response to this new need. In communities like Tulsa and Oklahoma City, with a long-standing immigrant presence, the sudden growth in the Spanish-speaking population led to the restoration of English-immersion programs that had been created when the first Vietnamese refugees settled in Oklahoma in the 1970s. Across the state, hospitals, schools, and other community-based organization scrambled to keep up with the demand for services from newly arriving immigrants who did not speak English.

Employers and business owners welcomed the growing immigrant community which provided them with critical workers who were also new consumers of Oklahoma products and services. A number of Latino/a-owned businesses were established in low-income neighborhoods with a high number of newly arrived immigrants, and as they prospered they stabilized and revitalized once-declining areas.

Not everyone in Oklahoma has been welcoming or tolerant of Oklahoma's new immigrants and, by mid-2000, a backlash against the state's growing Latino/a immigrant population had emerged and ultimately led to a ballot initiative to make English the official language of Oklahoma. The ballot measure, which was eventually defeated, would have prohibited state money from being spent on translations of documents or interpreters for government services. The proponents of the initiative all conceded that providing services to non-English-speaking residents was not a significant challenge for the state—either logistically or financially—at the time the measure was introduced nor was there any evidence that the measure was motivated by a specific intent to punish or discourage undocumented immigration to Oklahoma. Rather, the measure was likely a response to dramatic increases in the Latino/a immigrant population in the state, and critics of the initiative contended that the real intent was to stop the immigration of all Latino/as to Oklahoma. This measure would be followed by a number of other efforts by state and local officials in Oklahoma over the next dozen years to respond to the changing complexion of Oklahoma's immigrant community.

TOPICAL ESSAYS

Development, Relief, and Education for Alien Minors Act Oklahoma

Development, Relief, and Education for Alien Minors (DREAM) Act Oklahoma (DAOK) is a local affiliate of United We Dream, a national immigrant youth advocacy network founded in 2008 to ensure equal access to higher education for immigrant youth. DAOK members work to educate the public and lawmakers about the benefits of passing the DREAM Act, federal bipartisan legislation first introduced in 2001. The DREAM Act would make qualifying undocumented immigrant youth eligible for a six-year conditional path to citizenship that requires, among other things, the completion of a college degree or two years of military service. While Oklahoma congressional representatives and senators have almost universally opposed the passage of the DREAM Act, DAOK members have been successful in other efforts to enhance immigrant youth access to education in Oklahoma. DAOK members' efforts were instrumental in defeating efforts of the Oklahoma state legislature in 2011 to repeal in-state tuition benefits for undocumented immigrant students at state colleges and universities. In addition, after the June 2012 announcement by the Obama administration of a program to allow certain undocumented immigrant students to apply for temporary immigration relief, DAOK also played a critical role in educating immigrant students in Oklahoma about the application and eligibility requirements for this program.

Guymon, Oklahoma

Guymon, a city of 11,500 people in the center of the Oklahoma panhandle, is the one of the most ethnically diverse cities in the state and the only city in Oklahoma where Latino/as are a majority. Guymon's significant Latino/a immigrant population are linked substantially to the opening of a large hog slaughterhouse and processing facility owned by Seaboard Foods in 1995. Unable to hire enough workers locally, Seaboard recruited immigrant workers to fill many of the more than 2,000 jobs at that facility. Seaboard's immigrant employees are of diverse origins, including workers from Eritrea, Ethiopia, Somalia, Sudan, Burma, Laos, and Vietnam. The vast majority, however, had come from Mexico, Guatemala, Honduras, and elsewhere in Central and South America. Before the arrival of the Seaboard facility, Guymon already had a Latino/a population that was many times larger than the state average, but the influx of immigrant workers after the plant opened in 1995 had a transforming impact on the complexion of the Guymon community. According to the 2010 Census, 52 percent of Guymon residents are Latino/a, compared to 9 percent for the state as a whole. Additionally, 26 percent of the residents of Guymon are foreign-born and 39.9 percent of the households speak a language other than English at home, as compared to statewide rates of 5.4 and 9 percent, respectively. Guymon's diversity is remarkable even in comparison to figures for the United States as a whole, where 12.8 percent of the population is foreign-born, 16.7 percent is Latino/a, and 20.3 percent of households speak a language other than English. Given the prevalence of undocumented workers in the meat-processing industry, generally, it is likely that some percentage of the immigrant workers at Seaboard are undocumented and were not counted in the U.S. Census, so the actual numbers may be greater. Local law enforcement agencies at one point estimated that half of the population of Guymon were undocumented immigrants and complained that federal immigration agencies had little interest in taking custody of immigration violators apprehended by Guymon law enforcement officers. In late 2012, U.S. ICE announced an investigation at the Seaboard facility in Guymon but no further information was available and no arrests were made. The demographic change in Guymon since the mid-1990s is reflected most notably in the Guymon Public Schools, which have classrooms bursting beyond capacity with students, the majority of whom do not speak English as a first language. The change in the business community is also apparent, with Spanish-language signs; stores selling quinceañera dresses, tortillas, and other Mexican goods and groceries; and a growing number of Latino/a-owned businesses. By any measure, the influx of immigrant workers and their families to Guymon has created an economic boom for the community, even if the rapid demographic shift has brought its own set of challenges.

HUMAN TRAFFICKING AND THE JOHN PICKLE COMPANY

In 2001, the John Pickle Company, a Tulsa-based oil industry parts manufacturer, recruited and brought to the United States a group of 53 highly skilled workers, including high-tech welders, fitters, electricians, engineers, and cooks, from India to work in the Pickle facility in Tulsa. The men, most of whom left behind families and secure jobs in India, were promised a two-year position with the Pickle Company, with attractive pay and working conditions, health insurance, housing, and the possibility of lawful permanent residence in the future. When they arrived, the workers' immigration documents were taken by the employer and they were subjected to a number of abuses, including working long hours at much less than minimum wage, living in a run-down and overcrowded dormitory on the company's property without adequate meals, and being prevented from leaving the company grounds outside of working hours by intimidation and threats of deportation. When the workers complained, several were fired and put on a plane to India. Eventually, with the help of a local minister, five of the workers were able to escape, tell their story, and get help for themselves and those who remained. Four months after arriving, all of the workers had left the facility. The workers, later joined by the Equal Employment Opportunity Commission, filed suit against the John Pickle Company alleging that the company had subjected them to fraud, false imprisonment, violations of the Fair Labor Standards Act, and discrimination under Title VII of the Civil Rights Act.

In 2006, a federal judge in Tulsa ruled that the John Pickle Company had subjected the workers to fraud and deceit, inadequate pay, substandard living conditions, false imprisonment, lockdowns with an armed guard, phone tapping, food rationing, restrictions on freedom to worship, degrading job assignments, ethnic slurs, intimidation, the nonpayment of wages earned, and civil rights violations based on national origin and ethnicity, and awarded the workers almost $1.3 million. The workers eventually obtained visas which allowed them to remain in the United States and to bring their families from India. John Pickle's Tulsa plant shut down in late 2002 and, in late 2012, the company had still failed to pay the workers as ordered by the court.

Immigration Enforcement at the Tulsa County Jail

In July 2007, an agreement was entered into between the Tulsa County Sheriff's Office and U.S. ICE The agreement authorizes up to 40 designated sheriff's deputies, after completing four weeks of training, to perform federal immigration law enforcement functions under the supervision of ICE officers. In the first year of operation, 287(g) detention officers in the Tulsa County Jail detained 1,777 immigrants, of whom more than 1,300 have been removed or placed in removal proceedings (Vaughn and Edwards 2009). Between 2007 and late 2012, the Tulsa 287(g) officers reportedly detained and turned over to federal immigration officials more than 14,000 noncitizens.

The Tulsa County Sheriff also entered into an intergovernmental service agreement with ICE which allows the Sheriff's Office to provide detention facilities at the Tulsa County Jail for immigrants detained pending removal proceedings. ICE pays the jail $54.13 per day for each inmate held only on immigration charges and the Sheriff Department acknowledges that the jail agreement with ICE is a moneymaker for them. In August 2008, when a U.S. Department of Justice report revealed a high number of detainee deaths, unsanitary conditions, and excessive use of force at the Oklahoma County Jail, the Tulsa County Jail became the primary immigration detention facility in Oklahoma. The Tulsa County jail has 94 beds for immigration detainees, and they are almost always filled.

Oklahoma Taxpayer and Citizen Protection Act (HB 1804)

The Oklahoma Taxpayer and Citizen Protection Act (HB 1804) passed the Oklahoma legislature with an overwhelming bipartisan majority and was signed into law by Governor Brad Henry in May 2007. At the time it went into effect, HB

Undocumented inmates are seen loading a bus at the John Lilley Correctional Center near Boley, Oklahoma, on July 23, 2009. The inmates were among 22 who were handed over to custody of the U.S. Immigration and Customs Enforcement as part of a new state law that allowed inmates to be transferred for deportation if they are imprisoned for a nonviolent offense and served at least one-third of their prison sentence. Despite their nonviolent offenses, this will mean that they are put in detention (with no constitutional rights) and then deported. (AP Photo/Oklahoma House of Representatives)

1804 was widely regarded as a model state bill for targeting undocumented immigration and was described by supporters and in the media as the toughest, most punitive undocumented immigration bill in the nation. The law bars undocumented immigrants from receiving public assistance; makes it a state crime to transport, harbor, or shelter undocumented immigrants; penalizes employers who hire undocumented immigrants; restricts undocumented immigrants' access to all forms of official identification; prevents undocumented immigrant students from receiving state-funded financial aid or scholarships; and encourages local law enforcement agencies to train with federal authorities so they can assist in the apprehension of undocumented immigrants. A number of the provisions in HB 1804 mirrored existing federal immigration law. In particular, federal law had already prohibited undocumented immigrant access to public benefits for more than a decade and, since 1986, had provided sanctions for employers of undocumented immigrant workers.

Even before it went into effect on November 1, 2007, HB 1804 created fear and apprehension within Oklahoma's immigrant communities, and concern among individuals and organizations providing services to immigrants about what HB 1804 required and how it would be enforced. Three legal challenges to HB 1804 were filed almost immediately, two alleging that the statute violates the U.S. Constitution and is preempted by federal law and one raising claims under the Oklahoma Constitution. In February 2010, the Tenth Circuit Court of Appeals determined that two provisions of HB 1804, relating to the employment of undocumented immigrants, were unlawful and could not be enforced. In June 2011, the Oklahoma Supreme Court found that a third provision of HB 1804, denying bail to undocumented immigrants charged with felonies or with driving under the influence, violated the Oklahoma Constitution. The remaining provisions of HB 1804 remain in effect. However, more than six years after implementation of HB 1804, it is unclear whether any subsequent increase in immigration enforcement in Oklahoma is attributable to HB 1804 or, instead, to the implementation of federal immigration enforcement programs such as the Secure Communities Program and 287(g) cooperative agreements between U.S. ICE and local law enforcement agencies. With respect to the goal of driving undocumented immigrants from the state, HB 1804 seems also to have ultimately failed given the increase in Oklahoma's undocumented immigrant population since 2007.

There is no doubt that HB 1804 and subsequent efforts by state lawmakers to pass restrictive immigration-related laws have created a climate of fear in immigrant communities, but it appears that the overall lack of enforcement of HB 1804 and the recently thriving state economy have in the end helped to prevent the once-predicted exodus of immigrants from the state.

RESIDENT TUITION FOR UNDOCUMENTED STUDENTS AND HB 1559

In May 2003, the Oklahoma legislature approved and the governor signed a new law allowing certain undocumented immigrant students to attend Oklahoma state colleges and universities at in-state tuition rates and to apply for state financial aid. This law was HB 1559, 2003 O.S.L. 70–3242, 49th Leg., 1st Sess. (hereinafter HB 1559). The law provided this benefit to students who had lived in Oklahoma for at least two years before graduating from high school or obtaining a GED. The inspiration for the bill came from various reports and news accounts of talented high school students and long-time residents of Oklahoma who were accepted at state universities but would have been unable to attend without a change in the law. The bill's sponsor in the House of Representatives, Kevin Calvey, and other supporters of the bill argued that the qualifying students were Oklahomans and future Americans and that offering this opportunity to them was the right thing to do. Despite some opposition from legislators who objected to the cost of the program and who argued that it encouraged and rewarded illegal behavior, the bill passed both houses of the legislature with an overwhelming majority. At the time, Oklahoma was one of only four states providing this benefit to undocumented students.

NOTABLE FIGURES/GROUPS

IMMIGRATION REFORM FOR OKLAHOMA NOW

Immigration Reform for Oklahoma Now (IRON) is a group formed in 2004 to oppose the "illegal alien invasion of America." IRON is a self-described bipartisan citizens group formed for the purpose of educating Oklahoma lawmakers and taxpayers about the costs of undocumented immigration and of calling for the enforcement of existing immigration laws and an end to public subsidies and benefits to undocumented immigrants. Carol Helm, IRON president and founder, worked closely with Representative Randy Terrill and other members of the Oklahoma legislature to secure passage of the Oklahoma Taxpayer and Citizen Protection Act (HB 1804) in 2007. IRON has been heavily involved in lobbying state legislators to introduce or support legislation to fight what Helm calls "the illegal alien invasion."

In addition to HB 1804, IRON has supported legislation declaring English the official state language of Oklahoma, a state constitutional amendment, ultimately declared unconstitutional, barring state courts from considering international or sharia law in their rulings, and a law requiring the Oklahoma State Department of Corrections to release nonviolent undocumented immigrant inmates who have served at least one-third of their state prison sentences to U.S. ICE for deportation. In 2012, IRON called on state elected officials to take action in opposition to the Obama administration's June 2012 announcement of a policy providing for temporary relief from deportation for certain undocumented noncitizen residents who have arrived in the United States as children. Carol Helm has taken IRON's message and strategies to citizen groups and legislators around the country to assist them in efforts to enact similar legislation in their states.

JOHN SULLIVAN (1965–)

John A. Sullivan was the U.S. representative for Oklahoma's First Congressional District from 2002 to 2012. Sullivan, a Republican, was initially elected in a special election months after September 11, 2001. Throughout his tenure in Congress, Sullivan focused his energy on increasing the number of immigration enforcement officers in Oklahoma and involving state and local police in immigration enforcement in the state. Soon after taking office, Sullivan criticized federal ICE officials who claimed that the apprehension of student visa violators and immigrants identified in routine traffic stops were not enforcement priorities for the agency. He pushed for the establishment of a permanent ICE presence in Tulsa and for a more formal and active role for local law enforcement agencies in the

Oklahoma former state representative Randy Terrill, left, R-Moore, and his attorney, Chris Eulberg, right, listen to opening statements in his bribery trial in Oklahoma City on October 22, 2013. Terrill is charged with offering to set up former state senator Debbe Leftwich, D-Oklahoma City, with an $80,000-a-year job at the state medical examiner's office in exchange for Leftwich's promise to withdraw as a candidate for reelection in 2010. Terrill worked closely with the group IRON to stop the immigration "invasion" and to pass anti-immigration measures. (AP Photo/Sue Ogrocki)

enforcement of federal immigration law. In 2003, Sullivan supported the Clear Law Enforcement for Criminal Alien Removal (CLEAR) Act and the related Senate Bill, the Homeland Security Enhancement Act (HSEA), which both called for increased involvement of state and local governments in the enforcement of federal immigration laws. In early 2004, as the debate over border security and related immigration reforms heated up, Sullivan and other members of the largely Republican Oklahoma congressional delegation called for border enforcement first, and opposed President George W. Bush's temporary worker proposals and related proposals which provided a mechanism for undocumented immigrants to obtain legal status.

Sullivan introduced the Secure Our Nation's Interior Act of 2005, a bill that explicitly clarified the inherent authority of state and local law enforcement agencies to enforce federal immigration laws (H.R. 4079, Section 3, 109th Cong. 2005) Sullivan's bill was supported by the anti-immigration groups Federation for American Immigration Reform (FAIR) and NumbersUSA, which had consistently maintained that local arrest authority was a critical component of successful immigration enforcement. While advocating for federal legislation to enable all state and local police to enforce federal immigration law, Sullivan also worked for three years to establish an agreement between U.S. ICE and certain Oklahoma law enforcement agencies that would allow local officers to receive training and be authorized to enforce federal immigration law. Such agreements, known as 287(g) agreements, had been authorized by federal law since 1996, but in 2005 only two states had signed agreements in place. Sullivan argued that 287(g) agreements were a necessity, but some Oklahoma law enforcement officials were skeptical about the program, including the chief of the Tulsa Police, who expressed concern that the program would send the wrong message to Tulsa's Latino/a community and discourage crime victims and witnesses from working with police. Eventually, both the Tulsa Police Department and the State Highway Patrol declined to participate in the 287(g) program, but in July 2007, Sullivan secured the participation of the Tulsa County Sheriff's Office in the 287(g) program. In September 2008, Sullivan also announced that he had secured the establishment of a permanent ICE office in Tulsa, which would be located in the Tulsa County Jail.

Sullivan was a very vocal opponent of the Obama administration's legal challenge to Arizona's Senate Bill (SB) 1070 and the administration's proposal to downsize the 287(g) program. In response, he supported congressional legislation in 2012 that would prohibit federal funding for lawsuits seeking to invalidate state laws that support the enforcement of federal immigration laws and that would prevent the administration from terminating any 287(g) agreements. In June 2012, Sullivan lost the Republican primary to Tea Party candidate Jim Bridenstine.

RANDY TERRILL, (1969–)

Randy Terrill is a former member of the Oklahoma House of Representatives elected to his first term in 2004. A conservative Republican, Terrill was the author and primary sponsor of the Oklahoma Taxpayer and Citizen Protection Act (HB 1804), a comprehensive state law purporting to combat undocumented immigration in Oklahoma. At the time the law was passed in 2007, it was considered the strictest state immigration law in the country. In presenting the bill, Terrill criticized the federal government for not enforcing federal immigration laws and promised that his bill would succeed in stemming undocumented immigration where the federal government had failed. An outspoken proponent of state involvement in immigration regulation and enforcement, Terrill sponsored a number of other restrictionist immigration-related measures including bills declaring English the state's official language, eliminating the availability of a Spanish-language driver's license exam, and defining Oklahoma citizenship to exclude children born in the United States to certain noncitizen parents. Terrill's efforts have had the backing of national and local anti-immigration groups, including the FAIR, the Immigration Reform Law Institute (IRLI), and IRON. Terrill's efforts in 2011 to pass an even stricter immigration measure that he referred to as "Arizona-plus," referencing Arizona's controversial SB 1070, encountered strong opposition from community-based, religious, and civil rights groups and ultimately failed. Terrill, who was the subject of a corruption investigation in 2010 and subsequent felony bribery charges, did not seek reelection to the Oklahoma legislature in 2012.

BIBLIOGRAPHY

Baker, Rhoda. "Our Lives Are Here: Why People from around the World Come to Live in Tulsa." *Tulsa World*, November 8, 1991. lawprofessors.typepad.com/files/oklahoma taxpayer.doc. Accessed August 8, 2014.

Balderrama, Francisco E., and Raymond Rodriguez. *Decade of Betrayal: Mexican Repatriation in the 1930s*. Albuquerque: University of New Mexico Press 1995.

Barlett, Donald L., and James B. Steele. "The Empire of the Pigs." *Time Magazine*, June 24, 2001. http://www.time.com/time/magazine/article/0,9171,140572,00.html. Accessed January 4, 2013.

Bell, Lee. "The Changing Face of Guymon." *Tulsa World*, April 27, 2007. http://www.tulsaworld.com/news/article.aspx?articleID=070429_1_A1_hHisp84735. Accessed March 4, 2013.

Boisson, Steven. "Immigrants the Last Time America Sent Her Own Packing." HISTORYNET, July 27, 2006. http://www.historynet.com/immigrants-the-last-time-america-sent-her-own-packing.htm. Accessed March 13, 2013.

Branstetter, Ziva. "Local Officials Could Fight Illegal Alien Crime." *Tulsa World*, August 20, 2004, A11.

Brewer, Graham Lee. "The New Majority at Guymon." *Oklahoma Watch*, September 24, 2012. http://www.publicradiotulsa.org/post/new-majority-guymon. Accessed March 12, 2013.

Brewer, Graham Lee. "A Panhandle Explosion." *Oklahoma Watch*, September 23, 2012. http://oklahomawatch.org/2012/09/23/a-panhandle-explosion. Accessed March 4, 2013.

Brewer, Graham Lee. "Seaboard Started It All—Meat Processing Plant Served As Community Catalyst." *Enid News and Eagle*, September 26, 2012. http://enidnews.com/localnews/x1241971685/Seaboard-started-it-all. Accessed March 4, 2013.

Brunkow, Angie. "Bridging the Cultural Gap with More Hispanics in Class, Schools Reaching Out to Help." *Omaha World Herald*, August 30, 2001.

Census Viewer Maps and Data Links. http://censusviewer.com/free-maps-and-data-links/. Accessed March 12, 2013.

"The Competition." Narrated by Ira Glass. *This American Life*, Public Radio International, Transcript November 30, 2007. http://www.thisamericanlife.org/radio archives/episode/344/transcript. Accessed March 4, 2013.

Dean, Brian, and John Estus. "County Looks to Ease Jail Crowds." *The Oklahoman*, August 6, 2008. http://newsok.com/oklahoma-county-looks-to-ease-jail-crowds/article/3279547. Accessed March 29, 2014.

Driscoll, Barbara A. *The Tracks North: The Railroad Bracero Program of World War II*. Austin: University of Texas, 1999.

Gillham, Omer. "La Mayoría de los Oklahomeros No Pueden Leer Esto. Ellos Solamente ven Palabras que no Quieren Decir Nada." *Tulsa World*, April 26, 1999, A13.

Gillham, Omer. "Sinking Their Teeth into the American Dream." *Tulsa World*, April 27, 1999, A1.

Graham, Ginnie. "English Only Plan Draws Heat." *Tulsa World*, July 16, 2000, A11.

Graham, Ginnie. "Hispanics on Rise." *Tulsa World*, May 1, 2008, A1.

Graham, Ginnie. "Senator Seeks to Abandon Petition." *Tulsa World*, February 1, 2001, A9.

Gray, Jim. "State Question on 'English Only' Turns Back the Clock on Race Relations." *Native American Times*, August 31, 2000, C2.

Immigration Policy Center. New Americans in Oklahoma, January 2012. http://www.immigrationpolicy.org/sites/default/files/docs/New_Americans_in_Oklahoma_2012.pdf. Accessed March 14, 2013.

Johnson, Kevin R. "The Forgotten 'Repatriation' of Persons of Mexican Ancestry and Lessons for the 'War on Terror.'" *Pace Law Review* 26, no. 1 (Fall 2005). http://digitalcommons.pace.edu/plr/vol26/iss1/1/. Accessed August 22, 2014.

Jones, Todd. "Tulsa Deputies Say They're Not Picking on Anyone." *The Columbus Dispatch*, September 10, 2008. http://www.conlamic.org/press_detail.php?press_id=151. Accessed October 1, 2013.

Krehbiel, Randy. "Sullivan Fights for Funds for Tulsa Jail." *Tulsa World*, June 9, 2012, A1.

Krocker, Marvin E. "In Death You Shall Not Wear It Either: The Persecution of Mennonite Pacifists in Oklahoma." In Davis D. Joyce, ed. *An Oklahoma I Had Never Seen Before: Alternative Views of Oklahoma History*. Norman: University of Oklahoma Press 1998, pp. 80–91.

Levy, Larry. "How the ICE Has Melted in Tulsa; Deputies Are Now Getting Immigrant Training." *The Oklahoman*, August 22, 2007, A15.

Martindale, Rob. "State's Population Rises for Third Straight Year." *Tulsa World*, January 18, 1994, N1.

McCormick, Elizabeth M. "The Oklahoma Taxpayer and Citizen Protection Act: Blowing Off Steam or Setting Wildfires?" *Georgetown Immigration Law Journal* 23 (2009): 293–363.

Migration Policy Institute. *2011 American Community Survey and Census Data on the Foreign Born by State.* 2012. http://www.migrationinformation.org/datahub/acscensus. cfm. Accessed March 13, 2013.

Migration Policy Institute. *Oklahoma Social & Demographic Characteristics.* 2012. http://www. migrationinformation.org/DataHub/state.cfm?ID=OK. Accessed October 12, 2013.

Muse-Orlinoff, Leah. "Staying Put but Still in the Shadows, Undocumented Immigrants Remain in the Country Despite Strict Laws." Center for American Progress, February 2012. http://www.americanprogress.org/wp-content/uploads/issues/2012/02/pdf /mexico_immigration.pdf. Accessed March 12, 2013.

Passel, Jeffrey S., and D'Vera Cohn. Unauthorized Immigrant Population: National and State Trends, Migration Policy Institute. 2010. http://www.pewhispanic.org/files /reports/133.pdf. Accessed March 14, 2013.

Pew Hispanic Center. *Statistical Portrait of the Foreign Born in the United States 2006.* January 2008. http://pewhispanic.org/files/factsheets/foreignborn2006/Table-12.pdf. Accessed March 13, 2013.

Rappleye, Charles. "Mexico, America and the Continental Divide." *Virginia Quarterly Review* 61 (April 1, 2007). http://www.highbeam.com/doc/1P3-1256577891.html. Accessed August 22, 2014.

Scaperlanda, Michael A. "Human Trafficking in the Heartland: Greed, Visa Fraud, and the Saga of 53 Indian Nationals 'Enslaved' by a Tulsa Company." *Loyola University Chicago International Law Review* 2 (2006): 219–44.

Smith, Michael M. "Hispanics." *Encyclopedia of Oklahoma History and Culture.* http:// digital.library.okstate.edu/encyclopedia/entries/H/HI014.html. Accessed March 4, 2013.

Smith, Michael M. *The Mexicans in Oklahoma.* Norman: University of Oklahoma Press, 1980.

"State and County QuickFacts/Oklahoma Quick Links." U.S. Bureau of the Census. 2012. http://quickfacts.census.gov/qfd/states/40000lk.html. Accessed: March 4, 2013.

Tichenor, Daniel J. *Dividing Lines: The Politics of Immigration Control in America.* Princeton, NJ: Princeton University Press, 2002.

U.S. Equal Employment Opportunity Commission. Press Release. "EEOC Sues Pickle Manufacturing Company for Discrimination against Workers from India, Low Wages, Mistreatment, Harsh Living Conditions Lead to Federal Suit on Behalf of Immigrants." January 2, 2003. http://www.eeoc.gov/eeoc/newsroom/release/archive/1–2–03.html. Accessed March 4, 2013.

Vaughn, Jessica, and James R. Edwards Jr. "The 287(g) Program: Protecting Home Towns and Homeland, Center for Immigration Studies." Center for Immigration Studies, October 2009. http://www.cis.org/287greport. Accessed March 12, 2013.

Walker, Devona. "In Places like Guymon, New Law Is a Challenge." *The Oklahoman,* October 16, 2007. Accessed at 2007 WLNR 20302485.

Warner, Richard S. "Barbed Wire and Nazilagers: PW Camps in Oklahoma." *The Chronicles of Oklahoma* 37 (Spring 1986). http://www.rootsweb.ancestry.com/~okmurray /stories/barbed_wire_and_nazilagers.htm. Accessed August 8, 2014.

Wishart, David. *Encyclopedia of the Great Plains*. Lincoln: University of Nebraska Press, 2004.

Wright, Peter. "Viva La Communidad." *Oklahoma Gazette*, November 7, 2012. http://npaper-wehaa.com/oklahoma-gazette/2012/11/07/s1/#?article=1725907. Accessed March 14, 2013.

Zizzo, David. "English Only Debate Galvanizes Opposing Factions." *The Sunday Oklahoman*, August 13, 2000, 1A.

37

OREGON

Bob Bussel

CHRONOLOGY

1859	Oregon gains statehood.
1866	Oregon legislature passes sweeping miscegenation law barring blacks from marrying whites, Chinese, or native Hawaiians.
1869	Workers in Oregon City form a White Laborers Association to oust their Chinese workers who had replaced them.
1869	Bernard Goldsmith, a German Jewish immigrant, is elected mayor of Portland.
1872	Oregon legislature establishes a Board of Immigration to attract new residents.
1887	Thirty-four Chinese miners are murdered by horse thieves northeast of Enterprise, Oregon, along the Snake River.
1903	Oregon Bureau of Labor is established by Oregon legislature and directed to collect data on Chinese and Japanese employment and land ownership.
1905	Neighborhood House, an affiliate of the National Council of Jewish Women, is established in Portland to assist Jewish immigrants in adjusting to American life.
1907	Mob storms quarters of Japanese workers in Woodburn and seeks their dismissal, claiming they work for wages that whites will not tolerate and take their jobs away.
1917	Finnish shipyard workers strike in Astoria, prompting Oregon governor to send in troops.
1919	Hood River Anti-Asiatic Association is formed.

1923	Oregon legislature passes "Alien Land Law" barring noncitizens from land ownership. This law is especially aimed at Japanese landowners in the Hood River region.
1924	Mob of 300 storms Toledo, Oregon mill, where Japanese were brought in to perform work that whites refused to do.
1925	Oregon legislature creates State Department of Americanization, which is directed to organize local councils that offer English instruction and prepare foreigners to become naturalized citizens.
1944	Bracero Program reaches its peak employment in Oregon with over 4,600 Mexicans being employed as farmworkers.
1945	Hood River American Legion removes the names of Japanese soldiers from a public "honor roll" of local servicemen, provoking nationwide criticism condemning this action.
1945	Oregon legislature approves resolution urging federal government to prevent Japanese internees from returning to state before conclusion of World War II.
1949	Oregon Supreme Court overturns Alien Land Law.
1951	Oregon legislature repeals earlier mandate directing Bureau of Labor to track Chinese and Japanese employment.
1955	Rural Oregon farmers Bertha and Harry Holt bring 12 "GI Babies" to the United States from Korea and subsequently launch Holt International Children's Services, an organization specializing in international adoption.
1957	Oregon Bureau of Labor report estimates the presence of nearly 12,000 Spanish-speaking farmworkers in Oregon.
1975	Immigrant Refugee and Community Organization is formed to help integrate Oregon's growing immigrant and refugee population.
1985	Pineros y Campesinos Unidos del Noroeste (PCUN) is founded as a union for Oregon farmworkers and tree planters.
1995	CAUSA, an immigrant rights organization, is founded by farmworkers, immigrants, and their allies to counter anti-immigrant ballot measures prepared for circulation to Oregon voters.
2006	Immigrant rights rallies occur in April and May at Oregon state capitol involving thousands of people.
2007	Federal agents arrest 167 workers at the Fresh Del Monte plant in North Portland during an immigration raid.
2008	Oregon voters reject the ballot initiative seeking to limit bilingual education and promote what backers called "English immersion."
2008	Oregon legislature passes law requiring proof of citizenship or legal status to obtain an Oregon driver's license.
2011	Oregon State Senate approves tuition equity bill, but legislation does not come to a vote in the Oregon House of Representatives.

HISTORICAL OVERVIEW

Statehood to World War II

As one of the most racially homogenous states in the nation, Oregon has had an especially volatile history in its relations with people of color and an enduring ambivalence in its attitude toward immigrants. Oregon was the only non-slave state admitted to the Union with a constitutional provision barring blacks and after it gained statehood in 1859, continued to erect barriers aimed at preserving white hegemony in social, political, and economic affairs. This strong antipathy toward people of color and the accompanying desire to assert white supremacy, legitimated through law and reinforced by custom, set the tone for how Oregonians would evaluate the credentials of immigrants seeking to enter their new state.

Coupled with this belief in white superiority and an abiding distrust of people from different racial and ethnic backgrounds, many Oregonians also believed that their state was a special place whose pristine environment, pioneer ethos, and social harmony would be subverted by immigrants from unfamiliar lands. These convictions led Oregon's early political and civic leaders to distinguish between "desirable" and "undesirable" immigrants, resulting in a deeply ambivalent attitude toward immigration that has persisted into contemporary times. From the outset, Oregon's political and business leaders valued immigrants from northern Europe, who often came with financial resources, specific skills, and "industrious habits" that quickly made them valued social and economic contributors. For two other groups of late nineteenth-century immigrants, however, Oregon was distinctly unwelcoming, and the response of Oregonians to arrivals from China and Japan represented a disturbing episode in the state's encounters with newcomers. Like others in neighboring states on the West Coast, many Oregonians viewed Chinese and Japanese immigrants with suspicion, enacting laws to restrict their economic activity, and sometimes resorting to violence to eliminate them as economic competitors.

At the same time, other Oregonians were more respectful of immigrant customs and sensibilities. The Portland Americanization Council had over 100 member organizations and, at its eighth annual reception, in 1929, it honored naturalized citizens by featuring immigrants singing both folk songs from their native countries and patriotic American tunes. Although Americanization advocates could be heavy-handed in their efforts to encourage immigrant assimilation, their activities also represented a genuine attempt to help immigrants enter the social and civic mainstream. And in 1945, after the Hood River, Oregon American Legion removed the names of Japanese soldiers from a public "honor roll" of local residents serving in the military, many Oregonians joined the chorus of nationwide criticism condemning this action.

WORLD WAR II TO THE PRESENT

In the postwar years, several of Oregon's most prominent political leaders embraced the causes of refugee relief and comprehensive immigration reform that dismantled the discriminatory national origins quota system established in the 1920s. Many of their constituents, however, remained reluctant to reopen the gates to immigration and expand Oregon's ethnic, racial, and religious diversity. Moreover, as in the past, a strong appetite for cheap imported labor spurred both new immigration and fresh conflicts.

Following World War II, Oregon agricultural interests grew more dependent on Mexican and other foreign-born labor as native-born workers moved to less arduous and better-paying employment, leaving labor shortages in the fields. Like earlier generations of immigrants to Oregon, Mexicans were attracted by the availability of economic opportunity and increasingly found their way into occupations

Paulina Eyman, left, chats with friends in Woodburn, Oregon, on October 21, 2001. Eyman, now 51, arrived in Oregon from Turkey when she was 13-years old and has remained a member of the tightknit Old Believers community. (AP Photo/Greg Wahl-Stephens)

besides farm labor, including food-processing, manufacturing, construction, and small businesses. They also began to develop institutions to improve their living and working conditions. In 1953, Mexican immigrants in Nyssa formed an organization called Siempre Adelante to seek fair treatment after a white youth killed a Mexican, and the crime went unpunished. Subsequently, activists launched an aggressive and energetic farmworkers union, PCUN (or Farm Workers United of the Northwest), along with a host of community and church-sponsored organizations that provided social services, job training, and housing for farmworkers. During the postwar era, Mexicans and other Latino immigrants firmly established themselves as a visible presence in Oregon. The state's expanded dependence on imported Mexican labor—from legal immigrants and *braceros* to undocumented workers—had recast its demography.

Following the passage of the Immigration Reform Act of 1965, Oregon became a leading destination point for refugees fleeing turmoil and upheaval in their homelands, attracting émigrés from the Soviet Union, Southeast Asia, and Africa. The total number of immigrants from the Soviet Union remained small in Oregon until the mid-1960s when two religious groups that split off from the Russian Orthodox Church—Old Believers and Molokans—arrived as refugees. After first journeying to Latin America, Russian Old Believer immigrants received visas when a private foundation funded their trip from Brazil to the Willamette Valley, and local social service organizations and churches provided assurances that they would help the newcomers adapt to their new environment.

The migration of Russians and Ukrainians accelerated in the late 1980s after Soviet president Mikhail Gorbachev began permitting those seeking greater religious freedom to leave. This new sanction for Russian and Ukrainian migration has made the Portland metro area one of the largest areas of settlement for Slavic immigrants in the United States. In contrast to earlier immigrants to Oregon, post-Soviet era Russians and Ukrainians are all members of fundamentalist religious sects who came to the United States seeking greater freedom to practice their faith. Many who arrived in the 1990s were granted refugee status under legislation passed a decade earlier, and this status granted them access to numerous services and subsidies, including assistance with employment, housing, and education. Russian-speaking refugees also found a strong network of churches that catered to their spiritual needs and provided them with a much-needed sense of community and cohesiveness. Their transition has been further eased by social sympathy for their refugee status and the sense that they are legitimate, desirable immigrants whose presence affirms the nation's social generosity and commitment to being a haven for oppressed people seeking freedom. In addition, as Caucasian peoples, these immigrants more readily blended with the existing population and did not spark the kind of ethnic or racial antagonism that dogged the Chinese and Japanese a century earlier.

Besides Russians and Ukrainians, refugees from Southeast Asia and Africa have moved to Oregon since the late 1970s, mostly to the Portland metropolitan area. The social disorder following American withdrawal from Vietnam in 1975 led Vietnamese, Laotians, and Cambodians to seek refuge abroad, while civil strife in Ethiopia, Somalia, Liberia, and the Democratic Republic of the Congo prompted residents to flee these countries. Like the Russians and the Ukrainians, these groups of refugees received assistance from church-sponsored agencies and other private organizations. Vietnamese refugees drew on family and kinship networks to ease their adaptation, and Africans organized individual ethnic associations to provide needed services and support.

Southeast Asians and Africans have also begun to establish their own businesses, often serving ethnic constituencies. Although these groups have faced some ethnic and racially based hostility, their strong support networks have enabled them to make important strides toward gaining social acceptance. However, following the events of September 11, 2001, these immigrants and refugees have experienced greater social scrutiny and have begun to develop new organizations to defend their rights and enable them to speak more effectively in the civic and political arena.

As refugees and immigrants from Asia, Europe, and Africa made new homes in Oregon, most popular and political attention (both in Oregon and across the nation) focused after the 1970s on Latino immigration, especially from Mexico. Whether recruited through community social networks or following existing migrant streams as individuals, increasing numbers of Mexicans came to Oregon first as seasonal farm laborers and later as more settled residents. The passage of the Immigration Reform and Control Act (IRCA) in 1986 provided an impetus for organizing the state's farmworkers with PCUN, Oregon's farmworkers union, doubling its membership in just one month. Although applications for legal status under IRCA fell short of the state's expectations, both legal and undocumented immigration across the U.S.–Mexican border continued unabated due to strong economic incentives and powerful family and community ties. In the past two decades, indigenous workers from the state of Oaxaca have also swelled Oregon's immigrant population. Although their migration began several decades before the passage of the North American Free-Trade Agreement in 1994, Oaxacans left in greater numbers following rising food prices and stiff economic competition from American farmers that drove many of them off the land. At least 14 different indigenous ethnic groups from Guatemala and Mexico now reside in Oregon and have developed home-town associations, soccer clubs, and other organizations to aid their process of adaptation. They also began to organize for rights to language translation in courts, schools, and hospitals.

During the past decade, controversial policy choices about undocumented immigrants have proven as contentious for Oregonians as they have elsewhere in the country. During the spring of 2006, a series of immigrant rights rallies occurred in Oregon to protest congressional proposals that took a hard line on illegal immigration. Significantly, many immigrant workers who participated in these rallies or wore white shirts on the job to call attention to immigration issues received support from their employers, especially in the nursery, restaurant, and dairy industries. "The workers and employers have a good relationship," explained a spokesman for the Oregon Restaurant Association, which joined with other employer groups and immigrant rights advocates to press for legislation that would grant undocumented immigrants a pathway to citizenship (Skidmore 2006).

Yet as an alliance formed among Oregon businesses, unions, ethnic associations, and religious groups in favor of comprehensive immigration reform, opponents mobilized to promote tough measures against undocumented immigrants. Indeed, Oregonians for Immigration Reform, a group favoring crackdowns on undocumented immigrants, claimed that its membership doubled in the wake of May Day immigrant rallies in 2006. In the months that followed, advocates and opponents of undocumented immigrants clashed openly at day labor pickup sites from Cornelius to Portland. These confrontations began when the Oregon chapter of the Minuteman Civil Defense Corps and Oregonians for Immigration Reform sent boisterous, flag-waving protestors to intimidate contractors and homeowners attempting to hire day laborers. Immigrant rights groups soon joined the day laborers, and police attempted to maintain order as the two sides hurled insults and rocks at each other. In rural Columbia County, voters approved measures to restrict undocumented immigrants' access to employment, an action later struck down by a county judge.

Throughout Oregon, immigrants and their second- and third-generation successors are increasingly becoming involved in the political arena. Groups like PCUN in the Woodburn and Salem areas have engaged in extensive voter registration activities and are mobilizing immigrants to participate in the political process. In 2009, school board members in Hillsboro, a community with a 30 percent Latino population, appointed the district's first Latina to serve in a newly vacated position. In the past two years, a coalition of community organizations, nonprofit organizations, and foundations have allied to establish the Oregon Latino Agenda for Action, which aims to increase the political visibility of Latinos and enable them to speak with a more unified voice. Latinos are gaining greater political respect from public officials in Oregon, who have proven increasingly willing to support pro-immigrant legislation and speak out publicly in favor of immigrant rights.

Controversy over immigration in Oregon reflects familiar concerns and new preoccupations. The question of legality, which had been somewhat less prominent in earlier debates over immigration, now dominates social discussion. As the most visible group in Oregon favoring immigration restriction has argued, illegal immigration "lowers our moral and civic values by encouraging disregard for the law." This sense of violation dovetails with the profound economic insecurity experienced by many Oregonians who have seen their standard of living erode in a free-trade, global economy and a lingering recession. These fears are accompanied by the uneasiness that Oregonians have traditionally felt when encountering people from different ethnic or racial backgrounds. Delores Hickey, a 70-year-old resident of Independence, told *The Oregonian* in 2009 that, "today's immigrants have no pride (in the United States) and don't assimilate." "I look around," Hickey explained, and "I'm not part of America anymore" (Oregonians for Immigration Reform 2007; Hickey 2009).

Proponents of immigration take a more optimistic view. They observe that whatever costs may be associated with immigration are outweighed by the economic and social contributions of immigrants and express confidence in the state's ability to integrate them into Oregon's economic and civic life. They also note that immigrants deeply value the concepts of work, faith, and family; encourage their children to embrace the opportunities available to them in their new culture; and are seeking to become more vitally involved in civic and community affairs. In a 2006 resolution, the Portland City Council embraced this perspective, affirming "its commitment to the inclusion of immigrants and refugees in civic and public life" and creating a task force to advise the city on how this objective might best be achieved. And in a March 2010 article, David Leslie, executive director of Ecumenical Ministries of Oregon, offered a liberal Protestant rationale for supporting immigrants and immigration reform: "The growing ecumenical call for comprehensive immigration reform is based on the recognition that our current immigration policies diminish a person's humanity and are contrary to the call of the Gospel to welcome and treat the stranger—the immigrant—with the full respect that he or she deserves as a child of God" (City of Portland Resolution 2006; Leslie, 2010).

As Oregonians debate anew whether they should adopt an open-arms or arms-length approach toward immigration, they do so in the context of a foreign-born population that has increased from 4.5 to 9.7 percent of the state's total population between 1990 and 2010. An estimated 125,000–175,000 of these residents are undocumented. And with the recent passage of legislation in Arizona and elsewhere granting local authorities the power to question and detain persons whom they suspect lack official status, some Oregon political leaders and members of the public have again been clamoring for additional state and local action to restrict undocumented immigration. Oregonians will face complicated choices as they weigh the costs and benefits of immigration and consider, as one *The Oregonian* editorial posed the question in 1924, whether they are willing to accept immigrants "not only as workmen but as citizens and neighbors." They will make these choices in the context of a complex historical legacy that should leave little illusion about the difficulties of the challenges that lie ahead (Ayre, 2006; Migration Policy Institute, 2012).

TOPICAL ESSAYS

OREGON'S POST–WORLD WAR II SHIFT TOWARD LIBERAL PLURALISM AND IMMIGRANT INTEGRATION

By the mid- twentieth century, Oregon's immigration experience was a potent reflection of the nativism and contradictions that lay at the heart of official policies and popular sentiment since World War I. In the years following the enactment of national origins quotas in the 1920s, immigration from southern and eastern Europe slowed to a trickle. After Asian immigrants were denied entry, the remaining Asian Americans in Oregon were often subjected to brutal discrimination, reaching a crescendo with the removal and internment of thousands of Japanese Americans and aliens during World War II. Nonetheless, while the gates were closed to most European and nearly all Asian newcomers, Mexican immigrants, guest workers, and backdoor entrants continued to supply cheap, exploitable labor that fueled Oregon's economic progress and prosperity.

At the same time as Mexican labor migration was beginning to remake Oregon's demographics, several of the state's most prominent representatives in Congress, especially Senators Wayne Morse and Richard Neuberger, along with Representative Al Ullman, advocated a more welcoming approach to immigration that contrasted sharply with the restrictive and frequently nativist approaches that had guided many of their predecessors. During the 1950s and 1960s, these leaders championed refugee relief and comprehensive immigration reform that ultimately dismantled the discriminatory national origins quota system. Morse, Neuberger, and Ullman were guided by both moral and foreign policy imperatives. In 1956, when members of the American Legion lobbied Morse to maintain draconian immigration restrictions in order "to protect our country against undesirable people," the senator responded that existing quotas undermined U.S. interests in the Cold War struggle against the Soviet Union. "I must say frankly that I have been greatly disturbed by the bad effect of [immigration restriction] upon our standing in many areas of the world," Morse explained. "In the countries of southern and eastern Europe, and particularly in Greece and Italy where the Communist menace is always present and always seeking to capitalize on American mistakes and misfortunes, the racial and ethnic discriminations in the Act have been very damaging." Richard Neuberger echoed these views and went on to highlight the moral and economic dimensions of the issue. "The United States has a tradition of offering sanctuary to the oppressed," he noted. "Each immigrant is not only a jobholder, but he and his family are also consumers who buy goods and service." (Letter of Ansell Morehouse to Wayne Morse 1956; Letter of

Wayne Morse to Ansell Morehouse 1956; Letter of Richard Neuberger to "Dear Friend" 1959).

Throughout the accelerating debate on immigration reform in the 1960s, the vast majority of letters that ordinary Oregonians wrote to Morse, Neuberger, and Ullman vehemently opposed any expansion in refugee and immigrant admissions. Reacting to the growing demand for civil rights and the continuation of Cold War tensions, many of these constituents were unabashed in their hostility toward potential newcomers. They insisted that the United States should be "a nation . . . built on race" and "a land of Northwestern Europeans"; warned that reform would result in the country being "flooded" with "Asiatics and Negroes" who would "help the communists take over America"; and predicted that the demise of national origins quotas would open "our floodgates to hoards of the most undesirable peoples of the world." Fearing that a political shift toward racial egalitarianism and an influx of immigrants from unfamiliar lands might spark even greater social unrest, many white Oregonians regarded liberalization of immigration laws as unmistakable evidence that their privileged status and the nation's security were under siege (Letter of Dail Delaney to Senator Morse 1965; Letter of Downing to Wayne Morse 1964; Letter of Reilly to Wayne Morse 1964; Letter of Watford Reed to Wayne Morse 1965).

The growing commitment to cultural pluralism, civic inclusion, and human rights was not limited to Oregon's congressional representatives. In addition to ethnic, religious, and business groups, other Oregonians also embraced the causes of refugee relief and immigration reform. Harry and Bertha Holt, farmers in the rural town of Creswell, reacted sympathetically to a 1954 presentation about the plight of unwanted Korean orphans—so-called GI Babies—left behind by U.S. troops. With the backing of their six children, the Holts resolved to adopt eight of these abandoned "GI Babies." However, because existing immigration and refugee law prevented them from doing so, Harry Holt asked his senators for help. Neuberger and Morse shepherded special legislation through Congress that enabled the Holts to bring home the eight Korean children. In October, 1955, Harry Holt returned to Portland from Korea with 12 "GI Babies," eight of whom were legally adopted by the Holt family and another four who were adopted by other families. The Holt family became 16, and refugee relief had made its way to rural Oregon (*King's Business Magazine* 1955; Wisner 1955).

Morse and Neuberger continued to spearhead broader immigration reform efforts in Washington. In the late 1950s, both senators joined 11 of their colleagues in pressing for major revision of the 1952 McCarran-Walter Act, a Cold War-inspired law that upheld the restrictive national origins system established in the 1920s.Neuberger was a keynote speaker at a "Rally for a Fair Immigration Law" held at New York's Carnegie Hall sponsored by religious groups, ethnic associations, unions, and the Americans for Democratic Action. When the

House Committee on Un-American Activities questioned Neuberger's exchanges with the Clatsop County Committee for Protection of Foreign Born, he issued a blistering counterattack. "I hope it has not become un-American to suggest that the McCarran-Walter Act requires revision in the name of justice, fairness, humanity, and the long-standing heritage of our country," he declared. "In the event that any such notion prevails, I should like to cite the fact that the President of the United States—as well as a great many Members of both the Senate and the House—believe our immigration code needs a complete and thorough overhaul." During the same period, Wayne Morse continued to promote legislation that would "abandon racial and religious restriction as the foundation of our quota system" and significantly expand immigrant and refugee admissions. Each month, he obtained from the Justice Department a list with the names and addresses of "aliens naturalized in Oregon," to whom he wrote warm congratulatory letters on behalf of the nation and the state (Senate Bill 1206; Flier; Letter of Neuberger to Clatsop County 1957; Letter of Morse to Committee for the Protection of Oregon's Foreign Born 1960).

In 1965, Congress enacted sweeping immigration reform legislation as part of President Lyndon Johnson's Great Society juggernaut. Spurred by the Civil Rights Movement's demands for social equality and Soviet criticism that the United States' immigration policy advanced racial and ethnic favoritism, the new Immigration and Nationality Act reversed the discriminatory effects of the 1924 National Origins Act by lifting its quotas and allowing expanded immigration from southern and eastern Europe as well as Asia. The law established a new preference system for immigrant admissions that placed particular value on family reunification, with additional visas reserved for refugees and those with special job skills.

While many of his constituents remained hostile to the welcoming approach embodied in these reforms, Wayne Morse vigorously defended a more open immigration policy. Responding to one irate constituent in an October 1965 letter, Morse noted that "one hundred years ago, many long-time citizens of the United States were saying the same things about Irish immigrants that you are saying about eastern Europeans and Cubans. I think our country and our economy are strong and healthy enough to welcome these people and be helped by them." A year earlier, he told a detractor that he opposed "basing our immigration quotas on the concept of a 'racially pure' Anglo Saxon breed," denouncing this thinking as "discredited form of history that we should put behind us." Representative Al Ullman expressed similar views, arguing that, "the United States has been greatly benefited by having citizens of every ethnic background." Morse's and Ullman's unwavering support for immigration reform in the face of constituent opposition signaled a shift among the state's political leaders toward greater cultural pluralism and social tolerance aimed at aligning Oregon with the spirit of civic inclusion that was transforming America during the 1960s (Letter of Delaney to Morse 1965; Letter of Morse to K.C. Stevens 1964; Letter of Ullman to Laurence 1963).

With the passage of the Immigration Act of 1965, the cosmopolitan optimism of Richard Neuberger, Wayne Morse, and Al Ullman triumphed. Both the nation and Oregon have seen immigration increase dramatically over the past four decades, with Oregon becoming a leading destination point for refugees fleeing turmoil and upheaval in their homelands.

Beginning in the mid-1970s with the end of the Vietnam War, growing numbers of refugees from Indochina flocked to Oregon. A decade-and-a-half later, after Mikhail Gorbachev loosened restrictions on immigration and allowed those seeking greater religious freedom to depart, Russians and Ukrainians swelled the ranks of an earlier group of Slavic arrivals that had first settled in Oregon during the 1950s and 1960s. Toward the latter part of the 1990s, civil strife in Africa created yet another group of persons seeking protection from persecution and physical harm, leading refugees from Somalia, Ethiopia, the Congo, and other African countries to arrive in Oregon in increasing numbers. As a result of these successive migrations, by the first decade of the twenty-first century, Oregon ranked 11th nationally among all states as a resettlement destination for refugees, and Portland had the 12th-largest refugee population among American cities. At first imperceptibly and later more visibly, the face of Oregon had begun to change, as refugees obtained jobs and started businesses, established churches and community institutions, sent their children to school, and increasingly participated in community affairs.

As Oregon's largest city and one whose immigrant and refugee population has swelled over the past three decades, Portland has at both the community and governmental level undertaken several notable initiatives aimed at facilitating the integration process. Two key organizations, the Immigrant and Refugee Community Organization (IRCO) and the Center for Intercultural Organizing (CIO), have played vital roles in helping immigrants become economically, socially, and civically acclimated. For three decades, IRCO has provided job training, English instruction, and support for children and families. More recently, it has sought to increase immigrant civic participation through a joint program with the city of Portland that works to familiarize immigrants with government functions and encourage them to serve on boards and committees of public institutions. Founded after 9/11 amid the appearance of rising anti-Muslim sentiment, CIO has focused on helping immigrants and refugees assert their rights and engage more effectively and confidently in the political process. In 2010, it expanded its efforts to promote greater immigrant political and civic participation to the Portland suburb of Beaverton, a community with a sizable immigrant and refugee population.

The city of Portland has assumed a strong integrationist approach in response to its growing immigrant and refugee population. In 2006, Portland mayor Tom Potter convened a task force on immigrants and refugees that a year later offered a series of recommendations aimed at making the city a more welcoming environment for newcomers. Among its recommendations, the task force proposed the creation of an Office of Human Relations charged with combating discrimination and bigotry. Established in 2008, this office has a "New Portlanders" program whose mission is to develop "a set of strategic processes and practical approaches to integrate our newcomer communities into the life of the city." The city also sponsored the creation of a day-laborers center in 2008, prompted by the efforts of the VOZ Workers Education Project. For the past decade, VOZ has helped organize a mostly immigrant constituency of workers who seek temporary unskilled employment by soliciting jobs on street corners. Working with city officials and community allies, VOZ now administers a safe, secure site where day laborers can seek work in an orderly fashion under fair conditions and become accepted members of the surrounding community. All of these efforts have, in the words of the Office of Human Relations' New Portlanders program, helped immigrants become a more integral part of "the life of the city."

Both business and labor interests have also become deeply engaged in the integration process. In the Portland metropolitan area, there are approximately 400 businesses owned by Slavic immigrants, and an estimated 6,000 Latino-owned businesses. Support structures such as the Hispanic Metropolitan Chamber of

Aeryca Steinbauer, coordinator of CAUSA, an Oregon immigrants' advocacy group, speaks on a Spanish language call-in program on June 26, 2007. The program was broadcast from KPCN, a short-range station in Woodburn, Oregon. Steinbauer cohosted the show *Conectete con CAUSA* (*Get in Touch with CAUSA*). (AP Photo/Rick Bowmer)

Commerce in Portland, and the Latino Business Network in Lane County have emerged to support immigrant entrepreneurs. These organizations help aspiring businessmen and women understand basic business principles and find markets for their goods and services.

Labor unions are another institution that historically have played an important role in helping immigrants achieve economic mobility, civic confidence, and social acceptance. In Oregon, immigrants who work in various types of care giving (nursing homes, child care, foster care and home healthcare) are becoming union members in increasing numbers. Unions such as the Laborers and the Carpenters have been active in attempting to organize immigrant workers in the construction trades and in other occupations, while the Oregon's American Federation of Labor and Congress of Industrial Organizations and several of its affiliates have cultivated a close relationship with CAUSA, an energetic statewide advocate for immigrant rights. To be sure, some union leaders and members share the ambivalence of other Oregonians toward immigrants, especially those lacking legal status who they view as threats to their jobs and hard-won living standards. Yet, unions in Oregon have also spoken out vocally on behalf of comprehensive immigration reform, supported legislation aimed at curbing abuse of immigrants by employers, and recognized that establishing relationships with immigrants will be key to their future relevance and viability.

Institutions of higher education in Oregon are also playing a much more active role in the integration process through their efforts to recruit more Latino students. Between 2004 and 2009, Latino enrollment increased by 73 percent at Western Oregon University, the highest percentage among institutions in the Oregon University System. According to one study, this increase was "the result of deliberate, purposeful work by the university," including conscious efforts to provide financial and academic support. In October 2010, Portland State University (PSU) announced a $350,000 program to recruit and support Latino students. PSU president Wim Wiewel, who was accompanied by Portland's mayor at a press conference announcing this new undertaking, explained the university's action as long overdue: "This is an important part of the community that we have not been paying enough attention to." Other universities in Oregon are now launching similar initiatives (Graves 2010; Pardington 2009).

These increasing attempts to support outreach and equity suggest that the shift toward liberal pluralism and immigrant acceptance promoted by Wayne Morse and Richard Neuberger has gained approval among many of Oregon's key decision-making constituencies. Although some Oregonians continue to question the benefits of immigration and especially the presence of undocumented immigrants, a solid segment of Oregon's community and political leaders now agree that conscious efforts to promote immigrant integration will contribute significantly to Oregon's future success as a twenty-first-century state.

NOTABLE GROUPS

CAUSA

CAUSA is a group representing Latina/os throughout the state. They are the "largest Latino[a] civil and human rights organization in the Pacific Northwest." (CAUSA n.d.) This group promotes civic participation, public education, and policy reform related to immigrant issues regarding education, housing, health, work conditions and wages, and general safety concerns. Two campaigns in the year 2014 organized an Immigrant Action Day in April, to raise public awareness of immigrant needs and problems. They also supported the issuance of state driver's cards but this measure must be approved by a referendum, which will be held in November 2014. CAUSA works with other groups in the state to advocate for better public policy while also serving as a key source of information in immigrant communities.

BIBLIOGRAPHY

Ayre, Art. "Unauthorized Immigrants Working in Oregon." Oregon Employment Department, April 28, 2006.

Baker, Linda. "Russian Immigrants Love New Lives in USA." *Portland Business Journal*, February 4, 2000. http://www.bizjournals.com/portland/stories/2000/02/07/story3.html?page=all. Accessed August 22, 2014.

Bermudez, Esmeralda. "Tempers Collide on Immigration." *The Oregonian*, August 31, 2006, pp. A1, A7.

Bussel, Robert, ed. "Understanding the Immigrant Experience in Oregon." Labor Education and Research Center, University of Oregon, 2009.

Bussel, Robert, and Daniel Tichenor. "Trouble in Paradise: A Historical Perspective on Immigration in Oregon." Unpublished Essay, 2011.

Calavita, Kitty. *Inside the State: The Bracero Program, Illegal Immigrants, and the Bracero Program*. New York: Routledge, 1992.

CAUSA. Oregon's Immigrant Rights Organization. CAUSA Webpage. http://causaoregon.org/about/. Accessed February 25, 2014.

Center for Intercultural Organizing, and Bridgetown Voices. "Uniting Cultures in Portland: Bridging the Gaps in City Policy." Report by 2006 Politics of Immigration Capstone, Portland State University, 2006.

City of Portland Resolution, October 18, 2006.

Cowen, Lauren "Immigration Law's Uncertainty Spurs 'Organizing' Efforts." *The Oregonian*, November 20, 1986, pp. B1, B3.

Dolores Hickey interview. *The Oregonian*, June 20, 2009. http://www.oregonlive.com/opinion/index.ssf/2009/06/dolores_hickey_70_independence.html. Accessed March 29, 2014.

Ellis, Barnes C. "Immigration Law Fails to Meet Hopes." *The Oregonian*, February 15, 1988, pp. A1, B8.

Final Report of the War Relocation Authority Northwest Area Office. 1946. Part II. In Marvin Gavin Pursinger Papers, Oregon Historical Society.

Flier. "Citywide Rally for a Fair Immigration Law." Immigration Folder, Box 11. Richard Neuberger Papers, Special Collections, University of Oregon. June 10, 1955.

Friesen, S. "Columbia County Immigration Measure Declared Unenforceable." *The Oregonian*, April 13, 2009. http://www.oregonlive.com/news/index.ssf/2009/04/columbia_county_immigration_me.html. Accessed August 23, 2014.

Gonzalez-Berry, Erlinda, and Marcela Mendoza. *Mexicanos in Oregon: Their Stories, Their Lives*. Corvallis: Oregon State University Press, 2010.

Graves, B. "Portland State University Launches Initiative to Recruit and Retain More Latino Students." *The Oregonian*, October 4, 2010. http://www.oregonlive.com/education/index.ssf/2010/10/portland_state_university_laun.html. August 23, 2014.

Green, Amy "Protesters Target Day-Labor Site in Portland." *The Oregonian*, October 15, 2006, p. B2.

Haley, R. "IRCO: Doorway to Assimilation." www.midcountymemo.com/sept06. Accessed March 29, 2014.

Hardwick, S.W. "Far from Home: Slavic Refugees and the Changing Face of Oregon." Commonplace Lecture, Oregon Council for the Humanities, May 19, 2007.

Hardwick, S.W., and J.E. Meacham. "Heterolocalism, Networks of Ethnicity, and Refugee Communities in the Pacific Northwest: The Portland Story." *The Professional Geographer* 57, no. 4 (2005): 539–57.

Hume, Susan E., and Susan W. Hardwick. "African, Russian, and Ukrainian Refugee Settlement in Portland, Oregon." *The Geographical Review* 95, no. 2 (April 2005): 194–95.

Leslie, David. "D.C. Rally to Press for Immigration Reform." *Ethics Daily*, March 18, 2010. http://www.ethicsdaily.com/news.php?viewStory=15780. Accessed March 29, 2014.

Letter of Al Ullman to Virginia Laurence. August 6, 1963. Al Ullman Papers, Special Collections, University of Oregon.

Letter of Ansell Morehouse to Wayne Morse. February 29, 1956, A83, Special Collections, Wayne Morse Papers, Special Collections, University of Oregon.

Letter of Dail Delaney to Senator Morse. October 5, 1965, Box 60, Wayne Morse Papers, Special Collections, University of Oregon.

Letter of Mr. and Mrs. G.S. Reilly to Wayne Morse. July 6, 1964. Series L, Box 12, File 86. Wayne Morse Papers, Special Collections, University of Oregon.

Letter of R. Downing to Wayne Morse. August 7, 1964. Series L, Box 12, File 86. Wayne Morse Papers, Special Collections, University of Oregon.

Letter of Richard Neuberger on Letter Written on January 19, 1956 to Clatsop County, Oregon, Committee for Protection of the Foreign Born. 1957. Immigration—Walter-McCarran Act File, Box 11. Richard Neuberger Papers, Special Collections, University of Oregon.

Letter of Richard Neuberger to "Dear Friend." August 19, 1959. Richard Neuberger Papers, Box 11, Special Collections, University of Oregon.

Letter of Virginia Laurence to "Dear Sir" [Al Ullman]. July 24, 1963, Box 26, File 32, Al Ullman Papers, Special Collections, University of Oregon.

Letter of Watford Reed to Wayne Morse. August 27, 1965. Series L, Box 12, File 86. Wayne Morse Papers, Special Collections, University of Oregon.

Letter of Wayne Morse to Ansell Morehouse. March 22, 1956. A83, Special Collections, Wayne Morse Papers, Special Collections, University of Oregon.

Letter of Wayne Morse to the Committee for the Protection of Oregon's Foreign Born. March 24, 1960, A60, Immigration Folder, Wayne Morse Center. Special Collections, University of Oregon.

Letter of Wayne Morse to K.C. Stevens. October 7, 1964, Series L, Box 12, File 86. Wayne Morse Papers. Special Collections, University of Oregon.

Loew, Tracy. "Latino Summit Sets Action Plan." *Salem Statesman-Journal*, October 18, 2010, p. 1C.

McLagen, Elizabeth. *A Peculiar Paradise: A History of Blacks in Oregon*. Portland: The Georgian Press, 1980, pp. 26–31, 57–74.

Migration Policy Institute. "Oregon Fact Sheet." 2012. www.migrationinformation/org/datahub/state.ctm?ID. Accessed March 29, 2014.

"Newcomers Find Homes in Willamette Valley." *The Oregonian*, January 2, 1965, 11.

Oregon Bureau of Labor. "*Vámonos pal Norte* ("*Let's Go North*"): *A Social Profile of the Spanish Speaking Migratory Farm Laborer*." (1958): 6, 18, 21.

Oregonians for Immigration Reform Website. www.oregonir.org. Accessed March 29, 2014.

Pardington, Suzanne. "Oregon Universities Try to Recruit More Latino Students." *The Oregonian*, November 15, 2009. http://www.oregonlive.com/education/index.ssf/2009/11/oregon_universities_try_to_rec.html. Accessed August 8, 2014.

Pascoe, Peggy. "A Mistake to Simmer the Question Down to Black and White." In Jun Xing Erlinda Gonzales-Berry, Patti Sakurai, Robert D. Thompson, and Kurt Peters, eds. *Seeing Color: Indigenous Peoples and Racialized Ethnic Minorities in Oregon*. Latham, MD: University Press of America, Inc., 2007, pp. 27–30.

"People." *King's Business Magazine* (December 1955): 7.

Peterson del Mar, David. *Oregon's Promise: An Interpretive History*. Corvallis: Oregon State University Press, 2002, 33–34, 49–51, 62.

"Russian Immigrants Arrive in Portland." *The Oregonian*, December 4, 1964, 10.

Sakurai, P., M. Mendoza, and L. Stephen. "Asian and Mexican Oregonians: Their Ethnic Diversity." Unpublished Essays, 2011.

Senate Bill 1206. 84th Congress, Immigration Folder, Box 11. Richard Neuberger Papers, Special Collections, University of Oregon. 1955.

Shoemaker, Kent "An Open Letter to W. Sherman Burgoyne." *Hood River News*, January 26, 1945, p. 10.

Singer, Audrey, and Jill H. Wilson. *From 'There to Here': Refugee Resettlement in Metropolitan America*. Washington, DC: The Brookings Institution, 2006.

Skidmore, Sarah "Rally Organizers Vow More Work on Immigration Issues." *Press State and Local Wire*, May 2, 2006. Psuvanguard.com/author/sarah-skidmore-associated-press/. Accessed August 26, 2014.

Superintendent of Public Instruction. Correspondence (II) File, Oregon State Americanization Commission Files, 1925–1932, Oregon State Archives, Salem.

Tichenor, Daniel. *Dividing Lines: The Politics of Immigration Control in America*. Princeton, NJ: Princeton University Press, 2002.

Vendrell, C. "Listening to the People." In E. Gamboa, and C.M. Buan, eds. *Nosotros: The Hispanic People of Oregon*. Portland: Oregon Council for the Humanities, 1995, p. 144.

Wisner, D. "A Bright Spot." *The Wesleyan Missionary*, December, 1955, 22.

Wozniacka, Gosia. "Voters Target Illegal Hiring." *The Oregonian*, November 7, 2008. http://www.oregonlive.com/news/index.ssf/2008/11/voters_go_after_businesses_tha.html. Accessed August 8, 2014.

38

PENNSYLVANIA

Adam McGlynn

CHRONOLOGY

1643   The first European settlement in Pennsylvania is created at Tinicum Island by Governor Johan Printz of New Sweden.

1655   Peter Stuyvesant, governor of New Netherlands takes control of New Sweden, making it part of the Dutch colony in the New World.

1664   The English seize control of the Dutch territory in the Delaware River region in the name of the Duke of York, brother to the king of England.

1681   The Charter of Pennsylvania is signed by the king of England, granting William Penn control of the new territory of Pennsylvania which Penn plans to use as a safe haven for his fellow, persecuted English Quakers. Penn views the territory as a potential utopian society which would be "a free colony for all mankind." While the majority of Quakers who would immigrate to Pennsylvania are of English descent, they are followed by numerous Welsh and Dutch Quakers through the beginning of the 1700s.

1708   An influx of Germans from the Rhineland begins arriving in Pennsylvania due to the devastation in the wake of the War of Spanish Succession fought by France and England.

1717   The Scotch-Irish begin a sustained movement of people into Pennsylvania spurred by a lack of availability of affordable housing.

1740   A second wave of Scotch Irish immigrants descends upon Pennsylvania due to an Irish famine.

1766	Following the French and Indian War, Irish immigration begins to increase, reaching a high of 1,400 immigrants a year.
1780	The Pennsylvania Gradual Abolition Act is passed, making Pennsylvania the first state to enact an emancipation law in the United States.
1840s	Another wave of Irish immigrants descends upon Pennsylvania after the Irish Potato Famine.
1860	The free African American population has increased to 57,000 from only 6,500 in 1790. Philadelphia has the largest free African American population in the North.
1900	During the 10-year period that coincides with the beginning of the new century, Pennsylvania has its largest population increase in the commonwealth's history as new immigrants arrive from eastern and southern Europe.
1917	Migration of African Americans from the South increases due to decreased European immigration during World War I.
1924	The U.S. government passes the Immigration Act of 1924 which creates quotas to limit immigration from southern and eastern Europe, a source of much of Pennsylvania's immigrant population at the time.
1952	Over 24,000 displaced Europeans from World War II settle in Pennsylvania by the expiration of the U.S. government's Displaced Persons Act.
2006	The city of Hazleton is among the first subnational governments to adopt legislation which allows the city to impose sanctions for hiring undocumented immigrants or for renting housing to them.
2010	State representative Daryl Metcalfe introduces House Bill (HB) 2479, which, similar to the much-publicized Arizona Senate Bill (SB) 1070, would charge immigrants with a crime for not carrying proper documentation at all times to prove that they are in the United States legally.
2011	As the new chair of the State Government Committee, Representative Metcalfe introduces a package of legislation to address immigration issues in Pennsylvania called "National Security Begins at Home."

HISTORICAL OVERVIEW

EARLY HISTORY TO WORLD WAR II

While the story of the United States is a story of immigration, Pennsylvania epitomizes this more than many of the other states. Unlike New York and other territories which were developed due to geographical or natural resources, Pennsylvania was created and first developed primarily as a place for citizens of other countries to enjoy a utopian society. At the centerpiece of this society was a protection of religious freedom, jury trials, and freedom of the press as codified in William Penn's *First Frame of Government*. Beginning in 1681, Penn's fellow English Quakers immigrated to Pennsylvania under its promise of religious freedom after being persecuted in England. At the founding of Pennsylvania, approximately 60,000 Quakers resided in England. They were the most persecuted religion in England as 10,000 of its adherents had been jailed in the 20 years preceding the creation of Pennsylvania. They felt the wrath of the English Crown more than others as their abhorrence for hierarchy; refusal to partake in religious ritual, pay tithes, take oaths in court, engage in sports, singing, or dancing; and their promotion of pacifism were viewed as "subversive and dangerous to society" (Klein and Hoogenboom 1973, 18). William Penn, son of the admiral Sir William Penn, had been jailed multiple times for his Quaker beliefs. At the time of Admiral Sir William Penn's death, the British Crown owed him £16,000. As repayment of this debt, William Penn's request for the territory between Maryland and New York was granted by King Charles II and the immigration of Quakers to this safe haven in the New World began.

The first wave of non-English settlers began in the early 1700s as the Rhineland Germans arrived and settled north and west of Philadelphia in the counties of Northampton, Berks, Lancaster, and Lehigh where they "transformed this region into a rich farming country, contributing greatly to the expanding prosperity of the province" (Pennsylvania General Assembly 2011). These German immigrants left their homeland not only to avoid the War of Spanish Succession but also to escape the persecution of their Protestant religion. Following the Germans, were the Scotch Irish who began to arrive in 1717, first due to "rack renting, or the practice by a landlord of raising the rent on expiration of the lease" (Klein and Hoogenboom 1973, 40). Klein and Hoogenboom go on to identify multiple successive waves of Scotch Irish immigration first due to religious differences as many Protestants fled Ireland for Pennsylvania and then because of famine. Further, by the 1770s, pervasive economic despair has enveloped Ireland as the economic situation of those left behind after the previous emigration continually worsened. By 1776, the Scotch Irish were one-quarter of the commonwealth's population and while some settled near the Germans, others began to settle in central and western Pennsylvania. While the English-born Quakers, Germans, and Scotch Irish accounted for the vast majority of the commonwealth's population, there were French Huguenot, Dutch, Swedish, and Finnish settlers as well in pre-Revolution Pennsylvania; however many of them intermarried and were blended into the dominant groups. The Pennsylvania Assembly was dominated by the Quakers and their leadership was supported by German members of the body. Their alliance lasted up until the 1750s when conflicts surrounding the French and Indian War and the passage of a militia bill split the

Wiliam Penn. Engraved by J. Posselwhite from the print by J. Hall. (Library of Congress)

alliance and saw Germans align with the Scotch Irish in the assembly.

German immigration into the United States peaked in 1749 when approximately 9,500 immigrants arrived at the Port of Philadelphia. Irish immigration, on the other hand, continued but on an inconsistent basis through the rest of the century largely due to the conditions in Ireland, but also due to the French and Indian and then Revolutionary Wars which served to reduce immigration into the country in the late 1700s. While many of the first Irish immigrants were Protestant, Irish immigration increased rapidly in the nineteenth century when Irish Catholics began to leave their homeland in droves with 5 million Irish coming to the United States from 1820 to 1920 (Kenny 2003). The influx of Irish immigrants helped increase the commonwealth's population by no less than 25 percent per decade in the first half of the nineteenth century. These Irish immigrants settled throughout eastern Pennsylvania taking jobs, working on the railroads, and in coal mines. As their population increased, so did the political influence of the Irish, especially in Philadelphia, where they helped Democrats carry numerous statewide elections, leading to a nativist backlash in the form of the Know-Nothing Party who pledged "to destroy Catholicism in America, to stop foreign immigration, and to disenfranchise naturalized citizens" (Klein and Hoogenboom 1973, 150). The rise of the Republican Party and continued conflicts over slavery led to the dissolution of the Know-Nothing Party leading up to the Civil War, which upon its conclusion ushered in an era of even greater immigration into Pennsylvania.

As discussed in greater detail below in this chapter, Pennsylvania's rich endowment of natural resources, including coal deposits and iron ore, helped fuel immigration into the commonwealth after the Civil War. Unlike the 1700s and the first half of the 1800s, this new wave of immigration featured people from southern and eastern Europe, many of whom settled in the central and western parts of the state such as Steelton and Pittsburgh where their unskilled labor was most in demand. This immigration significantly changed the ethnic makeup of the commonwealth, with just one example being that the commonwealth received one-half of all Slavic immigrants who entered the United States between 1880 and 1920.

From 1890 to 1910, the Italian population of Philadelphia increased from 6,799 to 76,734. Overall, the commonwealth saw its overall population increase from just over 2.9 million people in 1860 to 9.6 million people in 1930. While these new immigrants came because of the availability of jobs, they also struggled underneath the power of their employers. Throughout the commonwealth from the coal mines in northeast to the steel factories in the west, there were company towns, where employers held a monopoly on jobs and in many cases also on housing, commerce, and government. As John Bodnar explains, in the city of Steelton, "Pennsylvania Steel employed over one-half of all residents in the town" and notes that, "[t]hroughout the fifty years after 1870 a high company official usually served as president of the town council" (Bodnar 1977, 7).

The Immigration Act of 1924 was passed in response to the significant number of southern and eastern Europeans entering the country and to eugenic concerns of this time period. In an essay written at the time, Robert Ward claimed, "there was no question of the racial superiority of the northwestern Europeans or of the racial inferiority of southeastern Europeans" (Ward 1924, 107). As further evidence that this law was meant to limit immigration from southern and eastern Europe, Ward cited a report from the House of Representatives which claimed a goal of the law to be to preserve racial homogeneity in the United States and defended the use of 1890 Census data as the basis for estimating the number of immigrants that could immigrate to the United States. As the 1890 Census occurred prior to mass immigration from eastern and southern Europe, using this census data served to allow the United States to limit the number of immigrants from these regions. As much of the commonwealth's new immigrant population was from these regions, the law served to limit the number of new immigrants in the coming decades. The next major migration of new residents into the commonwealth occurred in the aftermath of World War II.

WORLD WAR II TO THE PRESENT

By the end of World War II, there were nearly 1 million displaced Europeans, including some 250,000 European Jews who managed to survive the war in Russia and Poland. In response, the Displaced Persons Act of 1948 was proposed, which called for up to 205,000 displaced Europeans to immigrate to the United States. The bill was finally passed two years later and "[w]hen the act finally expired in 1952, the United States had accepted 380,000 people under its provisions, or approximately 40 percent of the displaced persons registered in Europe" (Burstin 1989, 77). Over 24,000 people entered Pennsylvania in this period, third to only New York and Illinois. In her study of the Polish experience in Pittsburgh after the war, Burstin found that both groups faced challengers upon their arrival. The Jewish community had a more organized and extensive response to the new immigrants as compared to the Christians in the area as they set up the Jewish Social Services Board and the United Vocational and Employment Service to aid the new arrivals. Despite these efforts, however, Polish Jews in Pittsburgh were more likely to say that they felt isolated (possibly due to the language barrier) and had a harder time adjusting than their Christian counterparts.

The demographics of Pennsylvania next began to change in the 1980s with a movement of Latinos and Asians into the commonwealth. For example, Kennett Square, a suburb of Philadelphia, saw its migrant population grow starting in the mid-1990s as Mexicans moved to the area to work in the mushroom industry. Compared to other states with major metropolitan areas, however, the impact of immigration in Pennsylvania was minor throughout the 1980s and early 1990s. A report by Philadelphia Federal Reserve economist Albert Saiz found that approximately 155,000 immigrants entered Philadelphia from 1983 to 1997, compared to over 1 million immigrants entering New York and Los Angeles and over 359,000 in Washington, D.C., demonstrating the minor impact immigration has had in Philadelphia and the commonwealth overall. The effects of immigration in Pennsylvania at the time also proved to be different than what had been observed in other cities

Some of 50 German Jewish refugee children whose ocean passage was paid by a local lawyer enjoy a game of leap frog in Philadelphia at the suburban estate where they will remain until foster homes are found for them, June 5, 1939. All came under immigration quotas. (AP Photo)

and what was going on currently, as greater efforts were made to include Mexican immigrants in communities like Kennett Square. Diaz-Barriga (2008) discusses how the area's annual Mushroom Festival includes a mariachi band and highlights the benefits of the mushroom industry and their workers to the region although the relationship later soured as these workers begin to unionize in the early 1990s.

This minor growth in the immigrant population was corrected at the turn of the century, when the immigrant population in both the Philadelphia and eastern half of the commonwealth exploded. From 2000 to 2010, the Latino population in the commonwealth jumped 82.6 percent, while the Asian population increased 58.8 percent. Without population growth among these two ethnic groups (and African Americans whose population increases by 12.5 percent), Pennsylvania's population would have remained stagnant as the Anglo population dropped 0.7 percent in this time period. The population growth has been centered primarily in the eastern portion of the state. The director of the Pennsylvania State Data Center, Sue Copella credits the growth to Philadelphia serving as a "reemerging gateway" for immigration as multiple ethnic groups migrated up from other Mid-Atlantic cities like Baltimore and moved west from New York City where they first settled in the United States (Matza and Duchneskie 2011, B01).Another possible reason for the growth among Latinos, according to Nelson Carrasquillo, the director of the Farmworkers Support Committee in Pennsylvania, was that federal immigration reform in 1986 granted amnesty to many of the farmworkers in the commonwealth like those of Kennett Square and in recent years they have finally saved enough money to start bringing their relatives into the commonwealth, helping to spur the population growth. This recent increase in immigration was significant as Philadelphia saw a net gain in population for the first time in 60 years with the results of the 2010 Census.

According to a Brookings Institution report (Singer et al. 2008), the Philadelphia region has had the most diverse set of immigrants coming into the commonwealth with 39 percent coming from Asia, 28 percent from Latin America and the Caribbean, 23 percent from Europe, and 8 percent from Africa. The report goes on to explain that nearly 60 percent of the region's foreign-born population has arrived in the area since 1990 and even though an increase in foreign-born residents usually places stress on a city's resources and poses a challenge to policymakers, immigration to Philadelphia has also been an economic benefit as 75 percent of the labor force growth in Philadelphia has been attributed to immigrants. Overall, the Brookings (Singer et al. 2008) report cites the uniqueness of recent immigration to Philadelphia compared to other metropolitan areas:

> Philadelphia's very diverse foreign-born residents defy generalizations on a number of demographic, social and economic characteristics. They depart from their U.S.-born and minority counterparts with regard to age distribution and they have differ-

ent educational and occupational profiles. In some respects they share characteristics of U.S.-born minorities, such as on individual income levels and some occupations, but in other ways their labor market attributes resemble the native-born white population. Most importantly, immigrants have a range of human capital and skills that seem to be meeting the demands of the Philadelphia labor market. (Singer et al. 2008, 29)

The growth in Philadelphia is only part of the recent immigration story in Pennsylvania, however. The unique geography of the eastern part of the state has spurred population growth from the Pocono Mountains in the northeast down to Philadelphia. The Latino population growth has centered in the northeastern part of the state and Philadelphia, while the Asian population growth has centered in Philadelphia and its surrounding counties. In the northeastern part of the state, access to Interstate 80 allows immigrants easy access to family and friends in the New York City area and has spurred migration to the Pocono Mountains. Also, the reduced cost of living in Pennsylvania serves as an additional motivation for relocation among Latinos, Asians and African Americans. Construction companies and economic development organizations seized on this fact starting in the 1990s when they advertised on New York City area radio stations touting the ability to own a home in Pennsylvania for less than they were renting an apartment in New York City. This in conjunction with a desire to get out of New York City after the events of 9/11 led thousands of African Americans and Latinos to relocate to northeastern Pennsylvania.

The population growth of Latinos and Asians, despite it possibly saving Pennsylvania from losing two congressional seats, rather than one, has not been widely accepted among the commonwealth's residents. As discussed in the following section, Hazleton adopted a statute to make it impossible for undocumented immigrants to find housing and employment in the city. The city went from being under 10 percent Latino to over one-third Latino from 2000 to 2010, and while this growth was credited with leading to several new businesses, concern over crime and the provision of social services led to this anti-immigrant backlash. Other areas, like Altoona, followed suit with their own laws, even though their foreign-born population accounted for less than 1 percent of their total population.

TOPICAL ESSAYS

Industrialization and Immigration in Pennsylvania, 1850–1940

By 1940, Pennsylvania was the second most-populated state in the country after New York. While much of the attention paid to swells of immigrants coming to the United States was focused on New York and Ellis Island, Pennsylvania's population boomed in this era as well, because while immigrants arrived in New York, many headed west to Pennsylvania for jobs. The discovery of abundant natural resources in the early and mid-1800s fueled the migration of new immigrants to the commonwealth. Extensive reserves of anthracite (hard coal) found in the eastern part of the state and soft coal in the western part of the state led to Pennsylvania becoming the country's leading producer of coal. In the eastern part of the state alone, three separate regions of coal production developed and the increased coal production fueled the need for greater transportation options. While these coal-producing regions were located near many of the commonwealth's prominent rivers, such as the Susquehanna, Schuykill, and Lehigh, these waterways had limited capacity and their construction almost bankrupted the state, thus fueling the need for the construction of railroads. By the start of the Civil War, the commonwealth had over 2,500 miles of railroad; more than any other state. The various railroad lines were ultimately consolidated under the single Pennsylvania Railroad monopoly which features lines from the major cities in the Midwest such as Chicago, St. Louis, and Cleveland through Pennsylvania and New Jersey and across the Hudson River into New York.

One of the reasons that the railroad industry flourished so quickly was the presence of iron ore in the central and western parts of the commonwealth. Anthracite iron was first produced in the Lehigh Valley and with the advances made in steel production such as the Bessemer process, several other steel towns in central and western Pennsylvania, such as Steelton and Johnstown, quickly developed. In 1859, Edwin Drake drilled the first successful oil well in Titusville, setting off an oil rush in northwestern Pennsylvania, which returns us to the issue of immigration: the bountiful natural resources Pennsylvania possessed and the continual need for an expanded transportation infrastructure to move these materials provided numerous employment opportunities for new immigrants who then came to the commonwealth in droves.

The Anthracite coal miners working in the eastern counties of Luzerne and Schuykill first consisted of primarily Irish Americans. Mining was dangerous work as aside from the daily exposure to smoke and dust, there was always the risk of death from a mine collapse. James Rodechko (1973) chronicles the hard times faced by most Irish Americans in the Anthracite coal region of Pennsylvania in his chapter, "The Irish American Society." Despite the volume of coal production, many Irish American families living in this region of the commonwealth still fell victim to poverty and many young boys took jobs in the mines to help make ends meet in their families. Mine owners who also controlled the stores and what passed as affordable housing ensured that the majority of miners' pay went back into their pockets. As in other states, Rodechko explains that the Irish were at the bottom of the social ladder in Pennsylvania, with some employers refusing to employ anyone of Irish descent and others willing to fire Irish workers if an English, Welsh, or

U.S.-born worker could be hired. The sources of this discrimination were the traditional stereotypes such as demeaning Irish intelligence, questioning their Catholicism, and of course the labeling that too many Irishmen were alcoholics.

In response to their social and economic troubles, the Irish attempted to form civic organizations which would increase their political clout and possibly improve their poor treatment by employers. These groups included the immigrant aid society called the Ancient Order of Hibernians (AOH); the Workingmen's Benevolent Association (WBA), a coal miner's union; and the Molly Maguires, a group which may have shared some membership with both the Hibernians and the WBA but unlike the other two was willing to use intimidation and violence to improve the treatment of Irish coal miners. Challenges from the coal mine owners; competition from other ethnic groups; a lack of a strong Irish press to promote their plight; and conflict between the AOH (Ancient Order of Hibernians), WBA and the Molly Maguires limited the ability of the Irish to improve their station in the Anthracite coal region and as a result, many relocated to other parts of Pennsylvania or other states for better economic opportunities. There remains much debate about the role, activities, and legacy of these three Irish organizations. First, questions remain on how intertwined the membership of these organizations were. More striking is the second question of how violent the Molly Maguires actually were and whether their activities were exaggerated by the mine owners who wanted to quash any resistance to their ability to turn a profit. Harold Aurand (1971) cites the debate over whether the Mollies, as they were called, were labor leaders or criminals and goes on to explain that either way, the highlight of this era in history was that the supposed members of the Mollies who were arrested and put to death for their activities did not occur by the hands of the Commonwealth of Pennsylvania but by private detectives and a private corporation whose economic interests were best served by the Molly Maguires being put out of existence.

In Philadelphia, Russians, Irish, Italians, and the Germans were the most prevalent groups of immigrants to be found. Without the natural resources of the cities to the north and west of them, Philadelphia thrived in garment manufacturing. At the time, one-third of the city's population worked in textile and clothing manufacturing. Similar to their brethren in the coal-mining industry, garment workers suffered under horrible working conditions. While there were some standards for operation and cleanliness in sweatshops in the late 1800s, families could manufacture garments in their own homes. These home shops were paid per garment and thus husbands, wives, and children worked tirelessly to produce finished products only to earn about $8.50 for a 60-hour work week when there was demand, which is only about half of the year. Overall, they found this equated to an income of $188.10 per year, with the average garment work family spending $108 of this on rent for three rooms.

Compared to other cities in the northeast and the commonwealth, Philadelphia's immigrant population was influenced by its larger population of African Americans as compared to other northeastern cities, as this caused the many Polish immigrants who entered the United States at the Port of Philadelphia not to stay in the city. Golab (1998) explains that while Pennsylvania received more Eastern European immigrants than any other state, "[t]he Polish immigrant who wished to settle in Philadelphia had to compete with the Irish and the Negroes who were there before him and with the Italians and Jews who arrived with him" (Golab 1998, 210).Another significant factor influencing the population of the Philadelphia was that the city had a more developed economy than the rest of the commonwealth. For example, in fields such as printing and publishing and leather manufacturing, highly skilled labor was needed and the vast majority of people in these fields were born in the United States. Overall then Poles and Italians had better employment opportunities in other areas of commonwealth, especially in western Pennsylvania, where jobs working in the railroad, coal or steel industry did not require the skills needed for many jobs in Philadelphia. The Italians who did stay in Philadelphia worked mainly in construction, while the Polish worked the limited number of steel and iron jobs that did exist.

The unskilled workers who struggled in Philadelphia found more opportunity in Pittsburgh but faced significant competition for the available positions there. While the vast majority of workers in the Pittsburgh area were semiskilled or unskilled at the beginning of the twentieth century, Andrew Carnegie and other employers in the region had their managers pay strict attention to controlling costs which yielded: declining wages, a workday which increased to 12 hours, and workforce reductions when possible. Despite these challenges, immigrants continued to travel to western Pennsylvania as the wages there far surpassed what was available in Europe. For example, Bodnar (1985) found that an English bricklayer could make only 30 percent of the salary that a bricklayer in Pennsylvania would and that overall wages and working hours were better in Pittsburgh than in English cities.

The higher wages and growing steel and iron sectors increased Pittsburgh's population in the latter half of the 1800s with immigrants from England, Ireland, and Germany, as in many other parts of the country. However, by the turn of the century, members of these countries of origin groups declined and the city saw drastic increases in the number of Polish, Italian, and African American residents. Between 1890 and 1900, the population of these groups increased by 318 percent, 219 percent and 96.5 percent, respectively. Each of the three groups arrived under different pretenses. Bodnar, Simon and Weber (1982) explain that African Americans seeking to escape the limited economic opportunities of sharecropping and political oppression in the South migrated north and based on word of mouth from friends and relatives regarding employment opportunities and wages settled in Pittsburgh. They go on to explain that Poles, like African Americans, came to Pittsburgh after leaving their farming origins. They migrated to Pittsburgh due to several factors, including overpopulation and social stratification, as land reform policies meant to allow peasants to own property only exacerbated the divide between the middle and lower classes in places like Prussia. The Italians who wound up in Pittsburgh were similar to the African Americans in relying on kinship in choosing where they settled and were similar to both African Americans and the Polish in seeking social advancement and economic opportunity. However, the authors find that unlike the other groups, Italians were more likely to be open to returning to their place of origin and appeared to look at Pittsburgh as a means to an economic end and not necessarily as a permanent destination.

Kinship was incredibly important to all three groups as a method for procuring employment as friends and family vouching for potential employees went much further than the content of an employment application in getting work. The Polish were far more successful in getting work in the steel industry than other ethnic groups, and the discrimination faced by African Americans limited their options to work as laborers such as janitors or in service positions such as waiters, porters, or domestic servant. Italians did not face the same discrimination as African Americans and fared better in employment because a higher percentage of Italians immigrants were skilled laborers. While Bodnar, Simon, and Weber (1982) find different employment experiences for these three groups, they shared a similar fate in that all three "received the least desirable land—that with the highest density, that with the oldest and most deteriorating housing, or that located on the most formidable terrain" (Bodnar, Simon, and Weber 1982, 70). Overall, the experience of immigrants to Pittsburgh did not turn out as many immigrants would have hoped. While there were greater employment opportunities, the African Americans, Italians, and Polish who flocked to Pittsburgh at the end of the nineteenth and beginning of the twentieth century faced varying levels of discrimination and had difficulty moving beyond the ranks of unskilled laborers. Thousands of immigrants, especially Italians, repatriated and succeeded in making more money than when they left their homeland. However, for those who stayed in the United States, there was a mixed record of improving their station in life by moving up the ranks to skilled labor positions and from blue-collar to white-collar positions.

The Illegal Immigration Relief Act and National Security Begins at Home

In the absence of comprehensive federal immigration reform, the city of Hazleton, Pennsylvania, adopted the Illegal Immigration Relief Act, to address problems of crime, school crowding, rising hospital costs, and extra demand for city services which it blamed on a growing undocumented immigrant population.

The city's population had grown approximately 30 percent to 32,000 residents largely from an influx of Latino/as from New York and New Jersey. As a former coal-mining town, this helped revitalize Hazleton as new residents led to new businesses. However, a shooting by two undocumented immigrants in May 2006 served as the catalyst for the Illegal Immigration Relief Act. The act required landlords to verify the citizenship of their current and prospective tenants to ensure that they were allowed to legally reside in the United States. Landlords could be fined $1,000 per day for renting to an undocumented immigrant and faced the loss of their building permits for continued noncompliance. Landlords were assisted in checking the immigration status of future tenants by the ordinance placing the city Code Enforcement Office in charge of issuing occupancy permits for individuals looking for rent in the city for the first time that could provide documentation of their legal status. Businesses as well faced similar fines and loss of permits for employing undocumented workers.

The importance of the Hazleton law is that it started a trend in states and cities around the country which looked to the city as a model for how to deal with their own perceived problems with undocumented immigration. For example, a National Council of State Legislatures survey conducted in April 2007 found that over 1,100 bills had been filed in the state legislatures concerning undocumented immigration, more than double the previous year. Then mayor, now Congressman Louis Barletta, estimated that half of the 10,000 Latino/as living in Hazleton left in response to the ordinance. The key question concerning this and similar legislation was twofold. First, did the enforcement of these laws violate the equal protection clause of the Fourteenth Amendment of the Constitution and second, were states and localities superseding federal authority in trying to regulate immigration? In an interview aired on the CBS program *60 Minutes*, former mayor Barletta disputed these arguments, claiming that the city was not regulating who could enter the country or even punishing undocumented immigrants as the consequences of the law would fall on landlords and employers.

The American Civil Liberties Union (ACLU), the Puerto Rican Legal Defense and Education Fund (PRLDEF), and several other groups were able to get an injunction approved which prevented the law from taking effect until ruled upon by the courts. The case of *Lozano et al. v. City of Hazleton* challenging the law was first heard in the Middle District of Pennsylvania, where Judge James M. Munley ruled the law unconstitutional in 2007. The case continued to receive national attention, not only because Hazleton's law is the first of its kind, but also because it brought together some rather strange bedfellows. Among those who filed amicus briefs in favor of the plaintiffs were the U.S. Chamber of Commerce and the Mexican American Legal Defense and Education Fund (MALDEF). Knowing the political affiliations of these groups, it is rare to find an issue where the U.S. Chamber of Commerce agreed with the ACLU, PRLDEF, and MALDEF. However, given that many Latino businesses closed up shop after the law was passed and the negative effect this had on the Hazleton economy and the economy of other municipalities who would pass similar laws, it made sense that they would side with the plaintiffs.

In 2010, the U.S. Court of Appeals for the Third Circuit in Pennsylvania heard the case and the three-judge panel unanimously upheld Judge Munley's decision that the law be thrown out because it was preempted by federal immigration law. However, in June 2011, after being appealed to the U.S. Supreme Court, the case was remanded back to the Third Circuit for review given the decision of the Supreme Court in *Chamber of Commerce v. Whiting*. In the *Whiting* case, the Supreme Court voted 5–3 to uphold an Arizona law which required employers in the state to only hire immigrants authorized to work in the United States and check the immigration status of their workers with the E-Verify system. Given these events, we should expect Hazleton's law as well of those of the cities who copy it to be upheld.

More recently, state representative Daryl Metcalfe has been at the forefront of the anti-undocumented immigration movement in Pennsylvania and has introduced a package of legislation totaling 14 bills called "National Security Begins at Home" to address the perceived issue. The legislative package includes making English the official language of the commonwealth and a law similar to Arizona SB 1070, which would require police to question anyone suspected of not being in the United States legally. Also included is a bill which disputes the Fourteenth Amendment's granting citizenship to anyone born on U.S. soil. In introducing this legislation, Metcalfe states, "When you're granting citizenship to the children of foreign nationals who are here without our permission and here temporarily, you've created a situation that's undermining the United States of America, undermining our citizenship for those who truly want to immigrate to our country in the right way and pursue the American dream with a proper work ethic rather than steal the American dream, as illegal aliens have been attempting to do" (Metcalfe 2011). The Republicans' sweep of the 2010 election gives Representative Metcalfe the chairmanship of the House State Government committee, which gives him an institutional platform to address immigration policy in the commonwealth. At the time of this writing, the committee has moved its first bill, HB 439 to the full House for consideration. This bill would allow the state to cancel the permanent license of any employer who hires an undocumented immigrant. Despite the dedication of Representative Metcalfe to this legislative package, it is unlikely that much of it will become law as the leadership of the Republican Party has identified other issues as their legislative priorities in 2011–2012 term.

In closing, given its cost of living and proximity to major population centers, we should expect immigration to increase in Pennsylvania as we progress into the twenty-first century. At the same time, we should also expect to see this increased level of immigration stay in the public eye and, in response, we should expect the commonwealth to be at the forefront of the anti-undocumented immigration movement.

NOTABLE GROUPS

PENNSYLVANIA IMMIGRATION RESOURCE CENTER

The Pennsylvania Immigration Resource Center is an immigrant advocate group in York that first began in 1993. In June of 1993, a ship carrying 286 Chinese nationals ran aground and many were sent to York jails to be held while they sought asylum. Their treatment and general rightlessness provoked community outrage and this group was formed to reflect the community's "shared commitment to the words inscribed on the Supreme Court entrance: *Equal Access to Justice*" (Pennsylvania Immigration Resource Center n.d.). Since then, this group has fought for immigrants who are the most vulnerable to exploitation and legal issues, including detainees. Among other services, this group provides legal information to individuals in detention as well as immigrants in the broader community. It also provides pro bono legal assistance, when needed, and pro se assistance, often drawing on partnerships with law schools and universities. They also specialize in aid to victims of domestic violence and victims of sexual assault and other crimes. Given its aims and work, it can foster greater ties to the community and cultivate greater civic education.

BIBLIOGRAPHY

Aurand, Harold W. *From the Molly Maguires to the United Mine Workers: The Social Ecology of an Industrial Union, 1869–1897.* Philadelphia: Temple University Press, 1971.

Barletta, Lou. "60 Minutes Interview." November 19, 2006. http://www.cbsnews.com/video/watch/?id=2100599n. Accessed March 29, 2014.

Bodnar, John E. *Immigration and Industrialization: Ethnicity in an American Mill Town, 1870–1940.* Pittsburgh: University of Pittsburgh Press, 1977.

Bodnar, John E. *The Transplanted: A History of Immigrants in Urban America.* Bloomington: Indiana University Press, 1985.

Bodnar, John, Roger Simon, and Michael P. Weber. *Lives of Their Own: Blacks, Italians and Poles in Pittsburgh, 1900–1960.* Urbana: University of Illinois Press, 1982.

Burstin, Barbara Stern. *After the Holocaust: The Migration of Polish Jews and Christians to Pittsburgh.* Pittsburgh: University of Pittsburgh Press, 1989.

Diaz-Barriga, Miguel. "Distracción: Notes on Cultural Citizenship, Visual Ethnography, and Mexican Migration to Pennsylvania." *Visual Anthropology Review* 24, no. 2 (2008): 133–47.

Dickinson, Joan Younger. "Aspects of Italian Immigration to Philadelphia." *The Pennsylvania Magazine of History and Biography* 90, no. 4 (1966): 445–65.

Frank, Howard. "Terrorism Reshaped the Poconos." *Pocono Record*, September 11, 2011, A1.

Golab, Caroline. "The Immigrant and the City: Poles, Italians, and Jews in Philadelphia, 1870–1920." In A. F. Davis, and M. H. Haller, eds. *The Peoples of Philadelphia: A History of Ethnic Groups and Lower-Class Life, 1790–1940*. Philadelphia: University of Pennsylvania Press, 1998, pp. 203–32.

Hamill, Sean D. "Altoona, with No immigrant Problem, Decides to Solve It." *New York Times*, December 7, 2006, A34.

Kaye, Jeffrey. "Re-Living Our Immigrant Past: From Hazleton to Arizona and Back Again." Immigration Policy Center, May 21, 2010. http://www.immigrationpolicy.org/perspectives/re-living-our-immigrant-past-hazleton-arizona-and-back-again. Accessed March 29, 2014.

Kenny, Kevin. "Diaspora and Comparison: The Global Irish as a Case Study." *The Journal of American History* 90, no. 1 (2003): 134–62.

Klein, Philip S, and Ari Hoogenboom. *A History of Pennsylvania*. New York: McGraw Hill, 1973.

Lattanzi Shutika, Debra. "Bridging the Community: Nativism, Activism, and the Politics of Inclusion in a Mexican Settlement in Pennsylvania." In V. Zuniga, and R. Hernandez-Leon, eds. *New Directions: Mexican Immigration in the United States*. New York: Russell Sage Foundation, 2005, pp. 103–32.

Matza, Michael. "Hearings Start on Immigrant Crackdown Package." *The Philadelphia Inquirer*, August 31, 2011, B05.

Matza, Michael, and J. Duchneskie. "Immigrant Surge: Why Area Grew; Affordability Is Credited for Luring the Latinos and Asiana Who Gave the Phila. Region a Census Boost." *The Philadelphia Inquirer*, March 13, 2011, B01.

Metcalfe, Daryl. "National Security Begins at Home Press Conference." March 1, 2011. http://www.repmetcalfe.com/Immigration.aspx. Accessed March 29, 2014.

Novack, J. "Immigration Shootout at the Local Corral." Forbes.com, July 19, 2007. http://www.forbes.com/2007/07/18/immigration-arizona-congress-biz-beltway-cz_jn_0719beltway.html. Accessed March 29, 2014.

Pennsylvania General Assembly. "Pennsylvania History." 2011. http://www.legis .state.pa.us/WU01/VC/visitor_info/pa_history/pa_history.htm. Accessed March 29, 2014.

Pennsylvania Immigration Resource Center. Pennsylvania Immigration Resource Center Website. http://www.pirclaw.org/about_us/history. Accessed February 25, 2014.

Price, J. Howard. "Towns Take a Local Approach to Blocking Illegal Aliens." *The Washington Times*, September 26, 2006, A03.

Richey, Warren. "Supreme Court Demands Review of Ruling in Anti-Illegal Immigration Case." *The Christian Science Monitor*, June 11, 2011. http://www .csmonitor.com/USA/Justice/2011/0606/Supreme-Court-demands-review-of-ruling-in-anti-illegal-immigration-case. Accessed March 29, 2014.

Rodechko, J. P. "Irish-American Society in the Pennsylvania Anthracite Region: 1870–1880." In J. E. Bodnar, ed. *The Ethnic Experience in Pennsylvania*. Lewisburg, PA: Bucknell University Press, 1973, pp. 19–38.

Rubinkam, Michael. "Hispanics Flee PA Town Before Crackdown." *Washington Post*, October 31, 2006. http://www.washingtonpost.com/wp-dyn/content/article/2006/10/31/AR2006103100712.html. Accessed March 29, 2014.

Saiz, Albert. "The Impact of Immigration on American Cities: an Introduction to the Issues." *Business Review, Federal Reserve Bank of Philadelphia* 2003 (Q4): 14–23.

Scolforo, Mark. "PA Town Enforces Illegal Immigrant Rule." July 14, 2006. http://www.washingtonpost.com/wp-dyn/content/article/2006/07/14/AR2006071400175_pf.html. Accessed March 29, 2014.

Singer, Audrey, Domenic Vitiello, Michael Katz, and David Park. *Recent Immigration to Philadelphia: Regional Change in a Re-Emerging Gateway*. Washington, DC: Brookings, 2008.

Ward, Robert DeC. "Our New Immigration Policy." *Foreign Affairs* 3, no. 1 (1924): 99–110.

Wokeck, Marianne S. "German and Irish Immigration to Colonial Philadelphia." *Proceedings of the American Philosophical Society* 133, no. 2 (1989): 128–43.

39

RHODE ISLAND

Florio Raffaele

CHRONOLOGY

1636	Colonization begins with Roger Williams after being banished for his religious views in Massachusetts colony. Williams settles in Great Salt Cove, land given to him by Native Americans.
1638	Ann Hutchinson, William Coddington, John Clark, and Philip Sherman settle on Aquidneck Island (then known as Rhode Island) purchased by the natives, who call it Pocasset.
1642	Samuel Gorton obtains native lands at Shawomet.
1643	Roger Williams publishes *A Key into the Language of America*.
1644	Portsmouth, Newport, and Providence unite for Independence as the Colony of Rhode Island and Providence Plantations.
1648	Samuel Gorton receives land for his settlement.
1652	The colony passes the first abolition of slavery in the 13 colonies.
1663	Royal Charter is issued.
1675	King Phillip's War begins.
1675 (December)	The Massacre at the Great Swamp.
1686	King James II makes Rhode Island part of New England and appoints Governor Edmund Andros, who suspends the colony's charter.
1688	William of Orange and his wife Mary, the daughter of James II, become king and queen of England as William III and Mary II.
1693	William and Mary extend Rhode Island's territory three miles east and northeast of Narragansett Bay; this conflicts with claims of Plymouth colony and it results in various transfers of territory between Massachusetts and Rhode Island.

1709	First Rhode Island ship to carry slaves sets out.
1755	About 11 percent of Rhode Island's total population (about 5,000 individuals) is black; in Newport, the number is 30 percent.
1774	Stephen Hopkins introduces a bill that eliminates the importation of slaves into the colony. This is one of the first anti-slave laws in the United States.
1784 (February)	Rhode Island legislature passes measure to slowly emancipate slaves, part of which makes children of slaves born after March 1 free.
1790	Samuel Slater founds the first textile mill in the United States in Pawtucket Rhode Island. He becomes known as the father of the Industrial Revolution.
1829	About 60 percent of white males are not eligible to vote.
1836–1914	Over 30 million Europeans migrate to the United States. The death rate on these transatlantic voyages is high, during which one in seven travelers die.
1842	Thomas Dorr creates a liberal constitution that is passed by popular referendum.
1859	Three-quarters of the whaling industry is housed in Warren where the significant majority of sailors are islanders from the Azores or Cape Verde, many of whom arrive in Rhode Island with their own ships.
1875	The Supreme Court declares that regulation of U.S. immigration is the responsibility of the federal government.
1882	The Chinese Exclusion Act, which prohibits certain laborers from immigrating to the United States, is enacted.
1885/1887	The Alien Contract Labor law, which prohibits certain laborers from immigrating to the United States, is enacted.
1891	The federal government assumes the task of inspecting, admitting, rejecting, and processing all immigrants seeking admission to the United States.
1892	On January 2, a new federal U.S. immigration station opens on Ellis Island in New York Harbor.
1898–1924	About 100,000 immigrants arrive in Rhode Island.
1903	The Immigration Act of 1903 (also known as the Anarchist Exclusion Act) restates the 1891 provisions concerning land borders and calls for rules covering entry as well as inspection of aliens crossing the Mexican border.
1907	The U.S. Immigration Act of 1907 reorganizes the states bordering Mexico (Arizona, New Mexico, and a large part of Texas) into Mexican Border District to stem the flow of immigrants into the United States.
1907	Peak of European immigration; 1,285,349 persons enter the country.
1910	About 13.5 million immigrants are living in the United States.

1917–1924	The number of U.S. immigration visas granted is reduced; they are now allocated on the basis of national origin.
1921	Congress passes the Emergency Quota Act.
1924	The Immigration Act of 1924 reduces the number of U.S. immigration visas and allocates them on the basis of national origin.
1935	The so-called Bloodless Revolution ends the decades-long dominance of the Republican Party in the state and begins a still-continuing Democratic Party dominance.
1938	The Great New England Hurricane strikes Rhode Island shores during high tide compounded by a full moon and the autumnal equinox.
1940	The Alien Registration Act requires all foreigners (non-U.S. citizens) within the United States to register with the government and receive an Alien Registration Receipt Card (the predecessor of the "Green Card").
1950	The Internal Security Act, which renders the Alien Registration Receipt Card even more valuable, is passed. Immigrants with legal status have their cards replaced with what generally became known as the "green card" (Form I-151).
1952	The McCarran-Walter Act establishes the modern-day U.S. immigration system. It refines the already-established quota system which imposes limits on a per-country basis. It also establishes the preference system that gives priority to family members and people with special skills.
1965	The Immigration and Nationality Act of 1965 ("Hart-Celler Act"): equalizes the quota system. By equalizing the quotas and allowing for family reunification, the act results in new immigration from non-European nations, which later changes the ethnic makeup of the United States.
1968	Immigration Act eliminates U.S. immigration discrimination based on race, place of birth, sex, and residence. It also officially abolishes restrictions on "Oriental" U.S. immigration.
1971	State income tax is enacted as a temporary measure.
1976	Immigration Act eliminates preferential treatment for residents of the Western Hemisphere.
1980	Refugee Act establishes a general policy governing the admission of refugees.
1986	Immigrant Act focuses on curtailing undocumented U.S. immigration. It legalized hundreds of thousands of undocumented immigrants and for this reason, the 1986 Immigrant Act is commonly known as the 1986 Immigration Amnesty. It also introduces the employer sanctions program which fines employers for hiring undocumented workers. It also passes tough laws to prevent bogus marriage fraud (this is later amended).

1990	George H.W. Bush signs the Immigration Act of 1990, which increases legal immigration to the United States by 40 percent. It establishes an annual limit for certain categories of immigrants. It also aims at helping U.S. businesses attract skilled foreign workers; thus, it expands the business-class categories to favor persons who can make educational, professional, or financial contributions. It creates the Immigrant Investor Program.
2000–2006	Rhode Island's immigrant population increases by 15.1 percent between 2000 and 2006.
2001	Studies conducted by the Urban Institute indicate that a rise in crowded housing often correlates with an increase in the number of immigrant residents.
2001	The USA Patriot Act is passed; it aims to unite and strengthen the country by providing appropriate tools required to intercept and obstruct terrorism.
2003 (March 1)	The U.S. Immigration and Naturalization Service becomes part of the Department of Homeland Security. The department's new U.S. Citizenship and Immigration Services function is to handle U.S. immigration services and benefits, including citizenship, applications for permanent residence, non-immigrant applications, asylum, and refugee services. U.S. immigration enforcement functions are now under the Department's Border and Transportation Security Directorate, known as the Bureau of U.S. Immigration and Customs Enforcement.
2005	Housing authorities determine over 6,000 of Rhode Island households to be crowded or severely crowded.
2008	Rhode Island lawmakers propose a series of measures aimed at undocumented immigrants.
2010 (November 2)	A referendum appears on the state's ballot to drop "and Providence Plantations" from the state's official name—Rhode Island and Providence Plantations—because some claimed that the term "Plantations" harkens back to the slave trade, which accounted for a large portion of the state's economy in the eighteenth century. Others argue that it is the equivalent to the English-period term "colony"; 78 percent vote to keep the name as is.
2013	One in eight Rhode Islanders is foreign-born, with about half of them being naturalized citizens.

HISTORICAL OVERVIEW

Colonization

Permanent European settlement in the colony which would come to be known as the State of Rhode Island and Providence Plantations began in 1636 when Roger Williams arrived, having been banished from Massachusetts Bay Colony for preaching contrary religious views. He founded Providence Plantations on the land he received as a gift from Chief Sachem Canonicus of the Narragansett in the state's present-day capital city, Providence. Williams was followed by several others: in 1638, Anne Hutchinson and her followers purchased land from the Narragansett on Aquidneck Island (present-day Portsmouth) and found Rhode Island Colony. The next year William Coddington and John Clarke established a second settlement on the same island (present-day Newport). In 1642, Samuel Gorton purchased the Shawomet Plantation from the tribe, renaming it with its present name, Warwick, in 1648 after the earl of Warwick who defended Gorton's rights against the courts of Massachusetts Bay Colony.

By this time the state's colonies had united as Rhode Island and Providence Plantations and it had become notorious for its progressive laws, which made it a popular destination and at times, a safe-haven for newcomers. With laws against witch trials, chattel slavery, servitude for indebtedness, religious persecution, and other common aspects of colonial culture, the colony experienced rapid growth. It had one of only eight chartered colonial colleges and a robust maritime industry which contributed to population growth. The eighteenth century witnessed major growth but under different circumstances. The French soldiers, most notoriously those serving under the Compte de Rochambeau, stationed in Newport during the Revolution changed the ethnic makeup of Rhode Island, bringing for the first time a Catholic presence which would eventually come to dominate the religious composition of the state. Another factor, and one which was often overlooked, was the slave population which peaked in that century. By the time of the Revolution, Rhode Island had almost twice as many slaves per capita than any other state in New England. In some agrarian areas in the southern part of the state, it was estimated that as high as one in three people there was a slave. During the Revolution, Rhode Island formed its first black regiment and started to offer slave holders in other colonies $150 per released slave to fight for the colony. After the war, surviving black soldiers were given freedom in the young state and a stipend of $20. It had also been suggested that Rhode Island merchants in the second half of the eighteenth century maintained around three-quarters of the 13 colonies' total slave trade. Beginning in 1774, laws were enacted to end slavery in Rhode Island; however, controversy emerged among the state's merchants as Narragansett Bay became the Triangle Trade's northern hub. The wealthiest of these, in particular John Brown and George DeWolf, continued the trade illegally even after a society of abolitionists was formed in 1789 to help enforce the laws.

The state found its next source of economic development in 1790 when Samuel Slater, the Father of the American Industrial Revolution entered a contract with Moses Brown. Brown was a slave-owner-turned-abolitionist and brother of John Brown (for whom Brown University was named), one of the state's wealthiest slave traders and the first to be prosecuted for slave importation. He developed a factory model that was based on Arkwright's design in England and which came to be known as the "Rhode Island System." Large-scale, diversified manufacturing capability in Rhode Island mills at the outbreak of the Civil War turned into huge profits as the state became a major supplier to the Union Army. Increased production continued after the war and new waves of immigration increased sharply. Factories became a magnet for new immigrants throughout the nineteenth century and by the turn of the twentieth century Rhode Island was one the leading industrialist states in the country. The 1860s to 1880s showed an interesting mix of newcomers. A large influx of immigrants from England was evident in the suburban neighborhoods bordering the factories. Many of these were here specifically to capitalize on the state's industry, bringing manufacturing expertise and serving as foremen, managers, agents, mill owners, and corporate representatives. Also during these years, workers began arriving in large numbers from Ireland, Germany, Sweden, and Quebec. After 1880, and until the nativist tensions of the early 1920s, most newcomers to Rhode Island were from southern and eastern Europe and the Mediterranean. During the first half of the twentieth century, immigrant communities commonly based in or around the many mill villages scattered throughout the state helped the state to become the second-most densely populated in the United States today (New Jersey was first).

CURRENT IMMIGRATION

Rhode Island's growth is due largely to its historic popularity as a destination for immigrants. It is still one of the states with the most foreign-born citizens per capita. For this reason, it boasts an ethnically diverse population, rich in public heritage. The three-largest ancestry groups are Italian and Irish which each makes up 19 percent of the total population, followed by French Canadian which comes close at 17.3 percent. The British account for 12 percent, Latino for 11 percent, and Portuguese at 8.7 percent which gives the state the highest percentage of Portuguese Americans in the country. The last decade, however, has shown an increasing population loss as a result of domestic migration. New immigration during that time has helped keep the population at a consistent, almost balanced number; although the 1 percent increase in population between 2000 and 2007 is far below the national average which stands at 9.9 percent

U.S. Census reports indicated that in 2010, 134,335 or 12.8 percent, of the state's population was foreign-born. The organization said that 47.6 percent of these have been naturalized and claims that there are 35,000 immigrants with an undocumented status. The current number of foreign-born people living in the state was the highest since 1940 when there were 138,878; it was still rather shy of the state's peak in 1910 at 179,141 (the total population in 1910, however, was less than half of its present number). The most significant groups in current immigration trends are from Portugal (17.6 percent), Dominican Republic (13.7 percent), and Guatemala (7.6 percent), although those from Columbia, Italy, Canada, Cambodia, the United Kingdom, China, and Laos make up another 22.7 percent.

The relatively high naturalization rates in Rhode Island may be indicative of an older, more permanent settlement and may also suggest a higher degree of assimilation. It is important to consider the waves of immigration which preceded World War II. Ethnic enclaves remained strong in term of heritage and identity, providing later waves of immigrants with common geographic roots with a friendly host environment, often times providing the linguistic and cultural resources, and even the necessary services to enable a smooth transition.

TOPICAL ESSAYS

NATIVE AMERICANS

Public archaeologists in Rhode Island are hesitant to assign a date to the arrival of the state's first settlers. A review of related literature reveals evidence of human activity ranging between 3,000 and 8,000 years ago; however, a clear shift from nomadic foraging to permanent coastal settlements emerged around the year 1000 BCE and these remained consistent until the arrival of the Europeans which began in 1524 with Giovanni Verrazano and increased rapidly as members of the Massachusetts colonies began migrating into present-day Rhode Island in the 1630s. The major Native American groups that permanently settled at that time included the Narragansett (by the far the majority in number and in total acreage within the state) and the Wampanoag (eastern Rhode Island and southwestern Massachusetts). Verrazano described them: "These people are the most beautiful and have the most civil customs that we have found on this voyage. They are taller than we are . . . the face is clear-cut . . . the eyes are black, and alert, and their manner is sweet and gentle, very like the manner of the ancients" (Beade et al. 1999, 16). The language, described by Roger Williams, and subsequently named by him after the state's largest tribe—the Narragansett was thought to be an Algonquian dialect. Spoken by the tribe and its smaller neighbors, Narragansett shared linguistic similarities with Mohegan (spoken by the Pequot in nearby Connecticut) and Wampanoag.

There were several smaller groups noted in the early accounts of colonists, most notably the Niantic (Rhode Island's southern coastline), the Cowesett (Greenwich Bay and its surrounding woodlands), and the Nipmuc (the northwestern woodlands). Unfortunate circumstances culminating in King Phillip's War of 1675 between the colonists and Native Americans which brought 40 years of peaceful cohabitation to a violent end, forced members of these groups to either be absorbed into the larger neighboring tribes or driven into the dense woodlands of

Connecticut and Massachusetts. The war began with a series of hostilities between the Wampanoag and the colonists from Plymouth. The colony's surprise attack on an important Narragansett village at Great Swamp in South Kingston, Rhode Island (December 1675) brought the tribe into the bloody war which eventually came to consume all of the state's Native American population with the exception of the Niantic tribe who remain neutral. The war left the tribes completely debilitated as families who survived the battles and the famines and diseases which followed sought refuge with the Niantic along the state's south coast. As a result, individual identity and traditional heritage associated with prewar tribes was lost and the group became known in general terms as simply the Narragansett.

Even though the tribe's oral history placed Narragansett ancestors in Rhode Island 30,000 years ago, in terms of negotiating identity, the past 30 years had become the setting for a dramatic scene. The consolidation of Rhode Island tribes in colonial times, the reduction of tribal lands to 15,000 acres by the turn of the nineteenth century, and the state's detribalization policy completed in 1884, all threatened the tribe's sense of collective heritage. With tribal structure officially disbanded and all government sanctioned lands within the boundaries of Rhode Island revoked, the Narragansett were dispersed throughout Rhode Island communities and found themselves counted as African Americans in census reports. In 1975, the tribe sued the State of Rhode Island for the restoration of 32,000 acres of land; in an out-of-court settlement, in 1978, they received 18,000 acres to be legally held by the Narragansett Indian Land Management Corporation as long as the Narragansett remained legally unrecognized. In April 1983, the tribe gained federal recognition as a sovereign nation and by the end of 1985 their land was designated as a tribal reservation. There are currently 2,400 members of the tribe who, by tribal policy, had traced their lineage to the tribal roll at the time of detribalization in the 1880s. Education programs are in place to help preserve the oral tradition, the language, and other cultural artifacts.

African Americans

In 1709, the First Rhode Island ship to carry slaves set out. Over the next 98 years, according to historian Jay Courghtry, no less than 934 trips were made transporting 106,544 slaves to the colonies. Many remained in southern Rhode Island plantations, but the vast majority was sold to slave dealers at various ports throughout the state, the busiest of which was Newport's Bannister Wharf. By 1755, 11 percent of Rhode Island's total population (about 5,000 individuals) was black; in Newport, the number was 30 percent. After 1784, it became illegal to buy slaves. Freed slaves began working as coopers, rope makers, housewrights, shipwrights, furniture makers, cooks, and sailors. As the whaling industry reached its peak, many black Rhode Islanders found jobs onboard these fleets.

Many African Americans had established themselves in the middle class and professional employment within Rhode Island; however, the vast majority was confined to unskilled labor. As the state established itself as an industrial leader, mass immigration trends toward the end of the nineteenth century brought a renewed bleakness for the black community. The new arrivals from Europe were willing to work for incredibly low wages offered by the manufacturing industry, and the owners and foremen preferred to hire the white newcomers. After World War II, conditions improved somewhat for African Americans in Rhode Island; however, it was not until the Civil Rights Movement in the 1960s that the improvement became noticeable.

INDUSTRIALIZATION LEADS TO A REBIRTH OF ENGLISH IMMIGRATION

By the 1830s Rhode Island was the most industrialized state in the nation. Samuel Slater, a mechanic in England's Arkwright factory system, left his homeland with a discretely drawn-up plan to build a similar system in the United States. The young Slater was given the funds he needed by Moses Brown in Providence. His mill was built on the Blackstone River in present-day Pawtucket, and his experiment kicked off an industrial explosion in the state providing employment opportunities for newly arriving immigrants. Resulting from this was a revival of English immigration which quickly populated the burgeoning mill towns across the state. As these Englishmen became supervisors, foremen, partners, and even mill owners themselves, the workforce was replaced with Scottish and eventually Irish immigrants.

JEWS

The first recorded Jewish immigrant to come to Rhode Island was in 1678 and Rhode Island was the site of the second Jewish community established in the American colonies. A 1663 Rhode Island charter granted religious freedom to any individual, a freedom that the Jewish population had long been denied. In the Roger Williams's Providence, Jews were denied complete equality (including the right to vote) being labeled as "Resident Strangers" (Beade et al. 1999, 36). Although treated with indiscriminate suspicion after landing in Newport in 1658, Jews, over the course of the next century carved out a successful presence there, establishing the first synagogue in the colonies—Touro Synagogue. Jews in Newport established themselves as mercantile leaders, trading slaves and goods produced in the West Indies, especially sugar. The enclave reached its peak in 1770, but in 1776, when Newport became occupied by the British, their streak ended.

Azores and Cape Verde Islanders

The whaling industry, as one of Rhode Island's most significant economic boons, peaked in the first half of the nineteenth century. The two biggest ports for this trade were in the cities of Bristol and Warren. By 1859, three-quarters of the industry was housed in Warren where the significant majority of sailors were islanders from the Azores or Cape Verde, many of whom arrived in Rhode Island with their own ships.

As whaling declined, the Portuguese-speaking population settled along Rhode Island shores expanding into various facets of the maritime industry—fishing, shipbuilding, and working as longshoremen. Ethnic tension begins to emerge between the Azoreans and the darker-skinned Cape Verdeans, and they started to settle in separate communities—the former in Warren, Bristol, and Tiverton, and the latter in the Fox Point section of Providence, Pawtucket, and East Providence. Azoreans soon diversified into other industries such as carpentry and masonry; their darker-skinned compatriots faced difficulties integrating into skilled labor and were treated similarly to African Americans. They persevered in the maritime industry and eventually became the dominant ethnic group among longshoremen, gaining control of the industry in the Port of Providence.

French Canadians

This wave of Catholic immigrants from Quebec to Rhode Island began in the mid-nineteenth century. Lacking political power and respect under English Protestant rule in Canada, they were attracted to the propaganda promoted by Rhode Island mill recruiters and their promises for economic prosperity. The transition from an agricultural lifestyle to an urban, industrial one was at first very difficult, and many returned home within a few years. This discouragement eventually gave way to the steady flow of French Canadian immigrants and a tenacious sense of community.

Irish

The Irish established an earlier presence dating back to the days of the Revolution. However, Irish Catholics began arriving en masse in the 1830s, spurring anti-Irish hysteria by the end of the 1840s. Potato crop failures between 1845 and 1849 brought, according to historian Patrick Conley, an average of 100,000 Irish immigrants a year, a trend which continued for about eight years. By 1850, they were the largest ethnic group in the state and comprised 69 percent of foreign-born Rhode Islanders.

In the 1980 Census, the first to ask about a person's ancestry, 210,950 Rhode Islanders claimed to be of Irish descent. This represented more than 22 percent of the state's total population. Despite waves of French Canadian and Italian Immigrants, Irish Americans have been Rhode Island's numerically dominant ethnic group for over a century. Known for their loyalty to the Catholic Church, ironically most of the early Irish Rhode Islanders were Protestant, usually Baptist, Quakers, Presbyterians, or Anglicans. Those few who were Catholic lost their religious affiliation due to the lack of Catholic Clergy.

After the War of 1812, the first massive migration of Catholic Irish to America began. This was due to the loss of agriculture and the need to reorganize. The failures of the potato crop, combined with harsh British policies, in 1818 and 1822 provided more trouble and brought more waves of Irish immigrants. Between 1847 and 1854, over 100,000 Irish, mostly from the cottier class (farmers), immigrated to America. The migration of Irish immigrants through the decades from 1840 to 1870 was unequaled by any other immigrant population. From 1841 to 1850, 780,719 immigrated and from 1851 to 1860 that number rose to 914,119. Then it declined to 435,778 from 1861 to 1870, but they still were second only to Germans in that time period.

By 1875, the Catholic Irish had established settlements and churches in every urban and industrial area of Rhode Island. Once established in Rhode Island, the Irish grew both numerically and economically, proving they belonged in their new home and would have an impact on the future of the United States.

Latinos

Latin Americans began to arrive in Rhode Island in the 1790s, following the slave trade revolts in Santo Domingo and Guadalupe. Because of the close commercial ties created in Rhode Island during the slave trade, the refugees from these countries sought the familiarity of the area. However, their stay was very brief, and not long after their arrival the newly settled immigrants returned to their European homelands. The next influx of Latino immigrants was seen in the Colonial era, when Sephardic Jews, fleeing oppression from the Spanish government arrived. Again, most of these immigrants left, and by the early 1820s, there was no substantial amount of any Latino group present throughout the state.

Ukrainians

During the 1870s, Ukrainian immigration was sporadic. However from 1880 to World War I, it became more continuous. In 1899, the estimated number of Ukrainians was between 200,000 and 500,000. Before 1899 immigration authorities had not developed better ways to determine race and nationality, so many Ukrainians were classified as Russian or Austrian. This was evident in the 1920 Census as 6.1 percent of Rhode Island's Austrian population was indeed Ukrainian. From 1899 to 1930, of the 268,311 Ukrainian immigrants who entered America's ports, 2,041 came to Rhode Island. The most found entering Rhode Island in one year was 337 immigrants in 1913. Many Ukrainians were immigrating due to political oppression, especially around World War I. From 1920 to 1939, around 40,000 Ukrainians immigrated to the United States; however, those who tried to immigrate from Soviet-controlled provinces of Ukraine were not permitted into the country.

ITALIANS

The first recorded account of European immigration to Rhode Island was made in 1524 by the Italian explorer Giovanni da Verrazzano. Verrazzano noticed the similarities in size between the new land and the island of Rhodes, and so the name Rhode Island was created. The first census taken in the state in 1850 counted only 23 Italian-born residents living in the state. During this time, the new settlers found it difficult to farm as they did back in Italy, so many took jobs in textile factories across the state. By 1900, nearly 9,000 Italian-born natives were living in Rhode Island. No one knows how the Italian immigrant population had grown until when on Columbus Day in 1910 a somewhat endless stream of Italian immigrants flowed by the native Rhode Islanders. From 1898 to 1932, the U.S. commissioner of immigration counted nearly 55,000 Italians who arrived through the Port of Providence. Almost 51,000 of these were recorded to have been from parts of Southern Italy, showing that these people came here in search of economic and social prosperity. In 1920, one in five of the foreign-born immigrants living in Rhode Island was of Italian descent. This sudden rise in immigrant population frightened the American-born lawmakers of the United States, combined with the popularity of eugenics, and the National Origins Quota Act of 1924 was passed, marking the end of any future large-scale Italian immigration to Rhode Island.

GREEKS

Greek immigrants began arriving to Rhode Island in the 1890s; however, information regarding the earliest Greek migration to the state is scant. By 1910, there were around 1,300 Greeks living in communities of Providence, Pawtucket, and Newport. Between 1898 and 1932, Rhode Island was listed on the entrance documents of 4,201 immigrants arriving from Greece as their destination. One of the first major community-based movements for Greeks in Rhode Island was to establish suitable places of worship to accommodate their Orthodox Church services, a task which was accomplished in each of the three identified enclaves in a very short amount of time. Most of these immigrants arrived illiterate and unfamiliar with the English language, seeking employment in the fishing industry, mills, restaurants, markets, and produce companies.

By mid-century, Greeks in Rhode Island had effectively maintained cultural identity through their network of well-established churches, social clubs, and Greek language schools. They had also risen substantially in socioeconomic status as restaurateurs, importers of Greek goods, and purveyors of markets and shops. They were also known to effectively raise funds to support social activist movements in their homeland during its various crises. After Greece was occupied during World War II, the Rhode Island Greek community, under the leadership of Anthony Spiritos, launched the War Bond Relief drive. Over $50,000 was raised in Providence and Pawtucket alone, which contributed to the $2.5 million raised from various sources across the United States.

THE COUNTRY CLOSES ITS DOORS

Between 1898 and 1924, over 100,000 immigrants arrived in Rhode Island; the two peak years, 1913 and 1914, alone brought in 27,000. These numbers were not particular to Rhode Island and across the country Americans began to develop a sense of xenophobia which was reflected in the immigration laws which followed this burst of new arrivals. The National Origins Act of 1924 was perhaps the most significant of these laws. With the subsequent depression of the late '20s and throughout the '1930s ethnic minorities suffered tremendously and there seemed to be no sense of urgency in demands for immigration reform which would reopen the gateway. In Rhode Island, in particular, the Hurricane of 1938, the first major one since 1869, struck Rhode Island shores during high tide compounded by a full moon and the autumnal equinox. Coastal villages were completed lost to the 16-foot swells, and Downtown Providence, the capital city's commercial center, was submerged in 13 feet of sea water and Rhode Island suffered more fatalities than any other state in New England. The recovery, which lasted until the early 1950s, was halted by yet another crisis, this time a global one—World War II.

A NEW WAVE OF IMMIGRATION AFTER WORLD WAR II

It is not until the 1960s, after the federal repeal of quota laws (i.e., the equalization of the quotas), that Rhode Island would become home to new international arrivals. A series of studies conducted by researchers at Brown University in the 1950s demonstrated that immigration during the early wave (1870–1910) was largely responsible for its economic growth during that time. Kurt Mayer and Sidney Goldstein claimed that migration accounted for two-thirds of the Rhode Island's population growth, thus arguing: "It is considerably cheaper and quicker to import a workforce than to grow one" (Mayer and Goldstein 1958, 16). Their statistics revealed that by 1905, "descendents of Yankee pioneers became a numerical minority," and further revealed that "Roman Catholicism had become the faith of the majority" (Mayer and Goldstein 1958, 19). Although these studies were conducted in response to a suffering state economy, Mayer concluded: "[A]ny unbiased reader of Rhode Island's record must be much more impressed with the remarkable achievements of its people than with their failures" (Mayer 1953, 70). If nothing else can be gleaned from their conclusions, it seems clear that the Rhode Island was built on the work of its immigrants, and that in many ways it lived up to its founder's idea of Providence as "God's gift to a homeless people."

Italians

By the end of World War I, almost 13,000 Italians have returned to their homeland. Many reasons, including the xenophobic views of the natives and the Great Depression, could be to blame for this mass exodus of such a prevalent ethnic group. However, during this time, the Italians who remained in Rhode Island were determined to preserve their culture and heritage. Many faced the harsh criticisms of the native population, due to Italy's relations with Germany during the war. The Italians who attended Brown University were often called "carpet baggers." Still, areas such as Federal Hill commonly referred to as a "Little Italy" remained full of the original Italian culture and way of life. Families still taught their children traditional Italian values and so were able to keep their culture intact.

In the years following World War II, the Italian population in Federal Hill dropped almost 50 percent. Many factors, including poor housing standards and economic prosperity, enabled the now economically advantaged Italians to seek a better life in other less-crowded parts of the state. In 1970, the Italian population realized that their culture needed to be preserved. After the devastating effects of the two world wars, a council was formed in Federal Hill, with the goal of revitalizing Italian culture and ethnicity.

Greeks

In the years after the war, the Greek community continued to grow; however, communities began feeling a sense of concern about the loss of identity. The renewed postwar immigration spurt was not enough to offset the assimilation which had occurred over the preceding decades. By the early 1950s, ethnically Greek Rhode Islanders held a substantial share of the professional community, and became a presence in the political arena. The Americanization process became evident to community leaders who lamented the loss of the Greek language in the youth of the time. Second- and third-generation Greeks showed much less interest in the preservation of Greek language and culture and by the end of the 1950s Orthodox Church leaders were revising their liturgies, documents, and services in order to accommodate the non-Greek-speaking generation by integrating English with the Greek and in some cases replacing the traditional language altogether.

Ukrainians

The largest influx of Ukrainians to the United States was post–World War II. This was made up of individuals and families who had left Ukraine during the war, who usually were in German work camps and refused to go back to the communist rule of their homeland. In the beginning of 1948, there were about 85,000 Ukrainians who entered the United States. In 1952, another 33,000 were admitted and 8,000 more arrived in 1955. Today almost every state has a Ukrainian population.

Armenians

Though few in numbers, the Armenian people were among the millions of immigrants who immigrated to America and were one of the leading sources of labor that helped make America an industrial power. Coming in small numbers during the 1870s and 1880s, then increasing their numbers in the 1890s, Armenians were escaping the provinces of eastern Turkey. They worked in Rhode Island factories and mills and made a name for themselves through hard work, especially during the Great Depression of 1893. Many were able to move away from the factories and created their own small businesses; they adapted to American culture effortlessly and thrived while working with other ethnic backgrounds. From 1898 to 1932, new Armenian arrivals to the United States reflected 6,375 to Rhode Island. Mostly due to the strong community and foundation they had made their home in America.

The church was the center of Armenian life, due to living under the sway of Islam in Turkey. They were recognized as a religious entity and therefore the church became a symbol of their nationhood. In 1895, in Providence, Armenians established their own church. However, it was not until 1914 that services could be held frequently, due to the previous lack of pastors. Throughout the century Armenian people helped lead a religious awakening for all people, due to their tolerance of other faiths and the importance of community guided by faith. Through their faith and tradition of hard work, the Armenian people found a new home in the United States.

Arabic-Speaking People

The first known Arabic-speaking person to immigrate to Rhode Island was David Saaty in 1886. He worked at a watch-making shop and after saving up enough money to send for his brother, they started a watch repair business together. Many of the Arabic-speaking immigrants coming to Rhode Island were Christian; however, according to the 1910 Census, 20 Muslim names appeared and in the 1919 Rhode Island draft registry 24 names appeared. However, according to the 1910 Census, these Muslims were Turkish-speaking and unlike Syrian Christians were all single men or married men without their families. During 1911, a survey of Syrians in United States determined that Rhode Island, with 150 Muslims, was the largest community of Muslims in the United States.

Those considered Syrians in America were only classified so by their geographic origin, most were not even from Syria. Many are from villages in northern Lebanon and southeast Turkey. By 1914, those classified as Syrians immigrating to the United States consisted of 100,000 and by 1924 the number rose to 122,000. Due to the quota laws of 1921, 1924, and 1927, the number of people who immigrated from the Middle East was greatly limited. The number was reduced to 5,105 in 1921 to 1,595 in 1924 and was down to hundreds by 1925. The quota laws had effectively almost ended the immigration of Arabic-speaking people until 1965, when the law was changed.

Due to the effects of the quota laws, the Arabic-speaking population in Rhode Island was extremely small. Out of the 135,156 immigrants in Rhode Island by 1920, only 1,285 were Arabic-speaking and many called themselves Syrian even if that was not geographically accurate. By 1929, the number increased to 2,500 due to the first-generation of Americans with Arabic descent. Even with small numbers, they were able to establish themselves by World War I, creating a distinct ethnic community in Rhode Island where many of the same families live today. Today the Arabic-speaking community in Rhode Island has grown to some 6,000 to 7,000 people. Among them include those from Jordan, Palestine, the Persian Gulf, and Egypt, Muslims and Christians. For the most part, people from these areas came after 1965. Their ties to the pioneering Syrians were only through their cultural and linguistic heritage; many Muslim immigrants have yet to establish a religious institution parallel to the Christian churches.

Latino/as

Due to the Immigrant Quota Act in the 1920s and the economic instability in the United States, there was a large drop in the immigration population in Rhode Island. However, by mid-century the Quota Act was abolished and the rise of Spanish-speaking Latino/as began to rise throughout the state. The Latino/as who arrived during this time found it hard to integrate into their new lives. Rhode Island, in the past centuries, had merely been a stopping ground for any Latino/a immigrant. Therefore, there was little sense of community for these new arrivals. However, from 1960 to 1970, there was a rise in population from immigrants in nearly every Latin American country. The Mexican population jumped from 115 to over 400. The Columbian population also rose from just 23 to nearly 500. Most of the Latinos during this time, with the exception of Cubans, came to Rhode Island in search of a better life. The textile factories throughout Rhode Island offered a chance of economic and social advancement. The Cubans who arrived in Rhode Island during this time were seeking refuge from the Castro regime. Most of these Latinos who arrived here between 1960s and 1980s came on work visas that would only be approved by the Secretary of Labor, provided that there were enough jobs available for the native population. Because of this, the Latino population was expected to decrease over the next decades.

Nevertheless, the Latino population in Rhode Island had nearly quadrupled since the 1980s. This number could only be thought of as an estimate, because a large number of the Latino populations were undocumented, and there was no way to accurately record their numbers. According to the 2000 U.S. Census Bureau survey, there were 90,820 Latino/as living in Rhode Island. The 2010 survey counted 130,655 Latino/as in the state, which accounted for nearly 10 percent of the overall population. It was clear that this group had found their sense of community in Rhode Island. Many businesses across the state were owned by Latino/a families and their cultural presence was growing. However, the growing

Mayor James Diossa, right, chats with restaurant owner Sergio Tabares, left, in Central Falls, Rhode Island, on January 28, 2013. Diossa, the newly elected mayor of Central Falls, Rhode Island, is from a Colombian immigrant family. Many hope this mayor can help to change this beleaguered community. (AP Photo/Steven Senne)

Belmont Street Elementary School fourth grade teacher Bernadine Veiga, left, teaches mathematics to her Cape Verdean students, including Cindy Rodrigues, right, at the school on April 14, 2004. The class is a part of a structured English immersion program for students who learn English as a second language. Immigrants from Cape Verde settled primarily in Massachusetts, where this school is located, and Rhode Island. (AP Photo/Chitose Suzuki)

number and influence of this population is causing somewhat of an issue with the native population in Rhode Island. Many locals have accused the Latino population of taking jobs from the people that have been here for generations. In 2006, "A Day without an Immigrant" was celebrated by many Rhode Islanders across the state. The Latinos responded by boycotting school, work, and other aspects of social life. The boycotts were aimed to show that the Latinos had something positive to offer the state and to the people within. This group of people had shown a strong sense of perseverance and the ability to assimilate into a new way of life.

Upon their arrival in the early 1960s, the Latino/as had no historical background in this state. There was no community to connect with. In contrast, other ethnic groups such as the English and Portuguese had roots in this country. The Latino/as had to start anew, build a new life, social standing, and economic niche and had done so quite successfully. This group of people had something great to offer to the culturally diverse state of Rhode Island.

Among the first groups were Dominicans, followed by Puerto Ricans. Spanish-speaking immigrants trickled in slowly during the 1940s and 1950s, but the federal repeal of quota laws in 1965 brought Latinos from all over Latin America. For example, mill owners actively recruited workers from Colombia, successfully reviving the workforce in Rhode Island's already suffering manufacturing industry. Over the next two decades, political unrest in South and Central America helped swell the numbers of Spanish-speaking immigrants tremendously—first from Argentina, Chile, and El Salvador, followed by Nicaragua, Honduras, and Guatemala in the next decade. By the mid-1970s, bilingual signs were appearing in Rhode Island's institutions.

Southeast Asians

In the wake of conflict in Southeast Asia, Rhode Island's religious communities worked tirelessly to provide homes to displaced families and orphaned children from that area. The transition to life in Rhode Island was much more difficult for the Laotians, Cambodians, Hmongs, and Vietnamese than for other groups during that period. These groups were poorly understood among the state's population which lacked experience with the cultures and languages of Southeast Asia. Worsening the situation was the fact that, although lumped together categorically by their hosts, each group brought its own very distinct culture, language, and collective identity.

For these groups the only means for survival in their new home was to adopt a common language. Learning English became one of the most important objectives within these families making Southeast Asians a significant part of the textile and jewelry manufacturing workforce, and soon after giving them a presence in the state's colleges and professional economy.

NOTABLE FIGURES/GROUPS

MOSES BROWN (1738–1836)

According to the Rhode Island Historical Society, Moses Brown "was a fervent opponent of slavery, a proponent of education, religion and agriculture, and a prominent Quaker" (Rhode Island Historical Society 1995). Brown was born on September 23, 1738, in Providence, Rhode Island. He was the youngest son of his parents, James and Hope Brown. Moses's father died while his son was very young. Following his father's death, Moses Brown came into the care of his uncle Obadiah Brown and became his apprentice. In the early years, Brown was heavily involved in the spermaceti works. Additionally, the company was active in distilling rum and participated in merchant voyages including the transportation of slaves. The company's shares were divided amongst Moses and his three brothers. This newly formed company quickly became involved in the slave trade, with Moses as "an active partner" (Rhode Island Historical Society 1996). However, their exploits in the slave trade did not prove lucrative. Upon their ship's first voyage coming back from Africa, a large percentage of slaves caught diseases or were killed during unsuccessful mutinies. This single experience discouraged the firm from any further involvement in the slave trade. Later on in life, ironically, Brown became a powerful abolitionist, and a proponent of the anti-slavery movement in Rhode Island. Brown was often challenged for his radical ideas, especially from within his own family. Moses's brother John was among the most outspoken slave traders in Rhode Island at the time. This caused a rift within the Brown family. In addition to anti-slavery, Brown served as an aid for refugees displaced by the war and provided financial assistance for these families. Although in 1788, Brown refashioned himself as a businessman, venturing into textile production, alongside his partners, Smith Brown, his cousin, and William Almy, his future son-in-law. During this period, Brown became interested in a new British technique involving water power to propel the mills. In the War of 1812, Moses Brown became a powerful advocate of peace and became one of the founders of the Rhode Island Peace Society, in 1818.

PROGRESO LATINO

Progreso Latino, established in the 1970s, is based in Central Falls and serves Latina/o immigrants and other immigrant groups statewide. This group provides multiple services, including running a food pantry; providing educational information and referrals; helping with employment, housing, and more specific immigration needs, such as filing for deferred action, naturalization papers, and family reunification. This nonprofit organization's website has links to important information, public education referrals, and posts an electronic bulletin, *La Voz del Pueblo*, for members of the surrounding community. While the group is not on the cutting edge of policy or fighting for immigrant rights, it provides for basic needs and aids immigrants in a variety of ways.

BIBLIOGRAPHY

Aubin, Albert K. *The French in Rhode Island: A Brief History*. Providence: Rhode Island Publications Society, 1988.

Blejwas, Stanislaus A. *A Rhode Island Ethnic Group: Polish Americans*. Providence: Rhode Island American Polish Cultural Exchange Commission, 1995.

Coli, W. B., and R. Lobban, eds. *The Cape Verdeans in Rhode Island*. Providence: Rhode Island Publication Society, 1990.

Conley, Patrick T. *The Irish in Rhode Island: A Historical Appreciation*. Providence: Rhode Island Publications Society, 1986.

Conley, Patrick T. *Rhode Island in Rhetoric and Reflection: Public Addresses and Essays*. Providence: Rhode Island Publications Society, 2002.

Cunha, M. Rachel, and Susan A. Pacheco, eds. *The Portuguese in Rhode Island: A History*. Providence: Rhode Island Publications Society, 1985.

Doumato, Eleanor A. *The Arabic-Speaking People in Rhode Island: A Centenary Celebration*. Providence: Rhode Island Publications Society, 1986.

Foster, Geraldine S. *The Jews in Rhode Island: A Brief History*. Providence: Rhode Island Publications Society, 1985.

Gelenian, Ara Arthur. *The Armenians in Rhode Island: Ancient Roots to Represent Experiences*. Providence: Rhode Island Publications Society, 1985.

Itzigsohn, Jose. *Encountering American Faultlines: Race, Class, and the Dominican Experience in Providence*. New York: Russell Sage Foundation, 2009.

Kyriakou, Stephen, and Venetia Georas, eds. *The Greek People in Rhode Island: Three Communities, One Ethos, 1893–1993*. Providence: Rhode Island Publications Society, 1994.

Lind, Louise. *The Southeast Asians in Rhode Island: The New Americans*. Providence: Rhode Island Publications Society, 1989.

Mayer, Kurt B. *Economic Development and Population Growth in Rhode Island*. Providence: Brown University Press, 1953.

Mayer, Kurt, and Sidney Goldstein, eds. *Migration and Economic Development in Rhode Island*. Providence: Brown University Press, 1958.

Mowatt, John J. *The Ukrainians in Rhode Island: Faith and Determination*. Providence: Rhode Island Publications Society, 1988.

Pearlman, Joel. *Ethnic Differences: Schooling and Social Structure among the Irish, Italians, Jews, and Blacks in an American City, 1880–1935*. Cambridge: Cambridge University Press, 1988.

Progreso Latino. Progreso Latino Webpage. http://www.progresolatino.org. Accessed February 25, 2014.

Rhode Island Historical Society, "Moses Brown Papers," Catalogue Number MS 313, Processed by Pam Narbeth (1995), Posted by Rick Stattler 1996. http://www.rihs.org/mssinv/Mss313.htm. Accessed August 9, 2014.

Roseman Beade, Lisa, Donald Breed, Rhode Island Historical Society, and Providence Chamber of Commerce. *The Wealth of Nations: A People's History of Rhode Island*. Andover, MA: Community Communications Inc., 1999.

Santoro, Carmela E. *The Italians in Rhode Island: The Age of Exploration to the Present, 1524–1989*. Providence: Rhode Island Publications Society, 1990.

Sicklinger, Raymond L. *The Germans in Rhode Island: Pride and Perseverance, 1850–1985*. Providence: Rhode Island Publications Society, 1985.

40

SOUTH CAROLINA

Nicole Kalaf-Hughes

CHRONOLOGY

1607	British settlement of Virginia initiates conflict with Spain over lands along the South Atlantic Coast.
1629	King Charles I of England grants Sir Robert Heath the land between 31°N and 36°N latitude.
1663	King Charles II of England grants eight nobles (known as the Lords Proprietors) the land from "six and thirty degrees of the northern latitude, and to the west as far as the South Seas" and southerly, as "one and thirty degrees of northern latitude."
1665	Second grant expands the limits of the colony to the land between 29°N and 36° 30'N latitude and the Atlantic and Pacific oceans.
1670	Charles Town is founded.
1689	Philip Ludwell receives instructions to become the "Governor of Carolina" with a capitol in the city of Charleston.
1715	South Carolina successfully petitions British officials to become a royal colony.
1719	During the Revolution of 1719, the Proprietary government is overthrown in a nonviolent coup. The British Crown then purchases the South Carolina colony back from the Lords Proprietors.
1729	Carolina is divided into northern and southern provinces and the separate royal colonies of North and South Carolina are established.
1735	Northern and southern colonies agree to a boundary beginning 30 miles southwest of the mouth of the Cape Fear River and extend to the 35th parallel. From there, a line would run west to the Pacific Ocean.

1758	The Cherokee War begins over tensions and suspected betrayals between British settlers and the Cherokee.
1775	First skirmish of the Revolutionary War in South Carolina at Ninety Six.
1776	South Carolina becomes the first southern colony and second of the 13 colonies to draft a state constitution.
1778	South Carolina signs the Articles of Confederation.
1778	British troops land in Georgia and attack South Carolina in an effort to regain control.
1783	The Treaty of Paris officially ends the Revolutionary War.
1787	Georgia and South Carolina agree on state boundaries.
1788	South Carolina ratifies the U.S. Constitution.
1832	South Carolina state convention passes the Ordinance of Nullification, which declared the federal tariff laws unconstitutional and not to be enforced in the state of South Carolina.
1833	In response to the Ordinance of Nullification, Congress passes the so-called Force Bill authorizing President Andrew Jackson to use whatever power necessary to enforce federal tariffs.
1852	First vote for South Carolina to secede from the Union fails at the state convention.
1856	South Carolina congressman Preston Brooks beats Massachusetts senator Charles Sumner in response to Sumner's speech attacking slavery.
1860	South Carolina votes to secede from the Union with all 169 delegates to the convention voting in favor of secession.
1861	Confederate Troops fire on Fort Sumter in Charleston Harbor beginning the Civil War.
1863	The Emancipation Proclamation takes effect in the portions of South Carolina under Union occupation.
1865	General William T. Sherman marches troops through South Carolina burning plantations and the city of Charleston.
1877	President Rutherford B. Hayes (a Republican) withdraws troops from South Carolina in exchange for Democratic support. The "Compromise of 1877" results in white Southerners reclaiming power in state government.
1881–83	A state's Bureau of Immigration is established but shuts down after two years.
1890s	An economic recession hits the state, and racist policies and segregation increase.
1890	Benjamin Tillman, an outspoken racist, is elected governor of South Carolina.
1890–1914	This period is an era of disenfranchisement, with the introduction of poll taxes and literacy tests; the number of African American legislators diminishes in this time period.
1895	Jim Crow laws are adopted in the state.

Early 1900s	The economy revives as the textile industry develops and farming revives for a brief period. Some effort is made to attract immigrant workers to the state.
1906	European immigration to the state includes individuals from Austria, Belgium, the Netherlands, and Spain.
1914	Considerable out-migration of African Americans, known as the Great Migration, begins, due to economic recession and racism.
1920s	Economic recession and cotton crop failure hit the state. The Ku Klux Klan becomes increasingly active in South Carolina and in the United States.
1951–55	Governor James F. Byrnes reduces the power of the Ku Klux Klan, expands public education, and abolishes the poll tax.
1961	Nine black Friendship Junior College students take seats at a whites-only lunch counter at a restaurant in Rock Hill, South Carolina.
1962	Clemson University is required to admit its first African American student, Harvey Gantt.
1964	Democrat dominance begins to decline in state politics.
1965	Voting Rights Act is passed by Congress outlawing discriminatory voting practices and requiring certain states (including South Carolina) to "preclear" election changes with the Department of Justice.
1966	South Carolina challenges the preclearance requirement of the Voting Rights Act of 1965. In *South Carolina v. Katzenbach* (1966) the U.S. Supreme Court rejects the challenge and finds it to be a valid exercise of Congress's power under the Fifteenth Amendment.
1968	South Carolina state troopers fire on a crowd of students protesting the denial of students from a mostly black college into Orangeburg, South Carolina's only bowling alley. Three students are killed and more than 30 are injured.
1972	The state legislature is reapportioned into single member-districts resulting in a decrease in representation for rural areas and an increase in opportunity for minority representation.
1986	The Immigration Reform and Control Act (IRCA) is passed by Congress. Legislation results in legalization of 2.3 million immigrants across the United States.
1996	Operations Gatekeeper and Hold-the-Line result in the redirection of undocumented immigrants from traditional destination states in the Southwest to new locations along the Atlantic coast.
2008	South Carolina legislature passes House Bill (HB) 4400 to improve immigration enforcement.
2011	South Carolina legislature passes Senate Bill (SB) 20 allowing local law enforcement officers to check immigration status after stopping people for another offense.
2011	A federal judge blocks part of SB 20 due to conflicts with the federal government's exclusive right to legislate immigration.

HISTORICAL OVERVIEW

Studies of ethnicity in South Carolina have traditionally been thought of on a black/white dimension. The state's geographic position in the South and history of civil rights actions, such as those by the Friendship Nine and the Orangeburg Massacre, are often highlighted in discussions of minority relations in the state. However, since the 1970s the increase in immigration to South Carolina has resulted in a shift away from an understanding of ethnicity as black/white, and moved the state toward a much more ethnically and racially diverse community.

The rapid increase in the foreign-born population is evident when considering data from the U.S. Census Bureau. The percentage of the South Carolina population identifying as foreign-born has increased from 1.4 percent in 1990 to 2.9 percent in 2000 to 4.4 percent in 2010. While this number is lower than the national average (nationwide, 2.4 percent identify as foreign-born), the foreign-born population in South Carolina has increased at a much higher rate than the national average. In fact, though the percentage increase in people identifying as foreign-born in the United States between 1990 and 2010 was about 102 percent, the percentage increase for the same time period in South Carolina was about 336 percent. These numbers are striking in and of themselves and present an interesting puzzle when we consider the fact that most of South Carolina's history was spent trying to attract immigrants with little to no success. What factors have changed in South Carolina to prompt an unprecedented increase in immigration over the past 40 years?

Immigration in South Carolina dates back to the 1670 settlement of the colony, and as a result of European immigration, South Carolina's population was majority white by 1860. Following emancipation and the end of the Civil War, South Carolina's population was mostly African American by 1870. In an effort to attract more Anglo immigrants and recreate a white majority in the state, South Carolina appointed a commissioner of immigration, John A. Wagner of Charleston, whose task was to attract white, northern European immigrants.

In 1881, South Carolina bolstered efforts to attract white immigrants once again when the state general assembly established the Bureau of Immigration. The Bureau advertised to European immigrants who had just arrived in New York City, organized cheap transportation to South Carolina, and offered translator services to work with the immigrants. The bureau managed to bring about 800 people; however, many did not stay in the state long after their arrival.

In the early twentieth century, South Carolina tried to bolster white immigration once again. Focusing solely on Northern Europeans, South Carolina recruited immigrants to replace blacks in the fields and work in the textile industry. The Cotton Manufacturers Association went so far as to pay immigrant fares in order to recruit new employees directly from Europe. The result was a few hundred

German, Austrian, and French immigrants; however, many of them left the state after arrival. The process of prepaying immigrants' passage to the United States was discontinued soon after.

Immigration to South Carolina was further hindered in the 1920s through the establishment of the federal quota system. In 1940, the foreign-born population of South Carolina was 4,979 down from 5,358 in 1930; 6,582 in 1920; and over 5,000 less than it had been in 1860. During the same time period, the state's total population increased from 1,683,724 in 1920 to 1,899,804 in 1940. The combined effect of an increasing population with a decrease in immigrants resulted in a population more homogenous than the state had seen even before the Civil War.

In 1970, the tide began to turn and the foreign-born population in South Carolina began to climb again. The return of immigrants to the area could be attributed to a variety of factors including the rapid population growth and subsequent need for workers, economic crises and a lack of jobs in countries of origin, and the passage of immigration policy measures in the United States that affected both increasing legal residents and encouraging undocumented residents to move away from traditional destination states in the West. The result of these changes was a drastic increase in the Latino and Asian foreign-born population.

Today, immigrants and their children comprise a rapidly growing share of the population and electorate in South Carolina. South Carolina is not alone in observing a rapid growth of immigrant populations. In fact, the entire Southeast has grown at a faster rate than the United States as a whole since 1960. South Carolina specifically has grown at a faster rate than the rest of the United States since 1970.

The needs of South Carolina's growing population have fueled demand for a larger pool of workers—many of whom are foreign-born. In fact, according to the U.S. Census Bureau, the majority of Asian and Latino persons in South Carolina are foreign-born. Of the approximately 176,000 foreign-born residents in South Carolina, about 54 percent are from the Americas, and 85 percent of those persons are from Central and South America.

A second factor responsible for the increasing immigrant populations in South Carolina since the 1970s could be attributed to a change in destination for new immigrants. This change could be due to a need for workers, as previously mentioned or problems in an immigrant's home country, but was also due in part to a change in policy at the southern border.

The first of these immigration policy measures to increase the flow of immigrants into South Carolina was the IRCA (Immigration Reform and Control Act) passed by Congress in 1986. Proposed by Kentucky Democrat Romano Mazzoli and Wyoming Republican Alan Simpson, the IRCA sought to control undocumented immigration to the United States through increased appropriations for enforcement of existing immigration law and a one-time amnesty for certain undocumented residents. With increased funding for enforcement, the law authorized weak employer sanctions for knowingly hiring or employing an undocumented worker. Additionally, the law legalized some undocumented immigrants who had been continuously present in the United States since 1982 and provided for family reunification. This aspect of the legislation resulted in the legalization of approximately 2.3 million people who had been living in the United States and allowed them to send for immediate family members. As traditional migrant-receiving areas became overcrowded, newly legalized Mexican migrants felt the freedom to relocate to other areas of the country that provided more economic opportunity, such as South Carolina.

In addition to the growing documented population, with the increasing economic pressure from abroad, many companies simply decided to stay local and hire low-cost immigrant workers. This offered opportunities to the many migrant workers who for years had been traveling through the region to work in the agricultural industry, who instead chose to take year-round jobs in the region.

Beyond changes to policy dealing with immigrants already residing in the United States, many of the more recent policies that affected immigration to South Carolina dealt with the question of undocumented immigrants. South Carolinians generally agreed that undocumented immigration was an important issue. However, the high level of attention paid to undocumented migration in other states directly impacted the number of undocumented residents of South Carolina. In fact, the second policy measures to increase the flow of migrants to South Carolina were the direct changes to federal enforcement of the border in Texas and California.

During the early 1990s, states sharing a border with Mexico, especially California, felt increasing pressure from voters to address concerns regarding undocumented immigration. The Clinton administration responded through two key changes to border enforcement: Operation Hold-the-Line (1993), which increased the number of Border Patrol agents in the El Paso sector in Texas, and Operation Gatekeeper (1994), which increased border security along the California–Mexico border. In October of the same year, California voters passed Proposition 187 (later deemed unconstitutional by the courts), which denied undocumented migrants access to social services such as education and non-emergency medical care. Four years later, they followed with Proposition 227 to end the state's bilingual education programs. These policies, combined with the changes to enforcement at the border, created a less hospitable environment in the traditional destination states in the West.

Operation Hold-the-Line and Operation Gatekeeper had the unintended effect of shifting undocumented immigration further east to the more rugged area of the U.S.–Mexico border, in particular Arizona. Additionally, because the Border Patrol implemented a catch-and-release policy for most non-Mexican apprehensions during this time, many, if caught, simply left the border region and moved upward and eastward throughout the United States (Johnson 2004), contributing to an expansion of the non-Mexican population in non-border states, such as South Carolina. Today, people originating from Latin America comprise the largest percentage of foreign-born in the South Carolina at 52.3 percent; considerably larger than the 3 percent of foreign-born South Carolinians originating from Africa, 16.6 percent originating from Europe, and 24.1 percent originating from Asia. Combine these changes with the fact that immigrant social networks are one of the best predictors of new destinations for the foreign-born, and there is an increased likelihood for a growing immigrant population in South Carolina. In a study conducted by the University of South Carolina examining Mexican immigrants to South Carolina, approximately 95 percent of respondents explained that they left Mexico to improve their economic situation, and about 62 percent of migrants based their decision to come to South Carolina on friends or family already in the state.

The growing number of foreign-born residents in South Carolina has implications in terms of political participation and economics. As the numbers of foreign-born in South Carolina are growing, so too are the levels of immigrant political participation. About 35.1 percent of immigrants were naturalized U.S. citizens in 2007, meaning they were eligible to vote. In the 2008 presidential election, 1.3 percent of all registered voters in South Carolina were naturalized citizens or the U.S.-born children of immigrants.

Immigrants were also a key component of South Carolina's economy. And according to the U.S. Census Bureau, immigrants comprised 5.4 percent of the state's workforce in 2007. Approximately 2.2 percent of the state's workforce was also comprised of undocumented immigrants. However, it is worth noting that it is notoriously difficult to create an accurate count of undocumented migrants in the United States and this number is a rough estimate that could be an underestimation of the actual number. According to the Pew Hispanic Center, most undocumented immigrants in the South were Latino. In the case of South Carolina, about half of all Latinos in South Carolina were American-born, but of the foreign-born Latinos, the majority was not citizens. Based on these rough numbers, it is estimated that if all undocumented immigrants were removed from South Carolina, the state would lose close to $2 billion in expenditures, $782 million in economic output, and about 12,000 jobs.

In addition to Asian and Latino immigrants, South Carolina has seen a steady increase in the number of refugees resettled in the area since 2006. The year 2010 alone saw the resettlement of immigrants from Afghanistan, Bhutan, Burma, Iraq, Iran, Eritrea, Lebanon, Somalia, Vietnam, and Russia. While the number of refugees in the overall population is still very small (approximately 0.003 percent of the South Carolina population), their diverse backgrounds, increasing numbers, and challenges with native South Carolinians make them a population worth noting. In fact, South Carolina earned national attention in 2004 when residents in the town of Cayce fought the settlement of Somali Bantus in their community based on their Muslim heritage.

Despite the economic and political activities of immigrants in South Carolina, their rapid population growth combined with the focus on the "illegality" of immigration has resulted in efforts to restrict immigration to the state—a drastic change from the policies of the past 40 years. April 10, 2006, saw millions of people nationwide and 4,000 people in Charleston, South Carolina, participate in protests over proposed changes to immigration policy found in The Border Protection, Anti-Terrorism, and Illegal Immigration Control Act of 2005 (House Report [HR] 4437) passed by the U.S. House of Representatives on December 16, 2005. This bill included provisions for, among other things, increased fencing along the southern border and increased penalties for employing or transporting undocumented migrants and mandates that employers verify legal status of their employees. Though this bill failed in the Senate and was therefore not sent to the president to be signed into law, the sentiments reflected in this bill and its success in the House spurred political activity from immigrants and immigrant supporters at unprecedented levels.

In addition to federal efforts at immigration reform, state legislatures have proposed policy changes. The year 2011 saw the South Carolina state legislature pass legislation (SB 20) requiring local police to check the immigration status of people they suspected of being in the country illegally after stopping them for another offense. The law made it a crime to knowingly transport or harbor an undocumented immigrant, and set up a unit within the state police to deal with immigration issues and serve as a liaison between local and federal officials. This act was similar to the legislation enacted by other states, most notably SB 1070 in Arizona. Judges had already blocked parts of similar laws enacted in Georgia, Arizona, Utah, and Indiana aimed at trying to deter undocumented immigrants from coming to those states. On December 23, 2011, a U.S. district judge temporarily blocked parts of South Carolina's measure from going into effect on January 1, 2012, ruling that the federal government had exclusive constitutional authority to legislate immigration. The ruling states that South Carolina could not require police officers to verify the immigration status of a person they stopped for even a minor traffic violation. The ruling also barred South Carolina from making it a felony for anyone to knowingly harbor or transport an undocumented immigrant. Finally, the ruling barred the state from requiring immigrants to carry federal alien registration documents, as this type of registration was under the purview of the federal government.

In conclusion, recent immigration to South Carolina mirrors much of the Southeast, particularly neighbors North Carolina and Georgia. Latino and Asian immigrants, as well as U.S.-born minorities, account for a large and growing share of the economy in the state. In fact, the number of Mexican-born residents of South Carolina has increased by approximately 300 percent since 1990. Immigrants make up 4.3 percent of the state's population and more than one-third of immigrants in South Carolina are naturalized U.S. citizens who are eligible to vote. Despite legislation seeking to limit the number of immigrants to South Carolina, with the recent growth of the immigrant population and increasing levels of political participation, the political importance and community involvement of the so-called New Americans is only expected to grow in years to come.

TOPICAL ESSAYS

CAYCE, SOUTH CAROLINA

The town of Cayce, South Carolina gained national media attention in May 2003 when the planned resettlement of 10,000 to 12,000 Somali Bantu refugees by the State Department in about 50 U.S. cities drew criticism from local residents. An article appeared in *The State*, a local newspaper, titled "Lost Tribe Finding a Home in Columbia." The article discussed the planned resettlement of

Margaret Todd, center, serves green beans to Helema Magano, 11, a Somali Bantu refugee during a dinner hosted by the South Carolina Baptist Convention on December 16, 2004, in Columbia, South Carolina. Christmas celebrations in most of South Carolina involve visits from Santa and presents under the tree, but these traditions are new to the state's growing immigrant population for many reasons beyond geographical displacement, including religious differences and lack of consumerism in the sending country. (AP Photo/ Mary Ann Chastain)

approximately 120 Somali refugees into the city of Cayce (population 12,500), and highlighted cultural differences that would need to be overcome to successfully integrate into society. Supporters and opponents of the plan debated the proposal's merits via letters to the editor and town meetings. The school district serving the town of Cayce was particularly vocal in the dissent citing the financial burden on the system, the possibility that the district's English as a second language program would be overwhelmed, and fear that the refugees would drag down district test scores. The situation in the community became so tense that the U.S. State Department revised the plan and decided in favor of settling the Somali refugees in nearby Columbia, South Carolina (population 129, 272), citing the lack of community support in Cayce.

HB 4400 (2008)

HB 4400 was passed by the South Carolina state legislature and was signed by Governor Mark Sanford on June 4, 2008. The bill required employers to verify whether their employees were legally authorized to work in the United States; classified the falsification of documents as a felony and imposed a fine or prison sentence if caught; authorized state law enforcement officers to enforce immigration laws; made knowingly harboring or transporting undocumented immigrants a felony; allowed jailors to attempt to determine whether prisons had been lawfully admitted into the United States; allowed employees, who proved that they were terminated and were knowingly replaced by an undocumented immigrant, to file a civil suit; and prohibited undocumented immigrants from attending public higher-education institutions.

HR 4437 (2005)

Also known as the Border Protection, Anti-Terrorism, and Illegal Immigration Control Act of 2005, this bill, proposed by Representative James Sensenbrenner (R-WI, 5), was designed to make "unlawful presence" in the United States a felony. It also included: criminal penalties for anyone who knowingly assisted an undocumented individual, or was undocumented themselves; expedited removal without appearance before an immigration judge; increased fencing along the southern border; delegation of immigration enforcement to local officials; increased penalties for asylum seekers convicted of minor offenses; authority to detain aliens deemed dangerous; refusal to admit immigrants from countries who do not accept the return of criminal aliens; and elimination of the diversity visa lottery program. This bill passed the House of Representatives but died in the Senate.

HR 4437 prompted nationwide rallies in 2006 in support of immigrant rights. Mobilized by Spanish language media, millions of immigrants and immigrant supporters (both documented and undocumented) took part nationwide. Though the largest protests were in Chicago (March 10, 2006) and Los Angeles (March 25, 2006), 4,000 people marched in Charleston, South Carolina, in support of immigrant rights.

IMMIGRATION REFORM AND CONTROL ACT

Also known as the Simpson-Mazzoli Act, the IRCA of 1986 reformed U.S. immigration law in order to control undocumented immigration, granted resident alien status to certain immigrants already in the country, and reformed legal immigration. The act amended the Immigration and Nationality Act (1965) to make it unlawful to hire or continue to employ a person who was in the country without authorization to work. It also allowed foreigners who have lived in the United States since January 1, 1982 to apply for resident alien status and granted legal status to certain seasonal agricultural workers. The IRCA resulted in an increase in migration from Mexico through amnesty programs and family reunification plans.

SB 20 (2011)

Governor Nikki Hayley signed SB 20 into law on June 27, 2011. The key provision of this legislation authorized law enforcement officers to determine the immigration status of individuals they detain. The law required a state or local law enforcement officer to determine the immigration status of any individual lawfully detained or investigated if he or she has a "reasonable suspicion" that the individual is not lawfully present in the United States; required that an individual who produced a valid picture ID issued by a federal, state, or tribal government agency to be presumed to be lawfully present in the United States; authorized a law enforcement officer to transfer custody of an individual he or she has detained to the Illegal Immigration Enforcement Unit of the South Carolina Department of Public Safety or the U.S. Immigration and Customs Enforcement, if the officer determined that the individual was not lawfully present in the United States; prohibited law enforcement officers from making an "independent judgment" or from considering race, color, or national origin when making determinations regarding an individual's immigration status; prohibited transporting or harboring within South Carolina of undocumented immigrants, punishable by a fine; required undocumented immigrants of at least 18 years of age to always have in their possession their federal certificates of registration, a violation of which was subject to punishment; and established the Illegal Immigration Enforcement Unit within the South Carolina Department of Public Safety, which was to have the purpose of enforcing federal and state immigration laws.

SB 20 was scheduled to go into effect on January 1, 2012. On October 31, 2011 the U.S. Department of Justice filed a motion to enjoin South Carolina's law in the U.S. District Court for the District of South Carolina, Charleston division. The motion sought to prevent some aspects of the law from going into effect in 2012 and argued that South Carolina's immigration provisions were preempted by federal law and therefore violated the Supremacy Clause of the U.S. Constitution. On December 22, 2011, a U.S. district judge temporarily blocked parts of South Carolina's measure, ruling that the federal government had exclusive constitutional authority to legislate immigration. The ruling stated that South Carolina could not require police officers to verify the immigration status of a person they stopped for even a minor traffic violation. The ruling also barred South Carolina from making it a felony for anyone to knowingly harbor or transport an undocumented immigrant. Finally, the ruling also barred the state from requiring immigrants to carry federal alien registration documents, as this type of registration was under the purview of the federal government.

Secure Communities Program (2010)

Secure Communities is a deportation program that relies on integrated databases and partnerships between federal, state, and local law enforcement officers. The goals of the program are to rely on information-sharing and identify criminal aliens, prioritize enforcement actions and ensure the apprehension and removal of dangerous foreigners. This program is unique compared to other recent immigration policy as it is an administrative program and not created through Congress, and therefore not subject to a congressional vote.

Under the Secure Communities Program, South Carolina has identified 3,778 undocumented migrants and deported 1,025 since the program was introduced in the state in 2010.

South Carolina v. Katzenbach (1966)

South Carolina v. Katzenbach (1966) was a U.S. Supreme Court decision in which South Carolina challenged the preclearance provisions in Sections 4 and 5 of the Voting Rights Act. The Court rejected the challenge on the grounds that the Voting Rights Act was a valid exercise of congressional power under the enforcement clause of the Fifteenth Amendment.

Voting Rights Act (1965)

President Lyndon Johnson signed this landmark legislation into law on August 6, 1965. The Voting Rights Act outlawed the discriminatory voting practices adopted in many southern states after the Civil War to skirt the requirements of the Fourteenth and Fifteenth Amendments to the Constitution. This legislation established extensive federal oversight of election administration, such that states with a history of discriminatory voting practices (measured as less than 50 percent of eligible population being registered to vote) could not implement any changes to electoral law, including the changing of registration requirements or legislative districts, without first obtaining the approval of the Department of Justice, a process known as preclearance. The states covered by this legislation were mostly in the South.

The Voting Rights Act included three major provisions applicable to South Carolina: Sections 2, 5, and 203 (added in 1975). Section 2 prohibited voting practices or procedures that discriminated on the basis of race, color, or linguistic minority. Section 2 was a permanent provision and has no expiration date. Section 5 was enacted in 1965 as temporary legislation set to expire in 1970 and applicable only to certain states meeting the following qualifications: as of November 1, 1964, states employing a "test or device" restricting the opportunity to register and vote, and states where less than 50 percent of the eligible population was registered to vote as of November 1, 1964. The following states became "covered jurisdictions" in their entirety: Alabama, Alaska, Georgia, Louisiana, Mississippi, South Carolina, and Virginia. Section 5 froze any proposed changes to election practices or procedures in covered states until an administrative review by the U.S. attorney general or after a lawsuit before the U.S. District Court for the District of Columbia. The proposed change would be approved if it has been shown to be free of discriminatory purpose or effect. If the proposed change had not been shown to be free of discriminatory purpose and effect, the attorney general may block implementation.

The provisions set forth in Section 5 were extended for an additional five years in 1970, and for an additional 7 years beginning in 1975. The 1975 changes broadened the Voting Rights Act to address voting discrimination against members of language-minority groups. Section 203 required certain covered jurisdictions to provide bilingual written materials and other assistance if members of a single-language minority constituted more than 5 percent of the citizens of voting age. The addition of protections for linguistic minorities resulted in adding coverage of Alaska, Arizona, and Texas in their entirety, and parts of California, Florida, Michigan, New York, North Carolina, and South Dakota to those states already covered by the Voting Rights Act.

Section 5 of the Voting Rights Act was extended for an additional 25 years in 1982, and again in 2006, indicating the continued need to protect minority voting rights for both ethnic and linguistic minorities.

NOTABLE FIGURES/GROUPS

Nikki Haley (1972–)

Nikki Haley, a Republican, is South Carolina's first woman and first Indian American governor (2011–). She served as a member of the South Carolina House of Representatives for the 87th District from 2005 to 2010. As the daughter of legal immigrants from India, Haley had garnered national attention for her support of HB 4400, South Carolina's 2008 immigration law that covered employee verification and increased penalties for violations of immigration law, and SB 20, a bill that authorizes law enforcement officers to determine the immigration status of individuals they detain. This legislation is currently being challenged in court by the federal government on the grounds that this type of immigration enforcement is beyond the scope of state powers. In December 2011, a federal court blocked parts of this legislation from going into effect. Hayley votes in favor of HB 4400 as a member of the South Carolina House of Representatives in 2008 and approved SB 20 as governor.

Governor Nikki Haley thanks her family as she delivers her first State of the State address at the South Carolina statehouse in Columbia, South Carolina, on January 19, 2011. Haley, the daughter of Sikh immigrants from India who grew up in rural South Carolina and became the first female governor of her state, is currently writing a memoir. (AP Photo/Brett Flashnick)

Pasos

Pasos is a group that serves the Latina/o community and aims at preventive health measures as well as access to medical treatment, connecting health issues to equality and community empowerment. This includes fostering a context in which individuals can make their own decisions as well as have access to public education. The Columbia-based group is housed at the Arnold School of Public Health, University of South Carolina, and works in partnership with other organizations and universities to achieve these goals. Adopting a grassroots approach to their advocacy, they have formed teams of promotores (community health workers) to provide public education and referrals. Others provide one-on-one information and are attentive to cultural differences and language. One project they have worked on was to research Latina/o family needs for maternal and child-health resources, assessing what support and services could be provided. They also work in partnership with local groups to help victims of domestic violence in a culturally sensitive way. This group plays an important role in their approach to helping immigrants, their research, and the services they provide.

JAMES STROM THURMOND (1902–2003)

Strom Thurmond was a governor of South Carolina, 1948 presidential candidate for the States Rights Democratic Party, and a U.S. senator representing South Carolina from 1954 to 2003. He started his tenure in the Senate as a Democrat, and switched parties in 1964 becoming a Republican out of opposition to the 1964 Civil Rights Act. Aside from his tenure in office, Strom Thurmond was most famous for his position against Civil Rights Legislation, as he held the record for the longest filibuster ever held by a lone senator. His efforts to oppose the Civil Rights Act of 1957 resulted in a filibuster of 24 hours and 18 minutes, nonstop. Though he claimed his position against Civil Rights was due to an opposition to excessive federal authority, he took positions against the desegregation of the armed forces and southern schools.

Through the 1970s, Strom Thurmond took more moderate positions on Civil Rights, appointing an African American to his staff and voting to make the birthday of Martin Luther King Jr. a federal holiday in South Carolina. Toward the end of his career, Strom Thurmond took numerous positions in support of temporary migrants working in the United States, voting yes on bills allowing more farmworkers into the United States and expanding the visa program for skilled workers. However, his support of a 1998 bill limiting welfare and food stamp assistance to legal immigrants and their children could be seen to echo his earlier positions against Civil Rights Legislation.

BIBLIOGRAPHY

Bondo, Mark A. "Addressing Immigration in South Carolina." *Institute for Public Service and Policy Research, University of South Carolina* 6, no. 1 (2008). http://ipspr.sc.edu/ejournal/ejmay08/Immigration%20in%20South%20Carolina.pdf. Accessed August 9, 2014.

Chourey, Sarita. "Refugees Find Hope in South Carolina's Services." *The Augusta Chronicle*, September 13, 2010. http://chronicle.augusta.com/news/metro/2010-09-13/refugees-find-hope-south-carolinas-services. Accessed August 9, 2014.

Durand, J., Douglas Massey, and F. Charvet. "The Changing Geography of Mexican Immigration to the United States: 1910–2000." *Social Science Quarterly* 81 (2000): 1–15.

Edgar, Walter. *South Carolina: A History*. Columbia: University of South Carolina Press, 1998.

Gleeson, David. "Immigration." In Walter Edgar, ed. *The South Carolina Encyclopedia*. Columbia: University of South Carolina Press, 2006, pp. 473–74.

Hernandez-Leon, Ruben, and Victor Zuniga. "Mexican Immigrant Communities in the South and Social Capital: the Case of Dalton, Georgia." U.C. San Diego Center for Comparative Immigration Studies, Working Paper 64, 2002.

Johnson, Kevin. "Border Patrol Catches, Then Releases, Illegal." *USA Today*, February 2, 2004. http://usatoday30.usatoday.com/news/nation/2004-02-02-border-cover_x .htm. Accessed August 9, 2014.

Johnson-Webb, Karen D. "Employer Recruitment and Hispanic Labor Migration: North Carolina Urban Areas at the End of the Millennium." *The Professional Geographer* 54 (2002): 406–21.

Kochhar, Rakesh, Roberto Suro, and Sonya Tafoya. *The New Latino South: The Context and Consequences of Rapid Population Growth*. Washington, DC: Pew Hispanic Center, 2005.

Kovacik, Charles F., and John J. Winberry. *South Carolina: A Geography*. Boulder, CO: Westview Press, 1987.

Lacy, Elaine C. *Mexican Immigrants in South Carolina: A Profile*. Columbia: Consortium for Latino Immigration Studies, University of South Carolina, 2007.

Mohl, Raymond A. "Mexican Immigration/Migration to Alabama." In Mary Odem, and Elaine Lacy, eds. *Mexican Immigration to the U.S. Southeast: Impact and Challenges*. Atlanta: Instituto de Mexico, 2005, pp. 85–108.

Murphy, A. D., C. Blanchard, and J. A. Hill, eds. *Latino Workers in the Contemporary South*. Athens: University of Georgia Press, 2001.

Nevins, Joseph. *Operation Gatekeeper: The Rise of the Illegal Alien and the Making of the U.S.-Mexico Boundary*. New York: Routledge, 2002.

Odem, Mary, and Elaine Lacy, eds. *Mexican Immigration to the U.S. Southeast: Impact and Challenges*. Atlanta: Instituto de Mexico, 2005.

Office of Refugee Resettlement. "Refugee Arrival Data by Country of Origin and State of Initial Resettlement." 2010. http://www.acf.hhs.gov/programs/orr/data/refugee_arrival _data.htm. Accessed March 29, 2014.

Paral, Rob, and Associates. *The New American Electorate: The Growing Political Power of Immigrants and Their Children*. Washington, DC: Immigration Policy Center, American Immigration Law Foundation, 2008.

PASOS. PASOS Webpage. http://www.scpasos.org/our-values/. Accessed February 25, 2014.

Passel, Jeffrey. *Estimating the Size of the Undocumented Population*. Washington, DC: Pew Hispanic Center, 2005.

Passel, Jeffrey, and D'Vera Cohn. *A Portrait of Undocumented Immigrants in the United States*. Washington, DC: Pew Hispanic Center, 2009.

The Perryman Group. *An Essential Resource: An Analysis of the Economic Impact of Undocumented Workers on Business Activity in the US with Estimated Effects by State and by Industry*. Waco, TX: The Perryman Group, 2008.

Phillips, N. "Winthrop/ETV Poll: Illegal Immigrants—Let Them Stay? SC Divided." *The State*, February 24, 2008. http://www.thestate.com/2008/08/21/493989/latest-winthropetv-poll-results.html/. Accessed August 9, 2014.

Schmid, C. "Immigration and Asian and Hispanic Minorities in the New South: An Exploration of History, Attitudes, and Demographic Trends." *Sociological Spectrum* 23 (2003): 129–57.

Schunk, Donald, and Douglas Woodward. *A Profile of the Diversified South Carolina Economy.* Columbia: Darla Moore School of Business, University of South Carolina, 2000.

U.S. Bureau of the Census. 2006. *American Community Survey.* Washington, DC: U.S. Bureau of the Census.

U.S. Bureau of the Census. 1940. *Census of Population.* Washington, DC: U.S. Bureau of the Census.

U.S. Bureau of the Census. 2010. *Census of Population.* Washington, DC: U.S. Bureau of the Census.

Young, Richard D. "The Growing Hispanic Population in South Carolina: Trends and Issues." Columbia: Institute for Public Service and Policy Research, University of South Carolina, 2005.

41

SOUTH DAKOTA

Wenqian Dai

CHRONOLOGY

1804	The Lewis and Clark Expedition arrive in South Dakota.
1817	An American fur trading post is set up at present-day Fort Pierre, beginning the continuous American settlement of this area.
1851	Treaty of Traverse des Sioux is signed. The Santee Sioux agree to cede all the lands east of the Big Sioux River, except for a 10-mile reservation area stretching along the Minnesota River eastward from Big Stone Lake and Lake Traverse.
1855	The American Army buys Fort Pierre and establishes a military post.
1856	General Harney decides to locate a new military post and lays out Fort Randall. Fort Pierre and Fort Randall are the first military posts to be established in South Dakota.
1857	A townsite location is sought by the representatives of white settler groups at the falls of Big Sioux to establish the prospective capital of the new territory. This townsite is named Sioux Falls.
1858	Under the Yankton Treaty of 1858, the Yankton tribe withdraws to a reservation tract of 400,000 acres along the east bank of the Missouri in the present Charles Mix County. The ceded land opens Dakota Territory for white settlers.
1859 (July 10)	This date is regarded as the official opening of Dakota Territory.
1861	The U.S. Congress passes a bill creating Dakota Territory. President James Buchanan signs this bill on March 2, 1861.
1862	The Homestead Act of 1862 is signed into law by President Abraham Lincoln.

1863	The first Norwegian Lutheran Church in the state is the St. Paul congregation located north of Elk Point in Union county.
1868	The Laramie Treaty terminates the hostilities between the Native Americans and the white settlers. The entire Powder River Country is given back to the tribes. The military posts within the unceded regions are removed and the Bozeman Road leading to the mines is closed. The Native Americans withdraw all opposition to the construction of the Union Pacific and stop attacking emigrant trains.
1869	The first group of Bohemian immigrants arrives in South Dakota and establishes their first settlement west of Yankton.
1870	Bohemians establish their first trade center Zizkov west of Utica.
1872	The first rail line crosses the Big Sioux River into Dakota Territory at Yankton.
1872	A homestead lot is assigned to the Catholic Bohemian Literary Society. The town is named Tabor and is the first town settled entirely by Bohemians.
1873	German Russian immigrants (Mennonite and Hutterites) arrive and settle in South Dakota.
1874	Custer's expedition discovers gold mines in the Black Hills. The gold fever brings another wave of immigration into South Dakota.
1874–1879	Russian Hutterites move to the area, some establishing new colonies such as Bon Homme and Wolf Creek.
1877	The Black Hills Treaty is signed by which the American Indians gives up the Black Hills. This treaty opens the west of the state to the settlers.
1877	Chinese immigrants arrive in Deadwood.
1878	The Finnish pastor Torsten Estensen and his Apostolic Lutheran followers establish Poinsett in Brookings County.
1878	A group of white miners organize the Caucasian League and Miners' Union to obstruct Chinese employment.
1883	About 300 Welsh immigrants settle in a town called Powell in Edmunds County.
1889	President Benjamin Harrison signs the proclamation officially admitting South Dakota as a state of the United States on November 2, 1889.
1891	The Norwegian Singers' Association of America, originally organized as the Northwestern Scandinavian Singers' Association is organized in Sioux Falls.
1897	The first lodge of the Western Bohemian Fraternal Association is organized in South Dakota.
1900	A group of African American farmers establishes the colony of Blair in Sully County.
1906	Sons of Norway, a fraternal organization for men and women of Norwegian birth and descent, develops its first lodge in South Dakota at

	Sioux Falls. Columbus Larsson founds the towns Columbus and Larson (1906, 1907) which are both initially inhabited by Norwegians only.
1910	The Chinatown in Deadwood has largely dispersed by 1910.
1910–1915	Last of the major waves of Germans and Russians enter the state.
1912	Norwegian student, Ludvig Holby, introduces ski jumping to Augustana College, where he is a student. He helps to plan the first Nordic competition in 1912.
1913	Oscar Micheaux publishes his novel, *The Conquest: The Story of a Negro Pioneer* that is based on his own experience as an African American homesteader in South Dakota.
1914–1918	German Hutterites are subjected to harassment and ill-treatment in South Dakota during World War I and many of the Hutterite communities move to Canada.
1918	Oscar Micheaux produces his first film, *The Homesteader* by adapting his first novel, *The Conquest: The Story of a Negro Pioneer*.
1920	Last year of the greatest wave of Norwegian immigrant settlement in South Dakota.
1930–1940	Because of economic depression, the state's population declines.
1934	Four more Hutterite colonies leave the state due to prejudice.
1935	Last wave of Chinese settler out-migration back to China occurs.
1936	The first Czechoslovak Day held by the Western Bohemian Fraternal Association lodges in South Dakota is held at Gregory.
1941	The USS *South Dakota* sails; it is later renamed *Battleship X*.
1944	The Pick-Sloan Flood Control Act is passed; four dams are provided for in the act.
1950s	The state enjoys an economic revival, and rural areas are increasingly wired for electricity.
1957	Research demonstrates that about 1,870 Hutterites remain in the state.
1973	Wounded Knee is occupied by the American Indian Movement as they protest policies toward Native Americans.
1980	The U.S. Supreme Court supports Sioux claims for land in the Black Hills, ordering compensation. The Sioux demand the land rather than monetary compensation.
1990s	The state sees a revival of agricultural enterprises.
1991–1998	A new wave of immigrants arrives in the state. Most are from Ethiopia, the former Soviet Union (Russia), and the Sudan.
2003	Somali refugees start to resettle in Sioux Falls.
2009	The SD S 17, Drivers Licensing Provisions, is enacted.
2010	Three legislations are enacted: SD H 1079, Birth Certificate Reissuance for Adoptions; SD H 1107, Commercial Driver's License; and SD H 1260, Federal Law Enforcement Officer.
2010	Asians take the place of Europeans to be the largest foreign-born group in South Dakota.

2011	SD S 32, Sex Offender Registration Regulations, are enacted.
2011	State legislators introduce three anti-undocumented immigration bills: House Bill (HB) 1198, Senate Bill (SB) 156, and HB 1199. HB 1198 would authorize law enforcement officers to make reasonable attempts to check a suspect's immigration status when they enforce other laws. SB 156 would penalize the employers who knowingly hire undocumented workers. HB 1199 challenges the automatic U.S. citizenship granted to the children of undocumented immigrants. All three bills fail to pass.
2011	The 50,000th Bhutanese refugee leave Nepal and arrive in South Dakota on August 1 for resettlement.
2012	Legislators introduce three anti-undocumented immigration bills: HB 1238, HB 1139, and SB 155. HB 1238 would require the employers to use the E-Verify system and set up penalties for hiring undocumented workers. HB 1139 is proposed to crack down on the use of stolen identification by undocumented immigrants. SB 155 intends to penalize employment of undocumented foreigners. All three measures fail to pass.

HISTORICAL OVERVIEW

Prior to statehood and widespread white settlements, American Indians (Sioux tribes, also called Dakota tribes) lived in the area that became South Dakota. The Lewis and Clark Expedition arrived in South Dakota in 1804. The expedition team passed the mouth of the Big Sioux and made camp on the South Dakota side of the Missouri near Elk Pointe, South Dakota, in August. This expedition provided early information about the territory that became Dakota Territory later. The westward progression of the American frontier brought immigrant pioneers to Dakota Territory. From the 1840s through the 1860s, some migrants came north into Dakota Territory during their westward migration across the central plains to the West Coast. The Yankton Treaty of 1858 with the Yankton Sioux made room for white settlers between Missouri and the Big Sioux. Dakota Territory officially opened for the settlers on July 10, 1859. The majority of pre-statehood settlers came from nearby states: Nebraska, Iowa, Minnesota, Wisconsin and Illinois. The proportion of immigrants among the inhabitants in Dakota Territory increased strikingly. "The census of 1860 listed a relatively large number of foreign-born among the inhabitants of the area later included in Dakota Territory. The aggregate native population numbered 3,063; the aggregate foreign, 1,774" (Johansen 1937, 6). The 1860 Census district included the area between the western boundary of the state of Minnesota and Iowa and the Missouri River. To the north, the border of the district was the international boundary; to the west, the boundary of the district was indefinite. Dakota Territory was created by act of Congress on March 2, 1861.

The first major influx of immigrants to South Dakota came in the 1860s. The east-river area (the east of the Missouri River) was ceded to the federal government by the Native American tribes who originally resided in this area, according to the treaties of 1851, 1858, 1868, and 1873. The Homestead Act of 1862 that granted an applicant ownership of 160 acres of undeveloped federal land west of the Mississippi River at no cost attracted immigrants into South Dakota. The railroads facilitated the settlers migrating and settling in South Dakota. Social and religious pressures, wars, and famines in Europe pushed Europeans to immigrate to United States to seek better fortunes at the same time. The Homesteaders came from eastern and midwestern states. New York Colony was the largest organized immigration group to settle in Dakota during the early 1860s. Nearly 100 families enrolled in the "Fee Homestead Association of Central New York" and reached nearby Yankton, South Dakota, in 1864. Probably 30 families settled in South Dakota permanently in the end.

The west-river area (the west of the Missouri River) was placed on the market much later. Custer's military expedition through the Black Hills in 1874 discovered gold mines, which stimulated another wave of immigration into South Dakota. The bulk of miners and other workers migrated into South Dakota, including the Irish, Cornish, and Chinese. The Black Hills Treaty of 1877 officially opened the west of the state to the settlers. There was a great trek of immigrants into the west-river area partly recruited from older settlements and partly from abroad in the first decade of twentieth century.

The Homestead Act, railroad development, and gold fever led to the "Great Dakota Boom" between 1870 and 1890. The foreign-born population in South Dakota reached its peak in 1910 with slightly more than 100,000 immigrants. It has declined since then. South Dakota was largely agricultural and rural. Many of the early immigrants to South Dakota were farmers and the majority of them resided in the rural areas. The immigrants constituted a larger proportion of the population in the east-river part than it did in the west-river area (Johansen 1936, 34). The early immigrants to South Dakota were predominantly from countries of northwest and central Europe, that is, Germans, Irish and Scandinavians, in particular. The majority of Scandinavian immigrants were Norwegian. There were also Swedes, Danes, and Finns. The Germans were another dominant ethnic group and became the most widespread of all the ethnic groups. The five largest ancestry groups in South Dakota are German (40.7 percent), Norwegian (15.3 percent), Irish (10.4 percent), Native American (8.2 percent), and English (7.1 percent).

Norwegian Immigrants

Norwegian immigrants were the majority of the early immigrants to South Dakota and the earliest and the largest foreign group in the state. "The Norwegians constituted the most numerous foreign nationality in the frontier settlements in 1860. They were among the first white settlers in South Dakota" (Johansen 1937, 8). There were 1,167 Norwegians residing in South Dakota in 1870, according to the 1870 Census, which constituted 28.6 percent of all foreign-born population in this state. The reasons for the influx of Norwegian immigrants to South Dakota were complex, including political, social, and economic aspects. Politically, Norway that was under the charge of Denmark first and then Sweden until 1905 was lacking forward-looking policies due to the subjected position. Demographically, the death rate, especially the infant death rate declined significantly after the demographic transition. Yet, the decline of the birth rate lagged, which made it more difficult for the individual farmer families with more adult children. These families were motivated to immigrate to Dakota Territory by their intense desire for homestead land. They came in large families or larger kinship groups.

Norwegians established their Lutheran congregations and churches during their first decade of settlement in South Dakota. The majority of these churches continued to function to the present. Norwegian immigrants and their descendants also established church-related institutions, for instance, the Augustana College in Sioux Falls, general hospitals, old people's homes, orphanage, and shelter for unmarried mothers. These institutions were fully assimilated. They not only served the Norwegian communities but also the larger American constituency. They reflected the strength of Norwegians in the state. "In consequence of their numbers and their social solidarity, the Norwegians have exerted a strong influence upon the development and form of community life the state" (Johansen 1937, 12).

Norwegians also developed other organizations to help their co-ethnic group members, to preserve their social and cultural heritage, and to serve the local community. Sons of Norway, a fraternal organization for men and women of Norwegian birth and descent, developed its first lodge in South Dakota in 1906. Another association, "Bygdelag" was known among Norwegians based on the immigrants from the same valley or district in Norway. These associations organized in sense of original communities devoted their activities mainly to biographical, genealogical, and historical studies and did much to foster Norwegian songs and music and promote skiing. The Norwegian Singers' Association of America, originally organized as the Northwestern Scandinavian Singer's Association was organized in Sioux Falls in 1891. This association helped cultivate and promote vocal music and choral singing.

Other Scandinavian Immigrants

Swedish immigrants came to the state later than the Norwegians did and their settlements were more scattered through the state. The Swedes began arriving in the state in 1868. Unlike the Norwegians who stayed within the framework of the Lutheran synods, the Swedes were divided among four or five principal denominations. They were the first to grow sugar beets and one of the first to grown alfulfu in the state.

The first Danes came to Dakota Territory shortly after the Civil War. More Danes immigrated into South Dakota in the years following the disastrous war with Germany in 1864, and in the 1880s and 1890s. They laid the foundation for one of its largest settlements in the United States in early 1870s in Turner County. The Danish Brotherhood in America and the Danish Sisterhood in America were organized by the Danish immigrant societies to provide aid to its members, keep its cultural heritage, and strengthen its members to obey the laws of the United States. The Danish culture is most evident in Viborg, a community in Turner County. The Danish Festival Days in Viborg celebrate the Danish heritage each year on the third weekend in July.

Finnish immigrants constituted a very small proportion of population in South Dakota, less than half percent of the state population. Pastor Torsten Estensen and his Apostolic Lutheran followers established Poinsett in Brookings County in 1878. Then about 200 Finns migrated to that area between 1878 and 1890. The gold rush brought Finnish miners to the Black Hills. Finns settled in concentrated groups.

English-Speaking Immigrants

English-speaking immigrants to South Dakota included the Irish, Welsh, Cornish, Scottish, and British. The English-speaking immigrants were among the earliest ones to the United States. They were also among the earliest settlers in Dakota Territory. They reached their highest number in South Dakota in 1890. The British settled mostly in urban areas and worked as shopkeepers, craftsmen, and laborers. They were also farmers and ranchers. The Irish, Cornish, and Scottish did not generally settle in large groups. They came as single families or individuals. One exception was a town named Powell in Edmunds County where about 300 Welsh immigrants settled in 1883. Irish and Cornish miners flocked to the Black Hills during the gold rush. They often held top jobs underground in the mines, due to their English ability and working experiences.

German Immigrants

German Americans are the largest ancestry group in South Dakota. In 2011, the population with German origin was 342,251 or 41.5 percent of the overall population in this state (2011American Community Survey 1-Year Estimate). German remains the second-most spoken language in the state. They are also the most widespread ethnic group in the state. People of German origin can be found in every county and town in the state. A majority of German immigrants to South Dakota came from Russia and included two prominent groups: the Mennonites and the Hutterites. A group of German farmers migrated to Russia in the 1760s when Empress Catherine the Great granted them the privileges of free land, religious freedom, and deferment from military service. When the series of privileges were revoked in the 1860s, many of these German farmers sought to move to America. The first group of Mennonite families settled near Yankton in 1873. The Hutterites also arrived and settled in Bon Homme, Hutchinson, Turner, and Yankton counties in the same year. They brought various winter wheat seeds, which helped South Dakota become a major wheat producer.

Mennonites owned individual property and Hutterites lived in commune colonies and were well known for their unique collectivist community organization. The Hutterite colonies were characterized by seclusion and isolation, being not only physically but also socially and culturally isolated. The Hutterites believed in isolation and their contacts with the outside were "largely limited to business relationships" (Johansen 1937, 37). The Hutterite communities were self-sufficient and had a highly developed division of labor where residents incorporated together to support their community and shared the food and other possession together. The communities took responsibility for many family functions, such as cooking and dining and education.

Czech (Bohemian) Immigrants

The long-term effects of being conquered and suffering oppression motivated the large immigration from Bohemia to the United States. The first group of Bohemian immigrants arrived in South Dakota in 1869 and established their first settlement west of Yankton. Many also settled in Bon Homme, Charles Mix, Gregory, Tripp, Brule, and Jackson counties. Brule County was opened to settlers in 1880. About half of the population in this county was at one time of Bohemian birth or origin. The first town settled entirely by Bohemians was Tabor. A homestead lot was assigned to the Catholic Bohemian Literary Society in 1872. The town was named Tabor. Tabor began to prosper in 1900 when the Milwaukee railroad established a station in the town. Bohemians established their first trade center Zizkov, four miles west of Utica in 1870. Their successful apple and cherry orchards contributed to the fruit-planting industry in the state.

The Bohemians were predominantly Roman Catholics. A small proportion was Protestants. They developed a strong system of social organization. The Bohemians in South Dakota had organized 20 lodges of the Western Bohemian Fraternal Association, four lodges of the Czechoslovak society of America, and five "Sokol" societies by 1937. The members of these organizations provided aid to one another when one was in need and received help from their lodge. These organizations were a strong source of cultural and social activities. They sponsored educational programs to further the continuation of Czech language and culture among the younger generation. Almost every lodge had a dramatic club, the young members of which usually presented plays in Czech language. Members also benefited from the library service. The Western Bohemian Fraternal Association lodges in South Dakota held the first Czechoslovak day at Gregory in 1936. Thousands of the members in the South Dakota lodges and delegates from the lodges of the neighboring states participated in this celebration. They had a parade and presented dances and drills in national costume and plays. The governor of South Dakota gave an address.

CHINESE IMMIGRANTS

Thousands of Chinese migrated to the United States in the mid-nineteenth century when the gold mines were discovered in California. The construction of the transcontinental railroad in the mid-1860s provided the Chinese thousands of jobs. They comprised 80 percent of the railway's workforce. The railroad also brought them far beyond California into the American West, including the Black Hills of Dakota Territory. The Chinese arrived in Deadwood Gulch with thousands of other migrants during the gold rush in Black Hills to take advantage of the economic opportunities.

Most of the Chinese arrived in large groups in 1877. It was estimated to be up to 400 Chinese in Deadwood, which made them the largest and most dominant ethnic group in the Gulch's early years. They established a Chinatown in Deadwood, elected their own mayor and council, and established a police force and fire department. Many Chinese immigrants extracted gold from those abandoned placer mines to make a living. Yet their work was not limited to mining. They largely ran businesses that served the local mining population, such as laundries, retail shops, hotels, restaurants, and domestic services in the white communities, which placed them among the region's self-employed middle class.

The Chinese preserved and celebrated their native customs and traditions, such as Chinese New Year. They welcomed the whites into their business and holiday celebration events. These events became a part of the local culture. The Chinese also became assimilated into the dominant culture. They attended the local multicultural celebrations. The *Black Hills Daily Times* praised their patriotism for their donation to the July 4 fund in 1879. They adopted the American conduct and lifestyle, wearing western dress, taking American names, sending their children to public schools, and learning English. Their significant assimilation resulted in their economic success and great acceptance by the local dominant population.

Nevertheless, the increasing popularity of racism and the perceived threat that the Chinese posed to white jobs stimulated white resentment toward Chinese. A group of white miners organized the Caucasian League and Miners' Union in 1878 to obstruct Chinese employment. Yet, the hostilities were short-lived. The Chinese community had largely dispersed by 1910 after the gold rush subsided. Some returned to China and others moved to larger cities in the United States.

African American Migrants

There were 94 African Americans in Dakota Territory in 1870. Black soldiers served at the Forts Meade, Randall, and Hale to protect railroad and surveying crews, cut wood and assist settlers in the times of disaster. African Americans also migrated to Black Hills during the gold rush and they were generally accepted into the local community. A group of African American farmers established the colony of Blair in Sully County in 1900. Many of these farm families were forced to leave South Dakota during the 1930s by the grasshopper infestations, drought, and financial hardship.

Contemporary Immigration in South Dakota

Most Recent Immigration Characteristics

South Dakota had a population of 814,180 in 2010 with the fifth-lowest population density in the United States. This state is largely rural. The number of foreign-born residents in this state was 22,238 (2.7 percent) in 2010, ranking 47th out of the 50 states. The percentage of immigrants in this state increased from 1.1 percent in 1990 to 1.8 percent in 2000 to 2.7 percent in 2010. It experienced a 64.7 percent increase in the percentage of immigrants from 2000 to 2010, ranking seventh in the United States. About 9 out of 10 children (91.2 percent) with immigrant parents were U.S. citizens in 2009. In 2010, the naturalization rate in South Dakota was 40.8 percent and 48.1 percent of the foreign-born population entered the United States after 2000. In 2010, 1.3 percent (or 5,742) of registered voters were "New Americans," naturalized citizens or the U.S.-born children of immigrants who were raised during the current era of immigration since 1965.

The Latino/a share of the state's overall population grew from 0.8 percent in 1990 to 1.4 percent in 2000 to 2.7 percent in 2010.The percentage of Asian population grew 0.4 percent in 1990 to 0.6 percent in 2000 to 0.9 percent in 2010. Asians became the largest immigrant group in 2010 and Latino immigrants were the second-largest group. Europeans were the largest foreign-born group in South Dakota until 2010.

Table 7   Origin of Foreign-Born Population in South Dakota, 2010

Region	Percentage of Immigrants in SD
Asia	29.40
Latin America	25.80
Africa	21.30
Europe	19.00
Canada	4.40
Oceania	0.10

Source: 2010 ACS 1-Year Estimate Summary Files, U.S. Census Bureau
American FactFinder.

Geographic Concentration

The majority of the foreign-born populations in South Dakota live in Sioux Falls, the center of the east river area in 2010. Sioux Falls has been called the "Ellis Island of the Great Plains" (*The World* August 20, 2009). Sioux Falls had 13,693 out of the overall 22,238 immigrants in South Dakota (61.5 percent). This share jumped from 47.2 to 61.5 percent between 2000 and 2010. The other big city in the state and the center of the west river area, Rapid City, shared 5.8 percent of the state's foreign-born populations at the same time. Its share of immigrants was 16.6 percent in 2000.

The geographic concentration of immigrants in Sioux Falls can be attributed to the new wave of refugee immigrants into South Dakota since 2000. Sioux Falls is where the primary resettlement agency in the state, Lutheran Social Services (LSS) of South Dakota, is located and is the main hub for the refugees. "A study last year [2002] by the Center for Immigration Studies in Washington, D.C., showed Minnehaha County had the fastest-growing percentage of foreign-born residents of any metropolitan area in the nation. Driven by Lutheran Social Services' refugee-resettlement programs, the foreign-born population more than doubled in Sioux Falls in the 1990s" (*Rapid City Journal* July 27, 2003). A number of Somali and Sudanese refugees have resettled in Sioux Falls since 2000. Falls Community Health, which partnered with LSS to provide medical care to the new arrival refugees, estimated that about 400 refugees were resettled in Sioux Falls every year. The refugees comprise the majority of the city's foreign-born population. Big employers in the city, such as the University of South Dakota Medical Center, Sanford Hospital, Citibank, and Augustana College, also attract the immigrants to Sioux Falls.

Assimilation

English proficiency is often viewed as an important indicator of assimilation. Speaking English well not only promotes immigrants' assimilation into U.S.

society but also arguably helps improve their socioeconomic status and achieve success. In South Dakota, 7.5 percent of the overall state population (5 years and over) did not speak English at home and 2.1 percent did not speak English well in this state in 2010. Among the immigrants, 6.7 percent of naturalized citizens could not speak English or did not speak English well and 27.6 percent of noncitizens showed limited English proficiency. Most of the children (88.4 percent) with immigrant parents were considered English proficient as of 2009.

Asian immigrants had the lowest rate of limited English proficiency among all four ethnic groups in South Dakota, according to the 2010 American Community Survey 1-Year Estimate (IPUMS-USA). While naturalized citizens were all proficient in English, 14.6 percent of their noncitizens did not speak English well in 2010. Latino/a immigrants and other immigrants of color also showed a pronounced percentage of limited English proficiency. All black immigrants who were naturalized to be U.S. citizens spoke English well, but almost half of their new arrivals, who were noncitizens, had a problem of limited English proficiency. Latino/a naturalized citizens were even worse off than their noncitizen counterparts, with regard to English proficiency. It was notable that 2 percent of Latino/a native-born citizens in South Dakota did not speak English well.

Educational attainment is another dimension of integration. It is related to English proficiency. Immigrants in South Dakota have both higher and lower levels of education than American-born individuals. Among the population 18 years and over in South Dakota, immigrants, especially naturalized citizens showed a higher percentage of having less than a high-school diploma in 2010 than did American-born individuals. They, however, were more likely to have a graduate or professional degree at the same time. A notable difference was that noncitizens' rate of a graduate or professional degree was even more than twice of that of the native-born residents.

Anglo and Asian immigrants were more likely to complete high school than immigrants of color were in South Dakota in 2010. Latino/a immigrants were the most disadvantaged group with regard to educational attainment. They had the highest high school dropout rate. Their percentage of having a college degree was only

Table 8 Limited English Proficiency of Immigrants in South Dakota, 2010

	White	Black	Hispanic	Asian
Naturalized Citizen	2.80	0.00	26.69	0.00
N	4,403	1,198	1,877	2,777
Non-Citizen	20.00	47.90	21.10	14.60
N	3,733	4,212	2,877	2,485

Source: 2010 ACS 1-Year Estimate, IPUMS-USA.

Table 9 Educational Attainment of Immigrants (18 Years and over) in South Dakota

| | White | | Black | | Hispanic | | Asian | |
	Naturalized Citizen	Noncitizen	Naturalized Citizen	Noncitizen	Naturalized Citizen	Noncitizen	Naturalized Citizen	Noncitizen
Less Than a High-School Diploma	25.85	13.96	57.35	0	33.08	37.69	18.56	9.25
High School Diploma	24.86	43.28	14.61	28.02	43.42	27.23	0	15.44
Some College	30.08 p	17.23	16.69	4.70	0	28.06	44.06	14.36
College	9.35	4.24	11.35	67.28	16.09	0	31.20	17.93
Postgraduate	9.86	21.29	0	0	7.41	7.02	6.19	43.02
N	3467	3447	1198	2534	1877	2776	1859	1762

Source: 2010 ACS 1-Year Estimate, IPUMS-USA.

higher than that of white immigrants. Their postgraduate educational achievement could only surpass the achievement of immigrants of color. Immigrants of color who were naturalized to be the U.S. citizens also showed a dramatic high school dropout rate. Immigrants of color who were not U.S. citizens, however, were much better off than their naturalized counterparts. They have an outstanding rate of college degree, the top one among all four racial groups of immigrants. Asian immigrants outperformed all the other three groups, regarding educational attainment. Their high school dropout rates were lower than other groups, except the immigrants of color who were not the U.S. citizens. They also showed a strikingly high rate of postgraduate degree. Over 4 out 10 Asian immigrants who were not the U.S. citizens had a postgraduate degree in this state in 2010.

Economic Status

Median household income of the foreign-born population in South Dakota ($53,200) was slightly lower than that of the native-born citizens ($59,200) in 2010. Among the immigrants, naturalized citizens were economically much better off than noncitizens. The former's median household income was $75,100, while the latter earned a median household income of $36,000. This gap indicates that the foreign-born who arrived earlier earned more than the most recent immigrants. Black and Asian immigrants were disadvantaged at earnings while white immigrants stood out of all racial groups with a pronounced high income. The median household income for white, immigrants of color, Latino/a, and Asian immigrants was $70,900, $31,700, $53,200, and $35,400, respectively. The disadvantage of Black and Asian immigrant with regard to earnings could result from the fact that a significant number of them are refugees in South Dakota.

Asians comprised 0.9 percent of the population in South Dakota in 2010 and owned 0.6 percent of businesses in the state. Black and Latino/a population were underrepresented among business owners. The percentages of black-and Latino/a-owned business were much less than their proportion in the overall population. Asians and Latino/as own 452 and 595 firms, respectively, in 2012, though the percentages are small. South Dakota's 595 Latino-owned businesses had sales and receipts of $317.4 million and employed 1,206 people in 2007, the past year for which data are available. The state's 452 Asian-owned businesses had sales and receipts of $203.8 million and employed 2,837 people in 2007, according to the U.S. Census Bureau's Survey of Business Owners. The amount of sales and employment size illustrated immigrants' integration into the state's business sector.

Immigrants had a slightly higher percentage of poverty than the native-born population in South Dakota in 2010. The 2010 American Community Survey 1-Year Estimate reported that 17.6 percent of foreign-born population and 14.9

percent of native-born residents in South Dakota lived in poverty (IPUMS-USA 2010). Among the immigrants, naturalized citizens had higher incomes and a better standard of living. About 18 percent of naturalized citizens and 27 percent of noncitizens lived below the poverty line in South Dakota in 2009. This difference can be attributed to the naturalized citizens' longer residence in this country. Immigrants have to be legal permanent residents for at least five years before they are eligible for naturalization. Then the naturalized citizens experience a longer period of integration to improve their socioeconomic status. Naturalizing also has a "self selection" effect on immigrants. Only those who can pass the citizenship test and expect a better life in the United States choose to be naturalized.

Refugee Immigrants

South Dakota is home to a growing refugee population. The state has taken 3,781 refugees from 34 different countries from 2000 to 2011, according to the U.S. Department of Health and Human Services, Office of Refugee Resettlement. The majority of the refugees are from Somalia (606), Sudan (462), Bhutan (434), Burma (404), and the former Yugoslavia (262) (including Bosnia and Herzegovina, Croatia, Macedonia, Serbia and Montenegro, Kosovo, and Slovenia). Sioux Falls is the main hub for the refugees. South and North Dakota are becoming a center for the resettlement of refugees. As stated above, Sioux Falls has been called the "Ellis Island of the Great Plains" (*The World* August 20, 2009). LSS of South Dakota, located in Sioux Falls, is the primary resettlement agency operating in the state. LSS Refugee and Immigration Programs provide a wide range of services for the newcomers. The Multi-Cultural Center of Sioux Falls identified 65 different languages being spoken in Sioux Falls in 2004.

These newcomer groups have expanded the area's cultural diversity. They brought their own cultural heritage with them to their new community, often leaving their homeland with little knowledge of English and customs of the American society. Resettlement and adjustment could be a difficult challenge for them and the local communities as well. The schools in Sioux Falls have struggled to provide help for the new arrival students to learn English and get assimilated into the state's culture. Dakotaland Federal Credit Union (FCU) partnered with LSS of South Dakota in 2009 to provide financial management workshops to help the Karen refugee community in Huron, South Dakota. Many of those Karen refugees came from refugee camps or impoverished areas in Burma with limited knowledge of English and lack of familiarity with basic financial management in a complex market economy. These Karen immigrants attained better knowledge of financial management and home ownership concepts after participating in the workshops. Additionally, partnering with LSS, Falls Community Health has a refugee health program to offer medical care to the new arrival refugees in Sioux Falls with

Table 10   Total Refugee Arrivals to South Dakota (2000–2011)

Year	Number of Refugees
Year 2000	378
Year 2001	298
Year 2002	107
Year 2003	159
Year 2004	329
Year 2005	214
Year 2006	179
Year 2007	219
Year 2008	317
Year 2009	536
Year 2010	555
Year 2011	490

Source: U.S. Department of Health and Human Services, Office of
Refugee Resettlement.

language-interpreting service. The refugees can have a physical examination and
screening to identify their illness and receive immunization and preventive care.

Undocumented Immigrants

South Dakota has a very small proportion of undocumented immigrants. As of
2010, the anti-immigration group Federation for American Immigration Reform
(FAIR) estimated the state's undocumented population size to be about 5,000 or
0.6 percent of the overall population. South Dakota is one of the 10 states with the
lowest density of undocumented population. The cost of undocumented population was estimated to be $33,306,846 by FAIR in 2009. The undocumented im-
migrants constituted less than 1.5 percent of the state's workforce in 2010. They
work in the logging industry, farms, and food-processing factories.

The farms and food-processing industry are of a great value to the state's economy. The farmers and the food production business owners complain that the
unworkable immigration laws force them to employ undocumented workers. The
H2A guest worker program was designed for seasonal work only and the job of
milking cows that is performed every day is not qualified for this category. The
dairy farms then are not allowed to use this visa system to bring foreign employees, who they can pay less and force to work longer hours. They have to
make a choice from a reliable but possibly undocumented worker or an American
worker who is unwilling to put up with low pay and physically intensive labor. On

June 29, 2012, *The Wall Street Journal* reported a dairy farm in Brookings, South Dakota, that allegedly had to make this choice. This farm was under the scrutiny of the U.S. Department of Labor for its use of the H2A visas to bring foreign employees. The law enforcement agents entered the farm to check the information of the employees and interrogate them to build a case against the owner. The farm owner paid thousands of dollars for the H2A visa petitions and expected to receive more legal bills because of the scrutiny of the Department of Labor. Yet, this farm probably would not face this challenge if they had not applied for the working visas and just employed the possible undocumented workers.

U.S. attorney Brendan Johnson announced, on September 27, 2012, that prosecutors charged four logging companies in Black Hills (Munoz Logging and Construction, Black Hills Thinning, Escalante Logging, and SM Logging) with defrauding the federal government by circumventing contract requirements and employing undocumented workers. Another five people were accused of harboring undocumented immigrants. The indictment said that the four companies have employed undocumented workers since 2008 to secure their profit and ensure a lower bid to win the federal contracts. Twenty-three undocumented workers in the companies have been arrested or deported since 2009. Eighteen people were arrested during the investigation. Johnson said the indictment shows his office's commitment to enforcing the nation's immigration laws. "This includes limiting the demand for undocumented workers by prosecuting employers who knowingly hire illegal workers," he said in a news release (Eaton 2012).

TOPICAL ESSAYS

IMMIGRATION POLICIES AND LEGISLATION

South Dakota has a continued Republican dominance in the governor's office and the state legislature. The state legislature has enacted eight law bills concerning immigration since 2008. The Driver Licensing Provisions Bill (SD S 17) enacted in 2009 clarifies the definition of lawful status and requires documentation of legal residence status to obtain a driver's license or state-issued ID. Three legislative acts that could impact immigrants were enacted in 2010, including the Birth Certificate Reissuance for Adoptions Bill (SD H 1079), Commercial Driver License Bill (SD H 1107), and Federal Law Enforcement Officer Bill (SD H 1260). The Birth Certificate Reissuance for Adoptions Bill requires the proof of the child's immigration to issue a new birth certificate in an adoption of a foreign-born child. The Commercial Driver License Bill asks for the documents of lawful presence to renew a nonresidential commercial driver's license. The Federal Law Enforcement Officer Bill expands the definition of federal law enforcement to include all officers and employees of the Federal Bureau of Investigation, the Drug Enforcement Administration, the U.S. Marshall Service, the Internal Revenue Service, the Secret

Service, the Bureau of Alcohol, Tobacco and Firearms, the U.S. Postal Inspection Service, the Federal Protective Service, the Immigration and Customs Enforcement Office of Investigations, and the National Park Service. The Sex Offender Registration Regulations Bill (SD S 32) enacted in 2011 requires sex offenders to register their immigration documents with the state.

South Dakota joined other states in support of Arizona's immigration law. Attorney General Marty Jackley and Governor Mike Rounds filed a friend-of-the court brief with officials from other states supporting Arizona's law against the federal lawsuit in July 2010. State legislators introduced three bills to address undocumented immigration in 2011. HB 1198 would authorize law enforcement officers to make reasonable attempts to check a suspect's immigration status when they enforce other laws. It would also be illegal to transport or conceal undocumented workers. This bill was killed in the House State Affairs Committee. SB 156 was aimed to crack down the employment of undocumented workers in South Dakota. The employers who knowingly hire undocumented workers would be penalized. This bill passed the Senate but narrowly failed in the House. The third measure (HB 1199) challenged the automatic U.S. citizenship granted to the children of undocumented immigrants born in U.S. by the Fourteenth Amendment of the U.S. Constitution. It is intended to encourage Congress to propose a change in the Fourteenth Amendment. This bill was shot down in the House State Affairs Committee.

Legislators continued to introduce more anti-undocumented immigration bills in 2012. HB 1238 would require the employers to use the E-Verify system and set up penalties for hiring of undocumented workers. Another bill (HB 1139) was proposed to revise the ID theft rules to crack down the use of stolen ID by undocumented immigrants. Both bills were defeated in the House Commerce and Energy Committee. The other attempt penalizing employment of undocumented aliens (SB 155) failed in the Senate.

These anti-undocumented immigration bills met opposition from the local business associations, some legislators and governmental agencies, and American Civil Liberties Union and some other local community organizations, such as the Spanish Speaking Community Association of Sioux Falls, the Sioux Falls Diversity Council, and the Catholic Presentation Sisters. Furthermore, the local businesses warned that these bills could drive up their cost, send the jobs to other states, and confuse them already trying to comply with federal laws. Those bills were also criticized for the extra work and spending it could bring the government, the potential to be challenged in court, and racial profiling.

Lawmakers pondered new bills after the Supreme Court made the ruling over the Arizona immigration law. Representative Manny Steele (R-Sioux Falls) who was a sponsor of several anti-illegal immigration bills said that he would pay close attention to what Supreme Court ruled unconstitutional, if he introduces new legislation addressing undocumented immigration in 2013. Senator Craig Tieszen (R-Rapid City), another active legislator going after hiring of undocumented workers, said that the Supreme Court's ruling concerned him and it might impede his efforts because there were others who would be scared off by the ruling.

KAREN COMMUNITY IN HURON

There is a small Karen community in Huron, South Dakota. The Karens are an indigenous ethnic minority group who reside in southern and southeastern Burma and have been persecuted by the country's ruling military government. The Karens came to the United States as political refugees. Some of them left the refugee camps

Representative Scott Ecklund, R-Brandon, a physician and sponsor of the bill to provide prenatal care to immigrant women who are not citizens, speaks during a committee hearing on February 6, 2014, in Pierre, South Dakota. The South Dakota House Health and Human Services Committee passed a measure that would provide prenatal care to low-income women who are in the country without documentation. (Jill Kokesh/AP/Corbis)

in Thailand which is a neighbor country of Burma. About 34,000 Karen refugees have settled in the United States, and about 4,000 of them live in St. Paul, Minnesota, one of the primary settlement sites, according to the Friends of the Karen People of Burma. About 1,000 Karens lived in Huron, South Dakota in 2011 and 400 to 500 of them worked at Dakota Provisions, a local turkey-processing plant. The business and community leaders in Aberdeen, South Dakota, also expect to add more than 1,000 jobs in 2012 and hope to attract these immigrants from Burma to meet that demand.

The Karen immigrants have been welcomed and were helped by the local community to get resettled and integrated into the local community. Dakotaland FCU offered tailored financial management workshop for the Karen people with translated materials and an interpreter. Dakotaland FCU expanded this workshop, thanks to a grant from the National Credit Union Foundation. James Valley Health Center, a local branch of Horizon Health Care, Inc., provides tailor-made access to care and offers language translation services to the Karen members. First Baptist Church of Huron was left with a dwindling, aging congregation when the young people moved to other parts of the country for better jobs. The Karen people and families started to join the church in 2007. Those new Karen members brought a new life to the "dying" church and helped replace the missing generations and revitalize the church congregation.

Sah Lay Lay Wah was born to her Karen parents in a refugee camp in Thailand. She stayed in two camps before she began her trip to the United States at the age of 23. She took the education programs in the camps offered by the Thai government. She speaks three languages. Her husband, Blue, heard of a town called Huron in South Dakota where they could find a job and have a safe home to raise their children. After arriving in Huron, Blue worked for Dakota Provisions and Wah joined the staff at Dakotaland FCU as a translator. She interpreted for her fellow Karen immigrants who could not speak English but needed to open accounts and apply for loans through the credit union. Wah and Blue were approved to buy their first home in 2011.

Tha Dah and Kyu Klu came to the United States in 2008 from a refugee camp in 2008. They traveled with their immediate family members and got resettled in Louisville, Kentucky. They were married in 2009. Then they got the news that a Karen community was setting in Huron, South Dakota, and there were employment opportunities in a local turkey-processing plant, Dakota Provisions. The couple and Kyu Klu's family moved to Huron, South Dakota. They attended the First Baptist Church in Huron and learned of the Individual Development Accounts (IDA) program there that could offer them a loan to purchase a home, car, or invest in a business or future education. They decided to save to buy a house. Their application was approved with the help of an IDA counselor from Lutheran Social Services. They purchased their first home in 2011. They were proud of their achievements within three years in the United States.

Bhutanese Refugees

Jai Prasad Sunuwar arrived in South Dakota on August 1, 2011, and became the 50,000th Bhutanese refugee who was resettled from Nepal to the United States and several other western countries, which marked a milestone of this resettlement process. Bhutanese refugees, largely of Nepali Lhotshampa ethnic origin and speaking Nepali, were perceived as a threat to sovereignty by the Bhutanese government which believes in ethnic nationalism and wants ethnic homogeneity. They were forcefully expelled to the Nepalese border region and made to stay in the refugee camps in Nepal. The UN High Commissioner for Refugees (UNHCR) launched a program to help these refugees resettled in the western countries in 2007. In that year, the Bush administration assistant secretary of state for Population, Refugees and Migration, Ellen Sauerbrey gave the green light for the United States to resettle 60,000 Bhutanese in the United States over 5 years. The United States resettled more than 42,000 Bhutanese refugees from 2007 to 2011, with several hundred coming to South Dakota. There were 434 Bhutanese refugees arriving in South Dakota in total from 2000 to 2011. The U.S. ambassador to Nepal Scott H. DeLisi said that the United States is expected to resettle more of the refugees still in Nepal.

Somalis in Sioux Falls

Somali refugees started being resettled in Sioux Falls in 2003. "As many as 150 refugees from the African country of Somalia will settle in Sioux Falls over the next two years. It would be the largest group to be relocated in Sioux Falls since the 2001 terrorist attacks" (*Rapid City Journal* July 27, 2003). The first group of Somalis was Bantus who are a persecuted minority in Somalia, with little to no resources because of their highly persecuted status. These Bantu families would join a large population of refugees already in Sioux Falls. Bantus were the descendants of slaves who were abducted a century ago from their homes in Tanzania and Mozambique. Many are Muslims and many have larger families, with four children on average, being accustomed to live in community lifestyle. The LSS staff members helped them get resettled and adjusted to the modern lifestyle once they arrived, arranging housing and providing household belongings, food, English classes, and job-replacement assistance. Sioux Falls School District had some of its staff members study the Somali Bantu culture. The influx of Muslim population has caused some local peoples' concerns at the same time. They questioned the necessity of building four mosques in Sioux Falls and were worried that this city will evolve into a "Tuula" (a village in Somali) by the growing Muslim Somali population in this city.

Sudanese in Sioux Falls

Thousands of Sudanese fled during the second Civil War from 1983 to 2005. Most of them were South Sudanese. Some of them were fortunately admitted into the United States as refugees. An estimated 30,000 unaccompanied children were displaced or orphaned during the war, who were called "Lost Boys/Girls of Sudan." These unaccompanied children fled religious and ethnic persecution and sought asylum in the refugee camps in South Sudan, Ethiopia, and Kenya. Girls are not allowed to stay alone, according to Sudanese culture. They were placed with their surviving family members or other Sudanese families. The resettlement program to the United States initiated in 1999 accepted refugee applications from children who were orphans only. The "Lost Girls" were not considered orphans since they had been with these families for years. Few of them then were eligible for the resettlement program to the United States. Approximately 3800 "Lost Boys" were allowed to resettle in the United States in 2001, as part of a program established by the U.S. government and the UNHCR. This program was halted after the September 11 terrorist attack and was resumed in 2004. Omaha, Nebraska, had the largest population of Sudanese refugees (about 7,000 people) in the United States by 2006. This program brought some Sudanese refugees to Sioux Falls, South Dakota. Today there are about 3,000 to 4,000 South Sudanese in Sioux Falls. They received help for resettlement from LSS that provides educational classes, cash assistance, and access to healthcare services. Many of these refugees are seeking to return to and rebuild their war-torn country after South Sudan became an independent state in 2011.

The transition to American life has not been easy for the Sudanese. Language is a problem. Many things get better and easier after these newest Americans grasp enough English. They face different lifestyles, ways to raise children, and gender relationships in the family. They need to learn how to live in an apartment with modern electronic appliances, such as refrigerators and microwaves. They cannot allow their children to play outside on the street all day when the traffic speed is 30 miles per hour or even faster. They do not understand the laws in their new country. Drunk driving and domestic violence are illegal in the United States but are acceptable in the Sudan. The husband and wife are believed to be equal in a marriage here, while the wife is considered as husband's private property according to traditional Sudanese culture. Despite these cultural barriers, many of these Sudanese have overcome these challenges and embrace a new way of life in Sioux Falls successfully.

Many of those older Sudanese who are at least 30 years and have lived through the Civil War in their native country, however, have more difficulty in getting Americanized. The Civil War memories and horror of their past experiences in the war have led them to despair. They are unable to separate themselves from their depression and post-traumatic stress disorder (PTSD). Peter Reng and at least a dozen Sudanese men spend their days in Whittier Park in the summer. They carry alcohol and enjoy the relief that it brings to them. They live on the street or in the shelter for the homeless. Reng was a boy soldier by age 9 and got shot three times in his neck and head. He suffers from stomach and back problems and from his memories. "When I drink, I sleep," Reng says, "When I pass out, I do not have the nightmares" (*Argus Leader* October 13, 2012). Lana Smith with Avera Behavioral Health counsels refugees and works with as many as 15 homeless Sudanese refugees. "The common thread with these Sudanese men who end up on the street is that they have alcohol problems," she says. "It is primarily because they suffer from PTSD and are self-medicating with alcohol. Through that process, they end up losing their jobs" (*Argus Leader* October 13, 2012).

Using domestic violence as a coping mechanism for their stress and depression is not uncommon among the refugees. The occurrence of domestic violence can also be attributed to culture. Men consider their wives as their private property and believe it is their right to be abusive. Women are expected to perform all household chores in South Sudan. "In South Sudan, when a man pays a dowry, so many cattle, to marry a woman, she basically becomes his property," Jal says. "He then is free to do with her what he wants. That's not the way it works here

[Sioux Falls]." (*Argus Leader* October 13, 2012). David Jal is a South Sudanese refugee and a probation officer in Sioux Falls

The gender relationship and the parent–child relationship are under change for these Sudanese immigrant families. Although parents struggle with the English language, their children get assimilated and Americanized fast. The balance of power in homes can shift. While parents cook their native food, try to keep their cultural heritage, and expect to move back to South Sudan someday, children like to eat American food, celebrate American holidays, and consider themselves Americans and do not want to go back to their native country. "Unfortunately, it seems like often that parents become the minority in their house," Bullen Furula, the head of the South Sudan Community Corp. says. "If the parents are not strong, the kids want to change the parents. An example is the food. When they are small, we all eat the food we did as Africans. But as our kids grow, they call it African food. They want hamburgers. They want pizza. You see it becomes a tough fight between parents and kids" (Young "Refugee Shadows Fade with Distance" 2012). Juliana Kor took her children to a celebration of her Shuluk heritage and exposed her children to native Sudanese songs, dance, and food. Her husband returned to Sudan in 2008 with a plan to start a business. She wanted to go back too but her children argued that life is better in Sioux Falls than it is in Africa and they would like to stay in the United States.

Most of these resettled Sudanese are from South Sudan and are Christians. For some of them, the animosity toward Muslims forged by a radical Muslim-led Sudan government bent on wiping out the Christian Southerners has not been forgotten. Some do not want their children to be friends with Muslim classmates, neighbors, or any Muslim. Some even called their public school principal to keep their children away from Muslim classmates. Garang Deng Akot has such a deep animus toward the Muslim-led Sudan government that he sends his children to St. Lambert Catholic School in Sioux Falls where they will not associate with any Muslim. "In America, I know the Muslims and Christians are not going to attack each other, but we know each other; we are enemies," Atem Juowei says. "It would be a big issue for me. At O'Gorman, I know the children will make friends with Christians, not Muslims. There are no Muslims in that school" (Young "Refugee Shadows Fade with Distance" 2012). Many of the South Sudanese, however, choose to forgive. They think that Muslim and Christian Sudanese children are both innocent and could be friends. Deborah Deng who watched her village destroyed by the Sudanese forces decided to let her anger go and not to prevent her daughter from making friends with Muslim children. Sudanese children, particularly those in public schools, usually have no problem with getting along with Muslims or Christians. Soliman Soliman, a senior at Washington High School from a Muslim family, insists that he has Christian friends in Sioux Falls.

Many resettled Sudanese in Sioux Falls considered returning to their native land to create jobs and business, build schools and hospitals, and dig wells and deliver water to villages after the Republic of South Sudan declared independence in July 2011. Probation officer David Jal and a dozen of his fellow refugees fly back and forth to South Sudan with their friends from South Dakota on personal missions to rebuild this war-torn country. Jal helped dig wells and delivered corn grinders to his native village of Dunyal in eastern South Sudan. He is working to raise money to build a school. Sam Kuach, Elijah Yuek, and friends at Prairie Hills Covenant Church plan to build a church in Nasir, South Sudan. Atem Jowei, Lisa Marie Johnson, and supporters at Holy Spirit Catholic Church are working on a library in Paliau. Members of Hillcrest Church work to bring water and education to Kalalayi village. Some Sudanese even returned and began to pursue their entrepreneurial plans before the independence of South Sudan. James Kong left Sioux Falls in 2005 to start a restaurant business. Eka John, a long-time employee of South Dakota Public Broadcasting returned to South Sudan in April 2011 to help build a broadcasting network.

Czech Days

Tabor's Czech Days is an annual ethnic festival to celebrate Czechoslovakian heritage. The three days' celebration events bring as many as 10,000 people to Tabor, a town established entirely by Czech/Bohemian immigrants, every June to enjoy a parade, Czech dance and music, traditional costumes, delicious Czech food, entertainment, kolache baking demonstration, and coronation of Czech Days Queen. There is also a "heritage walk" in the Vancura Memorial Park Mini Czech Village as a means of recognizing heritage, organizations, families, and ancestry. Their 65th annual Czech Days celebration was held in June 2013. It continues to be one of the largest and longest-running celebrations of the Czechoslovakian heritage in the United States.

NOTABLE GROUPS

Lutheran Social Services of South Dakota

LSS of South Dakota is a religion-based group in Sioux Falls. The organization was founded in 1920 to aid girls and women who became pregnant out of wedlock. Since then, their mission and services have broadly expanded. Their refugee resettlement program began in 1948, aiding individuals fleeing persecution in World War II. Their continuous service to refugees since then has helped numerous individuals and families and these services were expanded to Huron and Aberdeen in 2009. Given the range of services this group provides any individual, they are particularly helpful and understanding of what refugees have experienced and what challenges they face in a new country. The group offers case management, job referrals and information, interpreters' services, and English classes. In addition to helping refugees resettle in this area, LSS also serves immigrants in the community and is certified by the Board of Immigration Appeals and provides accredited immigration legal services. The group aims at helping individuals integrate into the community, helping family reunification, and ensuring that legal applications are filed appropriately.

BIBLIOGRAPHY

Ababovic, Marijana. "Karen Family Thrive in Huron, South Dakota." Institute for Social and Economic Development, December 19, 2011. www.isedsolutions.org/blog/refugee-ida/karen-family-thrives-huron-south-dakota. Accessed May 1, 2013.

2010 American Community Survey 1-Year Estimate Data (IPUMS-USA). http://usa.ipums.org/usa/. Accessed June 20, 2013.

2010 American Community Survey 1-Year Estimate Summary Files. U.S. Census Bureau American FactFinder. factfinder2.census.gov/faces/nav/jsf/pages/index.xhtml. Accessed June 20, 2013.

Anderson, Grant K. "Deadwood's Chinatown." *South Dakota History* 5, no. 3 (Summer 1975): 266–85.

Aware, Qudir. *Languages and Dialects Spoken in Sioux Falls*. Sioux Falls, SD: Multi-Cultural Center, 2004.

Bankston, Carl L., ed. *Encyclopedia of American Immigration*. Hackensack, NJ: Salem Press, 2010.

Bennett, Carl. "Oscar Micheaux." Silent Era Website. www.silentera.com/people/directors/Micheaux-Oscar.html. Accessed June 20, 2013.

Bernson, Sara L., and Robert J. Eggers. "Black People in South Dakota History." *South Dakota History* 7, no. 3 (Summer., 1977): 241–70.

Camarota, Steven A., and John Keeley. "The New Ellis Islands: Examining Non-Traditional Areas of Immigrant Settlement in the 1990s." Center for Immigration Studies, 2001. http://www.cis.org/ImmigrantSettlement1990s. Accessed June 20, 2013.

Davies, Williams D. "Touring the Welsh Settlements of South Dakota, 1891." *South Dakota History* 10, no. 3 (Summer 1980): 223–40.

Deadwood's Adams Museum. "Digging Deadwood: Understanding Chinatown." Deadwood, SD: Adams Museum & House, Inc., 2007.

Dvorak, Joseph A. *History of the Czechs in the State of South Dakota*. Tabor, SD: Czech Heritage Preservation Society, Inc., 1920.

Eaton, Kristi. "Feds Charge 9 with Using Illegal Workers." *Associated Press*, September 27, 2012. http://www.alipac.us/f12/s-d-feds-charge-9-using-undocumented-workers-264566/. Accessed June 20, 2013.

"The Ellis Island of the Great Plains." *The World*, August 20, 2009, www.theworld.org/2009/08/the-ellis-island-of-the-great-plains. Accessed June 20, 2013.

Fennelly, Katherine, Allison Boyle, Silvana Hackett, Marie Kurth, Robert Painter, Julia Pea-sley, Meredith Stocking, Nate Thompson, Morgan Winters, and Lisa Ziegler. "South Dakota." Midwest Coalition on Immigration and the Region's Future, University of Minnesota, 2012. immigrationtaskforce.hhh.umn.edu/south-dakota. Accessed March 29, 2014.

"Financial Workshops from NCUF Grantee Helping Karen Refugees in South Dakota." Credit Unions National Association, February 15, 2011. www.ncuf.coop/home/news /subnews/dakotaland_financial_workshops.aspx. Accessed June 20, 2013.

Fisher, Claude S., and Michael Hout. "Where Americans Came from: Race, Immigration, and Ancestry." In *Century of Difference: How America Changed in the Last One Hundred Years*. New York: Russell Sage Foundation, 2006: pp. 42–43.

"The Foreign-Born Population: 2000, Census 2000 Brief." U.S. Census Bureau, 2003. www .census.gov/prod/2003pubs/c2kbr-34.pdf. Accessed June 20, 2013.

Frelick, Bill. "For Bhutan's Refugees, There's No Place like Home." *Global Post*, March 30, 2011. www.globalpost.com/dispatch/news/opinion/110330/bhutan-refugees-nepal. Accessed June 20, 2013.

Grant, Kelli. "Refugees Find Home & Medical Care." Keloland Website. Sioux Falls, SD, October 13, 2010. www.keloland.com/healthbeat/newsdetail6387.cfm?Id=105901. Accessed June 20, 2013.

"Immigration Facts in South Dakota." Federation for American Immigration Reform, n.d. www.fairus.org/states/south-dakota. Accessed June 20, 2013.

"Immigration to South Dakota." U.S. Immigration Support. n.d. www.usimmigrationsup-port.org/southdakota.html. Accessed June 20, 2013.

Jimenez, Thomas R. "Immigrants in the United States: How Well Are They Integrating into Society?" Migration Policy Institute, 2011. www.migrationpolicy.org/pubs /integration-Jimenez.pdf. Accessed June 20, 2013.

Johansen, John P. *Immigrant Settlements and Social Organization in South Dakota*. Brookings: Agricultural Experiment Station, South Dakota State College of Agriculture and Mechanical Arts, 1937.

Johansen, John P. *Immigrants and Their Children in South Dakota*. Brookings: Agricultural Experiment Station, South Dakota State College of Agriculture and Mechanical Arts, 1936.

Kemp, David. *The Irish in Dakota*. Sioux Falls, SD: Rushmore House, 1992.

Lambert, Judy. "British Have Agricultural History in SD." *Argus Leader*, Sioux Falls, October 18, 2005. http://history.sd.gov/museum/education/Immigrants.pdf. Accessed August 13, 2014.

Lutheran Social Services of South Dakota. Lutheran Social Services of South Dakota Web-page. http://www.lsssd.org/about_us/vision.html. Accessed February 26, 2014.

MPI Data Hub. "South Dakota." Migration Policy Institute Webpage. http://www .migrationpolicy.org/data/state-profiles/state/demographics/SD. Accessed June 20, 2013.

Natalie-Lees, Jeff. "Workers Wanted in Aberdeen: Business, Community Leaders Begin Effort to Fill City's Labor Needs." *Aberdeen New*, August 12, 2011. articles.aberdeen news.com/2011–08–12/news/29882859_1_huron-jim-barringer-aberdeen-area -diversity-committee. Accessed June 20, 2013.

National Conference of State Legislatures. www.ncsl.org/issues-research/immig/immigration-laws-database.aspx. Accessed March 29, 2014.

Negstad, Joanne. "Sioux Falls Shows Its Heart by Offering Help to Immigrants." *Argus Leader*, Sioux Falls, August 7, 2005. http://history.sd.gov/museum/education/Immi grants.pdf. Accessed August 13, 2014.

"The New American Electorate: The Growing Political Power of Immigrants and Their Children." Immigration Policy Center, 2010. www.immigrationpolicy.org/sites/default/files/docs/New_American_Electorate_101410.pdf. Accessed June 20, 2013.

"New Americans in South Dakota: The Economic Power of Immigrants, Latinos and Asians in the Mount Rushmore State." Immigration Policy Center, 2012. www.immigra tionpolicy.org/sites/default/files/docs/New_Americans_in_South_Dakota_2012.pdf. Accessed June 20, 2013.

Oien, Iver I., H. A. Ustrud, M. G. Opsahl, and J. O. Asen, eds. Emily Brende Sittig and Clara Brende Christenson (translators), and H. S. Hileboe (writing Introduction). *Norwegian Pioneers History of Minnehaha County, SD*. Sioux Falls, SD: Historical Organization's Publication, 1928.

Olsen, Olga S. *A Historical Study of the Danish in South Dakota*. Vermillion, SD: University Press, 1940.

Passel, Jeffery S., and D'Vera Cohn. "Unauthorized Immigrant Population: National and State Trends, 2010." Pew Hispanic Center, 2011. www.pewhispanic.org/files/reports/133.pdf. Accessed June 20, 2013.

Peterson, August. *History of the Swedes Who Settled in Clay County, South Dakota and Their Biographies*. Self-Published, South Dakota: S.I. Peterson, 1947.

Post, Marv. "The Immigration Cops Go after a Dairy Farm." *The Wall Street Journal*, June 29, 2012. online.wsj.com/article/SB10001424052702304870304577488973455967032.html. Accessed June 20, 2013.

"Refugees Headed for Sioux Falls." *Rapid City Journal*, July 27, 2003. rapidcityjournal.com/news/state-and-regional/article_924923f5-f008–5bfe-a7ba-db42336ad8e8.html. Accessed June 20, 2013.

"50,000th Resettled Bhutanese Refugee Arrives in South Dakota." Refugee Resettlement Watch, August 18, 2011. refugeeresettlementwatch.wordpress.com/2011/08/18/50000th-resettled-bhutanese-refugee-arrives-in-south-dakota. Accessed June 20, 2013.

"Resettlement Program for Refugees from Bhutan Passes 50,000 Mark." UN Office of the High Commissioner for Refugees, August 17, 2011. www.unhcr.org/4e4bea789.html. Accessed June 20, 2013.

Satterlee, James. *The Hutterites: A Study in Cultural Diversit*. Brookings: Department of Rural Sociology, South Dakota State University, 1993.

Schell, Herbert S. "The German Heritage in South Dakota." *American German Review* 35, no. 5 (June/July 1961): 5–10.

Schell, Herbert S. *History of South Dakota*. 4th ed., Revised. Pierre: South Dakota State Historical Society Press, 2004.

Schone, Tammi. "Diversity within a South Dakota Rural Community." U.S. Department of Agriculture Website. May 10, 2012. blogs.usda.gov/2012/05/10/diversity-within-a-south-dakota-rural-community. Accessed June 20, 2013.

Singer, Audrey, and Jill H. Wilson. "From 'There' to 'Here': Refugee Resettlement in Metropolitan America." Brookings Institution, 2006. www.brookings.edu/~/media/files/rc/reports/2006/09demographics_singer/20060925_singer.pdf. Accessed June 20, 2013.

"South Dakota Immigrants: South Dakota State Historical Society Education Kit." history.sd.gov/museum/education/Immigrants.pdf. Accessed June 20, 2013.

Stupnik, Cynthia Anne Frank. *Steppes to Neu Odessa: Germans from Russia Who Settled in Odessa Township, Dakota Territory, 1872–1876*. Bowie, MD: Heritage Books, 1996.

Torma, Carolyn. *The Landscape of Finnish Settlement in South Dakota*. Vermillion, SD: State Historical Preservation Center, 1985.

Winchester, Cody. "Indicted Companies Won Big Forestry Contracts." *Argus Leade*, Sioux Falls, September 29, 2012. www.argusleader.com/article/DF/20120929/NEWS/309290040/Indicted-companies-won-big-forestry-contracts.Accessed June 20, 2013.

Young, Steve. "Hutterite Farms in South Dakota." *Argus Leader*, Sioux Falls, November 17, 2003. http://library.ndsu.edu/grhc/articles/newspapers/news/young5.html. Accessed February 26, 2014.

Young, Steve. "Refugee Shadows Fade with Distance." *Argus Leader*, Sioux Falls, October 9, 2012. www.argusleader.com/article/20121010/NEWS/310100022/Refugee-shadows-fade-distance. Accessed June 20, 2013.

Young, Steve. "South Dakota to South Sudan: Family Connections Strong despite Distance." *Argus Leader*, Sioux Falls, October 4, 2012. www.argusleader.com/article/20121004/NEWS/310040040/South-Dakota-South-Sudan-Family-connections-strong-despite-distance. Accessed June 20, 2013.

Young, Steve. "South Sudan: Hope and Faith Fight with Futility." *Argus Leader*, Sioux Falls, October 21, 2012. www.argusleader.com/article/20121021/NEWS/310210033/South-Sudan-Hope-faithfight-futility. Accessed June 20, 2013.

Young, Steve. "South Sudanese Refugees: New World, New Roles." *Argus Leader*, Sioux Falls, October 3 2012. www.argusleader.com/article/20121014/NEWS/310140010/South-Sudanese-refugees-New-world-new-roles. Accessed June 20, 2013.

42

TENNESSEE

Julia Skinner

CHRONOLOGY

1730s and 1740s	Scotch Irish settlers from the Irish province of Ulster begin coming to the United States.
1763	The English gain control of what would become Tennessee, and settlers begin moving westward to occupy the new territory.
1796	Tennessee becomes the 16th state to enter the Union.
1830	Volunteers from Tennessee go to Texas to fight alongside U.S. immigrants living in Mexican territory after the Mexican government tries to prevent further immigration.
1868	Hermann Bokum, the state's Commissioner of Immigration, publishes a handbook about Tennessee for immigrants to encourage them to move there and settle.
Early 1900s	Bureau of Immigration is created in Tennessee.
1905	Interstate conference is held in Chattanooga to discuss how to attract "desirable white immigrants" to the Southeast.
1910–1930	Decline in immigrant miners in Tennessee.
1924	Johnson-Reed Act, which creates yearly immigration quotas based on country of origin, is passed in the U.S. Congress with the help of Tennessee congressman William Vaile.
1942–1964	Tennessee growers participate in the Bracero Program, a guest worker program hiring Mexican workers for labor-intensive employment in agriculture.
1976	First wave of Kurdish immigrants, fleeing from failed Iraqi Kurdish Revolution, arrives at Fort Campbell army base, and many settle in the Nashville area.

1979	Second wave of Kurdish immigration arrives in the area, this time mostly Iranian Kurds fleeing the Khomeini Revolution.
1991–1992	Third and largest wave of Kurdish immigration reaches Nashville, as refugees flee genocide in Iraq.
1991–1992	Somali refugees, fleeing war and famine, come to the United States, some settling in the town of Shelbyville to work at a Tyson food-processing facility.
1996–1997	Final wave of Kurdish immigration occurs as a result of Civil War.
2000	U.S. Census data shows Tennessee as the 16th most populous state in the nation.
2001	Theresa Harmon forms Tennesseans for Responsible Immigration Policy (TNRIP), which becomes the state's largest anti-immigration group.
2001	Tennessee becomes the first state to grant driver's licenses to undocumented residents.
2004	Due to political pressure, the government changes licensing for undocumented residents from a driver's license to a certificate.
2006	The program to allow undocumented residents to be granted driving certificates is cancelled after it is discovered that busloads of immigrants from other states are being brought in to get Tennessee certificates.
2006	Senator Bill Ketron testifies before Congress about undocumented immigration in the state.
2007	Local elected officials in Nashville approve an English-only measure for the city, which is later vetoed by Mayor Bill Purcell.
2009	The Obama administration sends a directive to the sheriff in Nashville, asking him to release nonviolent criminals from among the 6,000 people he has charged with immigration crimes in the previous two-and-a-half years.
2009 (January)	Voters in Nashville reject another attempt to pass an English-only law in the city.
2011 (July)	The Refugee Absorptive Capacity Act, also called the Tracy Refugee bill, is signed into law.

HISTORICAL OVERVIEW

Eighteenth and Nineteenth Centuries

In 1796, Tennessee became the 16th state to enter the Union. It was also the 16th most populous state in the United States, according to the 2000 Census. Even though there has been immigration to the state, it has seen relatively less than other parts of the country. The first white settlers to come to the Tennessee territory were primarily English and Scotch Irish who came west from Virginia and North Carolina. A good number of these individuals came from several counties in

North Carolina after Tennessee was granted statehood. Many Scotch Irish came to the United States from the province of Ulster in the 1730s and 1740s, some of whom later settled in Tennessee. King George's proclamation, in 1763, made the Mississippi River the boundary between French and English colonies. On October 7, 1763, everything east of the river, except New Orleans, was ceded to the English, and the crown's ownership of this new land helped accelerate the flow of immigrants into what would become eastern Tennessee.

During Tennessee's early years, many of the people who came to the territory and early state were Presbyterians, and several Presbyterian ministers settled in the state to preach. The settlements of North and South Holston became the first settlements in the territory, as outlined in the Treaty of Hard Labor in 1768 and in a survey of the land in 1771, during which time it was still considered part of Virginia. In the 1760s and 1770s, there was a clear delineation between the cultures of eastern and western Tennessee. East Tennessee consisted mainly of English and Scottish Highlanders, who owned plantations and slaves. The west was populated by Scotch Irish and Germans who owned small farms on which only they and their families labored. Eastern Tennessee residents had commercial ties with England and coastal colonies, while the western portion of the state had a very restricted market. Many people began to move into western Tennessee during this time to escape repressive government and to build a better life.

Several decades later, in 1830, Tennesseans became involved in an immigration dispute in which U.S. immigrants were forbidden by the Mexican government from settling in what is now Texas. Many Tennesseans were sympathetic toward the U.S. citizens in Texas, and concerned residents from around Tennessee met to discuss how best to help the Texans. As a result of support raised around the state, hundreds of armed young men left to volunteer in fighting with the Texans.

Before the Civil War, Tennessee was a state that did not actively seek to invite immigrants to visit and settle. Those planters living in middle and western Tennessee discouraged the prewar movement of immigrants to areas that were at that time considered in the western part of the country. While many western governors encouraged immigration, no governor from 1849 to 1860 did so. However, after the war, views on immigration changed as the state experienced a shortage of laborers, and every governor from 1865 to 1881 supported immigration to the state.

In 1868, Hermann Bokum, the commissioner of immigration for the state, published *The Tennessee Hand-book and Immigrant's Guide* to educate immigrants about the state and encourage them to consider settling there. The handbook gave in-depth information about the geography of the state, descriptions of counties, and an overview of agriculture and industry. He also discussed the immigrants who have already settled in the state. According to Bokum, Irish immigrants have

Kurdish immigrant Hasain Dhahir, left, purchases bread from Salah Osman, part owner of Judy's International Market in Nashville, Tennessee, on January 26, 2005. There are an estimated 8,000 Kurds living in Nashville, in a place they call Little Kurdistan. Kurds can cast ballots in Iraq's national elections beginning Friday and running through Sunday thanks to the International Organization for Migration's effort to allow expatriates to vote. (AP Photo/John Russell)

settled in the larger cities and in towns along railroad lines. English, Scotch, and Welsh immigrants were mostly found in mining districts, and German immigrants lived mostly in larger cities but some were in rural areas.

Bokum spent a good deal of time speaking of the positive qualities of the state, and reassuring readers that most Tennessee residents supported immigration, "and are likely to treat the immigrant with courtesy and kindness" (Bokum 1868, 109). He also said that the state was desperate for robust, healthy laborers whose work, and whose participation in the Tennessee economy, would be a great benefit for the state. Bokum also elaborated on a desire to have an influx of white residents come to the state, especially in the central and western portions, where there were higher numbers of African American residents who had been slaves less than a decade before. Bokum says, "The influx of a white population into the State is likely, in a few years, to remove many of the difficulties which now surround this [slavery] question, and to act as a healthy stimulus on all classes of society" (Bokum 1868, 126). Like Bokum, many other authors of contemporary publications from Tennessee spoke of the importance of immigration, although some were less charming in stating their qualifications. In a report from one state agency, the importance of immigration as a way to improve the economy was stressed: "We want more people. We want not the scum that floats off from Northern countries—not the refuse of Castle Garden, but the choice of European yeomanry" (McWhirter 1887, 560).

Several decades later, in 1890, the largest group of foreign-born Tennesseans came from Germany (5,364), the next largest were from Ireland (5,016) and England (2,852).Tennessee had a large agricultural industry at the turn of the century, with over 900,000 acres of cotton planted in 1901. A 1901 report of the U.S. Congress indicated that many of these crops were maintained by immigrants, affirming these residents' importance to Tennessee society. Immigrants were encouraged to settle along railways by a number of railroad companies, and were encouraged to settle in certain areas by corporations and individuals.

Even though immigrants were encouraged to come to Tennessee, the welcome was only extended to some immigrants, and others, such as Russian Jews, met with resistance. One committee member said of their settlements in Tennessee: "They are very undesirable, being in poor physical condition and largely paupers." He recommended that a reading test be administered to these immigrants, arguing that it "would exclude such Jews only temporarily, for they would soon learn to read some passage" (U.S. House of Representatives 1901, lxix). This same report discussed Finnish immigrants more positively and gave a glowing report of the success of those who had settled in Hickman County. The state commissioner of agriculture gave his thoughts on immigration to the state, and made several observations about immigrants and farming. He felt that German and Swiss farmers were the most efficient workers, and indicated that "our farmers do not oppose, but favor, the influx of the right kind of foreigners into the State" (U.S. House of Representatives 1901, 565).

Twentieth and Twenty-First Centuries

The state's Bureau of Immigration was founded in the early years of the twentieth century. Interstate conferences were also held around the southern United States to discuss ways of attracting "desirable white immigrants," including one held in Chattanooga in 1905 (Warne 1916, 304–05). Foreign-born Tennessee residents were still subject to additional examination during this time. In 1914, Tennessee was one of the 27 states favoring the adoption of a literacy test as a method for restricting immigration. Immigrants continued to arrive in southern states, many through the port of New Orleans before heading elsewhere in the region. In 1916, the Commissioner of Immigration based there reported that immigration numbers were up slightly and included some Chinese and Japanese immigrants, most from unspecified countries.

From 1910 to 1930, the number of immigrants employed in coal mining dropped from 323,669 to 175,898, while the numbers of African American and native-born white laborers increased. Part of the reason was because Tennessee, along with Kentucky and Alabama, offered some of the lowest coal wages in the country, thus attracting relatively few immigrants.

In 1924, the U.S. legislature passes the Johnson-Reed Act, which established an annual quota for immigration based on the national origin of current U.S. residents, and which favored those from Western Europe. Tennessee congressman William Vaile supported the measure, saying it would help immigrants "become assimilated to our language, customs, and institutions" and "blend thoroughly into our body politic" (Powell 2005, 166). After World War II, the country of Israel was established in the Middle East. Many immigrants came to the new country and the nation's leaders required assistance to create an industrial economy. Many U.S. and European businesses stepped in to help, including Tennessee's General Shoe Corporation, based in Nashville, which sent experts overseas to help build a manufacturing plant.

In 1990, the largest groups of foreign-born Tennessee residents came from Germany, the United Kingdom, and Canada. Immigration into Tennessee accelerated by the mid-1990s. In fact, the city of Nashville has ranked first among U.S. cities for the number of new immigrants since 1990. Latino immigrants have been the largest group to enter the country recently and have become a more integral part of the population, with the number of births from Latino/a parents rising at least 40 percent in 2003. However, Latinos are not the only group of new immigrants to the state. In 1999, statistics also show that Asian Indian and Chinese individuals made up 8 and 5 percent, respectively, of the new immigrant population in the state.

Tennessee is still seeing a rise in Latino/a immigration, as it and many of its southern neighbors continue to attract people from Central and South America. Currently, Latinos account for approximately 45 percent of the state's foreign-born population. Many of these immigrants have settled in the state's three largest cities: Memphis, Nashville, and Knoxville. Many smaller towns with factories and processing plants have also seen an increase in immigration. Refugees from Somalia, Burma, and Egypt have also moved into Shelbyville and Bedford County in recent years to be closer to the Tyson Foods facility.

Debate has surrounded immigration into Tennessee in the present day. In 2001, Tennessee became the first state to grant driver's licenses to undocumented residents, which brought the issue of immigration into the forefront. After the September 11, 2001, attacks, the licensing debate became even more heated, as critics argued that the law could provide "driver's licenses for terrorists." Because of political pressure, the licenses were changed to "certificates" in 2004, and the program ended altogether in 2006 (Moser 2008). Senator Bill Ketron was opposed to the licensing program and testified before Congress on the matter. In 2006, he shared accounts of immigrants coming to the state to obtain licenses and felt that undocumented immigration to the state was high due to TennCare, the state-sponsored healthcare plan. He insisted that it was hard to tell how much Medicaid was disbursed to undocumented immigrants but felt it was very clear that emergency rooms had provided a good deal of care to these individuals. He also felt that immigrants were drawn by a growing number of jobs in the state.

While many Tennesseans welcome the new residents, some are resistant to growing immigrant populations. Some of this resistance to inclusive immigration reform comes from what has been called "the new Southern nativism," which may be a reaction against "another diminution of white privilege." Many nativists feel that their towns are transforming overnight, and feel that their world is changing quickly and they are powerless to stop it. This is particularly true in towns that had not seen much rapid change previously (Moser 2008). Contrary to those groups seeking to limit immigration, several groups have been created in response to a lack of immigrant services and advocacy in Tennessee. One of these is the Tennessee Immigrant and Refugee Rights Coalition (TIRRC), which has a diverse staff working together to address the needs of varying immigrant groups. TIRRC is described as a "statewide, immigrant and refugee-led collaboration" with the goals of empowering and advocating immigrants while creating a positive atmosphere that recognizes their contributions to Tennessee life (TIRRC 2011a). Another group is the Center for Refugees and Immigrants of Tennessee, which works with new Americans to find and secure employment, provides tutoring to students, and other community-building programs. While debate may continue over the best way to approach immigration in Tennessee, it is clearly an issue many are passionate about and one that has sparked discussion and involvement from across the spectrum of politics and personal experience.

TOPICAL ESSAYS

Somali Immigrants in Tennessee

Somali refugees fled their country in recent years to escape an ongoing war, and many went to Kenya before relocating. Refugees began coming to the United States approximately 20 years ago, many to escape famine from 1991 to 1992. In the past 10 years, over 50,000 refugees from Somalia have come to the United States. Many Somali refugees came to the town of Shelbyville to work at the Tyson chicken-processing plant. Abdul Farah, who has worked with Somali refugees, says that many have to leave their family behind to seek a better life. Farah says refugees face many obstacles, including language barriers, cultural differences, and a lack of job experience from working only as a farmer or having only lived in a refugee camp. Many Somali refugees around the United States seek ways to help during more recent famines that took place in 2011, and many were concerned for the people in their native country after having fled wars and famines only a decade or two before.

Somali refugees have joined an increasingly diverse population in Shelbyville, and have taken part in activities to bring together the Somali and Latino/a immigrant communities. Some have criticized the community's treatment of new refugees to Shelbyville, saying that native-born residents are unwelcoming to those who have resettled to work at the Tyson chicken-processing plant and that residents accuse immigrants of stealing jobs. However, the community's native-born and foreign-born populations have come together at local events and community building activities and are even the subject of a documentary.

Islamic Center of Murfreesboro

In 2010, the Regional Planning Commission of Rutherford County approved plans for a building that would become the Islamic Center of Murfreesboro. The new building would replace the Center's smaller site, which had become so crowded that it could no longer serve all the worshippers. The Islamic Center's mission, in addition to serving as a religious center, was to unite community members from a variety of backgrounds and to provide education about Islam and Muslims to others in the community. The group also provided a weekend school to provide Islamic education for children, as well as a listing of Muslim-owned businesses in the area. The center was set to begin construction in August 2011.

A group of Murfreesboro residents filed suit against the county, but Chancellor Robert Corlew ruled that the mosque's construction was not a threat. The plaintiffs were still given the chance to argue that the county violated the state's public notice law by not properly advertising the meeting where they approved the plans. The attorney for this group warned the Islamic Center that building in August could be problematic. This was because the case was still ongoing and if the 17 plaintiffs were to win, any construction already completed would be torn down. The plaintiffs and other residents also took part in protests against the new mosque. Others took a more extreme stance on the new building. Republican presidential candidate Herman Cain opposed the building of the mosque, suggesting that it would be a way to "sneak Shariah law into our laws" and that it was an "infringement and abuse of our freedom of religion" (Stockard 2011). While there may have been opposition, Islamic Center members have encouraged open communication with the community, which may lead to understanding and acceptance.

Refugee Absorptive Capacity Act (2011)

The Refugee Absorptive Capacity Act, also called the Tracy refugee bill, was signed into law in July 2011. The goal of the bill, originally created by Tennessee state senator Jim Tracy, was to make sure that local communities would be able to absorb new refugees. The law required Catholic Charities, the state's refugee placement agency, to meet quarterly with local governments to plan placement of refugees in advance of their arrival in their new communities. In 2008, the state of Tennessee withdrew from providing refugee services, instead appointing Catholic Charities to take over placement.

The goal was to make sure that communities and local economies could absorb new workers, residents, and students without spreading resources too thin. The bill's language indicated that it seeks to "insure that a refugee is not placed or resettled in an area highly impacted by the presence of refugees or comparable populations," that the federal government would take into account the state's recommendations for placement, and that there should be close cooperation between the state resettlement agency, local governments, and voluntary groups prior to the placement of refugees (Tennessee House of Representatives 2011, 1). Governments can also request a moratorium on new resettlement activities.

The law was criticized by immigrant rights groups, and was called an "unprecedented attack on refugees" (Mosely 2011). One concern was that the new law could create a hostile environment for new refugees, rather than encouraging communication among the individuals, settlement agencies, and the towns where they would live. Other critics added the law to a list of legislation under consideration in 2011 that would make settlement in the United States more difficult for foreign-born persons. These included a law requiring that parents present a child's Social Security number, birth certificate, or visa in order to enroll in public school. Other legislation would keep people without such papers from enrolling in the University of Tennessee system, while another would provide driving tests only in the English language. One journalist (Hargrove 2011) said the biggest problem with such laws, in addition to infringing on others' rights, was the fact that immigration was a part of foreign policy, and that overly restrictive laws could hurt the United States in the long run.

Kurdish Immigrants in Tennessee

Kurdish immigrants have joined an increasing number of others who see Tennessee as an immigrant destination. "Little Kurdistan," located in Nashville, is home to the nation's largest Kurdish population, consisting of approximately 11,000 people. Most of the Kurds here are from Iraq, although some have emigrated from other countries. The Kurds come from Iran, Iraq, Syria, and Turkey, and have for years been an ostracized group, who are not allowed to practice or share aspects of their language or culture in the same way as other ethnic groups in the Middle East.

Kurdish immigration began in 1976, when the first wave of Kurdish immigrants fled the failed revolution in Iraqi Kurdistan. They arrived at the nearby Fort Campbell army base, and many stayed in the area because of Nashville's booming economy. In 1979, another wave of Kurdish immigration took place as Kurdish Iranians fled the revolution led by Ayatollah Khomeini. The third and largest wave of Kurdish immigration took place from 1991 to 1992 as refugees fled from Saddam Hussein's genocide against Iraqi Kurds. Many Kurds fled to neighboring countries before relocating to the United States. The final wave of Kurdish immigration took place in response to a Civil War in Iraqi Kurdistan in 1996 and 1997. These immigrants were brought to the United States and assisted by a number of nonprofit agencies. The U.S. government paid to help resettle them in various communities around the country, including Nashville.

Kurdish immigrants lived mostly in the southern area of Nashville. The sizeable Kurdish population resulted in the creation of local infrastructure, including a mosque and international market, to help Kurds here keep their culture and traditions alive in the United States. Some Kurdish youth have also become involved in a gang called the Kurdish Pride Gang, thought to be the only Kurdish gang in the United States. The gang has been a source of great frustration for the Kurdish community in Nashville and elsewhere, where members have worked hard to build a good reputation and become a respected part of American society. Like many other ethnic groups, Nashville's Kurdish population is diverse and includes business owners and students (Emery 2007). Other states with major Kurdish populations include California, Virginia, Massachusetts, New Jersey, Texas, and New York.

Bilingual Education in Tennessee

The state government has created programs to assist immigrant children, although these are not exclusively related to bilingual education. One of these is the Migrant Education Program, the goal of which is to provide educational funding to assist children whose parents have relocated to find employment in agriculture or fishing industries, and which has resulted in a disruption to the child's education. Grants are given to school programs that assist these children in meeting curriculum requirements and learning outcomes.

Tennessee state senator Bill Ketron testified before Congress in 2006 that one of the common concerns he had heard from constituents was the difficulty the K-12 system had in accommodating a huge influx of students who are in the country undocumented, particularly those who do not yet speak or read English. The city of Nashville has been one place where bilingual education has frequently come under fire, with an English-only proposal being brought forth three times to city voters. In 2007, local elected officials approved such a measure, but it was vetoed by Mayor Bill Purcell.

While there has been opposition to bilingual education in the state, there has also been a good deal of support. The TIRRC was a major supporter of bilingual education and was integral in the defeat of the 2009 English-only referendum in the city of Nashville. The proposition was put before Nashville voters and lost by approximately 10,000 votes. This referendum was heavily criticized, with *The Nashville Tennessean* publishing an editorial that decries the measure as discriminatory and damaging. The editors also worried that it would marginalize non-English speakers and prevent them from assimilating and participating in society.

Latino/a Immigrants in Tennessee

From last part of the twentieth century through the beginning of the twenty-first century, Tennessee saw an increase in immigration from Central and South America. Between 1990 and 2000, the Latino/a population in the state doubled. Many Latinos have settled in Memphis, Nashville, and Knoxville, although many others have moved to smaller towns to pursue employment in manufacturing and food-processing industries.

Part of this is because of Tennessee's central location in relation to the majority of the U.S. population, 70 percent of which are a day's drive from the eastern part of the state. As a result, many food-processing plants and manufacturers have located their operations in this area, resulting in many labor-intensive jobs looking to hire Latino/a workers. However, Latino/as from a variety of backgrounds have come to the state to pursue employment across all sectors and have been drawn by scientific research institutions, a booming service industry, and a relatively low cost of living.

The rise in immigration to Tennessee began in the mid-1990s and increased so dramatically that the city of Nashville was ranked first among U.S. cities for the number of new immigrants. While Latino/a immigrants have sometimes been associated with agricultural labor, a number of immigrants, including many in Tennessee, were employed in the "new economy" of service, distribution, and construction jobs (Mendoza, Cicsel, and Smith 2001, 3). Research completed in 2001 indicates that recent Latino immigrants are younger and more highly educated than their predecessors and shows that more women and children are immigrating to the state than before. Latino immigrants have become a well-established group in the state in the early 2000s, as the number of births from Latino/a parents rose over 40 percent in 2003. Latino immigrants continue to come to the state and recent statistics indicate that they account for around 45 percent of the state's first-generation immigrants.

NOTABLE FIGURES/GROUPS

SENATOR BILL FRIST (1952–) AND THE MCCAIN-KENNEDY BILL

Senator Bill Frist of Tennessee was a Republican Senate majority leader who left his position after the 2006 election. Frist was accused of being uninterested in politics and unable to work on tough issues after his handling of immigration reform in 2006. The reform bill, introduced by senators Edward Kennedy and John McCain, and thus called the McCain-Kennedy bill, would introduce sweeping changes to the U.S. approach to immigration, including the building of a fence along the Mexican border, increasing the number of border patrol personnel, and discouraging employers from hiring undocumented workers. The bill was first introduced in 2005 and a revised, and less strict, version of the bill was introduced in early 2007. Frist introduced the bill for a vote before many felt that negotiations over its measures were finalized. To help negotiations later on, another measure, called the Hagel-Martinez plan, was introduced that would allow undocumented immigrants to remain in the country provided that they pay a fine, work for a number of years, and learn English.

TENNESSEE IMMIGRANT AND REFUGEE RIGHTS COALITION

The TIRRC is a statewide advocacy group in Tennessee. It is an immigrant and refugee-led organization that seeks to empower immigrants and advocate for immigrants who have settled in the state, and to make Tennessee a place that values their contributions to society. TIRRC has assisted immigrants and refugees in the state in a variety of ways, including speaking about the issues associated with enforcement of Immigration and Customs Enforcement's program, known as 287(g). In 2009, the Obama administration sent a directive to a Nashville sheriff who charged 6,000 people with immigration crimes in a two-and-a-half year period. The sheriff was told to release all nonviolent offenders, which was seen as a move to reassert federal authority over immigration reform.

When asked about 287(g), TIRRC executive director Stephen Fotopulos says that the program was there to help address concerns over violent criminals but has also resulted in the arrest and detention of undocumented immigrants over minor violations, including fishing without a license. TIRRC has been instrumentally involved with a number of other immigration-related issues in Tennessee. These include the defeat of the "English-only" referendum that is proposed in Nashville, co-founding the Southeast Immigrant Rights Network (which includes a number of immigrant advocacy programs in the southeastern United States), securing funding for education for immigrant children, and helping new voters engage in civic life.

Juana Villegas, center, and her son, Gael Carachure, 3, lead a march to the Tennessee Supreme Court building on June 14, 2012, in Nashville, Tennessee. In 2008, Villegas was jailed in Nashville and kept in shackles while in labor with Gael. During the march, inside the Supreme Court chamber, a Nashville immigration attorney argued that the Davidson County sheriff should be barred from participating in a federal program that lets deputies perform some of the duties of immigration agents. (AP Photo/Mark Humphrey)

Theresa Harmon

Theresa Harmon has been described as "Tennessee's most vociferous anti-immigration organizer" (Moser 2008). Harmon was born and raised in Tennessee, and her work is informed by what she sees as major issues arising from the large number of undocumented Latino/a residents in the state and in her hometown of Nashville. In one interview, she indicated that there was an important distinction between immigrants who arrived legally, who she feels want to assimilate, and those who arrive without documentation, who she says are primarily motivated by financial concerns and who are transforming her hometown into something unfamiliar. In response, she formed TNRIP in 2001, which became the state's largest anti-immigration group.

Harmon considers many of her political beliefs to be liberal and feels that her stance against undocumented immigration is in line with these views. As she says, "This immigration is driven by corporations who want more workers to exploit. It's killing working-class people, especially black folks. You can't tell me there's not a problem that needs solving here" (Moser 2008). The TNRIP blog has many heated and passionately written posts that discuss all undocumented immigration as problematic for a number of reasons, including alleged increased crime rates and a purported reduction in quality of life (Tennesseans for Responsible Immigration Policy 2007). While the group's blog had many posts from 2007, there were none from more recent times, suggesting that Harmon and TNRIP no longer feel it necessary to have an online presence. Harmon has represented TNRIP elsewhere, though, both in writing and in citations of her views in conservative articles on anti-immigration news sites that supported Arizona's strict 2010 immigration laws and other immigration restrictions (Baldwin 2010; *The Phil Valentine Show* 2006).

BIBLIOGRAPHY

Baldwin, Chuck. "Arizona State Has It Right." *News with Views*, April 30, 2010. http://www.newswithviews.com/baldwin/baldwin586.htm. Accessed March 29, 2014.

Bentley, Blanche. "Tennessee Scotch Irish Ancestry." *Tennessee Historical Magazine* 5, no. 4 (1920): 201–11.

Beutler, Brian. "Capitol Hill: Sour Mashed." *American Prospect* 17, no. 11 (2006): 11–13.

Bokum, Hermann. *The Tennessee Hand-Book and Immigrant's Guide*. Philadelphia: J.B. Lippincott & Co, 1868.

Center for Refugees and Immigrants of Tennessee. "Programs." 2011. http://www.centerforrefugees.org/index.php?option=com_content&view=article&id=15&Itemid=19. Accessed March 29, 2014.

Center for Refugees and Immigrants of Tennessee. "Services." 2011. http://www.centerforrefugees.org/index.php?option=com_content&view=article&id=5&Itemid=2. Accessed March 29, 2014.

CNN. "GOP Senators Offer Immigration Plan." 2006. http://articles.cnn.com/2006–04–05/politics/immigration_1_immigration-bill-illegal-immigrants-legal-status?_s=PM:POLITICS. Accessed March 29, 2014.

Committee on Energy and Commerce, U.S. House of Representatives. *Examining the Impact of Illegal Immigration on the Medicaid Program and our Healthcare Delivery System*. Washington, DC: U.S. Government Printing Office, 2006.

Corlew, Robert E. *Tennessee: A Short History*. Knoxville: University of Tennessee Press, 1981.

Drever, Anita. "Tennessee: A New Destination for Latina and Latino Immigrants." In Fran Ansley, and Jon Shefner, eds. *Global Connections, Local Receptions: New Latino Immigration to the Southeastern United States*. Knoxville: University of TN Press, 2009, pp. 65–86.

"Editorials: Enter McCain-Kennedy." *The Washington Post*, May 14, 2005. http://www.washingtonpost.com/wp-dyn/content/article/2005/05/13/AR2005051301483.html. Accessed March 29, 2014.

Emery, Theo. "In Nashville, a Street Gang Emerges in a Kurdish Enclave." *New York Times*, July 15, 2007. http://www.nytimes.com/2007/07/15/us/15gangs1.html?_r=0. Accessed August 11, 2014.

Fishback, Price Van Meter. *The Economic Welfare of Bituminous Coal Miners, 1890–1930*. New York: Oxford University Press, 1992.

Foote, William Henry. "Sketches of North Carolina, Historical and Biographical, Illustrative of the Principles of a Portion of Her Early Settlers." 1846. http://docsouth.unc.edu/nc/foote/foote.html. Accessed March 29, 2014.

Goodpasture, A. V. "Why the First Settlers of Tennessee Were from Virginia." *Tennessee Historical Magazine* 5, no. 4 (1920): 229–32.

Gunter, Michael M. *The Kurdish Predicament in Iraq: A Political Analysis.* New York: St. Martin's Press, 1999.

Harris, Pat. "City of Nashville Rejects English-only Law." *Reuters,* January 22, 2009. http://www.reuters.com/article/2009/01/23/us-usa-english-nashville-idUS-TRE50M11420090123. Accessed August 11, 2014.

Hargrove, Brantley. "Seven New State Bills Posturing over Illegal Immigration Could Leave a Bad Taste." *Nashville Scene,* April 21, 2011. http://www.nashvillescene.com/nashville/seven-new-state-bills-posturing-over-illegal-immigration-could-leave-a-bad-taste/Content?oid=2388836. Accessed August 11, 2014.

Islamic Center of Murfreesboro. "About us." 2011. http://www.icmtn.org/about.html. Accessed March 29, 2014.

Islamic Center of Murfreesboro. "Islamic School." 2011. http://www.icmtn.org/school.html. Accessed March 29, 2014.

Islamic Center of Murfreesboro. "Services." 2011. http://www.icmtn.org/services.html. Accessed March 29, 2014.

"Israel Faces the Facts of Life." A Photographic Essay by Robert Capa. *Life,* May 14, 1951, p. 116.

Jonnson, Patrik. "Illegal Immigrants Netted by Local Police Could Be Released." *Christian Science Monitor,* June 23, 2009. http://www.csmonitor.com/USA/Politics/2009/0623/illegal-immigrants-netted-by-local-police-could-be-released. Accessed March 29, 2014.

Karimi, Hero. "The Kurdish Immigrant Experience and a Growing American Community." 2010. http://www.kurdishherald.com/issue/v002/001/article04.php. Accessed March 29, 2014.

Klein, Rick. "Kennedy, McCain Try Again on Immigration." *Boston Globe,* February 28, 2007. http://www.boston.com/news/nation/washington/articles/2007/02/28/kennedy_mccain_try_again_on_immigration/. Accessed March 29, 2014.

McWhirter, A. J. *Biennial Report of the Commissioner of Agriculture, Statistics and Mines of the State of Tennessee.* Nashville: Marshall & Bruce, 1887.

Mendoza, Marcel, David H. Cicsel, and Barbara Ellen Smith. *Latino Immigrants in Memphis, Tennessee: Their Local Economic Impact.* Memphis: The University of Memphis Center for Research on Women, 2001.

Mohammed, Zaineb. "Somali Media Rally behind Famine Relief." *New American Media,* July 28, 2011. http://newamericamedia.org/2011/07/somali-media-rally-behind-famine-relie.php. Accessed March 29, 2014.

Mosely, Brian. "Refugees' Impact Being Documented." *Shelbyville Times-Gazette,* November 7, 2008. http://www.t-g.com/story/1476426.html. Accessed March 29, 2014.

Mosely, Brian. "Tracy Refugee Bill Attacked by Rights Group." *Shelbyville Times-Gazette,* July 13, 2011. http://www.t-g.com/story/1741393.html. Accessed March 29, 2014.

Moser, Bob. "Blue Dixie: Awakening the South's Democratic Majority." 2008. http://books
.google.com/books?id=PZusu6chFOMC&lpg=PT171&dq=tennessee%20immigratio
n&pg=PT3#v=onepage&q&f=false. Accessed March 29, 2014.

Peck, Barbara. *Tennessee: The Volunteer State*. Milwaukee: World Almanac Library, 2002.

The Phil Valentine Show. "Minuteman Co-Founder Headlining Illegal Immigration Town
Hall Meeting." 2006. http://www.philvalentine.com/DemagnetizeAmericaTownhall
Meeting.htm. Accessed March 29, 2014.

Powell, John. *Encyclopedia of North American Immigration*. New York: Facts on File, 2005.

Smietana, Bob. "Murfreesboro Mosque Opponent Caution against Groundbreak-
ing." *The Tennessean*, July 18, 2011. http://www.knoxnews.com/news/2011/jul/18/
murfreesboro-mosque-opponents-caution-against-grou/. Accessed March 29, 2014.

Smith, Heather A., and Owen J. Furuseth. *Latinos in the New South: Transformations of Place*.
Burlington, VT: Ashgate Publishing, 2006.

Stockard, Sam. "Cain 'Truly Sorry' for Mosque Comments" *The Daily News Journal*, July 29, 2011. http://pqasb.pqarchiver.com/dnj/access/2413563181.
html?FMT=ABSanddate= Jul+29%2C+2011. Accessed August 23, 2014.

Stonehouse, Merlin. *John Wesley North and the Reform Frontier*. Minneapolis: University
of Minnesota, 1965.

Swarns, Rachel L. "As Senators Debate Immigration Bill, Frist Offers His Own." *New
York Times*, March 17, 2006. http://www.nytimes.com/2006/03/17/politics/17immig.
html?_r=0. Accessed March 29, 2014.

Tennesseans for Responsible Immigration Policy. "Tennesseans for Responsible Immigration Policies." 2007. http://tnrip.livejournal.com/. Accessed March 29, 2014.

Tennessee Department of Education. "Federal Programs: Title I, Part C-Migrant Education." 2011. http://www.tn.gov/education/fedprog/fpmigrant.shtml. Accessed March
29, 2014.

Tennessee House of Representatives. "House Bill 1632." 2011. www.capitol.tn.gov
/Bills/107/Bill/HB1632.pdf. Accessed March 29, 2014.

Tennessee Immigrant and Refugee Rights Coalition (TIRRC). "About Us." 2011a. http://www
.tnimmigrant.org/about-us/. Accessed March 29, 2014.

TIRCC. "Tennessee Immigrant and Refugee Rights Coalition." 2011b. http://www.tnimmigrant
.org/. Accessed March 29, 2014.

U.S. Department of Labor. *Annual Report of the Commissioner General of Immigration to the
Secretary of Labor*. Washington, DC: Government Printing Office, 1916.

U.S. House of Representatives. *Reports of the Industrial Commission Immigration and Education, Volume XV*. Washington, DC: Government Printing Office, 1901.

Warne, Frank Julian. *The Tide of Immigration*. New York: D. Appleton and Company, 1916.

Yildiz, Kerim, and Georgina Fryer. *The Kurds: Culture and Language Rights*. London: Kurdish Human Rights Project, 2004.

43

TEXAS

William P. Kladky

CHRONOLOGY

1519   Spanish explorer Alonso Álvarez de Piñeda (1494–1520) maps the Texas coastline.

1528   Alvar Núñez Cabeza de Vaca (1488/1490–1557/1558) and his Spanish crew begin exploration of the Southwest.

1598   The land drained by the Rio Grande is claimed by Juan de Oñate (1550–1626) for Spain.

1685   French explorer René-Robert Cavelier, sieur de La Salle (1643–1687), searching for the Mississippi River's mouth, lands in Texas and establishes Fort St. Louis in Victoria County.

1689   After Spanish general Alonso de León's expedition finds the remains of Fort St. Louis, the Spanish begin establishing missions and settlements in east Texas.

1731   Fifty-five Canary Islanders arrive in San Antonio to establish San Fernando de Béxar.

1779   A group of settlers led by Antonio Gil Ybarbo establishes Nacogdoches near an abandoned mission site.

1813   The Spanish government grants Moses Austin (1761–1821) permission to establish a colony in the Texas region.

1829   The first of several large groups of Irish immigrants arrives in south Texas.

1830   The Mexican government temporarily outlaws legal immigration into Texas from the United States except in special cases.

1831   The first German family arrives in Texas, settling in Austin County.

1839	Cherokees are ejected from Texas at the Battle of the Neches River in Van Zandt County.
1840s	The largest numbers of German immigrants arrive.
1845	The first Norwegian settlement is founded as Normandy in Henderson County.
1848	The treaty ending the war with Mexico is signed, setting the international boundary.
1854	Two reservations are established for American Indians in northwest Texas.
1856	The first Arabic-speaking individuals arrive as camel tenders.
1859	American Indians on northwest Texas reservations are moved by the federal government to reservations in Indian Territory (now Oklahoma).
1873	The Houston and Texas Central Railway reaches the Red River, creating the first all-rail route from Texas to St. Louis and the East, greatly facilitating immigration.
1874	The Southern Plains Indians are defeated in the Battle of Palo Duro Canyon, and their resettlement in reservations begins the development of the western part of the state.
1880s	Italian immigrants arrive in substantial numbers.
1880	Lebanese and Syrian families begin coming from the Ottoman Turkish Empire to flee religious discrimination.
1890s	A surge in immigration from Mexico intensifies.
1903	Thirty colonists from Japan arrive in Webster in southern Harris County, with other families soon coming to work in rice production.
1920s	A San Antonio Chamber of Commerce official admits that they are "dependent upon the Mexican farm-labor supply."
1930s	Approximately 100,000 Latino/as immigrate back to Mexico in search of economic opportunities during the Great Depression.
1950s	Muslim immigrants from Lebanon and Syria arrive, fleeing the postwar turmoil in the Middle East.
1958	The integrated circuit is successfully tested in Dallas, beginning the semiconductor and electronic age as well as an economic boom that attracts many immigrants and migrants.
1960s	Over half of San Antonio's 750,000 person population is Spanish-speaking.
1963	After President John F. Kennedy (1917–1963) is assassinated in Dallas on November 22, Vice President Lyndon B. Johnson (1908–1973) of Stonewall, Texas, becomes the 36th U.S. president.
1970s and 1980s	The state's economic prosperity draws many new immigrants and migrants.
1988	George H. W. Bush (1924–) of Houston is elected president of the United States.

| 2009 | Texas has the second-highest estimated number of undocumented immigrants of all the states: 1.9 million. |
| 2013 | A bill is introduced into the Texas legislature that would allow undocumented immigrants to drive legally and purchase insurance in Texas if they pass a driving test and a criminal background check, submit fingerprints, and prove state residency. Another bill would prohibit law enforcement from asking crime victims and witnesses about their immigration status. |

HISTORICAL OVERVIEW

PRE-1800

Italy, Spain, and France were the initial explorers and settlers of Texas. Italians were part of the earliest Spanish exploration, employed by the Spanish court. Most were from Sicily and Naples, provinces formerly controlled by Spain. Coronado's 1541 journey across the High Plains included soldiers named Loro, Napolitano, and Romano. In 1629, two Spanish missionaries from New Mexico traveled to San Angelo to teach the Jumano Indians about Christianity. While they did not make many converts, the missions they established at San Antonio and La Bahia eventually led to the development of ranching and a growing settlement.

The rivals to the Spanish were the French. French explorers—such as René-Robert Cavelier, sieur de La Salle (1643–1687)—had been exploring Texas for decades. To facilitate more expansion, they set up Fort St. Louis in Victoria County. Attempting to block French westward expansion, the Spanish in 1719 tried to settle 200 families from the Canary Islands in Texas. The first (and only) group of 56, led by Juan Leal Goraz (1676–1743), arrived in San Antonio in 1731. Goraz was named the first mayor of the new civilian government, and descendants of the Canary Islanders still live in the San Antonio area.

San Antonio began growing in the late 1720s and early 1730s as the Spanish consolidated their missions, which also increased the number of Indians and support associated with the work of the missions. Ex-soldiers began settling in the area and marrying local women, a pattern that was repeated often. Beginning in the 1730s, the Spanish settlers and the Lipan Apaches battled. The Apaches were offended by the Spanish missionary activity, and struck at San Antonio when it began to infringe on Apache territory. This was complicated when the Comanches came from the Great Basin region of the west to Texas in 1719. The Comanches put pressure on the Apaches, who then fought with the Spanish.

There were sporadic attempts by Mexican ranchers to expand into Texas throughout this period. In the 1750s, some took root. One example in Webb and Zapata counties was a *hacienda* called Nuestra Señora de los Dolores, which had 3,000 cattle; 3,400 horses; and 2,650 mules and donkeys, tended by 30 families.

In 1760, the Spanish-speaking population of San Antonio, the largest settlement in Texas, was only about 1,000. Other missions were negligible, and dependent upon Mexico City for support.

Spain's decision to join France in the Great War for the Empire (1754–1763) against England influenced Texas immigration. Spain took control of Louisiana in 1766, and changed the mission policy to one favoring trade and suppressing hostile Native Americans. As of the 1770s, according to the commandant of the Interior Provinces of New Spain, Texas had "two presidios, seven missions, and an errant population of scarcely 4,000 persons." Indeed, the first census of Spanish settlements in 1777 discovered but 3,103 in Texas. Approximately one-fourth were Coahuiltecan Indians, and another quarter were mixed race (either mestizos [Spanish and Indian] or mulattoes [Spanish and African]) (Campbell 2003, 73–75, 79).

The rapid growth of the United States, especially after independence, translated into settler demand for the vast, fertile lands of Texas. Spain first tried to deal with this by promoting immigration and regulating commerce. Having failed to lure colonists from Spain or New Spain to populate Texas, the Spanish Crown now turned to U.S. citizens and encouraged immigration by making generous land grants and water access. The rather questionable theory was that a wall of American settlers would protect Texas from being overrun by Americans. By the 1790s, the crown reversed its immigration policy. It was concerned that the U.S. traders would ally with the American Indians along the Red River, and would threaten the Spanish order. In 1792, a Spanish Census discovered that Texas had 1,600 residents, including 449 free blacks. Around this time, Italian merchants immigrated to serve the growing population.

EARLY NINETEENTH CENTURY

Spain's grip on Texas ended soon after it signed the 1800 Treaty of Ildefonso, by which it returned Louisiana to France. In 1803, Napoleon sold Louisiana to the United States, and poorly defended Texas became Mexico's border province with the United States. Thomas Jefferson claimed he had bought all the way to the Rio Grande, but Spain disagreed. Subsequent U.S. efforts in 1804 and 1806 to explore the region were frustrated by the Spanish. Later in 1806, American lieutenant Zebulon M. Pike (1778–1813) explored the Colorado River before being arrested by Spanish soldiers. His report praising Texas's fertile soil and wildlife stimulated more Americans to lust for Texas land.

In 1813, the Spanish government granted Moses Austin permission to establish a colony in the Texas area. After he died, his son, Stephen F. Austin (1793–1836), continued the colonizing effort. After Austin's death, his son took over. The "Old Three Hundred" Catholic families of Houston included several Irish. The slaves brought by some of these settlers eventually became ranch workers and small landowners.

Around 1815, families began to immigrate to Texas from Louisiana, across the Sabine River, and into San Augustine east of Nacogdoches. A trading post was set up at Pecan Point in 1815, and farmers from Tennessee arrived. The Anglo-American phrase "Gone to Texas" popped up, as these illegal squatters came searching for land. Spanish officials let them alone as long as they did not get involved in politics, or harass the American Indians excessively.

After the United States abandoned its claims to Texas in the 1819 Transcontinental Treaty in exchange for Spain ceding Florida and the Oregon territories, Spain began a defensive immigration policy to secure its northern possessions. Enormous land grants were issued to agents called empresarios, who were required to bring over 100 families as settlers within six years. Those who agreed to become Catholics and Mexican citizens received approximately 4,500 acres of land for $100. Although the colonization plan was supposed to entice Mexican, American, and European settlers, most immigrants to Texas were thousands of U.S. citizens who rushed into the area.

In 1821, the Adams-Onis Treaty set the boundary between Louisiana and Texas. Spain hoped that this would ease immigration pressures on Texas. Soon, though, the establishment of a constitutional monarchy in Mexico later in 1821 led to the Mexican authorities assuming control of Texas.

By the early 1820s, Texas was already ethnically diverse. Latino/a ranchers and farmers were settled in the Nacogdoches area, and Anglos lived in small towns and farms from the Red River to the Neches. American Indians still outnumbered everyone else. More Mexican families arrived in 1824, beneficiaries of generous land grants. Many of the Anglo settlers had purchased land at 1 to 10 cents an acre from speculators who had no legal title. While the Mexican national government was worried about the political impact, local authorities welcomed the resulting economic boom.

Two pairs of Irish entrepreneurs started colonies in 1828 in San Antonio and the Gulf Coast, which were settled by Irish, Mexican, and other nationalities. In 1829, the first of several large groups of Irish immigrants arrived in southern Texas. Such movement was temporarily curtailed by the Mexican government in 1830, when it outlawed virtually all legal immigration into Texas from the United States.

During the 1820s, Austin brought about 1,500 Anglo families to Texas. By the early 1830s, there were 20,000 English-speaking settlers and their slaves in Texas compared to only about 4,000 Spanish speakers. In 1831, the first German family arrived, settling in Austin County, and their letter to a friend in Germany describing Texas as an earthly Eden convinced more families to migrate to southeastern Texas. The older cities of San Antonio, Nacogdoches, and Victoria also have Italian families who date back to this period.

TEXAS INDEPENDENCE TO THE CIVIL WAR

Immigrants to Texas helped it become independent. Many Irish fought in Texas's war of independence against Mexico, including 12 who died defending the Alamo in 1836. About 100 Irish-born soldiers were in the Battle of San Jacinto, as well as Italian-born Prospero Bernardi (1794–ca. 1837). The first constitution of the Republic of Texas stated that slaves would be their owner's property, that the Texas Congress could not prohibit the immigration of slaveholders bringing their property, and that slaves could be imported from the United States.

Some of the Irish worked as sutlers and teamsters with the U.S. Army during the Mexican War. An Irish neighborhood near the Alamo in San Antonio was called Irish Flat. Some remained in the army, while others became artisans, merchants, and politicians. Other Irish came to Texas to work on the railroads later in the century. At least 87 Irish settled in the Peters Colony in north-central Texas in the 1840s.

While many early Scandinavian immigrants came directly to Texas from Europe, the Swedes mainly came from other U.S. states. Swen Magnus Swenson (1816–1896) is called the father of Swedish immigration to Texas because many Swedes who arrived afterward were either related to or supported financially by him. He continued to help Swedes move to the state, especially to work on his northwest Texas ranches.

By the 1840s, the first Cajuns began moving across the Sabine River into Texas. The first U.S. Census in Texas in 1850 found 600 "Franco-Louisianans." The largest immigration of Germans came in the 1840s when the Adelsverein (Society for the Protection of German Immigrants in Texas) organized at Biebrich near Mainz. It helped many immigrate to central Texas and found New Braunfels and Fredericksburg. The German language was extensively used in these areas.

In 1845, the first Norwegian settlement was founded, as Johan Reinert Reiersen (1810–1864) brought a group to what they called Normandy in Henderson County. Many families moved in 1848 from the lowlands of the Neches River tributaries to higher altitude at Four Mile Prairie and Prairieville. The desire for more land drove some to found Norse in 1853–1854. Johannes Nordboe (1768–1855), the first permanent Norwegian settler, arrived in Galveston after nine years in New York. Many others were recruited by Cleng Peerson (1783–1865), who promoted immigration in his newspaper, and published a book that inspired even more Norwegian immigration.

After the 1848 Treaty of Guadalupe Hidalgo ended the Mexican–American War (1846–1848), immigration continued to increase. In 1849, Rev. Josef Arnost Bergmann (1797–1877) left his Czech homeland to minister to German Protestants in Austin County. His letter praising Texas published in the *Moravské Noviny* stimulated more to immigrate, and he is known as the "father" of Czech immigration to Texas.

The first U.S. Census in Texas in 1850 found 154,034 whites; 58,161 slaves; and 1,403 Irish. The largest Anglo grouping was the Germans with about 20,000. There also were over 100 Norwegians southeast of Dallas. During the 1850s, the state's population essentially doubled to 421,294 whites (a 173.5 percent leap since 1850) and 182,921 slaves (up 214.5 percent). There were 3,480 Irish. Soon these were joined by other European immigrants. In 1851, the first 16 Czech immigrant families arrived, with more coming in the next three years to mostly settle in the central plains south of Austin at Cat Spring. From there, they expanded to New Ulm and Nelsonville in Austin County and Fayette County. About 100 Polish families founded Panna Maria southeast of San Antonio in 1854, sponsored by an already-settled Polish priest. Some 700 more Polish immigrants arrived in the next couple years, and they began several other small towns. Most Czech immigrants settled around Fayetteville, the "cradle of Czech immigration" in Texas. There also were Czechs at Dubina, Bluff (Hostyn), and Mulberry (Praha). By the Civil War, there were about 700 Czechs in Texas.

Friction erupted when many of the recent European immigrants sided with the Union cause in the Civil War. The community was split, though, with those who settled in cotton country who had accepted slavery as an institution either volunteering for the Confederate Army or accepting conscription.

Post-Civil War Era

The butchering of numerous American Indians during the Civil War strengthened the Indian reform movement, and led to the policy adoption of pacification of native tribes rather than elimination. After the Civil War, strong European immigration continued. Two Texans traveled to Denmark and promoted central Texas as fine farming land. By the late 1870s, several Danish families settled in Lee County, called Little Denmark, and in Rocky Hill in Gillespie County. The largest Danish settlement started in 1894 at Danevang in Wharton County. Most had first immigrated to north-central United States, with a minority coming directly to Texas from Denmark.

In 1868, landowners in Del Rio formed a company to begin the first large-scale irrigation in Texas. This produced even more immigration, as formerly dry land became farmable. Several infrastructure improvements made during this period greatly helped immigrants travel to and around in Texas. The canal system was completed in 1871. In 1873, the Houston and Texas Central Railway reached the Red River, creating the first all-rail route from Texas to St. Louis and the East.

Free African Americans began to arrive in Texas during the 1870s and 1880s, coming from the American South in search of employment in the mines, sawmills, and timber camps. While 1874 marked the end of Reconstruction when a Democrat became Texas governor, it also was the year the Southern Plains Indians were defeated in the Battle of Palo Duro Canyon. Their consequent resettlement in several official reservations opened the western part of Texas to additional development. Immigrant and trade travel was further assisted by the continued expansion of railroads, such as the Texas and Pacific Railway which was extended to Sierra Blanca in west Texas.

During the 1870s and 1880s, Texas had another population boom, doubling during the 1870s to almost 1.6 million—three times the national rate. The urban population particularly grew, with major cities tripling their numbers. San Antonio went from 12,000 to 37,000, becoming the state's largest. Houston jumped from 9,000 to 27,000; Dallas from 3,000 to 38,000; and Fort Worth leapfrogged from 500 to 23,000 by 1890.

Much of this population growth came from immigration, with new groups arriving to add to Texas's mix of Anglo, Latino/a, and Germans. From being less than 200 in 1870, Italian immigrants began to arrive in the 1880s in substantial numbers. Most were farmers who settled in the Brazos Valley near Bryan, Galveston County, and the Red River Valley. Many worked in agriculture, with some forming small wineries, and others were miners and brick makers. So many Italians from Lombardy worked building a railroad in 1881 that went from Richmond and Rosenberg to Brownsville that it was known as the "Macaroni Line." In addition, Germans and Scandinavians were continuing to arrive, joining established communities.

Political oppression drove some immigrants. Texas was the destination of some Jews from the Diaspora, fleeing the eastern European pogroms. Rabbi Henry Cohen helped a number to relocate to the Galveston area. When ranching came to define Texas in the late 1800s, eager and ambitious Scots came directly from Edinburgh and Aberdeen to raise cattle and build railroads—and make money. The Lebanese and Syrian families who began coming to Texas around 1880 from the Ottoman Turkish Empire primarily were Maronites who were fleeing religious discrimination. The Lebanese assimilated quickly, settling across the state. Eventually, to preserve their culture, they started the Southern Federation of Syrian Lebanese American Clubs.

Others arrived for work and economic opportunity. The first Arabic-speaking individuals had arrived in 1856 as camel tenders. Part of a U.S. Army experiment, the camels were used before the Civil War as pack animals to transport materials between the Western military forts. Cajuns came to Texas as workers to cultivate rice in southeast Texas and to build the Southern Pacific Railroad line that ran from the Sabine River to Houston, where many settled. Louisiana's poor economy, destroyed during the Civil War, drove many Cajuns to seek work elsewhere. As more began living in Jefferson, Orange, and neighboring counties, a Cajun middle class emerged.

A second wave of Czech immigration followed in the 1870s and 1880s. These new arrivals lived on the coastal and Blackland prairies from Ellis County near Dallas in the north to Victoria County on the south. A third wave after 1900 moved eastward to Brazoria and Fort Bend counties near Houston.

The emergence of Texas as cattle country severely tested its reputation as a haven for immigrant farmers. Cowboy culture despised sheep farmers, for both practical and cultural reasons, and a number of immigrants—Germans and Scots especially—raised sheep. As cattle country became owned and controlled by eastern and foreign capital (e.g., Scottish and English). The rambunctious cowboys became employees and profitable sheep farming became big business. Some African American cowboys prospered in this new system, which was based on skilled labor and mutual respect. About one-quarter of the cowboys were blacks and one-quarter were Mexican (*vaqueros*).

Texas became an oil-producing state with the 1894 discovery of oil at Corsicana followed by the opening of a commercial field two years later. Many immigrants arrived to work the fields and the associated industries that developed.

The most significant immigration during this period was the powerful rise in Mexican arrivals that stretched for decades. There was a surge in immigration from Mexico during the 1890s. In 1887, the U.S. Census discovered 83,000 Latino/as. This essentially doubled by 1900, with approximately 50 percent from Mexico. Many were actively recruited by U.S. companies and a majority of workers were laying tracks for the Texas and Mexico Railroad during the 1880s, and migrated wherever there was work. Wherever they worked and lived, they were subject to intensive harassment and abject discrimination.

1900 to World War II

After 1900, immigration quickened and diversified. In 1903, Seito Saibara and 30 other colonists from Japan arrived in Webster in southern Harris County, with other families soon coming to work in rice cultivation. Colonies were started in Port Lavaca (Calhoun County), Fannett (Jefferson County), Terry (Orange County), Mackay and El Campo (Wharton County), and Alvin (Brazoria County) in the next two decades. A second wave of Japanese came from California in the 1920s to escape anti-Japanese harassment, mainly settling in the Lower Valley. Overall, Japanese families experienced less prejudice in Texas, perhaps because of their small numbers.

By 1910, there were 1,125 immigrants in Texas who had arrived "from Turkey in Asia," as the U.S. Bureau of the Census called the Ottoman Empire. Most were from Mount Lebanon and Greater Syria and chain-migrated from other states. The 1890s rapid increase in Mexican immigration to Texas continued during the first decade of the new century, with about 100,000 arriving. The surge was primarily stimulated by Mexico's economic stagnation and political oppression. Because the new immigrants were so poor, services were negligible and health conditions appalling. Adding to this, the Texas Rangers brutally and at times unfairly or indiscriminately targeted Mexicans for punishment and harassment.

After World War I, the three largest foreign-born groups in Texas were from Mexico (69.2 percent), Germany (8.6 percent), and Czechoslovakia (3.6 percent). The number of Czech "foreign white stock" (speaking Czech at home) in 1940 was 62,680. Many moved into Texas's urban areas, which grew rapidly during this period. The percentage of Texans living in metropolitan areas grew from 17.1 percent in 1900 to 41.0 percent in 1939.

In 1910, Texas received 55.5 percent of all Mexican immigration to the United States. During 1910–1920, another 264,503 Mexican immigrants came, joined by 165,044 more in the 1920s. Not legally monitored, the new arrivals were fleeing economic exploitation and political turmoil. The development of the Mexican International Railroad line linking Eagle Pass, Texas, with Durango significantly facilitated this movement. Many immigrants were agricultural laborers under 44 years of age.

Unfortunately, the new arrivals face obstacles in learning English and many were undereducated. They were hired for labor-intensive, low-tier work: as maids, pecan shellers, and cigar makers. Thus, these immigrants faced numerous obstacles to integration. Within a few years, Mexican immigrants dominated south Texas, constituting up to 70 percent of some communities. The reaction of many native Texas residents was racist, seeing the Mexican in the same negative light as they did African Americans. Under their control, all south Texas public schools segregated Mexicans and social harassment was common. The reaction of the later arrivals to Texas from other states and countries was much more positive toward Mexican immigrants. However, segregation continued after World War II and even today, major desegregation cases have been fought.

In 1921, the Texas legislature, following similar legislation in California and other western states, limited Japanese land ownership. Saburo Arai, a Houston businessman, led the Japanese Association to successfully have the bill exempt all Japanese who were already state residents.

However, they were not about to limit the number of Mexicans who were coming to Texas to work the low-paying, mostly periodic jobs essential to the state's growth. In the 1920s, a San Antonio Chamber of Commerce official admitted that they were "dependent upon the Mexican farm-labor supply." Another Texas official estimated, in 1928, that 75 percent of all construction workers in the state were Mexican. Many worked in the cotton industry, which was an important industry in Texas, producing one-third of all the cotton picked in the United States in 1922. Because employment in agriculture and construction was sporadic, Mexicans continued to migrate as economic conditions warranted. Their advancement in the occupations was curtailed because of rampant, accepted racial and ethnic discrimination. For example, in 1920 only 5 percent of Mexicans were in professional and managerial occupations compared to 30 percent of the Anglos.

The Great Depression caused economic hardship for most, especially immigrants. Filipinos lost their jobs to migrating whites searching for work, and returned to the Philippines. Similarly, Tejanos immigrated back to Mexico in search of economic opportunities, with a total of about 100,000 crossing back over the border. African Americans headed west to California, part of the migration from the South.

In the World War II years, Texans were hostile toward the Japanese but did not repeat World War I era German oppression. Germans were now Texans. But the few Japanese—some 400 in 1940—were targeted instead. Under a federal policy at the beginning of the war with Japan, several thousand Japanese were brought to Texas to internment camps at Kennedy and Crystal City in South Texas and Seagoville outside Dallas. Many were Japanese Americans from the West Coast and others were Japanese alien residents of Latin American countries. About 6,000 persons were involved, the majority of whom were of Japanese descent, although some German families from Latin America were also housed in the camps. After the war, most of the internees left the state but a few elected to stay.

After World War II, Texas attracted immigrants for different reasons. The state's healthy economy drew many. For example, the rise of shrimping attracted Cajuns to the better fishing grounds off the Texas Gulf Coast. Japanese migrants came for another reason. Many who had been displaced and had lost their California properties, then placed in relocation centers throughout the United States during the war, chose to relocate to Texas. The new Japanese Texan population of the 1950s moved into the booming cities, finding employment in business and working mostly in the professions. Some came to escape political oppression. For instance, Muslim immigrants from Lebanon and Syria who were fleeing the postwar turmoil in the Middle East came during the unsettled period after the war.

Late Twentieth Century: A Diverse State

Texas has always been a diverse state. However, that diversity has not always been encouraged or tolerated. To some extent, the state's intergroup relations improved after World War II. Official segregation was lifted in many areas and the state's manufacture-based booming economy translated into ample opportunities for many. The state's population leaped some 45 percent during the period between 1950 and 1970 to 11,196,730, the fourth-highest in the United States. African Americans grew 43 percent to 1.4 million (to 12 percent of the state) and the Latino population doubled to over 2 million (18 percent). Texas was still primarily a southern state in heritage and outlook. A strong majority of the native-born population has southern roots, and more of those born elsewhere came from the American South than from the rest of the country combined.

For many reasons, ethnic Mexicans largely have been left out of Texas's post-war prosperity and advances. In the 1960s, a small middle class did emerge, composed of the many Mexican immigrants who had settled in the state. However, by most standards of prosperity, ethnic Mexican lagged far behind. Most could not speak English, had few skills and negligible education, were subject to discrimination, and so were confined to the lowest-level jobs. The ethnic Mexican became unique in American immigrant history: a native-born citizen who was really a foreigner in his or her own country. This has persisted even after 1950.

The other major (and minor) immigrant groups have done extremely well in comparison, even though this sort of comparison is unfair given different circumstances, treatment, and so on. In particular, Mexicans have been singled out for increased border enforcement and labor exploitation, not to mention racial or ethnic discrimination and thus any sort of assessment must take these particular obstacles into account. There are Czechs across the state, though they have tended to remain geographically concentrated. The 1990 Census found 282,562 with Czech ancestry. The Italians in Texas are the sixth-largest ethnic group in the state, according to figures from the 1990 U.S. Census. Of the total population of 16.9 million, Italians or part-Italians comprised 441,256. Many arrived in the last half of the twentieth century when professionals and business workers were attracted or transferred to Texas in the booming job market. Swedish Texans are the tenth-largest ethnic group, according to both the 1990 and 2000 censuses. Scandinavians included 155,949 Swedish; 137,342 Norwegians; and 50,689 Danish in 2007.

The state's economic prosperity during the 1970s and 1980s continued to draw many new immigrants and migrants. Texas's oil industry boom was the major economic engine, but manufacturing and agriculture also prospered. "Gone to Texas" became the cry of many yet again, as numerous laid-off workers from the "Frostbelt" flocked to Houston, Dallas, and San Antonio. In the 1980s, the finance and real-estate industries instead led Texas's economic prosperity and the state continued to gain migrants and immigrants. Many Asians arrived in the Gulf Coast from Vietnam, the Philippines, and China to work in the shrimp-fishing industry. The 15,172 Japanese Texans found in 1990 were a small percentage of the state's population. Over two-thirds lived in the Houston, San Antonio, and Dallas-Fort Worth metros. By the 1980s, Cajun professionals and engineers in telecommunications, petroleum, and construction migrated from Louisiana to Texas. As of 2000, there were over 375,000 Cajuns in Texas.

In the 1990s Texas still rode an economic crest, this time with cotton, computer manufacture, and Rio Grande trade via North American Free-Trade Agreement (NAFTA) changes. The population growth during these decades brought immigrants of more diversity than previously. Latinos jumped 54 percent in the 1990s to 6.7 million. Asian population grew the fastest, though to only 500,000 statewide. African American population increased 23 percent to about 2.4 million in 2000. The state neared having a non-white majority population. Houston's already was, with 29 percent Anglo, 39 percent Latino, 25 percent black, and 7 percent Asian. The U.S. Census Bureau estimated in 2000 that there were 29,518 Texans of Lebanese and Syrian ancestry. The Asian population growth has mostly happened in west Houston, Fort Bend County southwest of Houston, the Dallas suburbs, and near Fort Worth. The largest numbers are from Vietnam, South Asia, China, the Philippines, Korea, and Japan.

The Immigration Reform and Control Act of 1986—which made it illegal for employers to hire undocumented workers, legalized some seasonal agricultural undocumented immigrants, and legalized undocumented immigrants who entered before 1982—has impacted immigration to Texas. However, it has largely contributed to one already-established trend. The destination of Mexican immigration has changed from the five traditional gateway states—including Texas as the second largest—to a variety of new states. The decline actually began in 1960 when Texas received 35.9 percent during the so-called the Bracero era, to 26.5 percent in 1970, followed by only 16.7 percent in 1996. While Texas still receives many immigrants, many more are traveling elsewhere in the United States.

TWENTY-FIRST CENTURY: UNDOCUMENTED IMMIGRANTS AND
RECENT ANTI-IMMIGRANT ACTIONS

Since Mexican immigration began to increase rapidly in the early twentieth century, Texas has been sharply divided regarding its advisability, impact, and best way to deal with it. The nineteenth-century immigrants had been primarily "Anglos"—from Germany, Scandinavia, other parts of Europe. But Mexicans were allegedly different in the social imaginary, despite sharing a border—including a border that had shifted. Even before the Depression hit in the 1920s, nativists were alarmed at the high Mexican immigration levels and birthrates, despite the constant demand for their labor. Added to these economic concerns was the popularity of pseudoscientific racism—that is eugenics—which posited that somatic features (e.g., darker skin) were correlated with lower intelligence, fewer work skills, and other allegedly biologically inferior traits. Many, including the president of Harvard University, signed a petition to Congress in 1927 advocating adding Mexico to the national origins quota system to preserve the nation's genetic purity. The eugenic origin of much of policy at this time is now considered a blot on the U.S. historical record as a democracy.

Today, undocumented immigration significantly impacts Texas. According to the Department of Homeland Security, with 1.68 million undocumented

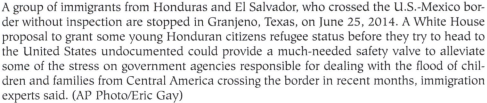

A group of immigrants from Honduras and El Salvador, who crossed the U.S.-Mexico border without inspection are stopped in Granjeno, Texas, on June 25, 2014. A White House proposal to grant some young Honduran citizens refugee status before they try to head to the United States undocumented could provide a much-needed safety valve to alleviate some of the stress on government agencies responsible for dealing with the flood of children and families from Central America crossing the border in recent months, immigration experts said. (AP Photo/Eric Gay)

immigrants, Texas had the second-highest estimated number of undocumented immigrants of all the states in 2009—15.5 percent of the nation's total. With 1,254 miles of border, the most in the United States, Texas (and California) is the most affected by shifts in undocumented entry (entry without inspection), federal policy, and associated economic conditions. There has been debate about whether undocumented immigration is a net plus or negative for state coffers. According to a 2006 report by the Texas comptroller, undocumented immigrants paid some $424.7 million more to the state government in fees and taxes than that was spent in educating, caring for, and incarcerating them. Locally, however, governments and hospitals spent almost $1 billion more than they received from the immigrants. The report has been criticized roundly by immigration opponents.

The U.S. government's 2006–2010 construction of a border wall in Texas to control Mexican immigration—as mandated in the Secure Fence Act of 2006 and the Consolidated Appropriations Act for FY2008—has generated widespread opposition. Most of Texas's fence is in the Rio Grande Valley, covering 70 miles of a 100-mile distance. Most of the fence is being built not along the border but inland, which angers many landowners. Students and public school teachers have organized well-attended protest marches. A coalition of mayors from border towns and cities has also initiated litigation. The County of El Paso and the Ysleta del Sur tribe, among others, filed a lawsuit challenging the constitutionality of the government's waiver of environmental and other standards. Despite this opposition, the barriers were built as part of three larger "Operations" to combat transportation of illegal drugs from Latin America and undocumented immigration: "Operation Hold-the-Line" in Texas and two others in California and Arizona.

Support for anti-immigrant legislation in Texas has risen and fallen in the past decade. In Texas's 2010 legislative session, several bills modeled after Arizona's controversial Senate Bill 1070 law were filed but not passed. One of the bills, House Bill 17, would have created the offense of "Criminal Trespass by Illegal Aliens" and have undocumented individuals arrested by state and local police officers. Other proposals would have imposed sanctions against "sanctuary cities," required state agencies to report financial costs related to undocumented immigrants, and required school districts to report the number of undocumented immigrants attending school. One legislator also filed a bill, again not enacted, to have police ask about someone's immigration status and arrest based on the answer. Another proposed bill would have required all Texas government agencies to use E-Verify to verify workers' immigration status. Texas governor Rick Perry was attacked while contesting the Republican presidential nomination in 2011 for his advocacy for giving in-state university tuition to undocumented immigrants attending Texas high schools.

There were over 50 immigration bills introduced in the 82nd Texas legislature in 2013, but it did not pass a "sanctuary cities" bill that would have stopped funding to cities not having their police asking the immigration status of people they arrest. Opposition was led by business leaders, because they needed the workers, and critics who said it would lead to racial profiling.

It can be argued that the growing political strength of the Latino/a population has changed the state's usually conservative approach to immigration. At the same time, attitudes of immigrants do change the longer one is a resident of the United States. One 1980s study of Hidalgo County, Texas, found that upper-income and third-generation Mexican immigrants were more likely to support sanctions on employers who hire undocumented immigrants than those who had recently arrived. Additionally, it was found that 49 percent of Latino/a Texans support amnesty for undocumented immigrants, compared to almost 90 percent approval by Latino/a community leaders.

TOPICAL ESSAYS

The Coming Latino/a Dominance

Continuing Latino/a legal and undocumented immigration to Texas, coupled with the new immigrants' higher birth rates, is about to make Texas predominantly a Latino/a state. It is expected that this will occur soon. In fact, the Texas state demographer has projected that the number of Latino/as in the state will surpass Anglos by 2040—even without migration. Migration gains will probably continue, though perhaps not at 2011s pace, where 54.6 percent were inbound compared to 45.4 percent outbound.

The coming Latino/a dominance in Texas has been predictable because of the surge in Latino/a immigration that began in the 1890s has continued, not to mention a shared border and transnational processes that have occurred since the beginning of this state's history. By the 1960s, over half of San Antonio's 750,000 population was Spanish-speaking. In 2010, Texas has both the second-largest population of any state with 25,145,561 (an increase of 4.1 million since 2000, the highest numerical change) as well as the fifth-highest percentage of undocumented immigrants of any state—6 percent of the population. The primary factors driving the steady immigration are the demand for low-paid labor in the United States and some displacement occurring in Mexico because of NAFTA.

Representative Marc Veasey, D-Texas, walks out of the U.S. Courthouse on July 14, 2014, in San Antonio. The U.S. Justice Department told judges in a trial that Texas lawmakers carefully crafted electoral maps marginalizing minority voters despite the state's exploding Latino and Latina population in a deliberate effort to racially discriminate and protect conservative incumbents. (AP Photo/Eric Gay)

It will be very interesting to see if Texas's long-established culture of ambivalence toward immigrants (particularly those considered racial Others), low taxes, and scarce public services, will continue in the future. Texas has long been guilty of ethnocentrism and the state had the highest percentage of residents native to the state where they live in 2012: 75.8 percent. The political establishment in Texas has repeatedly fought efforts to decrease its Anglo-dominant conservative power. Every change that has happened in the twentieth century has been forced upon the state. Women were virtually the last to get basic freedoms and rights for African Americans were forced upon the government despite its strenuous objections and defiance. People with disabilities have received less assistance on a per capita and enumerative basis than most other states, and all of the wealthier states. Additionally, too much of the Texas justice system has often been proven to be corrupt, resistant to change, and hostile to Latino/a and African American interests. While Texas always has been diverse, it continues to struggle with pluralism. All of its resources will be tested as it becomes primarily a Latino/a state.

NOTABLE GROUPS

Esperanza Peace and Justice Center

The Esperanza Peace and Justice Center is based in San Antonio and advocates on a broad range of issues pertaining to immigrants and individuals of Mexican and Central American descent. Going beyond reform-oriented groups, this center fights wage discrimination, residential segregation, sexism, and heteronormativity. Beyond a model of isolated individualism, they fight on behalf of social justice and fostering community. They work in cooperation with groups like the San Antonio Lesbian Gay Assembly and Chicanos against Military Intervention in Latin America, fostering the ability of various groups to engage in civic activity. They provide public education, support and host the arts, and run an Environmental Justice Project. Since 1998, the latter project has analyzed the connection between residential segregation, racism, and environmental waste, the location of landfills, and pollution. The group provides a necessary base for multiple policy issues and for fighting *de jure* discrimination.

BIBLIOGRAPHY

Barta, Carolyn. "82nd Legislature Cuts School Funds, State Jobs." *Texas Almanac*, 2011. http://www.texasalmanac.com/topics/government/82nd-legislature-cuts-school-funds-state-jobs. Accessed March 15, 2013.

Berlin, Ira. *The Making of African America: The Four Great Migrations*. New York: Viking, 2010.

Billington, Ray Allen, and Martin Ridge. *Westward Expansion: A History of the American Frontier.* New York: Macmillan Publishing Company, 1982.

Campbell, Randolph B. *Gone to Texas: A History of the Lone Star State.* New York: Oxford University Press, 2003.

Curtis, Gregory. "Lone Star Nation." *American History* 46 (2011): 46–49.

Curtis, Gregory. "What They Did Wrong." *Texas Monthly* 22 (1994): 5.

Devine, T. M. *To the Ends of the Earth: Scotland's Global Diaspora 1750–2010.* London: Smithsonian Books, 2011.

Dinnerstein, Leonard, Roger L. Nichols, and David M. Reimers. *Natives and Strangers: A Multicultural History of Americans.* New York: Oxford University Press, 1996.

Durand, Jorge, Douglas S. Massey, and Fernando Charvet. "The Changing Geography of Mexican Immigration to the United States, 1910–1996." *Social Science Quarterly* 81 (2000): 2–15.

Esperanza Peace and Justice Center. Esperanza Peace and Justice Center Webpage. http://www.esperanzacenter.org/. Accessed February 27, 2014.

Fehrenbach, T. R. *Lone Star: A History of Texas and the Texans.* New York: American Legacy Press, 1968.

Gilman, Denise. "Seeking Breaches in the Wall: An International Human Rights Law Challenge to the Texas-Mexico Border Wall." *Texas International Law Journal* 46 (2011): 257–93.

Gonzalez, Juan. *Harvest of Empire: A History of Latinos in America.* New York: Viking, 2000.

Hanner, Kenneth. "Texas Takes on Illegal Immigration in the Arizona Way." *Human Events* 66 (2010): 15.

Haley, James L. *Passionate Nation: The Epic History of Texas.* New York: Simon & Schuster, 2006.

Haynes, Sam W. " 'To Colonize 500 Families . . . Catholics, and of Good Morals': Stephen Austin and the Anglo-American Immigration to Texas, June 4, 1825." *OAH Magazine of History* 6 (2005): 57.

Jones, Richard C. "Using U.S. Immigration Data: Undocumented Migration from Mexico to South Texas." *Journal of Geography* 83 (1984): 58–64.

Miller, Richard K., and Associates. *Consumer Behavior 2013.* Richard K. Miller and Associates, Loganville, GA: 2012.

Moore, Michael Rugeley. "Peter Martin: A Stockraiser of the Republic Period." In Sara R. Massey, ed. *Black Cowboys of Texas.* College Station: Texas A&M University Press, 2000, pp. 39–48.

Plocheck, Robert. "Czech Texans." Texas Almanac, Texas State Historical Association, 2001. http://www.texasalmanac.com/topics/culture/czech/czech-texans. Accessed March 29, 2014.

Plocheck, Robert. "German Texans." Texas Almanac, Texas State Historical Association, 1997. http://www.texasalmanac.com/topics/culture/german/german-texans. Accessed March 29, 2014.

Plocheck, Robert. "Italian Texans." Texas Almanac, Texas State Historical Association, 2003. http://www.texasalmanac.com/topics/culture/italian/italian-texans. Accessed March 29, 2014.

Ramos, Mary G. "The First Official Permanent Civilian Settlement." Texas Almanac, Texas State Historical Association, 1993. http://www.texasalmanac.com/topics/history/first-official-permanent-civilian-settlement. Accessed March 15, 2013.

Ramos, Mary G. "Oil and Texas: A Cultural History." Texas Almanac, Texas State Historical Association, 2001. http://www.texasalmanac.com/topics/business/oil-and-texas-cultural-history. Accessed March 29, 2014.

Sacnz, Rogelio, and Edit Colberg. "Sustenance Organization and Net Migration in Small Texas Nonmetropolitan Communities, 1960–1980." *Rural Sociology* 53 (1988): 334–45.

Salamon, Jeff. "Everything You Ever Wanted to Know about Illegal Immigration." *Texas Monthly* 38 (2010): 144–49.

Skerry, Peter. *Mexican Americans: The Ambivalent Minority*. New York: The Free Press /Macmillan, 1993.

Sowell, Thomas. *Ethnic America: A History*. New York: Basic Books, 1981.

Takaki, Ronald. *A Different Mirror: A History of Multicultural America*. New York: Little, Brown, 2008.

Texas State Historical Association. "Timeline of Texas History." Texas Almanac, 2001. http://www.texasalmanac.com/topics/business/oil-and-texas-cultural-history. Accessed March 30, 2013.

Weissert, Will, Associated Press. "Texas Dems Want Immigration Talks Back at Capitol." *El Paso Times*, February 13, 2013. http://www.elpasotimes.com/texas/ci_22584334/texas-dems-want-immigration-talks-back-at-capitol. Accessed March 30, 2013.

44

UTAH

John Howell and Luke Perry

CHRONOLOGY

1776	Two Spanish priests, Father Silvestre Velez de Escalante and his superior Francisco Atanasio Dominguez start from Sante Fe to explore Utah.
1821	Mexico wins independence from Spain and claims Utah.
1822–1829	William H. Ashley's exploration and discovery of a central route to the Pacific allows trappers to enter northern Utah. Amongst those to respond are such legendary men as Jim Becwourth, Tom Fitzpatrick, David Jackson, Hugh Glass, Jim Bridger, and Jedediah Smith.
1824	Jim Bridger discovers the Great Salt Lake.
1826	Jedediah Smith leads expeditions to California and Nevada.
1832	Antoine Robidoux builds a trading post in the Utah Basin.
1841	Captain John Bartleson leads the first wagon train of settlers, including Nancy Kelsey, across Utah to California. Nancy Kelsey is the first white woman to see Utah.
1843	John C. Fremont and Kit Carson explore the Great Basin.
1844–1845	Miles Goodyear builds Fort Buenaventura, near present-day Ogden.
1846	The first party of Mormon settlers arrives in the Salt Lake Valley, led by Brigham Young.
1848	The United States wins the Mexican War. The Treaty of Guadalupe-Hidalgo cedes Utah to the United States.
1850	The Utah Territory is established.
1853	The Walker War with the Ute Indians begins over slavery among the American Indians.

1865–1868	The Ute Blackhawk War marks the last major Indian conflict in Utah.
1896	Utah becomes the 46th state to enter the Union.
1942	The Topaz Internment Camp for Japanese Americans is established near Delta.
1944	The first Utah chapter of the National Association for the Advancement of Colored People is established.
1976	John Ulibarri becomes the first Latino to serve in the Utah state legislature.
1986	Mark Maryboy becomes the first Native American to serve as a County Commissioner, representing San Juan County.
2001	George Garwood is elected mayor of South Ogden as Utah's first black mayor.
2009	Mia Love is elected mayor of Saratoga Springs as Utah's first black female mayor.
2010	The Utah Compact, a statement of principles on immigration, is signed. The Utah Compact is supported by immigration advocates, business leaders, and the Latter-day Saints (LDS) Church.
2013	The foreign-born comprise 8.4 percent of the state's population, with about one-third of them being naturalized citizens.

HISTORICAL OVERVIEW

EARLY UTAH AND THE MORMON SETTLEMENT

Utah was named after the Utes, Native American people whose lands once stretched from modern Salt Lake City to Denver down to the pueblo cultures of New Mexico. The life of the Utes began to change dramatically with the Mexican War. The United States took control of the territory with the Treaty of Guadalupe Hidalgo in 1848. This was a major defeat for the Spanish-speaking people of the South with whom the Utes had negotiated treaties and conducted trade.

The first European expeditions into the Great Basin were primarily military efforts to map the American West. Originally, there was little interest in the basin due to the lack of an internal drainage system. Waters were drained into the Great Salt Lake and eventually were evaporated into salt. Many unskilled immigrants migrated to the basin in the nineteenth century, stayed, and became farmers. This typically constituted a step up in social standing compared to their experiences in Europe.

The Mormons arrived in 1847 and established their base settlement in the Salt Lake valley. Mormon leaders chose followers from established households and new immigrants to settle the surrounding territories. Throughout the 1830s and the 1840s the Mormons migrated west after discovering golden plates that became *The Book of Mormon*. Joseph Smith and his followers faced violent opposition

Utah governor Gary Herbert, center, at a bill signing ceremony in Salt Lake City, Utah, on March 15, 2011. Herbert signed sweeping immigration reforms into law, leaving a long-lasting backlash across the conservative state. (HO/Reuters/Corbis)

in their attempts to establish a communitarian Mormon society. Mormons were forced out of Missouri, and then Illinois, where a mob killed Smith in 1844 while he was incarcerated on treason charges. No religious group in the nineteenth century had suffered more discrimination in the United States than the Mormons.

Several locations for a Western exodus were considered, including Texas, California, and Oregon. After Smith's death, church authorities decided to relocate to Utah, which was controlled by Mexico at the time. The hope was that this location would be sufficiently isolated in the wilderness to protect Mormons from outside influences and sufficiently unattractive to potential settlers to avoid previous troubles. In 1846, Brigham Young led over 3,000 Mormons West toward what would be called Zion. Arrival in the Salt Lake Valley on July 24, 1847, is commemorated in present-day Utah as a state and religious holiday, referred to as Pioneer Day.

Mormons settled in the most fertile areas of Ute land on the western border of their territories. These settlements were theocratic communities with a regulated cooperative economic system based in agriculture. Church literature emphasized economic opportunities in the Great Basin and the spiritual benefits of the religion. Beginning in the 1850s, overseas immigrants emigrated at a rate of approximately 3,000 per year. Over 90 percent of early immigrants were from Great Britain and Scandinavia.

Mormons relied on the Perpetual Emigrating Fund to assist poor converts in relocating to the Great Basin through loans and subsidization of related costs. Immigrants embarked in a tightly organized process that typically began with sailing from Liverpool to New Orleans, then ferrying up the Mississippi River, and journeying by wagon to Utah. This changed with the completion of the transcontinental railroad in 1869, which connected the territory with the rest of the country and helped shape the current boundaries of the state. The 1860s was the decade with the largest influx of immigrants to Utah. By 1870, over 30 percent of all Utah residents were foreign-born. By 1890, immigrants and their children constituted two-thirds of Utah's population.

Upon reaching Utah, Mormon immigrants were re-baptized and were able to become full participants in building a temporal and spiritual community through their religious convictions and daily work. Individual experiences varied from satisfaction and spiritual fulfillment to disillusionment and desertion. Mormons coped with internal division, apostasy, federal pressures to end polygamy, and struggles maintaining self-sustaining colonies throughout the settlement during the remainder of the nineteenth century.

Mormon leaders hoped to name the new territory Deseret, a word in *The Book of Mormon* that referred to the honeybee, which symbolized cooperative industry. Congress rejected this proposal, though the beehive later became the official state seal of Utah. The Mormons began to apply for statehood in 1850 and were repeatedly denied until 1896, when Utah became the 45th state in the Union. The practice of polygamy was officially outlawed as a condition of statehood. Today, several hundred thousand polygamists live in Utah. The informal position of law enforcement is to not enforce these laws unless children are in danger.

SECOND WAVE OF IMMIGRANTS

The development of the transcontinental railroad provided the opportunity to mine large quantities of coal, gold, silver, and copper. This attracted non-Mormon European immigrants in addition to many Chinese employees of the Central Pacific Railroad who remained in the area after the railroad was complete. English-speaking immigrants experienced upward mobility and decreasingly worked in mines. New immigrants from the Mediterranean, the Balkans, and to a lesser degree, Asia and the Middle East, filled these positions. Labor agents recruited gangs of unskilled laborers who would work for lower wages than Americans typically would. Italians, Finns, Slavs, Greeks, and Mexicans immigrated to Utah in large numbers. Two of the most prominent labor agents were Leonidas Skliris from Greece, who arranged for thousands of Serbians, Albanians, and Lebanese to emigrate to Utah, and Daigoro Hashimoto from Japan, who made arrangements for thousands of Koreans.

In contrast to Mormon pioneers, who crossed the plains and developed roads through forested mountains, new immigrants arrived by boxcar and occasionally by coach, typically from urban ghettos of large cites. The social environment was challenging. Government officials implemented a head tax and jailed aspiring workers for vagrancy. Existing workers were fearful that foreigners would take their jobs. These immigrants sought to make enough money to overcome poverty and return to their home countries with some capital to pursue a better occupation.

The first and second waves of Utah immigrants differed in several ways. The first wave of immigrants from the British Isles and Northern Europe were inspired by a grand vision of the Mormon pioneers. The second wave of immigrants from the Mediterranean and the Balkans encountered labor agents by chance and quickly found themselves at a mining camp that happened to be in Utah. These immigrants were often criticized or looked down upon for their "foreign looks" and "tainted blood." The nationwide view that immigrants from the Balkans and Mediterranean were inferior is deeper in Utah than in the country at large. Mormons preferred to hire fellow Mormons but the supply of willing workers did not meet the demand for manual labor.

In contrast to their predecessors, these immigrants were highly mobile and often moved in and out of the state depending on the availability of work. Company boardinghouses were scarce. Workers often worked in isolation laying track, building bridges or mining, and sleeping in tents, railroad cars, or self-made shacks made from gunpowder boxes. Five-year residency requirements for citizenship were not met in large numbers until the early 1920s. Differing national groups formed their own communities within the large enclave of Mormondom. In contrast to the Mormons, who often kept journals, history was spoken and sung.

Utah's foreign population peaked prior to World War I. Mining and railroad employment were at their height. Greeks and Italians were the largest ethnic groups and accounted for over 11 percent of the state's foreign-born population. During the beginning of the twentieth century, nearly 50,000 Mormons emigrated to the Intermountain West from the British Isles and 30,000 from Scandinavia. Smaller groups of Germans, Swiss, and French came as well.

Many immigrants returned home after earning a satisfactory amount of money. For example, from 1908 to 1920, approximately 5,000 Southern European immigrants returned to their native lands from Utah, mostly to Greece and Italy. The return rate of immigrants from Southern Italy was 49 percent and 30 percent from Northern Italy. This was comparatively higher than other countries in Europe, such as England, which experienced an 8 percent return rate, and Germany, which experienced 4 percent.

The Great Depression initiated a period of acceptance for immigrants in Utah. National loyalty to places of origin gave way to increased concern for life in America. This acceptance solidified with World War II and the military service conducted by second-generation immigrants. One notable exception was people of Japanese ancestry, who were interned at the Topaz relocation center in Millard County. The relaxation of immigration quotas after the war contributed to an increase of diversity in Utah. This was coupled with Mormon missionary efforts and an emphasis on preserving Utah's cultural heritage.

Beginning in the 1960s, the Mormon Church began encouraging converts to remain in their homelands and build churches, rather than migrate to Utah. Consequently, the majority of Mormons today live outside of the United States. The post–World War II era witnessed a resurgence of immigration to Utah, notably from Canada and the Netherlands. The Dutch government provided financial assistance to emigrants out of concerns surrounding overcrowding. Utah's Latino population grew between 1910 and 1930, due to immigration from Mexico, dropped during the Great Depression, and grew again after World War II. Most postwar Latino immigrants came from Colorado or New Mexico, rather than Mexico.

Southeast Asians resettled in Utah, beginning in the 1970s. From 1980 to 1986, over 9,000 refugees came to Utah. During this time, Utah was second only to Washington D.C. and Washington State in terms of resettled Southeast Asian refugees as a percentage of the overall population. At the same time, British roots remained strong. In 1970, Utah was the only state in which the United Kingdom was the most predominant ethnic origin for immigrants and their children.

Immigrants retained in part their languages and cultural heritage while assimilating to the norms of society at large. The 1990 U.S. Census data revealed that over 120,000 Utah residents over the age of five spoke a language other than English at home. About 87 percent of these people also spoke English "well" or "very well." Spanish was spoken at home by nearly 52,000 people and German by over 11,000 people.

Utah is unique in maintaining the numerical predominance of the Mormon Church, in the face of several periods of immigration. Mormons have comprised a minimum of 70 percent of Utah's population since the 1960s after a low of 60 percent in 1920. Mormons have a higher birthrate than Utah citizens at large, are less inclined to leave Utah, and contribute to their numbers in-state with regular proselytizing.

As a whole, the historical narrative of Utah immigration begins and ends with the LDS. Early church members were instrumental in the development of the state. The institution remained central to Utah's identity, culture, and politics. At the same time, immigration patterns in Utah have undergone several waves after the original Anglo-Saxon settlement in the mid-nineteenth century. Late nineteenth-century and early twentieth century immigration included various Southern Europeans. Mid-to-late twentieth-century immigration includes significant numbers of Southeast Asians and Latino/as.

TOPICAL ESSAYS

STATUS OF IMMIGRATION IN UTAH TODAY

Utah mirrors the United States as a whole in that immigration has been an important issue in recent years. The state also mirrors America in that it owes its existence and character to immigration. Ideologically, Utah is one of the most conservative states and is also one of the most partisan in its electoral support of Republican candidates. Immigration is commonly seen as an issue that has a distinct partisan and ideological split, with Democrats and liberals supporting laws that are more favorable to immigration and Republicans and conservatives supporting more restrictions on immigration.

Recent developments in immigration law have not necessarily followed this conventional wisdom. Legislation passed and signed into law in 2011 has not reflected a strong partisan split and is supported by Republican governor Gary Herbert. This bipartisan approach has attracted the attention of other states, which have suggested that they may use Utah's approach as a basis for dealing with immigration.

UTAH DEMOGRAPHICS

By comparison to most states, Utah is fairly homogeneous racially and ethnically. According to 2009 Census population estimates, Utah's population is 92.7 percent Anglo, as compared with 79.6 percent nationally. White persons not Latino/a amounted to 81.2 percent, and persons of Latino/a origin registered 12.3 percent. This number is not far from the national figure of 15.8 percent. When considering census data, it is important to note that persons may report as both Anglo and of Latino/a or Hispanic origin.

The Pew Hispanic Center is an excellent source of information on undocumented immigrants. The Pew Hispanic Center issues reports on many issues related to the Latino population, including reports on immigration, both legal and undocumented. In a 2010 report, the Pew Hispanic Center estimated Utah's "undocumented immigrant" population to be 110,000. This number represented a slight drop from the 2007 peak of 120,000, and mirrored the national trend which also saw a peak in undocumented immigrants in 2007 (www.pewhispanic.org 2010). The U.S. Census Bureau estimated Utah's 2009 population to be 2,784,572, meaning that Utah's undocumented immigrant population was approximately 3.9 percent of the state's population (U.S. Census Bureau 2010). About 3.9 percent was considerably lower that the undocumented immigrant populations of the nearby states of Arizona, California, and Nevada, which have 6.1, 6.9 , and 7.2 percent respectively. Utah's undocumented immigrant population was slightly higher than the national percentage of 3.6 percent.

THE UTAH COMPACT

A statement on immigration in Utah was drafted in 2010. Although not a specific objective, many saw this statement as a response to the vitriolic debate over immigration in Arizona. The Utah Compact was developed by government leaders, business leaders, interest groups, and individuals who wanted a comprehensive approach to the subject. Developers of the Utah Compact state the following:

> The Compact is based on Utah values and we urge our leaders to use these guiding principles as they address the complex challenges associated with a broken national immigration system. The Compact has broad support from community leaders, business associations, law enforcement officers and members of Utah's religious community.

> The Utah Compact was based upon five broad principles:

> - *Federal Solutions:* Immigration is a federal policy issue between the federal government and other countries—not Utah and other countries. We urge Utah's congressional delegation, and others, to lead efforts to strengthen federal laws and protect our national borders. We urge state leaders to adopt reasonable policies addressing immigrants in Utah.
> - *Law Enforcement:* We respect the rule of law and support law enforcement's professional judgment and discretion. Local law enforcement resources should focus on criminal activities, not civil violations of federal code.
> - *Families:* Strong families are the foundation of successful communities. We oppose policies that unnecessarily separate families. We champion policies that support families and improve the health, education and well-being of all Utah children.
> - *Economy:* Utah is best served by a free-market philosophy that maximizes individual freedom and opportunity. We acknowledge the economic role immigrants play as workers and taxpayers. Utah's immigration policies must reaffirm our global reputation as a welcoming and business-friendly state.
> - *A Free Society:* Immigrants are integrated into communities across Utah. We must adopt a humane approach to this reality, reflecting our unique culture, history and spirit of inclusion. The way we treat immigrants will say more about us as a free society and less about our immigrant neighbors. Utah should always be a place that welcomes people of goodwill. (The Utah Compact—Read the Utah Compact 2010)

The broad appeal of the Utah Compact could and still can be seen in each of its parts. Those who were concerned about state authority preempting national authority can look to the section on "Federal Solutions." Supporters of strengthening the borders and enforcing existing laws should also be encouraged by this section. The law enforcement community may be pleased that their time will not be occupied with enforcing federal immigration laws, which is a concern expressed by some in Arizona. The section on Strengthening "Families" appeals to the strong support of family life as outlined in statements from the LDS Church. The "Economy" section recognizes the inescapable fact that undocumented immigrants do have an impact on the state's economy and appeals to business interests.

Michael O. Leavitt, former Republican governor of Utah and secretary of health and human services under President George W. Bush, saw the Utah Compact as the basis for a national policy on immigration. Leavitt cited the nonpolitical origin of the Utah Compact as the basis of its appeal. The Utah Compact was endorsed by a wide variety of people and organizations with leanings toward both the Republican and Democratic Parties. Leavitt notes that the Utah Compact had been praised by such publications with divergent ideological views, citing the *New York Times* and the *Wall Street Journal* as examples.

Other states have taken note of the Utah Compact and have adopted similar approaches. Indiana and Maine have adopted Utah-style compacts, and other states such as Kansas, Texas, and Florida are considering similar approaches. A national version of the Utah Compact has already been largely written. Utah attorney general Mark Shurtleff touts "America's Compact" as a national comprehensive solution to immigration. Shurtleff hoped to see America's Compact signed by June 2011 but clearly, no comprehensive immigration reform has been passed.

The fate of the Utah Compact and legislation based upon it is uncertain. Leavitt echoes the federalism battle that has been prominent in Arizona in noting that the federal courts may conclude that Utah's new immigration statutes encroach upon enumerated federal powers.

INFLUENCE OF THE LDS CHURCH

The U.S. Constitution bars any state from recognizing an official state religion. However, Utah is one of a handful of states that does have a dominant religious culture. Only three states have a population in which the majority of residents are of one religious faith or denomination: Rhode Island is 51 percent Roman Catholic, Mississippi is 55 percent Baptist, and Utah is 57 percent Church of Jesus Christ of Latter-Day Saints. Often referred to as Mormons, the church leadership prefers the full title but recognizes the use of the shortened term LDS. Recognizing that LDS is certainly not an "established religion" by state government and that the Utah state constitution specifically forbids such an establishment, it is important to understand that the culture and laws of the state are influenced by the LDS Church.

The leadership of the LDS Church has had a strong inclination to remain silent on overtly political issues, preferring to allow its adherents to use their own conscience and beliefs in such matters. Many were surprised when the church chose to enter the debate over immigration. In 2010, the LDS Church issued the following statement in support of the Utah Compact:

> We follow Jesus Christ by loving our neighbors. The Savior taught that the meaning of "neighbor" includes all of God's children, in all places, at all times. We recognize an ever-present need to strengthen families. Families are meant to be together. Forced separation of working parents from their children weakens families and damages society. We acknowledge that every nation has the right to enforce its laws and secure its borders. All persons subject to a nation's laws are accountable for their acts in relation to them. Public officials should create and administer laws that reflect the best of our aspirations as a just and caring society. Such laws will properly balance love for neighbors, family cohesion, and the observance of just and enforceable laws. (Immigration-LDS Newsroom 2010)

Recent Utah Legislation

The 2011 Utah legislative session produced a number of proposals and four important pieces of legislation that are enacted into law. Each in its own way mirrored the Utah Compact and its goals.

House Bill (HB) 116, sponsored by state representative Bill Wright (R-Holden), was enacted into law with Governor Gary Herbert's signature on March 15, 2011. This bill was by far the more controversial of the two, and resulted in a great deal of attention from other states and from national proponents of a comprehensive approach to immigration reform. The bill, titled the "Utah Immigration Accountability and Enforcement Act," established a Guest Worker Program for undocumented immigrants, to be administered by the Utah Department of Workforce Services. To be eligible for the Guest Worker Program, a person must:

- Be 18 year of age or older or, if younger than 18 years of age, have the permission of a parent or guardian to obtain a guest worker permit;
- Live in the state of Utah, but not be lawfully present in the United States;
- Have worked or lived in the Unites States prior to May 10, 2011;
- Provide accurate contact information and regularly update such information;
- Provide documentation of a contract for hire under which the undocumented individual will begin providing services within at least 30 days of the day on which the undocumented individual obtains the guest worker permit;
- Agree to a criminal background check and not have been convicted of a felony;
- Provide evidence of good health;

- Be covered by a basic health insurance plan or provide evidence satisfactory to the department that the individual has no past due medical debt and agrees to have no medical debt that is past due during the term of the permit; and
- Hold a driving privilege card or provide evidence satisfactory to the department that the undocumented individual will not drive a motor vehicle while in the state of Utah. (Utah State Legislature 2011)

The Utah Immigration Accountability and Enforcement Act was passed by the Utah House of Representatives by a vote of 43–28 with 4 Not Voting. The bill was supported by a majority of both Democrats (14–3) and Republicans (29–25) (Project Vote Smart 2011). Many hailed the bill as a model for other states and for the U.S. government, not only due to its pro-immigrant and pro-business content but due to its bipartisan support. Referring to the Utah Compact, the Guest Worker Program was supportive of its goals of promoting a free-market economy and of promoting a free society.

Praise for the Utah Guest Worker Program came from both ends of the political spectrum. Jason Riley, writing for the business-oriented *Wall Street Journal*, remarked, "Apparently, there are still some conservative lawmakers left who don't abandon free-market principles in favor of reactionary populism when the topic turns to immigration" (Riley 2011). Ali Noorani, executive director of the Washington, D.C.-based National Immigration Forum, wrote, "The leadership in Utah, through the Compact, changed the debate around the country. It's clear the Compact has struck a chord with the silent majority that wants reform" (Loftin 2011).

While many praised the new Utah Guest Worker Program, others were not so enthusiastic. Soon after the bill became law, opponents of the new guest worker law launched a website seeking to repeal it. State representative Chris Herrod (R-Provo), referred to the law as providing amnesty to undocumented immigrants. Utah County Republican state delegate Brandon Beckham, who worked with the Utah Coalition on Illegal Immigration developing the petition, said that Governor Herbert should not have signed the bill as it was unconstitutional and would draw more undocumented immigrants to Utah. Beckham also sounded an ominous note for the governor's political future, saying, "As GOP delegates, we support the governor and everything he's done up until now. If he signs the bill, I don't think he's going to muster enough delegate support to make it past convention" (Daley 2011a).

Criticism also came from the political Left, which was traditionally the supporter of less-restrictive immigration laws. Froma Harrop, writing for the *Columbus Dispatch*, argued that one group that would suffer at the hands of the Utah Compact and the Utah Guest Worker Program were the American-born workers of Utah. Harrop writes, "Perhaps we can accurately call the Utah Compact 'pro-immigrant and pro-business.' Sadly, it's not pro-labor. But who asked the workers anyway?" (Harrop 2011).

As a companion to the Utah Guest Worker Program, the legislature also passed HB 497.This act, titled the Utah Illegal Immigration Enforcement Act, in some ways mirrored the well-publicized Arizona Senate Bill 1070 but is more moderate. Provisions of the act include the following:

- Requiring that an officer verify the immigration status of a person arrested for a felony or a class A misdemeanor and a person booked for class B or C misdemeanors and requiring that an officer attempt to verify immigration status for a person detained for a class B or C misdemeanor;
- Requiring that an officer may not consider race, color, or national origin, except as permitted by Utah and United States constitutions; and
- Requiring verification of immigration status regarding application for public services or benefits provided by a state or local government agency. (Utah State Legislature 2011)

The Utah Illegal Immigration Enforcement Act proved to be far more partisan that the Guest Worker Program. The bill passed the Utah House by a 59–15 vote, with Republicans voting Yea by 57–0 and Democrats voting Nay by 15–2. Referring to the Utah Compact, the Utah Illegal Immigration Enforcement Act was supportive of its goal of giving state and local law enforcement the tools it needed to enforce the law.

Criticism of the Utah Illegal Immigration Enforcement Act came mostly from the political Left. Ira Mehlman, media spokesman for the anti-immigration group Federation for American Immigration Reform, opposed all four recently passed Utah immigration laws. Mehlman sees the laws as an intrusion on federal authority and calls on an appropriate legal response. "What we'd like to see is the same sort of legal action that the Justice Department took against Arizona last year," said Mehlman in an interview with the Christian News Service (Mbom 2011).

In addition to the Guest Worker Program and the Utah Illegal Immigration Enforcement Act, the 2011 Utah legislature also passed two other pieces of legislation that did not draw as much attention. HB 466 established a partnership with the Mexican state of Nuevo León to allow workers to come to Utah using federal visas. HB 469 allowed Utah citizens to sponsor foreign nationals to live in Utah.

Public Opinion in Utah

Public opinion on HB 116, the Guest Worker Program, and HB 497, the enforcement law, is supportive of both. According to a poll by the opinion research firm Dan Jones & Associates, 54 percent of Utahans believe that enforcement by local police is either "definitely" or "probably" worth the expenditure of additional resources. About 71 percent of Utahans either "strongly" or "somewhat" favor state-issued work permits for undocumented immigrants (Daley 2011b).

Conclusion

The Utah Compact and the Guest Worker Program have placed Utah squarely on the front lines in the immigration debate in America. Utah's efforts are an example of the federal system of government at work, with the states operating as 50 separate policy laboratories. Recently passed legislation has been praised and criticized by both liberals and conservatives. Immigration has been and remains firmly rooted in the age-old federalism debate. The new laws will doubtless face federal court challenges, which may or may not be successful. Wendy Sefsaf, spokeswoman for the Washington, D.C.-based Immigration Policy Center, sums up the debate and Utah's role in it, saying, "I think, if anything, what it really can do and what we should celebrate is the way in which Utah has handled the issue and that has opened the door to change the debate" (Montero 2011a).

NOTABLE GROUPS

Catholic Community Services of Utah

The Catholic Community Services of Utah is based in Salt Lake City and aids both immigrants and refugees. They facilitate refugee resettlement (regardless of religion or belief) and administer basic legal help, connect refugees to employers, and provide information and referrals for basic services. This office was established in 1945 and opened a Vincentian thrift shop in 1967, as well as a soup kitchen for the homeless. The group initiated its Refugee Resettlement Program in 1974, under the guidance of Terence M. Moor and began to aid unaccompanied minor refugees the next year. Their service outreach expanded to immigrants in 1981. Today, they continue running these multiple programs, helping those who need it most.

BIBLIOGRAPHY

Booth, Fowler R., A. Hertzke, and L. Olson. *Religion and Politics in America: Faith, Culture, and Strategic Choices.* Boulder, CO: Westview Press, 2010.

Carson, S. "European Immigration into America's Great Basin, 1850–1870." *The Journal of Interdisciplinary History* 34, no. 4 (2004): 569–94.

Catholic Community Services of Utah. Catholic Community Services of Utah Webpage. http://www.ccsutah.org/programs/immigration-and-refugee-resettlement. Accessed February 27, 2014.

Daley, John. "Immigration Bills' Foes Turn up Heat." *Desert News*, March 15, 2011a. http://www.deseretnews.com/article/700118569/Immigration-bills-foes-turn-up-heat.html?pg=all. August 11, 2014.

Daley, John. *Poll: Utahns Undecided on Immigration Solution*. KSL.com, February 21, 2011b. http://www.ksl.com/?nid=833&sid=14463232. Accessed February 22, 2011.

Fox, Jeffrey. *Latter Day Political Views*. New York: Lexington Books, 2006.

Harrop, Froma. "Utah Immigration Deal Exploits Workers." *Columbus Dispatch*, March 12, 2011. http://www.dispatch.com/content/stories/editorials/2011/03/12/utah-immigration-deal-exploits-workers.html. August 11, 2014.

Immigration-LDS Newsroom. 2010. http://newsroom.lds.org/official statement/immigration. Accessed March 29, 2014.

Jensen, Richard. "Immigration to Utah." In *Utah History Encyclopedia*. Salt Lake City: University of Utah Press, 1994.

Leavitt, Michael O. "Utah Compact Provides Starting Point for Congress." *Desert News*, April 10, 2011. http://www.deseretnews.com/article/700125632/Utah-Compact-provides-starting-point-for-Congress.html?pg=all. August 11, 2014.

Loftin, Josh. *Public Opinion Online*. 2011. http://www.publicopiniononline.com/fdcp?unique=1302802354687. Accessed March 29, 2014.

Mbom, Lambert. *Utah Immigration Laws Go Too Far, FAIR Says*. March 18, 2011. http://www.cnsnews.com/news/article/utah-immigration-laws-go-too-far-fair-says.htm. Accessed March 29, 2014.

Montero, David. "Group Says Utah's Immigration Reform Will Be Tough Sell." *Salt Lake Tribune*, April 12, 2011a. http://www.sltrib.com/sltrib/politics/51614025-90/congress-department-enforcement-federal.html.csp. August 11, 2014.

Montero, David. "Supporters Push for National Version of Utah Compact." *Salt Lake Tribune*, April 6, 2011b. http://www.sltrib.com/sltrib/politics/51569783-90/compact-utah-immigration-america.html.csp. August 11, 2014.

Montero, David. "Utahns Launch Website to Repeal Guest-Worker Law." *Salt Lake Tribune*, March 30, 2011c. http://www.sltrib.com/sltrib/politics/51530973-90/bill-guest-herbert-immigrants.html.csp. Accessed August 11, 2014.

Olson, John Alden. "Proselytism, Immigration, and Settlement of Foreign Converts to the Mormon Culture in Zion." *Journal of the West* 6, no. 2 (1967): 189–204.

Ostling, R., and J. Ostling. *Mormon America: The Power and the Promise*. New York: Harper Collins, 1999.

Ostman, Kim. "From Finland to Zion: Immigration to Utah in the 19th Century." *The Journal of Mormon History* 36, no. 4, (2010): 166–207.

Papanikolas, Helen. *The Peoples of Utah*. Salt Lake City: Utah Historical Society, 1976.

Project Vote Smart. 2011. http://www.votesmart.org/issue_keyvote_member.php?cs_id=33637 and http://www.votesmart.org/ussue_keyvote_member.php?cs_id=34285. Accessed March 29, 2014.

Riley, Jason. "Utah Seeks a Better Way on Illegal Immigration." *Wall Street Journal*, March 5, 2011. http://online.wsj.com/news/articles/SB1000142405274870358000457618052252139701 8. Accessed August 11, 2014.

U.S. Census Bureau. 2010. quickfacts.census.gov. 2010. http://quickfacts.census.gov/qfd/. Accessed March 29, 2014.

"The Utah Compact—Read the Utah Compact." 2010. http://www.theutahcompact.com. Accessed March 29, 2014.

45

VERMONT

William P. Kladky

CHRONOLOGY

1535	The French explorer Jacques Cartier (1491–1557) becomes the first European to see Vermont.
1609	Samuel de Champlain (1574–1635), a French explorer coming from Quebec, discovers Lake Champlain.
1616	The Dutch government claims all the land between the Connecticut and Delaware Rivers, including Vermont.
1620	King James I issues a charter to the Plymouth Company claiming all land between the Atlantic and the Pacific Oceans (including Vermont).
1666	The French military constructs Fort Ste. Anne on Isle LaMotte, the site of the first white settlement.
1676	The King of France authorizes the first grants of land on Lake Champlain.
1690	The British build a small fort at Chimney Point.
1724	The British make Vermont's first permanent settlement at Fort Dummer, named after acting governor William Dummer (1677–1761) of Massachusetts, in what is now Brattleboro.
1731	Under Seigneur Gilles Hocquart (1694–1783), the French build a fort and begin settlement at Chimney Point.
1734	The French construct Fort St. Frederic which gives them control of the New France/Vermont border region in the Lake Champlain Valley.
1741	King George II rules that New Hampshire's southern border is along the Merrimack River until it turns north, with the border then going due west to New York.

1749	Governor Benning Wentworth (1696–1770) makes the first New Hampshire grant for the town of Bennington.
1759	The French abandon their settlement at Chimney Point.
1760	The Crown Point Military Road from Springfield to Chimney Point is completed across Vermont.
1761	In a bitter land jurisdiction dispute with New York, Governor Wentworth resumes giving New Hampshire Grants.
1764	The Privy Council decides that the Connecticut River is the boundary between New Hampshire and New York.
1770	The Green Mountain Boys organize to protect New Hampshire Grants.
1772	Windsor takes out its second town charter to become part of the Royal Colony of New York.
1774	The Scottish American Land Company brings Scottish settlers to Ryegate & Barnet.
1775	Ethan Allen (1738–1789) leads the settlers and the Green Mountain Boys to capture Fort Ticonderoga.
1776	The American military constructs the Mount Independence fort in Orwell.
1777	Vermont declares itself a republic in Windsor, adopting its first constitution with universal male suffrage, public schools, and abolishing slavery.
1778	The first general assembly establishes two counties, Bennington (west) and Unity (east), as well as votes to confiscate and sell Tory estates to fund a militia.
1779	The Bayley–Hazen Military Road stretches from Peacham to Lowell. The state establishes property rights for women, as well as the first state seal, designed by Ira Allen and cut by Reuben Dean.
1780	Led by the British, the last major Indian raid occurs in Royalton.
1781	The government of Massachusetts gives up all of its claims to Vermont.
1783	Vermont relinquishes all of its claims to towns in New York and New Hampshire.
1785	The first marble quarry opens in Dorset.
1786	Vermont asks 100 Shays supporters at Shaftsbury to leave the state.
1787	Castleton, Vermont's first college, opens, with a charter from the general assembly.
1789	New York agrees to negotiate with Vermont about the question of statehood.
1791	Vermont becomes the 14th state, and the University of Vermont is chartered.
1805	The state chooses Montpelier as its capital.
1810	The U.S. Census finds that there are 217,895 people in Vermont.
1823	The Champlain Canal opens, connecting Lake Champlain and the Hudson River. Alexander Twilight becomes the first African American to earn a college degree at Middlebury College.

1826	Horace Greeley of West Haven begins his first newspaper apprenticeship at the Northern Spectator in Poultney.
1834	The Vermont Anti-Slavery Society is formed.
1837	John Deere patents the steel plow, and Thomas Davenport patents the first electric motor.
1845	The Vermont Central Railroad Company is incorporated.
1850	The Vermont legislature passes an act to oppose the operation of the Fugitive Slave Act and sends protests to other state legislatures.
1855	Vermont elects its first Republican governor.
1864	The Confederates stage the St. Albans Raid, the northern-most Civil War battle.
1865	The State Agricultural College opens at the University of Vermont as a Land Grant College.
1876	The Vermont legislature incorporates Mary Fletcher Hospital, the first nonprofit voluntary hospital founded by a secular woman.
1881	Chester A. Arthur of Fairfield, vice president of the United States, becomes 21st president of the United States upon the assassination of President James Garfield.
1898	The first state highway commissioner is authorized.
1900	The U.S. Census identifies 343,641 people in Vermont.
1911	The Vermont Senate rejects the full voting franchise for women.
1920	The U.S. Census finds that Vermont's population is 352,428.
1921	Edna Beard (1877–1928) of Orange becomes Vermont's first congressional representative.
1923	J. Calvin Coolidge Jr. (1872–1933) of Plymouth becomes the 30th U.S. president upon the death of President Warren G. Harding. The state adopts a gasoline tax and begins regulation of airplanes.
1930	The U.S. Census finds 359,611 people in Vermont.
1934	The U.S. Supreme Court decides that the low-water mark on the western side of the Connecticut River is the Vermont border.
1936	A statewide referendum defeats a Green Mountain Parkway proposal.
1941–1945	Over 50,000 Vermonters enlist or are drafted into military service, with 1,233 casualties.
1950	The U.S. Census discovers that there are 377,747 people in Vermont.
1953	The SS *Ticonderoga* makes the last steamboat trip on Lake Champlain.
1954	Vermont elects Consuelo Northrop Bailey (1899–1976) of Burlington as the first woman lieutenant governor.
1962	Vermont elects its first Democratic governor, Philip H. Hoff (1924–) of Burlington, in over 100 years.
1963	The Stowe-Morrisville Airport, the first state-owned airport, opens.

1964	Victory, Granby, and Jamaica become the last towns in the state to receive electricity.
1968	Vermont bans billboards.
1971	The Vermont state legislature strengthens the state law against discrimination in hiring based on gender.
1984	Voters elect Madeleine M. Kunin (1933–) of Burlington as the first female governor of Vermont.
1999-Present	Undocumented Mexican workers are a significant part of dairy employees in Vermont.
2000	Vermont's Civil Unions Law, giving same-sex couples rights and responsibilities similar to marriage, takes effect. The U.S. Census finds 608,827 people in Vermont.
2011	Protestors acting on behalf of the Vermont Migrant Solidarity Project of the Vermont Workers' Center denounce the arrest of undocumented migrant workers in Vermont.
2012	The legislature passes and the governor signs a bill making driver's licenses and ID cards available to everyone.
2013	The foreign-born comprise 3.9 percent of the population, with well over half being naturalized citizens.

HISTORICAL OVERVIEW

BEFORE EUROPEAN EXPLORATION

Vermont was home to the nation of various Algonquian-speaking tribes, including the Mohican and Abenaki, and the Iroquois nation. Through numerous wars in the seventeenth century, the Iroquois become dominant. But that was until European exploration began in earnest. Numbering about 4,000, the Native Americans then were caught between the two rival European powers, France and Great Britain, switching their allegiance from one to the other. Most Abenaki allied with France, which had some successes in converting them to Catholicism. When the British were triumphant, this alliance resulted in the Abenaki's decline, and thus began the expansion of English farm settlements northward along the Connecticut River Valley into Vermont.

While Vermont was initially explored and chartered by the Dutch in 1616, the British claimed the same area in 1620. After a struggle, in 1664, the British drove the Dutch away. The new British royal colony of New York simply assumed the boundaries of the Dutch New Netherlands, which led to a serious boundary dispute in the 1770s. The population grew very slowly. Indian trails were the basis of most of Vermont's early roads until the 1790s when significant upgrading began. The military built some of these roads during wartime to connect forts or to facilitate defense or invasion.

Eighteenth Century

The first permanent settlement, Fort Dummer was built in 1724 (near current Brattleboro) to protect the first real British settlement in Vermont (Windham County). Trading posts were set up by the Massachusetts authorities to encourage Indian cooperation, but conflicts continued. At the time, there were some Dutch settlers on the Hoosic River and near Emerald Lake, but they did not stay.

The conclusion of the long-lasting French and Indian Wars (which began in 1689) in 1760 led to increased British farming and fur hunting settlement in the upper Connecticut River Valley, including Vermont. The cessation of the violence was welcomed, as some 1,196 English settlers had been captured and taken to Canada from New England during the Wars. With the signing of the Treaty of Paris in 1783, British settlers poured in. Scotch settlers arrived in 1773 as part of the Scottish American Land Company. Many new immigrants came for jobs, their trek somewhat aided by the slow development of the road system.

Vermont's eventual joining the American Revolution began in an effort to protect the legal ownership of settlers' properties from New York. Families who settled in the Grants (as the New Hampshire titled lands are known) were confident that if they moved their families, built farms, and worked the land, their claims would be honored. But in a prolonged dispute between the royal counties of New Hampshire and New York, England's King George III (1738–1820) ruled in favor of New York in 1764. When New York then issued titles to the same land as the Grants and when these Yorkers (i.e., the New York landholders) arrived to claim their land, they were violently harassed by the "Green Mountain Boys." The Green Mountain Boys destroyed the few Yorker homes and drove away the inhabitants. The Grants dispute led to the Westminster Massacre (or Riots) of March 13, 1775. Viewed by some historians as the first battle of the American Revolution, several protesting Grant holders were killed by British troops.

Vermont then resolved to become a state. At the statehood convention held in Westminster in 1777, the first name chosen for the state was "New Connecticut." It was changed to Vermont when the conventioneers were informed that it was duplicating another territory's name. The Vermont Constitution was rather unique in two basic ways. First, though it utilized the Pennsylvania Constitution as a model with a general assembly and other standard features, Vermont also had a Bill of Rights that abolished slavery and gave voting rights to all freemen. Thus, Vermont's Constitution was the first to outlaw adult slavery. Second, Vermont was the only state to separate a person's financial situation from their eligibility to vote. Other states used property ownership or tax-paying status, but Vermont did not. Free blacks were also enfranchised in the state, one of only six to do so.

There remained two problems that prevented Vermont's joining the new nation. The Grants-Yorkers dispute still was not settled. In addition, border disputes over 16 towns arose with New Hampshire. After learning that the U.S. Congress was intending to side against its interests, Vermont was so angered it began negotiating in 1780–1781 with Great Britain to join Canada, and even tried to annex lands from New Hampshire. After long negotiations, New York and Vermont settled their differences in 1790. The U.S. Congress intervened and had a commission decide the states' land problems. This resulted in Vermont paying $30,000 to settle the claims and keeping the land. With this, Vermont ratified the U.S. Constitution and on March 4, 1791, became the 14th state.

After statehood, infrastructure improvements increased in Vermont. Under a 1797 law, over half of landowners in a town had to agree to a tax assessment to pay for road construction. Another way to build roads was for a private person or company to be given a charter to do so and then collect a toll. Understandably, toll roads were hated by many, and some were inspired to build a "shunpike" which bypassed a toll road.

Nineteenth Century

Around 1800, Vermont consisted mostly of farmers. As it has been earlier, farming in the state was essentially based on self-sufficiency. The state's population was young, with over 50 percent under 16 years. Between 1800 and 1820, Vermont was changing from a frontier into a settled society. The state alternated between periods of very slow growth and a rapidly surging population. From 1790 to 1830, Vermont's population increased a startling 225 percent, making it one of the fastest-growing states. This was accompanied by significant migrations between different parts of the state, primarily from the already settled south to the north, as well as from the elevated areas to the valleys. Land values spiked 170 percent during the 1791–1806 period because of the increased population's demand for property. Migration was increasing because of the availability of jobs in new industries. During this time, the state became a major iron producer. Vergennes' Monkton Iron Company was one of the largest in the nation in 1813. Transportation improvements also helped. Probably the first canal in the United States was built around Bellows Falls in 1802. Several other canals were constructed and operated during this time.

However, immigration dropped considerably in the 1810s because embargoes against Canadian trade before the upcoming war with England hurt business, stimulating some out-migration. The state's location on the national border was proving a hindrance as well as a help. Disease also caused population declines, along with 1811s severe floods.

Fortunately, the state's agricultural sector was growing steadily, aided by technological improvements. When Merino sheep were brought into Vermont in 1811, sheep farming changed. Many farms were merged to gain the higher profitability of the large-scale raising of sheep. This was helped by road improvements, which spiked after counties were given the authority to assess taxes for road construction in 1827. Development of Burlington and the state were also assisted by the opening of the 60-mile Champlain Canal in 1823.

By 1837, there were over 1 million sheep—mostly on very large farms—whose wool was being shipped to the Massachusetts and Vermont textile mills. This economic development was aided by advances in education and transportation, as well as land-inheritance policies that produced smaller and smaller farms that were unsustainable. The opening of the Erie Canal and access to western markets also pushed agriculture in a decidedly commercial direction.

But there were negatives associated with the development of commercial farming. The flourishing wool industry's demand for larger and larger acreage increased land prices. Many young, would-be farmers could not pay the higher prices, and out-migrated to more affordable lands in the West. During the 1830s and 1840s, Vermont had its first substantial out-migration. Emigrants left for southern Michigan, northern Illinois, and southeastern Wisconsin. Moreover, the wool-driven agricultural boom was short-lasting, and it led to deforestation and environmental problems. The collapse of Vermont's wool industry in the 1840s also spurred out-migration.

Vermonters very reluctantly supported the War of 1812. One strong reason for its reticence was that the federal trade embargoes stopped all legal trade with Canada, retarding commerce. After the war, though, trade commenced again and the state continued its slow population growth.

In 1840, Vermont's population was 291,948, and its largest town was Burlington. Plank roads (i.e., a dirt road covered with a series of planks) were constructed and utilized during this period, lasting until roughly 1861. This type of road proved too expensive to maintain, and companies eventually graveled or macadamized the roads. During the early 1840s, a utopian community was established at Putney by John Humphrey Noyes (1811–1886), but later moved to Oneida, New York. A few migrants trickled in to live in that experiment that practiced (very) complex marriage, male continence, and spiritual self-improvement.

The construction of railroads occurred comparatively later in Vermont history in the 1840s. This primarily was because of the state's relative paucity of population and industry but was aggravated by fierce competition between the railroad companies. When railroads arrived, growth was spotty, as towns expanded along the routes but shrank inland. The population did increase in a few cities and towns, but overall there was stagnation.

Out-migration was a problem. The West's gold rush in the later 1840s stimulated out-migration, and by 1850, some 11,000 Vermonters were in California. Many have gone to other western states as well. The 1870 Census found that Montana had 227 Vermont- and New Hampshire-born residents, with most having arrived via migration with temporary stays in several other states ("chain migration"). An indication that more out-migrants were on the way was the formation of Kansas emigration societies in Montpelier, Rutland, and Randolph.

At the same time, Vermont shared in the increase in national immigration in the latter 1840s and 1850s. Most new arrivals in the state came to work. Vermont's first industrial workers were mostly female Yankees who had moved into towns from farms. New industries were started in Guilford, Brattleboro, and Springfield, among others. Mostly English and Scotch immigrants owned these first mines, factories, and railroads. In turn, they hired new immigrants as their manual laborers. Many immigrants came from Europe and other areas in North America. French Canadians—pushed from Quebec by a poor economy, farming failures, and discrimination—immigrated to Vermont to work on farms, mills, and in the scale industry. After Thaddeus Fairbanks (1796–1886) patented the platform scale for weighing hemp in 1821, his E&T Fairbanks Company began manufacturing scales and hiring workers.

Immigration and travel within—and from—Vermont was aided greatly by substantial railroad development. In the late 1840s, the Rutland and Burlington Railroad and the Vermont Central Railroad expanded. In 1850, the Connecticut and Passumpsic River Railroad was completed. Some types of immigrants faced abject discrimination, even from their fellow immigrants. Whatever their education and experience, though, the Irish and the African Americans became domestic servants and the lowest status manual laborers. While Italians, French Canadians, Swedes, Scots, and Welsh were recruited to work in the growing industries, the Irish did the very difficult work building the railroads. This immigration influx kept the population stable but resulted in marked social changes. The majority lived near their work in the urban areas. Their foreign customs, languages, and religions were very different from the Yankees. This led to a surge of nativism among existing residents, which included the burning of Burlington's first Catholic Church in 1838. The ongoing immigration spurred over 100 members of the Vermont House to belong to the Know-Nothing Party in 1850. Other nativism followed.

The 1850 Census discovered that 10 percent of the state's population was foreign-born, and some 15,377 Irish residents were foreign-born, the largest grouping. Most lived and worked in railroad towns such as Bellows Falls, Northfield, Rutland, Burlington, and St. Albans. Irish women mostly were employed as mill workers, domestic servants, and farm help. There were approximately 14,000 Québécois immigrants in Vermont in 1850, most resident in the northwestern counties. They comprised 14 percent of the population of Burlington and Colchester. Vermont's population would have decreased during this period if not for these immigrants.

Beginning with the 1850s, Vermont's farm population expanded after the introduction of ice-cooled railroad cars permitted dairy products to be shipped to distant markets. By 1860, Burlington was Vermont's major commercial and manufacturing city. It also was the most ethnically diverse with 2,165 foreign-born of its 7,716 population.

During the Civil War, the state sent about 11 percent of its men to fight, suffering 5,000 casualties. Many others did not return to Vermont after hostilities ended, creating a labor shortage that further hampered development. Railroad development quickened and consolidated after the war was concluded, assisting and benefiting from the rise of the lumber industry. The Central Vermont Railroad became the largest in New England, with 793 miles of track and two steamship lines in four states. Immigration also increased. The state's foreign-born population swelled to an historic high of 14 percent during 1870–1910. The first German Jews came to Vermont around 1850 to the Poultney area. In the early 1870s, Russian Jews migrated to Burlington, mostly working as peddlers and they eventually built many businesses and the state's first synagogue.

Around this time, Vermont also received its first minor wave of aesthetic tourism. This was inspired by the state's beautiful landscape, the Hudson River school of painters, and the writings of the Transcendentalists. The railroads also advertised the state's beauty to attract riders, and the state government became the first in the nation to have a "Bureau of Publicity" (Klyza and Trombulak 1999, 107).

But the state's population continued to go through boom and slow-growth intervals. In the 1850s, the population rose only 0.3 percent, but jumped 4.9 percent in the 1860s to 330,551. In the 1870s, the population increased a paltry 0.5 percent and rural towns actually lost population. Improvements kept coming, though. In the late 1880s, improvements to the Clarendon and Pittsford Railroad, owned by the Vermont Marble Company, connected the quarries to markets around the country. There was also a new immigration surge, with Russians and Poles coming to Springfield to work the machine shops. Immigrants came to serve in the military, for the high wages, or because of religious persecution. Resultantly, the state's population rose to 332,286 in 1880.

There was another slowdown during the 1880s, plagued by the economic depression. Out-migration rose again. By the 1880s, only 58 percent of native-born Vermonters lived in the state. The state tried to help, enticing Italian marble carvers to come to Proctor. But stagnation was the norm. During that decade, the state's population grew by only 136 to 332,422 by 1890. Vermont's level of out-migration reached a peak in the late 1890s, with 81 percent of its towns experiencing population declines in this period.

The growth in state's tourism helped slightly to reverse the trend. The state also made infrastructure improvements in an attempt to stir development. In 1885, an electric railway was constructed in Burlington. Several other electric railways were built in Barre, Bennington, Brattleboro, and Montpelier in the 1880s and 1890s. By 1898, tourism, financed by the railroads, was growing steadily. The tourism, though, did not produce many new residents.

Facing continued stagnation during the 1890s, Vermont recruited northern Europeans, mostly Swedes, to work in the abandoned farms. Swedish stonecutters worked Beebe's granite mines. Brattleboro had sufficient Swedish immigrants by 1893 to have a Swedish Lutheran Church. Barre became known as the "Italian Swiss Colony" due to the numerous Swedish stonecutters who had arrived. Others also came for employment. English copper miners worked the Ely mines in the 1880s. Finnish immigrants, escaping famine and forced army service, came to the Chester-Mt. Holly area to farm or to work in the Ludlow mills. Welsh immigrants arrived to work in the Fair Haven-Castleton-Poultney slate mines.

Increasing numbers and varieties of immigrants also began arriving from southern and eastern Europe but were not as welcomed into the community. Industries in Brattleboro, Burlington, Springfield, and Windsor attracted workers fleeing depressed Spain and Portugal. Some Christian immigrants from Greece and Lebanon also settled in. Peddling was the way many worked; many Greeks worked in the restaurant industry. Chain migration characterized many of their treks. More Italian immigrants went to Barre to work in the granite industry and to White River for the railroad industry. The population of Italians increased from 7 in 1890 to 4,594 by 1910.

Russians and Poles came to Bellows Falls, Springfield, Morrisville, Proctor, and West Rutland to work in the granite, marble, and scale industries. Many fled political oppression, with chain migration being the usual pattern. The first Russians came to Springfield in the 1890s to work in the Slack shoddy mill (i.e., a mill where lower-quality woolen cloth was made from the fibers that were produced by grinding woolen rags). After James Hartness (1861–1934) moved his revolving hydraulic engine (a water pump with interchangeable parts) to Springfield, the town became a major manufacturing center as workers made Hartness's turret lathe. Thousands of immigrants came to work, including many Russians.

Unfortunately, this strong state and national immigration led many "old immigrants," the business owners and government officials to advocate for restrictive immigration. In 1891, strict control of immigrants began and Vermont had a role. Vermont U.S. senator William P. Dillingham (1843–1923) especially railed against immigration, and his first speech in 1902 stimulated the national debate over restricting Chinese immigration. Dillingham was chair of the now-notorious Dillingham Commission from 1907 to 1911, which proposed eugenic immigration policies that were adopted in the following years.

1900 to World War II

As the century turned, more of Vermont's immigrants lived in rural areas than in towns and cities. The state's immigration totals were lower than most other states, and the population was comparatively slow-growing. Some modernization had occurred. Railroads were the dominant means of transportation in the state with over 1,000 track miles crisscrossing Vermont by 1900. But the advent of the automobile transformed Vermont. The state began legally restricting vehicle operation in 1902. There were only 275 autos in the state in 1905, but their owners started a club (Cheyney 1976, 218; Harrison 2006, 55). Along with continued immigration, Vermont also had a slight increase in the numbers of African American at the beginning of the twentieth century. In the 1910s and 1920s, the state comprised 0.5 percent African American.

Unsurprisingly, the developing uproar over national immigration policies extended to Vermont during this time. Though Irish, French Canadians, and Italian immigrants—among many others from various nations—were essential for the state's continuing growth, these new arrivals were allegedly different. Their Catholic religion, different languages, and odd cultural traditions stirred racial and ethnic prejudices. This was worsened by the fact that the immigrants were competitors for jobs and housing, particularly in periods of economic stagnation. Resultantly, the Ku Klux Klan (KKK) was swelled by hundreds of Vermont residents in the 1920s. In Montpelier and Burlington, the KKK burned crosses and conducted raids on Catholic cemeteries and churches. The response was swift and effective. City ordinances banned meetings of those wearing masks or disguises, and there were coordinated boycotts of business owners who were KKK members. The KKK subsequently lost its membership and power.

The state's love affair with the automobile continued to flourish. During the 1920s, the number of cars in the state tripled to about 90,000. More cars quickly translated into demands for better and more roads, and the state obliged. New businesses sprang up to utilize the automobile. The first passenger bus line began in 1922, and a boom in travel ensued. Many truck routes were also operating in the state by the end of the 1920s, aiding development.

But as the state's population increased and bucolic land use turned commercial and residential, concern for the environment deepened. Founded in 1910, Vermont's Green Mountain Club played a vital role in publicizing, making accessible, and preserving the state's hills. The club's expanding membership was responsible for opening and maintaining trails and building shelters.

The great flood of 1927 devastated the state, causing some $21 million of damage. Vermont's roads, bridges, and railways were devastated. In response, the state legislature passed an $8.5 million bond issue and secured over $2.5 million from the federal government. The funds greatly aided the state's recovery.

Two years later, the Great Depression struck hardest in Vermont's cities. Soaring unemployment in the 1930s led to shrinking tax lists and spiking costs for poor relief. Several cities and towns requested the state to seek federal aid to help with their payroll costs. The federal Civilian Conservation Corps (CCC) and the Public Works Administration were crucial in modernizing the state's infrastructure and providing jobs. The Farm Security Administration and Works Progress Administration helped the rural areas, as did the government's control of milk prices and rural electrification. The CCC made Vermont's mountains and forests accessible, and employed 11,243 during 1933–1942. They built bridges, dams, and roadways, cut trails to mountains, and opened up state forests. However, environmental concerns stirred the state's voters to reject the federal government's $18 million offer to build the Green Mountain Parkway across the Mountains from Massachusetts to Canada.

Steady, though small, immigration during the 1930s helped the state deal with the Depression. In the 1930s, some 30 percent of Vermont's rural residents were either first- or second-generation immigrants. Some 39 percent were French Canadian and 18 percent were British or Irish. The 1920s level of immigration had been significant for Vermont but not compared to other states or the nation as a whole. Vermont was the most homogenous state in 1930, with some 72 percent being native-born. Because of new immigration laws, the World Wars, and the Great Depression, the state's relatively small immigration virtually stopped in this decade. More emigrated than entered. Afterward, the majority of immigrants were female. Most had been solicited—along with African Americans—as workers in industry.

In 1936, Vermont was one of only two states that voted for the Republican Alfred M. Landon (1887–1987) against President Franklin D. Roosevelt. Vermont reinforced its particular reputation when it declared war on Germany in September, 1941-three months ahead of the official declaration by the U.S. government. This was done by the legislature to award service members a financial bonus for serving.

THE INTERSTATE HIGHWAY SYSTEM

The construction of the interstate highway system to Vermont brought tremendous changes. Like railroads in the previous century, this new transportation system was a major factor in the transformation of the state. It brought to the state economic development, urban growth, and new and different people. By 1950, the state had developed a good but limited road system linking its cities, towns, and recreational areas. Travel to other states was long and laborious. While many came for the summer to Vermont's camps and lakes, they did not settle permanently. The development of businesses and industries were hampered because of the extended time periods that have to be factored into their work. Railroads provided interstate service, but this was only good if the plant was located near a station or line.

Unlike the railroads, the interstates led more people to settle in the state as permanent residents, reversing the trend of the past century. Interstate construction occurred between 1957 and 1982, resulting in the 381 miles of Interstates 89, 91, and 93. The development of the system finished off most railroad service in Vermont, and there was little passenger service by the 1960s. But the interstate highway system made Vermont a much quicker and easier commute for many distant regions. Accompanying this, though, was increasing and conflicting demands on the land which caused environmental problems.

These transportation changes accompanied other changes affecting much of Vermont during the 1950s and 1960s. Agricultural concentration continued, the number of industrial jobs fell, and white-collar professional and service employment grew. As in the rest of New England, textile mills and the machine-tool industry were the major employers in the early 1950s. By the 1970s, IBM and the ski industry employed more than any other in Vermont. During the accompanying population boom between 1960 and 1990, new types of immigrants and migrants arrived: professionals, "hippies," "ski bums," and prosperous second-home owners who decided to become permanent residents. Racially, the state was one of the whitest states with only small numbers of minorities in the cities. Tensions increased between newcomers and natives over land use and politics.

Skiing in Vermont changed dramatically with the coming of the interstate highway system, beginning in the 1950s. In 1947, the state had only seven major ski areas, but by 1970 there were 34. The state saw skiing as economic development, spending over $30 million in the 1950s and 1960s on the expanding industry. It worked. The increasing popularity of skiing brought Vermont new jobs and an attractive image. A typical story was the development of the town of Stowe. A farming area, Stowe became a tourist destination after the Civil War. After the transportation improvements in the twentieth century, the summer tourist season expanded. Many now come during the fall foliage season as well in the winter to ski. Businesses expanded and the population increased. Stowe now has become the "Ski Capital of the East," and is a resort community almost all year.

Concerns about the environment have led to the state's enactment of much important environmental legislation. Billboards were banned in 1968, and in 1970, the Vermont state legislature passed Act 250, the first major land development control act, as well as Act 252 which set water quality standards. In 1972, a bottle deposit law was enacted to control litter. Act 200, strengthening local, regional, and state planning efforts, was passed in 1988. Many held that Act 250 has been successful in controlling and improving the quality of development in the state, but has weaknesses that have allowed inappropriate economic development.

THE VARIETY OF RECENT IMMIGRATION

Immigration to Vermont has changed in recent decades. During the 1980s and 1990s, the Vermont Refugee Assistance (VRA) provided assistance to immigrants fleeing Chile, El Salvador, Lebanon, Ethiopia, Somalia, and other countries. During 1988–1989, for example, it placed approximately 300 refugees with host families until they could legally enter Canada. In 2003, the VRA ceased operation because of lack of resources to handle the great influx.

Since the 1990s, Vermont's foreign-born population has increased through immigration and from children born to immigrants. Estimates have found that immigration and immigrant births added 1,250 to the population annually or 52.2 percent of the population change. The 2000 U.S. Census discovered 23,245 immigrant residents, the nation's 24th highest, showing a 32.5 percent growth during the 1990s. The native population grew 7.4 percent during these years. The proportion of non-English speakers at home increased to 5.8 percent from 5.3 percent in 1990, with 35.9 percent speaking English less than very well.

This surge of new immigrants has made Vermont's 2000 naturalization rate of 53.6 percent significantly higher than the national average of 40.1 percent. The state's rate has fallen from 60.7 percent in 1990. Vermont's slow rate of immigration means it was still occupied by many of its earliest European immigrants. In 2000, some 42.6 percent of Vermont residents claimed German heritage, making it one of the states with the most significant amount of individuals with German ancestry. In 2006, Vermont's immigrant population was estimated to be 27,525 or

A Hispanic man works at a dairy farm in Fairfield, Vermont, on March 5, 2009. If not for the hard work of foreign workers from Mexico and Central America, Vermont's dairy farms would dry up entirely. (AP Photo/Toby Talbot)

3.8 percent of the state population. The majority of immigrants were from Canada (34.0 percent), the United Kingdom (7.5 percent), and Germany (7.2 percent). Bosnia and Herzegovina, China, Vietnam, Korea, India, France, and Poland comprise 22.2 percent of the immigrants. Overall, Vermont's immigrant population increased by 30.7 percent between 2000 and 2006.

Vermont has seen an increase in its undocumented immigrant population in the 2007–2012 period. Most have come to work in the farms. In 2007, the conservative, anti-immigration group Federation for American Immigration Reform estimated that there were 5,000 undocumented aliens in the state or 0.8 percent of the total population. In 2010, the Vermont State Conference on Migrant Farmworkers criticized the nation's immigration policy as failing agricultural workers and employers.

According to the Vermont Migrant Education Program, few in Vermont are aware that Mexican labor was even present in the state. In 2010, over 50 percent of the migrant labor population was Latino/a, mostly young men without families. As of 2009, there were 1,043 dairy farms in Vermont, of which 116 have foreign workers. About 11 percent of farmworkers in Vermont are female, a higher than average number.

TOPICAL ESSAYS

Recent Anti-Immigrant Protests

Vermont certainly has not been immune to the anti-immigrant protests that have spread across the nation. As opposed to the situation in a number of states, the Vermont governor and various state and community organizations have supported immigrant rights. This was consistent with recent state political history, which has tended in the liberal direction. An example of these progressive tendencies was that Vermont was one of only three states that did not disenfranchise convicted felons.

Community activists in Vermont have protested the arrest of undocumented immigrant farmworkers in 2011. The protesters, on behalf of the Vermont Migrant Solidarity Project of the Vermont Workers' Center, stand in solidarity with the arrested workers to protest the "violation of anti-bias policing, (and an) unjust immigration policy." This stemmed from a purported racial profiling police stop in Middlesex by Vermont State Police that detected an alleged undocumented immigrant (Varricchio 2011). In response, Vermont governor Peter Shumlin (1956–) showed sympathy for immigrants' plight, noting that Vermont farmers cannot survive without workers from outside America. The state's Republican Party immediately attacked the governor's statement.

In 2011, the Vermont Farm Bureau announced that it supported year-round guest workers and opposed "inconsistent and heavy handed enforcement by the

Danilo Lopez, left, talks about his deportation issue with Governor Peter Shumlin, right, in Montpelier, Vermont, on June 5, 2013. Lopez, at the center of the push to get Vermont drivers' licenses for undocumented farmworkers, is now getting support from his fellow activists in his battle against deportation. (AP Photo/Toby Talbot)

INS [Immigration and Naturalization Service] of cases involving undocumented farm workers." The bureau also was in favor of simplifying visa procedures for farmworkers, the recognition of the human rights of persons who entered this country seeking work, decreased penalties against employers who hired foreign workers, and a path to citizenship for such laborers (Vermont Farm Bureau 2011).

Polls about the general public's feelings have been mixed. A 2012 Pulse Opinion Poll of Vermont Voters on Immigration Policy found that 55 percent believe that undocumented immigration negatively affected Vermont; 68 percent opposed in-state tuition subsidies and/or admission of undocumented aliens to public universities; 49 percent supported state involvement in immigration enforcement, similar to policies enacted in Arizona and other states; 44 percent supported reducing overall immigration to the United States, and 9 percent supported increasing immigration.

The Vermont state legislature passed a bill in 2012 (S 238) to make driver's licenses and ID cards available to everyone. In a spirited public debate, the bill was attacked by the *Green Mountain Outlook*, several citizen groups, and others.

After passing the legislature, the bill was signed by the governor on May 1, 2012. For the future, it remains to be seen if the state will embrace its new immigrants as Vermonters as it has done, however reluctantly at times, throughout its history.

NOTABLE GROUPS

MIGRANT JUSTICE

Migrant Justice advocates on behalf of migrant dairy farmers, many of whom are from Mexico and Central America. This group was established between 2009 and 2010 when migrant dairy farmers shared stories of their jobs and lives with students and teachers in several Vermont high-school Spanish classes. Part of these accounts involved the death of a dairy worker at the end of 2009—this project helped to return his body to Mexico and filmed a documentary, *Silenced Voices*, about this group of "invisible" workers. From 2011 to 2012, the group began to challenge unfair or discriminatory state and local policies that were criminalizing immigration. They have identified five areas of policy that they want to implement or change. First, they call for truly neutral policing. Second, they oppose Secure Communities as a failed project that has targeted the wrong people. Third, they are fighting to include migrant farmworkers in the Universal Healthcare system. Fourth, they want to improve employment and housing conditions in this industry and fifth, they are concerned with transportation issues and are advocating expanded eligibility for driver's licenses. Together with other groups that help these workers procure transportation, food, and basic necessities, this organization reflects and advocates on behalf of a relatively invisible and powerless group of workers. At least one of their goals has been met: on November 20 2014, President Obama ended the Secure Communities Program.

BIBLIOGRAPHY

Addison County Migrant Coalition. Addison County Migrant Coalition Webpage. http://www .addisoncoalition.org/Addison_Coalition/Welcome.html.   Accessed   February 27, 2014.

Bromage, Andy. "Shumlin Says VT Should 'Look the Other Way' on Illegal Immigration, Republicans Pounce." Blurt: Seven Days Staff Blog, September 16, 2011. http://7d. blogs.com/blurt/2011/09/shumlin-says-vermont-should-look-the-other-way-on-illegal-immigration-republicans-pounce.html. Accessed March 29, 2014.

Cheyney, Cora. *Vermont: The State with the Storybook Past*. Brattleboro, VT: Stephen Green Press, 1976.

Dillon, John. "'Above Ground' Railroad: Vermonters Feed, House Refugees as They Flee to Canada." *The Sunday Times*, 13, January 8, 1989, 1.

"Driving towards Justice: Vermont Migrant Rights Campaign Wins Licenses." sbynews. com. http://sbynews.blogspot.com/2012/04/driving-towards-justice-vermont-migrant .html. Accessed March 29, 2014.

English Heritage. "Shoddy Mill." National Monuments Record Thesauri, 1999. http://thesaurus.english-heritage.org.uk/thesaurus_term.asp?thes_no=1&term_no=93312. Accessed March 29, 2014.

Federation for American Immigration Reform. "Vermont Poll Data." 2012. http://www.fairus.org/default.aspx?PageID=12667557&A=SearchResult&SearchID=2306528&ObjectID=12667557&ObjectType=1. Accessed March 29, 2014.

Geggis, Anne. "Group Seals Immigration Cracks: Refugees Given Shelter En Route." *Burlington Free Press*, September, 1990. http://vtimmigrationandasylum.org/sites/default/files/Group%20seals%20immigration%20cracks,%20Burlington%20Press%20Press,%201990.pdf. Accessed March 29, 2014.

Guma, Greg. *The Vermont Way*. 2012. http://vermontway.blogspot.com/2011/10/boom-and-bust-in-quarry-towns.html. Accessed March 29, 2014.

Guyette, E. A. "Behind the White Veil: A History of Vermont's Ethnic Groups." In *Many Cultures, One People: A Multicultural Handbook for Teachers*. Middlebury, VT: Vermont Folklife, 1992, pp. 17–27.

Guyette, E. A. "Immigration to Vermont: 1840 to 1930." Southeast Vermont Community Learning Collaborative, 2012. http://www.flowofhistory.org/themes/movement_settlement/immigration.php. Accessed March 29, 2014.

Guyette, E. A. "Stories of Forced Migrations to Vermont." Southeast Vermont Community Learning Collaborative, 2012. http://www.flowofhistory.org/themes/movement_settlement/immigration.php. Accessed March 29, 2014.

Harrison, Blake. *The View from Vermont: Tourism and the Making of an American Rural Landscape*. Lebanon, NH: University of Vermont Press/University Press of New England, 2006.

Hiltzik, Michael. *The New Deal: A Modern History*. New York: Free Press, 2011.

"Immigration to Vermont." USimmigration support.org. http://www.usimmigrationsupport.org/vermont.html. Accessed March 29, 2014.

Johnson, Paul. *A History of the American People*. New York: Harper Perennial, 1997.

Keyssar, Alexander. *The Right to Vote: The Contested History of Democracy in the United States*. New York: Basic Books, 2000.

Klyza, Christopher McGrory, and Stephen C. Trombulak. *The Story of Vermont: A Natural and Cultural History*. Hanover, NH: Middlebury College Press, 1999.

Marcy, Darren, and Cristina Kumka. "Legislature Considers IDs for Farm Workers." *Vermont Today*, February 2, 2012. http://rutlandherald.typepad.com/vermonttoday/2012/02/legislature-considers-ids-for-farm-workers.html. Accessed March 29, 2014.

Merrill, Perry H. *Vermont under Four Flags: A History of the Green Mountain State 1635–1975*. Montpelier, VT: Merrill, 1975.

Migrant Justice. Migrant Justice Webpage. http://www.vtmigrantfarmworkersolidarity.org/node/172. Accessed February 27, 2014.

Murphy, Ronald Chase. *Irish Famine Immigrants in the State of Vermont. Gravestone Inscriptions*. New York: Clearfield, 2009.

Rooker, Sara. "Gathering and Interactions of Peoples, Cultures, and Ideas: Migration from Vermont." Southeast Vermont Community Learning Collaborative, 2012. http://www.flowofhistory.org/themes/movement_settlement/vtmigration.php. Accessed March 29, 2014.

Searls, Paul M. *Two Vermonts: Geography and Identity, 1865–1910*. Hanover, NH: University of New Hampshire Press, 2006.

Starr, Tena. "Vermonters Say Immigration Policy Is Failing Migrant Workers, Dairy Farms." vtdigger.org, April 26, 2010. http://vtdigger.org/2010/04/26/vermonters-say immigration -policy-is-failing-migrant-workers-dairy-farms/. Accessed March 29, 2014.

Stein, Mark. *How the States Got Their Shapes*. New York: Harper, 2008.

Stowe Historical Society. *A Brief History of Stowe*. Stowe, VT: Stowe Historical Society, 1983.

Suozzo, Andrea. "Migrant Driver's License Bill Advances in House." *Addison County Independent*, April 12, 2012. http://www.addisonindependent.com/?q=node/11437. Accessed March 29, 2014.

"Threats and Responses: Immigration; Vermont Refugee Aid Group Says Policy Thins Resources." *New York Times*, March 13, 2003, 17.

Varricchio, Louis. "From the Editor: Illegal Immigration in Vermont." *Green Mountain Outlook*, Middlebury, VT, April 12, 2012. http://www.gmoutlook.com/news/2012/apr/12 /editor-illegal-immigration-vermont/. Accessed March 29, 2014.

Varricchio, Louis. "Vermont Incident Sparks Protest of U.S. Immigration Policy." *New Market Press*, Middlebury, VT, September 19, 2011. http://www.newmarketpressvt.com /news/2011/sep/19/vermont-incident-sparks-protest-us-immigration-pol/. Accessed March 29, 2014.

Vermont Department of Tourism and Marketing. "The Geography of Vermont, 2012." http://www.vermontvacation.com/About%20Vermont/Geography.aspx. Accessed March 29, 2014.

Vermont Farm Bureau. "2011 VFTB Legislative Priorities." http://www.vtfb.org /vermont-farm-bureau-legislative-priorities.html. Accessed March 29, 2014.

Vermont Historical Society. "The Transformation of Vermont." 2006. http://freedomand-unity.org/vt_transition/vt_transformation.html. Accessed March 29, 2014.

Vermont Historical Society. "Vermont Railroad Timeline." 2006. http://freedomandunity. org/1800s/rr_timeline_88_94.html. Accessed March 29, 2014.

46

VIRGINIA

Kendall Funk and Francisco I. Pedraza

CHRONOLOGY

1584	Philip Armadas and Arthur Barlow arrive on the Atlantic Coast and name the region "Virginia" in honor of British Queen Elizabeth I.
1587	The first English child is born in North America, in Roanoke: Virginia Dare.
1606	Virginia is divided into parts and one part is overseen by the London Company and the other by the Plymouth Company. The first ships organized by the London Company arrive in December 1606.
1607	Jamestown becomes the first English colony.
1612	King James I issues the third charter of the Virginia Company and this charter is in force until 1624.
1619	Indentured Africans arrive in Jamestown.
1622	English colonists are attacked by Powhatans.
1623	The British lure Powhatans to a feast and poison their drinks, massacring the survivors.
1644	More settlers are attacked and killed by the Powhatans.
1683–1775	Major wave of German settlement occurs in this area. Many entered Philadelphia and eventually settle in Virginia.
1700s	Increased European settlement occurs as the British call for greater European settlement of foreign Protestants, including French Calvinists, German Lutherans and Pietists, Scotch Irish Presbyterians, Dutch Calvinists, Swiss, and some Swedes. Ongoing conflicts with Native Americans throughout this time period.
1715–1775	Scotch Irish arrive and eventually settle in Virginia.

1754	French and Indian War begins.
1774	White settlers attack unarmed members of the Mingo chief's family; the attack results in a prolonged conflict.
1776	On January 2, four British ships attack Norfolk. Fires and looting occur in Norfolk.
1781	General Benedict Arnold leads British troops into an attack on Richmond.
1786	Religious toleration is established.
1790	About 28 percent of free Virginians are German.
1831	Nat Turner's Rebellion, a slave uprising, erupts in southern Virginia.
1849	Successful slave escape from Virginia is performed by Henry "Box" Brown.
1859	John Brown leads unsuccessful slave rebellion at Harper's Ferry.
1861	Virginia secedes from the Union.
1865	General Robert E. Lee becomes general-in-chief of all Confederate Forces. In April, Union forces occupy Richmond.
1869	Virginia ratifies the Fourteenth and Fifteenth Amendments to the Constitution.
1870	Reconstruction ends in the commonwealth and Virginia is re-admitted to the U.S. Senate and House.
1882	Roanoke is formed.
1931	United Textile Workers strike at Schoolfield mills for roughly four months.
1940	Eighty Jewish refugees fleeing the Nazis arrive in Norfolk. They eventually receive visas to stay in the United States.
1959	Key legal battles over school integration occur. Desegregation begins in February.
1960	Important civil rights protests are staged by students from Virginia Union University.
1968	Poor People's March through Richmond to Washington, D.C, takes place.
1980	The Refugee Act of 1980 is enacted. It systematizes refugee process and codifies asylum status. About 10 million permanent immigrants are admitted legally to the United States. This is enacted in response to Vietnamese and Cuban refugee crisis.
1986	The Immigration Reform and Control Act (IRCA) of 1986 allows most undocumented immigrants who have resided in the United States continuously since January 1, 1982 to apply for legal status; it prohibits employers from hiring undocumented immigrants; and mandates penalties for violations. IRCA creates the 287(g) program that later allows local police forces to aid Immigration and Customs Enforcement (ICE) in immigration matters.
1989	United Mine Workers hold a rally in Norton. César Chavez delivers a speech to the thousands in attendance.

1990	The Immigration Act of 1990 sets an annual ceiling of 700,000 immigrants per year to enter the United States for the next three years and an annual ceiling of 675,000 per year for every year after.
1990	The foreign-born population comprises 5.0 percent of Virginia's total population. Latinos comprise 2.6 percent of the population, whereas Asians comprise 2.5 percent.
1996	The Illegal Immigration Reform and Immigrant Responsibility Act (IIRIRA) increases immigration enforcement and penalties for entering the country undocumented.
1996	The Welfare Reform Reconciliation Act cuts the availability of government aid to legal immigrants. The IIRIRA makes it easier to deport immigrants attempting to enter the United States without proper documents. IIRIRA is enacted, in part, as a response to the Oklahoma City bombing.
2000	On October 30, Congress passes the Child Citizenship Act of 2000 (PL 106–395), granting automatic U.S. citizenship to foreign-born biological and adopted children of American citizens.
2000	The foreign-born population comprises 8.1 percent of Virginia's total population.
2000	Latinos comprise 4.7 percent of the population, whereas Asians comprise 3.7 percent.
2001	The USA Patriot Act is enacted in October 2001 which broadens the discretion of law enforcement and immigration authorities in detaining and deporting immigrants suspected of terrorism-related activities.
2002	The Homeland Security Act of 2002 transfers the responsibilities of the Immigration and Naturalization Service (INS) from Department of Justice to Department of Homeland Security.
2002	The U.S. Patriot Act is considered by Congress to restrict the flow of immigrants and potential terrorists into the United States.
2006	The immigrant population comprises approximately 4.3 percent of the state's population. The largest immigrant populations come from El Salvador (8.9 percent), Korea (6.0 percent), and the Philippines (5.9 percent).
2008	The Virginia General Assembly passes a bill prohibiting contractors from knowingly employing an undocumented immigrant.
2008	For the 2008 presidential election, Latinos comprise 2.0 percent, and Asians 3.7 percent, of Virginia voters. This number is roughly equivalent to the margin of victory by which Obama defeats McCain in Virginia.
2008	A report by the Perryman Group finds that the removal of all undocumented immigrants from Virginia in 2008 would have a significant impact on the state's economy including a loss of $11.2 billion in economic activity and $5.5 billion loss in gross state product.

2010	In September, there are protests outside Richmond's Department of Motor Vehicles against Governor Bob McDonalds's move to restrict immigrants from obtaining valid driver's license.
2010	Virginia General Assembly passes a bill requiring state agencies and those newly hired to perform work in the state to use the E-Verify Program.
2010	The foreign-born population comprises 11.4 percent of Virginia's total population.
2010	Immigrants make up 15 percent of Virginia's workforce with 3.9 percent of these workers being undocumented immigrants.
2011	ICE "enforcement sweep" in conjunction with federal, state, and local police leads to the arrest of over 160 foreign nationals—most of them allegedly undocumented immigrants with criminal records—in northern Virginia.
2011	Virginia's House Bill (HB) 1651 restricts the issuance of driver's licenses, permits, and special identification cards to U.S. citizens only.

HISTORICAL OVERVIEW

Virginia claims heritage to numerous political debates that stretch far back to the founding of the United States. The issue of immigration is no exception. For example, Virginia takes rightful credit for opposition to the infamous Alien and Sedition Acts of 1798, largely through the pens of Thomas Jefferson and James Madison, who authored the Virginia and Kentucky Resolves. Like the debates of yesteryear, contemporary immigration debates in Virginia can be distilled to a concern for how the introduction of foreign elements risk compromising what makes America great today. In the late 1700s the ideas motivating the French Revolution were viewed as anathema to those of the new American Republic. In the early 1900s Catholic, Orthodox, and Jewish traditions were cast in sharp contrast to the virtues of Protestantism that underpinned the nation's moral character and high regard for individual rights. By 1900, the foreign-born population by birthplace was topped by Germany with 25 percent, Ireland with 20 percent, England with 19 percent, Russia and Scotland each with 7 percent, Canada with 6 percent, and rounded out with nominal shares from Italy, China and other European countries. For most of the Virginia commonwealth's history, immigrants have moved from Europe, and that trend changed considerably in the second half of the twentieth century.

It was only since 1970 that the foreign-born population in Virginia had exceeded more than 1 in 100 residents. In 2010, 1 in 10 Virginia residents were foreign-born, with newcomers from all over the globe, and in particular from Latin America and Asia. Whereas Europeans made up about 13 percent of immigrants residing in Virginia, over three-quarters of Virginia's foreign-born population were from Asia and Latin America. The vibrant growth of contemporary immigration trends accounted for a full quarter of Virginia's population growth from 2000 to 2010, and contributed to the rich diversity that we see in the Commonwealth today.

In terms of demographic changes, contemporary immigration coincided with at least three patterns in Virginia: population growth, aging and diversity. The overall population of Virginia was growing. Between 2000 and 2010, Virginia's population grew by 13 percent to reach 8 million, exceeding the 10 percent growth at the national level. The bulk of population growth in Virginia was occurring in the Northern Virginia, Hampton Roads and Richmond regions of the state, urban areas with the highest concentration of immigrants. Other, more rural, regions of Virginia have experienced population loss. This pattern of population decline is likely to continue in the Eastern Virginia, Southside and Southwest regions of the state, where large proportions of residents are aged 65 or older. By contrast, the population in Northern Virginia has been younger, growing faster, and highly diverse with respect to nativity, language, and ethnicity.

Cesar Perales, left, with the Puerto Rican Legal Defense and Education Fund, and Eduardo Ferrer, with the Howry LLP law firm, speak about a lawsuit being filed by Latinos in Prince William County, Virginia, against the county in an attempt to halt the implementation of a resolution that aims to deny a wide range of public services to undocumented immigrants in 2007. (AP Photo/Jacquelyn Martin)

About 40 percent of the immigrant population in Virginia is from countries in Asia, and 36 percent is from countries in Latin America. While the share of the foreign-born in Virginia that are from these two different regions of the world is similar, there are striking socioeconomic differences between Asian and Latin American newcomers to the state. According to the University of Virginia's Weldon Cooper Center for Public Service, over one-quarter of the foreign-born population in Virginia has limited proficiency in the English language. Over 60 percent of immigrants from Latin America speak English less than "very well," compared to about 40 percent of those of Asian origins. Asian immigrants in Virginia are the most likely of all foreign-born groups to hold bachelor's degrees and to have at least a high-school diploma or equivalent. By contrast, immigrants from Latin

America have completed far less formal education than any other foreign-born groups. The differences in education are reflected in economic disparities. At just over $71,000 per year, immigrants born in Asia top median household income in Virginia in 2006, exceeding the $55,800 figure for U.S.-born Virginians, and the $50,700 level for immigrants born in Latin America. Reports by the Cooper Center for Public Service suggest that Latin American immigrants are primarily employed in low-wage construction and extraction occupations, whereas recent Asian immigrants are overrepresented in higher-paying physical, social, and life science occupations. The demographic shifts in Virginia that are described above serve as a backdrop to contemporary responses to immigration in the state.

The response to immigration comes from government institutions and the general public. Although comprehensive national immigration reform has been tabled several times since 2000, a broader federal policy initiative that gives state and local officials a central role in immigration law enforcement has developed across the country. Virginia is not alone in experiencing contemporary immigration. Several counties and municipalities in Virginia have joined national agencies in cross-deputization, efforts which empower local police officials to enforce federal immigration policy. The most widespread cross-deputization efforts have been the *Secure Communities* and *287(g)* programs, the implementation of which began in

Attorney Loc Pfeiffer works in his office in Richmond, Virginia, on October 21, 2008, presidential election. Pfeiffer, 41, who arrived from Vietnam at age 6, said the election was a new topic because of a younger Asian generation with fresh attitudes. (AP Photo/Steve Helber)

several northern counties of Virginia in 2007 and 2008 (and which has just ended in November of 2014). Other state and local immigrant policy innovations in Virginia focus on labor market access, discriminatory housing ordinances, business hiring practices, and access to driver's licenses and special permits. On balance, the government response to immigration has been restrictive since 2006. This restrictive pattern in government policy has been reflected in the Virginia public. Over the course of the latter half of the 2000s, the views of ordinary Virginian toward immigrants have shifted away from majority support to majority opposition for expansionist policies.

TOPICAL ESSAYS

CONTEMPORARY RESPONSES TO IMMIGRANTS BY VIRGINIA'S STATE AND LOCAL GOVERNMENTS

Government responses to immigrants vary considerably from state to state and from one locale to another. In the absence of a unifying federal immigration policy, and in response to local constituent demands, state and local officials in Virginia have crafted a variety of response to immigrants. Similarly, no central database of subnational responses to immigrants exists. In an effort to catalogue the various responses in Virginia in a systematic and rigorous way, we leveraged multiple strategies. We suspect that readers of this volume, and especially those interested in Virginia's immigration story, are interested in the details of how and where we collected information to include in our entry. In the spirit of transparency and responding to that particular demand, we share a summary of our data collection methods.

Data Collection Methods

Table 11 was constructed through the use of various means and resources. We began our research by taking stock of a sample of articles and Internet blogs that bring to light specific examples of local responses to immigration. These articles provided us with an idea of the different ways in which cities may respond to immigration at the local level. The sample articles are obtained from Immigration Impact, a project of the American Immigration Council (www.immigrationimpact.com). After acquiring a general idea of the various ways in which locales may respond to immigration, we refined our search to identify locales with specific types of responses to immigration.

To identify locales with negative responses to immigration, we searched for the phrase "local anti-immigration policies" in Google. The search yielded a report published in 2007 by Mexican American Legal Defense and Education Fund (MALDEF) titled "List of Local Anti-Immigrant Legislation." The information provided by MALDEF gave us a sort of template from which we were able to originate Table 11. After the general search in Google was performed, specific websites of organizations such as the Southern Poverty Law Center, Migration Policy Institute, Progressive States Network, TRAC Immigration, Immigration Policy Center, Center for Community Change, and the National Immigration Law Center were investigated to find reports and information regarding local responses to immigration.

The National Immigration Law Center's website, www.nilc.org, yielded a report titled "Laws, Resolutions, and Policies Instituted across the U.S. Limiting Enforcement of Immigration Laws by State and Local Authorities" that was published in 2008. This report contains descriptive information regarding cities and states that would be considered "Sanctuary Cities" or "Sanctuary States." We also used the websites www.sanctuarycities.info and www.ojjpac.org to identify other locales that have implemented the so-called sanctuary policies, or mandates and policies restricting the enforcement of federal immigration laws.

Information regarding local police coordination with federal enforcement officers was obtained from the U.S. ICE website, www.ice.gov. All locales that have federal partnership programs in effect with ICE through Memorandum of Agreements (MOA) were thus identified and recorded in Table 11. We also came across two other sources that aided us significantly in the construction of Table 11, the *Database of Recent Local Ordinances on Immigration* provided by Fair Immigration Reform Movement in 2007 and the *List of Local Ordinances* produced by Puerto Rican Legal Defense and Education Fund in 2008.

The information collected from each of the sources was then incorporated into one coherent document which we named the "Table of Local Responses to Immigration." Table 11 is organized by state and then broken down into specific cities and counties. For most every city and county, we have provided detailed information on the pieces of legislation present within that respective locale. Specifics about each piece of legislation, such as the date of proposal or passage, status of the legislation, and a description of the policy, are documented and can be found in the table. To further progress our research efforts, we analyzed data from the Latino National Survey (LNS) conducted in 2006. We looked into the number of respondents from each city surveyed in the LNS as an indicator to predict which cities may have proposed local immigration ordinances. Within each state, we have elected to examine seven cities. These cities had the highest numbers of respondents within each state, suggesting that there is a large Latino population and therefore a greater probability that there will also be a large immigrant population. The website www.sanctuarycities.info was again used to determine if any of the selected cities had implemented any sanctuary-type policies. To determine if the remaining cities had implemented any immigration-related ordinances, we conducted a search through Google using the city name, state abbreviation, and the term "immig* ordinance." We then browsed the results produced from the search to identify any news of the city passing or proposing an ordinance in response to immigration. If a news story was identified, we recorded the website and corresponding URL as a potential source of information. The selected cities will be further investigated in the time to come.

Attitudes toward Immigrants and Immigration among Virginia's Public

Responses to immigrants and immigration are not limited to official government policy. Contemporary immigrants are embedded in real communities and the bulk of their day-to-day interactions are with other community members at work and school, in stores and restaurants, and public spaces like parks on the weekends and roadways during commuting hours. In this section, we scratch the surface of the mass public's response to immigrants as measured in public opinion surveys.

Virginia Public Attitudes toward Immigrants from Public Opinion Surveys

Like the residents of many other states, a broader national debate focused the attention of Virginians in the spring of 2006, when immigrants and immigrant advocates took the nation by surprise with hundreds of peaceful marches organized across the United States. The catalyst for those marches was widely acknowledged to be U.S. House Resolution (HR) 4437, a proposal sponsored by Republican U.S. representative Jim Sensenbrenner of Wisconsin. Sensenbrenner's proposal, The Border Protection, Anti-Terrorism and Illegal Immigration Control Act of 2005, HR 4437, called for a number of controversial provisions, including the construction of a 700-mile fence along the U.S.–Mexico border, a requirement that federal officials take custody of undocumented persons detained by local authorities, and shifted the violation of several immigration laws from civil to criminal offenses. In 2006, the Cooperative Congressional Election Study (CCES), an academic survey fielded across the United States, collected information on over more than 31,000 Americans, including a representative sample of 827 registered voters in Virginia. In the 2006 study, 34 percent of Virginians support HR 4437, and about 36 percent opposed a pathway to citizenship for undocumented immigrants. One year later, in 2007, support for HR 4437 increased among Virginians to 39 percent and 50 percent expressed opposition to providing a pathway to citizenship.

By 2010, according to the CCES, 62 percent of Virginians opposed granting legal status to undocumented immigrants, and 71 percent opposed increasing the number of guest workers who entered the United States. The restrictive sentiment in Virginia was of particular consequence to the business community, as evidenced by 74 percent in support of fining businesses that hired undocumented

Table 11   Local Responses to Immigration in Virginia

Location	Status	Date	Description
Alexandria			Possible Sanctuary City.
Culpeper	Passed	08/07/07	Proposal to make English as the official language.
Culpeper	Rejected	10/17/06	Proposal for hiring a special officer to aggressively enforce existing zoning codes in hopes of limiting the number of families living in single-family dwellings, an issue that targeted the Latino community.
Culpeper	Rejected	10/17/06	Proposal for Code Enforcer and Letter Writing Campaign to Congress.
Culpeper	Pending	9/18/06	Councilman proposed housing ordinance based on original Hazleton ordinance during Town Committee Meeting
Culpeper	Under consideration		Memorandum of understanding with ICE.
Culpeper	Under Consideration		Immigration taskforce that would research the impact of undocumented immigrants in their community and determine what they can and cannot do regarding passage of an anti-immigrant ordinance. Sponsored by Councilman Jenkins.
Fairfax County			Possible Sanctuary City.
Harrisonburg	Under Consideration		Immigration taskforce. Councilwoman Carolyn Frank asked for research on the impact of immigration.
Herndon	Passed	09/03/07	Fairfax County announces that it will stop funding the Herndon day-labor center because the current operator does not require documents.
Herndon		08/29/07	Fairfax Circuit Court judge Leslie Alden ruled that Herndon's anti-solicitation ordinance was unconstitutional. City is still undecided if to appeal.
Herndon		08/22/07	Mayor Steve DeBeneditts of Herndon has setup a meeting on August 22, 2007 with county officials to try to get the county to reinstate funding. The city of Herndon will take over the worker site temporarily. The city will require that workers that use the site show documentation of their status.

Table 11 (*Continued*)

Location	Status	Date	Description
Herndon	Under Consideration	07/02/07	Two proposals have been received to ban undocumented immigrants from day-labor centers in the town.
Herndon	In Effect	03/21/07	ICE MOA with Herndon Police Department; task force
Herndon	Tabled	12/06	English language ordinance
Herndon	Under Consideration	10/05/06	Occupancy restriction ordinance and anti-day laborer ordinance (according to *Arizona Republic* article: "MESA seeks immigration answers").
Herndon	In Effect	Since 2005	Anti-solicitation ordinance that bans motorists and day laborers from discussing employment in the street.
Herndon			UNDER CONSIDERATION: English only. PASSED: Illegal to hire resolution. Have asked state for legislation to allow them to enforce federal law. Resolution to deny business licenses and town contracts to anyone not able to prove his or her U.S. citizenship. Must provide evidence to the town government that all their employees are in the country legally.
Loudoun County	In Effect	03/21/08	ICE MOA with Loudoun County Sheriff's Office; task force
Loudoun County	Passed		Proposal to start checking driver's license, fine businesses that hire undocumented immigrants, and deny city services to undocumented immigrants.
Manassas	In Effect	03/21/08	ICE MOA with Manassas Police Department; task force
Manassas		04/04/07	Group formed to lobby for anti-immigrant laws
Manassas	Repealed	12/12/06	Ordinance passed on December 6, 2006 was repealed by the city council
Manassas	Passed	12/06/06	Proposed ordinance that would change the legal definition of a family in the city's zoning code to only include immediate family members, excluding uncles, aunts, cousins, and others, targeting the growing Latino population.
Manassas	Passed		Business license ordinance
Manassas Park	In Effect	03/10/08	ICE MOA with Manassas Park Police Department; task force

(*Continued*)

Table 11   (*Continued*)

Location	Status	Date	Description
Prince William County	In Effect	02/26/08	ICE MOA with Prince William County Police Department; task force
Prince William County	In Effect	02/26/08	ICE MOA with Prince William County Sheriff's Office; task force
Prince William County	Passed	07/10/07	Resolution passed directing police to develop procedures to enforce immigration laws and develop criteria to deny city services to undocumented immigrants.
Prince William County	In Effect	07/09/07	ICE MOA with Prince William-Manassas Regional Jail; jail enforcement
Prince William County	Under Consideration		Considering sending a bill to Congress for the cost of undocumented immigration in Prince William County. Board county supervisors called for a wide-ranging study to determine how much money undocumented immigrants are costing the county. Report from January /16, 2007. It determined that it spends about $3 million each year to provide services to undocumented immigrants. At the same time, the study found the cost was far "outweighed by the economic benefit and money that this segment of the population brings into the county."
Rockingham County	In Effect	04/25/07	ICE MOA with Rockingham County Sheriff's Office; jail enforcement
Shenandoah County	In Effect	05/10/07	ICE MOA with Shenandoah County Sheriff's Office; jail enforcement and task force
Spotsylvania	Tabled		Maximum occupancy ordinance and seeking to deny city services to undocumented immigrants.
Virginia Beach			Possible Sanctuary City
Waynesboro	Pending	09/12/06	Proposed ordinance that would fine landlords and employers for aiding undocumented immigrants. City attorney will examine other cities' ordinances.

Table 12   Immigration Policies from the Commonwealth of Virginia

Bill	Status	Date	Description
Senate Bill (SB) 1049	Passed	03/25/11	Public Procurement Act; state agencies to include in contract that contractor use E-Verify Program. Introduced by George L. Barker
HB 1651	Passed	03/23/11	Driver's licenses, permits, and special IDs to be issued only to U.S. citizens. Introduced by John A. Cosgrove
HJ 822	Passed	02/22/11	Commending those who have immigrated to the United States while adhering to the immigration laws. Introduced by L. Scott Lingamfelter
HB 1430	Tabled	02/22/11	Arresting officer to ascertain citizenship of arrestee even if arrestee is not committed to jail. Introduced by David B. Albo
HB 1421	Tabled	02/22/11	Immigration laws, federal; enforcement by state, political subdivisions, or localities (Commonwealth and its political subdivisions may not limit or restrict the enforcement of federal immigration laws). Introduced by David B. Albo
HB 1465	Tabled	02/22/11	Higher educational institutes; policies prohibiting admission of undocumented aliens. Introduced by Christopher K. Peace
HB 1934	Tabled	02/22/11	Immigration laws; state police to enter into agreement with U.S. ICE (superintendent of state police to seek to enter MOA with ICE). Introduced by Jackson H. Miller
HB 1775	Tabled	02/22/11	Students; school boards to report to Board of Education the number of students enrolled in English as second language. Introduced by C. Todd Gilbert
HB 1895	Tabled	02/08/11	Undocumented immigrants; document verification for employment and penalty for false representation. Introduced by Vivian E. Watts
SB 1328		02/07/11	Magistrates; ascertaining citizenship of arrested persons. Introduced by Mark R. Herring PASSED senate by indefinitely in Courts of Justice
HR 46		01/31/11	State sovereignty; Congress urged to honor Tenth Amendment of U.S. Constitution. Introduced by Christopher K. Peace. PASSED in House of Delegates
HB 737	Passed	04/11/10	E-Verify Program; requires state agencies and those newly hired to perform work in state. Introduced by David B. Albo

(Continued)

Table 12   Immigration Policies from the Commonwealth of Virginia

Bill	Status	Date	Description
HB 2580	Passed	03/30/09	Undocumented immigrants; removes code provision that prohibits an arrest thereof more frequently (revises code provision that prohibits an arrest of an undocumented alien [who has been previously convicted of a felony and deported] more frequently than once every six months to allow arrests within the six-month period when confirmation has been received from ICE that the arrested person will be taken into federal custody). Introduced by Jackson H. Miller
SB 1436	Tabled	02/28/09	Crime victims; no law enforcement officer shall inquire into immigration status of victim of crime. Introduced by Janet D. Howell
HB 1689	Tabled	01/21/09	Undocumented aliens; fraudulently assisting undocumented aliens and penalty provisions (assisting an undocumented alien is Class 1 misdemeanor) Introduced by Robert Tata
SJ 26	Tabled	12/05/08	Undocumented immigration; attorney general to pursue all remedies through litigation for reimbursement. Introduced by Charles J. Colgan
HB 1558	Tabled	12/04/08	Public Procurement Act; verification of legal presence of contractors for employment. Introduced by Benjamin L. Cline
SB 517 HB 1298	Passed	04/14/08	Contractors; shall not knowingly employ undocumented alien. Introduced by Ken T. Cuccinelli
HB 1249	Tabled	02/12/08	Unfair employment practices; discharging employees when undocumented aliens are employed. Introduced by Timothy D. Hugo
HB 2688	Tabled	02/19/07	Workers' compensation; benefits paid to undocumented aliens; penalties provisions (makes employer and not workers' compensation insurance carrier liable for payment of workers' compensation benefits payable to undocumented alien). Introduced by John S. Reid
HB 2376	Tabled	02/08/95	Social services for undocumented aliens (prohibits the expenditure of state funds to provide social services to undocumented aliens and provides for reporting such individuals to INS). Introduced by S. Vance Wilkins Jr.

immigrants. The most onerous state and local policy measures targeting undocumented immigrants were those empowering local law enforcement officials to ask individuals about their immigration status. On that matter, public support was split in Virginia, with roughly half in support and half in opposition. According to the CCES data, contemporary immigration attitudes in Virginia have shifted in a more restrictive direction, since the immigration marches of 2006. The pattern in more restrictive attitudes among the public was consistent with the shift in state and local immigrant policy that developed during the same years.

Latino/a Attitudes toward Immigration or View of Local Response to Immigrants

Perhaps even more significant than the general attitude of the public in Virginia is the particular attitude held by the Latino population. To gain a fuller understanding of Virginia's local response to immigration, we explore these particular attitudes through an analysis of data obtained from the LNS conducted in 2006. Included in our dataset are a total of 238 respondents from the state of Virginia and the Washington, D.C., Metro area. Of the 238 respondents, 176 are residents of Virginia, while 62 respondents live in the D.C. Metro area.

The issue of undocumented immigration has always been particularly relevant to Latinos. This statement is supported by the LNS data in which 43 percent of Latinos living in Virginia identified undocumented immigration as the most important issue facing Latinos today. Likewise, undocumented immigration was ranked the third most important problem facing the United States in 2006. Since immigration is of particular significance to Latinos, most Latinos hold strong opinions toward the issue. When asked how welcoming the general public of Virginia is toward Latino immigrants, over 50 percent of respondents reported that the general public was welcoming or very welcoming (respondents from D.C. Metro area only). Within the Latino population, a whopping 92 percent of respondents replied that immigrants today strengthen our country rather than pose a burden on the welfare system and the economy.

Regarding policy preference on undocumented immigration, more than 75 percent of respondents favored the immediate legalization of current undocumented immigrants or a guest worker program leading to legalization eventually. Additionally, over 75 percent of Latino respondents were opposed to the statement "undocumented immigrants attending college should be charged a higher tuition rate at state colleges and universities even if they grew up and graduated high-school in the state." Given the data gathered from the LNS, we may assume that Latinos in Virginia are generally welcoming toward new immigrants and are supportive of policy measures that are beneficial to undocumented immigrants.

NOTABLE GROUPS

DREAMers of Virginia

Established in 2012, DREAMers of Virginia is a group that advocates for immigrant youth who are eligible to attend schools and want to pursue post-secondary education. It is a statewide group that gives Deferred Action clinics, provides information, and mobilizes the immigration reform movement. The group supports in-state tuition for DREAMers and provides high school outreach for immigrant youth. In addition to running clinics and providing public information, they also organize rallies and community meetings to foster civic education and engagement. Their website has a helpful scholarship database for all immigrant youth and a Dream College Database to identify colleges and universities that support DREAMers. The group offers internships, paid positions, and volunteer opportunities for any individual, regardless of legal status, to participate and help immigrant youth to become educated and lead a successful life in their country of residence.

BIBLIOGRAPHY

Clapp, Susan. "Virginia's Foreign Born Population." *Stat Chat*, July Newsletter, July 2008. http://www.coopercenter.org/institute. Accessed March 29, 2014.

Dreamers of Virginia. Dreamers of Virginia Webpage. http://www.dreamersofvirginia.com/#. Accessed February 28, 2014.

Fair Immigration Reform Movement (FIRM). "Database of Recent Local Ordinances on Immigration." www.fairimmigration.org. Accessed March 29, 2014.

Hopkins, Daniel J. "Politicized Places: Explaining Where and When Immigrants Provoke Local Opposition." *American Political Science Review* 104, no. 1, (2010): 40–60.

Immigration Policy Center. "New Americans in Virginia." www.immigrationpolicy.org/just-facts/new-americans-virginia. Accessed March 29, 2014.

Judicial Watch. "Illegal Immigration." www.judicialwatch.org/immigration-problems. Accessed March 29, 2014.

Mexican American Legal Defense and Education Fund. "Anti-Immigrant State Legislation and Ordinances."www.maldef.org/immigration/public_policy/state_legislation_ordinances/index.html. Accessed March 29, 2014.

National Immigration Law Center. "Laws, Resolutions, and Policies Instituted Across the U.S. Limiting Enforcement of Immigration Laws by State and Local Authorities." www.nilc.org. Accessed March 29, 2014.

NumbersUSA: For Lower Immigration Numbers. *Sanctuary Laws*. www.numbersusa.com/content/learn/national-security/sanctuary-laws.html. Accessed March 29, 2014.

Ohio Jobs and Justice PAC. *The Original List of Sanctuary Cities, USA*. www.ojjpac.org/sanctuary.asp. Accessed March 29, 2014.

Perreira, Krista. *Immigration Timeline*. http://www.unc.edu/~perreira/198timeline.html. Accessed March 29, 2014.

The Perryman Group. "An Essential Resource: An Analysis of the Economic Impact of Undocumented Workers on Business Activity in the US with Estimated Effects by State and by Industry." 2008. www.americanslorimmigrationreform.com/files/Impact_of_the_Undocumented_Workforce.pdf. Accessed March 29, 2014.

Petriello, Gene. *Protest Outside Richmond DMV Over Licenses, Immigration*. NBC12 (Richmond, VA), September 22, 2010. www.nbc12.com/story/13198798/protest-outside-richmond-dmv-over-immigration-and-licenses?redirected=true.   Accessed   March 29, 2014.

Pew Hispanic Center. "Unauthorized Immigrant Population: National and State Trends." 2010. www.pewhispanic.org/files/reports/133.pdf. Accessed March 29, 2014.

Puerto Rican Legal Defense and Education Fund. "List of Local Anti-Immigrant Ordinances."   www.aliadownloads.org/advo/PRLDEF-ListOfLocalOrdinances.xls.   Accessed March 29, 2014.

"Sanctuary Cities and States Protecting Illegal Aliens in the United States." Sanctuary Cities in Virginia. www.sanctuarycities.info/sanctuary_state_virginia.htm. Accessed March 29, 2014.

Seghetti, Lisa, Karma Ester, and Michael John Garcia. "Enforcing Immigration Law: the Role of State and Local Law Enforcement." *Congressional Research Service Report for Congress*, 2009. Retrieved through the Library of Congress website www.loc.gov. Accessed March 29, 2014.

Tippet, Rebecca, and University of Virginia, Virginia Institute of Government. "Virginia's Changing Population." *The Column*, Fall 2011 Newsletter. http://www.coopercenter.org/institute. Accessed March 29, 2014.

U.S. Census Bureau. *The Foreign-Born Population: 2000*. www.census.gov/prod/2003pubs/c2kbr-34.pdf. Accessed March 29, 2014.

U.S. Immigration and Customs Enforcement. "Fact Sheet: Delegation of Immigration Authority Section 287(g) Immigration and Nationality Act." www.ice.gov/news/library/f actsheets/ 287g.htm. Accessed March 29, 2014.

U.S. Immigration Support. "Immigration to Virginia." www.usimmigrationsupport.org/virginia.html. Accessed March 29, 2014.

Virginia General Assembly. "Legislative Information System." www.leg1.state.va.us. Accessed March 29, 2014.

47

WASHINGTON

K. Jurée Capers and Francisco I. Pedraza

CHRONOLOGY

1700s	Early exploration by British explorers and Spanish.
1790	With threats of war from the British, Spain opens the Pacific Northwest territories to other nations.
1805	Lewis and Clark Expedition travels from the eastern part of what is now Washington to the Pacific Ocean.
1811	First Hawaiian laborers settle in the Pacific Northwest.
1850s–1890s	First Latino, mainly Mexican immigrants, arrive in Washington. Territory and surrounding Pacific Northwest areas provide mining and ranching opportunities.
1853–1863	Set of territorial law restricts Chinese immigrants. They are banned from voting, testifying in court cases involving whites, and are subject to poll taxes.
1880	Establishment of Seattle International District, urban multiethnic neighborhood with residents of Chinese and Japanese heritage. Beginning in 1930s through the 1970s, Korean, Filipino, and Vietnamese diaspora join.
1886	The Alien Land Law barring Asians from owning land is passed. Violence against Chinese immigrants erupts in Tacoma, Seattle, and other Washington Territory towns.
1889	Washington becomes the 42nd state of the Union.
1895	Influx of Scandinavian immigrants begins, lasting through 1915, making Scandinavians the largest foreign-born ethnic group in Washington.

1907	Gentleman's agreement between U.S. and Japan governments ends the immigration of Japanese workers to the United States.
1915	Chongwa Benevolent Association is established as one of the first Chinese advocacy groups in Washington.
1933	Cannery Workers' and Farm Laborers' Union, the first Filipino immigrant-led union, is created in Seattle.
1940s	Washington immigrant (Mexican American) communities, particularly in the Columbia River Basin region (includes Yakima Valley in Washington) begin to grow with the increased demand for agricultural labor but there is a decline in laborers triggered by World War II.
1942	Washington State is designated an "exclusion zone" by U.S. military commanders under authorization of President Roosevelt's Executive Order 9066, effectively prohibiting residency in the state by Japanese Americans because they are considered "enemy aliens."
1942–1947	Agreement between the United States and Mexico leads to a wave of contract workers, or *braceros*, to the region to harvest crops and assist in the railway industry in Washington and the Pacific Northwest. Many work in the Wenatchee Valley, Yakima Valley, Pasco Mt. Vernon, and Walla Walla areas of Washington.
1960s–1970s	Latinos, experiencing a heightened amount of discrimination, join the Civil Rights Movement and establish the Chicano Movement in Washington. Washington experiences the most activity in the movement within the Pacific Northwest.
1962	The first Asian American is elected to the Seattle City Council.
1967	The Mexican American Federation is established as an advocate group for Mexican community development and political empowerment.
1969	United Mexican American Students march in Seattle for Latino civil rights.
1969–1970	Latino farm and migrant workers strike in the Yakima Valley area of Washington.
1970s	Washington experiences a surge in Latino civil rights organizations.
1971–1972	The Washington State Commission on Hispanic Affairs and State Asian Advisory Council are created under Governor Evans's executive order to improve public policy development and government service delivery to immigrant communities.
1972	Farm Workers Clinic is established as the main healthcare provider for migrant and seasonal farmworkers. (It becomes an incorporated, nonprofit organization in 1978.)
1972	El Centro de la Raza is created to provide social services to Latinos in the Seattle area.
1972	National Organization of U.S. Filipino American citizens is established.
1978	Sea Mar (Clínica de la Comunidad) is created to serve Latinos with medical, dental, and behavioral health services.

1986	César Chávez leads a march for improved working conditions on farms in the Yakima Valley.
1990s	Economic and political turmoil in Latin American countries drives large Latino immigrant influx in Washington.
1995	Based on the United Farm Workers of Washington State's efforts, the first union contract for farmworkers is established with Chateau Ste. Michelle winery.
1996	Gary Locke becomes Washington's first Asian American governor and the first Asian American governor in the United States.
1997	The International District Village Square in Seattle, Washington, is completed, which houses social services agencies, a community health clinic, housing for elderly, and daycare facility.
2000	Japanese American owned Uwajimaya, the largest Asian grocery story in the Pacific Northwest completes the new Uwajimaya Village in the heart of Seattle's International District.
2001	Hate-Free Zone (HFZ) is established as a leading immigrant advocacy group. Washington declares itself a "Hate-Free State."
2002	Civic organizations such as Washington Chapter of American Civil Liberties Union (WA-ACLU) and One America (formerly HFZ) force the state legislature to abandon a wiretapping bill and anti-terrorism legislative package.
2003	Advocacy groups successfully push the Seattle City Council to pass a nationwide ordinance to prohibit city employees from asking about one's immigration status.
2006 (April 11)	About 15,000, mainly Latino residents—citizens and undocumented residents—march the streets of Seattle advocating for immigrant rights.
2006 (May 1)	In response to federal legislation aimed to criminalize undocumented immigrants, thousands march in Yakima and in Seattle for immigrant rights. Marchers and community leaders advocate for a clearer path to citizenship, family unification assistance, and workplace and civil-rights protections.
2007	Seattle's mayor instituted policies on foreign language interpretation and translation services for immigrants in city government.
2008	Partnership between One America (Formerly Hate Free Zone) and Governor Gregoire leads to an executive order establishing a policy council on immigrant integration and legislature financial support to create the New Americans Citizenship Program.
2009	King County council members pass a local law to continue service provision to immigrants, regardless of citizenship status.
2011	Respect Washington's efforts to include Initiative 1122 regarding restrictions to immigrants' rights on the November ballot fails.
2011	Voters reject Loren Nichols, a Kennewick City Council candidate promoting a restrictive immigrant agenda. His bid draws more attention to the environment and citizen response.

HISTORICAL OVERVIEW

The state of Washington boasts deep historical immigration roots. Human beings migrating by land from present-day Alaska or possibly by boat from the Pacific Islands arrived to what is now the state of Washington millennia ago. Their descendants received explorers from Spain and Britain in the 1700s, often with catastrophic consequence to their populations with the introduction of European diseases like smallpox. Spain was the first European nation to stake claim to the Pacific Northwest, including present-day Washington. Under threat of war from Britain, in 1790, Spain opened the Pacific Northwest territories to other nations, and by 1805 Lewis and Clark Expedition traversed from the eastern part of what is now Washington to the Pacific Ocean. Although Spain, until 1819, and Britain, until 1846, exercised legal claims to territories in the Pacific Northwest, American immigrants established fur trading and sawmill companies throughout Washington in the first half of the 1800s. A booming American settler economy, fierce conflict between settlers and First Nations tribes, the Pig War between the United States and Great Britain, and the arrival of Chinese immigrants, all occurred under the governance of the Washington territorial legislature in the second half of the 1800s. Originally part of the territory of Oregon created by the U.S. Congress in 1848, the state of Washington that we know today gained statehood in 1889.

Following the enactment of the Chinese Exclusion Act of 1882 by the U.S. Congress, anti-Chinese riots erupted in the state of Washington. The riots culminated in the forced deportation of Chinese immigrants from the cities of Seattle and Tacoma by Washington whites and First Nations people. The Washington constitution of 1889 prohibited the sale of lands to "aliens ineligible for citizenship," a policy excluding Asians who were the only immigrants ineligible to become naturalized U.S. citizens. Washington state policymakers passed additional laws in 1921 banning leasing rights to Asian immigrants and, in 1923, denying property ownership for U.S.-born citizens who were the children of Japanese and Chinese immigrants. Previously unfettered immigration from Asia to the United States declined shortly after with the 1907 Gentleman's agreement between the governments of Japan and the United States, and came to a standstill with the passage of the 1924 Johnson-Reed Act that established quotas by country of origin. While existing Chinese and Japanese diaspora sustained a presence in Washington, their overall numbers declined relative to other immigrants groups.

At the dawn of the twentieth century, Washington state population grew by 120 percent, and much of that growth can be credited to an influx of immigrants from Sweden, Finland, and Norway. Immigrants from Nordic countries entered Washington and settled primarily in Seattle, Tacoma, and other towns in the Puget Sound area. By 1910, Scandinavians composed 25 percent of immigrants in Washington state, followed closely by Germans at 17 percent and Canadians at 16 percent. The vibrant immigrant-driven growth in the early 1900s helped to build Washington's economy. Three of the most prominent legacies of Scandinavian immigration included the north Seattle neighborhood of Ballard, the Nordic Heritage Museum in Ballard, and the Department of Scandinavian Studies at the University of Washington, Seattle.

An especially dark period of Washington history was the relocation and internment of Japanese Americans in 1942. Immediately after the Japanese bombing of Pearl Harbor in December 1941, President Roosevelt reasoned that Japanese Americans, even those born in the United States, represented an "enemy within." Roosevelt's Executive Order 9066 authorized the forced imprisonment of over 14,000 Washington citizens of Japanese heritage, a gross violation of constitutional rights as not a single case of espionage or sabotage was pursued. In 1948, and a generation later, in 1988 and 1992 the descendants of wrongfully interned Japanese Americans lobbied the U.S. government for formal reparations to individuals wrongfully imprisoned. The Seattle City Council passed a reparations ordinance in 1984 compensating five city council employees who were terminated because of their Japanese heritage to the tune of $5,000 each. White farmers capitalized on the internment of Japanese Americans, buying properties from Japanese American farmers who were forced to sell at discounted prices, and by leveraging U.S. government-sponsored contract labor programs with Mexico during and after World War II.

The national Bracero Program of the early 1940s revived the Latino pioneering legacy of the late 1700s Spanish settlements, composed primarily of Mexican settlers, in Neah Bay, the most Northwest point of Washington state. Like the Mexican mulepackers of the mid-1800s who made mining enterprises in eastern Washington possible in the absence of fully formed railroad networks, *braceros* in the 1940s filled labor shortages in eastern and central Washington that rendered agricultural business profitable. By the 1950s, Chicano labor from Texas and Mountain West states like Idaho, Utah, Wyoming, and Colorado, began to shift away from circular migratory patterns and to settle permanently in the Yakima Valley in central Washington. By the 1960s, Latino populations west of the Cascade Mountains developed in Seattle and cities in the greater Puget Sound area.

Permanent Chicano settlements in Washington mixed with a history of racial discrimination in the labor markets to produce civic and political activism. Chicano students and farmworkers joined national grape boycotts between 1968 and 1970, and organized several strikes in the Yakima Valley. Their efforts paved the way for social services organizations like the United Farm Workers Clinic (1972) in Yakima, and El Centro de La Raza or The Center for All Races (1972) and the community clinic, Sea Mar (1978), in Seattle. Latino civic activism continued into the 1980s and 1990s during a revival of the farmworkers movement. The newly unionized farmworkers of Washington joined the national United Farm Workers union led by César Chávez and Dolores Huerta, and secured the first union contract for farmworkers in 1995 with Chateau St. Michelle winery. In 1994, community activists in Seattle formed Casa Latina, a worker center directing services to Latino immigrant laborers that included classes in English-language training, workers' rights, immigration laws, parenting skills, and health education.

Immigrant-derived communities have been central to the demographic developments in Washington since 1970. Although the share of the foreign-born in Washington's population reached a twentieth-century low in 1970 at 4.6 percent, the federal Hart-Celler Act of 1965 equalized national origin quotas and revived immigration flows. Newcomers from Asia and Latin America constituted the largest share of immigrants to Washington State since 1970. The share of the population that was foreign-born in Washington increased to 6 percent in 1980, then to 7 percent in 1990, 10 percent in 2000 and was estimated to be 13 percent as of 2011. Within the Washington foreign-born population, 40 percent was born in Asia, and this figure has held steady from 1990 to 2010. By contrast, Washington immigrants born in Europe have declined from 24 percent in 1990 to 18 percent in 2010, and those born in Latin American countries have increased from 18 percent in 1990 to 30 percent in 2010. While the largest share of the foreign-born

New Washington state Supreme Court justice Mary Yu recites an oath during her swearing-in to the bench on May 20, 2014, in Olympia, Washington. Yu stood with supporters Anne Levinson, left, Ruth Woo and Phyllis Gutierrez Kenney. Yu, a former King County Superior Court judge, was sworn in as the newest member of the court, marking the first time the high court has had an openly gay justice. Yu, whose mother is from Mexico and father is from China, is also the first Asian American and first female Latina member of the court. (AP Photo/Elaine Thompson)

population in Washington has been from Asia, since 1980, Mexico was the top origin country, followed by the Philippines and Canada. In 2009, one in four Washington immigrants were born in Mexico, and no other country of origin alone constituted a share that was greater than 1 in 14. According to the 2010 U.S. Census one in three Washingtonians self-reported as non-white, 16 percent as Latino/a, 13 percent as African American, 5 percent as Asian American, 1 percent as First Nations or Native American, and less than 1 percent as native Hawaiian or Pacific Islander.

The history of Washington State has been a history of immigration. Newcomers of yesteryear occupied center stage in Washington's major social, political, and economic developments through the nineteenth and twentieth centuries, and the same can be said of newcomers today. The issue of immigration has always linked newcomers to members of the receiving community. In Washington that linkage continues to be grounds of contestation as evidenced by the response to immigration from state and local government, civic organizations, and the public.

TOPICAL ESSAYS

The Contemporary State of Immigration in Washington State

A watershed moment in U.S. history was the September 11, 2001, attacks on the World Trade Center in New York City. The political fallout of the 9/11 attacks had serious consequences for contemporary immigrant communities in the state of Washington. Public fervor reminiscent of the "enemy within" rhetoric directed toward Chinese American and Japanese American communities in the 1800s and 1900s, now targeted Muslim Americans and undocumented immigrants in the first decade of the 2000s. State and local officials across the country, including those in Washington, began to feel pressure to respond to alarmist concerns about Muslim American and undocumented immigrant communities. In the state of Washington, most of the contemporary tensions between immigrant restrictionists and immigrant advocates were being expressed in two immigrant-related policy debates. The first was about cross-deputization programs that focused on the role of local law enforcement officers, and the second was about E-Verify, an Internet-based employment eligibility program that focused on employer compliance with immigration laws.

Cross-Deputization and Local Government Responses to Immigration in Washington

The statutory root of cross-deputization was Section 287(g) of the 1996 Immigration and Nationality Act. The act authorized state and local officers to screen people for immigration status, issue detainers to hold them on immigration

Malisa Taing, 8, holds a sign as she stands with others in a small demonstration in front of the federal courthouse on June 17, 1999, in Seattle. Taing was participating in a protest of the indefinite detention of people by the Immigration and Naturalization Service. Malisa's brother had been held in INS detention for more than two years. (AP Photo/Elaine Thompson)

violations, and generate the charges that would begin the process of their removal from the United States. In practice, 287(g) programs have come in three forms. One is a jail model in which immigration status is screened only after an individual is charged with a crime (i.e., not a violation of a civil law like immigration rules). The more controversial model involves a task force of police officials who are charged with screening for immigration status while on patrol. A third model is a hybrid of the first two. In 2009, the Department of Homeland Security announced a nationwide initiative to establish jail models of cross-deputization programs, part of the Secure Communities Program, in every county in every state of the country by 2013. Overall, local governments in Washington have rejected proposals to establish any 287(g)-related programs (and the program is now defunct, as of November 2014).

Contrary to the popular conception that the federal government has failed to act on the issue of undocumented immigration, the development of cross-deputization programs indicates widespread action by the federal government in partnership with state and local law enforcement officials. A major justification and motivation for such programs is that federal resources fall short of what is needed to adequately enforce immigration law. From the point of view of federal agencies, leveraging local police resources represents a potential multiplier effect that boosts federal resources with a far greater impact on immigration law enforcement. From the point of view of local police agencies, cross-deputization programs inappropriately shift the enforcement burden of federal laws to the local level, and undermine the relationships that local police cultivate with communities that enable police to keep the public safe. Since 9/11 there have been several high-profile workplace raids conducted by the Immigration and Customs Enforcement (ICE) agency in the state of Washington. However, relative to other states, officials in Washington have, in general, rejected proposals to partner with federal agencies in order to enforce federal immigration laws.

Local legislation targeting undocumented immigrants has been rejected or anticipated in several local jurisdictions in Washington. In 2002, the Seattle Police Department issued a directive prohibiting screening of civil immigration status by police officers. A Seattle city ordinance the following year has extended this prohibition to all city employees and has clarified that police officers are only permitted to inquire about immigration status for those individuals who have been charged with a felony. In 2004, a Seattle city resolution further reinforced earlier legislation by interpreting that immigration status screening by municipal police, barring any criminal activity, is a federal civil violation, prohibiting police officers from initiating police action based solely on an individual's civil immigration status. By a vote of 5 to 4, council members of King County, the larger jurisdiction that includes Seattle, passed into law in 2009, the commitment to continue providing services to residents without regard to citizenship status. Supporting council members of the county's "don't ask" policy say that the measure discourages racial profiling. Support from law enforcement officials stems from concerns that without the law people would be afraid to come forward as victims, and health officials say denying health care on the basis of citizenship is bad medicine and not cost-effective.

On the other side of the state, the city of Kennewick rejected legislative proposals in 2006 that would make it illegal to employ or rent housing to an undocumented immigrant. That same year Kennewick rejected a proposal to establish English as the official language of the city. In 2007, Kennewick officials rejected similar proposals that mete out a $1,000 fine to landlords for each undocumented migrant living in an apartment, and allow the city to deny business licenses to those who do business with undocumented immigrants. Just as immigrant restrictionist proposals have been rejected by policymakers in Kennewick, at least one candidate running an anti-immigrant campaign in 2011 was rejected by voters. Loren Nichols gained notoriety as a Kennewick City Council candidate the summer before the November 2011 city elections, when he advocated for capital punishment to undocumented immigrants who currently reside in the United States and that undocumented immigrants entering the United States be shot at the border. Although Kennewick voters rejected Nichols's bid for a council position, the city was poised to adopt E-Verify, the federal-sponsored employment eligibility program.

E-Verify and State and Local Government Responses to
Immigration in Washington

The issue of cross-deputization has played out primarily at the local level of politics in the state of Washington, and has remained off of the state legislative policy agenda. By contrast, E-Verify has been at the center of contemporary policy debate in Washington at the local and state levels. E-Verify is an online database cross-reference program designed for employers to identify whether a person is eligible for employment in the United States. Some states like Arizona and Mississippi mandate that employers use the program, and in the state of Washington such a mandate is not in place, though public offices and private enterprises can voluntarily make use of E-Verify. The E-Verify movement by a handful of local governments has a supporting counterpart in a statewide citizen initiative, both of which have generated an opposition proposal in the state legislature.

As of January 2012, 3 counties and 11 cities in Washington State mandated the use of E-Verify by its contractors. Clark County in the southwestern part of the state spearheaded the movement by local governments to use E-Verify, though some cities within the county have resisted using the program. The use of E-Verify by local governments remains a contested issue at the local and state levels. In January 2012, the Kennewick City Council voted on whether to mandate the use of E-Verify Program, and approved/rejected the measure. State officials for their part, including state representative Phyllis Gutierrez Kenney (D-Seattle) and Washington governor Christine Gregoire, offer conditional support to the E-Verify Program if the federal government passes a broader immigration policy reform. Governor Gregoire has sided with the opposition to E-Verify as part of a broader campaign to support the growers' industry in the state. In summer 2010, Governor Gregoire toured farmlands in eastern Washington and made public statements calling on the U.S. Congress to pass immigration reform that meets the needs of Washington's $35 billion agriculture industry. Governor Gregoire along with a delegation of Washington farm group representatives flew to Washington D.C. to lobby members of Congress to oppose a Republican bill that mandated employers to use E-Verify. Approximately 92,000 workers were needed for seasonal harvests in Washington and about two out of three farmworkers lacked proper employment documents. The fact that so many of Washington's farmworkers were and are undocumented has set the stage for the rare coalition focusing on opposition to E-Verify between Washington growers and immigrant advocates. Currently, Washington state does not mandate the use of E-Verify, and state representative Kenney sponsored House Bill (HB) 2568 to stop cities and counties from requiring employers to use E-Verify. Despite support from immigrant advocates and the powerful farming lobby in the state, HB 2568 died in the state House chamber in February 2012.

Although cross-deputization has not been a state or local legislative priority, responses by the federal government to undocumented immigration in Washington state made news headlines on several occasions in the late 2000s. For example, in 2009, a car engine repair firm in Bellingham was the target of the first worksite raid under the Obama administration. The raid targeted workers rather than the employer, a practice inconsistent with the announced priorities of the Obama administration to target undocumented immigrants engaging in crime and employers who hired undocumented laborers. News accounts indicated that the raid took the owner of the firm by surprise because a previous intervention by the federal government at the firm did not go any further than a notice of an I-9 audit (the forms that workers submit to employers verifying employment eligibility). Two years later, a series of raids of mobile homes in Ellensburg by ICE agents led to 30 arrests related to immigration law. The raids renewed debate in Washington on the role of local law enforcement agencies because ICE officials have relied on help from local police to coordinate the raids.

The worksite and homesite raids in Washington stood in sharp contrast to the "I-9 audit" approach by ICE, whereby employers were given notice that federal agents will be evaluating the legal eligibility of employees. The most prominent I-9 audit in Washington State occurred in 2009, and involved the fruit growers industry. News accounts reported that orchard owners released hundreds of workers and this has impacted every fall harvest since 2010. Growers desperate for workers to take near-record-breaking crops off of trees have turned to unemployed workers in the state, inmates from nearby minimum-security prisons, and guest workers from Jamaica. The challenge that growers face is that labor drawn from the first pool is simply not up to the task and tends to quit after a few days, while labor from prisons and Jamaica is very costly. In all cases, growers underscore that harvesting fruit requires skill and they estimate lower yields from using any of the available alternative labor relative to what they might extract from the more experienced undocumented farmworkers.

Governor Gregoire's official position on immigration is advocacy for federal immigration reform that provides for a guest worker program and a pathway to citizenship. In broader efforts to secure the economic vitality of Washington, Governor Gregoire created the state's New Americans Policy Council in 2008 and invited several prominent leaders of civic organizations in Washington to join the Council (New Americans Policy Council 2009). To date, the council's major achievement is a report detailing a set of policy recommendations for integrating newcomers into the state's fabric of social, political, and economic life.

Major Players/Actors in Washington Immigration Policy

Immigration Advocates

Civic and service organizations have played a significant role in shaping a positive climate toward immigrants in Washington. A host of organizations in the state focus specifically on serving immigrants. Many others advocate on the behalf of immigrants as a constituency of the broader community that the organization serves. Organizations such as the Northwest Immigrant Rights Project and the Washington Chapter of the American Immigration Lawyers Association (AILA) specifically focus on immigrants and work to provide them with legal services and aid them in the naturalization process. These two groups in particular work closely to represent detainees in the Northwest Detention Center (NDC), a prison facility that holds immigrants waiting for further legal processing, built in 2004 on the tide flats and toxic-waste dump area of Tacoma, Washington. Other civic organizations, like El Centro de la Raza and Casa Latina, offer immigrants educational support through tutoring and bilingual or English as a second language (ESL) education courses, financial support through food bank goods, subsidized housing, and employment opportunities. The Washington State Migrant Council offers similar services with a special emphasis on migrant, seasonal and farm-working immigrants.

Groups like the Washington Community Action Network, Community to Community Development, and the Alliance for a Just Society are Washington-based organizations that serve the broader population but also emphasize immigration or immigrant rights in their mission or "issues of interest." For example, Community to Community Development focuses broadly on serving people of color, women, poor, and low-income communities in the program areas of "participatory democracy, food justice and movement building." As a part of their "Participatory Democracy" sector, they have developed the "Immigration Justice Project" to end the marginalization of immigrants and their families and combat the unfair hostility and discrimination immigrants experience from anti-immigrant organizations. Since 2005, this project has maintained solidarity vigils, hosted educational workshops and presentations to raise awareness about ICE abuses and immigrants' rights, and partnered with other organizations in lobbying fair immigration reform. Similarly, the Alliance for a Just Society cites a mission of service to all people to ensure them equal access to opportunity and protection from discrimination and oppression. Under this mission, the coalition works to address these issues in health care, economic justice, and immigration.

National organizations—for example, ACLU—also serve immigrants in Washington through local chapters working on projects related to immigrants or immigration. The WA-ACLU dedicates a division of its services to "combating public and private discrimination against immigrants." They provide legal services via class action suits and lobby for pro-immigrant legislation in the state legislature.

These organizations are also known for their political activity and advocacy. As a response to the U.S. government's stricter immigration policies, many groups have heightened their political involvement and empowered immigrants to do the same. Northwestern Immigrants Rights Project initiated more programs and assistance for immigrants to ensure equal rights. The Washington Community Action Network currently hosts workshops on immigration policy and immigrant rights. El Comité Pro-Reforma Migratoria Y Justicia Social is responsible for some of the most successful immigrant rights marches in Washington as a response to Congress's policies that affected and specifically targeted immigrants.

Most notable, One America, formerly HFZ, was created in 2001 by Pramila Jayapal as a response to the discrimination and backlash directed toward immigrants after the 9/11 attacks. One America is leading the way in changing the social, political, and economic environment for all immigrants in Washington. As the largest immigrant advocacy organization in Washington, One America is active in organizing and engaging immigrants politically and providing research for policymakers and political leaders on immigrant issues and immigration policy. One America has been instrumental in educating policymakers and the public about issues salient to the immigrant community. For example, in 2008, One America coauthored the scathing critique of the NDC in Tacoma (Seattle University School of Law and One America 2008). The main charge in the report was that the NDC fell short of National Detention Standards and International Human Rights in the areas of legal due process, treatment by guards, medical care, mental care, and general living conditions. A later report authored exclusively by One America in 2009 detailed immigrant contributions to Washington's economy, and highlighted the role of immigrants in Washington as taxpayers, consumers, and workers in several industries. Finally, most recently, several leaders in the One America organization accepted an invitation from Governor Gregoire to join the New Americans Policy Council in 2008. The council issued a detailed report recommending, among other initiatives, a statewide English language-learning campaign, the dedication of resources to encourage citizenship, and to provide immigrant and refugee professionals with a pathway to career re-entry. Table 13 captures some of the active organizations in Washington.

Immigration Restrictionists

Despite a strong and dominant presence of support and advocacy groups in Washington for immigrants, the state is not without its share of organized immigration restrictionists. Although debunked currently, Washington has been the home of the Washington Minuteman Civil Defense Corporation until 2010. This citizens' organization's primary mission was to secure the borders and coastal boundaries of the United States from "unlawful and undocumented entry of individuals, contraband, and foreign military through civil protest, demonstration and lobbying all levels of government" (MinutemanHQ.com 2011). The group actively lobbied against the Development, Relief, and Education for Alien Minors Act and against providing any form of amnesty to immigrants and lobbied for stronger border control via fencing, technology, or an increase in border agents. Its more radical and militant offshoot, Minuteman American Defense, served a similar purpose

Table 13 Washington State's Civic Organizations

Name	Year Established	Purpose/Mission	Website
Chong Wa Benevolent Association in Washington	1915	Chong Wa Benevolent Association is a Chinese advocacy organization that promotes Chinese culture and welfare in Washington's communities. They sponsor programs such as a Chinese language school, citizenship classes, and Chinese cultural activities.	http://www.chongwa.org/ChongWa/index.shtml
ACLU of Washington State-Immigrants' Rights Project	1931 (WA Chapter created) 1987 (national division on immigration created)	Among a host of other issues, the ACLU of Washington works to combat both public and private discrimination against immigrants through legal action. They lobby against discriminatory border control methods, immigrant detention techniques and police practices, and are strong supporters of pro-immigrant legislation.	http://www.aclu-wa.org/issues/immigrant-rights http://www.aclu.org/immigrants-rights/about-aclus-immigrants-rights-project
AILA—Washington Chapter	1946 (chartering of WA chapter unknown)	AILA is a nonpartisan, not-for-profit association of attorneys and law professors who practice and teach immigration law, while working as grassroots immigration advocates. The Washington Chapter of AILA sponsors continuing legal education seminars and conferences, organizes a statewide naturalization day, and promotes pro bono efforts to serve immigrants.	http://www.ailawa.org/
Washington Community Action Network	1970	The Washington Community Action Network is a grassroots organization (and part of the Alliance for a Just Society) working to achieve racial, social, and economic justice in Washington. Immigration reform is considered one of the core racial and economic issues; for immigrants, they have worked to ensure that seasonal farmworkers receive the same health benefits as other workers.	http://washington-can.org/wordpress/

Organization	Year	Description	URL
El Centro de la Raza: Center for People of All Races	1972	The mission of El Centro de la Raza centers on unity, empowerment, justice, and equality for all racial and economic groups. They are providers of advocacy support and services such as bilingual and multicultural childcare, mentoring, and tutoring; hot meals and food bank goods; housing; subsidized healthcare; and courses on citizenship, homeownership, and financial literacy in the Latino community.	http://www.elcentro delaraza.com/
The Federation for American Immigration Reform (FAIR)	1979	FAIR's mission is to examine immigration trends and its effects; educate others on these effects, and advocate for policies aimed at reducing immigration such as border patrol and criminalizing undocumented immigration.	http://www.fairus. org
Northwest Immigrant Rights Project	1984	The Northwest Immigrant Rights Project works primarily toward helping immigrants becoming legalized in Washington. They offer legal services to low-income immigrants and educate them on immigration law.	http://www.nwirp. org/Home aspx
Casa Latina	1994	Starting with a group of community activist serving homeless Latinos, Casa Latina has grown into full service worker organization. Their current mission is "empower Latino immigrants through educational and economic opportunities." They teach ESL, workers' rights, and immigration law courses and provide employment opportunities and job skills training.	http://www.casa-la-tina.org/
Alliance for a Just Society (formerly the Northwest Federation of Community Organizations)	1999	The Alliance for Just Society is an eight-state coalition group that focuses on addressing economic, racial and social inequalities through state partnerships and regional and national campaigns. Their projects and issues include immigration, health care and economic justice.	http://alliancefora-justsociety.org
El Comité Pro-Reforma Migratoria Y Justicia Social (formerly El Comité Pro-Amnistia General Y Justicia Social)	1999	El Comité Pro Reforma Migratoria Y Justicia Social is a social justice, grassroots organization that focuses on civil, labor, and human rights. One of their largest efforts is providing social justice for Latino immigrant workers in Washington; however, they also work with labor unions and faith groups to promote rights for all immigrants.	http://elcomitewa. wordpress.com/

Table 13 Washington State's Civic Organizations

Name	Year Established	Purpose/Mission	Website
One America (formerly HFZ)	2001	As the largest immigrant advocacy organization in Washington, One America's mission is to advance democracy and justice by empowering immigrant communities and collaborating with allies. They work in the areas of immigration reform, civic engagement and participation among immigrants, and immigrant community organizing.	http://weareoneamerica.org/
Community to Community Development—Immigrant Justice Project	2005	Community to Community Development is a grassroots organization aimed at building social justice movements through inclusive strategies and strategic alliances. Their projects include partnerships with immigrant communities and leaders to "end the marginalization of immigrants and their families," promoting food justice and ecofeminism.	http://foodjustice.org
Washington State Migrant Council	n/a	Washington State Migrant Council is a nonprofit corporation that seeks to improve the quality of life for migrant, seasonal, farmworkers, and rural poor families through human service opportunities. It offers head start programs, childcare services, and nutritional aid for children in 11 counties around Washington.	http://www.wsmconline.org/index.phtml
Grassroots of Yakima Valley	n/a	Grassroots of Yakima Valley's goal is to increase awareness about undocumented immigration and U.S. foreign policies related to immigration. Their objectives include securing the U.S. borders, eliminating any form of amnesty for undocumented immigrants, and demanding greater government transparency in treaty negotiations among others.	http://grassrootsofyakimavalley.com/
Washingtonians for Immigration Reform	n/a	Washingtonians for Immigration Reform is a nonprofit organization advocating for the reform and enforcement of stronger immigration laws at the federal and state levels. They argue that immigration strains the U.S. economic, social, and environmental systems.	http://www.wfir.org/
Respect Washington	n/a	Respect Washington, "home of Washington State's E-Verify Citizens' Initiative," focuses on changing immigration laws and eliminating immigration corruption through petitions, legislative initiatives, and research. They are large proponents of making E-Verify mandatory for all employers.	http://www.respectwashington.us/

in Washington but is most known for its more extreme tactics and targeted focus on Latino immigrant narcotic traffickers and dealers.

Currently, active anti-immigration groups include Washington State Citizens for Immigration Control, Respect Washington and Washingtonians for Immigration Reform, among others. These groups advocate for more restrictive immigration laws that aim to reduce the number of foreign-born residents in the United States. Such organizations are critical of both federal and state government immigration policies and frequently cite economic, social, and environmental strains that increases in immigration pose to the United States and American citizens. Working both independently and with national anti-immigration organizations, members frequently petition local, state, and federal leaders for changes in immigration laws and restrictions on services and aid provided to noncitizens.

The organization Respect Washington spearheaded the 2008 citizen-based proposal, Initiative 409. Initiative 409, and its 2011 reincarnation, Initiative 1122, included measures to prohibit the state from issuing driver's license to undocumented immigrants, requiring immigration status screening by state agencies delivering services, compelling all local jurisdictions to cooperate with federal authorities in enforcing immigration laws, and making mandatory the use of the E-Verify Program. Respect Washington advocates failed to gather sufficient signatures to merit inclusion of Initiative 409 and Initiative 1122 on the November ballot in 2008 and 2011, respectively. The organization has declared intentions to continue their efforts in 2012.

Lastly, national organizations such as Eagle Forum, FAIR, and Pro English have also made their presence and position known in the state of Washington. Pro English and FAIR are national organizations that have rallied around Washington state legislation that negatively affects immigrants or restricts immigration. For example, Pro English leaders, members, and supporters lobbied for state legislation to make English Washington's official language, a move that would limit bilingual education in schools and bilingual and translation services in public service organizations. This move would adversely affect the immigrant population and many have viewed it as anti-immigrant legislation. The proposed legislation was defeated and Washington has remained one of the 19 states without an official state language. Similarly, FAIR has partnered with local anti-immigration groups such as Respect Washington to contest legislation that designated Washington as a "Sanctuary City" and city council aid used to fund pro-immigrant organizations.

Washington Public Attitudes toward Immigrants and Immigration

In addition to official governmental policy, the contemporary state of life for Washington's immigrants is shaped by the public. Contemporary immigrants live in real communities and interact with other community members at work and school, in stores and restaurants, and public spaces like parks on the weekends and roadways during commuting hours. In this section we scratch the surface of the mass public's response to immigrants as measured in public opinion surveys.

Since 2006, the Washington Poll housed in the Center for Survey Research at the University of Washington has had a finger on the pulse of Washington public opinion. Survey data collected in 2011 of Washington voters shows that 35 percent agree that immigration is changing the culture in the United States for the worse, and 60 percent say that they hold an unfavorable view toward undocumented immigrants, in particular. Attitudes toward immigrants in the context of a broader American community is more split, with 50 percent of voters declaring that welcoming immigrants into U.S. society, even immigrants who entered without authorization, makes America better off in the long run. Of particular interest to policymakers and commentators is whether these views translate into clear majority positions in favor of policy alternatives.

According to the Washington Poll, registered voters in Washington are not becoming less restrictive when it comes to federal immigration policy alternatives. Between 2006 and 2011, no more than 16 percent say that government policy should be to "make all illegal immigrants felons and send them back to their home country." The immigration policy most preferred by Washington voters was a pathway to citizenship for undocumented immigrants, increasing from 46 percent in 2006 to 52 percent by 2011 (Barreto and Parker 2011). These figures suggest that Washington voters are becoming less restrictive. To help put these figures of Washington voter opinions into context, a Gallup Poll reports that over the same time period, about 60 percent of all adults in the United States prefer a policy that provides undocumented immigrants with a pathway to citizenship. The two survey sources are not directly comparable because the Gallup is examining the attitudes of the entire adult population in the country, whereas the Washington Poll samples only from registered voters in the state of Washington.

When it comes to attitudes toward state and local policy alternatives, voters in Washington are slightly more complex. On one hand, the policy on the minds of most Americans is Arizona's controversial state policy that calls on local law enforcement officers to ask the immigration status of individuals suspected of being undocumented. On this matter, 52 percent of Washington voters support Arizona's policy, which mirrors the nationwide average support of 51 percent according to the Gallup Poll. However, this bare majority in Washington should be viewed next to the full 82 percent of Washington voters who oppose racial profiling by police officers as a strategy for identifying undocumented immigrants. Even among the 52 percent who support Arizona's policy, 74 percent disapprove of racial profiling. While Washington voters may be split on whether local police should shoulder the burden of enforcing federal immigration law, four in five take the issue with how the policy is most likely to be implemented.

LATINO/AS' ATTITUDES TOWARD IMMIGRATION

Perhaps even more significant than the general attitude of the public in Washington is the particular attitude held by the Latino population. Latinos make up about 9.6 percent of the population in Washington, with 34 percent of this population comprising foreign-born Latinos. The 2006 Latino National Survey (LNS) dataset includes 403 Washington Latino respondents of which 280 are immigrants and a variety of questions that tap into their political attitudes. The 2006 LNS data suggest that Latinos in Washington generally hold strong and positive opinions toward immigrants and immigration. Assessments of immigrants show that a majority of Latinos in Washington view immigrants in a positive light—contributing and strengthening the country rather than representing a burden to the welfare system and economy. This general orientation may be underpinning Latinos' evaluations of anti-immigrant organizations in the state and perceptions of the general public toward immigrants.

Shortly after the 9/11 attacks, citizen vigilante organizations formed in Washington state to protest what they viewed as a porous U.S.–Canadian border (several of the 9/11 airplane hijackers entered the United States through Canada). The Minute-Man association gained notoriety in Washington State and the 2006 LNS asked Latinos their opinions toward anti-immigrant activities in the state. A majority of Washington Latino/as, 52 percent, indicate that activities by civilian border patrol organizations have created greater hostility toward immigrants and Latino/as in the state, and a smaller 8 percent of the respondents viewed civilian border patrol efforts as a valid method to improving border control. Washington Latino/as are split regarding whether the general public in Washington is welcoming (or very welcoming) to immigrants. About 35 percent of Latino/as viewed discriminatory treatment as a result of their ethnicity or immigrant status, while another 35 percent of the respondents reported being discriminated against for related ethnic or immigrant characteristics such as their accent, nationality, and skin color.

Latino/as in Washington are generally supportive of immigration policies that benefit immigrants. For example, about 53 percent of Latino/as support immigration reform that immediately legalizes undocumented immigrants or provides a pathway to eventual normalized immigration status over time through a guest worker program. Additionally, over 77 percent of Latino/as oppose policies that charge undocumented students a higher tuition rate to attend state colleges and universities. To put these attitudes into perspective, it is worth noting that only 9 percent of Washington Latinos identified undocumented immigration as the most important issue facing Latinos today, and ranked it the fourth-most important problem facing the United States in 2006.Overall, the LNS data indicate that Washington and Latino/as in the state are generally welcoming toward new immigrants and are supportive of policy measures that are beneficial to undocumented immigrants.

NOTABLE GROUPS

GENERATION PROGRESS

Generation Progress, formerly Campus Progress, is a student-led group that provides information about many areas of immigration and immigration policy, particularly as they affect student immigrants. The group targets people aged 18–35 and encourages developing leadership skills and grassroots political organizing. The three broad areas that concern this group are economic justice, human and civil rights, and democracy. While all three of these areas pertain to immigrants, they link human and civil rights to immigration policy and reform in particular. Generation Progress publishes informative articles on immigration issues; for example, how they pertain to students who often qualify for Deferred Action Childhood Arrivals. The group uses social media, leadership meetings, and holds summits on immigration issues to develop advocacy skills and foster civic participation for this age group. They target an important population, particularly because many immigrants from mixed status families are in this age group and will become voters in the next few decades.

BIBLIOGRAPHY

Barreto, Matt A., and Christopher Parker. "2011 Washington Poll." 2011. http://www.wash ingtonpoll.org/results.html. Accessed March 29, 2014.

Baretto, Matt A., and Christopher Parker. "The Washington Poll: Issues and Opinions May 2010." http://www.washingtonpoll.org/results/MAY2010.pdf. Accessed March 29, 2014.

Columbia River Basin Ethnic History Archive. "Mexican Americans in the Columbia Basin Historical Overview." http://archive.vancouver.wsu.edu/crbeha/ma/ma.htm. Accessed March 29, 2014.

Dizon, Jude Paul. "Washington State Students Advocate for Undocumented Peers." Generation Progress, January 31, 2014. http://genprogress.org/voices/2014/01/31/25103/washington-state-students-advocate-for-undocumented-peers/. Accessed February 28, 2014.

Dupler, Michelle. "Kennewick Council Poised to Adopt E-Verify." *Tri-City Herald*, January 15, 2012. http://www.tri-cityherald.com/2012/01/15/1787833/kennewick-council-poised-to-adopt.html. Accessed March 29, 2014.

Fraga, Luis R., John A. Garcia, Rodney Hero, Michael Jones-Correa, Valarie Martinez-Ebers, and Gary M. Segura. "Latino National Survey (LNS)." 2006 [Computer file], ICPSR20862-v4. Ann Arbor, MI: Inter-university Consortium for Political and Social Research [distributor], 2010–05–26. doi:10.3886/ICPSR20862.v4.

Fresco, C. "Cannery Workers' and Farm Laborers' Union 1933–39: Their Strength in Unity." Seattle Civil Rights and Labor History Project. http://depts.washington.edu/civilr/cwflu.htm. Accessed March 29, 2014.

Jayapal, Pramila, and Sarah Curry. "Building Washington's Future: Immigrant Workers' Contribution to Our State's Economy." http://weareoneamerica.org/immigrant-contributions-washingtons-economy-report. Accessed March 29, 2014.

Johnson, Anne. "Generation Progress." Generation Progress Website. http://genprogress.org/about/about-us/the-new-campus-progress-is-generation-progress/. Accessed February 28, 2014.

Jones, Jeffrey M. "More Americans Favor than Oppose Arizona Immigration Law." http://www.gallup.com/poll/127598/Americans-Favor-Oppose-Arizona-Immigration-Law.aspx. Accessed March 29, 2014.

"Latino History of Washington State." http://www.historylink.org/index.cfm?DisplayPage=output.cfm&File_Id=7901. HistoryLink.org. Accessed March 29, 2014.

MinutemanHQ.com. "About Us." 2011. http://www.minutemanhq.com/hq/aboutus.php. Accessed March 29, 2014.

New Americans Policy Council. "A Plan for Today, A Plan for Tomorrow." 2009. http://www.governor.wa.gov/priorities/diversity/report.pdf. Accessed March 29, 2014.

Sea Mar Community Health Centers. "Sea Mar Community Health Centers." http://www.seamar.org/. Accessed March 29, 2014.

Seattle University School of Law, and One America. "Voices from Detention: A Report on Human Rights Violations at the Northwest Detention Center in Tacoma." 2008. http://www.weareoneamerica.org/sites/default/files/OneAmerica_Detention_Report.pdf. Accessed March 29, 2014.

Washington State Commission on Asian Pacific American Affairs. "Selected Dates and Events of Asian Pacific American History," http://www.capaa.wa.gov/data/timeline.shtml. Accessed March 29, 2014.

Washington State Commission on Hispanic Affairs. "About Us." http://www.cha.wa.gov/?q=node/3. Accessed March 29, 2014.

Yakima Valley Farm Workers Clinic. "About Us." http://www.yvfwc.com/about.asp. Accessed March 29, 2014.

48

WEST VIRGINIA

Kathleen R. Arnold

CHRONOLOGY

1584	Queen Elizabeth I authorizes Sir Walter Raleigh's expedition. Part of his expedition arrives on Roanoke Island and they claim the land. Remaining settlers disappear without any trace.
1586	Colonists on Roanoke Island abandon the settlement because of their difficulties.
1606	A royal charter funds new exploration in this area.
1607–1776	The territory now known as West Virginia is first established as part of the Virginia Colony in 1607, controlled by the British. It is called Virginia to honor the Virgin Queen, Queen Elizabeth I.
1671	The New River and Kanawha Falls are discovered by a British search expedition. German and French explorers also enter this territory.
1700s	Scotch Irish and German settlers arrive in West Virginia. There are attempts at Swiss settlement during this time as well.
1722	Treaty of Albany claims that the Blue Ridge Mountains will mark the boundary of European settlement and acknowledges Iroquois rights in most of West Virginia. Shawnee and Cherokee also hunted in this area.
1727	Pennsylvania Germans found a settlement at New Mecklenburg (now Shepherdstown).
1730s	Germans, Welsh, Scots, Irish come to this area to settle.
1731	First settlement in what is now known as West Virginia by a Welsh explorer occurs.
1734	Virginia is established, including all of the territory that would become West Virginia.

1742	Coal is discovered at the Coal River.
1744	Treaty of Lancaster is signed.
1748	George Washington surveys land in western Virginia for the British.
1752	Treaty of Logstown is signed.
1754–1763	French and Indian War is fought.
1760s	Increased settlement patterns occurs. Many come through other states.
1761	Robert Harper begins operating a ferry (establishing what is now called Harpers Ferry).
1763	Proclamation of 1763 reaffirms Native American claims to the land.
1768	The Iroquois cede some territory to Britain (Treaty of Fort Stanwix).
1774	By the Treaty of Lochaber, Cherokee holdings in western Virginia are sold to the colony of Virginia. First British settlers come to Kanawha County area.
1776–1794	Prolonged skirmishes between Native Americans and European settlers are fought.
Early 1800s	Increasing divisions are seen between what is now called Virginia and what would become West Virginia.
1806	The first salt well is established in the Great Kanawha Valley.
1810	Oil is discovered in western Virginia.
1815	The country's first gas well is discovered in Charlestown, West Virginia.
Mid-1800s	German and Irish immigrants arrive directly to this area.
1859	Abolitionist John Brown attempts to lead an armed insurrection against the institution of slavery at Harpers Ferry. The effort fails and he is convicted of treason and sentenced to death.
1862	After lengthy debates, the territory known as West Virginia applies for admission to the Union as a state. They are granted permission for this application if they legislate a phasing out of slavery in their new state constitution.
1863	West Virginia is formed during the Civil War era, seceding from Virginia and becoming a Union state. It is the 35th state. Boundaries and former debts are not resolved at this time.
1863–1893	From statehood in 1863, West Virginia is one of most important coal-producing states, but particularly after 1893; production increases every year from 1863 to 1893.
1866	Anyone who aided the confederacy is denied citizenship. Their citizenship is later restored in 1871.
1870–1915	New York serves as a port of entry, where immigrants would arrive and then travel to West Virginia to work in the coal industry. During this time period, West Virginia becomes an important site of labor disputes.

1877	Baltimore and Ohio Railroad employees strike, protesting their wages.
Late 1800s	Greater numbers of immigrants arrive from Ireland, Hungary, Italy, and Poland. Some businesses conducted include beaver trapping and coal and salt mining.
1880s–1940s	Belgian glassblowers arrive in West Virginia. They settle with their families and maintain strong ties to their region.
1880	Coal strike occurs.
1881	Declaration that all citizens with the vote, including African Americans, can serve on juries is passed.
1885	Charleston becomes the state capital.
1892	Italians begin to arrive in coal mines and become one of most important labor forces. Many settle along the Monongahela River in Marion County. Poles, Slovaks, and Hungarians also arrive.
1896	Christopher Payne becomes the first African American in the state to be elected to the legislature.
1897	Miners continue to assert their right to unionize and fight for decent conditions. "Mother Jones" is a key leader in this struggle for workers' rights.
1905	Croatians begin to arrive to work in coal mines, mostly settling in Monongah.
1906	Significant number of mining accidents occurs this year.
1907	Mining accidents with over 400 deaths occur. The explosion attracts foreign laborers seeking work, including Austrians, Russians, Lithuanians, Slovenians, and Eastern Slavs. English, Scotch, and Welsh immigrants are often hired as mining management. This is a peak year of coal-mining production.
1907–1930s	Romanians, Macedonians, Spaniards, Greeks, and Syrians arrive, many without their families.
1910s	Belgian glassblowers become dominant in towns such as Salem and Clarksburg.
1912–1921	Prolonged conflicts occur between mine owners and miners who want the right to collective bargaining and safer conditions.
1912	Strike by the United Mine Workers of America leads to the imposition of martial law. Mother Jones continues to fight for miners' rights to decent wages and higher safety standards.
1914	Germany invades Belgium and Belgian glassblowing communities in West Virginia mobilize to help their country women and men.
1916	Women are denied the vote.
1919	Nationwide miners' strike begins.
1920	Matewan Massacre occurs in Mingo County, evidence of intense labor disputes mixed with racial tensions and divisions between immigrants and citizens. Federal troops are sent to guard the mines.

1920–1921	"Coal wars" take place as workers fight for basic labor rights.
1921	Violent skirmishes between workers and mine owners take place. Three Days Battle occurs between striking miners, state police, and coal company management. Battle of Blair Mountain also occurs—it is considered one of the largest armed protests on behalf of workers' rights.
1924	Mining accident kills 119 people.
1927	About 97 miners are killed in one accident.
1928	First African American woman—Minnie Buckingham Harper—is elected to the state legislature.
1940	About 91 people are killed in mining explosion.
World War II Era	There is high participation in World War II, including women volunteers from West Virginia. Labor strife continues during this time, particularly as the United Mine Workers continued to assert their rights to decent work conditions in this era.
1950s–1960s	There is less immigration to this area and more general population losses are seen with increasing unemployment, particularly in mining jobs. The 1950s mark a significant time period for out-migration.
1956	Women are allowed to serve on juries.
1960s	During the Vietnam War era, this state has the highest death rate as a result of this war of any state in the nation.
1966	Mining explosion occurs.
1968	Mining explosion occurs.
1969	Coal Mine Health and Safety Act law is passed.
1971	Major coal strike by roughly 40,000 miners takes place.
1976	Miners strike.
1981	Miners strike.
1990s	Population begins to increase and foreign investment from Japanese, Taiwanese, and British firms stimulate the economy. Service industries are established and expanded. Some immigration is seen in this area as the South becomes a new immigration gateway—particularly migration from Mexico—but still relatively lower numbers arrive in West Virginia compared to other southern states.
1996	West Virginia University College of Law Immigration Law Clinic is established to help immigrants and refugees.
2000-Present	Refugees from Eritrea, Vietnam, and Yugoslavia arrive.
2006	Mining tragedy occurs: 13 miners are trapped and one survives.
2010	Mining explosion kills 29. The longest-serving senator and member in the history of the U.S. Congress, Senator Robert Byrd, passes away.
2012	The West Virginia University College of Law Immigration Law Clinic helps a Syrian family gain asylum.
2013	West Virginia senators support comprehensive immigration reform, including a path for citizenship for some resident immigrants.

HISTORICAL OVERVIEW

Western Virginia to 1863

West Virginia is the 41st largest state and one of the least densely populated of all states. The state entered the Union in 1863, when it seceded from the state of Virginia and was accepted as the 35th state. The state had a strong history of immigration, particularly as coal, salt, and other natural resources were discovered but it also became one of the least populated states in the postwar period up until recently. Today, its population is still low and immigration numbers are correspondingly minimal, although increasing.

The territory of Virginia was first explored by the English in 1584, when Queen Elizabeth I authorized Sir Walter Raleigh's expedition to the Americas. A group from his expedition arrived on Roanoke Island and claimed the land, settling there for some time. Some colonists left in 1586, after enduring too many hardships, but others stayed behind. These settlers, called the Lost Colony, seemingly vanished into thin air—there was no trace of them after 1590. A new British expedition to this area was funded in 1606 and Virginia Colony was established in 1607. It was named Virginia to honor the Virgin Queen Elizabeth I. This territory remained under British control until 1776. Nevertheless, several other groups of explorers also traveled through the territory and established some settlements. A British search expedition founded New River and Kanawha Falls. German explorers also traveled through this area as well as French explorers in 1671. Scotch Irish arrived and more German settlers, as the area now known as West Virginia was settled. There were some attempts by the Swiss to settle but these attempts failed. Unsurprisingly, as these settlers increased in number, they began to negotiate with Native Americans. In 1722, the Treaty of Albany established the Blue Ridge Mountains as a border for European settlement, while the Iroquois are granted rights in most of what is now West Virginia. The Shawnee and Cherokee also hunted in this area.

In 1727, Pennsylvania German founded New Mecklenburg (now Shepherdstown) and more Germans, Welsh, Scots and Irish began to settle in what is now West Virginia in the 1730s. A Welsh explorer established the first settlement in the area now known as West Virginia. In 1742, coal was discovered at the Coal River. In 1748, George Washington surveyed the land in the western part of Virginia for the British. A few years later, the French and Indian War broke out (1754), lasting until 1763. Despite this conflict, settlement increased in this area.

In 1763, Robert Harper began operating his ferry, beginning what is now called Harpers Ferry. In this decade, Native American claims to the land were reaffirmed but the Iroquois gave some land to Britain in 1768, in the Treaty of Fort Stanwix. In 1774, British settlers arrived at Kanawha County. In the

Rosie Flores stands inside her Rincon Latino store on April 7, 2005, on Washington Street in Charles Town, West Virginia. Flores, whose husband is a jockey at Charles Town Races, owns the store that caters to the rising Latino and Latina population in the eastern panhandle town. (AP Photo/Dale Sparks)

same year, Cherokee territory is sold to Virginia. For nearly two decades (1776–1794), there were continuous battles and tensions between Native Americans and European settlers. Despite this strife, European settlement continued, particularly from two of Europe's main countries of emigration: Germany and Ireland. Natural resources were discovered—salt in 1806, oil in 1810, and gas in 1815.

After independence, tensions between the two parts of Virginia developed. The most important of these tensions arose from the fact that eastern parts of Virginia were slaveholding and therefore had more electoral representation from 1829 on, while the western counties did not use slave labor. Although some of these divisions were addressed at a state constitutional convention (1850–1851), residents of the western part of Virginia continued to feel politically unequal compared to inhabitants in the eastern part of Virginia. These differences were only exacerbated in the pre-Civil War and Civil War era. In 1859, abolitionist John Brown tried to organize a slave revolt at Harpers Ferry. He did not succeed and was sentenced to death.

Statehood to the Present

In 1861, as Virginia declared that it would secede from the North, the Wheeling Conventions were held to establish that West Virginia was a separate state. Under the leadership of Francis H. Pierpont, West Virginia applied for admission to the Union. They were given conditional membership, only if their new constitution phased out slavery. In the midst of the Civil War, West Virginia officially became a state in 1863, although some counties were still contested between Virginia and West Virginia. Unresolved issues regarding boundaries and shared debts also remained.

Despite these political difficulties, the state emerged as the most important coal producer in the nation for the next three decades. As one state report notes, there was an increase in coal production every year between 1863 and 1893. The coal mines employed individuals born in the area, including African Americans, and others were recruited by labor agencies from Pennsylvania and New York. Immigrants were increasingly recruited and others came through word-of-mouth recruiting. Some of the first immigrants to arrive were Poles, Slovaks, Northern Italians, and Hungarians (1892–1893). Italians, Slovaks and Poles were most often hired in mines along Monongahela River in Marion County. As more mines opened, more foreign workers came and were employed everywhere. Many settled around the Monongahela River in mining towns near Fairmont and Clarksburg. About 2,100 Italians were employed in 1892 and approximately 650 Poles and 650 Slovaks were hired at this time. In the next year, Hungarians began arriving and their numbers increased over time—many of them were recruited in northern cities or in Europe. Some immigrants came after fleeing labor tensions in Pennsylvania, particularly in 1894. As workers faced dangerous conditions, they began to organize in West Virginia and significant strikes occurred in mining towns in 1880 and 1897, for example. "Mother Jones," a key figure in labor history, was an important leader in this area.

From the post-Civil War Era to the beginning of World War I, otherwise known as the "Gilded Age," West Virginia's industries continued to attract immigrant labor and became the site of some of the most important labor struggles. Communities, like the industrial community on Virginius Island arose to meet the needs of employers and wage laborers. As Shackel and Palus (2008) note, unresolved racial divisions were often played on by employers, using one group to undercut—or threaten to undercut—the other. Added to the changing dynamics of the labor force and continuous arrival of immigrants was the emigration of Belgian glassblowers during this time. From the 1880s through World War II, pro-union Belgian glassblowers began to arrive in West Virginia as they left an increasingly repressive state and labor conditions in Belgium. Unlike other immigrant workers they were highly skilled, well paid, and traveled with their families. These workers were unique in the power they held and through their international union ties that linked their own efforts in the Charleroi region to other glassblowing centers in Europe and the United States. For example, they formed the Universal Federation in the 1880s to increase their mobility and worker solidarity in the profession. Thus, these workers had strong social supports and held fairs, musical events, and other community activities. They often returned to Belgium, maintaining loyalty more to their region and fellow glassblowers than to the country itself. Their union beliefs were founded on a mix of socialism, craft identity, and regional traditions. They were also unique in their gender equality: women worked alongside with men in glassblowing factories. Unfortunately, part of their assimilation into American culture was accepting gender segregation. Nevertheless, many were openly socialist when they settled in West Virginia towns.

As some mechanization began to change glassblowing techniques, Belgian workers were leaders in forming cooperatives to keep their skills alive and to protect workers from job loss. For instance, "in Clarksburg, West Virginia . . . several cooperatives made certain that 'all of their buildings [were] large and commodius' and that they attracted 'an excellent set of workers'" (Fones-Wolf 1996, 310). And "In the Adamston and North View sections of Clarksburg, for instance, stockholders in the cooperatives soon bought lots in the new neighborhoods around their plants and built their own homes, increasing the tax base and contributing to local boosterism" (Fones-Wolf 1996, 310). In Belgian neighborhoods of Salem and Clarksburg, West Virginia, workers held dinner theater in a mixed gender setting (even as women were increasingly banned from the workplace). As relatively privileged, white workers, they often distanced themselves from racial minorities and immigrant groups deemed racially inferior (particularly, Italians and Poles). However, with changes in the glassblowing industry and Germany's invasion of Belgium in 1914, workers' loyalties changed and they began to support their country at the same time that their neighborhoods became more mixed. In this way, their former communities began to break up as their social roles changed. They continued to be important in the glassblowing industry and continued to play key roles in efforts to unionize and in established unions: "among the leadership of the CIO-affiliated Federation of Flat Glass Workers in Clarksburg were some names familiar to those who remembered the francophone labor and socialist past of the town: Fernand and Jules Wery, Louis and Phil Malfregeot, Danton Caussin, Amil Gregoire, and Arthur Lorrant" (Fones-Wolf 1996, 314).

As coal mines continued to expand and hire laborers, Italians arrived in even greater numbers. Spaniards from Andalucía, Galicia, and Asturias also came to work in the mines (Hidalgo 1999). Croatians began arriving in greater numbers in 1905, mostly settling in Monongah.

Although mining was always dangerous, significant numbers of accidents occurred in 1906, and in 1907, there were over 400 deaths from one explosion.

The explosion attracted even more immigrants seeking work, including Austrians, Russians, Lithuanians, Slovenians, and Eastern Slavs. English, Scotch, and Welsh immigrants were often hired as mining management. From about 1907 through the interwar period, single male Romanians, Macedonians, Spaniards, Greeks, and Syrians also came to work. As a 1911 report states, "[T]he history of immigration to the community . . . is largely identical with the history of the development of the coal business in the locality" ("Recruitment of Immigrants: Immigrants in Industries" 1911). While immigrants in other states were often used as strikebreakers, this report holds that this did not happen in West Virginia (or, not as frequently). The greatest number of immigrants settled in Fayette and Raleigh counties. Many other immigrants worked in Pocahontas Field, which included McDowell, Mercer, Mingo, and Logan counties. This area developed even more when the railway was built. With better transportation, Hungarians, Slovaks, Italians, Russians, Lithuanians; Romanians, Croatians, Greeks, and Syrians came seeking work.

In 1912, the United Mine Workers of America conducted a strike, which was met with the imposition of martial law. Mother Jones continued to fight for miners' rights to decent wages and higher safety standards at this time. In 1919, a nationwide miners' strike was held and miners in West Virginia were an important part of this strike. Conflicts continued through the next decade, as workers fought for decent wages and safer, more humane conditions. In 1920, the famous Matewan Massacre (aka the Battle of Matewan) occurred in Mingo County, as portrayed in the film *Matewan*, directed by John Sayles (Sayles 1987; Zappia 2011). This particular incident was emblematic of broader issues, including inadequate work conditions, a job market often split along racial lines, immigrant-citizen tensions, and sometimes, state collusion with employers. This particular conflict was rooted in part by the actions of a detective agency, akin to today's private security firms, that came into the town of Matewan to evict several mining families from their homes. The chief of Police, Sid Hatfield confronted the detectives as armed miners began to surround them. Gunfire was exchanged and several detectives as well as three townspeople were killed. Federal troops were brought in to guard the mines after this fatal conflict. The next two years were marked by "coal wars," as miners continued to fight for collective bargaining rights. In 1921, the Three Days Battle broke out between striking miners, state police, and coal company management. The Battle of Blair Mountain also occurred in 1921—it was considered one of the largest armed protests on behalf of workers' rights.

In 1924, a mining accident killed 119 people. Three years later, 97 miners were killed in a single accident. Another major explosion occurred in 1940 when 91 workers were killed in a mining explosion. During the World War II era, there was high participation in the war. Miners who stayed behind continued fighting for their labor rights. The United Mine Workers were particularly active at this time.

In the next two decades, the state suffered some major population losses as unemployment increased. Mining jobs were lost and significant explosions occurred in 1966 and 1968. After years of struggles for workers' protections, the Coal Mine Health and Safety Act law was passed in 1969, but conditions were still difficult. In 1971, approximately 40,000 miners commenced a strike. They held another general strike in 1976 and yet another one in 1981. Unfortunately, mining tragedies continued to occur, notably in 2006 and again in 2009.

From the 1990s, the population began to increase and foreign investment has stimulated the state's economy. Some service industries have developed and the state has attracted a relatively minor immigration flow. They have also begun to accept some refugees, including individuals from Eritrea, Vietnam, and Yugoslavia who have gotten refugee status. Educational institutions have helped immigrants and refugees, particularly West Virginia University College of Law Immigration Law Clinic. In contrast to other states in this region, West Virginia political readers have apparently taken a more moderate and thoughtful approach to immigration reform, rather than enacting harsh anti-immigration policies like their neighbors.

TOPICAL ESSAYS

Recent Immigrant History

Given the rich history of immigration to this area, West Virginia's towns are still marked by this earlier heritage. For example, individuals of Belgian descent have maintained some buildings and institutions from the nineteenth century. Interestingly, "the ethnic identity of their descendants has become more Belgian and less Wallonian or Carolingian, but these children and grandchildren are more interested in visiting Charleroi or Jumet than Brussels" (Fones-Wolf 1996, 314). Places like Clarksburg, West Virginia, demonstrate this historical legacy. But new immigrants have begun to arrive .

Several recent studies have identified the South as a new destination site for immigrants, particularly those seeking agricultural work and other types of low-tier wage labor. While there has been a long history of hiring seasonal agricultural labor in many of these states, not to mention the legacy of enslaved, indentured, or low-paid service labor, West Virginia's trajectory has been different than other southern states. In 1996, the federal government ceded some of its power to the states, allowing the partial devolution of the regulation of immigration policy through the Anti-Terrorism and Effective Death Penalty Act and the Personal Responsibility and Work Opportunity Reconciliation Act (Varsanyi 2008). As southern states dealt with unresolved racial tensions of the past, combined with relatively minor increases in immigration, many introduced anti-immigration legislation at the state level and municipal efforts to punish landlords and employers who knowingly aided or conducted business with undocumented immigrants. In the post-9/11 era, these policies became increasingly restrictive (Winders 2007). In contrast, West Virginia's politics do not seem to have followed these regional trends. Challenging regional trends to criminalize some immigrants, West Virginia senators Rockefeller and Manchin have supported comprehensive immigration reform (the Border Security, Economic Opportunity, and Immigration Modernization Act), recognizing that immigrants needs pathways to legal residency and citizenship.

Although West Virginia is still a poor state, immigrants are beginning to come to this state because there are opportunities in retail, service, and construction. These migrants, many of whom are Latino, are arriving because housing is more affordable, jobs are relatively stable, and wages may be slightly higher. These changes have occurred since at least the year 2000 and have continued even after 2001, challenging the trend of reduced immigration to other areas in the post-9/11era. Interestingly, in a state that has an aging population, immigrants are not always arriving alone but bringing their families, including young children.

As of 2013, about 2 percent of all children in West Virginia have at least one immigrant parent. These families are from Mexico (17 percent), Western Europe (13 percent), and East Asia (12 percent). Immigrant families in the state are also from Central and Eastern Europe and the former USSR: 10 percent; South Central Asia: 9 percent; and Africa: 8 percent. Most of these immigrant parents have been long-term residents in the state and many (79 percent) are U.S. citizens. While language attainment for all immigrants in this state is high, about 93 percent of all immigrant children are fluent in English. Children in these families have considerable sources of strength—these families tend to stay intact for longer than American-born families and they tend to have strong community support. In a very poor state, they also share issues with long-term residents: overcrowded housing, low wages, and some obstacles to high educational attainment.

Refugees

Although a very small part of the population of immigrants, some refugees have been resettled in West Virginia. Nonprofit organizations (often religious groups) help to facilitate refugees' integration into communities, providing information and referrals for these groups. They also find sponsors who will help individuals and families to integrate into the community, find housing and find steady employment. At times, different nonprofit organizations work together to draw on community resources for refugees. One example was in 2010, when the resettlement director from the West Virginia Office of Catholic Charities Migration and Refugee Services—Kim Keene—worked together with Ann Weimer, a pastoral assistant at Sacred Heart Co-Cathedral Basilica to ask the community to donate bikes to refugees so that they could have steady transportation (Smith 2010). The two refugee groups they were trying to help were from Burma and Ethiopia and both were employed in the poultry industry.

Another important resource for immigrants and refugees is the West Virginia University College of Law Immigration Law Clinic. This clinic was established in 1996 and "the clinic serves foreign citizens who are facing deportation, asylum, and other immigration proceedings" (West Virginia University College of Law n.d.). This was the year when the United States initiated a system of mass detention and deportation and so this clinic was founded at an important time. The clinic has helped refugees in a variety of cases: "The Clinic has won political asylum for clients from Afghanistan, Iraq, Egypt, and Guinea, often pushing the law creatively in circumstances related to today's most pressing issues, such as gender persecution, social turmoil during democratic transition, and conflict in the Middle East" (West Virginia University College of Law n.d.). More broadly, it aids people who need any sort of immigration legal counsel but cannot afford it.

NOTABLE GROUPS

CATHOLIC CHARITIES MIGRATION AND REFUGEE SERVICES

Catholic Charities Migration and Refugee Services is an important group that provides services to the entire state. Among other services, it provides translation services, English language instruction, job placement, counseling and cultural orientation, immigration assistance, and other referrals and information. This organization aids refugees in finding appropriate sponsors and they arrange for cultural training for these sponsors, in which the latter are educated in the unique needs and traditions of the specific refugee group they are helping. Some translation and interpretation is provided in Vietnamese, Arabic, and Spanish. Beyond helping refugees, this organization also helps all immigrants to the state, including providing information and referrals to help get legal residency, providing legal counseling, and helping in naturalization applications, when possible.

BIBLIOGRAPHY

Blanchard, Victoria L., Nancy A. Denton, Donald J. Hernandez, and Suzanne E. Macartney. "Children in Immigrant Families in West Virginia Fact Sheet." Center for Social and Demographic Analysis, sponsored by the Annie E. Casey Foundation, September 2009. http://www.caseyfoundation.org/~/media/Pubs/Topics/Special%20 Interest%20Areas/Immigrants%20and%20Refugees/ChildreninImmigrantFamiliesinWestVirginia/AECF_immigrant_families_brief_west_virginia.pdf. Accessed December 13, 2013.

Catholic Charities West Virginia. Migration and Refugee Services Web page. http://www
.catholiccharitieswv.org/index.php?option=com_content&task=view&id=56&Ite
mid=66. Accessed December 13, 2013.

Fones-Wolf. "Transatlantic Craft Migrations and Transnationaol Spaces: Belgian Window
Glass Workers in America, 1880—1920." *Labor History* 45, no. 3 (Winter 1995–
1996): 299–321.

Gilroy, Marilyn. "More than Crossing Our Southern Border . . . Hispanics Find Jobs That
Shift Migration." *The Hispanic Outlook in Higher Education* 17 (February 2007):
49–53.

Hidalgo, Thomas Gene. "Reconstructing a History of Spanish Immigration in West Virginia: Implications for Multicultural Education." Electoral Doctoral Dissertations for
UMass Amherst, Scholar One site, Paper AAI9920609, January 1, 1999. http://schol-
arworks.umass.edu/dissertations/AAI9920609/. Accessed March 29, 2013.

Metro News Staff. "West Virginia Senators Help with Passage of Immigration Reform
Bill." *Metro News: The Voice of West Virginia*, June 27, 2013. http://wvmetronews
.com/2013/06/27/west-virginia-senators-help-with-passage-of-immigration-reform-
bill/. Accessed October 12, 2013.

"Recruitment of Immigrants: Immigrants in Industries." 61st Congress, 2nd Session, Senate Document no. 663. Part 1: Bituminous Coal Mining, GPO 1911. West Virginia
Archives and History site. http://www.wvculture.org/history/government/immigra
tion05.html. Accessed January 17, 2014.

Sayles, John. *Matewan* (Film). Cinecom Pictures, 1987.

Shackel, Paul A., and Matthew M. Palus. "The Gilded Age and Working-Class Industrial
Communities." *American Anthropologist* 108, no. 4 (2008): 828–41.

Smith, Charlotte Ferrell. "Bikes Needed for Refugee Poultry Workers." *Daily Mail*, Charleston, West Virginia, November 24, 2010. http://www.charlestondailymail.com/foodan
dliving/201011231038. Accessed December 13, 2013.

Varsanyi, Monica. "Rescaling the 'Alien,' Rescaling Personhood: Neoliberalism, Immigration and the State." *Annals of the Association of American Geographers* 98, no. 4
(2008): 877–96.

West Virginia Department of Health and Human Resources. Family Assistance: Refugee
Assistance Web page. http://www.wvdhhr.org/bcf/family_assistance/refugee.asp. Accessed December 13, 2013.

"West Virginia Emigration and Immigration." Family Search Website. https://familysearch
.org/learn/wiki/en/West_Virginia_Emigration_and_Immigration. Accessed October
12, 2013.

West Virginia University College of Law. "Immigration." West Virginia University College
of Law Website. http://www.law.wvu.edu/clinics/immigration. Accessed October 12,
2013.

Winders, Jamie. "Bringing Back the (B)order: Post-9/11 Politics of Immigration, Borders,
and Belonging in the Contemporary US South." *Antipode* (2007): 920–42.

Zappia, Charles A. "Labor, Race, and Ethnicity in the West Virginia Mines: Matewan."
Journal of American Ethnic History 30, no. 4 (Summer 2011): 44–50.

49

WISCONSIN

Lukasz Albanski

CHRONOLOGY

1634	Jean Nicolet, a French explorer, arrives in the Green Bay area.
1673	French explorers Father Jacques Marquette and Louis Joliet enter the Wisconsin area, traveling from Lake Michigan down Green Bay and the Fox River, and then, after a brief portage, down the Wisconsin River to the Mississippi.
1716	French explorers attack a Mesquakie Native American village to dominate the fur trade in the Wisconsin area.
1763	France loses the Seven Years' War (known as the French and Indian War in America) and cedes to Great Britain all its territory east of the Mississippi River.
1783	Wisconsin becomes a territorial possession of the United States after the end of the American Revolutionary War (1775–1783).
1820s	Increased migration to and settlement in this area occurs, particularly due to lead mining.
1822	Native American tribes—for example, Oneida, Stockbridge Munsee, and Brothertown—arrive in Wisconsin.
1825	U.S. government representatives and tribal leaders from 11 Native American tribes sign the Treaty of Prairie Du Chien, which allows for greater European settlement in this region.
1832	The Black Hawk War leads to the forced migration of the Native Americans from large parts of Wisconsin. Up this point, there is little European settlement in the territory.

1836	Wisconsin becomes organized as a territory. The prospect of their own homestead and mineral wealth draws American settlers and European immigrants to Wisconsin and results in the creation of an ethnic mosaic in the territory.
1840s	Norwegian settlers begin to arrive in Koshkonong; Welsh and Danish immigrants also begin to settle in the territory.
1845–1870	Swiss representatives from the Canton of Glarus purchase land for settlement and New Glarus becomes one of the most prominent areas of settlement in the territory; many of the Swiss work in dairy farming.
1848	Wisconsin becomes the 30th state; significant numbers of German immigrants begin to arrive through 1860.
1850	Immigration has increased to the point that one in three individuals in this state is foreign-born; settlers include Germans, Irish, Norwegians, and French Canadians.
1852–1855	The Wisconsin Commission of Emigration encourages European immigrants to settle in the state; pamphlets in German, Norwegian, Dutch, and English are distributed in Europe and advertisements are placed in newspapers.
1854	The Wisconsin State Supreme Court declares the Fugitive Slave Law—enacted as part of the Compromise of 1850—unconstitutional at the trial of Joshua Glover (a runaway slave from Missouri).
1854	Wisconsin's strong stand against the Kansas-Nebraska Bill provides a political platform for the formation of the new Republican Party, which is first organized in Ripon, Wisconsin.
1855	Anti-immigrant sentiment leads to the termination of the Commission of Emigration, but immigrants from Europe continue to arrive, including Finns, Danes, and Italians.
1860	Swedish immigrants begin settling in the state.
1861	The Civil War begins; the state raises over 90,000 troops for the Union war effort between 1861 and 1865, with most serving in the Western Theater.
1864	Belgian immigrants of northeastern Wisconsin riot in Green Bay when the government makes them eligible for the draft by forcing them to sign a Declaration of Intent to receive land. By declaring that they intended to become citizens eventually, they became liable to the draft.
1865–1875	A second wave of German immigration occurs.
1870	A wave of Polish immigration to the state begins. Increasing numbers of Swedish immigrants arrive from 1870 through the 1890s. Icelandic immigrants settle in the state to work in the fishing industry.
1875–1890	The last and most numerous wave of German immigration to the state occurs.

1886	The fight for an eight-hour day by workers leads to strikes and marches in Milwaukee. On May 5, troops fire on striking workers at the Bay View factory in Milwaukee.
1889	The Bennett Law is passed, requiring all school instruction to be in English; immigrant families protest.
1890	Italian and Czech immigrants arrive in the state.
1891	Because of protests by German immigrants, the Bennett Law is overturned.
1897	The Social Democratic Party (SPD) of Wisconsin is established. The SDP makes political efforts to unite the entire working class; many workers are of immigrant origins. Victor L. Berger (1860–1929) helps implement the minimum social reforms program in the state.
1900	Robert La Follette (1855–1925), a prominent reformer and leading progressive, is elected governor of Wisconsin as a Republican; he serves until 1906 when he enters the U.S. Senate.
1900	Swiss immigrants and their descendants are running close to 200 cheese factories in the state.
1906	Governor La Follette is elected to the U.S. Senate, where he serves until his death in 1925. His opposition to U.S. entry into World War I makes him popular with anti-war German Americans in the state, but unpopular with his colleagues and those who support the country's entry into the war in 1917.
1914–1918	Anti-German sentiment grows in the state (and country) during World War I, especially after U.S. entry into the war on the Allied side in 1917.
1919	Wisconsin ratifies the Nineteenth Amendment giving women the right to vote in federal elections.
1920	Slovak and Russian immigration into the state occurs.
1924	Senator La Follette runs as the Progressive Party presidential candidate in 1924; he finishes third behind Republican Calvin Coolidge and Democrat John W. Davis, winning 17 percent of the popular vote, but carrying only Wisconsin in the Electoral College.
1947	Joseph McCarthy (1908–1957) becomes a Republican U.S. senator from Wisconsin. McCarthy launches an anticommunist crusade to expose communists and their sympathizers in American political and social elites.
1950s–1960s	Mexican immigrants often work as seasonal migrant laborers in Wisconsin. In the 1950s, roughly 12,000 temporary workers arrive each summer to work on farms. The Bracero Program is also operating at this time, bringing Mexican workers to growers.
1965	Lloyd Barbie (1925–2002) files a lawsuit that challenges school segregation in Milwaukee. Housing discrimination is banned in 1965.
1967	Race riots in Milwaukee lead to the declaration of the state of emergency and to inner-city violence.

1970	Radical antiwar protests at the University of Wisconsin-Madison campus culminate in the Sterling Hall bombing incident, which results in one death.
Late 1970s–1980s	Hmong refugees from Laos begin to resettle in the state after the end of the Vietnam War.
1976	Federal judge John Reynolds rules that Milwaukee schools are illegally segregated.
1986	Tommy Thompson (1941–) is elected the 42nd governor of Wisconsin; he dominates state politics for 14 years, revitalizing the state's economy and reforming social welfare. In 2001, he becomes the secretary of Health and Human Services for the George W. Bush administration.
1990s	A new wave of Mexican immigration to the state begins. Some Cuban refugees as well as those fleeing wars in Central America begin to settle in Wisconsin. Refugees fleeing war and genocide in the former Yugoslavia also resettle in Wisconsin.
1998	Tammy Baldwin (1962–), a Democrat, becomes the first woman to be elected to Congress from Wisconsin.
2004	Gwen Moore (1951–), A Democrat, becomes the first African American to be elected to Congress from Wisconsin.
2008	Some Burmese, Burundi, Iraqi, and Somali refugees arrive.
2009	Bhutanese refugees begin to resettle in the state.
2011	Widespread protests in the state oppose the Wisconsin Budget Repair Bill, which limited the collective bargaining rights of some public employees.
2012	Congresswoman Tammy Baldwin is elected to the U.S. Senate, defeating former governor Tommy Thompson.
2014	Wisconsin now has the third-largest Hmong population in the United States.

HISTORICAL OVERVIEW

The territory of present-day Wisconsin was originally inhabited by the Algonquian, Ojibwe, Dakota Sioux, Ho-Chunk (Winnebago), Menominee, Potawatomi, Fox, and Sauk tribes. Some early French exploration occurred in the 1600s, mostly for fur trading. In 1716, French explorers attacked a Mesquakie village to take over the fur trade in that region. French traders continued to enter the area in the eighteenth century, but there was little settlement. In 1763, after their defeat in the French and Indian War, the French ceded their territory in North America, including Wisconsin, to Great Britain. The Wisconsin Territory passed to the United States at the end of the Revolutionary War in 1783, but remained under effective British control until the end of the War of 1812 in 1815, when a real American presence was established in the region. Although there had been some earlier European migration to the area, more permanent settlements began to be established from the 1820s on. During the same time period, Native American tribes fleeing repression in the East began to arrive in Wisconsin, including the Oneida, Stockbridge Munsee, and Brothertowns. In 1825, American officials and leaders representing 11 different Native American tribes signed the Treaty of Prairie Du Chien, which permitted greater European settlement in the region. An influx of Europeans into southwestern Wisconsin in the 1820s and 1830s increased tensions with the Native American groups in the area and led to the Black Hawk War of 1832, which led to further Indian removals in the region and encouraged greater European settlement.

In the 1840s, Danish, Norwegian, and Welsh settlers began to settle in this area. In 1845, two representatives from the Canton of Glarus bought land for the Swiss settlement in south-central Wisconsin; New Glarus being one of the main Swiss settlements. Swiss immigration into the area continued through 1870. The first wave of German immigrants also began arriving in the late 1840s and continued through at least 1860.

Wisconsin became the 30th state to enter the Union on May 29, 1848. Immigration continued in significant numbers in the first decade after statehood. By 1850, one in three individuals in the state had been born abroad. Increasing numbers of immigrants from Germany, Ireland, Norway, and Canada arrived in the state. From 1852 to 1855, the Wisconsin Commission of Emigration worked to attract European immigrants to the state. Pamphlets in German, Norwegian, Dutch, and English were distributed in Europe, including at ports, and advertisements were placed in newspapers. The growing influx of immigrants caused anti-immigration sentiment to emerge in the 1850s and the commission was closed in 1855. Nevertheless, immigrants continued arriving, including Finns, Danes, and Italians. Belgian immigrants settled in northeastern Wisconsin in the 1850s and 1860s.

In 1860, Swedish immigrants began arriving in Wisconsin and a second wave of German immigration occurred from 1865 to 1875. Polish immigrants also began arriving beginning in 1870 and more Swedish immigrants settled in the state through the 1890s. Icelandic immigrants also came to the state to work in fishing. A third large wave of German immigration occurred between 1875 and 1890. At this time, immigrants were also involved in fighting for workers' rights and Wisconsin was a key state in the labor rights movement. In 1886, the struggle for an eight-hour work day led to violence in the state when strikers were fired on by troops.

Despite the continuous waves of immigrants and their struggles for democracy, the Bennett Law was passed in 1889, requiring all school instructions to be in English. Immigrant families protested, particularly German immigrants, and the law was repealed in 1891. During this time period, Italian and Czech immigrants began arriving in the state. Workers continued fighting for their rights and the SDP was established in 1897. During the World War I, although anti-German sentiment was strong, some Germans continued to come to the state.

Dramatic changes in immigration policy and in the origins of immigrants coming to the United States occurred at the end of World War II in 1945. A large number of European immigrants, along with Holocaust survivors, came to the United States to seek political asylum after their traumatic experience of the war and the postwar order in Europe. At this time, fears arose that these refugees were impoverished and would require much public assistance. Cold War concerns about communism and political ideology were also voiced at this time. The large foreign-born share of Wisconsin's population comprised members of ethnic groups from countries that had benefited from the policies of the Third Reich or were currently under Communist regimes. The 1950 Census of population showed that the foreign-born population accounted for 7 percent of the total population in the state (218,234 foreign-born of a total population of 3,420,435). The lion's share of the foreign-born population in Wisconsin came from Germany (26.8 percent), Poland (11.6 percent), Norway (6.7 percent), Austria (5.6 percent), the Soviet Union (5.5 percent), Czechoslovakia (4.4 percent), and Italy (4.4 percent).

In the 1950s, public anxiety that the American way of life was coming under siege were launched by the anticommunist campaign of Wisconsin's U.S. senator Joseph McCarthy. Before McCarthyism got underway, Senator McCarthy announced in his well-known 1950 speech in Wheeling, West Virginia, that he had exposed communists in the State Department. To him, the political and cultural life of the United States had been polluted by communism, and, thus, he initiated the second "Red Scare" (the first having occurred immediately after World War I). Because of the fear-mongering of the time ("red baiting"), foreign-born citizens were subject to intense scrutiny in their everyday lives. In particular, immigrants from Central and Eastern Europe suffered from the stigma of being associated with communism.

Until the 1940s, immigration to Wisconsin from Central and Latin American had been low. Between 1940 and 1950, Latin American immigration to Wisconsin constantly increased, from 0.4 percent of the total foreign-born population in 1940 (961 people) to 0.8 percent in 1950 (1,712 people). In particular, labor shortages caused by World War II created a demand for agricultural workers from Mexico. The Mexican labor migration to Wisconsin was facilitated by the federal Bracero Program until its ending in 1964. Another Spanish-speaking group that arrived in Wisconsin at that time was Puerto Ricans, who were drawn to industrial jobs in Milwaukee, Kenosha, and Racine counties in southeastern Wisconsin.

Although Wisconsin had attracted people from diverse backgrounds before World War II, the state had a small population of visible minorities. Wisconsin received a tiny influx of Asian immigration in the nineteenth century, which was gradually reduced by the elimination of direct immigration from such countries as China, India, Japan, and the Philippines at the beginning of the twentieth century and during the "tribal twenties." However, the Immigration and Nationality Act of 1952 preserved racial quotas but added Cold War concerns to the law to create more obstacles to immigration. This situation changed with the Immigration Act of 1965, which equalized quotas, removing the eugenic basis of immigration ceilings. The act also provided for some opportunities for family reunification.

Wisconsin received many Hmong refugees from Laos in 1975. The Hmong were recruited during the Vietnam War as guerilla soldiers to fight the North Vietnamese. After the United States withdrew its soldiers from Vietnam, the Hmong were left to the hostile communist regime. Many Hmong people were forced to flee across the border to escape massive and brutal repression. Refugee camps in Thailand served as the site where the United States vetted asylum-seekers. By the 2010s, Wisconsin had the third-largest Hmong population in the country, after Minnesota and California.

Hmong immigrants, from left, Mai Chor Lee, Cher Vue, Song Her, Xia Thao, Xia Cha, and Sia Xiong Lee take a look at a Hmong story cloth that promotes seasonal safety tips at the Volunteers of America building in Minneapolis, on December 7, 2005. The new tapestry in Minnesota weaves a tale using pictures of a car stuck in a snowbank, mittens, and an icy lake to teach new Hmong immigrants how to stay safe during a brutal Minnesota winter. (AP Photo/Beth Schlanker)

Hundreds of people marched through Milwaukee on May 1, 2013, to a park along the Milwaukee River to call for immigration reform and better protections for immigrant workers. The march and rally were organized by Voces de la Frontera. (AP Photo/M.L. Johnson)

Changes in Europe in the late twentieth century (including the economic boom in Western Europe), combined with lower numerical ceilings for European entrants led to decreased immigration flows. In contrast, political upheavals, population growth and deteriorating economic conditions produced massive pressure to emigrate in Latin America and Asia. By the 1980s, the United States had restructured its economy and, consequently, there was a demand for workers in low-tier positions. The United States' role as a world leader and the last years of the Cold War were also influential in determining national debates on immigration and refugees.

The consequences of these changes are well illustrated by considering ethnic compositions of the Wisconsin population between 1950 and 2000. In 1950, the top 10 countries sending immigrants to Wisconsin were European countries and Canada; immigrants to the state were almost entirely Europeans or the descendants of Europeans. In 1970, the top 10 countries of birth for foreign-born population were still European countries and Canada, but the state's Asian and Latino/a population had grown significantly. By 2000, the top 10 sending countries included only three European countries (Germany, Poland, and the United Kingdom), Canada, five Asian countries (China, Laos, Korea, India, and Thailand),

and Mexico. The 2009 data showed that even more people from East Asia and Central and South America accounted for growing shares of the population in Wisconsin, while European groups were declining in numbers. The impact of new ethnic groups also became more visible in the state's economy, education system, and levels of consumer purchasing power.

TOPICAL ESSAYS

CURRENT CHANGES IN WISCONSIN POPULATION

The foreign-born share of Wisconsin's population has gradually increased since 1990. According to the U.S. Census Bureau, the foreign-born population of Wisconsin in 1990 (121,547) accounted for 2.5 percent of the state's total population (4,891,769). In 2000, the foreign-born share rose to 3.6 percent (193,751 foreign-born out of total population of 5,363,675), and to 4.5 percent in 2009 (256,085 foreign-born of a total population of 5,654,774). Immigration has played a major role in increasing the diversity of the population in Wisconsin by contributing to the growth of the Asian and Latino populations since the 1990s. In 2000, 32.4 percent of the Asian population and 33.9 percent of the Latino population were foreign-born, compared with 26.9 percent of the white population. The U.S. Census Bureau estimated in 2000 that the foreign-born population in Wisconsin consisted of 36.1 percent of the Anglo population, 2.3 percent of the black population, 0.3 percent of the American Indian population, 28.7 percent of the Asian population, and 32.6 percent of the Latino population. In 2009, the foreign-born population in the state was 26.7 percent of whites/Anglos, 4.1 percent of blacks, 0.4 percent of Native Americans, 28.8 percent of Asians, and 39.9 percent of Latino/as.

Nearly half of Wisconsin's foreign-born residents (42.8 percent, 109,633 people) were naturalized U.S. citizens in 2009, who were eligible to vote. The two largest groups of naturalized citizens were among the Anglo population (39.5 percent) and the Asian population (37.9 percent), while naturalized citizens among the Latino population accounted for 18.4 percent. According to the Center for Social and Demographic Analysis at the University of Albany, most children (86 percent) in Wisconsin's immigrant families were U.S. citizens in 2007. However, only 63 percent of children in immigrant families in Wisconsin had parents who were U.S. citizens, but most children (73 percent) had parents who have lived in the United States for 10 or more years.

The Latino share of Wisconsin's population rapidly grew from 1.9 percent (93,194 people of a total population of 4,891,769) in 1990 to 3.6 percent (192,291 people of a total population of 5,363,675) in 2000 to 5.3 percent (316,667 people of a total population of 5,654,774), while the Asian share of the population also grew from 1.1 percent (52,782 people) to 1.7 percent (88 763 people) in 2000 and to 2.1 percent (118,750 people). The white/Anglo share of Wisconsin's population slowly declined from 92.2 percent (4,512,523 people) in 1990 to 88.9 percent (4,769,857 people) to 88.4 percent (4,998,820 people) in 2009, while the black share of the population slightly increased from 5.0 percent (244,539 people) in 1990 to 5.7 percent (304,460 people) in 2000 to 6.0 percent (339,286 people) in 2009. The American Indian share of the population did not change from 0.9 percent in 1990 (39,387 people) to 0.9 percent (508,929 people) in 2009.

Although the foreign-born share in the state has been steadily increasing, Wisconsin's counties are likely to include homogenous neighborhoods with the same racial or ethnic identities. The U.S. Census Bureau estimated in 2000 that the diversity index for Wisconsin was very low, between 1 and 3 percent (except for the Milwaukee area). The index expresses the likelihood that two randomly selected people in a given area would differ by race or ethnicity. However, the whole region of Midwest had the lowest value of the index in the country. The research also showed which ethnic and racial minority groups represented the highest percentage of a county's population. Latinos were the largest minority group in the southern part of the state (except for Iowa, Dane and Rock counties, which were settled by the black population), while the highest concentration of Asians was in Marathon, Portage, Wood, Dunn, Chippewa, and Eau Claire counties. The American Indian population is clustered in the northern part of Wisconsin.

Racial and ethnic composition varies from metropolitan areas, to the suburbs, and to non-metropolitan areas. According to 2009 data from the U.S. Census Bureau, the Latino/a, Asian, and black populations are more likely than the Anglo and American Indian population to live in central cities. However, the Anglo population is by far more likely to live in metropolitan areas outside center cities. In 2009, Milwaukee (the largest city in Wisconsin) had the highest percentage of the Latino population (57.2 percent of 59,785) of the foreign-born population, while both the Anglo and black populations accounted for 44.8 percent and 40.3 percent of 545,242 native-born population in the city. In contrast, rural areas in Wisconsin were dominated by the Anglo population (96.3 percent of the native-born population and 70 percent of the foreign-born population). The Latino population in rural areas accounted for 21.9 percent of the foreign-born population.

While immigration has increased in Wisconsin, the native-born population is not increasing significantly. In 2009, the fertility rate among the American-born population was 53 (rate per 1,000 women), compared to 93 of the foreign-born population. The average Wisconsin's family size was 2.99 in 2009. However, the average foreign-born family size was 3.71, while average American-born family size was 2.95. The foreign-born population was likely to live in a married-couple household (59.7 percent) more than the native-born population (51.7 percent). The American-born population had a higher percentage of divorce than the foreign-born population. About 10.2 percent of the native-born population was divorced compared with 6.6 percent of the foreign-born population. Moreover, American-born parents (30 percent) were more likely to be single parents, compared to foreign-born parents (20 percent). However, the poverty rate of these native-born families was lower than of foreign-born families. Foreign-born families were more likely than native-born families to have another adult relative in the home. Therefore, average foreign-born household size (3.15) was higher than average native-born household size (2.38). Based on U.S. Census 2000 data, *American Demographics* described Latino families as living in traditional settings, where a solid majority of households belong to married-couple families. Asian families consisted of two or more people, most of whom were married-couple families. While Latinos and Asian families were traditionally family-oriented, other ethnic groups were more likely to live alone or live in unmarried-couple families.

Earnings from the labor market were the primary source of income for the majority of households. Most foreign-born households (86.7 percent) had earnings in 2009. This percentage was even higher for foreign-born residents' households (93.4 percent). In comparison with foreign-born households, 80.7 percent of American-born households were employed. Foreign-born households also had more workers than in American-born households (1.43 versus 1.22). Median annual income was the commonly used indicator to capture economic status for populations. In 2009, the median household income in Wisconsin was $49,993. However, the median American-born household income was roughly above $50,000, while median foreign-born household income was $46 380, but there was a significant gap between naturalized U.S. citizens ($54,929) and non-citizens ($38,917). The highest median income was in Asian households ($57 955) and Anglo households ($52,080), while other racial and ethnic households had a lower median income: Latinos ($36,980), American Indians ($33,671), and blacks ($25,807).

In 2009, the proportion of families in Wisconsin with incomes below 200 percent of the poverty line was 29.3 percent. However, roughly one-half (51.8 percent) of foreign-born families had an income below 200 percent of the poverty line, while naturalized U.S. citizens' families earned 28.1 percent, and American-born families earned 28.7 percent. Childhood poverty is a subject of particular concern, because it is also associated with inequality of opportunities and child development. The childhood poverty rate for American-born families was 14 percent, compared with 28.2 percent of foreign-born families with children. However, naturalized citizens' families had only 11.5 percent poverty rate. Poverty rates were relatively high for all children in single-parent families maintained by women (roughly 40 percent), but poverty rate for foreign-born families was considerably higher (54.5 percent). Despite their higher median income, the poverty rate among Asian families (9.6 percent) was higher than that of Anglo families (5.9 percent). However, the poverty rate of other racial and ethnic type families was much higher than these two populations (blacks: 33.7 percent, American Indian: 27.5 percent, and Latinos: 23 percent).

High housing cost burdens and crowding are the most often-used measures of adverse housing conditions. In 2009, American-born households with moderately high housing cost burdens (30 percent or more of one's income) accounted for 28.7 percent of 1,510,288 American-born owner-occupied housing units, compared to roughly 40 percent of foreign-born owner-occupied housing units (for naturalized U.S. citizens: 33 percent). Only 10 percent of the American-born population had fewer than three rooms, compared to 22.1 percent of the foreign-born population (the naturalized U.S. citizens: 11.1 percent). In addition, foreign-born families were more likely to live in overcrowded housing than American-born families (more than one person per room). Less than 2 percent of American-born families lived in overcrowded housing, compare to roughly 13 percent of foreign-born families and to 6.4 percent naturalized U.S. citizens' families.

Roughly one-third of the foreign-born population (30.3 percent) did not have any health insurance in 2009, compared to 8.4 percent of the American-born population. There was also a significant difference between Wisconsin's foreign-born residents, because those with U.S citizenship account only for 11.8 percent, while the percentage for others increased to 44.2 percent. The lowest percentage of uninsured was among the Anglo population, while the Latino population had three times higher percentage of uninsured individuals (7.7 percent versus 28.4 percent), and other racial and ethnic populations had approximately two times higher percentage of uninsured individuals (Asian: 13.5 percent, Blacks: 13.2 percent, American Indians: 16.8 percent).

The foreign-born population comprised 5.2 percent of Wisconsin's labor force in 2009 (164,287 workers). According to the class of workers, foreign-born workers accounted for: 5.4 percent of private salary workers, 3.9 percent of government workers, and 4.7 percent of self-employed workers in the state. According to occupation, foreign-born employees accounted for: 4.7 percent of employed in management and professionals occupations, 6.1 percent of employed in services, 3 percent of employed in sales, 2.2 percent of employed in farming, 3.8 percent of employed in construction and repair occupations, and 7.7 percent of employed in transportation occupations in the state. The foreign-born population comprised 6.5 percent of Wisconsin's unemployed (16,429 people). The unemployment rate for the foreign-born population was 5.6 percent, compared with 7.0 percent of the American-born population. The highest labor force participation rate was the Asian population (65 percent), while the Latino population approached the labor force participation rate of the Anglo population (63 and 64.5 percent, respectively). The lowest participation rates were the African American population (48.9 percent) and the American Indian population (53.5 percent). These two populations also had the highest unemployment rates (Blacks: 19.5 percent and

American Indians: 18.2 percent). Asians' unemployment rate (8.4 percent) was higher than Anglos' rate (7.1 percent), but lower than Latinos' rate (13.3 percent).

In addition to these other measures of well-being, there is a wage gap between men and women. While median annual earnings for men in Wisconsin were $44,812 in 2009, median annual earnings for women were far lower ($33,631). Median annual earnings for American-born and naturalized U.S. male residents even exceeded that of the total population (roughly above $45,000). However, in comparison with those two groups, foreign-born men earned much lower (less than $27,000) while the wages of American-born women were higher than those of naturalized U.S. female residents ($33,611 versus $29,878). Median annual earnings for foreign-born women were even lower ($24,258). The wage disparity between men and women appeared to rise for the American-born and the naturalized U.S. citizen populations rather than for long-term foreign residents. Some of the wage gap could be explained by occupational differences. American-born and naturalized U.S. residents of Wisconsin, as well as American-born women, were more likely to work in professional and managerial occupations and were less likely to work in "blue collar" occupations, compared with foreign-born women and immigrant men, who were more likely to be find themselves in lower tier (and less well paid) occupations. Therefore, long-term foreign residents who were often trapped in low tier positions had less social mobility than their naturalized or American-born counterparts. The wage gap among naturalized U.S. citizens was even more likely than among other populations to be affected by gendered socio-economic status than other factors.

The Sellig Center for Economic Growth at the University of Georgia estimated that total buying power in Wisconsin expanded by 41 percent from 2000 to 2009. That percentage change in the state's buying power resulted from increasing Asian and Latino buying power, which totaled $5.7 billion for the Latinos population and $3.0 billion for the Asian population in 2009 (Humphreys 2009). According to the U.S. Census Bureau's *Survey of Business Owners of 2007*, Wisconsin's 390,041 Anglo-owned businesses generated receipts of $214,264,039 and employed 1,204,480 people in 2007, while 6,785 Asian-owned businesses had receipts of $2,330,310 and employed 15,808 people and 5,619 Latino-owned businesses had receipts of $2,421,160 and employed 10,901 people. The state's 11,143 black-owned businesses had receipts of $972,452 and employed 12,892 people, compared with 2,515 American Indian-owned businesses which had receipts of $322,854 and employed 2,102 people. To compare with the U.S. Census Bureau's *Survey of Business Owners of 2002*, both Asian- and Latino-owned business had expanded to wield economic clout. Asian and Latino entrepreneurs and consumers added billions of dollars and thousands of jobs to Wisconsin's economy and thus they have contributed to the size and vitality of the state's market.

According to a report by the Pew Hispanic Center, published in 2009, undocumented immigrants comprised 1.8 percent of Wisconsin's labor force in 2008 (55,000 workers). The Pew Hispanic Center estimated that the number of undocumented immigrants in Wisconsin had substantially increased from 10,000 in 1990 to 85,000 in 2008. Wisconsin belongs to the states with a low-to-average percentage of undocumented immigrants among their foreign-born population. According to another report by The Perryman Group, published in 2008, undocumented immigrants in Wisconsin were integral to Wisconsin's services, construction, and farming sectors to fill shortages of workers in the lower-paid and skilled jobs. This group argues that if undocumented immigrants were removed, the state's economy would fail. Further, The Perryman Group claims (based on size of the U.S. economy in 2008) that attempts at removal of the undocumented would result in the overall losses of $2.6 billion in economic activity, $1.2 billion in gross state product, and approximately 14,579 jobs.

Another important factor in Wisconsin's economics is seasonal labor migrants. Before 2004, more than 5,000 migrants worked in temporary, seasonal positions. After 2004, their numbers began declining to less than 5,000 migrants per year. According to the 2009 Migrant Population Report by The Bureau of Migrant Labor Services, 3,637 migrant workers and 459 dependents arrived in Wisconsin to work in food-processing industries and agriculture. A 2003 study on the economic impact of migrant workers on Wisconsin's economy conducted by researchers from the University of Wisconsin-Madison found migrants' contribution to Wisconsin economy was that 417 jobs were created annually, generating about $14.9 million in income to Wisconsin's residents and business. Additionally, $8.7 million in revenues were generated, flowing to Wisconsin's state and local governments. According to the same study, more than 50 percent of earned wages were spent locally by migrants, while 47 percent of season's earning (14 percent of season's earning for workers with their families) was sent to support family members who were at home or to pay loans abroad.

Foreign students are another important group contributing to the well-being of the state. The NAFSA has assessed that 8,647 foreign students contributed $195,313,000 to the state's economy in tuition, fees, and living expenses for the 2008/2009 academic year. Most foreign students are enrolled at the University of Wisconsin-Madison (50 percent of all foreign students in the state, 4,243 students) and at the University of Wisconsin-Milwaukee (12 percent of all foreign students in the state, 1,074 students).

Educational attainment is usually treated as an important indicator of lifetime opportunities. Wisconsin's foreign-born students accounted for 2.2 percent of all students enrolled in elementary schools (or 14,782 students), 3.1 percent of all students enrolled in high schools (or 9,826 students), and 4.7 percent of all students enrolled in colleges and graduate schools (or 20,106) in 2009. The number of the foreign-born households with a college degree increased 47.3 percent between 2000 and 2009 (from 37,428 to 55,127), compared with 22.6 percent of the American-born households with a college degree (from 742,249 to 910,301). In 2009, foreign-born households with a college degree accounted for 1.4 percent of all households and 27.1 percent of total foreign-born households, compared with American-born households' 24.2 percent of all households and 25.6 percent of total American-born households. In contrast, the number of the foreign-born households with less than a high school diploma also increased 33.9 percent between 2000 and 2009 (from 48 816 to 65 357), while the number of American-born households with less than a high-school diploma went down to 32 percent (from 469,959 to 319,344). In 2009, the foreign-born households with less than a high school diploma accounted for 1.7 percent of all households and 32.1 percent of total foreign-born households, compared with American-born households' 8.5 percent of all households and 9 percent of total American-born households. However, naturalized U.S. citizens' households had higher percentage of college degree holders (30.8 percent), compared with 23.9 percent of noncitizens' households. At the same time, naturalized U.S. citizens' households with less than a high-school diploma accounted for 22.9 percent of total foreign-born households, while noncitizens' households had 40 percent. According to data from the Migration Policy Institute, the proportion of persons with lower educational attainment in Wisconsin constituted only 8.6 percent of the English-speaking population, 17.9 percent of the Indo-European language-speaking population, 22.3 percent of the Asian-speaking population, and 42.3 percent of the Spanish-speaking population. In contrast, the proportion of individuals with a bachelor's or higher degree comprised only 25.6 percent of the English-speaking population, 36.4 percent of the Indo-European language-speaking population, 38.7 percent of the Asian-speaking population, and 14.7 percent of the Spanish-speaking population. The 2003 National Assessment of Adult Literacy showed that 42.2 percent of U.S. adults had poor English-reading skills, compared with 73.2 percent of foreign-born adults. About 50 percent of U.S. adults had low English literacy, compared with 73.5 percent of foreign-born adults.

The foreign-born population's roots in Wisconsin are reflected in language fluency and citizenship. In 2009, 8.3 percent of households in Wisconsin had diverse language environments (438,692 households), while the majority of Wisconsin's households (4,855, 586) spoke only English. A smaller proportion (1.6 percent of foreign-born households) lived in linguistically isolated households (all persons age 14 and over in the household had limited English proficiency). The linguistically isolated households in Wisconsin constituted 21.7 percent of Spanish-speaking households, 19.8 percent of Asian language-speaking households, 9.9 percent of Indo-European language-speaking households, and 17.2 percent of households speaking other languages. The percentage of the foreign-born population in Wisconsin, which had limited English proficient, increased by 37.6 percent between 2000 and 2009 (from 86,155 households or 45.4 percent of total foreign-born households to 118,587 households or 46.9 percent of total foreign-born households). However, 78.3 percent of 99,980 children in families that speak a language other than English have English-language proficiency. The most predominant languages in foreign-born households are: Spanish (51.6 percent), German (8.2 percent), Hmong (7.9 percent), French (3.2 percent), and Chinese (3.2 percent). Among these linguistic groups, limited English-proficient households account for 50.3 percent of Chinese-speaking population, 46.9 percent of Hmong population, 45.2 percent of Spanish-speaking population, 20.7 percent of German-speaking population, and 17.5 percent of French-speaking population. According to the U.S. Census Bureau, Wisconsin's naturalized U.S. citizens in 2009 are less likely to speak English poorly than noncitizens (32.8 percent versus 57.4 percent). Their households constituted a higher percentage of households speaking only English than noncitizens' households (29.2 percent versus 10.2 percent) and lower percentage of linguistically isolated households than noncitizens' households (17.8 percent versus 38.4 percent). About 75 percent of naturalized U.S. citizens' families (38 179 families) lived in family-owned homes, compared with 37 percent of noncitizens' families (18 882 families) and with 69.6 percent of American-born families (1,510,553 families).

According to a report by Rob Paral and Associates published in 2008, the electoral power of Latinos and Asian voters has been growing in Wisconsin, since many "New Americans" account for an increasing share of the state's naturalized U.S. citizen population. In 2006, 3 percent of 2,947,938 registered voters in Wisconsin were either Latinos or of Asian origin. The U.S. Census Bureau reported that Wisconsin's voters in 2008 presidential election accounted for 91.6 percent of Anglo voters (2,682,000), 5 percent of black voters (145,000), 2.3 percent of Latinos voters (66,000), and 1.1 percent of Asian voters (31,000). The same report concluded that the growing political power of naturalized U.S. citizens and their children in the state exceeded electoral victory margins and thus their votes were often decisive in close elections such as the presidential race in 2004. In addition, Latino and Asian voters were likely to establish pivotal voting blocs in battleground states, even where their numbers were considerably smaller than those of other racial and ethnic groups.

Wisconsin's history as both an agricultural state and a key site of low-tier labor mean that mainstream views often hold that labor integration constitutes successful immigrant assimilation. These views also often associate perceived skill levels with the intrinsic qualities of the immigrants themselves. Although these assumptions are problematic, the statistics above indicate that the foreign-born have been very successful in their integration efforts, in a number of different spheres. In particular, immigrants who have naturalized have advanced economically and educationally. Indeed, their social and economic well-being is on par with or even exceeding that of the American-born population's educational attainment and economic achievement in the state. Regardless of their diverse origin, the majority of naturalized U.S. citizens speak English very well.

Although the population in Wisconsin is becoming more diverse, the proportions of persons with a mixed raced origin among the naturalized U.S. citizen population in Wisconsin is still very low (in comparison with the whole country). In 2009, only 0.6 percent of the naturalized U.S. citizen population was multiracial, compared with 1.6 percent of the American-born population and 1.1 percent of noncitizen population.

As indicated above, citizenship status strongly affects economic and social status, and plays an important role in explaining internal divisions among broadly defined ethnic and racial categories. In contrast, those who face numerous barriers to naturalization often suffer. They often have a lower relative socioeconomic status and fewer opportunities for educational advancement. When these barriers are recognized, civil society groups and policymakers could facilitate greater integration for all immigrants and not just the privileged.

To the degree that many do successfully naturalize, their voting power is increasingly important. As registered voters, they may use their political power to help other immigrants who are less privileged. Many may also cast their ballots against anti-immigrant political policies and nativist leaders in the state, although studies have also shown that the greatest anti-immigrant forces are often amongst the recently naturalized. According to the Pew Hispanic Center many Latino registered voters (75 percent) in 2008 viewed immigration as an important issue in their vote. They often linked immigration enforcement to racial profiling or distinctions based on alienage. When a Hartford Republican representative Don Pridemore introduced a bill in March 2011 that would require law enforcement officers to demand proof of legal presence in the country if they were suspected of a crime, many foreign-born residents protested this measure and were on alert for an "Arizona-like immigration law" or the possibility of Wisconsin's support for an "Arizona-style law."

Related to these issues, according to research by the Wisconsin Policy Research Institute published in 2007, Wisconsin's residents strongly opposed any state's benefits for undocumented immigrants. However, there was a dramatic shift on the question of allowing undocumented immigrant children to attend local public schools. The majority (46 percent) of respondents believed that younger children (often born in the United States) ought to be given similar opportunities as legal residents. Wisconsin's views on immigration appeared to be fairly typical of Americans' views. According to the most recent poll by the Gallup, released in June 9–12, 2011, although Americans still believe immigration is good for the country (59 percent), they are most likely to say immigration levels should be decreased

(43 percent).In general, Wisconsinites have positive views on immigration and its role in the state's history, but at the same time they doubt that there should be more of immigration into their state. The increasing focus on the foreign-born population's educational and economic advancement in Wisconsin means that undocumented immigrants who have low levels of schooling and income are less likely to be socially accepted. However, the changing makeup of the state's population might begin to more strongly advocate on behalf of the foreign-born.

NOTABLE GROUPS

Centro Legal

Centro Legal is a Milwaukee-based legal advocacy office that serves low-income immigrants of all ethnicities. Their mission is to help the poor navigate the legal system and maintain their families, homes, and jobs, if and when they have legal difficulties. Their legal representation is in the areas of family law and criminal misdemeanors, as well as offering *guardian ad litem* services for minors. They provide public outreach in English and Spanish regarding family law, educating individuals and other service providers. Although this group does not offer immigration services, it helps low-income immigrants and recently naturalized citizens to maintain what they have built.

BIBLIOGRAPHY

Bureau of Migrant Labor Services. "2009 Migrant Population Report." http://dwd.wisconsin
.gov/migrants/pdf/migrantpoprep2009.pdf. Accessed March 29, 2014.

Center for Social and Demographic Analysis. *Children in Immigrant Families in Wisconsin.* Albany, NY: University of Albany, SUNY, 2009.

Centro Legal. Centro Legal Webpage. http://centrolegalwisconsin.org/RecentNews.html. Accessed February 28, 2014.

Daniels, Roger. *Coming to America: A History of Emigration and Ethnicity in American Life.* 2nd ed. New York: Harper Perennial, 2002.

Gallup. "Americans Views on Immigration Holding Steady." 2011. http://www.gallup.com/poll/148154/Americans-Views-Immigration-Holding-Steady.aspx. Accessed March 29, 2014.

Humphreys, Jeffrey M. *The Multicultural Economy 2009.* Athens: Selig Center for Economic Growth, University of Georgia, 2009.

Koltyk, Jo Ann. *New Pioneers in the Heartland: Hmong Life in Wisconsin.* Needham Heights, MA: Allyn & Bacon, 1997.

Lopez, Mark H., and Susan Minushkin. *2008 National Survey of Latinos: Hispanics See Their Situation in the U.S. Deteriorating.* Washington DC: The Pew Hispanic Center, 2008.

Migration Policy Institute. "MPI Data Hub: Wisconsin: Language and Education." http://www
.migrationinformation.org/datahub/state2.cfm?ID=wi#5. Accessed March 29, 2014.

NAFSA: Association of International Educators. *The Economic Benefits of International Education to the United States for the 2008–2009 Academic Year: A Statistical Analysis*. Washington, DC: NAFSA: Association of International Educators, 2009.

Paral, Rob, and Associates. *The New American Electorate: The Growing Political Power of Immigrants and Their Children*. Washington, DC: Immigration Policy Center, American Immigration Law Foundation, 2008.

Passel, Jeffrey S., and D'Vera Cohn. *A Portrait of Unauthorized Immigrants in the United States*. Washington, DC: The Pew Charitable Trusts, 2009.

The Perryman Group. *An Essential Resource: An Analysis of the Economic Impact of Undocumented Workers on Business Activity in the US with Estimated Effects by State and by Industry*. Waco, TX: The Perryman Group, 2008.

Slesinger, Doris P., and Steven Deller. *Economic Impact of Migrant Workers on Wisconsin's Economy*. Madison: Center for Demography and Ecology, University of Wisconsin-Madison, 2003.

Thompson, William F. *The History of Wisconsin*. Vol. 6. Madison: State Historical Society of Wisconsin, 1990.

Wellner, Alison S. *Diversity in America: Supplement to American Demographics*. Washington DC: American Demographics, 2002.

Wisconsin Policy Research Institute. "2007 WPRI Poll." http://www.wpri.org/Reports /Volume%2020/poll/WCS12.07Rel1Web.pdf. Accessed March 29, 2014.

U.S. Census Bureau. *2000 American Community Survey*. http://factfinder.census.gov/servlet /SAFFFacts?_event=&geo_id=04000US55&_geoContext=01000US|04000US55&_ street=&_county=&_cityTown=&_state=04000US55&_zip=&_lang=en&_ sse=on&ActiveGeoDiv=&_useEV=&pctxt=fph&pgsl=040&_submenuId=factsheet_1&ds_ name=DEC_2000_SAFF&_ci_nbr=null&qr_name=null&reg=null%3Anull&_keyword=&_ industry=. Accessed March 29, 2014.

U.S. Census Bureau. *2009 American Community Survey*. http://factfinder.census.gov /servlet/STTable?_bm=y&-context=st&-qr_name=ACS_2009_1YR_G00_S0501&-ds_ name=ACS_2009_1YR_G00_&-CONTEXT=st&-tree_id=307&-redoLog=false&-geo_ id=04000US55&-format=&-_lang=en. Accessed March 29, 2014.

U.S. Census Bureau. *1950 Census of Population; Characteristics of the Population: Wisconsin*. Washington, DC: U.S. Government Printing Office, 1952.

U.S. Census Bureau. *1970 Census of Population; Characteristics of the Population: Wisconsin*. Washington, DC: U.S. Government Printing Office, 1973.

U.S. Census Bureau. *2003 The Foreign-Born Population*. http://www.census.gov /prod/2003pubs/c2kbr-34.pdf. Accessed March 29, 2014.

U.S. Census Bureau. *2008 Presidential Election: Popular Votes and Totals* (used data from Immigration Policy Center "New Americans in the Badger State"). http://www.immi grationpolicy.org/just-facts/new-americans-badger-state. Accessed March 29, 2014.

U.S. Census Bureau. *2002 Surveys of Business Owners*. http://www.census.gov/econ/sbo/02 /cbsof.html. Accessed March 29, 2014.

U.S. Census Bureau. *2007 Surveys of Business Owners*. http://www.census.gov/econ/sbo/. Accessed March 29, 2014.

50

WYOMING

Lilia Soto

CHRONOLOGY

1600s	Shoshonis, Utes, Crows, Cheyennes, and Arapahos enter Wyoming Territory.
1743	Francois and Louis-Joseph Verendrye are believed to have traveled through Big Horn Mountain.
1803	The United States acquires land from Louisiana Purchase that becomes part of the Wyoming Territory.
1805	French trader Francois Larocque travels through Power River and Clear Creek.
1807	John Colter visits Cody, Jackson Hole, Yellowstone.
1819	The United States acquires land from Spain that becomes part of the Wyoming Territory.
1830	Mountain men and fur traders pass through Wyoming.
1830	Oglala and Brulé Sioux enter Wyoming Territory.
1830s	West Coast travelers pass through the Wyoming route of the Oregon Trail.
1840s	There is some immigrant travel through Wyoming, but very little settlement.
1841–1868	The Emigrant Trail, which passes through Wyoming, is established and used.
1846	The United States acquires land from Great Britain that becomes part of Wyoming Territory.
1848	The United States acquires land from Mexico that became part of Wyoming Territory.

1850	The first school in Wyoming is established.
1851	Treaty of Fort Laramie is signed.
1859	Gold discovery in Colorado brings many people to the area of southeastern Wyoming.
1860s	Discovery of gold and railroad construction attract immigrants to Wyoming; Irish and Mexican workers arrive in the state.
1860	The Pony Express reaches Wyoming.
1867	Arrival of the Union Pacific Railroad Company.
1867	Cheyenne becomes the first settled town in Wyoming.
1868 (July 25)	Wyoming is organized as a U.S. territory of the United States; conversations for statehood begin immediately.
1868	Treaty of Fort Laramie is signed.
1868	Wind River Indian Reservation is established for the Shoshonis.
1869	Legislators adopt an act to protect married women under a separate category.
1869	Legislators adopt school law of equal pay for all teachers.
1869 (December 10)	Women of Wyoming Territory are granted the right to vote and to hold office.
1870s	British immigrants are the largest share of the foreign-born. Many are English Mormon settlers from Idaho, who begin to settle in Wyoming. Separately, Irish immigrants arrive to work on railroads. Some Presbyterian Scots also settle in this area. German immigrants work in the cattle industry and on railroads.
1870 (June)	Union Pacific announces the hiring of Chinese workers.
1870	The Arapahos are relocated to the Wind River Reservation.
1871	Susan B. Anthony visits Laramie, Wyoming.
1872	Yellowstone Park becomes the first national park in the United States.
1875	Chinese immigrants arrive to work on the Union Pacific Railroad; they are subjected to racial persecution.
1876 (June)	The Battle of Little Big Horn is fought in the Montana, but the campaign that leads up to it encompasses northern Wyoming.
1880s	Finnish immigrants work as miners in Uinta and Sweetwater counties.
1885 (September 2)	Rock Springs Massacre: anti-Chinese discrimination and violence break out in Rock Springs, including a massacre of 28 Chinese workers; 15 others are injured. More violence breaks out in surrounding areas. Leading up to the massacre, about 335 Chinese workers lived in this area. Some Chinese families had also settled in Evanston.
1887	The University of Wyoming is established.
1888	German Jews settle in Wyoming and Temple Emmanuel is established in Cheyenne.
1890 (January)	About 200 African Americans arrive from Ohio to work in the coalmines.

1890 (July 10)	Wyoming enters the Union as the 44th state.
1890–1910	Italian immigrants from Lombardy, Tuscany, and Piedmont come to Wyoming to work in the mining industry. Eastern Europeans also arrive from what is now the Czech Republic, Hungary, Poland, and the area that was once Yugoslavia.
1890–1910	Sheep raids occur, leading to sheep slaughter, vandalism, and some homicides.
1892 (April)	Johnson County War is fought.
1898	The Spanish American War is fought; three units from Wyoming volunteer for service.
1900	Largest wave of Mormon settlers comes to Wyoming. Native Americans continue to reside in the state, including members of the Arapaho, Cheyenne, Cree, Gros Ventre, Menominee, Sioux, Ute, and Ute Southern tribes. Greek immigrants also begin settling in the state.
1902	Basque settlers come to Wyoming, establishing sheepherding. Many live in Johnson County and Sweetwater.
1906	German Jews continue to settle in the state, many of them farming in areas like Huntley. Romanian Jews also farm in this area.
1910	Eastern European immigrants continue to arrive in the state until 1920, many working in mining.
1915–1916	Russians of Germanic descent settle in Worland and Lovell, many of whom work in the sugar beet industry. Others arrive in Goshen County.
1917	The United States enters World War I. About 6 percent of the state's population enters military service.
1922	The Greek Orthodox Church of Saints Constantine and Helen is built in Cheyenne.
1924	Mrs. Nellie Taylor Ross becomes the first female governor of the state of Wyoming.
1925	Nellie Tayloe Ross is elected governor, becoming the first woman to be elected governor in the United States.
1941 (December 7)	The United States enters World War II after the bombing of Pearl Harbor in Hawaii.
1942 (February 19)	President Franklin Roosevelt signs Executive Order 9066, providing for internment of Japanese Americans; Heart Mountain Relocation Center is established in Park County, becoming one of the 10 relocation centers for Japanese internees during World War II.
1943	Heart Mountain Relocation Center houses 10,767 detainees.
1945	Heart Mountain Relocation Center closes and most of its Japanese American internees move back to the West Coast.
1947 (October 24)	Under fear of "subversive activities," the University of Wyoming Board of Trustees assign a committee to review text books used in the Social Sciences.

1969 (October 16)	The Black 14 delivers letter to the president of the University of Wyoming and the Head Football Coach. They are subsequently removed from the team. The National Association for the Advancement of Colored People (NAACP) and American Civil Liberties Union (ACLU) file a suit in the *Williams v. Eaton* case. They lose the case on November 10, 1971.
1982	La Cultura Oral History Project produces 83 oral histories of Mexicans and Mexican Americans in Wyoming.
1990–2011	This period sees an increase in immigrant arrivals in the state.
1994	Wyoming is the leader in the coal industry.
1997	Under the direction of the Social Justice Research Center, the Symposium on Social Justice is established at the University of Wyoming. The name is changed to the Shepard Symposium in 2002.
1998 (October 6–7)	Matthew Shepard is tortured by Aaron McKinney and Russell Henderson. Shepard is pronounced dead on October 12, 1998.
2000	Radio Bilingüe is established in Laramie.
2000 (July 25)	Wyomingite Dick Cheney joins the Republican ticket for the 2000 presidential elections. Cheney is elected vice president in November.
2001 (September 16)	Eight students from the University of Wyoming Track Team are killed in an automobile accident.
2009 (October 29)	President Barack Obama signs the Hate Crimes Prevention Act, also known as the Matthew Shepard Act.
2013	The foreign-born comprise about 3.2 percent of the state's population, with about one-third being naturalized citizens.
2014	Campaign is launched to establish refugee resettlement in Wyoming, the only state that has no official refugee resettlement office.

HISTORICAL OVERVIEW

Nineteenth Century

The history of the "Equality State" narrates the lives of the pioneers in the making of Wyoming: the mountain men, fur trappers, and the French brothers who stumbled upon areas of the state. It also narrates the accomplishments for equality of the 1860s that earned Wyoming the name of the "Equality State." These successes became elevated, but when placed next to the Indian Wars—The Battle of Little Big Horn—or the Chinese Massacre, the "Equality State" of the 1860s did not seem so equal after all. Perhaps a follow-up question should be, equal to whom? As Michel Rolph Trouillot (1997) states, history is produced by the winners of history, those who make it to the archives, those who won. Narratives that continue to be recycled yield the same results, and these same results are complicit in the continuous silencing of other narratives. Narratives of the "Equality State" briefly mention the lives of American Indians, African Americans, Mexicans, and Asians. Such histories and contributions should be recognized, not as a footnote or as an additive sentence at the end of an extensive study, but as central to understanding the history of Wyoming. Their stories, as Phil Roberts (2007) so eloquently states, show that the state of Wyoming "has been the home to hundreds of different ethnic and economic groups and thousands of immigrants from around the world. Conflicts between these groups are an important part of the state's history." The histories of racialized groups show, as Roberts states, that, "Wyoming was not settled by cowboys exclusively nor was that group ever in the majority" (Roberts 2007, 3).

During the 1800s, legislators from what was then Wyoming Territory passed a series of laws and acts that assured equality for all its citizens. In 1869, the Wyoming Territory "adopted an 'act to protect Married Women in their separate property, and the enjoyment of the fruits of their labor'" (Larson 1978, 78). That same year, the legislators also "adopted a school law which provided that 'in the employment of teachers, no discrimination shall be made in the question of pay on account of sex when the persons are equally qualified'" (Larson 1978, 78). Legislators finished that year by granting women the right to vote on December 9, 1869. These laws and/or acts allowed for the Wyoming Territory to be named the "Equality State." Whether to attract settlers to populate the state, as questioned by Larson, these acts certainly granted women rights that were not too common in the United States.

During these celebratory moments, Native Americans were at constant war with the government and local authorities. The government policies of how to deal with the "Indian problem" of removal and displacement were certainly in place in the Wyoming Territory by the 1800s. By the time Wyoming became known as the "Equality State," the Wind River Reservation, originally to house Shoshonis, was already established. In the 1870s, the Shoshonis began to share their land with the Arapahos. During the 1800s, several treaties were made and broken between the U.S. government and the Native Americans. Perhaps one that stands out is the Battle of Little Big Horn of 1876 in the Montana and Northern Wyoming region over the Black Hills. Based on the Fort Laramie Treaty of 1868, the Black Hills were given to the Sioux. As part of the treaty, white settlement was not allowed. When gold was rumored to be in abundance, the government opened the area for all. A second event that took place around the same time as the three laws and acts for equality was the Chinese Rock Springs Massacre. Chinese were brought to Rock Springs to work on the railroads and coal mines. Employers used racialized Chinese's status as second-class citizens to pay them lower wages. White workers, angered by what they perceive as "preferential treatment," massacred 28 Chinese individuals and wounded 15 on September 2, 1885. When Chinese laborers returned to work 10 days later, they had to be protected by local authorities.

This period of conflict and success culminated with the entrance of Wyoming into the Union. On July 10, 1890, the "Equality State" became the 44th to enter the Union of the United States. The state population then was 60,000. The University of Wyoming opened its doors in 1887; the Johnson County War of 1892 seemed part of the nineteenth century, and Cheyenne—Wyoming's state capital—began to celebrate "Frontier Days" by 1897.

TWENTIETH AND TWENTY-FIRST CENTURIES

Wyoming is a young state and little conflict had been documented in the state until the 1940s, when Japanese Americans arrived at Heart Mountain. Gary Okihiro (2005) states that the internment of Japanese and Japanese Americans was not an isolated incident, rather, it was part of a historical anti-Japanese, anti-Asian, and "yellow peril" sentiment (Okihiro 2005, 103). The Paige Law of 1875, the Chinese Exclusion Act of 1882, the Gentlemen's Agreement Act of 1907, the Alien Land Laws of 1913 and 1920, the Asiatic Barred Zone of 1917, and the Tydings-McDuffie Act of 1934 were some of the anti-Asian immigration laws targeting Asian immigrants and Asian Americans that made Asians the perpetual foreigner within. The state of Wyoming was not immune to this sentiment.

After the bombing of Pearl Harbor and the United States' entrance into World War II, the War Relocation Authority (WRA) announced the forced relocation of Japanese and Japanese Americans to camps away from the West Coast. The removal and incarceration of Japanese—many of them U.S. citizens—was seen as "unique, unprecedented, and a radical departure from American ideals and principles" (Okihiro 2005, 102). Ten locations were chosen for the construction of the camps. In 1942, the WRA announced to Governor Smith that Heart Mountain in Park County would be one of the cities. By August 13, 1942, the first trainload arrived to the 456 barracks constructed for them. From the beginning, Wyomingites were not pleased as they did not want to "host" them, "Governor Smith and many others feared that the Japanese would like Wyoming [and] make [it] their postwar homes . . . and would deprive Wyoming citizens of jobs" (Larson 1954, 305). Once there, the Japanese and Japanese Americans began to create a community within Heart Mountain. They developed a newspaper, *The Heart Mountain Sentinel*, and created a hospital, stores, movie theaters, schools, and after-school programs for their children. Some Japanese were allowed to leave the camp temporarily for work on the sugar beet harvest, and others were allowed to go anywhere except the West Coast (Larson 1954, 301). At the end of the war, Japanese slowly started to leave Heart Mountain and many returned to the West Coast. Heart Mountain began to shut down and the last 250 evacuees left the camp by November 10, 1945. Many Japanese fled, like the Chinese after the Rock Springs Massacre. Most returned to the West Coast.

After the departure of Japanese and the closing of Heart Mountain, fear of "subversive activities" became a concern for the University of Wyoming's Board of Trustees. In 1947, they "appoint[ed] a special committee to examine all text books used in the social science department of the University" (Larson 1978, 597). The committee found no evidence of "subversive activities." The climate of World War II and the McCarthy era of the 1950s came to an end and in came the 1960s. At the national level, protests in colleges and universities demanding diversity in the faculty, courses, and student population led to the development of Ethnic Studies programs, such as African American Studies, Chicano Studies, American Indian Studies, Asian American Studies, and Women's Studies. The anti-war movement, Black Power, Feminist, American Indian, Chicano, and Asian movements were also very strong in colleges and universities. The University of Wyoming seemed far removed from these developments, at least that is how it seemed, until sports, race, and civil rights collided.

Football in Wyoming was very much a "source of pride to the Equality State" (Bullock 1996, 6). In the 1960s, there were plans to expand Memorial Stadium to seat all Wyomingites who lived in surrounding towns and eagerly traveled to Laramie for the home games. The head coach of the football team, Coach Eaton, had a very strict policy of not allowing "his players" to participate in any rallies or protests. Football players were seen as employees of the university. In 1969, there were 14 African American players on the football team who decided to challenge this policy.

In the late 1960s, a series of protests developed against Brigham Young University (BYU) and the Latter-day Saints' policy that still "denied Blacks full membership" (Bullock 1996, 5). College sport teams from the Western Association Conference refused to compete with BYU's athletes and a series of protests erupted. It began in 1969 when members of the track team from University of Texas at El Paso (UTEP) "refused to participate in a meet at Provo, Utah. The UTEP protest, resulting in the dismissal of eight Black athletes, gained national notoriety" (Bullock 1996, 6). This initial protest was followed by San Jose State University, University of New Mexico, and Arizona State University who refused to compete against BYU. The next major protest came from the University of Wyoming's football team.

With the assistance of a PhD candidate in math, Willie Black, leader of the Black Student Alliance, the "Black 14" wrote a letter to Coach Eaton and to the president of the University William D. Carlson. On the letter, the "Black 14" expressed their refusal to play the next game against BYU. After the letter and a conversation with the football players, Coach Eaton, with full support from the president, dismissed the "Black 14" from the team and canceled their scholarships. At a conference, President Carlson said that in Wyoming, football was more important than civil rights. The ACLU and NAACP decided to assist the "Black

14" and filed a suit based on the First and Fourteenth Amendment in the *Williams v. Eaton* case. By the time they went to court, most of the "Black 14" had left the university. They lost the case and the ACLU and NAACP did not appeal the decision. The football team, along with the coach, trustees, and lawyers argued that the releasing of students from the football team was based on "discipline and not on race" (Bullock 1996, 10). They too argued that students could protest but not employees and football players were considered employees of the university. After this incident, it took approximately 10 years for the University of Wyoming to diversify their football team.

The 1970s and 1980s were significantly quiet in the "Equality State." In the 1970s, the Wyoming State Archives published the first edited collection of essays on the European heritage. By the 1980s, the absence of Mexicans from Wyoming history was quite apparent. Mexicans had been present in the state of Wyoming since at least the late 1800s. Like other migrants, they arrived to work on the railroads, the coal mines, and the sugar beet industry. Forced to live in segregated communities, Mexicans began to make a life for themselves in Rock Springs, Torrington, Rawlins, and Cheyenne, among other towns. Their labor contributed to the making of the state. However, in T. A. Larson's (1978) *History of Wyoming*, there is very little mention of the presence of Mexicans. Like the British, Eastern Europeans, Italians, Basque immigrants, at the turn of the twentieth century, Mexican immigrants also began to make a life for themselves in the "Equality State." Unlike the aforementioned migrants, however, little is known about the presence of Mexicans in the great state of Wyoming.

Concerned about the lack of information on the Mexican presence, the Wyoming Council for the Humanities organized a meeting on March 12–13, 1982. The goal was to begin to fill in a gap in Wyoming history and to document the presence of Mexicans. Out of these meetings, was a set of interviews of Mexicans in Wyoming. A set of topics was designed and Wyoming was divided into five areas to target the whole state. Eighty-three interviews were completed and deposited at the Wyoming State Archives, Museum and Historical Department for those interested in further research. Known as La Cultura Oral History Project, the interviews "demonstrated that Wyoming Mexican American/Hispanics derive from three main historical sources of migration: from New Mexico/Southern Colorado, from Texas via Kansas and Nebraska, and from Mexico. Even today, the great majority of Wyoming Mexican/Hispanics migrate from these areas" (Bustamante-Rios and Vialpando 2001, 20). In 2001, the *Annals of Wyoming* published a special issue on Mexicans in Wyoming. Some of the articles featured in this special issue were pulled from La Cultura Project to show the presence of Mexican families. However, to this day, there is no comprehensive study on the presence— past and current—of Mexicans in Wyoming. The absence, erasure, or silencing of crucial characters in the making of the history of a place certainly challenges narratives of the "Equality State."

By the 1990s and 2000s, the event that took central stage was the killing of Matthew Shepard, a student at the University of Wyoming who was tortured on the night of October 6, 1998. He left the Fireside Lounge with Aaron McKinney and Russell Henderson and was found 18 hours later and pronounced dead on October 12, 1998. "The Laramie Project," first a play and then a film, along with other documentaries and books, fully documented the story. On October 29, 2009, President Barrack Obama signed the Hate Crimes Prevention Act also knows as the Matthew Shepard Act to prevent and punish any further hate crime.

The events that took place in the 1900s certainly force one to question the egalitarianism of the "Equality State." To cite Roberts (2007) once again, "[c]onflicts between these groups are an important part of the state's history" (Roberts 2007, 3). The Heart Mountain Wyoming Foundation was established in 1996 to preserve and remember the thousands of Japanese who were incarcerated. The Student Union at the University of Wyoming has a small cleat as a monument to remind students, faculty, staff, and the endless visitors that pass through of the stories of the "Black 14." La Cultura Oral History Project serves as a remedy to the erasure and silencing of Mexicans in Wyoming. Finally, each year the University of Wyoming's Social Justice Research Center sponsors the Shepard Symposium on social justice. These historical events must be considered along with the histories of the late 1800s that lead to the naming of Wyoming as the "Equality State." These stories are not separate but are intricately connected to the making of Wyoming history. Such stories allow us to see this history as complex and contradictory as all histories are.

TOPICAL ESSAYS

Migration to Wyoming

In the United States, certain states—New York, California, Texas, Illinois, and Florida, for example—have historically been immigrant destinations. In recent years, new gateway communities, South Carolina, Arkansas, and Alabama, to mention a few, have witnessed an increase in their population. The state of Wyoming has not been one of those states, perhaps with the exception of Teton County where the Mexican population has increased from 1 percent to 20 percent in 1990. Wyoming, however, has also experienced the arrival of migrants long before it became a territory, but always at a much lower scale.

During the 1600s, indigenous groups migrated into the territory. As well documented by Larson (1978), the Shoshonis and Utes entered Wyoming long before the 1700s. The Shoshonis and Utes were followed by the Crows, Cheyennes, and Arapahos in the eighteenth century and the Sioux in the nineteenth century. The indigenous groups inhabited the land until the arrival of the Europeans in the mid-1700s.

European migration into Wyoming coincides with both the mercantile and the industrial periods. The mercantile period brought travelers, mountain men, and fur traders to and through Wyoming. Though there is no evidence of the Spanish empire ever sending explorers to Wyoming, but Kansas, Nebraska, and Utah were visited. The first believed to have arrived in Wyoming were the Verendrye brothers. During the industrial period, mountain men and fur traders were believed to have passed through Wyoming along with "scientists, missionaries, and sportsmen, then emigrants bound for Oregon, California, or Utah" (Larson 1978, 9). The Oregon Trail, which passed through Wyoming, was the gateway for many migrants wanting to reach the West. John Charles Frémont, Stephen W. Kearly, Francis Parkman, Brigham Young, Howard Statsbury, F.T. Bryan, among others, were believed to have crossed through the state of Wyoming en route to California and Utah.

It was not until the Union Pacific Railroad Company came to the Wyoming Territory in the 1860s that a stable population of migrants began to settle in the dozen or so towns that sprung up alongside the railroad tracks. The Union Pacific Coal Company also brought migration to the state, as did the cattle boom, sheep herding, the sugar beet harvest, and the mineral boom.

All European migrants—whether British, Irish, or Southern/Eastern Europe—came to Wyoming for similar reasons: jobs and the opportunity for a better life. Of course, the context of arrival shaped their opportunities. Initially, most of these migrants worked on the railroads and in the mines. Some, like the British, were able to move up the ranks. Some groups were assumed to have assimilable traits—language and religion—therefore, experiencing a positive context of reception. The British, for example, spoke English and fared better than Russian Germans or Basques. Their race, however, facilitated their full assimilation with latter generations.

The first to arrive were the British, Irish, and Scottish. In fact, the British composed approximately one-fifth of the foreign-born population by 1870; their ability to speak English allowed for a smooth transition into the areas where they settled. The Irish made Rawlins, Casper, Rock Springs, Lander, and Torrington their home. These three groups of migrants worked on the mines and railroad tracks. With the arrival of other ethnic and racialized groups, the British, in particular, were promoted. Some began to work in the cattle industry and were very successful.

One of the groups who also labored in the mines and railroads were the Germans. The Germans came to Wyoming in two waves from two different groups: German natives and Russians of Germanic descent. Political, social, and economic reasons motivated them to move to the United States. Some wanted to avoid military obligations, others political unrest, and all had "the spirit of adventure" (Hodgson and Hills 1977, 38). The German natives arrived in the late 1800s, first to cities in the plains. By the 1970s, they comprised 19 percent of the foreign-born population. They also found work with the Union Pacific Railroad and in the cattle business. They settled in Cheyenne, Laramie, and Casper where they developed German societies that allowed them to retain their culture while simultaneously assimilating into American life. The second wave of Germans— the Russian Germans—arrived in the early 1900s and settled in the Big Horn Basin, Sheridan, and Laramie. They were recruited by the Great Western Sugar Company to work in the sugar beet harvest.

The groups that came after the British and the Germans began to experience a different context of reception both nationally and within the state. Nationally, anti-immigration laws whose targets were the "wrong kind of migrants" were already brewing. Within Wyoming, the Greeks, for example, became a target of the local Ku Klux Klan in the 1920s.

Migration continued during the industrial period and in came the Italians and the eastern Europeans. They arrived in the late 1800s and early 1900s, a turning point in immigration policy. This wave was considered a new one with "new immigrants." The Italian new immigrants usually arrived in the United States from southern Italy. The wave that arrived into Wyoming actually comes from the northern part of Italy. Their reasons for migration are similar to other groups: overcrowding, poor soil conditions, and the idea of a better life in the United States. They came to work in the railroads and the mines and mostly settled in Sweetwater, Laramie, and Uinta. They assimilated fairly fast as older Italians learned English in night school sponsored by organized labor and the young learned it in school. Eastern Europeans came to Wyoming between the 1910s and 1920s. They migrated for political, social, and economic reasons. Like the Italians and Germans, conditions in Eastern Europe and the dream of a better life in the United States pushed and pull them to the United States. Some had heard of work opportunities in Wyoming from friends and relatives who already lived there. Once they arrived, they were mostly employed in the coal mines and settled around Rock Springs, Torrington, Lander, and Sheridan. Though they assimilated rather quickly—the second generation has lost most of their culture and tradition—this group of migrants were certainly affected by the immigration acts of 1917 and 1924 that targeted the "wrong kind of immigrants."

The Greeks and the Basques settled in Cheyenne and Casper and in Buffalo, respectively. The Greeks first arrived in 1867 to help construct the Union Pacific Railroads. They became successful bar, grocery, and coffee house owners. The coffee houses in particular allowed them the space to retain their traditions. The Basques moved to Wyoming in 1902. Some first moved to California and South American before arriving in Wyoming. Those who went to South America became sheepherders. Once they migrated to Wyoming, they became sheepherders. Like the Greeks, they were able to retain their culture via food and language. They opened the Twenty-One Club that allowed them to socialize. The Basques had their own radio station in 1956 that broadcasted for almost 40 years.

None of the ethnically white immigrants experienced the same context of reception as the racialized migrants. The Chinese, Japanese, and Mexicans shared a similar story of migration to the Europeans: work, hopes for a better life, and recruitment. The Chinese came to Wyoming in 1869 to work on the railroads and the coal mines. From the moment they arrived, newspapers began to publish articles stating that Chinese were receiving higher wages and better treatment at the mines. The newspapers also argued that white workers were losing jobs to the privileged Chinese workers. In reality, Chinese were earning much less than what was assumed. They earned from $1.73 to $2.00, while whites earned from $2.50 to $3.00. Continuous labor disputes allowed the mining coal company to bring Chinese workers to Rock Springs to fill in labor demands. A high number of Chinese were brought in that by the 1870s—Rock Springs is the home to 40 percent of the total Chinese population in the state. As a racialized and undesired group, they were not welcomed. They mostly settled in the Bitter Creek area of Rock Springs. The anti-Chinese sentiment escalated and on September 2, 1885, whites killed 28 and wounded 15 in what has been called, the Chinese Massacre. Immediately after the massacre, many Chinese fled Wyoming. Ten days later, the coal mining company brought in

Miners of the Union Pacific Railroad Company shooting at a crowd of fleeing Chinese miners working for the Union Pacific. Published in 1885. (Library of Congress)

100 Chinese who reluctantly agreed to work. By October of that year, 720 Chinese were once again working on the coal mines. Slowly, they began to make a community. By the 1940s, Chinese began to celebrate the Chinese New Year that introduced their culture, tradition, and customs to the larger Rock Springs community.

The Japanese in Wyoming were also treated in a similar fashion to Chinese. Like the Germans, the Japanese came to Wyoming in two different waves, first as contract laborers and second as interned Japanese placed at Heart Mountain's concentration camp in 1942. The first came at the "turn of the century as railroad workers and coal miners." Most settled in the Rock Springs area of Wyoming and "came as contract laborers with low wages forced to live in company-owned housing" (Gardner 1996, 25). Their population slowly increased and by 1909, there were 436 Japanese in Rock Springs. The bombing of Pearl Harbor during World War II immediately altered their lives. First, those Japanese who lived in Wyoming have to register and, second, they are forbidden to work "within the vicinity of bridges, tunnels, and railroad facilities" (Gardner 1996, 27). Since most work on the mines and the railroads, they lost their jobs. The second wave was the Japanese and Japanese Americans who were brought to Heart Mountain after the signing of Executive Order 9066. Heart Mountain was one of the 10 relocation centers that functioned as concentration camps to house Japanese Americans (Chambers Noble 1996, 40). Following the executive order, Governor Nels H. Smith hired workers to construct 456 barracks to accommodate almost 11,000 people. By August 10, 1942, the first train of internees arrived to Heart Mountain. The last train left in November 1945. During this time, Heart Mountain became the third-largest city in Wyoming.

Mexicans came to Wyoming in several different waves and from different points of entry. Part of the state of Wyoming once belonged to the Spanish Empire, though as discussed above, there is no evidence of Spain ever sending explorers. There are records, however, of Mexicans living in Wyoming as early as the 1850s and 1860s. The first wave was traced to the early 1900s. Mexicans came from "three main historical sources of migration: from New Mexico/Southern Colorado, from Texas via Kansas and Nebraska, and from Mexico" (Bustamante-Rios and Vialpando 2001, 20). From Mexico, migrants usually came from the states of Chihuahua, Durango, Zacatecas, and Aguas Calientes. They came to work on the sugar beet harvest, railroads, and coal mines—the same as earlier waves of European migrants. Mexicans settled throughout the state including Worland, Torrington, Rock Springs, Rawlins, and Laramie. Like the Chinese and Japanese, Mexicans lived in segregated communities. They were not welcomed into restaurants or stores to purchase food supplies.

A second wave came in the 1940s with the Bracero Program—a labor agreement between Mexico and the United States that allowed Mexicans to legally work in the United States for a certain period of time to fill in the labor demands of

Simeon Malqui, 53, stands in the doorway of a trailer with a sheepherding dog on a sheep ranch near Wamsutter, Wyoming. Alone and miles from home, the immigrant sheepherder roams some of the West's most desolate and frigid landscapes, tending a flock for as little as $600 a month without a day off on the horizon. These are considered some of the most dangerous jobs in the United States. (AP Photo/Ivan Moreno)

World War II. Perhaps this could be considered a third wave, or a contemporary wave of Mexican immigration, but there were no comprehensive studies. We do know that Teton County had experienced a high increase of Mexican immigrants. We do not know how well they were adapting and/or assimilating into the community. Back in 1982, to remedy the gap of Mexicans in the making of Wyoming, the Wyoming Council of the Humanities met on March 1982 to rectify the omission. Perhaps what is needed is to once again study the contemporary impact, as the *La Cultura Oral History Project* did, of Mexicans in Wyoming. Conducting interviews would be a starting point.

Immigration to the state of Wyoming paralleled the history of immigration into the United States, though at a much lower scale. The four periods highlighted by Massey neatly follow the patterns of migration and context of reception each wave of immigrants encounters. It was jobs that brought all these immigrants to Wyoming and it was jobs that continue to have an impact on immigration. All these immigrant groups began working in the same industry: railroads, mines, and sugar beet harvest. Because these came during different moments, the context of reception, race, religion, and perceived likeliness of assimilation affected the way these were received in the "Equality State."

NOTABLE FIGURES

Bertine Bahige (1983–)

Bertine Bahige is from the Democratic Republic of Congo and in 1996, along with his sister, was kidnapped by a rebel group and forced to be a child soldier. He finally escaped two years later and made his way to the United States. With the aid of the United Nations, he resettled in Maryland where he learned English and worked. In 2006, the University of Wyoming offered him a scholarship, which he accepted. He moved there, graduated, and has remained in the state. He is now married, with two children, and teaches high-school math and coaches soccer. Since 2010, he has served as a delegate for the UN Refugee Congress and is using his position to influence the state to open a refugee resettlement office. In 2014, Wyoming is the only state in the nation that does not have a refugee resettlement program. He has begun working with the University's law school to draft a plan, including agencies that would work together to help refugees resettle. To Bahige, Wyoming is a far better place for refugees than crowded urban spaces: "When you come from nothing, it's not easy to find your way in a big community. That's the beauty of Wyoming: small and family oriented communities. If you fall, people will pick you up" (Roerink 2014).

BIBLIOGRAPHY

Barrett, James E. "The Black 14: *Williams v. Eaton*—A Personal Recollection." *Annals of Wyoming* 68, no. 3 (1996): 2–7.

Bullock, Clifford A. "Fired by Conscience: The Black 14 at the University of Wyoming and the Black Protest in the Western Athletic Conference, 1968–1970." *The Wyoming History Journal* 68, no. 1 (1996): 4–13.

Bustamante-Rios, Antonio. "Wyoming's Mexican Hispanics." *Annals of Wyoming* 73, no. 2 (2001): 2–9.

Bustamante-Rios, Antonio, and Jesse Vialpando. "La Cultura Oral History Project: Mexicano/Hispanic History in Wyoming." *Annals of Wyoming* 73, no. 2 (2001): 18–21.

Chambers Nobel, Antoinette. "Heart Mountain: Remembering the Camp." *Wyoming History Journal* 68, no. 2 (1996): 38–44.

Franco, Jere'. "Going the Distance: World War II and the Wind River Reservation." *Wyoming History Journal* 68, no. 2 (1996): 14–21.

Gardner, Dudley. "World War II and the Japanese of Southwest Wyoming." *Wyoming History Journal* 68, no. 2 (1996): 22–31.

Gardner, Dudley. "The Wyoming Experience: Chinese in Wyoming." http://uwacadewb.uwyo.edu/ROBERTSHISTORY/gardner_chinese_wyoming. Accessed March 29, 2014.

Hodgson, Donald, and Vivien Hills. "Dream and Fulfillment: Germans in Wyoming." In Gordon Olaf Hendrickson, ed. *Peopling the High Plains: Wyoming's European Heritage*. Cheyenne: Wyoming State Archives and Historical Department, 1977, pp. 35–66.

Kathka, David. "The Italian Experience." In Gordon Olaf Hendrickson, ed. *Peopling the High Plains: Wyoming's European Heritage*. Cheyenne: Wyoming State Archives and Historical Department, 1977, pp. 67–94.

Larson, T.A. *History of Wyoming*. 2nd ed. Lincoln: University of Nebraska Press, 1978.

Larson, T.A. *Wyoming's War Years, 1941–1945*. Cheyenne: Wyoming Historical Foundation, 1954.

Massey, Douglas. "Why Does Immigration Occur? A Theoretical Synthesis." In Charles Hirschman, Philip Kasinitz, and Josh DeWind, eds. *The Handbook of International Migration: The American Experience*. New York: Russell Sage, 1999, pp. 34–52.

Okihiro, Gary. *The Columbia Guide to Asian American History*. New York: Columbia University Press, 2005.

Paige, John C. "Country Squires and Laborers: British Immigrants in Wyoming." In Gordon Olaf Hendrickson, ed. *Peopling the High Plains: Wyoming's European Heritage*. Cheyenne: Wyoming State Archives and Historical Department, 1977, pp. 1–34.

Roberts, Phil. "Introduction to Readings in Wyoming (5th Revised Edition)." 2007. http://uwacadweb.uwyo.edu/ROBERTHISTORY/indrocution_to_readings_in_wyo.htm. Accessed March 29, 2014.

Roerink, Kyle. "Former Child Soldier Wants Refugee Office." *Stamford Advocate*, February 22, 2014. http://www.stamfordadvocate.com/news/article/Former-child-soldier-wants-Wyoming-refugee-office-5258658.php. Accessed February 28, 2014.

Talagan, Dean P. "Faith, Hard Work, and Family: The Story of the Wyoming Hellenes." In Gordon Olaf Hendrickson, ed. *Peopling the High Plains: Wyoming's European Heritage*. Cheyenne: Wyoming State Archives and Historical Department, 1977, pp. 149–68.

Trouillot, Michel Rolph. *Silencing the Past: Power and the Production of History*. Boston: Beacon Press, 1997.

Tuchman, Gary. "Mexican boom town . . . in Wyoming?" CNN Website. http://www.cnn.com/CNN/Programs/anderson.cooper.360/blog/2006/03/mexican-boom-town-in-wyoming.html. Accessed March 29, 2014.

SELECTED BIBLIOGRAPHY

Akram, Susan, and Kevin R. Johnson. "Migration and Regulation Goes Local: The Role of States in U.S. Immigration Policy: Race, Civil Rights, and Immigration Law after September 11, 2001: The Targeting of Arabs and Muslims." *New York University Annual Survey of American Law* 58, no. 295 (2002). http://papers.ssrn.com/sol3/papers.cfm?abstract_id=365261. Accessed March 17, 2014.

Andres Torres, ed. *Latinos in New England*. Philadelphia: Temple University Press, 2006.

Arnesen, Eric, Julie Greene, and Bruce Laurie. *Labor Histories: Class, Politics, and the Working Class Experience*. Champaign: University of Illinois Press, 1998.

Arnold, Kathleen R. *American Immigration after 1996: The Shifting Ground of Political Inclusion*. College Station: Penn State University Press, 2011.

Balderrama, Francisco E., and Raymond Rodriguez. *Decade of Betrayal: Mexican Repatriation in the 1930s*. Albuquerque: University of New Mexico Press 1995.

Bearce, Sara M. "Justice before Deportation: Idaho Should Guarantee Non-Citizens the Right to Know the Immigration Consequences of Pleading Guilty." *Idaho Law Review* 42, no. 3 (2005): 853–81.

Beechert, Edward D. *Working in Hawaii: A Labor History*. Honolulu: University of Hawai'i Press, 1985.

Bussel, Robert, ed. "Understanding the Immigrant Experience in Oregon." Labor Education and Research Center, University of Oregon, 2009.

Calavita, Kitty. *Inside the State: The Bracero Program, Illegal Immigrants, and the Bracero Program.* New York: Routledge, 1992.

Camayd-Freixas, Erik. "Statement of Dr. Erik Camayd-Freixas, Federally Certified Interpreter at the U.S. District Court for the Northern District of Iowa Regarding a Hearing on the Arrest, Prosecution, and Conviction of 297 Undocumented Workers in Postville, Iowa, from May 12 to 22, 2008." Before the Subcommittee on Immigration, Citizenship, Refugees, Border Security and International Law. July 24, 2008 at 11:00 a.m., 1310 Longworth House Office Building. http://judiciary.house.gov/hearings/pdf/Camayd-Freixas080724.pdf. Accessed March 17, 2014; http://www.kyoolee.net/Interpreting_the_Largest_ICE_Raid_in_History_-_Personal_Account.pdf. Accessed March 17, 2014.

Castro, Raul H., and Jack L. August Jr. *Adversity Is My Angel.* Fort Worth: Texas Christian University Press, 2009.

Cruz, José. *Identity and Power: Puerto Rican Politics and the Challenge of Ethnicity.* Philadelphia: Temple University Press, 1998.

Cruz, Wilfredo. *City of Dreams: Latino Immigration to Chicago.* Lanham, MD: University Press of America, 2007.

Daniels, Roger. *Asian America: Chinese and Japanese in the United States since 1850.* Seattle: University of Washington Press, 1988.

Doty, Roxanne. *Anti-Immigrantism in Western Democracies: Statecraft, Desire and the Politics of Exclusion.* New York and London: Routledge Press, 2003.

Dow, Mark. *American Gulag: Inside U.S. Immigration Prisons.* Los Angeles and Berkeley: University of California Press, 2004.

Driscoll, Barbara A. *The Tracks North: The Railroad Bracero Program of World War II.* Austin: University of Texas, 1999.

Ehrkamp, Patricia, and Caroline Nagel. "Immigration, Place of Worship and the Politics of Citizenship in the US South." *Transactions of the Institute of British Geographers* 37, no. 4 (2012): 624–38.

Frank Norris, "North to Alaska: An Overview of Immigrants to Alaska, 1867–1945." *Alaska Historical Commission Studies in History,* no. 121 (June 1984).

Gavett, Gretchen. "Why Three Governors Challenged Secure Communities." *Frontline,* October 18, 2011. http://icirr.org/content/why-three-governors-challenged-secure-communities. Accessed March 17, 2014.

Gilroy, Marilyn. "More than Crossing Our Southern Border . . . Hispanics Find Jobs That Shift Migration." *The Hispanic Outlook in Higher Education* 17 (February 2007): 49–53.

Glass, Ira. "The Competition." *This American Life.* Transcript. NPR: Public Radio International, November 30, 2007. http://www.thisamericanlife.org/radio-archives/episode/344/transcript. Accessed March 4, 2013.

Gonzalez-Berry, Erlinda, and Marcela Mendoza. *Mexicanos in Oregon: Their Stories, Their Lives*. Corvallis: Oregon State University Press, 2010.

Hardwick, S. W., and J. E. Meacham. "Heterolocalism, Networks of Ethnicity, and Refugee Communities in the Pacific Northwest: The Portland Story." *The Professional Geographer* 57, no. 4 (2005): 539–57.

Hayes-Batista, David E. *La Nueva California, Latinos in the Golden State*. Berkeley: University of California Press, 2004.

Hernández, César Cuauhtémoc García. "No Human Being Is Illegal." *Monthly Review*, June 2008. http://www.monthlyreview.org/080616garcia.php. Accessed March 17, 2014.

Hernandez, Kelly Lytle. "Mexican Immigration to the United States 1900–1999." Annenberg Foundation, n.d. http://www.learner.org/courses/amerhistory/pdf/Mexican_Immigration_L-One.pdf. Accessed March 17, 2014.

"History of Sí Se Puede." United Farm Workers, n.d. http://www.ufw.org/_board.php?mode=view&b_code=cc_his_research&b_no=5970&page=1&field=&key=&n=30. Accessed March 17, 2014.

Holli, Melvin and Peter d'A Jones. *Ethnic Chicago: A Multicultural Portrait*. 4th ed. Grand Rapids, Michigan: Eerdmans Publishing. 1995.

Honig, Bonnie. *Democracy and the Foreigner*. Princeton, NJ: Princeton University Press, 2001.

Immigrant and Worker Rights Coalition. "Immigrant and Worker Rights Coalition." 2011. http://wmciwr.blogspot.com/. Accessed March 17, 2014.

Johnson, Kevin R. "The Forgotten 'Repatriation' of Persons of Mexican Ancestry and Lessons for the 'War on Terror.'" *Pace Law Review* 26, no. 1 (Fall 2005): 1–26.

Johnson, Kevin R. "'Melting Pot' of Ring of Fire?: Assimilation and the Mexican-American Experience." LatCrit: Latinas/os and the Law: A Joint Symposium by *California Law Review* and *La Raza Law Journal*. *California Law Review* 85, no. 5 (October, 1997): 1259–313.

Johnson, Kevin R. "Race and Immigration Law and Enforcement: A Response to Is There a Plenary Power Doctrine?" *Geography Immigration* 289 (1999–2000): 289–305.

Junn, Jane, and Natalie Masuoka. "Asian American Identity: Shared Racial Status and Political Context." *Perspectives on Politics* 6, no. 8 (December 2008): 729–40.

Kanstroom, Daniel. *Deportation Nation*. Cambridge, MA: Harvard University Press, 2007.

King, Robert. "Should English Be the Law?" *The Atlantic Online*, April 1997. www.theatlantic.com/issues/97apr/english.htm. Accessed March 17, 2014.

La Botz, Dan. *Cesar Chavez and La Causa*. New York: Pearson Longman, 2006.

Maravillas, Anthony Rama. "Nixon in Nixonland." *Southern California Quarterly* 84 (Summer 2002): 169–81.

Martin, Philip. "Mexican Workers and U.S. Agriculture: The Revolving Door." *International Migration Review* 36, no. 4, Host Societies and the Reception of Immigrants: Institutions, Markets and Policies (Winter 2002): 1124–142.

McCormick, Elizabeth M. "The Oklahoma Taxpayer and Citizen Protection Act: Blowing Off Steam or Setting Wildfires?" *Georgetown Immigration Law Journal* 23 (2009): 293–363.

Mitchell, Chip. "Illinois County Defies Feds on Immigrant Detentions." *National Public Radio,* September 12, 2011. http://www.npr.org/2011/09/12/140407306/cook-county-ill-bucks-immigration-enforcement.   Accessed   November 9, 2011.

Nevins, Joseph. *Operation Gatekeeper: The Rise of the 'Illegal Alien' and the Making of the U.S.-Mexico Boundary.* New York and London: Routledge, 2002.

Ngai, Mae M. *Impossible Subjects.* Princeton, NJ: Princeton University Press, 2004.

"The Official Bracero Agreement." The Farmworkers Website. http://www.farmworkers.org/bpaccord.html. Accessed March 17, 2014.

Pallares, Amalia. "The Chicago Context." In Amalia Pallares, and Nilda Flores-Gonzalez, eds. ¡*Marcha! Latino Chicago and the Immigrant Rights Movement.* Urbana-Champaign: University of Illinois Press, 2010, pp. 37–64.

Perea, Juan F., ed. *Immigrants Out!: The New Nativism and the Anti-Immigrant Impulse in the United States.* New York: University Press, 1997.

Purkayastha, Bandana, ed. *Asian Americans in Connecticut Census 2000: Race, Ethnicity, Household and Family.* Asian American Studies Institute Research Paper Series vol. 3, no. 1. Storrs: University of Connecticut Press, 2004.

Robertson, Campbell. "After Ruling, Hispanics Flee an Alabama Town." *New York Times,* October 3, 2011. http://www.nytimes.com/2011/10/04/us/after-ruling-hispanics-flee-an-alabama-town.html?pagewanted=all&_r=0.   Accessed March 17, 2014.

Robertson, Campbell. "Alabama Immigration Law's Critics Question Target." *New York Times,* October 27, 2011. http://www.nytimes.com/2011/10/28/us/alabama-immigration-laws-critics-question-target.html?_r=1&scp=1&sq=alabama%20immigration%20law&st=cse. Accessed March 17, 2014.

Sassen, Saskia. "Bits of a New Immigration Reality: A Bad Fit with Current Policy." Border Battles: The U.S. Immigration Debates. ssrc.org, July 28, 2006. http://borderbattles.ssrc.org/Sassen/. Accessed March 17, 2014.

Sassen, Saskia. *Globalization and Its Discontents: Essays on the New Mobility of People and Money.* New York: New Press, 1998.

Sassen, Saskia. *Guests and Aliens.* New York: New Press, 1999.

Scaperlanda, Michael A. "Human Trafficking in the Heartland: Greed, Visa Fraud, and the Saga of 53 Indian Nationals 'Enslaved' by a Tulsa Company." *Loyola University Chicago International Law Review* 2 (2006): 219–44.

Shanks, Cheryl. *Immigration and Politics of American Sovereignty, 1890–1990.* Ann Arbor: University of Michigan Press, 2001.

Shaw, Randy. *Beyond the Fields: Cesar Chavez, the UFW and the Struggle for Justice in the 21st Century.* Berkeley and Los Angeles: University of California Press, 2008.

Shultz, Benjamin J. "Inside the Gilded Cage: The Lives of Latino Immigrant Males in Rural Central Kentucky." *Southeastern Geographer* 48, no. 2 (2008): 201–18.

Singer, Audrey, and Jill H. Wilson. *From "There to Here": Refugee Resettlement in Metropolitan America.* Washington, DC: The Brookings Institution, 2006.

Smith, Emily Rene. "Putting Down Roots: A Case Study of the Participation of Somali Bantu Refugees in the Global Gardens Refugee Farming Project in Boise, Idaho." MA Thesis. Presented to the Department of International Studies and the Graduate School of the University of Oregon, June 2011. https://scholarsbank.uoregon.edu/xmlui/handle/1794/11496. Accessed March 17, 2014.

Smith, Michael Peter. "Can You Imagine? Transnational Migration and the Globalization of Grassroots Politics." *Social Text* 39 (Summer 1994): 15–33.

Smith, Michael Peter. "The Two Faces of Transnational Citizenship." *Ethnic and Racial Studies* 30, no. 6 (November, 2007): 1096–116.

Takaki, Ronald. *Strangers from a Different Shore.* New York: Back Bay Books, 1998.

Varsanyi, Monica. "Rescaling the 'Alien,' Rescaling Personhood: Neoliberalism, Immigration and the State." *Annals of the Association of American Geographers* 98, no. 4 (2008): 877–96.

Varsanyi, Monica, ed. *Taking Local Control: Immigration Policy Activism in U.S. Cities and States.* Palo Alto, CA: Stanford University Press, 2010.

Wasem, Ruth Ellen. "U.S. Immigration Policy on Haitian Migrants." CRS Report for Congress, 2005. http://trac.syr.edu/immigration/library/P960.pdf. Accessed March 17, 2014.

Winders, Jamie. "Bringing Back the (B)order: Post-9/11 Politics of Immigration, Borders, and Belonging in the Contemporary US South." *Antipode* 39, no 5 (2007): 920–42.

About the Editor and Contributors

THE EDITOR

Kathleen R. Arnold is visiting assistant professor of political science at DePaul University in Chicago, specializing in political theory. Her research interests are statelessness, homelessness, and immigration. Her publications include *Homelessness, Citizenship and Identity* (State University of New York [SUNY] Press 2004); *America's New Working Class* (Penn State Press 2007); and *American Immigration after 1996: The Shifting Ground of Political Inclusion* (Penn State Press 2011).

CONTRIBUTORS

Lukasz Albanski is an assistant professor in the Institute of Education Sciences at the Pedagogical University of Cracow, Poland.

Gayle Kathleen Berardi is a professor of political science and co-director at the Center for Leadership and Community Development at Colorado State University, Pueblo.

Samantha Bryant is a doctoral student and teaching assistant in history at the University of Nebraska-Lincoln.

Bob Bussel is an associate professor of history and director of the Labor Education and Research Center at the University of Oregon, Eugene.

K. Jurée Capers is an assistant professor in public management and public policy at Georgia State University.

Wenqian Dai is an assistant professor of sociology at the University of South Dakota.

Kendall Funk is a doctoral student in political science and a research assistant for the Project for Equity, Representation, and Governance at Texas A & M University.

Sarah Garding is a postdoctoral researcher at the School of Interdisciplinary Area Studies and Nuffield College, University of Oxford.

Anne Gebelein is the associate director of El Instituto: Latino, Caribbean, and Latin American Studies Institute at the University of Connecticut.

John Howell is a professor at Southern Utah University.

Miriam Jimenez, PhD, teaches in political science at SUNY at Oswego.

Nicole Kalaf-Hughes is an assistant professor in political science at Bowling Green State University in Ohio.

William P. Kladky is affiliated with the American Institutes for Research and is an adjunct lecturer at the College of Notre Dame of Maryland. A PhD sociologist, he is the author of many articles and papers in the areas of American and European culture, history, religion, and race relations. Besides his teaching and research activities, he works in civil and human rights education/advocacy.

Jessica L. Lavariega-Monforti is a professor of political science at the University of Texas, Pan American.

Karey Leung, PhD, teaches political science at Rutgers University in New Brunswick, New Jersey.

Amy Lively is the internship coordinator for the School of Sustainability at Arizona State University.

Anthony Rama Maravillas is a professor at the College of DuPage, San Francisco Bay Area.

Elizabeth M. McCormick is an associate professor of law and director of the Immigrant Rights Project at the University of Tulsa College of Law.

Adam McGlynn is an assistant professor of political science at East Stroudsburg University in Pennsylvania.

Carla R. Monroe, PhD, is an associate editor for *Intercultural Education,* a journal based with the International Association of Intercultural Education.

Catherine Morrisey Ribeiro teaches at Arizona State University.

Katherine M. O'Flaherty teaches history at the University of Maine at Orono.

Francisco I. Pedraza is a Robert Wood Johnson scholar in Health Policy Research at the University of Michigan.

Luke Perry is an associate professor and chair person of the Department of Government and Politics at Utica College.

Candice Quinn, PhD is the editor-in-chief of *The International Social Science Review* and communications director of MN-ASAP.

John T. Radzilowski is a professor at the University of Alaska Southeast.

Florio Raffaele is a professor at Regis College in Massachusetts.

Darlene Xiomara Rodriguez is an assistant professor in political science at the University of North Carolina, Greensboro.

Julia Skinner is a doctoral candidate in information studies at Florida State University.

Lilia Soto is an assistant professor in American studies and Chicano studies at the University of Wyoming.

Maryam Stevenson is an assistant professor in the Department of History and Political Science at the University of Indianapolis.

John Tuman is chairperson and associate professor in the Department of Political Science and director of the Institute for Latin American Studies at the University of Nevada, Las Vegas.

Anduin Wilhide is a doctoral candidate in the Department of History at the University of Minnesota.

James Wren is a retired professor and independent scholar with numerous publications.

INDEX